Technology in Financial Markets

Technology in Financial Markets

Complex Change and Disruption

MARCO DELL'ERBA

OXFORD
UNIVERSITY PRESS

Great Clarendon Street, Oxford, OX2 6DP,
United Kingdom

Oxford University Press is a department of the University of Oxford.
It furthers the University's objective of excellence in research, scholarship,
and education by publishing worldwide. Oxford is a registered trade mark of
Oxford University Press in the UK and in certain other countries

© Marco Dell'Erba 2024

The moral rights of the author have been asserted

First Edition published in 2024

All rights reserved. No part of this publication may be reproduced, stored in
a retrieval system, or transmitted, in any form or by any means, without the
prior permission in writing of Oxford University Press, or as expressly permitted
by law, by licence or under terms agreed with the appropriate reprographics
rights organization. Enquiries concerning reproduction outside the scope of the
above should be sent to the Rights Department, Oxford University Press, at the
address above

You must not circulate this work in any other form
and you must impose this same condition on any acquirer

Public sector information reproduced under Open Government Licence v3.0
(http://www.nationalarchives.gov.uk/doc/open-government-licence/open-government-licence.htm)

Published in the United States of America by Oxford University Press
198 Madison Avenue, New York, NY 10016, United States of America

British Library Cataloguing in Publication Data
Data available

Library of Congress Control Number: 2023936362

ISBN 978–0–19–887361–7

DOI: 10.1093/oso/9780198873617.001.0001

Printed and bound by
CPI Group (UK) Ltd, Croydon, CR0 4YY

Links to third party websites are provided by Oxford in good faith and
for information only. Oxford disclaims any responsibility for the materials
contained in any third party website referenced in this work.

Preface: The Line of Disruption

'The line of disruption' is an oxymoron. The concept of a 'line' refers to a continuous succession of points that is infinite. The Oxford English Dictionary defines 'disruption' as 'a situation in which it is difficult for something to continue in the normal way; the act of stopping something from continuing in the normal way'. Synonyms for the word 'disruption' include 'interruption', 'break', 'separation', and 'severance'. How can disruption, or multiple disruptions, form a line?

When I was a child, I was always fascinated by the little red strips of firecrackers that street vendors sold during Christmas time, starting around the third week of December. In Italy these strips are called 'TricTrac', which has nothing to do with the word 'trick' as it relates to the more famous Halloween 'Trick or Treat'. It is a rather onomatopoeic word, echoing the noise of the continuous little deflagrations that TricTracs generate. The way TricTracs work is very simple. After lighting the little fuse at the very beginning, the strip of firecrackers keeps exploding for about 30 seconds, and kids enjoy the noise of the deflagrations.

If I have to identify a method or a single image to convey the chain of events that led to the transformations in the current financial, political, and regulatory frameworks, the most powerful image that comes to my mind is the red strip of firecrackers of my childhood. The word 'line' refers to a very minimalistic concept, and the action of tracing a line is a rather natural and easy task. Also, from a mathematical perspective, the concept of a line relates to the infinite and offers therefore a rather optimistic view.

Understanding the way one event triggers the other, or at least making the effort to do so, is vital for emphasizing the way specific changes are happening, how they may be instrumental to build something durable, and ultimately achieving a more sustainable (not in the environmental sense) economic and financial framework. I started to study corporate law in the aftermath of some of the biggest scandals in corporate governance and capital markets, and apparently this was only the beginning of a very significant transformation for modern capitalism. The generation of legal scholars that I am a part of has grown up in an era of scandals and crises. Enron and WorldCom in the United States and Parmalat in Europe proved to be of unusual magnitude and dominated the legal and regulatory debate. New scandals emerged, such as Bernie Madoff in the United States, a modern declination of the always effective Ponzi scheme, that ended in tragedy, with prison sentences and suicides. Finally, the financial crisis of 2008 was a spectacular deflagration or the beginning of the disruption, and its long fuse has extremely deep roots in the history of politics and capitalism. Law makers reacted with a heavy regulatory response, as they systematically did after every scandal or crisis.

The observation of this incessant regulatory activity certainly had profound consequences on my way of interpreting the facts and the reactions that they triggered. In particular, I was always astonished by the methodological approach of regulators when tackling these apparently new heterogeneous issues. Providing a new regulatory framework was the consequence of a systematic approach consisting of highlighting the novelties underlying the new wave of scandals, crises, and innovation. This has exacerbated misperceptions of the roles of regulation and the law in general, as these incessant initiatives have created a perception of law as a tool to solve an emergency.

After the financial crisis of 2008, the regulatory response intended to restore trust in financial markets and, more broadly, in capitalism. In addition to regulation, technology brought a further response, with Bitcoin and financial technology ('Fintech') emerging as disruptors within the financial system. Bitcoin's white paper, drafted by the fictitious 'Satoshi Nakamoto', appeared online in October 2008 (although it certainly was the result of years of study). This white paper provided a new alternative payment infrastructure and triggered a more systematic discussion around the underlying technology, blockchain technology (a subtype of distributed ledger technology, DLT), and its potential applications in capital markets. At the same time, other technologies that predated the explosion of blockchain, such as artificial intelligence (AI) and the Internet of Things (IoT), spread not only in high-futuristic laboratories but also in real life. The combination of these technologies favoured the establishment of new paradigms, such as Fintech and decentralized finance (DeFi), enhancing the discussion on viable ways to redistribute the functions of capitalism among different market actors and platforms.

The 'line of disruption' clarifies that the problems are always the same in commercial practices, capital markets, corporations, and financial networks. Understanding the nature of such problems is critical to maintaining this line as a proper *line*, instead of curving it, transforming it into a circle—a vicious cycle. It is for this reason that a specific point of the line is identified with shadow banking, and the final point of the analysis is what I identify as 'shadow central banking' and 'crypto shadow banking'.

In addition to the layer of the factual dimension, the 'line of disruption' is critical to emphasize another characteristic of the chain of events, which is also functional to better understand the relevance of the current changes. This is the increased interconnection between different fields that were traditionally approached and studied as separate. Such was the case in financial regulation, central banking and monetary policy, and corporate governance. The 'line of disruption' clarifies that the problems and innovations emerging at the payment system level—Bitcoin is an alternative payment system—propagated at different levels. These include a new way of contracting in commercial practices: capital formation with initial coin offerings (ICOs), and their evolution, as well as the way securities are issued and voted on, contributing to rethinking of the market infrastructure involved and corporate governance matters. At another level, ICOs and their volatility emphasize the monetary side of the issue, in particular the quest for stability in cryptocurrencies to absolve their function as a currency—serving as a medium of exchange, a unit of account, and a store of value. The discussion then propagates to the level of central banks, with private actors in a position to challenge them in an unprecedented way.

These transformations happening in the context of so-called cryptoeconomy and DeFi pose important questions regarding central banking and shadow banking. The emerging 'shadow central banking' and 'crypto shadow banking' share extremely dangerous similarities with the transformations in the financial system since the 1960s that led to the emergence and the establishment of shadow banking. This couples with an alarming lack of ratings, beyond credit ratings, and the possibility of identifying the real value of the new instruments populating new economic paradigms in a less discretionary manner. These are traditional problems, some of which led to the implosion of the financial system and which may still pose a serious threat to the cryptoeconomy and DeFi as emerging paradigms.

In the new technological environment, commercial practices, monetary policy, securities law issues, and corporate governance have become extremely interconnected parts of the same discussions.

In light of this, the purpose of my book is twofold. First, when referring to technology, financial innovation, and the relationship of the two with the law, there is always a problem of systematization. Therefore, one implicit—though obvious— objective of my book is to emphasize the problem of systematizing the disrupting novelties emerging from the new ecosystem and explain the role of the law in the transformative phases of the economy.

Second, the minimalism underlying the 'line of disruption' should serve to shed light on the chain of events that occurred over the past two to three decades, spanning from the financial crises and scandals to the technological developments related to cryptoeconomy. Furthermore, the 'line of disruption' should allow the more 'abstract' interconnection between traditionally different fields of studies and fields of policy to emerge. When it comes to policy, scholars and regulators seldom cooperate to identify the contours of a broader landscape. This happens particularly often in contexts such as monetary policy, corporate governance, financial and banking regulation, and technologies that are often perceived as distant and separate niches. In this context, complexity theory (or theories) emerges as an important tool to navigate the establishment of new paradigms, where interconnected networks relying on heterogeneous entities generate dynamic evolutions. Therefore, complexity theory is the underlying theoretical foundation sustaining the development of the line of disruption: international finance as a whole is a dynamic complex adaptive system, resulting from the multiple interconnections within the different subparts composing it, each of them being a dynamic complex adaptive system.

All of this should not only serve to solve the problems related to the emerging and the potential transition toward the nascent economic paradigm represented by cryptoeconomy, tokeneconomy, and decentralized finance, but should also be instrumental to another, more ambitious goal: developing an appropriate methodology for regulating any form of disruption. The 'next', but still contemporary, challenge is to design, build, and implement a sustainable economic and financial environment. After all, the challenges posed by technology and sustainability, and more generally any disruptive phenomena, are not very different, with problems related to adapting specific definitions, and an equally relevant interconnection between central banking, corporate governance, and financial law issues to optimize.

Acknowledgements

When I first encountered blockchain in 2016, it marked a special time in my life. I had unequivocally decided to pursue a future in academia and made the decision to move to the United States. Additionally, I had never visited Switzerland before. Little did I know that a few years later, I would find myself authoring a book on the cryptoeconomy, split between New York and Zurich.

My interest in blockchain stemmed from a pure intellectual curiosity, despite my usual aversion to technology. I distinctly recall my brother's coding prowess with an old Commodore 64, which I rarely approached except for playing car video games and Batman. Blockchain forced me to reconsider traditional legal and financial structures that I had always taken for granted, and it opened up avenues for philosophical, historical, and political considerations that were not strictly tied to technology. I would describe this topic as a time machine, compelling me to ensure a thorough understanding of the past so as to avoid any interpretative mistakes regarding the future and the presumed novelty underlying ongoing developments. I learned that nothing is entirely new and nothing is entirely old.

In the past few years, I have lived in Italy, France, the United Kingdom, Singapore, the Netherlands, the United States, and Switzerland. These international experiences have profoundly influenced my approach to the law and my interest in the cross-border aspects of various phenomena and developments. It is likely that these experiences also contribute to my interest for blockchain. New York, particularly New York University School of Law, and Zurich, specifically the Faculty of Law at the University of Zurich, served as the thriving hubs for my research. I have greatly benefited from these institutions and locations, each in their own unique ways, and I have cultivated a symbiotic relationship with my offices in 40 Washington Square South and 74 Ramistrasse. I am immensely grateful for the opportunities these institutions have provided me.

I am equally grateful to the mentors I have encountered along my journey: Edward B. Rock, Alain Pietrancosta, and Guido Ferrarini. I consider myself fortunate to have crossed paths with them at various stages of my career, and I am truly honoured they have become cherished friends.

I am particularly grateful to Rolf H. Weber, who generously dedicated his time to carefully read my work and provide invaluable advice on crucial points. His contributions have greatly enriched both my book and my growth as an academic. Additionally, I am sincerely grateful to my colleagues at the University of Zurich, in particular Kern Alexander, Thomas Gachter, Rolf Sethe, Christian Schwarzenegger, Sarah Summers, Brigitte Tag, and those in my research group for their support.

In the past few years, I have had the privilege of sharing wonderful discussions with numerous colleagues and friends. I would like to express my gratitude to Francesco Mauceri, Giovanni Patti, Stratos Pahis, Giuliano Castellano, Elio Taurino, Cosimo

Cascione, Roberto Tallarita, Robert Dilworth, Valmore Rojas Guerra, Andrea Guaccero, Jennifer Arlen, Laurent Laughlin, Troy A. McKenzie, Katja Langenbucher, Katharina Pistor, Alan Rechtshaffen, Kevin Werbach, Hanna Halaburda, Wolf-Georg Ringe, Yesha Yadav, Nizan Geslevich Pakin, Yuliya Guseva, Holger Spamann, Claudio J. Tessone, Dan Awrey, and Andrew Hinkes.

I am also grateful to Rachel Mullaly for her unwavering support and consistently constructive and positive advice throughout the entire process of publishing this book.

I am aware that I would have never pursued this career if I hadn't meet a special academic and researcher as my dear godfather Vincenzo Cuomo, and the unforgettable professor Berardino Libonati.

Finally, I want to thank Claudio and Miriana Dell'Erba, Tommaso Dell'Erba and his family, and my Eugenia for their love.

Contents

List of Figures	xvii
Table of Cases	xix
Table of Legislation	xxi
List of Abbreviations	xxix

1. The Underlying Complexities within the Line of Disruption   1
   Introduction   1
      A. An Oxymoron—One More   1
      B. Emergence Economies and Network Growth Economies   2
      C. The Need for a New Theoretical Framework to Understand the New Economic and Societal Transformations   3
      D. The Word 'Complexity' and Its Multiple Uses and Contexts   3
      E. The Structure of Chapter 1   6
     I. Complexity as a Science: Complexity of Adaptive Systems or Complexity Science *Tout Court*   6
      A. What Are Complex Adaptive Systems?   7
      B. The Scope of Complexity Science   10
      C. The Impact of Complexity on Legal Science   12
     II. Complexity in Capital Markets and Finance: A Structural (Static) Attribute of International Finance and the Basis for Alternative Views   15
      A. General Remarks   15
      B. Approaches to Complexity in Financial Markets   17
      C. An Alternative View on the Relationship between Financial Markets and Complexity   20
     III. How Does Innovation Come into Play When Analysing Complexity? Diving into the Relationship between Complexity and Technology   21
      A. Financial Innovation   21
        1. General Traits and Continuity of Financial Innovation over Time   21
        2. Transaction Meta-Technologies   22
      B. Disruptive Technologies: The Current Landscape   24
        1. Sustaining vs Disruptive Technologies   24
        2. The Main Disruptive Technologies   25
        3. Specific Discontinuities in the New Paradigms   28
      C. Disruptive Innovation (and Technology) as Regulatory Disruptive Innovations   29
        1. A Few Examples   29
        2. Approaches for Regulatory Disruptive Innovations   31
        3. Regulatory Disruption, Complexity, and the Idea of Dynamic Regulation   35

IV. Complexity as History-Dependency: The Historical Dimension of Transformations and Disruptive Innovations in International Finance 38
   A. The Shadow Banking System 42
      1. What Is the Shadow Banking System? 42
      2. Causes Leading to the Establishment of the Shadow Banking System 43
   B. The Financial Crisis of 2008: A Financial and a Corporate Scandal 44
   C. After the Financial Crisis 47
      1. Regulatory Response 47
      2. Technological Response 49
V. The Layers of Complexity 63
   A. The Three Basic Layers 64
   B. Evolving Complexity and Multidimensionality 65
      1. Intrinsic Evolution of Each Subpart 66
      2. Interaction between Each Subpart: Complexity as Multidimensionality 67
VI. The Structure of the Technological Implications and the Key Questions 68
   A. An Ascending Climax 68
   B. The Key Problems and the Two Dimensions 69
      1. The Static Component of the Problem 69
      2. The Dynamic Component of the Problem 70
   C. Limiting the Scope of the Analysis to Technology 73
Conclusion 74

2. **Starting from the Basics: Regulating Smart Contracts** 76
Introduction 76
  I. A New Technical and Infrastructural Environment for Contracting: Smart Contracts 81
   A. What Are Smart Contracts? 81
   B. The Role of Blockchain Platforms for Popularizing Smart Contracts and Increasing Their Complexity 87
      1. General Remarks 87
      2. Increasingly Complex Smart Contracts, Distributed Autonomous Organizations (DAOs), and 'The DAO Case' 88
  II. Towards a Regulatory Framework for Smart Contracts 90
   A. The Law and Economics of Smart Contracts 90
   B. The Legal Regime of Smart Contracts in the United States 93
      1. Uniform Commercial Code 93
      2. The Regulation of Smart Contracts under the Uniform Electronic Transaction Act (UETA), the Electronic Signature in Global and National Commerce Act (ESIGN), and the Uniform Computer Information Transaction Act (UCITA) 98
      3. The Regulation of Blockchain and Smart Contracts at the State Level 101

C. Europe	105
1. General Remarks	105
2. The Debate on Smart Contracts within the European Union	106
3. Mapping the Main Initiatives in Europe	110
III. Critical Considerations	115
A. Why Smart Contracts Are a Matter of Law	115
B. The Formation of the Agreement in the Context of Smart Contracts	118
C. The Problem of Regulatory Fragmentation and the Importance of Uniform Principles: Regulatory Fragmentation and Lex Cryptographia	120
D. The Importance of Self-Regulatory Organizations	124
E. Smart Contracts and Complexity	127
Conclusion	129
3. Enhancing Disruption: Smart Contracts in Capital Markets, or Initial Coin Offerings: Breached Promises and Relevant Consequences	130
Introduction	130
I. Key Aspects of ICOs and How They Evolved	133
A. The Structural Pattern	133
B. ICO Problems and Structural Adaptations	136
II. The Regulatory Debate on ICOs	139
A. United States	140
1. CFTC and SEC: Two Faces of the Same Coin	140
2. Recent Initiatives	147
B. European Union	149
C. Switzerland	152
III. Unsolved Issues Emerging from ICOs	156
A. The Best Regulatory Approach	156
1. Emerging Regulatory and Enforcement Patterns and the Difficulty to Effectively Compare Them	156
2. Implications of the Securities Enforcement beyond the 'Securities Space': The Problem of Stablecoins	162
3. Residual Concerns	166
B. The Breached Promises of ICOs	168
1. Financial Inclusion	168
2. Disintermediation of Venture Capitalists	170
3. Disintermediation of Market Infrastructures	172
IV. ICOs' Relevant Consequences	176
A. Consequences for Capital Market Structures	177
B. Consequences for the Creation of 'Mainstream' Digital Securities	179
1. Impact of Digital Securities on Corporate Offerings	180
2. Impact on Government Offerings	187
3. Potential Infrastructural Consequence of Digital Securities at the Level of Traditional Exchanges and Other Market Infrastructures	188

    C. Broader Consequences for Corporate Governance 192
        1. Ownership Transparency 193
        2. Shareholder Voting 194
        3. Real-Time Monitoring 199
        4. A Hypothetical Blockchain-Based Infrastructure for Corporate Governance 200
        5. Potential Problems of a Blockchain Solution 202
    D. The Impulse to the Development of Tokenized Crypto-Assets 208
        1. Crypto-Assets 209
        2. NFTs 211
    E. ICOs and Complexity 218
Conclusion 219

4. Disrupting Central Banking or Shadow Central Banking 221
Introduction 221
  I. Central Banking 225
    A. Goals and Mission of Central Banks 225
    B. Central Banks' Main Characteristics 228
    C. Traditional Money and Payment Systems 231
        1. Central Bank and Commercial Bank Money 231
        2. The Functions of Money 232
  II. Shadow Central Banking 234
    A. What Is Shadow Central Banking 234
        1. The Role of Technology 234
        2. Shadow Central Banking versus Private Central Banking 235
        3. Shadow Central Banking versus Shadow Banking 236
    B. New Forms of Money as the Main Source of Disruption 237
        1. E-Money and Pre-Bitcoin Digital Currencies 237
        2. Bitcoin 239
        3. Stablecoins 240
        4. Payments and DeFi 256
    C. Similarities in the Causes Leading to the Emergence of Shadow Banking and Shadow Central Banking 257
    D. The Reaction of Central Banks 259
        1. Central Bank Digital Currencies 259
        2. Public Debate and Experiments 263
  III. Critical Considerations 278
    A. An Old Paradigm? 279
        1. Private Central Banks 279
        2. A Pre-'Full-Faith-and-Credit' Paradigm 280
    B. Independence, Governance, and Corporate Governance in Shadow Central Banking 281
        1. Private Central Banks and Separation between Ownership and Control 281
        2. Corporate Governance 282

C. Potential Problems	286
1. Systemic Risk	286
2. Shadow Central Banking as Liquidity Provider and Lender of Last Resort: Structural Limits	293
3. Fragmented Network and Interoperability	297
D. Broader Regulatory Implications	298
E. Potential Scenarios	300
1. Scenario 1: Shadow Central Banking Replacing the Current Central Banking System	300
2. Scenario 2: Reducing or Eliminating Shadow Central Banking	303
3. Scenario 3: Effective Co-Existence between CBDCs Issued by Central Banks and Private Currencies	305
F. Shadow Central Banking and Complexity	306
Conclusion	308
5. Disrupting Shadow Banking or Crypto Shadow Banking	**309**
Introduction	309
I. Crypto Shadow Banking?	311
A. The Network of Crypto Shadow Banking	314
1. Crypto-Lending or DeFi Lending	314
2. (DeFi) Lending Platforms	315
3. Towards Non-Collateralized Loans? The Case of Flash Loans	316
4. Leverage in the Cryptoeconomy, Derivatives, and Other Instruments	317
5. Money Market Funds (MMFs) and Stablecoins	324
6. Private Funds	326
7. Prime Brokers and Custodians	327
8. Securitization and Tokenization	330
B. Similarities between Shadow Banking, Shadow Central Banking, and Crypto Shadow Banking	332
II. The Risks of Crypto Shadow Banking	335
A. Excessive Leverage and Opacity	335
B. Liquidity Risks	337
C. Technology-Related Risks	339
D. Rating Crypto-Assets	340
1. Credit Rating and Environmental Social Governance Rating	340
2. Rating Analysis in the Cryptoeconomy	343
E. From Speculation to the Creation of Financial Conglomerates	344
III. Regulatory Measures to Build a Sustainable Cryptoeconomic Ecosystem	346
A. Regulating Stablecoins as MMFs	346
B. Market Infrastructures	347
C. Crypto-Financial Products	350
D. Financial Conglomerates	350
E. The Discussion on Rating for Crypto-Assets	353
F. Facing Technological Risks in Crypto Shadow Banking	354
G. Crypto Shadow Banking and Complexity	355
Conclusion	356

Concluding Remarks: What's Next? . . . 358
  Introduction . . . 358
    I. Answering the Key Questions . . . 359
      A. The Static Component . . . 359
      B. The Dynamic Component . . . 360
      C. Complexity, Dynamic Regulation, and the Problem of Managing Disruption . . . 363
      D. Technological Disruption as a Case Study? The Case of Sustainability . . . 364
      E. The Intersection of Sustainability and Technology: Sustainable Digital Finance . . . 366
    II. What's Next? The Metaverse as a Synthetic Universe . . . 369
      A. What Is the Metaverse? . . . 369
      B. The Key Elements of the Metaverse . . . 371
      C. Market Developments in the Metaverse . . . 373
      D. Key Questions . . . 374
  Conclusion . . . 375

References . . . 377
Index . . . 431

List of Figures

1.1	*Digital Finance Cube*	63
1.2	The layers of complexity	64
1.3	Evolving complexity	66
1.4	An ascending climax	68
1.5	The line of disruption	71
3.1	The ascending climax of ICOs	177
5.1	Shadow banking vs crypto shadow banking	313

Table of Cases

EUROPEAN UNION

C-422/19 and C-423/19, Johannes Dietrich and Norbert Häring v Hessischer
    Rundfunk [2021] 276n.399
C-628/13, Jean-Bernard Lafonta v Autorité des marchés financiers [2015]

SWITZERLAND

FINMA Enforcement Proceeding Against E-Coins [2017]......................... 160–61
FINMA Enforcement Proceeding Against Envion [2019] 160–61

UNITED STATES

Appraisal of Dell, Inc., Re (2015) No. 9322-VCL, WL 4313206
    (Del. Ch. 30 July 2015)... 195, 195n.407
Coinflip Inc., Re (2015) CFTC No. 15–29, WL 5535736
    (17 September 2015) 140n.68, 141n.74, 251, 251n.224
Commodity Futures Trading Commission v Patrick K. McDonnell and
    CabbageTech Corp. d/b/a Coin DropOpens [2018] 287 F. Supp. 3d 213
    (E.D.N.Y. 2018).. 164
Dole Food Company, Inc., Re (2017) No. CV 8703-VCL, WL 624843
    (Del. Ch. 15 February 2017) 195, 195n.408
Gary Plastic Packaging Corp. v Merrill Lynch, Pierce, Fenner & Smith, Inc.
    [1985] 756 F.2d 230 (2d Cir. 1985) 145, 145n.103
Hill v Gateway [2000] 105 F.3d 1147 (7th Cir. 1997) 96n.131
Int'l Bhd of Teamsters v Daniel [1979] 439 U.S. 551............................... 142n.80
John Deaton et al. Petition for Writ of Mandamous against Elad Roisman as
    acting SEC Chairman (1 January 2021).................................... 158n.180
Marine Bank v Weaver [1982] 455 U.S. 551....................................... 142n.80
Reves v Ernst & Young [1990] 494 U.S. 56............................. 142n.80, 250n.218
SEC v C.M. Joiner Leasing Corporation [1943] 320 U.S. 344 .... 142n.82
SEC v Parmalat Finanziaria S.p.A. (29 December 2003) 46n.315
SEC v REcoin Group Foundation LLC (29 September 2017) 143–44, 143n.87
SEC v Telegram Group Inc. et al. [2020] No. 1:2019cv09439 S.D.N.Y................... 164
SEC v Unique Fin Concepts Inc. [1999] 196 F.3d 1195 (11th Cir. 1999) 143n.83
SEC v W.J. Howey Co [1946] 328 U.S. 293...................... 120n.299, 142nn.80–81,
                                                                                         143nn.83–84, 145n.102
SEC Complaint against REcoin Group Foundation, LLC,
    DRC Wold Inc. a/k/a Diamond Reserve Club and Maksim
    Zaslavskiy (29 September 2017).. 143–44
SEC Complaint against Ripple Labs, Inc., Bradley Garlinghouse and
    Christian A. Larsen (22 December 2020) 140, 146, 147n.113, 157, 166
SEC Complaint against Telegram Group Inc. and Ton Issuer Inc.
    (11 October 2019) 140, 164, 164n.216, 165–66, 362–63

SEC Order Instituting Cease-And-Desist Proceedings and Imposing a
    Cease-And-Desist Order Re Munchee Inc. [2017] Release No. 10445,
    118 SEC Docket 5, 36–38 (11 December 2017) 143–44, 143n.88
SEC Order Instituting Cease-And-Desist Proceedings, Making Findings
    and Imposing a Cease-And-Desist Order Re Zachary Coburn [2018]
    Release No. 84553, (8 November 2018)...144
Tcherepnin v Knight [1967] 389 U.S. 332 ....142n.80
United Housing Foundation Inc. v Forman [1975] 421 U.S. 837 .... 142n.80, 142n.82
Williamson v Tucker [1981] 645 F.2d 404 (5th Cir. 1981) 143n.83

Table of Legislation

INTERNATIONAL INSTRUMENTS

Basel Accord 1988 (Basel I) 40nn.271–72, 41, 43
Basel Accord 2004 (Basel II) ... 40nn.271–72, 41, 43, 189–90
Basel Accord 2010 (Basel III) 40nn.271–72, 41, 43, 133n.9, 189–90, 227–28
Basel Accord 2019 (Basel IV) 40n.271, 41, 43
Principles for Financial Market Infrastructures (PFMI) 243–44
Principles of European Contract Law ... 105
Art 2:101 .... 105n.206
Art 2:102 .... 105n.207
Art 2:103 .... 105n.207
Unidroit Principles of International Commercial Contracts (2016) 105, 105n.203, 105n.209
Principle 1.2 .... 105n.209
Principle 2.1.2 .... 105n.209
Principle 2.1.6 .... 105n.209
United Nations Convention on Contracts for the International Sale of Goods (CISG) (1980) 105, 105n.204
United Nations General Assembly Resolution 70/1, 'Transforming Our World: The 2030 Agenda for Sustainable Development' (21 October 2015) 365, 365n.6

G20 LEADERS' STATEMENTS

Paris Agreement (2016) 228
Pittsburgh (2009) 223
G20 Declaration of the Summit on Financial Markets and the World Economy (15 November 2008) 223n.13

EUROPEAN UNION

Treaties and Statutes

Statute of the European System of Central Banks
Art 16 275
Art 17 275
Art 20 274–75
Art 22 275
Treaty on the Functioning of the European Union (Consolidated Version) [2010] OJ C 83/47
Art 127(2) 274–75
Art 128 275
Art 128(1) 275–76
Art 128(2) 275
Art 130 .... 230–31, 230n.58
Art 133 276
Art 289 276

Regulations

Regulation 593/2008 of 17 June 2008 on the law applicable to contractual obligations (Rome I) [2008] OJ L 177/6 .... 110n.243
Regulation (EU) 1092/2010 of 24 November 2010 on European Union macro-prudential oversight of the financial system and establishing a European Systematic Risk Board [2010] OJ L 331/1 .... 48n.330, 49n.339
recital 13 .... 48n.330
Regulation (EU) 1210/2010 of 15 December 2010 concerning authentication of euro coins and handling of euro coins unfit for circulation [2010] OJ L 339/1 276
Art 3 .... 276n.402
Art 4 .... 276n.402

Regulation (EU) 236/2012 of 14 March 2012 on short selling and certain aspects of credit default swaps (Short Selling Regulation – SSR) [2012] OJ L 86/1 . . . . 48–49, 49n.332, 223, 223n.16, 351

Regulation (EU) 648/2012 of 4 July 2012 on OTC derivatives, central counterparties and trade repositories (European Market Infrastructure Regulation – EMIR) [2012] OJ L 201/1 . . . . 48–49, 49n.333, 223, 223n.17, 300, 351

Regulation (EU) 575/2013 on prudential requirements for credit institutions and investment firms [2013] OJ L 176/1
Art 4(1) 39n.263, 232n.74

Regulation (EU) 600/2014 of 15 May 2014 on markets in financial instruments (MiFIR) [2014] OJ L 173/84 . . . . . 48–49, 49n.337

Regulation (EU) 909/2014 of 23 July 2014 on improving securities settlement in the European Union and on central securities depositories [2014] OJ L 257/1 . . . . . 205–6, 206n.475

Regulation (EU) 910/2014 on electronic identification and trust services for electronic transactions in the internal market (eIDAS) [2014] OJ L 257/73 . . . . 107, 107n.225, 108–9, 108n.231
Art 3(10) 108n.229

Commission Delegated Regulation (EU) 2017/565 of 25 April 2016 supplementing Directive 2014/65/EU as regards organisational requirements and operating conditions for investment firms (MiFID Organisational Regulation) [2017] OJ L 87/1 . . . . 150–51, 251–52, 252n.231
Art 2 . . . . 150.134, 252n.230

Regulation (EU) 1131/2017 on Money Market Funds (MMF Regulation) [2017] OJ L 169/1 . . . . 324, 324n.111, 346, 346n.236

Commission Implementing Regulation (EU) 2018/1212 of 3 September 2018 laying down minimum requirements implementing the provisions of Directive 2007/36/EC as regards shareholder identification, the transmission of information and the facilitation of the exercise of shareholder rights (Shareholder Rights Directive Implementing Regulation) [2018] OJ L223/1 . . . . .195n.405
Recital 3 . . . . .195n.405
Recital 4 . . . . .195n.405

Regulation (EU) 2176/2019 on European Union macro-prudential oversight of the financial system and establishing a European Systematic Risk Board [2019] OJ L 334/146 . . . . .49n.339

Regulation (EU) 2020/1503 on European crowdfunding service providers for business [2020] OJ L 347/1 . . . . 158, 158n.183
recital 15. . . . . .158n.183

Regulation (EU) 2022/858 of 30 May 2022 on a pilot regime for market infrastructures based on distributed ledger technology [2022] OJ L 151/1 . . . . 176, 176n.283, 206, 206n.477, 349, 349n.243
recital 36. . . . . 206, 206n.479
Art 3 176
Art 3(1) 176n.284
Art 14(j) 206n.478

Regulation (EU) 2022/2554 of 14 December 2022 on digital operational resilience for the financial sector [2022] OJ L 333/1 . . . . 293, 293n.497, 354

Regulation (EU) 2023/1114 of 31 May 2023 on Markets in

Crypto-assets (MiCAR) [2023]
  OJ L 150/40 .... 32n.210, 35n.236,
    106, 106n.214, 151–52, 151n.144,
    164, 209, 212, 217–18, 252–54,
    252n.232, 254n.253, 273, 293,
    306, 330, 330n.153, 333,
    333n.175, 349, 352
  recital 6b 152n.147, 217n.553
  recital 6c.............212n.515, 217n.553
  recital 10.................. 252–53n.236
  recital 12a....................306n.572
  Art 3(1)(3)....................253n.237
  Art 3(1)(4)....................253n.242
  Art 32........................253n.239
  Art 33........................253n.240
  Art 34........................253n.241
  Art 39........................255n.259
  Art 39(1) 254n.253
  Art 41(1) 254n.254
  Art 41(3) 254n.255
  Art 43(1)(a)...................253n.244
  Art 44(2) 253n.245
  Art 44(3) 253n.246
  Art 44(4) 254n.247
  Art 44(5) 254n.248
  Art 50........................255n.260
  Art 52........................255n.257
  Art 68........................349n.244
Regulation (EU) on harmonised
  rules on fair access to and use of
  data (Data Act) [2023]
  Art 36......................... 109–10

Directives

Council Directive 85/374/EEC of
  25 July 1985 on the
  approximation of the laws,
  regulations and administrative
  provisions of the member
  states concerning liability for
  defective products [1985]
  OJ L 210/29 ....206n.480
Directive 2003/71/EC of 4 November
  2003 on the prospectus to be
  published when securities are
  offered to the public or admitted
  to trading (Prospectus Directive)
  [2003] OJ L 345/64...... 149, 149n.125
Directive 2004/39/EC of 21 April
  2004 on markets in financial
  instruments (MiFID)
  [2004] OJ L 145/1 ...... 48–49, 49n.335
Directive 2005/29/EC of 11 May 2005
  concerning unfair business-to-
  customer commercial practices in
  the internal market [2005]
  OJ L 149/22 ....150n.129
  recital 10................. 150, 150n.130
  art 2(c) 150n.131
Directive 2009/110/EC of 16
  September 2009 on the taking
  up, pursuit and prudential
  supervision of the business of
  electronic money institutions
  [2009] OJ L 267/7
  Art 2.........................237n.104
Directive 2011/61/EU of 8 June 2011
  on Alternative Investment Fund
  Managers (AIFMD) [2011] OJ L
  174/1 .... 47, 48–49, 48n.331, 124,
    149, 223, 223n.15,
    282, 327, 351
  Art 4(af)......................327n.134
  Art 21........................327n.135
Directive 2014/65/EU of 15 May
  2014 on markets in financial
  instruments (MiFID II) [2014]
  OJ L 173/349 .... 48–49, 49n.334,
    49n.336, 149, 217–18,
    251, 251n.229
  Art 4(1)(44)...................149n.127
  Annex I, Section C 149n.128,
    150–51, 251–52
Directive (EU) 2015/849 of 20 May
  2015 on the prevention of the use
  of the financial system for the
  purposes of money laundering or
  terrorist financing (Fourth Anti-
  Money Laundering Directive)
  [2015] OJ L 141/73 ...... 149, 149n.126
Directive (EU) 828/2017 of 17 May
  2017 amending Directive
  2007/36/EC as regards the
  encouragement of long-term
  shareholder engagement
  (Shareholders' Rights Directive
  II) [2017] OJ L 132/1 ....195n.405
  Art 3a(1) 195n.405
  Art 3a(2) 195n.405
  Art 3a(3) 195n.405

Directive (EU) 2018/843 of 30 May
2018 on the prevention of the use
of the financial system for the
purposes of money laundering or
terrorist financing [2018]
OJ L 156/43 . . . . .330n.154
Directive (EU) 2018/1972 of 11
December 2018 establishing
the European Electronic
Communications Code (Recast)
[2018] OJ L 321/36 . . . . 205–6, 205n.473
Art 63(2)(c) 206n.474

Resolutions

European Parliament, Resolution
2017/2772(RSP) of 3 October
2018 on distributed ledger
technologies and blockchains:
building trust
with disintermediation
[2018] OJ C 11/7
   Para 37 . . . . .108n.228
   Para 38 . . . . .106n.216
   Para 68 . . . . .106n.210

Recommendations

Commission Recommendation of
22 March 2010 on the scope and
effects of legal tender of euro
banknotes and coins [2010] OJ L
83/70 . . . . 275–76, 275n.398

NATIONAL LEGISLATION

China

People's Bank of China Law 303
Proposed People's Bank of China Law . . . 303
   Art 19 303
   Art 22 303–4

France

Décret d'application n° 2018–1226 du
24 décembre 2018 . . . . 271, 271n.370
Loi n° 2016-1691 du 9 décembre
2016 relative à la transparence,
à la lutte contre la corruption
et à la modernisation de la vie
économique. 183n.322
Art 120 . . . . .183n.323

Monetary and Financial Code 1999
(Code monétaire et financier)
   Art L. 54-10-1 2° 273
   Art L. 211-3 271
   Art L. 211-7 .271n.371
Ordonnance n° 2017-1674 du
8 décembre 2017 relative à
l'utilisation d'un dispositif
d'enregistrement électronique
partagé pour la représentation
et la transmission de titres
financiers 183n.324, 271, 271n.369

Germany

Act Implementing the Amending
Directive on the Fifth EU Anti-
Money Laundering Directive 330
Banking Act (Kreditwesengesetz –
KWG) 209n.494, 217–18, 330
   § 1(11)(11) .217n.555
Capital Investment Act
(Vermögensanlagengetz) 217–18
   Pt 1, Subsection 1, § 6 . . . . .218n.557
   Pt 1, § 1(2) 218n.556

Italy

Law No 12/2019
(12 February 2019) 113n.267
   Art 8-ter 113n.267
   Art 8-ter(2) .113n.268
Legislative Decree No 179/2012
(Decreto-Legge 18 ottobre
2012, n. 179)
   Art 16(4) 86n.62

Liechtenstein

Token and Trustworthy Technology
Service Providers Act (Law of
3 October 2019) 183, 210, 331–32
   Art 2(c) 210n.500,
                                      331n.166

Malta

Digital Innovation Authority
Act 2018 Ch 591 . . . . .114n.275
Innovative Technology Agreements
and Services Act 114
Virtual Financial Assets Act 2018 32–114
   Art 2(2) 114n.272

Switzerland

Anti-Money Laundering Act
  1997 (AMLA) (Bundesgesetz
  über die Bekämpfung der
  Geldwäscherei und der
  Terrorismusfinanzierung).... 154n.163,
          155, 160–61
  Art 2(2)(A)(3)................155n.169
  Art 2(3) 155n.169
Banking Act 1934 (Bundesgesetz über
  die Banken und Sparkassen) ...154n.163,
          155, 160–61
  Art 242a....................... 209
Botschaft zum Bundesgesetz zur
  Anpassung des Bundesrechts
  an Entwicklungen der Technik
  verteilter elektronischer Register
  vom 27 November 2019, BBl
  2020 233......... 185n.341, 186n.345,
          209n.492
Code of Obligations (CO) 1912
  (Obligationenrecht).........81–82, 111,
          112–13, 154n.163, 158–59,
          185n.342, 186
  Art 197....................... 111–12
  Art 369....................... 111–12
  Art 481......................256n.266
  Art 965......................153n.156
  Art 973c.........153n.157, 153–54n.160,
          185, 186
  Art 973c(3) 184n.329, 185n.342
  Art 973d..........153–54n.160, 185–86
Collective Investment Schemes
  Act 2006........ 155, 155n.168, 160–61
Federal Act on Debt Enforcement and
  Bankruptcy 1889 (Bundesgesetz
  über Schuldbetreibung und
  Konkurs)...................154n.163
Federal Act on Financial Services
  (FinSA) 2018
  Art 3(b) 153–54n.160, 186
Federal Act on Private International
  Law 1989 (Bundesgesetz über das
  Internationale Privatrecht) 154n.163
Federal Act on the Adaptation of
  Federal Law to Developments in
  Distributed Ledger Technology
  (DLT Law) 2020 (Bundesgesetz
  zur Anpassung des Bundesrechts
  an Entwicklungen der Technik
  verteilter elektronischer
  Register) 32n.209, 153–54n.160,
          154, 154nn.162–63, 176, 179,
          185, 185n.342, 186, 209, 348
Federal Act on the Swiss National
  Bank 2003 (Bundesgesetz über
  die Schweizerische
  Nationalbank)...............154n.163
  Section 3 ....228n.44
Federal Act on Debt Enforcement and
  Bankruptcy 1889 209
Federal Intermediated Securities Act
  (FISA) 2008 (Bundesgesetz über
  Bucheffekten) 154n.163, 186
  Art 3......................153n.159
  Art 4(2)(g)..................186n.347
Federal Law to Adapt Federal Law to
  Developments in Distributed
  Electronic Register Technology
  2019 (Bundesgesetz Entwurf zur
  Anpassung des Bundesrechts
  an Entwicklungen der Technik
  verteilter elektronischer
  Register) 179n.298, 185n.339
Financial Institutions Act 2018
  (Bundesgesetz über die
  Finanzinstitute) 154n.163
Financial Market Infrastructure Act
  (FMIA) 2015 (Bundesgesetz über
  die Finanzmarktinfrastrukturen
  und das Marktverhalten im
  Effekten- und
  Derivatehandel) 153–54, 154n.163,
          163, 186, 256, 256n.269, 283
  Art 2(b) 153–54n.160, 186
  Art 2(bbis)... 153–54n.160, 186, 186n.346
  Art 2(c)......................153n.158
  Art 73a...................... 176, 348
  Art 73c(1) 176n.282, 348n.242
Financial Market Infrastructure
  Ordinance 186
  Art 2(1) 153–54n.160
Financial Services Act
  (FinSA) 2018...............154n.163

United Kingdom

Electronic Money Regulations
  2011 .... 218, 218n.560

Financial Services and Markets Act
  2000 (Regulated Activities)
  Order 2001 218
  Pt III 218n.559
Money Laundering, Terrorist
  Financing and Transfer of Funds
  (Information on the Payer)
  Regulations 2017 ....218, 218n.562

United States of America
Arizona Revised Statutes 2022
  t 44 c 26 § 7003 ....102n.169
  t 44 c 26 § 7061 .... 102nn.169–70
Arizona State HR Bill 2603,
  Corporations; blockchain
  technology (3 April 2018) 187n.352
Bank Holding Company Act 1956
  Art 13 .... 288, 288n.468
  para 2 ....39n.263, 232n.74
Banking Act (Glass-Steagall Act)
  1933 ....48, 48n.327, 77n.9, 288
Blockchain Regulatory Certainty Act,
  U.S. HR Bill (23 March 2023) ... 148–49
California State Senate Bill 838
  (2017–2018), Corporate
  records: articles of incorporation:
  blockchain technology
  (28 September 2018) 187n.354
Colorado Securities Act 1961 ......187n.356
Colorado State Digital Token
  Act 2019....................187n.356
Commodity Exchange Act (CEA)
  1936 .... 140–41, 250–51, 251n.227
  § 1a(9) 141n.70, 141n.77, 250.221
  § 1a(47)(A) 251n.227
  § 4c(b) 140–41, 141n.72
  § 5h(a)(1)............. 140–41, 141n.73
  § 13-1 ....141n.77
Delaware General Corporation
  Law 1899
  §151 186–87
  §202 186–87
  §218 186–87
  §224 186–87
  §232 186–87
  §364 186–87
Delaware State Senate Bill 69 (2017–
  2018), An Act to Amend Title 8 of
  the Delaware Code Relating to the

General Corporation Law
  (21 July 2017) 186–87, 186n.350
Digital Commodity Exchange Act
  (DCEA), U.S. HR Bill 7614
  (28 April 2022) 148–49, 349
  Art 52(A) 149n.123
  Art 52(B) 149n.123
Dodd–Frank Wall Street Reform
  and Consumer Protection
  Act 2010....... 47, 47n.320, 48, 49, 223,
              223n.14, 228, 351
  § 111..........................49n.338
  § 118..........................49n.338
Electronic Signature in Global and
  National Commerce Act (E-sign
  Act) 2000 ...... 99, 99n.148, 100–1, 126
Executive Order on Ensuring
  Responsible Development of
  Digital Assets (President Biden)
  (9 March 2022) 147, 147n.114,
              217, 267–68
  Section 1 ....147n.115
  Section 2 ....147n.115
  Section 3 ....147n.116
Federal Reserve Act 1913........... 229–31
Gramm-Leach-Bliley Act 1999...... 48, 288
Illinois General Assembly, House
  Joint Resolution No 25 (12
  December 2017)...... 103–4, 104n.191
Investment Advisers
  Act 1940............... 299, 329n.147
  Rule 15c3-3 329
  Rule 206-4 329
  Rule 206(4)-2(c)(1) 328n.137
  Rule 206(4)-2(c)(3) 329n.142
Investment Company Act 1940...... 346–47
Maryland State Senate Bill 136,
  Corporations – Corporate
  Records and Electronic
  Transmission
  (30 April 2019) 187n.357
Massachusetts State Senate Bill 200,
  An Act relative to blockchain and
  cryptocurrencies (2019-2020)
  (9 January 2019) 187n.360
Montana State HR Bill 584,
  Generally revises laws
  relating to cryptocurrency
  (9 May 2019) 187n.359

National Banking Act 1863 229–30
Nevada State Senate Bill 163, Revises
 provisions relating to technology
 used by certain business entities
 (14 February 2019)...........187n.358
New York State Assembly Bill 8780,
 Allowing Signatures Secured
 Through Blockchain Technology
 to be Considered an Electronic
 Signature (2017–2018)... 103, 103n.180
 § 1, subdiv 6...................103n.181
 § 1, subdiv 7...................103n.182
New York State Assembly Bill 8783,
 Establishing a Task Force to Study
 and Report on The Potential
 Implementation of Blockchain
 Technology in State Record
 Keeping, Information Storage,
 and Service Delivery
 (2017–2018) 103nn.184–85
New York State Assembly Bill 8792,
 Study of the Use of Blockchain
 Technology in Elections
 (2017–2018) 103n.183
North Dakota Century Code 1960
 § 9-6-19 ....105n.200
Private Fund Investment Advisers
 Registration Act (PFIARA) 2010 ... 351
Restatement (Second) of the Law of
 Contracts 1981 ..... 94, 95–96, 105, 117
 § 1............................94n.113
 § 24...........................96n.126
Sarbanes–Oxley Act 2002 .... 46, 46n.313
Securities Act 1933........142n.80, 145–46,
 147–48
 s 2(a)(1) 141–42, 142n.80, 192, 249
 s 8A.......................... 143–44
 Reg A+........................ 138
 Reg D 138
 Reg S........................... 138
Securities Clarity Act, U.S. HR Bill
 (22 May 2023)................ 148–49
Securities Exchange Act 1934 148
 s 3(a)(1) 142n.80, 144
 s 3(a)(10) 144, 163n.209, 250
 Rule 3b-16................144, 144n.96
 Rule 3b-16(b) 144
 Rule 10b-5 ....159n.186
South Carolina State HR Bill 4351
 (2019–2020), SC Blockchain
 Industry Empowerment Act
 (28 March 2019).............187n.353
Statutes of Nevada 2017
 ch 391 s 1 ....102n.173
 ch 391 s 2 ....102n.174
 ch 391 s 4 ....102n.175
Tax Code 1986....................... 13
Texas State HR Bill 3608 (2019-2020),
 Relating to business entities
 (1 September 2019) 187n.355
Token Taxonomy Act, U.S. HR Bill
 1628 (8 March 2021)...147–49, 147n.117
Uniform Commercial Code
 (UCC) 1952............ 80–81, 83n.33,
 94, 95–96, 95n.122, 99n.148,
 101, 103, 105, 114–15, 118,
 119, 120, 122, 359
 § 1-201(b)(3)...................95n.123
 § 1-201(b)(12).................95n.122
 § 1-303 ....95n.123
 Art 2..... 81, 95–96, 96n.126, 99, 99n.148,
 117, 119, 119n.294
 § 2................................ 98
 § 2-204.................... 96, 101, 119
 § 2-204(1) 96n.129, 119n.296
 § 2-205........................... 96
 § 2-206....................... 96, 101
 § 2-206(1) 96n.130
 § 2-207....................... 97–98
 § 2-B........................... 101
 Art 2A 99, 99n.148
Uniform Computer Information
 Transactions Act (UCITA)
 1999 .... 101, 107
 §203(4)......................101n.166
 § 206.........................101n.166
Uniform Electronic Transactions
 Act (UETA) 1999 ...... 85–86, 99–101,
 99n.148, 100n.150, 107
 § 2(8) 86n.63, 101n.161
 § 5(b) 100nn.158–59
 § 12.........................100n.159
Uniform Regulation of Virtual-
 Currency Businesses Act
 (URVCBA) 2018........ 122, 122n.307
 § 103 cmt 1....................122n.308
Uniform Securities Act 2002........142n.80
 § 102(28) 142n.80
Vermont Statutes Annotated 2017
 t 12, ch 81 § 1913............ 102–3n.179

Volcker Rule (12 USC § 1851 (2010); 12 CFR § 248.1 et seq) ... 288, 288n.469, 351, 352
Wyoming Money Transmitter Act–virtual currency exemption, Wyoming State HR Bill 19 (7 March 2018).....187n.361
Wyoming Uniform Securities Act 2016....................187n.361
Wyoming State HR Bill 70, Commercial filing system (26 February 2019)...........105n.199
Wyoming State HR Bill 70, Open blockchain tokens-exemptions (12 March 2018)............187n.361
Wyoming State HR Bill 101, Electronic corporate records (12 March 2018)............187n.361

List of Abbreviations

ABCP	asset-backed commercial paper
ABS	asset-backed securities
ALI	American Law Institute
ATS	Alternative Trading System
BIS	Bank of International Settlements
CAS	complex adaptive system
CASPs	crypto-asset service providers
CBDCs	central bank digital currencies
CDO	collateralized debt obligation
CER	controllable electronic record
CFTC	Commodity Futures Trading Commission
CISG	United Nations Convention on Contracts for the International Sale of Goods
CRAs	credit rating agencies
CSD	Central Securities Depositors
CSRC	China Securities Regulatory Commission
DAO	distributed autonomous organization
DCEA	Digital Commodity Exchange Act
DLT	distributed ledger technology
EMIR	European Market Infrastructure Regulation
EMRs	Electronic Money Regulations
ESCB	European System of Central Banks
ESG	environmental social governance
ESIGN	Electronic Signature in Global and National Commerce Act
ESMA	European Securities and Market Authority
ESRB	European Systemic Risk Board
ETF	exchange-traded funds
ETN	exchange-traded notes
FATF	Financial Action Task Force
FCA	Financial Conduct Authority
FINMA	Swiss Financial Market Supervisory Authority
FISA	Federal Intermediated Securities Act
FSOC	Financial Stability Oversight Committee
HFT	high-frequency trading
ICO	initial coin offering
IEOs	initial exchange offerings
IGO	initial game offering
IMF	International Monetary Fund
IOSCO	International Organization of Securities Commissions
IoT	Internet of Things

ITASA	Innovative Technology Arrangements and Services Act
LSEG	London Stock Exchange Group Plc
MBS	mortgage-backed securities
MDIA	Malta Digital Innovation Authority
MiFID	Market in Financial Instruments Directive
MiFIR	Market in Financial Instruments Regulation
MLRs	Money Laundering Regulations
MMF	money market fund
NCBs	national central banks
NCCUSL	National Conference of Commissioners on Uniform State Laws
NFT	non-fungible token
NME	new monetary economics
PECL	Principles of European Contract Law
POS	proof-of-stake
POW	proof-of-work
RAO	Regulated Activities Order
SBF	Swiss Blockchain Federation
SCA	Securities Clarity Act
SDGs	Sustainable Development Goals
SDR	special drawing rights
SEC	Securities and Exchange Commission
SIFIs	systemically important financial institutions
SPEs	special purpose entities
SPV	special purpose vehicle
SSE	Shanghai Stock Exchange
SSR	Short Selling Regulation
STOs	Security Token Offerings
TBTF	too big to fail
TCM	token container model
UCC	Uniform Commercial Code
UCITA	Uniform Computer Information Transaction Act
UETA	Uniform Electronic Transaction Act
VFA	Maltese Virtual Financial Assets Act

1
The Underlying Complexities within the Line of Disruption

Introduction

A. An Oxymoron—One More

'The line of disruption' is an oxymoron based on the association between two implicitly opposite concepts: a line refers to a continuous succession of points, whereas 'disruption', a synonym for interruption, echoes the idea of a breaking point.[1]

The title of this first chapter adds another oxymoron. Here, this figure of speech is employed by associating the concept of 'complexity' with (again) the 'line'. The concept of a line is a rather minimalistic and intuitive one. On the contrary, the word 'complexity' is defined by the Oxford English Dictionary as '[t]he quality or condition of being complex'; it refers to the plural 'complexities' as 'an instance of complexity; a complication'.[2] The Oxford Learners Dictionary defines complexity by adding a few more elements, referring to complexity as 'the state of being formed of many parts; the state of being difficult to understand' and complexities as 'the features of a problem or situation that are difficult to understand'.[3]

Indeed, this second oxymoron emphasizes how rich and dense are the underlying theoretical, factual, and conceptual dimensions that support the apparently minimalistic mono-dimensionality underlying the line of disruption. More precisely, the line of disruption condenses in its minimalism significant evolutionary tensions and dynamics, which this chapter will make clearer and this book will fully develop.

After all, a line is not necessarily a straight line. As a fine Italian writer said in describing Italy, 'the shortest line between two points is the arabesque. We live in a network of arabesques'.[4] This image intuitively explains how the words 'complex' and 'line' are not necessarily in antithesis.

---

[1] See the Preface.
[2] See Oxford Dictionary, 'Complexity, n' (*OED Online*, OUP 2023) <https://www.oed.com/view/Entry/37689?rskey=cjcVW3&result=1&isAdvanced=false#eid> accessed 1 May 2023.
[3] See Oxford Learner's Dictionary, 'Complexity, n' (*OLD Online*, OUP 2023) <https://www.oxfordlearnersdictionaries.com/definition/english/complexity> accessed 4 April 2022.
[4] Ennio Flaiano, *La solitudine del satiro* (Rizzoli 1973).

B. Emergence Economies and Network Growth Economies

In the past decades significant changes have reshaped modern society, shifting towards a complex global system, with enhanced interactions among countries and continents.[5] Such a complex global system is the result of specific trends and forces, which include globalization, the mobility of capital and technological advancements, migration flows, and enhanced interactions based on infrastructures (shipping lanes, electricity grids, and computer networks).[6] Consistent with these broad societal transformations, the modern economy clearly followed a similar path[7] and moved toward a new paradigm, the 'network growth economy'.

Network growth economies are the result of what is identified with 'emergence economics', a broader category referring to how individual agents act through interconnected networks. By operating in significant networks, individuals are engaged in the evolutionary market processes of differentiating, selecting, and amplifying certain business plans and technologies, which in turn generate a host of emergent economic phenomena.[8] Because of their characteristics, the paradigm of 'emergence economics' (as well as network growth economies) should be characterized more as a complex system where change, evolution, and disequilibrium are essential elements. After all, this applies more broadly to human society, of which economy is only a specific manifestation.[9]

Within the label 'network growth economy', the words 'network' and 'growth' refer to two key structural characteristics of this paradigm and differentiate it from older economic structures. First, a network economy emerges following a bottom-up path of development that is free and unpredictable as a result of the numerous interactions between people in a highly connected marketplace, as networks are.[10] Second, in connection with the freedom and unpredictability characterizing the development of this system, today's growth economy relies on innovation as a central mechanism for generating value.[11] In recent years it has been possible to observe a gradual increase in the pace of development of innovation; it is nowadays exponential, clearly contributing to unpredictable systemic transformations.

Addressing the unpredictability of such systemic transformation is also essential to highlight another key characteristic of contemporary 'network growth economy' paradigms when confronting them with other paradigms. While more traditional economic paradigms rely on static and linear forms of growth moving towards

---

[5] See generally Miguel A. Centeno, Manish Nag, Thayer S. Patterson, Andrew Shaver, and A. Jason Windawi, 'The Emergence of Global Systematic Risk' (2015) 41 AnnRS 65.
[6] Ibid.
[7] See Ethiopis Tafara, 'Foreword: Observations about the Crisis and Reform' in Eilis Ferran, Niamh Maloney, Jennifer G. Hill, and John C. Coffee, Jr (eds), *The Regulatory Aftermath of the Global Financial Crisis* (CUP 2012) xi–xii.
[8] Richard S. Whitt and Stephen J. Schultze, 'The New "Emergence Economics" of Innovation and Growth, and What It Means for Communications Policy' (2009) 7 JTHTL 217, 22 (hereafter Whitt and Schultze, 'The New "Emergence Economics" of Innovation').
[9] Ibid, 226–227.
[10] Ibid, 221.
[11] Ibid, 221.

equilibrium, network growth economies are self-reinforcing, with the potential to multiply their effects in unexpected ways. Technological innovation contributes to future innovations and triggers network effects, with new users capable of bringing benefit to the rest of the network.[12]

C. The Need for a New Theoretical Framework to Understand the New Economic and Societal Transformations

In this new societal and economic environment, sciences, theories, and methodologies focusing on networks, stability, and dynamism to interpret the processes related to complex systems have gained traction. Among them, complexity science, network theory, and chaos theory have become increasingly important tools for understanding unprecedented changes affecting society at different levels, including public administration, policy, and governance.[13] Such theories originated from physics, mathematics, and informatics and were gradually applied to social sciences.

This gradual application to social sciences, starting from sociology and economics and more recently extending to law, exemplifies their inherent versatility. Because of this important characteristic, their approach may be a useful tool for developing a better comprehension of radical systemic transformations, which are essentially cross-sectorial and multidimensional. This is the case for the transformations induced by technology in economy and finance, as will be explained in the course of this book. Furthermore, such theories may also provide a valid theoretical background for identifying possible solutions to make new (or evolving) systems more resilient. Not surprisingly, these theories have gradually entered the lexicon of social scientists (and specifically of legal scholars and policy-makers). They have greatly contributed to spreading the use of the underlying concepts and key words beyond pure academic, policy, and research circles, and to their penetration of popular media and mainstream academic writing.[14]

D. The Word 'Complexity' and Its Multiple Uses and Contexts

As part of this trend, economy, finance, and modern financial markets were increasingly and recurrently described as complex[15] and dynamic.[16] The word 'complexity'

---

[12] Ibid, 221.
[13] See generally Göktuğ Morçöl and Aaron Wachhaus, 'Network and Complexity Theories: A Comparison and Prospects for a Synthesis' (2009) 31 ATP 44 (hereafter Morçöl and Wachhaus, 'Network and Complexity').
[14] Lawrence G. Baxter, 'Adaptive Regulation in the Amoral Bazaar' (2011) 128 SALJ 253, 260 (hereafter Baxter, 'Adaptive Regulation').
[15] See generally Dan Awrey, 'Complexity, Innovation and the Regulation of Modern Financial Markets' (2012) 2 HarvBusLRev 235 (hereafter Awrey, 'Regulation of Modern Financial Markets'). See also Kathryn Judge, 'Fragmentation Nodes: A Study in Financial Innovation, Complexity, and Systemic Risk' (2012) 64 StanLRev 657 (hereafter Judge, 'Fragmentation Nodes'). See also Steven L. Schwarcz, 'Regulating Complexity in Financial Markets' (2009) 87 WUnLRev 21 (hereafter Schwarcz, 'Regulating Complexity').
[16] See generally Dan Awrey and Kathryn Judge, 'Why Financial Regulation Keeps Falling Short' (2020) 61 BCLRev 2295 (hereafter Awrey and Judge, 'Financial Regulation Keeps Falling Short').

was increasingly associated with broad and general concepts related to finance and economics, and more recently to Fintech (a term referring to any technological application to deliver financial solutions)[17] and disruptive technologies.[18] This trend became especially evident in the aftermath of the financial crisis of 2008. After this event, regulators as well as legal and financial scholars focused their policy and academic analyses on the causes of the financial crisis. In this context, the growing complexity of the international financial system greatly contributed to increasing systemic risk[19] on a cross-border level and ultimately led to the financial crisis of 2008.[20]

A key question is the meaning of 'complexity'. From a scientific perspective, this term precisely refers to the concepts elaborated in the area of 'complexity of adaptive systems', which has emerged as an independent science, commonly referred to as complexity science. As will be explained in greater depth in this chapter, the focus of complexity science is the understanding of complex adaptive systems. Complex adaptive systems rely on different subparts that are in constant interaction, and the result of these interactions is the creation of changes and evolution as well as other more specific dynamics within the network. In the context of 'complexity science', concepts that were gradually applied to finance, such as contagion, feedback, and resilience,[21] are key conceptual pillars with a very precise meaning.

As this chapter will show, a closer analysis of academic and policy work in the area of financial regulation suggests that both scholars and policy-makers did not necessarily or explicitly refer to complexity science when describing the system as 'complex'. More precisely, notwithstanding the rigorous lexicon underlying complexity as a science, they often employed the word complexity *tout court* as a synonym for 'complicatedness' or 'complicated' to refer more generally to one of the key features of financial regulation, or financial markets, or their risks (in particular systemic risks), without necessarily offering a real theoretical foundation for the term.

The word 'complexity' was employed to refer to a broad range of institutions, instruments, and situations, with different degrees of specificity—for example, referring to market structures and specific financial instruments. As a consequence, complexity as applied to heterogeneous fields (in particular financial law) was often extremely far from the way in which scientists referred to it and almost never related to complexity science. Indeed, the vast majority of scholars (both legal and financial) have not dealt with a definition of complexity, and, not surprisingly, legal and financial formalizations of complexity as a concept are difficult to find.

Therefore, when dealing with complexity in capital markets and finance, it is crucial to distinguish two different meanings. A first one—as a synonymous for complicatedness—identifies a key structural characteristic of financial markets, where technology and innovation are drivers enhancing it. A second one indirectly

---

[17] For an analysis of Fintech, see Section IV.C.i.
[18] For an analysis of disruptive technologies, see Section III.B.
[19] See generally Judge, 'Fragmentation Nodes' (n 15). See also Hal S. Scott, 'The Reduction of Systemic Risk in the United States Financial System' (2010) 33 HarvJL&PubPol'y 671, 673.
[20] See Schwarcz, 'Regulating Complexity' (n 15) 212–213.
[21] See Stefano Battiston, Doyne J. Farmer, Andreas Flache, Diego Garlaschelli, Andrew G. Haldane, Hans Heesterbeek, Cars Hommes, Carlo Jaeger, Robert May, and Marten Scheffer, 'Complexity Theory and Financial Regulation' (2016) 351 Science 818, 818 (hereafter Battiston et al., 'Complexity Theory').

refers to the characterization of the whole financial system as a complex adaptive system, with specific dynamics and interactions emerging within its network. The two approaches are not necessarily mutually exclusive, but the underlying theoretical frameworks as well as the utilization of similar (or even the same) words may be slightly different.

In order to fully understand complexity not only as a structural (static) attribute but most of all for its dynamic implications, considering the relevance of complexity as a science is an essential step. Only an appropriate consideration of 'complex adaptive systems' and how their dynamism and change affect large networks offers the opportunity to better characterize the real meaning of complexity within capital markets beyond the pure static structural attribute. Furthermore, it offers unprecedented and underdeveloped opportunities for appropriately regulating capital markets, focusing on new forms of dynamic regulation as opposed to traditional immutable *ex post* regulations.

Capital markets are currently exposed to the exponential growth of disruptive technologies, in particular blockchain, artificial intelligence, and big data. Disruptive technologies strongly differ from sustaining technologies. According to Christensen, sustaining technologies contribute to improve product performances; therefore, established market actors can cope with them. On the contrary, disruptive technologies lead to significant changes, posing a threat for such established actors.[22] Disruptive technologies represent a major source of complexity themselves, in addition to the traditional financial innovation that was constantly developed in the context of financial markets. Understanding the traditional and new sources of complexity characterizing modern capital markets is an essential aspect of this chapter.

The concept of disruptive technology underlies the idea of innovation, which is connected to the two key features of financial markets, their dynamic complexity and structural complexity. Innovation contributes to both dynamism and structural complexity, and it is strongly related to the way financial markets and society develop and evolve. Throughout history, innovation has affected the way economic and financial cycles developed, making possible the creation of new markets, activities, and products. For this reason, although complexity and innovation are two different notions, dealing with complexity necessarily means dealing with innovation.

As will be explained further in the course of this chapter, and more extensively in the rest of the book, complexity in financial markets can be identified by the multidimensionality of the changes that have emerged in the past few years (as the idea of the line of disruption tries to emphasize). Such multidimensionality calls for embracing changes and dynamic interactions among fields of economy and of law, such as commercial practices (commercial law), financial markets (financial law), corporate governance (corporate law), central banks (central banking law), and, more generally, financial networks (and their regulation, touching upon shadow banking and systemic problems).

---

[22] See generally Clayton M. Christensen, *The Innovator's Dilemma: When New Technologies Cause Great Firms to Fail* (HBSP 2016) (hereafter Christensen, *The Innovator's Dilemma*).

E. The Structure of Chapter 1

This chapter focuses on identifying the meaning of complexity science and the characteristics of complex adaptive systems, and their relevance for this book. Complexity science might be an important tool for understanding the radical transformations happening in economy and finance. In proposing a complexity approach, this chapter considers the historic evolutions characterizing the past six decades of international finance, under the pressure of different forms of disruptive technologies, challenging market actors, and regulators. Because of the relevance of structured finance and its characteristic as a disruptive innovation,[23] the beginning of such transformations is identified as the emergence of the shadow banking system. The shadow banking system is a network of financial institutions and financial instruments contributing to the creation of credit, as well as maturity and liquidity transformation (all prerogatives of regulated credit institutions), without formally being authorized and regulated as a network of credit institutions. The financial crisis of 2008 led to specific regulatory and technological debates and developments, which this book especially emphasizes.

Furthermore, this chapter identifies the layers of complexity and highlights the multidimensionality of the evolving technological ecosystem as its key characteristic. Finally, it summarizes the two main components of the line of disruption. One static component is understanding how the existing regulatory paradigms fit with the new evolving framework, and one dynamic component emphasizes the way such multidimensionality is achieved, in the sense of understanding how one evolution triggers the following in another context.

I. Complexity as a Science: Complexity of Adaptive Systems or Complexity Science *Tout Court*

The concept of complexity has its roots in a methodological approach and an independent science—the science of complex adaptive systems, commonly known as 'complexity science'. Complexity science first emerged in physical sciences,[24] and scholars belonging to other fields gradually applied it to their own disciplines, in particular biological sciences (contributing to a revisiting of the Darwinist theory of evolution[25]), and in a second stage social sciences.[26]

---

[23] See Nathan Cortez, 'Regulating Disruptive Innovation' (2014) 29 BerkeleyTechLJ 175 (hereafter Cortez, 'Regulating Disruptive Innovation').

[24] See generally Brenda Zimmerman, Curt Lindberg, and Paul Plsek, 'A Complexity Science Primer: What Is Complexity Science and Why Should I Learn about It?' (*napcrg.org*, adapted from: Brenda Zimmerman, Curt Lindberg, and Paul Plsek, *Edgeware: Lessons from Complexity Science for Health Care Leaders*, VHA 1998) <https://www.napcrg.org/media/1278/beginner-complexity-science-module.pdf> accessed 2 April 2022 (hereafter Zimmerman et al., 'A Complexity Science Primer').

[25] See generally J. B. Ruhl, 'Fitness of Law: Using Complexity Theory to Describe the Evolution of Law and Society and Its Practical Meaning for Democracy' (1996) 49 VandLRev 1406.

[26] J. B. Ruhl, Daniel Martin Katz, and Michael J. Bommarito II, 'Harnessing Legal Complexity' (2017) 355 Science 1377, 1377 (hereafter Ruhl et al., 'Harnessing Legal Complexity').

The increased relevance of networks in international economy has favoured the application of complexity science to the economy[27] and finance,[28] and more recently to the context of legal research. Legal scholars have attempted to apply complexity to many branches of law, including administrative law[29] and environmental law,[30] law and economics,[31] financial law,[32] and financial regulation.[33]

The approach of complexity science strongly differs from that developed by traditional sciences, and it emphasizes specific aspects inherent to living systems that were generally neglected or understated in the context of traditional sciences.[34] Models in economics, management, and physics rely on the Newtonian scientific approach and principles. As Zimmerman and others suggest, the metaphor of the machine summarizes the entire conceptualization of Newtonian science.[35] Here different parts constitute the machine, and they respond to immutable external forces or rules, making the machines 'simple and predictable' and at the same time implying the exclusion of any form of self-determination.[36] This approach might not be optimal when dealing with living systems, where other dynamics emerge and such dynamics are essential for any system based on human behaviours.

In light of this, an important starting point is to understand how complexity science attempts to reframe the traditional Newtonian approach and how all of this could become relevant for the regulatory environment, especially in a situation of high dynamism and continuous evolution as in the case of international finance. The following subsections will clarify the key characteristics of complex adaptive systems, the scope of complexity science, and the impact of complexity on legal systems, which will be further analysed in the course of this chapter in relation to specific problems (as in the case of dynamic regulation).

A. What Are Complex Adaptive Systems?

Complexity science cannot be considered as a single theory, because it focuses on complex adaptive systems and on the way in which interactions and their self-determinations within such complex adaptive systems lead to change and dynamism. This explains not only the plurality of theories emerging within complexity science but also its inherent interdisciplinary nature related to the numerous fundamental questions that complex adaptive systems trigger.

---

[27] See generally Whitt and Schultze, 'The New "Emergence Economics" of Innovation' (n 8) 221.
[28] See Battiston et al., 'Complexity Theory' (n 21) 818.
[29] See generally Donald T. Hornstein, 'Complexity Theory, Adaptation, and Administrative Law' (2005) 54 DukeLJ 913.
[30] See generally Daniel A. Farber, 'Probabilities Behaving Badly: Complexity Theory and Environmental Uncertainty' (2003) 37 UCalDLRev 145 (hereafter Farber, 'Probabilities Behaving Badly').
[31] See Mark J. Roe, 'Chaos and Evolution in Law and Economics' (1995) 109 HarvLRev 64.
[32] See generally J. B. Ruhl, 'Managing Systemic Risk in Legal Systems' 89 IndLJ 559 (2014) (hereafter Ruhl, 'Managing Systemic Risk').
[33] See generally J. B. Ruhl, 'Financial Complexity: Regulating Regulation' (2016) 352 Science 301. See also Battiston et al., 'Complexity Theory' (n 21) 818.
[34] Zimmerman et al., 'A Complexity Science Primer' (n 24) 2.
[35] Ibid.
[36] Ibid.

Before diving into the analysis of complexity science, it is useful to more closely focus on the notion of 'complex adaptive systems'. Generally speaking, complex adaptive systems differ from highly adaptive complex systems, such as ecosystems, and non-adaptive complex systems, such as hurricanes.[37] The term 'complex adaptive system' identifies systems characterized by the presence of large networks where heterogeneous components interact on the basis of simple rules of operation without relying on central control.[38] These basic elements (large network, multiplicity of institutions and actors, and structural rules of operation) contribute to the emergence of 'complex collective behaviour, sophisticated information processing, and adaptation via learning or evolution'.[39]

The locution 'complex adaptive system' is an association of three different words and concepts. Starting with the word 'system', it refers to any object (abstract or concrete) studied in some fields and identifies 'a set of connected or interdependent' parts.[40] Examples of systems are almost infinite and comprise stock markets, human bodies, immune systems, termite colonies, and hospitals, and although systems strongly differ from one another they still share in common some patterns of behaviour, such as sustainability, viability, health, and innovation.[41] A system can be either complex or chaotic, simple or complicated,[42] and this leads to the analysis of the term 'complex'.

The adjective 'complex' is one of the possible attributes of a system, and it necessarily implies diversity, a concept referring to the multiplicity of connections among a broad range of elements.[43] A complex system differs from complicated systems, chaotic systems, and simple systems. Complex systems are highly composite, with large numbers of mutually interactive subunits 'whose repeated interactions result in rich, collective behaviours that feed back into the behaviour of the individual parts'.[44] On the contrary, complicated systems rely on numerous subunits with specific functional roles and responding to simple rules,[45] and simple systems are characterized by small numbers of subunits behaving in accordance with simple laws.[46] Chaotic systems can count only very few subunits, and their interaction could produce highly intricate dynamics.[47] Chaos generates 'complicated, aperiodic, seemingly random behaviour from the iteration of a simple rule',[48] where the concept of complicatedness differs from the concept of complexity, and such complicatedness is rather chaotic in mathematical terms: in the context of complex adaptive systems, simple interactions

---

[37] See J. B. Ruhl and Daniel Martin Katz, 'Measuring, Monitoring, and Managing Legal Complexity' (2011) 101 IowaLRev 191, 195 (hereafter Ruhl and Katz, 'Managing Legal Complexity'). See also J. B. Ruhl, 'Thinking of Environmental Law as a Complex Adaptive System: How to Clean Up the Environment by Making a Mess of Environmental Law' (1997) 34 HousLRev 933, 953–958.
[38] Melanie Mitchell, *Complexity: A Guided Tour* (OUP 2009) 12–13.
[39] Ibid.
[40] Zimmerman et al., 'A Complexity Science Primer' (n 24) 5.
[41] Ibid, 1.
[42] Dean Rickles, Penelope Hawe, and Alan Shiell, 'A Simple Guide to Chaos and Complexity' (2007) 61 JEp&CommHeal 93 (hereafter Rickles et al., 'Chaos and Complexity').
[43] Zimmerman et al., 'A Complexity Science Primer' (n 24) 5.
[44] Rickles et al., 'Chaos and Complexity' (n 42).
[45] Ibid.
[46] Ibid.
[47] Ibid.
[48] Ibid.

among subunits in the system generate collective dynamic behaviour, whereas chaotic systems are not necessarily complex, and vice versa.[49]

The second adjective, 'adaptive', refers to the fundamental property of complex systems to 'alter or change' and corresponds to the 'ability to learn from experience'.[50] Therefore, it is necessary to understand two further key characteristics of complex systems: their dynamism and their nonlinearity. First, dynamical systems are characterized by an evolution of their states and variables throughout time, following specific rules.[51] Dynamism is conceptually related to the reaction of 'adapting' to changes, and the subunits operating within the complex adaptive system do that through their interactions, also reflecting the two key elements of 'change and emergence'.[52] Second, nonlinear (dynamical) systems, as opposed to linear systems, are those systems that do not satisfy the superposition principle.[53] The superposition principle can be explained in the following terms: 'if A and B are both solutions for some system (ways in which the system could evolve), then so is their sum A + B—this implies that a linear system can be decomposed into its parts and each part solved separately to construct the full solution.'[54] The nonlinearity (and the superposition principle within it) clarifies the existence of a 'disproportionate relationship between variables' because a small change at the level of one variable may generate large (therefore disproportionate) changes at the level of the other variable.[55]

In light of these properties, it is now easier to understand that complex adaptive systems are inherently dynamic, and that dynamism is a distinctive feature of open systems, pursuing far-from-equilibrium conditions.[56] Nonlinearity and complexity are interrelated because nonlinearity coupled with dynamism explains how systems react to specific changes, leading either to disintegration or the pursuit of higher degrees of stability and order via self-organization. Self-organization assumes the nuance of distributed control in opposition to centralized control, and this contributes to reinforcing the capacity of the independent subparts populating the complex adaptive system to apprehend new strategies and moving towards new forms of adaptation.[57] In this context of decentralization, the continuous exchanges between the subparts preserve the coherence of the complex adaptive system.

The different subparts of the complex adaptive system are generally complex adaptive systems themselves. A tree is a living entity and at the same time is part of a forest, whereas both the tree and the forest might be complex adaptive systems.[58] As will be explained in the following sections, the construction of international finance responds to the same dynamics.[59] Such subparts are in continuous evolution and contribute

---

[49] Ibid.
[50] Zimmerman et al., 'A Complexity Science Primer' (n 24) 5.
[51] Ibid.
[52] Morçöl and Wachhaus, 'Network and Complexity' (n 13) 45.
[53] Rickles et al., 'Chaos and Complexity' (n 42).
[54] Ibid.
[55] Morçöl and Wachhaus, 'Network and Complexity' (n 13) 45, 49.
[56] See generally Ilya Prigogine and Isabelle Stengers, *Order Out of Chaos: Man's New Dialogue with Nature* (Verso 1984) (hereafter Prigogine and Stengers, *Order Out of Chaos*).
[57] See Zimmerman et al., 'A Complexity Science Primer' (n 24) 6.
[58] Ibid.
[59] See Section V.

to the evolution of the overall complex adaptive system, which is informed by diversity. In a complex adaptive system diversity contributes to strengthening the potential for future adaptations and to maintaining or even increasing the sustainability within such complex systems.[60]

An important trait in the way complex adaptive systems evolve is their 'history dependency'.[61] As Zimmerman et al. noted, although it may be trivial to realize that what came first affects the subsequent developments, traditional sciences as well as management theories tend to ignore this trait, and the foundational assumption in these fields is that systems pursue an equilibrium as a consequence of their 'equifinality' whereas, as noted earlier, complex adaptive systems pursue far-from-equilibriums.[62] Emphasizing the importance of the historical dimension helps to enhance the comprehension of complex adaptive systems and the trajectories of their future developments. This chapter will explicitly provide a historical contextualization of the transformations emerging in the financial system starting from the 1960s.

B. The Scope of Complexity Science

The terminological analysis of 'complexity adaptive systems' is essential for understanding the fundamental scope of complexity science. This science analyses the relevance of systems' effects, with a focus on the inter-agent connections and the system-wide effects emerging from such connections.[63] When applying complexity science to social systems, its approach is different from both small-number agent models (an example is bilateral game theory) and large-number models (which include rational law and economics models).[64] Indeed, the vast majority of social science models include 'either very few (typically two) or very many (often an infinity) agents to be tractable',[65] and these two models correspond to two extremes. However, both extremes still have in common the possibility of tracing the way agents interact. In fact, in a context where an agent interacts with few other agents, all agents' interactions and reactions can be directly traced. At the same time, in a situation characterized by

---

[60] See Zimmerman et al., 'A Complexity Science Primer' (n 24) 6.
[61] In the context of the evolutionary path of species, building on the distinction proposed by Eric Desjardins identifying two forms of historicity—dependence on initial conditions and path-dependency—Marc Ereshefsky notes: 'We can think of both of these notions as describing how events in the past affect a future event. According to the first notion of historicity, the probability of an out-come is largely a function of initial conditions. For example, the probability that Joe will die as a result of radiation exposure is largely a function of how much radiation he was exposed to at the Chernobyl nuclear power plant disaster. According to the second notion of historicity, path dependency, not only do initial conditions affect the probability of an outcome but so do events along the path, as well as the order of those events.' See Marc Ereshefsky, 'Species, Historicity, and Path Dependency' (2014) 81 PhilSci 714. See also Eric Desjardins, 'Historicity and Experimental Evolution' (2011) 26 Bio&Phil 339.
[62] See generally Prigogine and Stengers, *Order Out of Chaos* (n 56).
[63] See J. B. Ruhl and Daniel M. Katz, 'Harnessing the Complexity of Legal Systems for Governing Global Challenges' in Victor Valz (ed), *Global Challenges, Governance, and Complexity—Applications and Frontiers* (Elgar 2019) 149.
[64] See Ruhl and Katz, 'Managing Legal Complexity' (n 37) 202.
[65] John H. Miller and Scott E. Page, *Complex Adaptive Systems: An Introduction to Computational Models of Social Life* (PUP 2007) 221.

a significant multiplicity or an infinite number of agents, the possibility of identifying an average in the behaviour of the masses offers the opportunity to easily and indirectly trace agents' interactions and reactions.[66]

Traditional analytic tools fail in the space between these two extremes, or as explained by Ruhl and Katz: 'traditional models of inter-agent behaviour do not work well when there are too many interacting agents to fit neatly into bilateral models, but not enough agents to ignore idiosyncratic behaviour by averaging-out to an infinite-numbers "rational actor" model.'[67] In this situation, complexity science is a useful tool for 'building models for contexts in which agent heterogeneity and interrelatedness can and usually do influence outcomes'.[68]

Complexity theories also differ from network theories, although these two branches share some similarities and show a degree of complementarity in attempting to explain and clarify certain dynamics within networks of heterogeneous subparts. Both complexity and network theories have their roots in mathematics.[69] Furthermore, there are some commonalities when referring to the notions of networks and complex adaptive systems. Networks can be defined as 'stable and complex patterns of relationships among multiple interdependent and self-organizing elements'.[70] Therefore, networks and complex systems share in common the existence of multiple interdependent components and some degree of stability as a characteristic in the patterns of relationship in the two contexts. In addition, both networks and complex systems develop some forms of self-organization mechanisms in their pursuit of stability.[71] However, a key difference emerges when considering their approach and object: while network theories focus on the analysis of stability and structures, complexity theories tend to emphasize two further elements, change and emergence, to stress the importance of dynamism in this context.[72]

The 'dynamism' versus 'stability' dichotomy characterizing these two approaches echoes, and in a way replicates, a clear dichotomy traceable in philosophy and sociology. Critical thinkers such as Comte, Durkheim, and Weber developing structural functionalism researched the causes and facts underlying stable societies.[73] Interestingly, although structural functionalism is built on the concept of society as a complex system with multiple subparts operating together, it focuses exclusively on

---

[66] Ibid.
[67] See Ruhl and Katz, 'Managing Legal Complexity' (n 37) 202.
[68] Ibid.
[69] See generally Albert-László Barabasi, *Linked: The New Science of Networks* (Perseus 2002).
[70] Morçöl and Wachhaus, 'Network and Complexity' (n 13) 45.
[71] Ibid.
[72] Ibid. For an analysis of financial regulation adopting network theories, see Luca Enriques, Alessandro Romano, and Thom Wetzer, 'Network-Sensitive Financial Regulation' (2020) 45 JCorpL 351 (hereafter Enriques et al., 'Network-Sensitive Financial Regulation'). For an approach to corporate governance adopting network science, see Luca Enriques and Alessandro Romano, 'Institutional Investor Voting Behavior: A Network Theory Perspective' (2019) 1 UIllinoisLRev 223. For a first approach to disruptive technologies adopting a network science framework, see Anat Lior, 'The AI Accident Network: Artificial Intelligence Liability Meets Network Theory' (2020) 95 TulLRev 1103.
[73] See Raymond Boudon, 'Weber and Durkheim: Beyond the Differences a Common Important Paradigm?' (1995) 49 RIntlPh 22. See also Donald McIntosh, 'Max Weber as a Critical Theorist' (1983) 12 Th&Soc 69. See also Ralph Schroeder and Rich Ling, 'Durkheim and Weber on the Social Implications of New Information and Communication Technologies' (2014) 16 NM&S 789.

the stability among such subparts, without emphasizing at all the evolutionary dynamism, as complexity science does.

As opposed to structural functionalism, other scholars, such as historicists and evolutionists, considered the importance of understanding the changes happening within society. Karl Marx developed a framework for better understanding the dynamics related to social changes.[74] Historical materialism in particular emphasizes the centrality of the material reality for the theory of history, achieved through class struggle.[75] The roots of Marxist historicism develop from Hegel's theory of history, which was based on the spirit rather than on material reality,[76] and still identify some sort of dynamism within the society, although it is not as predominant as in Marx. Herbert Spencer applied Darwinism and evolutionism to society, in a view that highlights the similarities between the mechanics happening in nature and society.[77]

C. The Impact of Complexity on Legal Science

Different approaches to complexity science emerged in the legal scholarship, developing an analysis of the broad theoretical implications on the law and legal system. Other scholars have developed a framework for considering complexity in the context of more specific fields of law. Focusing here on the first approach, major theoretical problems are the characterization of legal systems as complex adaptive systems, the application of complexity theories to legal problems, and the need for a proper understanding of the laws of complexity.[78]

Part of the legal scholarship has tried to adapt complexity theories to legal systems, urging policy-makers to apply this theoretical framework to solve specific regulatory failures, such as the one leading to the financial crisis of 2008.[79] In doing this, legal scholars attempted to highlight or map the key legal concepts and to characterize legal systems as adaptive systems by identifying specific parallels between these two notions. Legal systems are interconnected and interactive networks, where a multiplicity of actors and institutions implement a broad range of activities, such as interpreting and enforcing laws, and do so by interacting with each other and relying on specific and highly interconnected instruments (including laws and regulations).[80]

From such an approach, those who characterized legal systems as adaptive systems have identified specific properties. First, the existence of feedback results from the way in which feedback is provided, generating flows as a response to issues. Second, legal systems, like any other adaptive system, rely on a mechanism of emergence, corresponding to unpredictable behaviour generated by the network. Finally, and

---

[74] Neil Smelser, *Karl Marx on Society and Social Change* (UCP 1973).
[75] See generally Karl Marx, *Capital* (1867).
[76] See generally Georg Wilhelm Friedrich Hegel, *The Phenomenology of Spirit* (Terry Pinkyard and Michael Baur eds, CUP 2018).
[77] See generally Robert G. Perrin, 'Herbert Spencer's Four Theories of Social Evolution' (1976) 81 AmJSoc 1339.
[78] Eric Kades, 'The Laws of Complexity and the Complexity of Laws: The Implications of Computational Complexity Theory for the Law' (1997) 49 RutgLRev 403.
[79] Ruhl et al., 'Harnessing Legal Complexity' (n 26) 1377.
[80] Ruhl and Katz, 'Managing Legal Complexity' (n 37) 203.

complementary to the second point, legal systems emerge as self-organized structures, dominated by spontaneous organization and relying on specific structural rules contributing to the stability of the system without a 'central controller' or plan, thereby revealing important traits of decentralization in their structures.

Beyond the categorization of legal systems as complex environments, Ruhl and Katz attempt to measure legal complexity. They take as an example the US Tax Code and the very common judgment referring to that Code as 'too complex'.[81] As they explain, this sentence underlies two different hypotheses. A first hypothesis is inherently descriptive and refers to the law as complex, requiring some definition of such legal complexity to be subsequently empirically testable.[82] A second hypothesis, the one referring to the adverb 'too' in the judgment 'too complex', is normative and requires an assessment of the optimal level of legal complexity, somehow measurable and comparable.[83] Ruhl and Katz point out the importance of defining legal complexity by adopting different angles and the importance of empirically testing such complexity by identifying attributes and variables relevant for complexity.

More generally, legal systems are tied to their regulatory targets through a process of 'perpetual coevolution', where coadaptive dynamics have contributed to increasing structures and sizes of many different regulations,[84] and such an increase in the size and structure of regulation has triggered consequential adaptations at the level of regulatory targets. Examples of this coadaptive dynamics are easily observable in the relationship between financial structures and regulation. Complexity at the level of regulation often translates into financial complexity, mostly determined by market participants' need to constantly cut the costs and complications that compliance with new regulations requires.[85] In the context of finance, a crucial development of this perpetual coevolution is the establishment of the shadow banking system, because of the predominant role (with other important factors) played by banking regulation coupled with significant deregulation in financial services.[86]

Until today, regulators and policy-makers did not use complexity science as a further tool to support the decision-making process, often because of the difficulties or rather a reluctance in characterizing legal systems as complex adaptive systems.[87] Beyond this ontological problem, the reserve shown towards complexity science is consistent with the difficulties of characterizing the integration of other methodologies and sciences when approaching the law.[88] Furthermore, the role of complexity for strengthening the policy process would lead to considering policy formation not as a static end result but rather as a continuous process[89] consistent with an approach

---

[81] See Ruhl and Katz, 'Managing Legal Complexity' (n 37) 193–194.
[82] Ibid.
[83] Ibid.
[84] Ruhl et al., 'Harnessing Legal Complexity' (n 26) 1377.
[85] Chester S. Spatt, 'Complexity of Regulation' (*Harvard Business Law Review Online*, 16 June 2012) <https://www.hblr.org/2012/06/complexity-of-regulation/> accessed 2 April 2022.
[86] See Section IV.A, when identifying regulation as one of the causes leading to the emergence of the shadow banking system.
[87] Ruhl et al., 'Harnessing Legal Complexity' (n 26) 1377.
[88] Similar difficulties can be observed when taking into account the introduction of a rigorous cost–benefit analysis before issuing specific regulations.
[89] Lawrence G. Baxter, 'Capture in Financial Regulation: Can We Channel It toward the Common Good' (2011) 21 CornellJL&PubPol'y 175, 188 (hereafter Baxter, 'Capture in Financial Regulation').

of adaptive management, which requires constant monitoring activities coupled with numerous interventions.[90] This is especially important when dealing with markets characterized by rapid changes, as in the case of information technology[91] and financial services.[92]

However, specific technological advancements might facilitate ways in which complexity science could enter into social sciences, notably in law. The exponential growth of data favours the creation of data sets in any discipline, including law. In this field, data sets could help to strengthen a quantitative historical analysis of the way legislative reforms have taken place and more precisely identify how they contributed to change legal systems and shape consequential evolutions at the level of regulated targets, such as the financial and technological industries.[93] In addition to data sets, predictive analytics applications[94] could contribute to accelerating potential complexity approaches to the law, especially on the side of private actors (such as market actors). They could focus on legislative amendments related to relevant statutory provisions or judicial decisions affecting the interpretation of specific rules (in both directions: either narrowing or broadening them), and could lead to specific adaptations anticipating such events.[95] In this sense, Ruhl has investigated the possibility that a complex adaptive system (CAS) predictive model could offer a contribution to understand the way legal systems and regulatory targets coevolve from the perspective of sharing systemic risk.[96]

Complexity science might also permeate legal systems via more indirect mechanisms as a consequence of a holistic multidisciplinary approach: social scientists could cooperate with academic economists, as well as pure complexity scientists, as part of a broader theoretical analysis where complexity theories provide a useful complement to current approaches and existing models.[97] This theoretical stage might lead to specific policy developments and methodologies, especially in financial regulation, to better understand the way the nodes within the financial network interact, and protect the system from financial and economic shocks. As Battiston and others have proposed, an 'ambitious option would be an online, financial-economic dashboard that integrates data, methods and indicators ... [to] monitor and stress-test the global socioeconomic and financial system in something close to real time, in a way similar to what is done with other complex systems such as weather systems or social networks'.[98]

---

[90] Farber, 'Probabilities Behaving Badly' (n 30) 148–149.
[91] Whitt and Schultze, 'The New "Emergence Economics" of Innovation' (n 8) 221.
[92] See Baxter, 'Adaptive Regulation' (n 14) 257–264.
[93] Ruhl et al., 'Harnessing Legal Complexity' (n 26) 1377.
[94] For an overview of predictive analytics, see Matthew Alan Waller and Stanley E. Fawcett, 'Data Science, Predictive Analytics, and Big Data: A Revolution that Will Transform Supply Chain Design and Management' (2013) 34 JBusLog 77 (hereafter Waller and Fawcett, 'Supply Chain Design and Management').
[95] Ibid.
[96] See Ruhl, 'Managing Systemic Risk' (n 32).
[97] See Battiston et al., 'Complexity Theory' (n 21) 819.
[98] Ibid.

II. Complexity in Capital Markets and Finance: A Structural (Static) Attribute of International Finance and the Basis for Alternative Views

A. General Remarks

As mentioned above, 'complexity' as a scientific approach and as an increasingly employed term spread in different disciplines and branches of the law. Among them, financial legal scholarship has more often used the word 'complexity'. The financial crisis of 2008 gave great impetus to studies focusing on 'financial complexity', and the analysis of financial complexity highlighted the possibility that it could have been one of the major causes of the crisis and more generally a threat to the financial system.[99] Furthermore, the thesis that previous financial regulations could have greatly contributed to increasing complexity rather than minimizing it also emerged, often in association with studies on systemic risk.[100] Also, the problem of complexity was analysed focusing on the way financial regulation dealt with specific financial instruments, including derivatives and structured products, which were a catalyst for such complexity.

These studies did not take into account the relationship between finance and the underlying concepts of complexity science, and do not refer to any of the key terms developed by complexity science, such as 'complex adaptive system' or interaction among the subparts. However, they implicitly refer to key concepts of complexity science, such as dynamism, as important characteristics of capital markets[101] and to the general representation of international finance as a dynamic network subject to specific forces. Therefore, these implicit references do not function to properly emphasize the evolutionary (therefore dynamic) tensions underlying such concepts.

Financial and financial legal scholars analyse complexity in different ways, by referring to broad concepts or by approaching narrower and more specific ambits. When approaching the general aspects of complexity and its relationship with broad concepts, scholars identified complexity as a key feature of modern finance, together with its dynamism,[102] and associated it with the general framework of capital markets[103] and financial regulation.[104] Alternatively, they analysed complexity as one of the causes that contributed to the financial crisis of 2008.[105] When applying complexity

---

[99] See generally Awrey, 'Regulation of Modern Financial Markets' (n 15).
[100] See generally Schwarcz, 'Regulating Complexity in Financial Markets' (n 15), and Awrey, 'Regulation of Modern Financial Markets' (n 15).
[101] See generally Awrey and Judge, 'Financial Regulation Keeps Falling Short' (n 16).
[102] Ibid.
[103] See generally Awrey, 'Regulation of Modern Financial Markets' (n 15), and Schwarcz, 'Regulating Complexity in Financial Markets' (n 15).
[104] Daniel M. Gallagher, 'Complexities of Capital Markets Regulation' (*HLS Forum on Corporate Governance*, 7 March 2013) <https://corpgov.law.harvard.edu/2013/03/07/complexities-of-capital-markets-regulation/> accessed 4 April 2022.
[105] See for example Schwarcz, 'Regulating Complexity in Financial Markets' (n 15). See also Steven Schwarz, 'Systemic risk' (2007) 97 GeoLJ 193. As the author explains, 'A contributing factor to the recent subprime crisis, for example, is allegedly that "[a] lot of institutional investors bought [mortgage backed] securities substantially based on their ratings [without fully understanding what they bought], in part because the market has become so complex".

to more specific ambits, traditional examples come from investment banking, leveraged finance, and structured products,[106] as well as the derivative industry and credit derivatives.[107]

Although financial and legal scholars refer to complexity and build theories to deal with complexity when regulating capital markets, it is difficult to identify a clear definition of it, both at a broad conceptual level and in relation to more specific situations, such as financial instruments.[108] Referring to financial legal scholarship, there is no formalization of 'financial complexity'. The terms 'complexity' and 'complex' are rather used as synonyms of 'complicatedness' and 'complicated'. Other social sciences, such as sociology, which employed complexity science much earlier than legal scholarship, underwent similar problems.[109]

In the context of financial literature, an example of the challenge to properly defining complexity with regard to specific financial instruments comes from 'complex securities': comparing derivatives with more elementary (only in principle) equity shares, Brunnemeier and Oehmke explain that 'while CDOs [collateralized debt obligations] are viewed by most as highly complex, equity shares of financial institutions, whose payoff structures are even more complicated, are often seen as less complex'.[110]

Financial complexity and the way specific concepts and terms are employed prove that these studies do not explicitly refer to, and sometimes even ignore, complexity science. Legal scholars seem to characterize and use the idea of financial complexity as a static, structural attribute of capital markets or the narrower entities and institutions with which they associate complexity. Based on the analysis provided of complexity science and its main concepts, the use of the word 'complexity' and the consequential description of financial systems as complex lead to the conclusion that legal scholars adopted an opposite approach. Because complexity is a structural attribute, it would be plausible to consider that this scholarship develops an approach that is closer to structural functionalism,[111] referring to complexity to better understand the stability of the financial system and its preservation, and the threats to such stability.

---

[106] See generally Claire Celerier and Boris Vallee, 'What Drives Financial Complexity? A Look into the Retail Market for Structured Products' (2013) 1013 Les Cahiers de Recherche—HEC Paris.

[107] See generally Dan Awrey, 'Complexity, Innovation and the Dynamics of OTC Derivatives Regulation' (DPhil thesis, University of Oxford, 17 September 2012) <https://ora.ox.ac.uk/objects/uuid:340dff47-0a78-43a8-85eb-c39b950e5153/download_file?file_format=pdf&safe_filename=THESIS01&type_of_work=The> accessed 4 April 2022.

[108] Markus K. Brunnermeier and Martin Oehmke, 'Complexity in Financial Markets' (2009) Princeton University Working Paper <https://scholar.princeton.edu/sites/default/files/complexity_0.pd> accessed 4 April 2022.

[109] As Read Bain remarked in the context of sociology, 'When we address ourselves to the task of analysing the concept of complexity as applied to social phenomena, we are at once faced with the vagueness and confusion that surrounds it. Like so many terms in constant use by sociologists, it means all things to all men. It is one of those indefinite blanket-terms that serve to conceal our scientific inadequacy.' See Read Bain, 'The Concept of Complexity in Sociology' (1929) 8 SocForces 222, 224.

[110] Ibid.

[111] See Section I.B.

B. Approaches to Complexity in Financial Markets

Different scholars have analysed complexity in capital markets, proposing complementary analyses which share in common a descriptive (static) approach, in a way antithetical to the basic idea of dynamism and evolution characterizing complexity science and more generally evolutionary approaches in science.

An example of this approach comes from Dan Awrey, who analysed the importance of complexity in the aftermath of the financial crisis of 2008. Awrey considers financial complexity by offering a theoretical economic framework coupled with an analysis of its main determinants.[112] The underlying economic framework relies on two variables: information costs and bounded rationality.[113] Information costs identify the costs generated by those activities related to 'searching for, acquiring, filtering, manipulating and analysing information'.[114] Bounded rationality instead encompasses both cognitive and temporal constraints that affect the ability of actors to process such information.[115] A hypothetical 'perfectly rational and fully informed actor' will be exempt from information costs, and no external factor will affect his bounded rationality,[116] whereas a real-world actor will need to understand complex financial instruments and navigate through the available (sometimes manipulated) information. In these conditions, the real-world actor will likely be exposed to other costs.

In Awrey's view, information costs and bounded rationality are instrumental to identifying two insights related to complexity. First, complexity is relative, depending on what an individual perceives as complex. Second, the tolerance for complexity is finite; therefore, irrespective of the levels related to information costs and bounded rationality pertaining to each individual, there is a threshold where high information costs and bounded rationality will likely 'render full comprehension impossible within a given timeframe'.[117] These two variables are functions of complexity, and specific drivers, or sources, affect such variables. According to Awrey, such variables encompass technology, opacity, interconnectedness, fragmentation, regulation, and reflexivity, and they all contribute to increasing complexity in financial markets.[118] Other sources of complexity within financial markets were identified in the creation of contingent and dynamic economic interests in the underlying assets, the competitiveness animating different categories of investors, and the long chain that separates an investor from the underlying assets that he owns through financial investment.[119]

Complementary to the explanation of an economic framework as well as of the main drivers of complexity in financial markets is an understanding of the different levels (or layers) of complexities existing in financial markets. Adhering to the model identified by Steven L. Schwarcz, three levels of complexities are especially relevant.

---

[112] Awrey, 'Regulation of Modern Financial Markets' (n 15) 241.
[113] Ibid.
[114] Ibid.
[115] Ibid.
[116] Ibid.
[117] Ibid.
[118] Ibid, 242–258.
[119] See generally Judge, 'Fragmentation Nodes' (n 15).

A first level comes from the assets underlying investment securities, as well as the way of originating such assets.[120] Underlying assets include mortgage loans and a broad range of securities, where each of these assets requires specific approaches in relation to modelling and the calculation of certain risks,[121] such as default risks and interest rate risks, and each asset has its own complexities at the level of contractual terms and conditions, as in the case of the subprime mortgage crisis.[122] The origination of these assets is an additional cause for concern, in particular when referring to mortgage-backed securities (MBSs) distributed to investors by different categories of conduits (including institutional investors and investment banks, among others) via securitizations, potentially leading to a failure at the level of lending standards.[123] The financial crisis of 2008 has shown the weaknesses related to such complexity.[124]

A second level of complexities relates to securities themselves. MBSs are an example of what is unanimously characterized as complex securities and include collateralized debt obligations (CDOs), generally owned by a special purpose vehicle (SPV),[125] and resulting from a pool of securities that investment banks put together starting from mortgage and other asset-backed securities (ABSs). Complex securities impact financial markets in different ways, in particular making the achievement of a fair disclosure more difficult.[126] Because of the lack of an efficient and fair disclosure, complex securities can be a threat in two different ways. First, they can harm investors in their ability to fully understand the consequences of specific investments,[127] thereby being exposed to unintended consequences without being fully aware of their fully rational decisions. Second, fair disclosure related to complex securities could be a cause for concern at a systemic level, contributing to the emergence of systemic risk favouring financial contagion and at the same time harming market integrity favouring frauds.[128]

A third level of complexity refers to modern financial markets as a whole, mostly depending on a sort of information uncertainty (notwithstanding disclosure and transparency obligations) partially driven by the 'indirect holding system', human interactive behaviours,[129] regulation, and interconnection of market participants.[130]

---

[120] Schwarcz, 'Regulating Complexity in Financial Markets' (n 15) 216.
[121] For an in-depth analysis of the problems related to financial modelling, see Thomas S. Y. Ho and Sang Bin Lee, *The Oxford Guide to Financial Modeling: Insitutions* (OUP 2004) 348.
[122] Schwarcz, 'Regulating Complexity in Financial Markets' (n 15) 216.
[123] Ibid, 218.
[124] See Section IV.B.
[125] SPVs have been the centre of many financial scandals, in particular the epochal Enron scandal. As already mentioned, in that context the corporate executives implemented sophisticated accounting tricks in relation to credit derivatives to artificially inflate the value of the company, and complacent (or inadequate) gatekeepers could not detect the fraud.
[126] See generally Steven L. Schwarcz, 'Rethinking the Disclosure Paradigm in a World of Complexity' (2004) UIllinoisLRev 1.
[127] See Schwarcz, 'Regulating Complexity in Financial Markets' (n 15) 223. See also Henry T. C. Hu, 'Misunderstood Derivatives: The Causes of Informational Failure and the Promise of Regulatory Incrementalism' 102 YaleLJ 1457 (1993).
[128] Schwarcz, 'Regulating Complexity in Financial Markets' (n 15) 223–227.
[129] Ibid. Schwarcz identifies a reason for concern (and complexity) in human interactive behaviours and explains how nonlinear feedback effects resulting from human interactions within financial markets lead to unintended consequences confuting a rigorous cause-and-effect approach, and more generally undermining an ability to predict, which is generally associated with specific roles in financial markets. The author identifies examples of this complexity in the context of real estate dynamics and securities trading.
[130] Ibid, 230–235.

An important characteristic of financial markets is that they do not generate or increase complexity *per se* but tend to do so for two main reasons. First, investors generally prefer financial investments in securities fulfilling their specific needs while at the same time granting higher returns. In this way, they contribute to the development of complex financial instruments.[131] Second, complex financial instruments are generally justified by a need to promote efficiency within capital markets.[132] Therefore, financial institutions have an incentive to pursue efficiency by structuring gradually more complex financial instruments.

Although complexity and financial innovation have emerged as two main features of modern finance, conventional financial theories did not take into account their relevance and failed to identify both complexity and financial innovation in their discourse.[133] As Awrey suggests, this might be consistent with a general mistake in the approach of neoclassical economists who failed to include the Second Law of Thermodynamics,[134] referring to entropy and open systems,[135] to explain specific trends towards disequilibrium. Entropy is not only a measure of a system's thermal energy, but it also serves to measure the molecular disorder, also referred to as randomness, of a system.[136] In economics, open systems also emphasize the interaction within a network as a source of change and dynamism.[137] Therefore, the notions of entropy and open system share affinities with the problems underlying complexity science and, more specifically, could be helpful for understanding dynamic complexity in finance.

This theoretical lack was also mirrored at the level of regulatory responses in the regulation of financial markets. Financial regulation simply failed in addressing such forces and this contributed to enhancing the financial crisis of 2008.[138] The way regulators approached financial derivatives exemplifies the lack of understanding about the importance of complexity and financial innovation, and regulators attempted to correct the system only after the financial crisis of 2008. Developments within the derivatives industry took place continuously over more than three decades, and the financial creativity surrounding such innovations was wrongly perceived as the solution to the regulatory and structural imperfections in financial markets.[139] In her fundamental contribution 'A Legal Theory of Finance', Katarina Pistor emphasizes that '[f]inancial systems comprise a complex, interdependent web of contractual obligations, or IOUs, that link market participants to one another', therefore the law plays a

---

[131] Ibid, 213.
[132] Ibid.
[133] See generally Awrey, 'Regulation of Modern Financial Markets' (n 15).
[134] For an explanation of the Second Law of Thermodynamics see NASA, 'Second Law of Thermodynamics' <https://www.grc.nasa.gov/WWW/K-12/airplane/thermo2.html> accessed 4 April 2022.
[135] See Whitt and Schultze, 'The New "Emergence Economics" of Innovation' (n 8) 226–227.
[136] Gordon W.F. Drake, 'Entropy', *Britannica* (last updated 28 April 2023) <https://www.britannica.com/science/entropy-physics> accessed 30 April 2023.
[137] See generally Victoria Chick and Sheila Dow, 'The Meaning of Open Systems' (2005) 12 JEconMeth 363.
[138] See generally Awrey, 'Regulation of Modern Financial Markets' (n 15).
[139] Ibid.

'critical role ... in the construction of financial markets', which are hierarchical, both at international and domestic levels.[140]

C. An Alternative View on the Relationship between Financial Markets and Complexity

Opening the conversation to complexity science in financial markets means a shift from referring to 'complexity' as a pure structural attribute to highlighting the dynamism that is intrinsic to capital markets.

A starting point would be identifying the dimension of international finance as a CAS. On the basis of the previous analysis of complex adaptive systems,[141] international finance is characterized as a large network, where heterogeneous components interact among themselves without a real central control. Although points of control exist (such as national central banks, securities regulators, and even national governments and supranational entities), the international dimension of finance escapes the paradigm of a strict dependence on one main point of central control. On this basis, international finance could likely be characterized as a CAS.

Focusing on international finance's heterogeneous components or subparts, they can be identified with different degrees of abstractness. A potential classification is the one referring to the key forces contributing to reshaping markets. Key determinants in this context are politics, economics, law, and finance. These are essential attributes when assessing the way corporate governance changes and evolves. Mark Roe explicitly considered how corporate governance is the result of different factors or forces, which he explicitly defined as 'determinants'.[142] The presence of these forces, and the influence they are capable of exercising, can be safely extended to the broader dimension of international finance, leading to important transformations.

To make it more concrete, these forces are the result of specific entities, both individual and collective, including (but not limited to): investors, politicians, regulators, central bankers, shareholders, stakeholders, scientists, national parties and movements, corporations, fund managers, investment bankers, gatekeepers, judges, technologists, and so on.

As this chapter (and more broadly this book) will explain in depth, another way to identify the different subparts would be to focus on the several 'dimensions' involved in the line of disruption, in particular the contractual (commercial) dimension, capital markets and corporate governance, and financial networks, at the two levels of central banking and shadow banking. The way in which these subparts interact leads to the pursuit of forms of evolution, where the role of innovation is essential in the way it contributes to dynamism and to the pursuit of 'far-from-equilibriums', consistent

---

[140] See Katharina Pistor, 'A Legal Theory of Finance' (2013) 41 JCompEcon 315, 317–320. For a broader analysis on the role of the law in codifying assets, see Katharina Pistor, *The Code of Capital* (PUP 2019).
[141] See Section I.A.
[142] Mark Roe, 'Political Determinants of Corporate Governance' (2003) Discussion Paper No. 451, Harvard John M. Olin Discussion Paper Series, iii <http://www.law.harvard.edu/programs/olin_center/papers/pdf/451.pdf> accessed 4 April 2022.

with the evolutionary paths characterizing complex adaptive systems. Innovation will be the core issue in Section III of this chapter.

In addition to the abovementioned key features of international finance as a CAS, it is also characterized by its 'history dependency'. History dependency is useful for contextualizing and better understanding the way heterogeneous forces interact and lead to specific evolutions.

The dynamic approach as a consequence of 'complexity' is an alternative and the way in which this chapter (and the rest of the book) will dive into the analysis of the line of disruption, as opposed to the exclusively static dimension characterizing most of the existing financial legal scholarship.

III. How Does Innovation Come into Play When Analysing Complexity? Diving into the Relationship between Complexity and Technology

As mentioned above, innovation is a structural attribute of emergence economies.[143] Through the lenses of complexity science, innovation is a significant form of evolution, which—especially in the case of disruptive innovations—leads to far-from-equilibriums (to adopt the lexicon developed in the context of complexity science), favouring increased forms of interconnection among all the subparts involved in any system.

When referring more specifically to financial markets, innovation contributes to increasing their structural complexity in the traditional sense elaborated by the financial legal scholarship, as well as to enhancing dynamic evolutionary paths,[144] as in the case of complex adaptive systems. Here innovation emerged in the form of pure financial innovation and was coupled with new forms of technological (disruptive) innovation. This section focuses on financial innovation and how it evolved in the new technological paradigms. Furthermore, it provides an overview of the most important disruptive technologies and the way their main characteristic, that of being 'regulatory' disruptive, affects regulatory strategies.

A. Financial Innovation

1. General Traits and Continuity of Financial Innovation over Time
Innovation is heterogeneous *per se* and, more broadly, innovation in capital markets involves three distinct forms of innovation: theoretical innovations (such as the well-known Black–Scholes option pricing model[145] or the Modigliani–Miller theorem for corporate finance[146]); technological innovations; and the emergence of new financial

---

[143] See Whitt and Schultze, 'The New "Emergence Economics" of Innovation' (n 8) 221.
[144] Awrey and Judge, 'Financial Regulation Keeps Falling Short' (n 16).
[145] Fischer Black and Myron Scholes, 'The Pricing of Options and Corporate Liabilities' (1973) 81 JPolEcon 637.
[146] Franco Modigliani and Merton H. Miller, 'The Cost of Capital, Corporation Finance and the Theory of Investment' (1958) 48 AmEconRev 261.

markets, institutions, and financial instruments.[147] The combination of such forms of innovation leads to significant changes in finance and capital markets,[148] and these evolutions can be traced at the level of market structures, implying both micro- and macro-economic transformations.[149]

Although financial innovation assumes different forms in the different historical eras, it is certainly not a novelty of modern times; rather, it is a continuous, incessant process. Revolutionary legal structures emerged in the Middle Ages, such as the creation of the corporation form as a tool to favour entrepreneurial investments,[150] as well as the scheme of the Commenda, which anticipated the structure of modern investment trusts and more generally of modern financial intermediation.[151] More recent examples of financial innovations are modern financial derivatives, structured products, securitizations, repurchase agreements, and trading techniques, including high-frequency and algorithmic trading. All these new structures and financial instruments started to proliferate in the twentieth century with the emergence of the shadow banking system and contributed to increasing both the penetration of financial innovation in many key areas, and its pace of development.

Financial innovation is characterized so much by its continuity that the reiteration of specific techniques can be traced even in the context of the new paradigms emerging with disruptive technologies applied to finance. In an effort to identify specific continuities between financial transformation happening in the last years and new disruptive technologies (in particular blockchain), Omarova has identified and formalized what she labelled as 'transaction meta-technologies'.[152] According to Omarova, transaction meta-technologies shaped the recent decades in finance and continue to be implemented in the context of new technologies.

2. Transaction Meta-Technologies

Transaction meta-technologies encompass different ways of structuring financial assets and transactions and all contribute to the 'constant growth and complexification of the financial market'.[153] Omarova identified four main meta-technologies, in particular pooling, layering, acceleration, and compression.[154] Their common

---

[147] Awrey and Judge, 'Financial Regulation Keeps Falling Short' (n 16).
[148] Ibid.
[149] See generally Saule T. Omarova, 'New Tech v. New Deal: Fintech as a Systemic Phenomenon' (2019) 36 YaleJonReg 735 (hereafter Omarova, 'New Tech v. New Deal').
[150] For a revolutionary overview on the history of the corporation form, see Germain Sicard, *The Origins of Corporations* (YUP 2015).
[151] The Commenda was an act on behalf of, but not in the name of, another: the commendator conferred to a tractator, generally a merchant, some amount that had to be employed for a certain time to pursue a performance, so that the commentator could have a gain. The tractator had full managerial powers. For a historical perspective, see Henry Hansmann, Reinier Kraakman, and Richard Squire, 'Law and the Rise of the Firm' (2006) 119 HarvLRev 1333 (discussing the commenda as a form of financing medieval maritime trade); Robert Yee, 'Financial Innovation and Commenda Contracts in Medieval Europe' (*The Vanderbilt Historical Review*, updated 21 December 2019) <https://www.vanderbilthistoricalreview.com/post/financial-innovation-and-commenda-contracts-in-medieval-europe> accessed 4 April 2022 (discussing commenda as a way to split labour and capital and diversify risk).
[152] Ibid.
[153] Omarova, 'New Tech v. New Deal' (n 149) 762.
[154] Ibid.

characteristic is that rather than identifying a specific product or transactions, they are 'system-level operational principles or core techniques that enable financial markets' continuous reproduction and expansion'.[155]

Pooling and layering are the two financial techniques that contribute to financial markets' structural complexity, whereas acceleration and compression impact the volume and velocity of trading.[156] Pooling refers to the financial technique of combining specific financial assets with the purpose of creating financial claims fully backed by the resulting pool.[157] Layering identifies the technique of synthesizing financial assets to generate a chain of linked claims that are structured on a hierarchical basis, where the financial performance of each layer depends on the other.[158] Securitizations[159] are an example of combined pooling and layering strategies.

Acceleration contributes to increasing the speed of transactions, thereby increasing the volume of transactions, as in the case of high-frequency trading (HFT), and compression is a way to simplify complex transactional structures by 'aggregating and compacting risk exposures and obligations associated with multiple trades in a manner that de facto transforms them into a single economic transaction', as in the case of multiple derivatives with the same counterparties substituted with one contract with a reduced notional amount.[160]

All these transaction meta-technologies have contributed to micro-economic changes, in the sense of affecting specific activities implemented in capital markets. At the same, time they have led to the emergence of new macro-economic dimensions. This continuous process has also taken place with the implementation of new disruptive technologies in finance, which have contributed to accelerating the pace and intensity of such transformations.[161]

As this book will show, disruptive technologies[162] (in particular blockchain) are contributing to redesign the way specific activities and transactions take place, as well as more general market structures. New disruptive technologies aim to implement a more systematic disintermediation (as in the case of blockchain technology), potentially leading to a redistribution of powers and roles within financial markets. Therefore, at a superior level, disruptive technologies enable the emergence of new macro-economic dimensions and equilibriums. Disruptive technologies do so by breaking down the financial services supply chains into discrete parts and disintermediating traditional functions, and this comes with significant uncertainty because risks and benefits are not perfectly known or predictable.[163] More broadly, this also means rethinking the potential shift towards a new financial environment. Indeed, although specific principles and structures are reiterated and perpetrated

---

[155] Ibid.
[156] Ibid, 764.
[157] Ibid, 762–763.
[158] Ibid, 763.
[159] For an analysis of securitizations, see Chapter 5, Section II. For an identification of the similarities between securitizations and tokenizations, see Chapter 5, Sections II and III.
[160] Omarova, 'New Tech v. New Deal' (n 149) 765–766.
[161] Ibid.
[162] See Section II.B.
[163] Christopher Brummer and Yesha Yadav, 'Fintech and Innovation Trilemma' (2019) 107 GeoLJ 235, 242 (hereafter Brummer and Yadav, 'Fintech and Innovation Trilemma').

within the new system, specific changes in the paradigm are radically new and could contribute to enhance structural complexity and trigger unforeseeable evolutions in an unprecedented way.

A useful example in the sense of the dual level transformations induced by disruptive technologies comes from blockchain technology. The same transaction meta-technologies of pooling, layering, acceleration, and compression can be traced in the blockchain-related implementations. Bitcoin and initial coin offerings (ICOs)[164] are both examples of asset synthetization with the digital representation or the tokenization of securities and assets, and distributed ledger technology (DLT)[165] as infrastructural technology could potentially amplify the magnitude of the trading.[166] In the post-trading phase, DLT will systematically speed up the settlement of transactions. While in the current framework the time for the settlements is T+3, and in some cases T+2 or T+1, referring to the time frame of three days to conclude the settlement of a transaction, blockchain technology-based market infrastructures enable an almost instantaneous T+0 settlement. At a superior level, because of its potential for decentralization and disintermediation, DLT (and in particular blockchain) promises to induce radical transformations of market structure and may lead to unprecedented systemic evolutions, which will include public powers and institutions, such as central banks, and their role in international economy.

B. Disruptive Technologies: The Current Landscape

1. Sustaining vs Disruptive Technologies

As noted at the beginning of this chapter, disruptive technologies strongly differ from sustaining technologies, in particular in the way established institutions may or may not react to them. According to Christensen, sustaining technologies contribute to improve product performances; therefore, established market actors can cope with them, whereas disruptive technologies lead to significant changes, posing a threat for established actors.[167] In fact, disruption refers to a process whereby new entrants are in the position to outperform established actors. As Christensen, Raynor, and McDonald explain:

> [A]s incumbents focus on improving their products and services for their most demanding (and usually most profitable) customers, they exceed the needs of some segments and ignore the needs of others. Entrants that prove disruptive begin by successfully targeting those overlooked segments, gaining a foothold by delivering more-suitable functionality—frequently at a lower price. Incumbents, chasing higher profitability in more-demanding segments, tend not to respond vigorously. Entrants

---

[164] For a broad analysis of initial coin offerings and the way they contributed to market transformations at different levels, please refer to Chapter 3.
[165] For an analysis of DLT and blockchain, see Section IV.C.2.b.
[166] Omarova, 'New Tech v. New Deal' (n 149) 771–782.
[167] See generally Christensen, *The Innovator's Dilemma* (n 22).

then move upmarket, delivering the performance that incumbents' mainstream customers require, while preserving the advantages that drove their early success.[168]

In recent years the process of disruption emerged with a special intensity because of a unique mix of disruptive technologies applied to many heterogeneous contexts, generating unprecedented structural transformations; this is especially the case for financial markets. Blockchain, coupled with artificial intelligence, big data, and other important technologies (which will be analysed in the following subparagraph), represented the major source of such disruption.

2. The Main Disruptive Technologies

Nowadays, the current landscape of disruptive technologies encompasses a mix of different and complementary technologies, the most important being blockchain, big data, artificial intelligence (and machine learning), mobile technologies, and the Internet of Things (IoT).

a. Blockchain technology

Blockchain technology will be analysed in greater depth in subsection III.B.2.a., but here it is worth mentioning its key characteristics and contextualizing it among the other disruptive technologies. Blockchain allows the creation of a decentralized network relying on the consensus of participants as a tool to validate the transactions, replacing the role of a decentralized authority. One of its main properties resides in the possibility to program smart contracts (analysed in Chapter 2), which are in principle self-executing forms of contracting.

b. Big data

Big data are characterized by the so-called 3Vs—volume, velocity, and variety—as identified by Doug Laney. Big data originate from different channels, such as business transactions, smart devices, and social media, and because of the heterogeneity of such sources they are extremely heterogeneous, too. The significant growth of such channels also involved the data flow to businesses, with an impact on the way they should be managed: almost in real time.[169]

As early as 2013, the Article 29 Working Party (a working group dissolved in 2018) highlighted that corporations, governments and other large organizations hold gigantic digital data sets extensively analysed using computer algorithms.[170] Big data proved to have the potential to identify more general trends and correlations, as well as to more directly affect individuals, posing privacy and transparency issues, and

---

[168] Clayton M. Christensen, Michael E. Raynor, and Rory McDonald, 'What Is Disruptive Innovation?' (*Harvard Business Review*, December 2015) <https://hbr.org/2015/12/what-is-disruptive-innovation> accessed 4 April 2022.

[169] SAS, 'Big Data: What It Is and Why It Matters' <https://www.sas.com/en_us/insights/big-data/what-is-big-data.html> accessed 4 April 2022. See also Thomas Erl, Wajid Khattak, and Paul Buhler, *Big Data Fundamentals: Concepts, Drivers & Techniques* (Pearson 2016).

[170] For an overview of the activities developed by the Article 29 Working Party, see generally Digital Watch Observatory, 'Article 29 Working Party' <https://dig.watch/actor/article-29-working-party> accessed 1 May 2023.

challenging the relationship between technology, human rights, and markets[171]—all issues that clearly fall outside the scope of this work. Big data have become a major concern also for financial regulators, because of their implications for the financial industry.[172]

c. *Artificial intelligence*
Artificial intelligence and machine learning (a branch of artificial intelligence) are functional to the analysis of complex, fast, and heterogeneous big data sets via complex mathematical algorithms and calculations.[173]

The term 'artificial intelligence' was coined in 1956, and the technology evolved over time along three clearly identifiable steps. A first stage of artificial intelligence was the one relying on so-called neural networks, which developed from 1943 on (the term 'artificial intelligence' was coined even before that), although the very first multi-layered structure was developed in 1976.[174] Neural networks replicate the neural structure of human neurons in the brain, relying on algorithms for the recognition of specific patterns and correlations in data.

In the 1980s, developments in machine learning opened up the second stage of artificial intelligence.[175] Machine learning is a method for analysing data, with the purpose of automating analytical model building, and as a branch of artificial intelligence it develops the key concept that systems learn from data.[176] Machine learning systems should be capable of identifying patterns as well as be in the position of making decisions, in a rather autonomous setting, without relying on human intervention.[177]

The third (contemporary) stage of artificial intelligence advancements involves so-called deep learning, a branch of machine learning with a focus on training computers for the performance of human-like tasks. While the previous paradigms essentially relied on recognizing specific patterns via data organization, deep learning

---

[171] For an overview of these issues, see European Data Protection Supervisor, 'Opinion 7/2015—Meeting the Challenges of Big Data' (19 November 2015) <https://edps.europa.eu/sites/edp/files/publication/15-11-19_big_data_en.pdf> accessed 4 April 2022.

[172] See also Joint Committee of the Supervisory Authorities, 'On the Use of Big Data by Financial Institutions' (2016) Joint Committee Discussion Paper 2016/86 <https://www.esma.europa.eu/sites/default/files/library/jc-2016-86_discussion_paper_big_data.pdf> accessed 4 April 2022 (hereafter 'On the Use of Big Data by Financial Institutions').

[173] SAS, 'Machine Learning: What It Is and Why It Matters' <https://www.sas.com/en_us/insights/analytics/machine-learning.html> accessed 4 April 2022 (hereafter SAS, 'Machine Learning'); see also Ethem Alpaydin, *Machine Learning: The New AI* (MIT Press 2016). See also SAS, 'Artificial Intelligence: What It Is and It Matters' <https://www.sas.com/en_us/insights/analytics/what-is-artificial-intelligence.html> accessed 4 April 2022; see also Thomas H. Davenport, Erik Brynjolfsson, Andrew McAfee, and H. James Wilson, *Artificial Intelligence* (HBR 2019); and Michael Haenlein and Andreas Kaplan, 'A Brief History of Artificial Intelligence: On the Past, Present, and Future of Artificial Intelligence' (2019) 61 CalManagRev 5.

[174] SAS, 'Neural Networks—What Are They and Why They Matter' <https://www.sas.com/en_us/insights/analytics/neural-networks.html> accessed 4 April 2022. See also Adrian Iustin Georgevici and Marius Terblanche, 'Neural Networks and Deep Learning: A Brief Introduction' (2019) 45 IntensiveCareMed 712; and Alexander Derry, Martin Krzywinski, and Naomi Altman, 'Neural Networks Primer' (2023) 20 NatMethods 165.

[175] Ibid.

[176] SAS, 'Machine Learning' (n 173).

[177] Ibid.

relies on specific parameters that are set up to achieve autonomy on the side of the computer, which will learn on its own by recognizing patterns on the basis of multi-layer processing.[178]

d. Mobile technologies
Mobile technologies mostly refer to 'portable two-way communications devices', and include computing devices (such as notebook computers, mobile telephones, and GPS-navigation devices) and the networking technology connecting these devices (wireless technologies),[179] favouring data sharing. Web-based financing, such as peer-to-peer (P2P) platforms and investment crowdfunding platforms, provide support for the development of electronic money transfers and direct financing of projects by small investors located in different areas of the world.

e. Internet of Things
The IoT, like DLT and mobile technologies, relies on connectivity, and it is structurally related to big data. The IoT consists of a platform of devices connected to the internet and to other devices, via sensors, through to an IoT platform in charge of integrating data originating from each device and developing analytics, identifying the relevant information for specific applications and needs.[180] The combination of such connected devices with platforms allows gathering information as well as analysing it and implementing actions for the purpose of supporting an individual with a specific task or learning from a process.[181] Data collection may be beneficial at the micro-economic level, for example to support the decisions of a buyer, while at the same time leading to some more general economic effects, such as increasing efficiency.

Broader economic effects can be achieved only with generalized adoption of the technology. A study by PwC has demonstrated that this is currently happening and gathered relevant data in this sense, concluding: 'Industrial manufacturers are using IoT across the business: 60% on projects within their facilities, 57% with supply chain and other partners, 42% with end consumers and 58% with their business customers. Their top focus areas are logistics (50%), supply chain (47%) and employee and customer operations (46%).'[182]

f. The metaverse
The term 'metaverse' has become extremely popular and is gaining traction with the increasing popularity of so-called non-fungible tokens (NFTs), representing digital or

---

[178] SAS, 'Deep Learning—What Is and Why It Matters' <https://www.sas.com/en_us/insights/analytics/deep-learning.html> accessed 4 April 2022. See also Ian Goodfellow, Yoshua Bengio, and Aaron Courville, *Deep Learning* (MIT Press 2016); and Yann LeCun, Yoshua Bengio, and Geoffrey Hinton, 'Deep Learning' (2015) 521 Nature 436.
[179] IBM, 'What Is Mobile Technology?' <https://www.ibm.com/topics/mobile-technology> accessed 4 April 2022.
[180] Jen Clark, 'What Is the Internet of Things (IoT)?' (*IBM Business Operations Blog*, 17 November 2016) <https://www.ibm.com/blogs/internet-of-things/what-is-the-iot/> accessed 4 April 2022.
[181] Matt Burgess, 'What Is the Internet of Things? WIRED Explains' (*Wired*, 16 February 2018) <https://www.wired.co.uk/article/internet-of-things-what-is-explained-iot> accessed 4 April 2022.
[182] PwC, 'IoT Makes Manufacturers "Smart"' (2019) https://www.pwc.com/us/en/services/consulting/technology/emerging-technology/iot-pov/manufacturing-iot-snapshot.html> accessed 4 April 2022.

physical assets. NFTs and the metaverse will be analysed in greater depth in the next chapters.

Neal Stephenson's novel *Snow Crash* featured the first reference to the metaverse. With this term the author identified an 'online environment that was a real place to its users'.[183] In the current debate, the metaverse is set to become a three-dimensional 'immersive internet of the future' in which people can connect through various devices.[184] The gaming industry, in particular through online games such as Fortnite, Roblex, and Second Life, proved capable to anticipate some of the key features currently discussed in the context of the metaverse and bring them into the discussion. Not surprisingly, it is currently heavily invested in the development of the metaverse, which has also attracted the attention of established tech institutions including Meta, the parent company controlling Facebook, Microsoft, and Nvidia.

So far, underdeveloped technical infrastructure has impeded the creation of the metaverse. However, key technologies, in particular the DLT and the instruments emerging in the context of decentralized finance (DeFi), the virtual world, virtual and augmented reality, and cyberspace could enable its further development.

3. Specific Discontinuities in the New Paradigms

While the abovementioned transaction meta-technologies are useful to identify specific continuities in finance, this new wave of disruptive technologies also comes with some peculiar characteristics, triggering specific discontinuities with the past.

Three main characteristics are especially important in this evolving landscape. First, unprecedented availability of data will likely impact the design and development of new Fintech products.[185] Big data combined with blockchain technologies increases the opportunity to generate, collect, and store much higher amounts of data compared to the past. Second, artificial intelligence and machine learning have penetrated many different aspects of finance.[186] Third, new market actors proposing business models based on disintermediation are capable of disrupting established financial institutions' methods of conducting business, in particular breaking the ability of such institutions to offer a broad range of financial services.[187]

These specific characteristics have two main effects. On the one hand, they exacerbate capital markets' methods of enhancing structural complexity. On the other hand, they challenge regulators in their ability to pursue three main objectives at the same time, exposing them to the 'trilemma' of innovation. These objectives include the provision of clear rules (or legal certainty), the pursuit of market integrity, and the need to support innovation without stifling it.[188] Fintech and disruptive innovations are posing this issue in an unprecedented way, due to the intensity and multiplicity of the

---

[183] Cory Ondrejka, 'Escaping the Gilded Cage: User Created Content and Building the Metaverse' (2004) 49 NYLSchLRev 81.
[184] Kevin Stankiewicz, 'Jim Cramer Says These 4 Companies Are the Best Ways to Invest in the Metaverse' (*CNBC*, 11 November 2021) <https://www.cnbc.com/2021/11/10/jim-cramer-says-these-4-companies-are-the-best-ways-to-invest-in-the-metaverse.html> accessed 4 April 2022.
[185] Brummer and Yadav, 'Fintech and Innovation Trilemma' (n 163) 264.
[186] Ibid, 265.
[187] Ibid, 269.
[188] Ibid.

changes brought by them. However, this has been a historical problem for regulators, who were forced to rethink their regulatory approaches in line with specific epochal changes in the twentieth century.[189]

C. Disruptive Innovation (and Technology) as Regulatory Disruptive Innovations

1. A Few Examples

When dealing with technology and innovation, all the constituencies of society, but in particular public authorities (governments, national authorities, central banks) as well as entrepreneurs and start-ups, play a crucial role, because innovation is essentially a collective process.[190]

In this collective process, nation-states can support innovations in different ways. Financing innovation is an important pillar, as Mariana Mazzucato emphasizes in using the expression 'Entrepreneurial State' to refer to the importance of the involvement of the state, which is often excluded from the narratives of innovation despite being investor of 'first resort'.[191] Furthermore, states can significantly contribute to the early adoption of technology,[192] as well as to the informational flow which is functional to understanding and applying new technologies in new fields.[193]

A fundamental duty of policy-makers is the provision of an appropriate regulatory framework as an essential pillar for technology to prosper, and to support the development of innovation as a collective process.[194] However, this is not an easy task, especially when dealing with disruptive innovation. As Mazzucato and others emphasize, the risk of not properly recognizing the collective process of innovation is that of 'a narrow group of private corporations and investors reaping the full returns of projects which the state helped to initiate and finance'.[195] As mentioned above, disruptive technologies proved to be economically and financially disruptive, promoting changes in the industry and opening new businesses to new market actors capable of replacing established institutions.

Not only are disruptive technologies economically and financially disruptive to the industries where they are introduced; they are also 'regulatory disruptive', challenging existing regulatory frameworks and legal categories,[196] and forcing policy makers to rethink their traditional regulatory approaches to react to the theoretical legal issues posed by innovation. Previous, though still recent, examples of disruptive innovations include the internet and the massive financial innovations introduced in capital

---

[189] Ibid.
[190] See Mariana Mazzucato, *The Value of Everything* (Penguin 2019) xi.
[191] See generally Mariana Mazzucato, *The Entrepreneurial State: Debunking Public vs. Private Sector Myths* (Penguin 2015) (hereafter Mazzuccato, *The Entrepreneurial State*).
[192] Michele Finck, *Blockchain Regulation and Governance in Europe* (CUP 2018) 148 (hereafter Finck, *Blockchain Regulation*).
[193] Ibid, 149–150.
[194] See generally Mazzucato, *The Entrepreneurial State* (n 191).
[195] Mariana Mazzucato, Rainer Kattel, and Josh Ryan-Collins, 'Challenge-Driven Innovation Policy: Towards a New Policy Toolkit' (2020) 20 JIndCompTrade 421, 421–437, 431.
[196] See generally Cortez, 'Regulating Disruptive Innovation' (n 23).

markets from the end of the 1990s to the financial crisis of 2008. The internet emerged in the 1980s and was massively adopted in the 1990s, and regulators reacted with the so-called do-no harm approach as a way to avoid stifling innovation with an undue and burdensome legislative intervention potentially detrimental for innovation.[197]

Another example comes from the financial structures implemented within the financial industry which greatly contributed to the financial crisis of 2008. Even this wave of financial innovations forced regulators to recalibrate their approach towards financial regulation.[198] Although financial innovation is a continuous process, the intensity of the innovations at that time had become difficult to manage for regulatory and supervisory authorities involved. Both in Europe and in the United States, regulators and supervisors were 'captured' by the financial industry, which was proposing increasingly sophisticated financial products (as in the case of derivative contracts) or functions (i.e., implementing highly sophisticated risk-management models). In this situation they could not challenge such activities by designing and implementing appropriate policy measures and enforcement actions (regulatory capture),[199] because they lacked a matching level of technical expertise and understanding. Only a major systemic failure (such as the financial crisis of 2008) would force governments to attempt to fill this gap and to radically change the traditional regulatory approach, based on systematic deregulation of financial services, in an attempt to regain control over market actors and their market practices.

When dealing with the most recent examples of disruptive technologies (in particular big data, artificial intelligence, and DLT), many of the problems seen in the past have resurged with greater intensity, mostly because the same greater intensity could also be found in the new wave of technological disruptive innovation.

Ex post facts-based, trial-and-error rule-making and the provision of immutable rules, generally identified as 'stable and presumptively optimal rules',[200] are regulatory strategies characterizing the vast majority of jurisdictions. Disruptive innovations in principle challenge both of them, for two main reasons: their pace of development is exponential, and it comes with substantially unknown and often unpredictable future developments.

These two strategies are, in principle, too slow to properly react to technological changes, and 'stable and presumptively optimal rule[s]' are not structurally tailored for providing regulatory solutions capable of anticipating the course of the events.[201] As will be shown below, these structural challenges have led some economists and

---

[197] See Marco Dell'Erba, 'From Inactivity to Full Enforcement: The Implementation of the "Do No Harm" Approach in Initial Coin Offerings' (2020) 26 MichTechLRev 175 (hereafter Dell'Erba, ' "Do No Harm" Approach in Initial Coin Offerings').
[198] See Cortez, 'Regulating Disruptive Innovation' (n 23) 176–177.
[199] See Financial Crisis Inquiry Commission, *Final Report of the National Commission on the Causes of the Financial & Economic Crisis in the U.S.—The Financial Crisis Inquiry Report* (2011) 234 <https://www.govinfo.gov/content/pkg/GPO-FCIC/pdf/GPO-FCIC.pdf> accessed 2 April 2022 (hereafter Inquiry Commission, *Financial Crisis Inquiry Report*). The Report analyses the reaction of multiple American agencies to the new financial innovations.
[200] See Wulf A. Kaal and Erik P. M. Vermeulen, 'How to Regulate Disruptive Innovation—From Facts to Data' (2017) 57 Jurimetrics 169, 185–188 (hereafter Kaal and Vermeulen, 'How to Regulate Disruptive Innovation').
[201] Ibid.

legal scholars to consider the possibility of a more dynamic approach to regulation, in an attempt to anticipate the challenges posed by such regulatory disruption instead of chasing them.[202]

2. Approaches for Regulatory Disruptive Innovations
a. *General considerations*
Regulators struggled to identify proper regulatory approaches for dealing with innovation, in particular for the enhanced difficulties of pursuing multiple goals that might be in conflict. The 'innovation trilemma' proves the difficulty, if not the impossibility, of pursuing market integrity while supporting innovation and providing clear rules.[203] Beyond these fundamental goals the situation becomes even more challenging for regulators when taking into account other policy objectives, which include consumer protection, privacy, and public welfare.[204]

In the context of these primary regulatory goals, a major critical point of the current regulatory framework refers to its inadequacy for identifying and supporting beneficial innovation, with the further negative consequences of generating permanent legal uncertainty and inconsistency.[205] The complexity of the current system makes the creation of new laws an extremely long process, resulting in an inadequate response due to the time sensitivity characterizing the regulation of disruptive innovations (which develop following an exponential pace) as opposed to other regulations.

In an attempt to mitigate economic and financial risks and to pursue multiple goals at the same time, policy-makers have implemented different strategies, trying to gradually integrate different complementary tools. Regulation might support the development of technology in different ways. In particular, it might contribute to pursuing solid legal certainty, create the basis for a new market to develop, ensure interoperability (a consistent and coherent system) between new technologies and existing laws, and ultimately foster users' trust in the mutated technological framework, thereby significantly contributing to its adoption.[206] Financial regulation and private law are both functional to the pursuit of this objective, while contributing to the protection of market actors, the market, and society more broadly.[207]

The debate on the most appropriate approach to achieve these goals remains topical. While regulators are considering new and increasingly sophisticated techniques (such as regulatory sandboxes and innovation hubs),[208] there is no definitive answer on which is the best way for regulating innovation.

When facing radically disruptive technologies, a first dilemma for regulators is whether the application of existing legal frameworks is adequate or whether new regulations are necessary. This is an old dilemma—the traditional debate between Lessig and Easterbrook (see Section VI)—and is always an important starting point. Here, as will be explained further in the course of this chapter, a key methodological question

---

[202] See Section III.C.3.
[203] See generally Brummer and Yadav, 'Fintech and Innovation Trilemma' (n 163).
[204] Kaal and Vermeulen, 'How to Regulate Disruptive Innovation' (n 200) 194.
[205] Ibid, 184.
[206] See Finck, *Blockchain Regulation* (n 192) 150–153.
[207] Philipp Paech, 'The Governance of Blockchain Financial Networks' (2017) 80 ModLRev 1073.
[208] See Section III.2.b and III.2.c.

is whether a hermeneutic process of interpretation mostly in the hands of judges and authorities (in the case of financial markets, national market authorities) is the best way to apply existing regulation to decide cases. If not, regulators will be the ones in charge of drafting new *ad hoc* regulations.

In the context of Fintech and disruptive technologies (in particular blockchain), the trend has rather consisted in the emergence of (or at least attempts at) new regulatory projects in different ambits and different jurisdictions. When looking at the regulation of blockchain technology, different countries have implemented new laws explicitly mentioning the new technology as well as specific new contractual or financial instruments originating from it. Switzerland recently passed a new Blockchain Law,[209] and in Europe and the United States there are regulatory measures and/or proposals for appropriately regulating ICOs and their multiple transformations (in particular security token offerings (STOs), and initial exchange offerings (IEOs)), as well as digital assets[210] and crypto-exchanges.[211] Furthermore, at the national level both in Europe and the United States, various states have opted for explicit regulation of smart contracts.[212]

b. *The problem of timing: the examples of 'wait and see' and guidelines issuance*

Not only do regulators face the dilemma of regulating versus applying the existing legal frameworks to disruptive technology; they also face the problem of 'when' to intervene, highlighting the importance of designing timely regulations. Consistent with the abovementioned 'do-no harm' approach, regulators should avoid, or at least minimize, the risk of stifling innovation with excessively restrictive rules issued at a very early stage of innovation, destroying the chances for technology to prosper. They should also avoid the opposite—reacting too late to innovations. A way to mitigate these risks comes from specific regulatory techniques, including 'wait and see' as well as the issuance of specific guidelines to address specific regulatory concerns.[213]

The 'wait and see' approach should not be a passive one; on the contrary, it should be characterized by an attempt to actively 'learn more about the innovation [doing] so while it remains sufficiently immature that we are not placing our objectives, stability, protection and integrity, at risk by not taking action'.[214] In the context of this approach, regulators shift towards active regulation only when innovation has reached

---

[209] Federal Act on the Adaptation of Federal Law to Developments in Distributed Ledger Technology (25 September 2020).
[210] See for example European Parliament legislative resolution of 20 April 2023 on the proposal for a regulation of the European Parliament and of the Council on Markets in Crypto-assets and amending Directive (EU) 2019/1937 (COM(2020)0593, C9-0306/2020, 2020/0265(COD)) <https://www.europarl.europa.eu/doceo/document/TA-9-2023-0117_EN.pdf> accessed 2 May 2023 (hereafter MiCAR).
[211] See Regulation (EU) 2022/858 of 30 May 2022 on a pilot regime for market infrastructures based on distributed ledger technology [2022] OJ L 151/1 (hereafter EU Pilot Regime on DLT). See also MiCAR (n 210).
[212] See Chapter 2.
[213] For a specific analysis of the negative consequences in the ICO market see Marco Dell'Erba, 'Initial Coin Offerings: The First Regulatory Responses' (2018) 14 NYUJL&Bus 1107.
[214] Patrick Armstrong, 'Financial Technology: ESMA's Approach, 4th Luxembourg FinTech Conference' (Speech at the 4th Luxembourg FinTech Conference, Luxembourg, 10 October 2018) <https://www.esma.europa.eu/sites/default/files/library/esma71-99-1051_speech_on_cryptoassets_-_pa.pdf> accessed 4 April 2022

III. COMPLEXITY AND TECHNOLOGY   33

a degree of maturity requiring them to do so. The European Securities and Market Authority (ESMA) has explicitly acknowledged the importance of a watchful strategy when dealing with blockchain technology.[215]

The complementary approach of issuing guidelines goes beyond 'policy' guidelines in the strictest sense and includes those issued to warn market actors about specific risks and to 'threaten' entrepreneurs engaged with disruptive innovations. Guidelines provide an invaluable advantage in the sense of enhanced flexibility as opposed to traditional rules.[216]

As will be explored in greater depth in the following chapters, there are prominent examples of this approach in different areas of financial law. With regard to policy guidelines, the Swiss Financial Market Supervisory Authority (FINMA) has systematically issued guidelines to rapidly and proactively address specific regulatory concerns raised by disruptive technologies, as in the case of ICOs and stablecoins, consistent with an established principle-based approach in that jurisdiction.[217]

With regard to guidelines in a broader sense, the Securities and Exchange Commission (SEC) in the United States provides a useful example. The SEC has waited for some time before taking a position on the role of existing securities laws or enforcing them in the context of ICOs, and the debate is still unsolved and ongoing at the time of writing. Since 2017, the SEC has opted to warn investors of the risks related to the nascent market of ICOs and to infringing existing securities laws, and actively engaged with issuing warnings to tech entrepreneurs,[218] before enforcing existing securities laws.

The example of the SEC is also useful for highlighting the similarities between the 'wait and see' approach and guidelines issuance.[219] Notably, both offer regulators the opportunity to combine the decision not to implement formal regulatory decisions with other, more informal forms of intervention, supporting the financial industry while protecting investors.

However, both 'wait and see' and guidelines issuance also come with some risks. The 'wait and see' approach might institutionalize a sort of inertia for regulators, opening up the possibility that new market actors relying on innovative technologies develop and conduct new businesses (whose volume could also be extremely relevant) while remaining substantially unregulated for a long time. Furthermore, contrary to the spirit of this approach, it can also be a source of uncertainty, detrimental for investors, who would perceive it as a threat for their initiatives.

Even the issuance of guidelines (which in the past was associated with a principle-based approach)[220] might contribute to increasing uncertainty among market actors instead of creating the basis for technology to prosper. The nature of this approach could potentially require multiple interventions from regulators, with a risk of contradictory assessments, which would likely lead to instability.[221]

---

[215] Ibid.
[216] See generally Tim Wu, 'Agency Threats' (2011) 60 DukeLJ 184.
[217] See Chapters 3 and 4.
[218] Ibid.
[219] See Chapter 3.
[220] See Julia Black, 'Forms and Paradoxes of Principles Based Regulation' (2008) 3 CMLJ 425 (hereafter Black, 'Forms and Paradoxes').
[221] Ibid.

c. Innovation hubs and regulatory sandboxes

The intensity of the technological changes that society and the economy have experienced in the past years has forced regulators to develop more advanced regulatory techniques, in an attempt to address key societal and economic concerns while trying to identify a path for the development and the adoption of such disruptive technologies. Innovation facilitators are a catalyst for innovation, and innovation hubs and regulatory sandboxes are the most representative of these. Although the two strategies are rather different, they still present a certain degree of complementarity.

Innovation hubs create points of contact for firms in need of solving specific regulatory uncertainties with competent authorities with regard to Fintech issues, to obtain non-binding guidance on licensing, registration, regulatory, and supervisory requirements of new financial products and services or even business models.[222] Innovation hubs are a way to institutionalize knowledge exchange between market actors and public authorities. The majority of the European member states opted for the establishment of innovation hubs, with this objective.[223] In Switzerland, FINMA created its own Fintech desk in 2016,[224] and many other regulators worldwide also implemented this strategy.[225] Among them, the SEC not only created the Fintech Hub (commonly referred to as FinHub) in 2018 as part of the Division of Corporation Finance, but transformed it in a stand-alone office.[226]

Regulatory sandboxes are settings designed to enable a selected group of highly innovative firms[227] to test their new financial products, financial services, or business models in accordance with a specific testing plan agreed to and monitored by a dedicated function of competent authorities.[228] Sandboxes may also imply the use of legally provided discretions by the relevant supervisors,[229] including temporary exemptions from specific regulations.[230] However, temporarily exempted market actors generally operate their business model in a restricted manner, which might include a controlled number of clients or risk exposure, as well as close regulatory supervision.[231] To some extent regulatory sandboxes are complementary to innovation hubs because even in this case regulators might provide some guidance to market actors as a consequence of

---

[222] See Radostina Parenti, 'FinTech: Regulatory Sandboxes and Innovation Hubs' (2020) <https://www.europarl.europa.eu/RegData/etudes/STUD/2020/652752/IPOL_STU(2020)652752_EN.pdf> accessed 22 April 2022 (hereafter Parenti, 'FinTech').

[223] Ibid, 8.

[224] FINMA, *Annual Report 2016* (December 2016) 28 <https://www.finma.ch/en/~/media/finma/dokumente/dokumentencenter/myfinma/finma-publikationen/geschaeftsbericht/20170404_fin_jb16.pdf?la=en> accessed 2 April 2022.

[225] See generally Dirk. A. Zetzsche, Ross P. Buckley, Douglas W. Arner, and Janos N. Barberis, 'Regulating a Revolution: From Regulatory Sandboxes to Smart Regulation' (2017) 23 FordhamJCorp&FinL 3 (hereafter Zetzsche et al., 'Regulating a Revolution').

[226] SEC, 'SEC Announces Office Focused on Innovation and Financial Technology' (3 December 2020) <https://www.sec.gov/news/press-release/2020-303> accessed 4 April 2022.

[227] Competent authorities generally design a test in order to assess whether a specific firm can 'play in the sandbox'. The test generally assesses the capacity of firms to prove their support for the financial services industry, be in the position of providing genuine innovation, and benefit consumers. See Zetzsche et al., 'Regulating a Revolution' (n 225).

[228] 'On the Use of Big Data by Financial Institutions' (n 172) 4.

[229] Ibid, 4.

[230] Finck, *Blockchain Regulation* (n 192) 158.

[231] Ibid.

an enhanced interaction and continuous exchange with competent authorities, where regulators increase their degree of understanding and provide more legal certainty to the financial industry.[232] In Switzerland, FINMA has adopted this approach, by creating a new licensing category for innovative companies since 2016, and has gradually adjusted the category with continuous interventions, affecting specific operations.[233] Other examples can be found in Singapore, Hong Kong, Taiwan, Australia, Canada, and the United Kingdom. Furthermore, the debate is advancing at European Union level, encouraging the creation of regulatory sandboxes[234] as a key pillar accompanying the new regulations for market infrastructures[235] and crypto-assets.[236] In the United States the creation of sandboxes has not reached unanimous consensus, notwithstanding the proposal of SEC Commissioner Peirce in some critical areas, such as cryptocurrencies.[237]

3. Regulatory Disruption, Complexity, and the Idea of Dynamic Regulation

While some of the mentioned regulatory approaches might display some degree of utility in supporting the growth of innovation, they still miss an important point, failing to emphasize specific elements directly and indirectly stemming from complexity approaches. Such elements may be beneficial for designing an appropriate, or at least complementary, regulatory approach to better deal with systematic disruptive innovation, which is becoming the new normal in today's society and today's legal systems.

As mentioned earlier, regulators and policy-makers did not use complexity science as a further tool to support the decision-making process, due to the difficulties—or, rather, a reluctance—in characterizing legal systems as complex adaptive systems,[238] as well as because of the challenges of applying new methodologies and sciences in an approach to the law.[239] When referring to financial markets, this might be especially surprising because of their inherent dynamism and continuous process of evolution,[240] which would in principle require an equally dynamic and continuous policy process,[241] with adaptive management, constant monitoring activities, and numerous interventions.[242]

If key elements of complexity are dynamism and change, dynamic regulation is an approach to regulation that would be consistent with complexity science and some of the key concepts developed in that context. Dynamic regulation's key characteristic is to be a continuous process coordinated by regulators who adapt to change instead of

---

[232] Ibid.
[233] FINMA, 'FinTech License and Sandbox: Adjustments to FINMA Circulars' (15 March 2019) <https://www.finma.ch/en/news/2019/03/20190315-mm-fintech/> accessed 4 April 2022.
[234] See Parenti, 'FinTech' (n 222).
[235] See EU Pilot Regime on DLT (n 211).
[236] See MiCAR (n 210).
[237] See Chapter 3.
[238] Ruhl et al., 'Harnessing Legal Complexity' (n 26) 1377.
[239] Similar difficulties can be observed when taking into the introduction of a rigorous cost–benefit analysis before issuing specific regulations.
[240] See Baxter, 'Adaptive Regulation' (n 14) 257–264.
[241] Baxter, 'Capture in Financial Regulation' (n 89) 188.
[242] Farber, 'Probabilities Behaving Badly' (n 30) 148–149.

intervening with *una tantum* regulations. Dynamic regulation has been extensively analysed in economics.[243] In broad terms, it identifies a specific approach to regulation as a phenomenon strongly interconnected with preceding and succeeding events, and is based on 'institution-specific and decentralised information to facilitate feedback effects for anticipatory rulemaking'.[244]

From a theoretical perspective, dynamic regulation subverts a key pillar of rule-making activity. Traditional rule-making processes are built on the idea that stable and presumptively optimal rules designed as a reaction to preceding events are the best approaches for policy-making activities. Dynamic regulation relies on a much stronger, more historicist, interpretation of the policy-making dimension as intrinsically interconnected with the historical relevance and sequence of the events happening in a certain environment.[245] Therefore, dynamic regulation not only considers the preceding events but also tries to anticipate future developments by being essentially adaptive.

An essential part of dynamic regulation as an adaptive tool is structurally connected to feedback effects, reposing on some of the key elements of complexity, including networks and enhanced interaction between different constituencies of the society.[246] In the policy-making context, feedback effects identify the way policy-makers react to different events, including 'institutional changes or private actors' reactions and counteractivities to institutional constraints'.[247] A clear explanation of feedback effects and their relationship to the law-making process comes from Nobel laureate Trygve Havelmo and his Nobel lecture:

> Starting with some existing society we could conceive of it as a structure of rules and regulations within which the members of society have to operate. Their response to these rules as individuals obeying them, produces economic results that would characterize society. As the results materialize they will stimulate the political process in society towards changing the rules of the game. In other words, the results of the

---

[243] For an economic analysis of dynamic regulation, see generally Tracy R. Lewis and Huseyin Yildirim, 'Learning by Doing and Dynamic Regulation' (2002) 33 RANDJEcon 22. Here the authors emphasize the notion of 'learning by doing'. For a deeper analysis of this point, see David P. Baron and David Besanko, 'Regulation and Information in a Continuing Relationship' (1984) 1 InfEconPol'y 267, and 'Commitment and Fairness in a Dynamic Regulatory Relationship' (1987) 54 RevEconStud 413. See also Stephane Auray, Thomas Mariotti, and Fabien Moizeau, 'Dynamic Regulation of Quality' (2011) 42 RANDJEcon 246. See also Edward J. Kane, 'Interaction of Financial and Regulatory Innovation' (1988) 78 AmEconRev 328.

[244] Kaal and Vermeulen, 'How to Regulate Disruptive Innovation' (n 200) 191.

[245] Ibid.

[246] Feedback effects were studied in different fields spanning from economics to informatics and applied to different fields of law. For a general analysis on different legislative approaches, with an emphasis on feedback effects, see Vincent Di Lorenzo, 'Legislative Chaos: An Exploratory Study' (1994) 12 YLPR 425 (hereafter Di Lorenzo, 'Legislative Chaos'). For an analysis of the application of network effects to other fields of the law, see Ben Depoorter, 'Law in the Shadow of Bargaining: The Feedback Effect of Civil Settlements' (2010) 95 CornellLRev 957. See also William L. Baldwin, 'The Feedback Effect of Business Conduct on Industry Structure' (1969) 12 JL&Econ 123. For an analysis of feedback effects, see Itay Goldstein, 'The Feedback Effect: How the Financial Markets Affect Decisions in the "Real Economy"' (*Knowledge at Wharton*, 24 October 2012) <https://knowledge.wharton.upenn.edu/article/the-feedback-effect-how-the-financial-markets-affect-decisions-in-the-real-economy/> accessed 4 April 2022. For an analysis of the political dimension of feedback effects, see David Easton, *A Systems Analysis of Political Life* (UCP 1979) 363–468.

[247] Kaal and Vermeulen, 'How to Regulate Disruptive Innovation' (n 200) 192.

individuals in a society responding in a certain way to the original rules of the game have a feedback effect upon these rules themselves.[248]

A basic feedback mechanism connecting institutions and regulatory outcomes is the interaction between rules and rule-making processes and their evolution over time.[249] If the outcome of such interaction is suboptimal, a traditional regulatory environment informed on stability would perpetuate such suboptimal levels, whereas in a framework informed by dynamic regulation, policy-makers would be in a better position to solve these problems.[250] Here institutions are in a position to establish whether rules should be applied and adapted to future conditions, relying on feedback effects to build such adaptation.[251]

In connection to this element, important potential benefits related to feedback effects reside in the enhancement of information for regulation. On the basis of increasingly 'institution-specific, decentralised and timely information' available to regulators, they may be in a position to flexibly and adaptively react to regulatory happenings relying on relevant feedback effects.[252] Therefore, the key promises of feedback effects are a decreased level of unforeseen contingencies in the rule-making process, coupled with its enhanced certainty. Because of such increased systemic interaction, dynamic regulation could also contribute to accelerating the legislative process, which could lead to more appropriate regulatory responses to disruptive innovation because of their time sensitivity.

The idea of dynamic regulation is not a new proposal connected to disruptive technologies. A 1994 study on different categories of legislative processes conducted in the United States by Di Lorenzo highlighted important characteristics related to feedback effects. In particular, the study identifies four main legislative factors on which feedback effects (and dynamic regulation) have an impact. Feedback effects had become prevalent in the legislative process in the form of constant flux.[253] Furthermore, feedbacks impact on legislative outcomes, making them more unpredictable and contributing to periods of legislative turbulence.[254] On the basis of these four factors, the study highlighted two shortcomings that should induce regulators to be cautious about the implementation of dynamic regulations as a tool to correct specific problems as they emerged in traditional approaches. A first point of concern is related to the timing and content of legislative decisions, because feedback effects may exacerbate their unpredictability—for example, increasing legislators' uncertainty in relation to the perception that new legislative actions are required—and the way in which available information emerging from feedbacks could be used and implemented.[255] A second element of concern is the overall complexity of the legislative actions that

---

[248] Trygve Havelmo, 'Econometrics and the Welfare State' (1997) 87 AmEconRev 13, 15.
[249] See Wulf A. Kaal, 'Evolution of Law: Dynamic Regulation in a New Institutional Economics Framework' in Wulf A. Kaal, Andreas Schwartze, and Matthias Schmidt (eds), *Festschrift Zu Ehren Von Christian Kirchner* (Mohr Siebeck 2014) 4.
[250] Ibid.
[251] Ibid, 4–5.
[252] Kaal and Vermeulen, 'How to Regulate Disruptive Innovation' (n 200) 192–193.
[253] Di Lorenzo, 'Legislative Chaos' (n 246) 467.
[254] Ibid.
[255] Ibid.

a system structurally based on feedbacks could display,[256] revealing some structural impracticability.

Disruptive technologies could contribute to strengthening the possibility of designing more dynamic regulatory environments. The quality and quantity of data allowing for better monitoring could favour the development of dynamic regulatory frameworks. As highlighted above, data sets could potentially favour the application of complexity science to social sciences. More specifically, data sets coupled with predictive sciences could be useful tools for enhancing forms of interaction between private and public actors and more generally optimizing feedback effects. Even in this context, data sets could be helpful to better assessing a quantitative historical analysis of the legislative reforms, identifying the way they changed legal systems and shape consequential evolutions at the level of regulated targets.[257] In addition to data sets, predictive analytics applications could also help regulators to structure better anticipatory provisions.[258]

IV. Complexity as History-Dependency: The Historical Dimension of Transformations and Disruptive Innovations in International Finance

As mentioned in the Introduction, complexity theories rely on the study of complex adaptive systems, and mainly focus on how their development takes place. A fundamental trait of their evolution is the 'history dependency', and this is mostly related to the achievement of stability by complex adaptive systems in the form of far-from-equilibriums. This view is antithetical to the way traditional sciences theorize and formalize the pursuit of static immutable forms of equilibrium, which are consistent with the equally static and invariable rules governing such equilibriums, as in the case of the Newtonian approach.

For the purposes of this book, opening a space for complexity theories necessarily requires an emphasis on the historic dimension of financial transformations to enhance comprehension of specific phenomena and their emergence in the economy and finance, and more broadly in the society. This is also functional to anticipate the trajectories of potential future developments, with the further possibility to employ this better understanding of the evolving events to develop potential regulatory solutions.

Westerns—especially Sergio Leone's *A Fistful of Dynamite*—teach that fuses can be of many types and length, and this variation mostly depends on the level of danger of the explosive attached to the fuses. Many different 'Time Zeroes' corresponding to the beginning of the fuse can be identified, and each of them would be a reasonable choice, because economic history and the developments happening in finance represent a continuous dimension. At the same time, many other 'Time Ones' corresponding to the deflagration of the explosive can be identified. This depends on two

---

[256] Ibid.
[257] Ruhl et al., 'Harnessing Legal Complexity' (n 26) 1377.
[258] See generally Waller and Fawcett, 'Supply Chain Design and Management' (n 94).

aspects. First, the economy and finance have proven to be cyclical, with phases of expansion, contraction, and crisis depending on heterogeneous factors, including politics, wars, speculations, and financial scandals. Second, financial innovation is not a novelty that emerged in recent decades.[259] Even Fintech did not in fact emerge in very recent years; its roots can be identified starting from the nineteenth century, more precisely in the 1860s.[260] In this continuity of transformation, the pace at which financial engineering and technological innovation were increasingly applied to financial markets and corporations has significantly accelerated in the past decades, becoming exponential in recent years.

Financial engineering became very important for the dynamics of financial markets as well as corporate governance (equity swaps are an example) and significantly contributed to the definitive establishment of new financial institutions and financial networks. In addition, the new 'layer' represented by technology further enhanced innovation and transformations, with increasingly powerful computers capable of managing and processing higher volumes of trading and complex investment decisions. Furthermore, technological innovation contributed to epochal 'infrastructural' transformations, such as the internet and the blockchain revolutions, and it has continued to reshape capital markets and corporate governance.

In this continuous dimension of economic, financial, and monetary transformations, a reasonable Time Zero for the purposes of this book may be the end of the 1960s or beginning of the 1970s, and an equally reasonable Time One could be the great financial crisis of 2008.

It is worth focusing now on the Time Zero. Since their emergence in the Middle Ages in the form of usury,[261] banks have been the centre of the financial system, and they played a prominent role in the shift from a feudal system based on an agricultural economy to a mercantile economy with faster economic cycles.[262] Banks further contributed to the shift towards new capitalistic paradigms, constantly adapting their businesses to new conditions, including the change from the gold standard to the new paradigms in the monetary economy.

Commercial banks' business model is based on maturity transformation. Banks[263] transform short-term liabilities (short-term debt of retail depositors and money markets) into medium and long-term loans.[264] Maturity transformation is completed with liquidity transformations by taking liquid short-term debt and transforming it into

---

[259] See Section III.
[260] See Section IV.C.3.c.
[261] See generally Jacques Le Goff, *Your Money or Your Life: Economy and Religion in the Middle Ages* (PUP 1988).
[262] See Jacques Le Goff, 'Church Time and Merchant Time in the Middle Ages' (1970) SSI 9 (4) 151, 153.
[263] Regulation (EU) 575/2013 of 26 June 2013 on prudential requirements for credit institutions and investment firms [2013] OJ L 176/1. Art 4.1 defines a credit institution as 'an undertaking the business of which is to take deposits or other repayable funds for the public and to grant credits for its own account'. In the United States, the Bank Holding Company Act 1956 (12 U.S. Code, s 1841, et seq.), para 2 defines a bank as an institution 'which both—(i) accepts demand deposits or deposits that the depositor may withdraw by check or similar means for payment to third parties or others; and (ii) is engaged in the business of making commercial loans'.
[264] John Armour, Dan Awrey, Paul Davies, Luca Enriques, Jeffrey N. Gordon, Colin Mayer, and Jennifer Payne, *Principles of Financial Regulation* (OUP 2016) 290 (hereafter Armour et al., *Principles of Financial Regulation*).

more risky illiquid loans, and with credit transformation, which consists of transforming deposits into riskier loans.[265] Different theories emerged to justify the role of banks in the economy. The generally accepted theory considers banks as intermediaries, focusing on their capacity to collect deposits from savers while distributing funding to a broad range of borrowers.[266] Therefore it denies that banks create money both individually (credit creation theory) and collectively (fractional reserve theory).[267] However, more recent studies have shown that it would be more correct to justify the activity of banks by adopting the credit creation approach[268] and that there is no empirical support for the fractional reserve or the intermediation theories.[269] By combining different operations, in particular deposit-taking and granting of loans, banks are in the unique position to 'invent new money in the form of fictitious customer deposits when purporting to engage in the act of lending'.[270]

Banking activity has traditionally been heavily regulated, especially since the inception of the Basel Accords,[271] with prudential regulations aimed at increasing capital requirements while also regulating liquidity, in an effort to control the risks emerging from liquidity, maturity, and credit transformations.[272]

Starting from Time Zero as defined above, new trends in the banking business have gradually emerged. Banks started to operate in a different manner, with an increased global dimension of capital markets where foreign exchange controls were liberalized.[273] In this changed paradigm, investors could change their investment strategies

---

[265] Ibid.

[266] See Kern Alexander, *Principles of Banking Regulation* (CUP 2019) 18 (hereafter Alexander, *Principles of Banking Regulation*).

[267] Richard A. Werner, 'How Do Banks Create Money, and Why Can Other Firms Not Do the Same? An Explanation for the Coexistence of Lending and Deposit-Taking' (2014) 36 IntlRevFinAn 71 (hereafter Werner, 'How Do Banks Create Money').

[268] See Michael McLeay, Amar Radia, and Ryland Thomas, 'Money in the Modern Economy: An Introduction' (2014) 54(1) Quarterly Bulletin 2014 Q1 4 <https://www.bankofengland.co.uk/-/media/boe/files/quarterly-bulletin/2014/money-in-the-modern-economy-an-introduction.pdf?la=en&hash=E43CDFDBB5A23D672F4D09B13DF135E6715EEDAC> accessed 4 April 2022. See also Michael McLeay, Amar Radia, and Ryland Thomas, 'Money Creation in the Modern Economy' (2014) 54(1) Quarterly Bulletin 2014 Q1 14 <https://www.bankofengland.co.uk/-/media/boe/files/quarterly-bulletin/2014/money-creation-in-the-modern-economy.pdf?la=en&hash=9A8788FD44A62D8BB927123544205CE476E01654> accessed 4 April 2022.

[269] Richard A. Werner, 'Can a Bank Create Money out of Nothing? Using Accounting Information to Test the Three Theories of Banking Empirically' (2014) 36 IntlRevFinAn 1.

[270] See Werner, 'How Do Banks Create Money' (n 267) 77. The author also considers that banks are the only institutions in the position of doing so because of their key characteristic in UK as exempt from the so-called Client Money Rules, preventing other firms from creating money in the same way. It was found that, in practice, only banks can issue money in this way.

[271] The Basel Committee on Banking Supervision has provided a series of Accords in 1988 (Basel I), in 2004 (Basel II), in 2010 (Basel III), in 2017 (colloquially referred to as Basel IV), to regulate banks via minimum standards. Although such standards apply exclusively to banks operating on an international scale, some major jurisdictions have opted for applying them to all the credit institutions, even the ones operating in local markets. See generally Armour et al., *Principles of Financial Regulation* (n 264) 295.

[272] In addition to pre-existing capital requirements introduced with Basel I and strengthened with Basel II, Basel III agreements introduced a Liquidity Coverage Ratio and the Net Stable Funding Ratio. For an overview see generally Basel Committee on Banking Supervision, 'Basel III: The Liquidity Coverage Ratio and Liquidity Risk Monitoring Tools' (January 2013) <https://www.bis.org/publ/bcbs238.pdf> accessed 4 April 2022, and Basel Committee on Banking Supervision, 'Basel III: The Net Stable Funding Ratio' (October 2014) <https://www.bis.org/bcbs/publ/d295.pdf> accessed 4 April 2022.

[273] Alexander, *Principles of Banking Regulation* (n 266) 24.

to pursue higher returns and diversification.[274] The basis for this shift was the proliferation of pension funds and life insurers in the United States and United Kingdom after the end of the Second World War.[275] A key characteristic of such institutions is that they do not need to rely on banks' intermediation services. Their customers and life insurers cannot 'receive or contract for liquid' claims, because such claims are connected to specific events happening in the future, and therefore pension funds and insurers do not need banks' liquidity and maturity transformation.[276] Furthermore, these institutions can afford their own investment advisers and typically invest only in high-rated instruments, without any need for monitoring or loan management, therefore eliminating the credit transformation-related services.[277] The emergence of such institutions and the increasing role of investment banks created the conditions for loan origination based on distribution of debt securities to institutional investors.[278]

Banking disintermediation (or market-based credit intermediation) as a trend and so-called shadow banking as a network then started to emerge, reducing the centrality of traditional banks within the economy and contributing to the emergence of new risks. Banking disintermediation occurs when corporations obtain funding from sources other than banks, whether these be non-bank lenders or alternative techniques such as issuing bonds.[279] Events such as financial and economic crises, as well as increased regulatory pressure (such as the Basel Accords, strengthening the capital ratios for banks), favoured the emergence of banking disintermediation.[280] As will be explained more in depth in the next paragraph, the shadow banking system comprises a series of heterogeneous instruments and institutions, substituting regulated credit institutions in the provision of specific credit services.

The increasing role of financial engineering and the massive creation of new financial derivatives contributed to the establishment of leveraged finance as a new paradigm based on complex derivatives and structured products. A clear result of these transformations consisted in the escalating growth of the shadow banking system, which led to structural transformations investing in international finance and international banking. The need for new funding to be channelled into the economy has continued to date, driving further change. This transformation was recently completed with the gradual inclusion of small investors through crowdfunding and peer-to-peer lending practices that became part of the new financial landscape.

The emergence of shadow banking had two effects. It led to increased financial—structural—complexity and interconnection, favouring riskier investments within the financial system, and the levels of legal uncertainty in financial regulation as a

---

[274] Ibid.
[275] Armour et al., *Principles of Financial Regulation* (n 264) 436.
[276] Ibid.
[277] Ibid, 437.
[278] Ibid.
[279] For an analysis of the transformations at the level of market structures and banking disintermediation, see Steven L. Schwarcz, 'Regulating Shadow Banking' (2012) 31 RevBank&FinL 619, 622–623. See also Charles K. Whitehead, 'The Evolution of Debt Covenants, the Credit Market, and Corporate Governance' (2009) 34 JCorpL 101, 133. See also Alexander, *Principles of Banking Regulation* (n 266) 26–27.
[280] For an overview of the pre-crisis financial architecture and an historical approach, see Rolf H. Weber and Douglas W. Arner, 'Toward a New Design for International Financial Regulation' (2007) 29 UPaJIntL 391.

consequence of the abovementioned connection to financial complexity.[281] The financial industry could create unregulated structures and financial instruments, which ultimately burst in the financial crisis of 2008.

The shadow banking system is a plausible starting point or Time Zero also because the massive financial innovations from the end of the 1990s up to the financial crisis of 2008, investing in and contributing to the system's definitive growth, can be considered one of the most striking examples of disruptive innovation in finance of modern times.[282] From the regulatory angle, such disruptive innovation in finance challenged regulators who struggled to identify appropriate regulatory tools to effectively deal with financial and economic risks emerging from these practices.

Starting from the development of the shadow banking system, this chapter focuses on the earlier dimension of the timeframe covered in this book and attempts to understand the basis for the new developments as they emerged in economic and finance under the pressure of new disruptive technologies, in particular blockchain technology. In this way, this chapter emphasizes the dynamic component of the book, identifying the salient points of the line of disruption that will be further developed in the following chapters.

A. The Shadow Banking System

1. What Is the Shadow Banking System?

The shadow banking system performs the economic functions generally associated with the banking system (regulated credit institutions).[283] The shadow banking system is a 'network of financial instruments and institutions', and its main mission consists of connecting 'commercial and consumer borrowers indirectly to investors in capital markets',[284] providing credit and liquidity transformation. Its growth led to significant changes in the financial system, where new entities using new financial instruments could compete with traditional banks and increase the pressure on the latter's traditional business model. As a consequence, banks suffered decreased profitability and had to exit the regulated perimeter of activities.

Heterogeneous institutions and financial instruments are part of this network. Investment banks, money market mutual funds, mortgage brokers, and private funds all play a role in the shadow banking system. These institutions often recur to securitizations as well as sale and repurchase agreements (repos), ABSs, CDOs, and

---

[281] See for example Daniel C. Hardy, 'Regulatory Capture in Banking' (2006) IMF Working Paper WP/06/34. See also Giovanni Dell'Ariccia and Robert Marquez, 'Competition among Regulators and Credit Market Integration' in Franklin Allen, Elena Carletti, Jan Pieter Krahnen, and Marcel Tyrell, *Liquidity and Crises* (OUP 2011).

[282] See generally Cortez, 'Regulating Disruptive Innovation' (n 23).

[283] See Gary Gorton and Andrew Metrick, 'Regulating the Shadow Banking System' (2010) 2010(2) Brookings Papers on Economic Activity 261 <https://www.brookings.edu/wp-content/uploads/2010/09/2010b_bpea_gorton.pdf> accessed 4 April 2022 (hereafter Gorton and Metrick, 'Regulating the Shadow Banking System'). On shadow banking, see generally Alexander, *Principles of Banking Regulation* (n 266) 293–306.

[284] Erik F. Gerding, 'The Shadow Banking System and Its Legal Origins' (2012) SSRN 3 <https://ssrn.com/abstract=1990816> accessed 4 April 2022 (hereafter Gerding, 'The Shadow Banking System').

asset-backed commercial paper (ABCP).[285] All of these instruments have peculiar characteristics that differentiate them from traditional credit instruments. Specifically, they serve a dual function, providing credit as well as transferring credit risk via capital markets.[286]

Shadow banking spreads assets (often illiquid) to investors, via multiple transformations in other financial products, which institutional investors, including money market funds, pension funds, and other institutional investors (generally all referred to as 'conduits') distribute to investors.

2. Causes Leading to the Establishment of the Shadow Banking System

The shadow banking system's extraordinary growth started in the United States in the 1960s, but it has become a global phenomenon, with significant developments in China now accounting for 16 per cent of the global assets.[287] Investment banks have dominated modern finance, performing key tasks in capital markets, such as providing advisory and underwriter services for firms, as well as other important tasks extremely relevant in the context of the shadow banking system.[288] Investment banks traditionally provide brokerage services and asset management and are engaged in proprietary trading—that is, trading and investing their own resources typically in a hedge fund or over-the-counter (OTC) derivatives—and in market-making activities.[289]

More recently, so-called collective investment schemes (including bond funds, hedge funds, money markets, and mixed funds) have registered impressive growth.[290] The main drivers of this shift in the banking market are the demand for collateral for financial transactions[291] and regulation, competition, and innovation. With regard to regulation, financial institutions in the shadow banking network were in a position to do their business outside of the scope of the regulatory framework created in the aftermath of the Great Depression.[292] Regulation and deregulation impacted the system in two ways. First, systematic deregulation of financial activities encouraged these activities, with prominent regulators and economists, including former Federal Reserve Chairman Alan Greenspan, favouring this approach.[293] Second, banking regulation such as the Basel Accords favoured credit risk transfer by imposing capital requirements that triggered banking disintermediation.[294]

Regulation also increased banks' costs and restrictions, thereby intensifying the competition between the profit margins of banks and specialist non-banks. Banks attempted to react to this heightened competition by acquiring these specialist

---

[285] See Gorton and Metrick, 'Regulating the Shadow Banking System' (n 283) 262.
[286] Ibid and Gerding, 'The Shadow Banking System' (n 284) 3.
[287] Jeff Cox, 'Shadow Banking Is Now a $52 Trillion Industry, Posing a Big Risk to the Financial System' (*CNBC*, 11 April 2019) <https://www.cnbc.com/2019/04/11/shadow-banking-is-now-a-52-trillion-industry-and-posing-risks.html> accessed 4 April 2022 (hereafter Cox, 'Shadow Banking').
[288] Armour et al., *Principles of Financial Regulation* (n 264) 35–36.
[289] Ibid, 36.
[290] Cox, 'Shadow Banking' (n 287).
[291] See Gorton and Metrick, 'Regulating the Shadow Banking System' (n 283) 267.
[292] Inquiry Commission, *Financial Crisis Inquiry Report* (n 199) 27.
[293] Ibid.
[294] Zoltan Pozsar, 'The Rise and Fall of the Shadow Banking System' (*Economy*, 2008) 14, 16 <https://www.economy.com/sbs> accessed 4 April 2022.

non-banks and shifted the focus of their credit intermediation toward these newly acquired, less regulated non-bank subsidiaries—or shadow banks.[295] Indeed, this strategy in part legitimized shadow banking because eventually these practices became widely accepted.

In addition to regulation and competition, innovation in capital markets, in the form of financial engineering, gave shadow banking a more prominent financial dimension. The commercial paper market was the first form of shadow banking to proliferate in the 1960s, followed by the 'repo' market in the 1970s and a gradual increasing use of leverage.[296] At the same time, risky loans started to spread, with banks (including commercial banks) lending money to companies and governments from emerging markets for diverse deals, including oil and gas, leveraged buyouts of corporations, or advancing money.[297] Innovations in securitization and credit risk transfers greatly contributed to the creation of the 'originate-to-distribute' model. This system was based on banks selling the loans they originated to broker-dealers, and the broker-dealers then pooling the underlying cash flows and credit risks. In doing this, broker-dealers used dedicated securities and distributed them to a subset of investors with 'unique risk appetites'.[298]

B. The Financial Crisis of 2008: A Financial and a Corporate Scandal

The financial crisis of 2008 revealed the structural deficiencies of a system based on risky loans favoured by off-balance-sheet financing based on derivatives, leverage, and short-term financing instruments (repos and commercial papers). The significant financial and economic interconnections amplified the danger of liquidity and counterparty risk and the lack of adequate structural mechanisms to disperse risk. This system generated 'too big to fail' (TBTF) entities, such as financial conglomerates, that catalysed new systemic risks and financial instability, which were exacerbated by high interconnection.

Extremely low interest rates favoured mortgage originators, who provided large amounts of money to subprime borrowers to purchase real-estate assets and, with the assistance of investment banks, arranged the necessary securitizations. These securitizations allowed the loan originators to sell the mortgages to SPVs, which in turn sold the resulting residential MBSs to pension funds, hedge funds, and banks.[299] In addition to MBSs, investment banks also created separate tranches of CDOs, resulting from combinations of mortgage-backed securities.[300] The result of this chain

---

[295] Zoltan Pozsar, Tobias Adrian, Adam Ashcraft, and Hayley Boesky, 'Shadow Banking' (July 2010) Federal Reserve Bank of New York—Staff Report No. 458 <https://www.newyorkfed.org/medialibrary/media/research/staff_reports/sr458_July_2010_version.pdf> accessed 4 April 2022 (hereafter Pozsar et al., 'Shadow Banking').
[296] See Inquiry Commission, *Financial Crisis Inquiry Report* (n 199) 34.
[297] Ibid, 35.
[298] Pozsar et al., 'Shadow Banking' (n 295) 22.
[299] See Stephen J. Choi and Adam C. Pritchard, *Securities Regulation, Cases and Analysis* (4th edn, Foundation Press 2015) 39.
[300] Ibid.

was an increased interconnection between heterogeneous financial institutions, which ultimately increased the levels of systemic risk. The fragility of the system was clear when the number of defaults on mortgages rised, simultaneously causing a decrease in the value of MBSs.[301] The massive exit of investors left financial institutions with an increased need for collateral to avoid insolvency. Sovereign states chose to rescue some while letting others fail, the latter category including giant investment banks such as Lehman Brothers.[302] The public intervention was necessary to avoid even more catastrophic consequences relating to spreading liquidity risk.

The financial crisis demonstrated the problem of managing financial conglomerates. This problem has two underlying issues: excessive interconnection and TBTF entities. The significant interactions between banks, insurance companies, and shadow banking entities contributed to enhancing and transmitting the different risks and severely affected the global financial system, in a situation where a lack of macroprudential tools and appropriate regulation and oversight at both the national and international level favoured opaque transactions.[303] TBTF entities encompass a broad range of institutions, including credit institutions, broker-dealers, insurance companies, government-sponsored enterprises, and hedge funds.[304] Among the credit institutions, an example of TBTF entities is 'universal' banks, active in a large sphere of activities and capable of providing a significant offer of financial services.[305] In a typical pre-crisis scenario, universal banks had ties with investment funds and their proprietary trading activities. Interconnection and financial conglomerates increased the systemic risks, especially in the form of liquidity and counterparty risks. Because of the variety of activities that shadow banking performs, shadow banking entities may be direct counterparties to banks in multiple ways, such as derivative and funding markets.[306] Conversely, banks may be exposed to shadow banking entities in many other ways, including 'common membership of a corporate group [and] the provision of explicit or implicit backstops or indirectly through their common exposures to assets'.[307] Furthermore, banks' liquidity support to off-balance sheet activities further increased liquidity and counterparty risks.[308]

Adopting a different angle, the financial crisis and the problems emerging at the level of the shadow banking system were the last 'corporate' scandals of a long series of

---

[301] Ibid.
[302] Ibid.
[303] See Jorge Abad, Marco D'Errico, Neill Killeen, Vera Luz, Tuomas Peltonen, Richard Portes, and Teresa Urbano, 'Mapping the Interconnectedness between EU Banks and Shadow Banking Entities' (2017) European Systemic Risk Board Working Paper Series No. 40, 1 <https://eba.europa.eu/sites/default/documents/files/documents/10180/1431348/5a5b092b-dc8b-4816-89e0-9673bd75d304/Mapping%20the%20interconnectedness%20between%20EU%20banks%20and%20shadow%20banking%20entities_paper.pdf?retry=1> accessed 4 April 2022 (hereafter Abad et al., 'Mapping the Interconnectedness'). See also Charles K. Whitehead, 'Destructive Coordination' (2011) 96 CornellLRev 323. For an approach highlighting the multiple interactions within the network, see Enriques et al., 'Network-Sensitive Financial Regulation' (n 72).
[304] See Nouriel Roubini and Stephen Mihm, *Crisiseconomics: A Crash Course in the Future of Finance* (Penguin 2010) 223–230.
[305] See Yesha Yadav, 'Too-Big-to-Fail Shareholders' (2018) 103 MinnLRev 587, 604.
[306] Abad et al., 'Mapping the Interconnectedness' (n 303) 1–2.
[307] Ibid.
[308] Ibid.

scandals affecting the financial system in the past two decades. Beyond the 'financial' dimension, in the financial crisis of 2008 corporate governance matters became extremely relevant at two levels. First, managers belonging to financial institutions implemented investment decisions in a position of conflicts of interest, such as unregulated proprietary trading. Second, in a similar though less sophisticated way, unscrupulous sellers of financial products or loan originators contributed to spreading subprime mortgages, which became the basis for massive securitizations. Specific remuneration policies that existed within the financial institutions favoured these mechanisms.[309]

An important season of corporate scandals opened with Michael Milken and the Drexel Burnham Lambert investment firm in 1988, followed by Enron and WorldCom in the United States and Parmalat and Cirio in Europe, and concluded with the more recent Goldman Sachs 'Abacus' scandal. The most representative corporate scandal is Enron, which was both an accounting and a securities fraud.[310] Enron executives put in place an articulated financial structure based on special purpose entities (SPEs) concluding a series of swaps among each other to artificially create economic value that in reality did not exist.[311] This ultimately led to a gigantic accounting fraud.[312] The US Congress reacted by enacting the Sarbanes–Oxley Act in 2002,[313] in the face of many critical voices.[314]

In Europe, the Parmalat scandal shares some similarities with the Enron scandal, although with specific differences related to the different shareholding structure. In the Parmalat scandal, which the SEC defined as 'one of the largest and most brazen corporate financial frauds in history',[315] the controlling shareholder pursued a strategy of systematic exploitation of the controlled company, without fulfilling its duties of monitoring the executives managing the corporation.[316] This situation, coupled with the lack of an effective and independent auditing function acting as a gatekeeper,[317] generated the most famous collapse in Italy. Italian regulators reacted with radical corporate law reform in 2003.

---

[309] See generally Grant Kirkpatrick, 'The Corporate Governance Lessons from the Financial Crisis' (2009) 1 OECD Financial Market Trends 1 <https://www.oecd.org/finance/financial-markets/42229620.pdf> accessed 4 April 2022. See also Lucian Bebchuk, 'Executive Pay and the Financial Crisis' (*World Bank Blogs*, 31 January 2012) <https://blogs.worldbank.org/allaboutfinance/executive-pay-and-the-financial-crisis> accessed 4 April 2022. See also Guido Ferrarini and Maria Cristina Ungureanu, 'Executive Pay at Ailing Banks and Beyond: A European Perspective' (2010) 5 CMLJ 2.

[310] William Bratton and Adam J. Levitin, 'A Transactional Genealogy of Scandal: From Michael Milken to Enron to Goldman Sachs' (2013) 86 SCalLRev 783, 786 (hereafter Bratton and Levitin, 'Transactional Genealogy of Scandal').

[311] Ibid.

[312] Ibid, pt IV.

[313] For an overview of the Sarbanes–Oxley Act, see Brian Kim, 'Sarbanes–Oxley Act' (2003) 40 HarvJLegis 235.

[314] For a critique see generally Larry Ribstein, 'Market vs. Regulatory Responses to Corporate Fraud: A Critique of the Sarbanes–Oxley Act of 2002' (2002) 28 JCorpL 1. See also Roberta Romano, 'Does the Sarbanes–Oxley Act Have a Future' (2009) 26 YaleJonReg 229.

[315] *Securities and Exchange Commission v Parmalat Finanziaria S.p.A.* [2003] Litigation Release No. 18527 <https://www.sec.gov/litigation/litreleases/lr18527.htm> accessed 4 April 2022.

[316] Guido Ferrarini and Paolo Giudici, 'Financial Scandals and the Role of Private Enforcement: The Parmalat Case' (2005) European Corporate Governance Institute (ECGI)—Law Working Paper 40/2005, 1 <https://ssrn.com/abstract=730403> accessed 4 April 2022.

[317] See generally John C. Coffee Jr, 'Understanding Enron: "It's the Gatekeepers, Stupid"' (2002) 57 BusLaw 1403.

The Bernie Madoff scandal was a classic Ponzi scheme, which contributed to the enactment of new regulation on private funds, as in the case of the Alternative Investment Fund Manager Directive (AIFMD) in Europe.[318] Discussing Madoff's fraud, Julia Black notes that this scandal proliferated in a context of 'prescriptive and detailed rules and with an aggressive approach to enforcement' and emphasizes the important role played by those in charge of enforcing these rules, who should understand the regulated activity.[319] This critique of the existing regulatory framework, which can be safely extended to the enactment of new regulations, critically exemplifies part of the distrust shown towards a regulatory solution to restore market integrity and investor confidence, which may generate alternative answers to crises and scandals. Finally, the Goldman Sachs 'Abacus' scandal further contributed to accelerate the enactment of the Dodd–Frank Wall Street Reform and Consumer Protection Act (Dodd–Frank Act).[320] Different financial regulators from different geographic areas and belonging to different legal traditions all reacted to these financial and corporate scandals in the same way, which consisted of enacting new regulations.

Recent developments, in particular the Wirecard scandal in Germany and the crash of crypto-exchange FTX, have reproposed similar problems in the context of Fintech companies. The Wirecard scandal originated from a series of corrupted business practices and reporting frauds, ultimately leading to the bankruptcy of the company.[321] FTX's management implemented an articulated business model, entering into a series of risky investments and proprietary trading, with significant conflicts of interests and no adequate corporate governance in place.[322] The two scandal showed the weakness of gatekeepers' networks.

C. After the Financial Crisis

1. Regulatory Response

Lehman Brothers filed for Chapter 11 (bankruptcy proceedings) on 15 September 2008.[323] The leaders of the Group of Twenty, commonly known as G20, met in

---

[318] On the Madoff scandal, see generally Peter G. Szilagyi and Chong Wei Wong, 'The Board of Directors in Hedge Fund Governance' (2012) (unpublished manuscript) <https://pdfs.semanticscholar.org/319d/c4d3c4bf92ad949208138b733b44cd491cca.pdf?_ga=2.257922315.1814225679.1589206661-1203352850.1589206661> accessed 4 April 2022.
[319] Black, 'Forms and Paradoxes' (n 220) 1044.
[320] Dodd–Frank Wall Street Reform and Consumer Protection Act 2010 (hereafter Dodd–Frank Act).
[321] Professor Katja Langenbucher, 'Wirecard and Lessons Learnt' (Public Hearing before the European Parliament Economic and Monetary Affairs (ECON) and Legal Affairs (JURI) Committees, 23 March 2021) <https://www.europarl.europa.eu/cmsdata/231679/02%20Langenbucher%20statement.pdf> accessed 30 April 2023. See also SAFE Finance Blog, 'Wirecard—A scandal at the right time' (20 August 2020) <https://safe-frankfurt.de/news-latest/safe-finance-blog/details/wirecard-a-scandal-at-the-right-time.html> accessed 30 April 2023.
[322] John J. Ray III, 'Declaration in Support of FTX Trading LTD Chapter 11 Petitions and First Day Pleadings' (17 November 2022) <https://s3.documentcloud.org/documents/23310507/ftx-bankruptcy-filing-john-j-ray-iii.pdf> accessed 30 April 2023. See also Marco Dell'Erba, 'Crypto-Trading Platforms as Exchanges' (2023) MichStLRev (forthcoming) <https://papers.ssrn.com/sol3/papers.cfm?abstract_id=4405361> accessed 26 April 2023.
[323] WSJ, 'Lehman Makes It Official in Overnight Chapter 11 Filing' (15 September 2008) <https://blogs.wsj.com/wallstreetcrisis/2008/09/15/lehman-makes-it-official/> accessed 4 April 2022.

Washington, DC on 31 October 2008, in an attempt to coordinate efforts to provide a unitary and adequate regulatory response within the financial system.[324]

What followed is well known. The system responded to these events by developing a traditional 'endogenous' reaction, and in Europe and the United States new regulatory initiatives took place.[325] All such newly enacted regulations adopted a macroprudential approach, which until the financial crisis had been marginal. Regulators considered shadow banking as one of the main causes of the financial crisis. Therefore, rigorous scrutiny and significant regulatory initiatives were implemented, including the Dodd–Frank Act[326] in the United States and a new regulatory framework in Europe.

The US Congress passed the Dodd–Frank Act in 2010. Among the numerous provisions, the Dodd–Frank Act strengthened the registration requirements provided for private funds in an attempt to more closely monitor their activities. One of the key regulatory measures adopted with the Dodd–Frank Act was the Volcker Rule, which re-introduced a structural restriction measure after the Graham–Leech–Bliley Act repealed the Glass–Steagall Act[327] in 1999, during the Clinton administration. Consistent with the purposes of the Glass–Steagall Act, the Volcker Rule limits banks' exposure to risky activities of private funds, and the consequent conflicts of interest, by banning proprietary trading activities.[328]

In Europe, the High-Level Group on Financial Supervision, chaired by Jacques de Larosière, published its de Larosière Report[329] in 2009. The report stressed the need to rethink the European Union's system of control at a macroprudential level and the importance of combining macroprudential and microprudential supervision to efficiently pursue financial stability.[330] The new European regulatory framework is the result of this approach. Apart from the rejection of rules similar to the Volcker Rule in Europe, European and US regulators adopted converging regulations in many respects. Consistent with the registration requirements introduced in the United States for private funds, the AIFMD[331] was the European response to the concerns that private funds (in particular hedge funds and private equity funds) generated during the

---

[324] On this matter see generally Rolf H. Weber, 'The Legitimacy of the G20 as a Global Financial Regulator' (2013) 28 Bank&FinLRev 389; and Rolf H. Weber, 'Multilayered Governance in International Financial Regulation and Supervision' (2010) 13 JIntlEconL 683.

[325] See generally Kevin Davis, 'Regulatory Responses to the Financial Sector Crisis' (2010) 19 GriffithLRev 117.

[326] See Bratton and Levitin, 'Transactional Genealogy of Scandal' (n 310) 786.

[327] The Banking Act 1933 (Glass–Steagall Act) passed in 1933 intended to separate investment banking from commercial banking activities. See Julia Maues, 'Banking Act of 1933 (Glass–Steagall)' (*Federal Reserve History*, 22 November 2013) <https://www.federalreservehistory.org/essays/glass_steagall_act> accessed 4 April 2022.

[328] See Charles K. Whitehead, 'The Volcker Rule and Evolving Financial Markets' (2011) 1 HarvBusLRev 39, 68.

[329] The High Level Group on Financial Supervision in the EU, *Report of the de Larosière Group* (2009) <https://ec.europa.eu/economy_finance/publications/pages/publication14527_en.pdf> accessed 4 April 2022.

[330] Regulation (EU) 1092/2010 of 24 November 2010 on European Union macro-prudential oversight of the financial system and establishing a European Systematic Risk Board [2010] OJ L 331/1 (hereafter EU Macro-Prudential Regulation). Recital n. 13 refers to para 148 of the Report of the de Larosière Group.

[331] Directive 2011/61/EU of 8 June 2011 on Alternative Investment Fund Managers [2011] OJ L 174/1.

financial crisis. The AIFMD focuses on the regulation of alternative investment fund managers (AIFMs), and European regulators opted for establishing more rigorous corporate governance requirements for AIFMs, in particular providing more rules for their investment strategies as an attempt to protect investors while safeguarding the overall system. Key pillars of the new regulatory framework are also the Short Selling Regulation (SSR),[332] which focuses on one of the most debated and controversial investment techniques, and the European Market Infrastructure Regulation (EMIR).[333] EMIR extended the mandate for clearing to a broader range of derivatives and expanded the scope[334] of the Market in Financial Instruments Directive (MiFID)[335] to off-exchange and OTC trading with the newly enacted MiFID II[336] and the Market in Financial Instruments Regulation (MiFIR).[337] These new regulations pursued different regulatory objectives, although they all promoted a macroprudential approach to supervision, combined with more rigorous investor protection at the microprudential level.

Both the United States and the European Union also created *ad hoc* institutions to increase macroprudential supervision: respectively, the Financial Stability Oversight Committee (FSOC), as part of the reforms introduced with the Dodd–Frank Act,[338] and the European Systemic Risk Board (ESRB).[339] The main objective of these institutions is supervision of systemic risks. Furthermore, both the US and European regulators implemented the creation of resolution authorities (Single Resolution Board and Orderly Resolution Authority, under the supervision of the Federal Deposit Insurance Corporation) to manage orderly failure of large financial firms as an alternative to traditional bankruptcy proceedings.

2. Technological Response

a. Bitcoin

A more comprehensive analysis of the magnitude of the consequences triggered by the financial crisis would take into account other events in addition to the regulatory answers provided in Europe, the United States, and to some extent internationally. The

---

[332] Regulation (EU) 236/2012 of 14 March 2012 on short selling and certain aspects of credit default swaps [2012] OJ L 86/1.
[333] Regulation (EU) 648/2012 of 4 July 2012 on OTC derivatives, central counterparties and trade repositories [2012] OJ L 201/1.
[334] For an analysis on the scope of MiFID II, see Niamh Moloney, 'MiFID II: Reshaping the Perimeter of EU Trading Market Regulation' (2012) 6 L&FinMktRev 327.
[335] Directive 2004/39/EC of 21 April 2004 on markets in financial instruments [2004] OJ L 145/1. For a brief historical analysis of MiFID, see Thomas Iseli, Alexander F. Wagner, and Rolf H. Weber, 'Legal and Economic Aspects of Best Execution in the Context of the Markets in Financial Instruments Directive (MiFID)' (2007) 1 L&FinMktRev 313.
[336] Directive 2014/65/EU of 15 May 2014 on markets in financial instruments [2014] OJ L 173/349.
[337] Regulation (EU) 600/2014 of 15 May 2014 on markets in financial instruments [2014] OJ L 173/84 (hereafter MiFIR).
[338] See Dodd–Frank Act (n 320) ss 111, 118. For an overview of the regulatory reaction to systemic risk in the United States, see generally John C. Coffee Jr, 'Systemic Risk after Dodd–Frank: Contingent Capital and the Need for Regulatory Strategies beyond Oversight' (2011) 111 ColumLRev 795.
[339] EU Macro-Prudential Regulation (n 330). This text was recently amended by Regulation (EU) 2019/2176 of 18 December 2019 amending Regulation (EU) No 1092/2010 on European Union macroprudential oversight of the financial system and establishing a European Systematic Risk Board [2019] OJ L 334/146.

previous section omitted a chronological element. Lehman Brothers filed for bankruptcy on 15 September 2008. Satoshi Nakamoto published 'Bitcoin: A Peer-to-Peer Electronic Cash System'[340] on 31 October 2008. The G20 leaders met in Washington, DC on 31 October 2008, in an attempt to coordinate efforts for a unitary and adequate regulatory response within the financial system. The dates of these events are not circumstantial[341] and lead to important considerations.

After Lehman Brothers' failure, the publication of Satoshi Nakamoto's white paper provided an answer to regulators from all jurisdictions as well as to the whole financial system. Satoshi Nakamoto proposed a self-sufficient payment system that could, in theory, bypass the existing financial system and the regulatory framework in place. The publication of the white paper generated a cascade of events, such as the application of the underlying blockchain technology, and, in particular, smart contracts, to a broad range of activities—including cryptocurrencies—leading to a proliferation of virtual currencies via ICOs.

As will be explained in greater depth in Chapter 4, Bitcoin has its roots in many different contexts belonging to different ideologies. Among them, 'cypherpunks' consider disruptive technology an alternative to political mobilization, where neoliberalism, counterculture, and technological determinism are melded.[342] These heterogeneous roots can be traced to previous experiences that precede Bitcoin, such as the first secure digital currency system,[343] based on a 'cryptographic blind signature',[344] created by David Chaum. This idea was the basis for Digicash, E-Gold (1996, backed by gold), and Liberty Reserve (2006),[345] and was further developed by Timothy May and Jim Bell—inspired by libertarian and anarchist ideas—and Nick Szabo's BitGold.[346] So-called laissez-faire banking favoured the emergence of new media of exchange, based on competition.[347]

Bitcoin implements an alternative view of the trust theory of money. It is a mechanism in which people make payments with confidence using a decentralized currency, and because they pay with it, money becomes the input of the system rather than the output.[348] When Bitcoin was presented in 2008, the main idea was to provide

---

[340] Satoshi Nakamoto, 'Bitcoin: A Peer-to-Peer Electronic Cash System' (31 October 2008) <https://bitcoin.org/bitcoin.pdf> accessed 4 April 2022.

[341] For an overview of blockchain (as well as Bitcoin and other trustless-based machines) as a response to the financial crisis, see Primavera De Filippi, Morshed Mannanc and Wessel Reijersd, 'Blockchain as a Confidence Machine: The Problem of Trust & Challenges of Governance' (2020) 62 TechSoc 1 (hereafter De Filippi et al., 'Blockchain as a Confidence Machine'): 'Blockchain technology was created as a response to the trust crisis that swept the world in the wake of the 2008 financial crisis. Bitcoin and other blockchain-based systems were presented as a "trustless" alternative to existing financial institutions and even governments.' Ibid, 1.

[342] See Rosa María Lastra and Jason Grant Allen, 'Virtual Currencies in the Eurosystem: Challenges Ahead' (2022) 52 IntlLaw 177.

[343] See Kevin Werbach, *The Blockchain and the New Architecture of Trust* (MIT Press 2018) 41 (hereafter Werbach, *The New Architecture of Trust*).

[344] FSBT.tech, 'What Is Electronic Money and Is It Real?' (*Medium*, 28 August 2018) <https://medium.com/fsbtapi/what-is-electronic-money-and-are-they-real-5277578bcbcd> accessed 4 April 2022.

[345] Ibid.

[346] Nick Szabo, 'BitGold' (*Unenumerated blogspot*, 27 December 2008) <http://unenumerated.blogspot.com/2005/12/bit-gold.html> accessed 4 April 2022.

[347] See F.X. Browne and David Cronin, 'Payment Technologies, Financial Innovation, and Laissez-Faire Banking' (1995) CatoJ 101.

[348] Werbach, *The New Architecture of Trust* (n 343) 41.

an alternative payment system that could bypass the existing centralized authorities, including existing central banks. In doing this, Bitcoin created a new form of trust based on a decentralized consensus and secured by cryptography. The debate on the nature and characteristics of this system permeated academia and, more slowly, the world of regulators and central bankers, although its purpose to disrupt the existing monetary and central banking systems was clear from its inception.

Bitcoin is the first cryptocurrency and an example of virtual currency (or digital money). According to the International Monetary Fund (IMF), the term 'virtual currency' refers to a digital representation of value, issued by private developers and denominated in their unit of account. It 'can be obtained, stored, accessed, and transacted electronically, and can be used for a variety of purposes'.[349] Bitcoin, like any other cryptocurrency that followed, is related to the activity of 'Bitcoin mining'. From a technical standpoint, Bitcoin mining, like the activity of mining any cryptocurrency, consists of extracting Bitcoin by solving complex computational mathematical problems, based on cryptography. As is very well known, Bitcoin is built on a specific type of DLT technology, blockchain, consisting of a chain of blocks in which each block represents a transaction and is attached to the preceding block with cryptographic keys, based on so-called consensus. Distributed consensus is a set of rules and procedures replacing the trusted validation system.[350] It regulates the process by which the majority, or the totality, of the network's validators reach an agreement on the state of a ledger, contributing to maintenance of a 'coherent set of facts between multiple participating nodes'.[351]

An important trait of Bitcoin is the proposal of a model which could be replicated. Indeed, just four years after the emergence of Bitcoin, J.R. Willett theorized the possibility of creating new coins *on top* of Bitcoin[352] and in 2013 Willett launched the first ICO, Mastercoin[353] (now Omni[354]). This contributed to opening a new era for the 'cryptoeconomy', giving rise to a multiplication of cryptocurrencies, also referred to as

---

[349] See Dong He, Karl Habermeier, Ross Leckow, Vikram Haksar, Yasmin Almeida, Mikari Kashima, Nadim Kyriakos-Saad, Hiroko Oura, Tahsin Saadi Sedik, Natalia Stetsenko, and Concepcion Verdugo-Yepes, 'Virtual Currencies and Beyond: Initial Considerations' (IMF Staff Discussion Note, January 2016) 7 <https://www.imf.org/external/pubs/ft/sdn/2016/sdn1603.pdf> accessed 4 April 2022.

[350] Hong Kong Applied Science & Technology Research Institute, 'Whitepaper on Distributed Ledger Technology' (2016) 5 <https://www.hkma.gov.hk/media/eng/doc/key-functions/financial-infrastructure/Whitepaper_On_Distributed_Ledger_Technology.pdf> accessed 4 April 2022 (hereafter HKASTRI, 'Whitepaper on DLT').

[351] Tim Swanson, 'Consensus-as-a-Service: A Brief Report on the Emergence of Permissioned, Distributed Ledger Systems' (6 April 2015) <http://www.ofnumbers.com/wp-content/uploads/2015/04/Permissioned-distributed-ledgers.pdf> accessed 4 April 2022.

[352] J. R. Willett, 'The Second Bitcoin Whitepaper' (2012) <https://cryptochainuni.com/wp-content/uploads/Mastercoin-2nd-Bitcoin-Whitepaper.pdf> accessed 4 April 2022. As Willett explains in the summary, 'We claim that the existing bitcoin network can be used as a protocol layer, on top of which new currency layers with new rules can be built ... We further claim that the new protocol layers ... [w]ill provide initial funds to hire developers to build software which implements the new protocol layers, and ... [w]ill richly reward early adopters of the new protocol.' Ibid, 1 (emphasis omitted).

[353] See Marco Dell'Erba, 'Initial Coin Offerings: The Response of Regulatory Authorities' (2018) 14 NYUJL&Bus 1107, 1136.

[354] See Laura Shin, 'Here's the Man Who Created ICOs and This Is the New Token He's Backing' (*Forbes*, 21 September 2017) <https://www.forbes.com/sites/laurashin/2017/09/21/heres-the-man-who-created-icos-and-this-is-the-new-token-hes-backing/#108e76ad1183> accessed 4 April 2022.

alternative coins, or altcoins. Conceptually, cryptocurrency mining is the beginning of the structural fragmentation of money creation in modern times, a function that has always been the prerogative of monetary policy and central banking.

The establishment of Bitcoin as a medium of exchange and unit of account, as well as its consequential role as a viable alternative to existing fiat currency for the execution of payments, was slower than the boom in market capitalization of Bitcoin and alternative coins in 2017 might have suggested. A high degree of volatility depending on speculation and specific structural characteristics of Bitcoin[355] impaired its establishment as a reliable alternative to fiat currencies.[356] As a consequence, the idea of creating stable cryptocurrencies, commonly referred to as 'stablecoins', emerged in the cryptoeconomy, and the possibility of global stablecoins developed by important tech giants raised concerns of regulators and central bankers.[357] The G7 stated that 'no global stablecoin project should begin operation until the legal, regulatory and oversight challenges and risks outlined above are adequately addressed, through appropriate designs and by adhering to regulation that is clear and proportionate to the risks'.[358] At the same time, stablecoins triggered a reaction from central bankers, who increased the level of debate on the possibility of launching central bank digital currencies (CBDCs), which will be analysed in the following chapters.

b. The underlying technological framework of Bitcoin: blockchain technology

Bitcoin has become extremely relevant, but not only for the importance that it has had at the monetary level: most of all, it has contributed to bringing attention to the underlying technology, blockchain technology, and more generally the role of disruptive technologies within economy and finance, and more generally within society.

Blockchain is a specific type of distributed ledger technology (DLT).[359] While in a normal distributed ledger, records are stored in a continuous ledger,[360] blockchain

---

[355] See Tommaso Mancini-Griffoli, Maria Soledad Martinez Peria, Itai Agur, Anil Ari, John Kiff, Adina Popescu, and Celine Rochon, 'Casting Light on Central Bank Digital Currency' (IMF Staff Discussion Note, 12 November 2018) <https://www.imf.org/en/Publications/Staff-Discussion-Notes/Issues/2018/11/13/Casting-Light-on-Central-Bank-Digital-Currencies-46233> accessed 4 April 2022.

[356] Nathan Sexer, 'State of Stablecoins 2018' (*Medium*, 24 July 2018) <https://media.consensys.net/the-state-of-stablecoins-2018-79ccb9988e63> accessed 4 April 2022.

[357] See Chapter 4.

[358] G7 Working Group on Stablecoins, 'Investigating the Impact of Global Stablecoins' (October 2019) 2 <https://www.bis.org/cpmi/publ/d187.pdf> accessed 4 April 2022.

[359] See for example BBVA, 'What Is the Difference between Blockchain and DLT' (3 May 2018) <https://www.bbva.com/en/difference-dlt-blockchain/> accessed 4 April 2022. In answering the question on the difference between blockchain and DLT, the post states that 'A blockchain, a chain of blocks, is a type of DLT. This is a case of a common phenomenon of name recognition causing confusion: when the success of a specific service, product, or application overtakes the "umbrella" to which it belongs and ends up devouring its namesake. In the same way not all sticky notes are Post-it, not all DLTs are blockchain'. In the same sense, see also R3, 'Blockchain/DLT101' <https://www.r3.com/blockchain-101/> accessed 4 April 2022. For a terminological analysis (not clarifying the relationship between DLT and blockchain), see Angela Walch, 'The Patch of the Blockchain Lexicon (and the Law)' (2017) 36 RevBank&FinL 713. See also Carla L. Reyes, 'If Rockefeller Were a Coder' (2019) 87 GWashLRev 373; and Carla L. Reyes, 'Conceptualizing Cryptolaw' (2017) 96 NebLRev 384.

[360] UK Government Chief Scientific Adviser, 'Distributed Ledger Technology: Beyond Block Chain' (2016) <https://assets.publishing.service.gov.uk/government/uploads/system/uploads/attachment_data/file/492972/gs-16-1-distributed-ledger-technology.pdf> accessed 4 April 2022.

implements a structure based on a series of blocks where each block contains a collection of transactions and is securely attached to the others.[361] Starting from the first block in the ledger, the 'genesis block', the following blocks are added, forming a chain.[362] This chain respects the chronological order of the transactions,[363] via complex cryptography ensuring security and integrity of the data. Furthermore, the resulting chain, representing a register of transactions, is considered to be the official record:[364] all transactions are immutably stored in that ledger, which is replicated among all validating nodes.[365]

Because blockchain is a subtype of DLT, the characteristics associated with DLT can be safely extended to blockchain. Therefore, this subparagraph will generally refer to DLTs. Regulators attempted to define DLT rather than blockchain. Multiple definitions of DLTs have been elaborated in different contexts and there is no one commonly accepted legal definition.[366] Among others, the International Organization of Securities Commissions (IOSCO) defines DLT as 'a consensus of replicated, shared, and synchronized digital data geographically spread across multiple sites, countries, and/or institutions. Distributed Ledger Technologies are technologies used to implement distributed ledgers.'[367] Irrespective of a legal definition, DLT combines different key features, in particular peer-to-peer (P2P) networking coupled with distributed data storage, where cryptography plays a key role in increasing the overall security of the system.[368]

A key concept is the ledger. Similar to accounting ledgers, electronic ledgers are updated whenever a transaction takes place. However, while accounting ledgers are overwritten, in the context of DLT the nodes (the system participants) exchange the transaction information that is subsequently added as a new ledger entry.[369] In

---

[361] HKASTRI, 'Whitepaper on DLT' (n 350).
[362] Ibid, 19.
[363] 'Distributed Ledger Technology' (2016) 1 In Focus 1 <https://www.ecb.europa.eu/paym/pdf/infocus/20160422_infocus_dlt.pdf> accessed 4 April 2022.
[364] Ibid. As Pinna and Ruttenberg explain in an article about DLTs, some of the characteristic features of DLTs can be found in earlier database technologies that have been developed since the 1990s, that is, in the field of master–master replication. These technologies allow a number of parties to update records in a common database, with conflicts being resolved by some form of consensus algorithm. It is possible that there will be a renewal of interest in technologies of this type, as a result of the current focus on shared databases (and distributed ledgers), and that they will, as a result, be updated and come to represent a competing alternative to DLTs. They could allow otherwise traditional databases designed to be shared among financial institutions to be updated non-centrally. Andrea Pinna and Wiebe Ruttenberg, 'Distributed Ledger Technologies in Securities Post-Trading' (2016) European Central Bank Occasional Paper Series, Paper No. 172, 10 <https://www.ecb.europa.eu/pub/pdf/scpops/ecbop172.en.pdf> accessed 4 April 2022 (hereafter Pinna and Ruttenberg, 'Distributed Ledger Technologies').
[365] See HKASTRI, 'Whitepaper on DLT' (n 350) 10 (describing the process by which a distributed ledger is updated).
[366] See David Mills, Kathy Wang, Brendan Malone, Anjana Ravi, Jeff Marquardt, Clinton Chen, Anton Badev, Timothy Brezinski, Linda Fahy, Kimberley Liao, Vanessa Kargenian, Max Ellithorpe, Wendy Ng, and Maria Bair, 'Distributed Ledger Technology in Payments, Clearing, and Settlement' (2016) Finance & Economics Discussion Series, Working Paper No. 095 <https://doi.org/10.17016/FEDS.2016.095> accessed 4 April 2022 (hereafter Mills et al, 'Distributed Ledger Technology') ('DLT is a term that has been used by the industry in a variety of ways and so does not have a single definition').
[367] IOSCO, *Research Report on Financial Technologies (Fintech)* (February 2017) 47 <https://www.iosco.org/library/pubdocs/pdf/IOSCOPD554.pdf> accessed 4 April 2022.
[368] Mills et al., 'Distributed Ledger Technology' (n 366) 3.
[369] See HKASTRI, 'Whitepaper on DLT' (n 350) 10 (describing the validation process by which new ledger entries are added).

addition, differently from accounting ledgers, electronic ledgers are 'collectively maintained'[370] by a shared or distributed network of participants.[371] Typically, the distributed network is a 'peer-to-peer' network, where each connected computer is a 'peer' node,[372] joining 'the network by connecting to one of the well-known peers, whose information has been made public. It then learns about other peers through the information received from this well-known node. At the same time, other nodes learn about this new node.'[373]

In a distributed or decentralized network, the intermediation of a centralized validation entity (a central bank or a clearinghouse) in charge of recording and validating the transactions is not necessary.[374] In this decentralized network,[375] DLT users dispose of specific information that identifies assets and their owners: information is distributed among users, who can implement a wide range of actions, without a trusted central counterparty acting as a validator.[376]

The DLT decentralized model substitutes the trusted central validation system with 'distributed consensus' on the new information added to the ledger.[377] Consensus is a set of rules and procedures regulating the process by which the majority, or also the totality, of the networks' validators reach an agreement on the state of a ledger, collectively maintaining a 'coherent set of facts between multiple participating nodes'.[378] The process of consensus can vary. Proof-of-work (POW) and proof-of-stake (POS) are the two main consensus mechanism. Bitcoin adopts POW, therefore the 'longest chain', the chain with the most POW, is the valid ledger.[379] Ethereum moved towards POS, and describes it in these terms: '[POS] requires users to stake their ETH to become a validator [users who need to stake more than 32 EHT] in the network. Validators are responsible for the same thing as miners in POW: ordering transactions

---

[370] Ibid.
[371] ESMA, *Report—The Distributed Ledger Technology Applied to Securities Markets* (2016) 8 <https://www.esma.europa.eu/sites/default/files/library/dlt_report_-_esma50-1121423017-285.pdf> accessed 4 April 2022 (hereafter ESMA, *Report on DLT*).
[372] See HKASTRI, 'Whitepaper on DLT' (n 350) 10.
[373] Ibid.
[374] See ESMA, *Report on DLT* (n 371) 8 (explaining that the 'uniqueness' of the distributed network is the fact that they are not maintained by a centralized entity or validation system).
[375] For an analysis of decentralization, see Vitalik Buterin, 'A Next-Generation Smart Contract and Decentralized Application Platform White Paper' (*Ethereum*, 2018) <https://ethereum.org/669c9e2e20273 10b6b3cdce6e1c52962/Ethereum_Whitepaper_-_Buterin_2014.pdf> accessed 30 April 2023 (hereafter Buterin, 'A Next-Generation Smart Contract') (providing a history and overview of the concept of decentralised currency and consensus).
[376] Pinna and Ruttenberg, 'Distributed Ledger Technologies' (n 364) 8.
[377] HKASTRI, 'Whitepaper on DLT' (n 350) 10. See generally also (*ex multis*) De Filippi et al., 'Blockchain as a Confidence Machine' (n 341).
[378] Tim Swanson, 'Consensus-as-a-Service: A Brief Report on the Emergence of Permissioned, Distributed Ledger Systems' 4 (*Great Wall of Numbers*, 2015) <https://www.ofnumbers.com/2015/04/06/consensus-as-a-service-a-brief-report-on-the-emergence-of-permissioned-distributed-ledger-systems/> accessed 4 April 2022.
[379] Ibid. Swanson notes that '[t]here are multiple alternative consensus mechanisms which have been developed over the past three decades. For instance, the Dijkstra Prize is an annual award for academic research on distributed computing. Some of the ideas and innovations from these proceedings have influenced both distributed databases which require fault tolerance (*i.e.*, Paxos from Leslie Lamport) and distributed economic consensus methods. The primary distinction between the former and latter is that of maturity in formalization, analysis and implementation.'

and creating new blocks so that all nodes can agree on the state of the network.'[380] DLT users reach consensus on a particular version of the distributed ledger, namely on the sequential order of transactions, with the consequence that 'there cannot be any doubt as to the users' respective holdings', replacing a central validation with 'a set of cryptographic[381] solutions and economic incentives that combine to prevent illicit updates and reconcile discrepancies'.[382] Concretely, in the process of 'distributed consensus', two distinct phases are (i) the 'validation' of each transaction and (ii) the 'broadcast & consensus'.[383] In the first phase, the nodes assess the validity of the new entries in a transaction block and the possibility of adding the new transaction block to the immutable ledger, ensuring the legitimacy of all the elements within the ledger.[384] In the 'broadcast & consensus' phase, validating nodes agree on a common view of the state of the ledger in relation to the new block.[385] The ledger produced can thus be considered authoritative, although its management is shared among users with conflicting incentives.[386]

DLT uses digital signature technology, a derivation of public-key cryptography, to verify the authenticity of transactions over the network and further increase its security.[387] Digital signature technology is an implementation of asymmetric key cryptography, which operates in substitution of a notary function, serving the purpose of certifying the authenticity of the transactions.[388] The digital signature is based on three algorithms. First, a key generation algorithm creates a pair of keys—a private signing key and public verification key—such that 'the private key may not be derived from the public key'.[389] Second, a signing algorithm executes the message while at the same time associating the private key of the sender with that message.[390] A third signature

---

[380] Hezhao, 'Proof-of-Stake (POS)' (*Ethereum*, 20 April 2022) <https://ethereum.org/en/developers/docs/consensus-mechanisms/pos/> accessed 20 April 2022. Ethereum identifies the following points as key improvements related to POS:

> better energy efficiency—you don't need to use lots of energy mining blocks lower barriers to entry; reduced hardware requirements—you don't need elite hardware to stand a chance of creating new blocks; stronger immunity to centralization—proof-of-stake should lead to more nodes in the network; stronger support for shard chains—a key upgrade in scaling the Ethereum network.

[381] Cryptography is 'computer-based encryption techniques such as public/private keys and hash functions, to store assets and validate transactions'. ESMA, *Report on DLT* (n 371) 8.
[382] Pinna and Ruttenberg, 'Distributed Ledger Technologies' (n 364) 9.
[383] HKASTRI, 'Whitepaper on DLT' (n 350) 10.
[384] Ibid. Such validation may consist in verifying that 'the sender of a transaction is the true owner of the asset being sold. For transactions containing a contract execution instruction, validating nodes will also execute the instruction that has been received and confirmed by the consensus process.'
[385] Ibid.
[386] An authoritative ledger with shared management presents unique problems because of the existence of bad faith users and bona fide users alike. See Pinna and Ruttenberg, 'Distributed Ledger Technologies' (n 364) 8.
[387] Charles Brennan and William Lunn, 'The Trust Disrupter' (*Finextra*, 3 August 2016) <https://www.finextra.com/finextra-downloads/newsdocs/document-1063851711.pdf> accessed 4 April 2022 (hereafter Brennan and Lunn, 'The Trust Disrupter') (finding 'blockchain more easily optimizable to different objectives').
[388] HKASTRI, 'Whitepaper on DLT' (n 350) 26.
[389] Brennan and Lunn, 'The Trust Disrupter' (n 387) 20.
[390] Ibid.

verification algorithm employs a public key and ensures that the correct private key served for signing the digest.[391] Conversely, anyone who does not possess that specific private key and tries to sign with another is immediately identified as a fraudulent individual.[392]

c. The new paradigms

i. Fintech At a broader level beyond the pure 'monetary' dimension connected to Bitcoin, most recent developments in Fintech are also related to the financial crisis of 2008, or at least related to it. Indeed, Fintech companies' founders are often experienced professionals who were employed in banking institutions and lost their jobs in the aftermath of the financial crisis.[393] They had a strong background in relation to 'connecting financial services with the new technologies to launch innovative companies and/or create new business models'.[394]

Fintech, a term coined in 1990, refers to any technological application to deliver financial solutions,[395] bringing more flexibility, security, efficiency, and opportunities when compared to traditional financial services.[396] Different from other labels such as digital finance and e-finance, Fintech emphasizes technological innovations and technological developments. Indeed, the majority of Fintech companies started operations in the information technology (IT) sector rather than the financial sector, and afterwards elaborated new solutions applicable to the financial industry.[397]

Fintech encompasses both start-up and established institutions,[398] and, consistent with Christensen's identification of disruptive vs sustaining innovation,[399] sustaining vs disruptive Fintech was also proposed.[400] Along a similar line, scholars highlighted that Fintech is not synonymous with 'techfin',[401] which in contrast identifies companies

---

[391] Ibid. For a definition of 'digest' see IBM, 'Message Digests and Digital Signatures' (31 March 2022) <https://www.ibm.com/docs/en/ibm-mq/7.5?topic=concepts-message-digests10510_.html> accessed 4 April 2022.

[392] HKASTRI, 'Whitepaper on DLT' (n 350) 26.

[393] See Amy King, 'Fintech: Throwing Down the Gauntlet to Financial Services' (*Unquote*, 17 January 2014) <https://www.unquote.com/unquote/analysis/74596/fintech-throwing-down-the-gauntlet-to-financial-services> accessed 4 April 2022.

[394] Peter Gomber, Jascha-Alexander Koch, and Michael Siering, 'Digital Finance and FinTech: Current Research and Future Research Directions' (2017) 87 JBusEcon 537, 541 (hereafter Gomber et al., 'Digital Finance and FinTech').

[395] See Marc Hochstein, 'Fintech (the Word, That Is) Evolves' (*American Banker*, 5 October 2015) <http://www.americanbanker.com/bankthink/fintech-the-word-that-is-evolves-1077098-1.html> accessed 4 April 2022.

[396] See Peter Lee, 'The Fintech Entrepreneurs Aiming to Reinvent Finance' (2015) 46 Euromoney 42.

[397] Gomber et al., 'Digital Finance and FinTech' (n 394) 540.

[398] Ibid.

[399] See Section III.B.

[400] Gomber et al., 'Digital Finance and FinTech' (n 394) 540.

[401] See generally Dirk A. Zetzsche, Ross P. Buckley, Douglas W. Arner, and Janos N. Barberis, 'From FinTech to TechFin: The Regulatory Challenges of Data-Driven Finance' (2018) 14 NYUJL&Bus 393. See also Jim Marous, 'The Future of Banking: Fintech or Techfin?' (*Forbes*, August 2018) <https://www.forbes.com/sites/jimmarous/2018/08/27/future-of-banking-fintech-or-techfin-technology/#5a44e415f2d5> accessed 4 April 2022.

that adapt existing financial capabilities to new technological transformations instead of innovating in a radical way, as Fintech companies do.[402]

Fintech also differs from digital finance, both being part of it and currently representing one of the most disruptive components within it.[403] According to Gomber, Koch, and Siering, Fintech is one of the three dimensions of what they call the 'Digital Finance Cube'.[404] This is the dimension of digital finance institutions, where Fintech companies and established institutions co-exist.[405]

Consistent with the scope of Bitcoin and blockchain, 'disruptive' Fintech's entrepreneurial initiatives intended to disrupt existing established financial institutions, cutting the costs for market actors and increasing transparency and financial inclusion. Bitcoin and blockchain certainly favoured the increasing importance of Fintech.[406]

The development of Fintech was gradual. Arner, Barberis, and Buckley suggest that this process started in 1866 and developed in three stages. A first phase of Fintech was identified in the period between 1866 and 1967, with new technologies including telegraph, railroads, and steamship contributing to the creation of new financial connections (and interconnections), and further technologies spreading after the Second World War, such as the global telex, that would create an embryonic globalized system which established itself and grew in the following decades.[407]

New technological advancements in the late 1960s and 1970s opened the way for the second phase of Fintech. New technologies revolutionized the payment systems, with the creation of the Inter-Bank Computer Bureau in UK, the US Clearing House Interbank Payments System, Fedwire, and the Society of Worldwide Interbank Financial Telecommunications (Swift).[408] At the same time, new problems and fragilities emerged, such as in the case of the so-called Black Monday of 1987 when extremely interconnected financial markets crashed all over the world, or in the case of Long Term Capital Management's collapse partially related to new computerized approaches to risk management.[409]

---

[402] See Greeninvest, 'Fintech, Green Finance And Developing Countries' (May 2017) 5 <http://unepinquiry.org/wp-content/uploads/2017/06/Fintech_Green_Finance_and_Developing_Countries-input-paper.pdf> accessed 4 April 2022 (hereafter Greeninvest, 'Fintech, Green Finance and Developing Countries').

[403] Gomber et al., 'Digital Finance and FinTech' (n 394) 540.

[404] Ibid, 542.

[405] Ibid.

[406] See Douglas W. Arner, Janos Barberis, and Ross P. Buckley, The Evolution of Fintech: A New Post-Crisis Paradigm? (2015) University of Hong Kong Faculty of Law, Research Paper No. 2015/047. See also Douglas W. Arner, Janos Barberis, and Ross P. Buckley, 'FinTech, RegTech and the Reconceptualization of Financial Regulation' (2017) 37 NWJIntlL&Bus 371. See also Christopher Brummer, 'Prologue to Daniel Gorfine, FinTech Innovation: Building a 21st Century Regulator' (November 2017) Georgetown University IIEL Issue Brief 11/2017 <https://www.law.georgetown.edu/iiel/wp-content/uploads/sites/8/2018/01/LabCFTC-Chris-Brummer-Dan-Gorfine-IIEL-Issue-Brief-November-2017-Accessible.pdf> accessed 4 April 2022. Here the author identifies peculiar characteristics of today's Fintech when comparing it with its predecessors. See also Dirk A. Zetzsche, Douglas W. Arner, Ross P. Buckley, and Rolf H. Weber, 'The Evolution and Future of Data-Driven Finance in the EU' (2020) 57 CMLRev 33.

[407] See generally Douglas W. Arner, Janos Barberis, and Ross P. Buckley, 'Fintech and Regtech in a Nutshell and the Future in a Sandbox' (2017) 3 CFA Research Foundations Brief <https://www.cfainstitute.org/en/research/foundation/2017/fintech-and-regtech-in-a-nutshell-and-the-future-in-a-sandbox> accessed 4 April 2022 (hereafter Arner et al., 'Fintech and Regtech in a Nutshell').

[408] Ibid, 5.

[409] Ibid, 5–6.

The third phase, starting with the financial crisis of 2008, corresponds to the massive implementation of an array of disruptive technologies in finance, contributing to the exponential pace by which technology develops and the degree of substitution within financial markets.[410]

In the current landscape, a common trait of Fintech companies is that they are technology companies entering the financial system, where they combine digital technologies (in particular big data analytics, machine learning, and artificial intelligence)[411] with financial services and consumer finance in innovative ways.[412] Beyond this similarity, the Fintech sector is highly diverse. Some companies open up new markets in the financial industry; others offer new solutions for existing products or services offered by banks, asset managers, or insurance companies.

Fintech developed in three different sectors of capital markets and banking. Many of these Fintech start-ups sought to disrupt the retail and commercial banking industries. Such firms include Revolut (currency exchange), Neon (digital banking and debit cards), Chime (services similar to checking accounts), Greenlight (smart debit cards for kids), Divvy (business-to-business payments and expenses platform), Nubank (a mobile bank focusing on unbanked and underbanked people living in Latin America), Petal (credit cards for those who do not meet the requirements for a credit line from traditional banks), and Brex (funding for start-ups).[413]

Many Fintech innovations also supported the growth of shadow banking. For example, technological developments had a dual effect. First, innovation initiated the emergence of new entities providing financial and banking services, consistent with what happened at the very beginning of the 'first wave' of shadow banking. Crowdfunding platforms, for example, intended to fund projects by individuals who would otherwise be unable to borrow money from traditional banks.

Second, both established institutions and new Fintech start-ups and consortia were able to identify solutions that supported the evolution of the 'classic' tools of shadow banking. In fact, the Depository Trust & Clearing Corporation and Digital Asset Holdings have considered the potential application of DLT to manage repo transactions,[414] and R3 Corda similarly explored the applicability of DLT to commercial paper transactions.[415] Both of these instruments played essential roles in the shadow banking system.

A third subcategory of Fintech developments contributed to the emergence of other initiatives in the context of payments and currencies, as in the case of Bitcoin and

---

[410] Ibid, 7.
[411] See generally Arner et al., 'Fintech and Regtech in a Nutshell' (n 407).
[412] See Greeninvest, 'Fintech, Green Finance and Developing Countries' (n 402) 5.
[413] Faisal Khan, 'Fintech Startups Are Disrupting the Banking Industry around the World' (*Medium*, 20 October 2018) <https://medium.com/datadriveninvestor/fintech-startups-are-disrupting-the-banking-industry-around-the-world-7d5ca5bb3cb8> accessed 4 April 2022.
[414] Anna Irrera, 'DTCC Completes Blockchain Repo Test' (*Reuters*, 27 February 2017) <https://www.reuters.com/article/us-dtcc-blockchain-repos/dtcc-completes-blockchain-repo-test-idUSKBN1661L9> accessed 4 April 2022. See also DTCC, 'DTCC & Digital Asset Move to Next Phase after Successful Proof-Of-Concept for Repo Transactions Using Distributed Ledger Technology' (27 February 2017) <https://www.dtcc.com/news/2017/february/27/dtcc-and-digital-asset-move-to-next-phase> accessed 4 April 2022.
[415] Yogita Khatri, '4 Banks Complete €100K Commercial Paper Transaction on R3's Corda' (*CoinDesk*, 6 December 2018) <https://www.coindesk.com/4-banks-complete-e100k-commercial-paper-transaction-on-r3s-corda> accessed 4 April 2022.

subsequent developments. The resulting new technological platforms may be a useful tool for central banks to review their policies and create a more modern ecosystem. At the same time, these new instruments and platforms empower private actors to do the same and use innovation for their own private entrepreneurial purposes. Now much more than in the past, private actors are in a position to compete with established public institutions, such as central banks. The initiatives by J.P. Morgan and the Libra Foundation (rebranded as Diem) to create their own digital currencies with a potentially global impact have made clear that this technology can directly affect the current structure of the monetary system and the role of central banks. The threat that these new Fintech developments pose to central banks is even stronger than that of Bitcoin, the 'original' disruptor.

ii. Cryptoeconomy, tokeneconomy, and decentralized finance (DeFi) With his white paper, Satoshi Nakamoto proposed a new payment system infrastructure and, with it, a new concept of digital money. One of the main characteristics of the 'new' money is that it is 'mined' by individuals and not issued by central banks, as modern money. Bitcoin's underlying technology, the blockchain technology, made this possible. As mentioned earlier, in principle blockchain implements full decentralization, created via a collective distributed 'consensus' that replaces the activity of a centralized authority acting as a central validator. In addition to decentralization, blockchain technology relies on an immutable ledger, implementing a new, stronger form of trust among the peers who are part of the network. Beyond this, blockchain enables the possibility of creating 'smart contracts' (as analysed in Chapter 2) that can be fully enforced without any human interaction. ICOs and their evolutions rely on smart contracts, and many other applications can be created relying on this digital platform, not only in finance but also in everyday life.

The possibility of replicating the model developed by Bitcoin through blockchain technology led to the multiplication of cryptocurrencies as well as digital tokens. The proliferation of cryptocurrencies and digital tokens led to the establishment of new paradigms, and with them new words to identify such paradigms were coined. A major consequence was the emergence of a new era, the one of 'cryptoeconomy', built on the underlying blockchain technology, and the other strictly associated with it, the 'tokeneconomy'.

The cryptoeconomy identifies a network of blockchain applications, adopting forms of digital cash.[416] In this way, the cryptoeconomy should implement a system based on decentralization, trust, and security among the different institutions involved.[417] The term 'tokeneconomy' refers to the 'token' itself, and its diffusion is associated with ICOs because ICO issuers distribute digital tokens.[418] Tokens may vary depending on

---

[416] See Darcy Allen, 'Discovering and Developing the Blockchain Cryptoeconomy' (2017) SSRN 1 <https://ssrn.com/abstract=2815255> accessed 4 April 2022.

[417] See generally Marcella Atzori, 'Blockchain Technology and Decentralized Governance: Is the State Still Necessary?' (2017) 6 JGov&Reg 1.

[418] See Swiss Federal Council, *Report on the Legal Framework for Distributed Ledger Technology and Blockchain in Switzerland* (14 December 2018) 32 <https://www.newsd.admin.ch/newsd/message/attachments/55153.pdf> accessed 4 April 2022.

the designing options, and beyond their legal characterization[419] tokens may have different functions (among the most important being payment tokens, utility tokens, and security tokens).

Another new term is 'decentralized finance' (DeFi), a movement emphasizing the characteristics of decentralization in finance, disrupting the more traditional approach designed around financial hubs.[420] There is no consensus on what DeFi is, nor on the notion of decentralization when applied to products, services, or activities.[421] The IOSCO refers to it as 'an important evolving and expanding technological innovation', although rather than a technological innovation itself, it might be characterized instead as a proper paradigm or emerging financial network, relying on specific technological innovations. The European Commission correctly defines DeFi as 'a newly emerging form of autonomous financial intermediation in a decentralised digital environment powered by software—smart contracts on public blockchain [involving] uncontrolled access to financial services on a quasi-anonymous basis using crypto-asset wallets'.[422] In DeFi, financial products, services, arrangements, and activities are developed relying on DLT, with the purpose of disintermediating and decentralizing 'legacy ecosystems by eliminating the need for some traditional financial intermediaries and centralized institutions'.[423]

The idea of decentralization in finance is not necessarily and structurally connected to blockchain or DLT. Before the emergence of blockchain, examples of decentralization can be identified in Skype, eMule, and Napster, which disrupted centralized paradigms in the telecommunications and music industries.[424] However, blockchain technology has contributed to increasing the traction of decentralization, because of the promise of implementing full decentralization, substituting the role of a centralized authority with distributed consensus.[425] DeFi relies on 'open financial infrastructures built upon public smart contract platforms',[426] as in the case of the Ethereum blockchain,[427] with no intermediaries or centralized institutions, substituted by decentralized applications (DApps). In this environment, smart contracts enforce the agreements, and the transactions are executed 'in a secure and deterministic way and

---

[419] See for example FINMA, 'Guidelines for Enquiries Regarding the Regulatory Framework for Initial Coin Offerings (ICOs)' (2018) <https://www.finma.ch/~/media/finma/dokumente/dokumentencenter/myfinma/1bewilligung/fintech/wegleitung-ico.pdf> accessed 22 April 2022 (hereafter FINMA, 'Guidelines for ICOs').

[420] Dirk A. Zetzsche, Douglas Arner, and Ross P. Buckley, 'Decentralized Finance' (2020) 6 JFinReg 172.

[421] IOSCO, *Decentralized Finance Report* (March 2022) 1 <https://www.iosco.org/library/pubdocs/pdf/IOSCOPD699.pdf> accessed 22 April 2022 (hereafter IOSCO, *Decentralized Finance*).

[422] European Commission, 'European Financial Stability and Integration Review 2022' (2022) <https://commission.europa.eu/system/files/2022-04/european-financial-stability-and-integration-review-2022_en.pdf> accessed 30 April 2023. This emphasis on automation is consistent with the concept of 'driverless finance' as analysed by Hilary J. Allen. See generally Hilary J. Allen, 'Driverless Finance' (2020) 10 HarvBusLRev 157. For a broader analysis see also Hilary J. Allen, *Driverless Finance: Fintech's Impact on Financial Stability* (OUP 2022).

[423] Ibid.

[424] See Wulf Kaal, 'Decentralization—A Primer on the New Economy' (2019) SSRN 6 <https://ssrn.com/abstract=3406323> accessed 4 April 2022.

[425] See Chapter 2.

[426] See Fabian Schär, 'Decentralized Finance: On Blockchain- and Smart Contract-Based Financial Markets' (2020) 103 FedResBankStLRev 153 (hereafter Schär, 'Decentralized Finance').

[427] Buterin, 'A Next-Generation Smart Contract' (n 375).

legitimate state changes persisted on a public blockchain'.[428] The resulting environment promises to be based on immutability and interoperability and to pursue transparency and equality in terms of access rights, without relying on market infrastructures such as custodians or clearing houses, whose tasks would become fully automatized, as a consequence of the implementation of smart contracts.[429]

DeFi is structured on a multilayer hierarchical structure (settlement, asset, protocol, application, and aggregation layers), in which the security of the superior lawyers depends on the ones below.[430] The basic layer, the settlement layer, is the technology itself, the DLT, where the consensus state is maintained. The settlement layer offers the opportunity to design and execute smart contracts for a broad range of activities, including offering, trading, lending, borrowing, and actively managing these assets.[431] Even end-user applications rely on smart contracts, and are fundamental for providing access and interoperability.[432] Therefore, the settlement layer operates as a common infrastructure where transactions are recorded, and market participants can store their assets. The second layer is the 'asset' layer. Here market participants create, offer, and transfer crypto-assets, including cryptocurrencies and digital tokens. The third layer is the 'smart contract' one, where smart contracts are designed for implementing the operational functionality of the DeFi products and services. Finally, the last 'application' layer is the one allowing the interaction among participants.[433]

Notwithstanding the promise of full decentralization, DeFi is still far from being fully implemented. As will be explained further in the following chapters, a vast majority of market actors (issuers creating stablecoins and private funds) and market infrastructures (such as crypto-exchanges) operate on a centralized basis, without benefiting from the substantial advantages that DeFi promises to bring. This mostly depends on the risks associated with DeFi at a very early stage of its implementation—especially in terms of cybersecurity—which are hard to overcome. Beyond cybersecurity, another major technical impediment relates to the limited number of transactions that can be executed on DeFi platforms, such as the most popular one, Ethereum, which processes 10–30 transactions per second instead of the 24,000 that a payment system such as Visa claims to process.[434]

It may be hard to establish whether cryptoeconomy, tokeneconomy, and DeFi are synonyms or whether they identify different—though complementary—aspects, and this second possibility may be more likely. While tokens, cryptocurrencies, and decentralization are structurally linked to one another, they are not exactly synonyms, and they refer to different aspects. Cryptocurrencies necessarily require the existence of tokens, although tokens do not necessarily imply the existence of a cryptocurrency. Furthermore, decentralization may be a common characteristic

---

[428] Schär, 'Decentralized Finance' (n 426) 2.
[429] Ibid.
[430] Ibid, 3–4.
[431] IOSCO, *Decentralized Finance* (n 421) 1–2.
[432] Ibid.
[433] Ibid.
[434] Ruaridh O'Donnell, 'In 2020, Will Decentralized Finance Finally Flourish in a Centralized World?' (*Nasdaq*, 27 November 2019) <https://www.nasdaq.com/articles/in-2020-will-decentralized-finance-finally-flourish-in-a-centralized-world-2019-11-27> accessed 4 April 2022.

for both cryptocurrencies and tokens, but tokens are not necessarily decentralized, with many of them being fully centralized. At the same time, DeFi shares some intersections with both tokeneconomy and cryptocurrency. Therefore, the three words identify three different dimensions, and at the same time are unified by a common intersection.

iii. Digital finance The emergence of these new paradigms makes the transition from traditional finance to digital finance more concrete. Digital finance broadly refers to the digitalization of the financial industry, encompassing electronics, products, and services of the financial sector, which span from credit and chip cards, to electronic exchange systems, to home banking and mobile and app services.[435] According to the Digital Finance Institute, digital finance start-ups are companies engaged in 'creating innovation for integrating distributed digital banking, mobile solutions and delivery platforms, micro-finance, payment solutions, peer-to-peer lending and crowd-funding'.[436] However, as with Fintech, even established institutions are part of this ecosystem.[437]

Digital finance is characterized by three main aspects.[438] First, a major shift in digital finance relates to data: compared to the past, in this new paradigm data is generally cheaper, more reliable, and abundant.[439] Second, in terms of structure digital finance generally attempts to systematically implement a full financial disintermediation, with beneficial consequences at the level of cost-cutting.[440] Third, digital finance is a driver for innovation at the level of financial products, private actors, and market structures: the crypto-revolution, peer-to-peer lending, and crowdfunding platforms[441] are all examples of these changes, where the emergence of new business models corresponded to the emergence of new market actors—new financial products—that drastically changed traditional market structures.

As mentioned above, digital finance differs from Fintech and other paradigms such as electronic finance (e-finance). E-finance generally refers to companies starting to use information and communication technology in the financial sector, whereas digital finance broadly identifies the general process of digitalization emerging within the financial industry.[442]

The best way to consider the multifaceted aspects of digital finance is by referring again to Gomber, Koch, and Siering's 'Digital Finance Cube' (see Figure 1.1) and its three dimensions; (i) digital finance business functions; (ii) relevant technologies and technological concepts, and (iii) institutions providing digital finance solutions.[443]

---

[435] Ibid, 539.
[436] Ibid, citing Digital Finance Institute, 'Innovation: Innovation Matters' (2015) <http://digifin.org/digital-finance-innovation/> accessed 4 April 2022.
[437] Gomber et al., 'Digital Finance and FinTech' (n 394) 539.
[438] UN Task Force on Digital Financing of the Sustainable Development Goals, 'People's Money: Harnessing Digitalization to Finance a Sustainable Future' (2020) <https://unsdg.un.org/resources/peoples-money-harnessing-digitalization-finance-sustainable-future> accessed 4 April 2022.
[439] Ibid.
[440] Ibid.
[441] Ibid.
[442] Gomber et al., 'Digital Finance and FinTech' (n 394) 541–542.
[443] Ibid, 541.

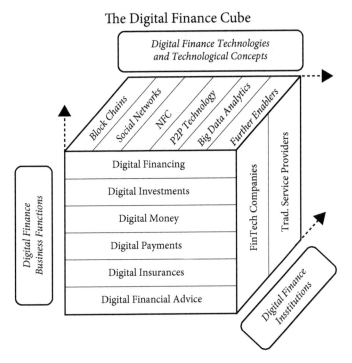

Fig. 1.1 *Digital Finance Cube*

By looking at the main elements constituting the three dimensions, the relationship between Fintech, cryptoeconomy, tokeneconomy, and digital finance becomes clearer. Some of Fintech's, cryptoeconomy's, and tokeneconomy's foundational functions, institutions, or technologies are part of this cube; therefore, they are part of digital finance and actively affect its development. Among all the elements mentioned within the cube, this book will deal with digital money, digital payments, and blockchain and will mention digital financing, social networks, peer-to-peer (P2P) technology, big data, and Fintech and established service providers.

V. The Layers of Complexity

Complexity and innovation are two different aspects in the context of financial regulation, and each has specific characteristics. As mentioned in Sections I and II, complexity might identify both a structural and a dynamic attribute, depending on the approach. Innovation is a key feature of emergence economies and one of the main drivers of complexity in modern financial markets. As mentioned earlier, dealing with either of the two likely implies dealing with the other. Although they are two different notions with different implications, they share in common the importance (or the need) for identification of a proper analytical framework for adequate intervention in different areas. Complexity science could provide valuable support for understanding the way transformations spread and how such transformations can be efficiently mapped, especially in an effort to identify the continuities and discontinuities with previous paradigms.

A. The Three Basic Layers

What are the key layers of complexity in the evolving capital markets scenario? Because capital markets are in constant evolution, they will include different paradigms that will co-exist, including, among others, traditional finance, cryptoeconomy, and DeFi. Both the layers and the underlying concepts are often interrelated under the incessant pressure of disruptive technology.

As Figure 1.2 suggests, a first layer is traditional finance, with an emphasis on leveraged finance and its networks, in particular shadow banking, and the way they are continuing to operate through different adaptations while being part of the economic and financial landscape. Therefore, in any attempt to understand financial complexity in an evolving context, key structures and instruments developing in traditional finance still require careful consideration. This is consistent with the emphasis that regulators put on the application of existing rules to new innovations. A focus on the continuity of traditional problems in apparently new structures might be helpful for developing an appropriate understanding of new phenomena in finance as well as for calibrating new regulatory initiatives.

A second layer of complexity is technology applied to traditional finance and the way it might trigger further transformations and complications. Traditional finance, as the first layer, is instrumental to developing a deeper understanding of specific structures in the evolved (technological) finance. After the identification of those problems that are structurally similar, this layer should focus on the analysis of the transformations induced by technology and verify the consistency or inconsistency with specific structures and networks developed in traditional finance. The examples of shadow central banking and crypto shadow banking analysed in Chapters 4 and 5 clarify how technology can be conducive to specific transformations whose underlying problems had already emerged in the past. This is also consistent with Omarova's theories on transaction meta-technologies, where there are specific structures and

Fig. 1.2 The layers of complexity

instruments that continue to be developed, irrespective of any technological advancements. Understanding the way new technologies enshrine on old structures is vital for any regulatory decision.

Finally, a third layer comes from technological advancements, in the broadest sense. This layer requires comprehension of the way technology as a new infrastructural environment works and can be conducive to new complexities, reshaping entire societal structures (including finance) and their operations under the emergence of new enhanced networks. An example could be the potential development of the metaverse as a synthetic universe.

The conceptualization through layers might be helpful for regulators and policymakers to elaborate appropriate regulatory measures that would deal with a revised and more dynamic concept of complexity in the financial markets context. Two important and distinct aspects of such conceptualization are the identification of (i) the layer (or the layers) in which transformations originate and (ii) the layer (or the layers) in which such transformations may or may not propagate. Understanding the layer(s) where evolutions originate and propagate might be relevant for regulators and policymakers to focus their intervention on the layer(s) involved.

In this regard, there might be two different scenarios. In a first scenario, not all the transformations would necessarily affect the totality of the layers at the same time. In a second scenario, such technological transformations might affect one of those layers with the two possibilities of (i) leading to a cascade effect on the totality of the layers or (ii) remaining confined within one specific layer. Therefore, layers are an opportunity for identifying a precise and traceable trajectory of the transformations. For this purpose, a further possibility might be the identification of sub-layers to potentially anticipate certain developments with adequate dynamic regulation in more specific areas.

B. Evolving Complexity and Multidimensionality

When trying to deal with complexity science and its categories more explicitly in the context of international finance, a first step is characterizing international finance as a CAS.[444] As mentioned above, modern financial markets are dynamic and constantly evolving networks, whose subparts (individuals and institutions) interact in different ways and contexts; such interactions trigger evolving patterns. A crucial problem is the identification of their subparts, to understand the way networks operate, expand, become increasingly interconnected, and ultimately evolve in a dynamic and adaptive manner. A plausible way to identify these subparts can be to refer to the contractual dimension, capital markets, corporate governance, central banks, and financial institutions organized in a network (shadow banking and its evolutions). Each of these subparts is a CAS *per se*, with internal interactions, emergence, and dynamic changes.

In the line of disruption, these subparts are analysed in two different ways.

---

[444] See ss II and III.

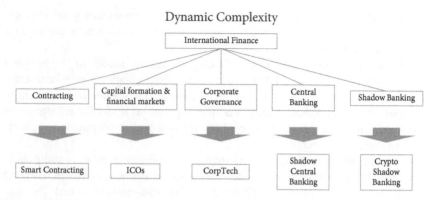

Fig. 1.3 Evolving complexity

1. Intrinsic Evolution of Each Subpart

A first angle from which to analyse the various subparts of international finance is by focusing on their intrinsic evolution. Indeed, each subpart evolved mostly under the pressure of disruptive technologies and in particular blockchain technology (especially relevant for the purposes of this book). Such subparts proved to be multiple sub-complex adaptive systems themselves (see Figure 1.3). The contractual dimension (at least in the context of digital performance)[445] is being revolutionized in the sense of technological 'smart-contracting'. Capital formation is affected by developments in the area of ICOs and their most promising transformations, namely IEOs and STOs. Technology also invades corporate governance, with multiple technologies revolutionizing the way the different constituencies interact, and the newly coined term CorpTech is an explicit reference to corporations and technology.[446] This book focuses on the transformations induced by blockchain in the area of digital securities (one of the consequences of ICOs) and maps the major potential changes happening in corporate governance. Central banks operate under the pressure of new market actors developing a new network, with the potential for playing a predominant role in international finance, as in the case of shadow central banking. Shadow banking also evolves or replicates itself, because of the mutated conditions, and becomes crypto shadow banking.

Each of these evolutions is consistent with the key characteristic of complex adaptive systems as 'history dependent'.[447] These evolutions are the result of specific innovations and events that contributed to reshaping the different contexts, triggering chain reactions. Specific inefficiencies, financial shocks, and crises as well as financial

---

[445] Rolf H. Weber, 'Smart Contracts: Do We Need New Legal Rules?' in Alberto De Franceschi and Reiner Schulze (eds), *Digital Revolution—New Challenges for the Law* (Nomos 2019): 'Smart contracts allow to "transfer" digitally referenced goods and services, not a performance in the real world.'

[446] See generally Luca Enriques and Dirk A. Zetzsche, 'Corporate Technologies and the Tech Nirvana Fallacy' (2020) 72 HastingsLJ 55. See also Howell E. Jackson and Margaret E. Tahyar, *Fintech Law: The Case Studies* (Harvard.edu, 2020) 10–22 <https://projects.iq.harvard.edu/fintechlaw/home> accessed 11 April 2022.

[447] See Zimmerman et al., 'A Complexity Science Primer' (n 24) 8.

scandals and the way policy-makers, market actors, and other constituencies of society reacted to such events are all examples contributing to reinforce the idea of an evolutionary pattern as 'history dependent'.

2. Interaction between Each Subpart: Complexity as Multidimensionality

A second more general point of analysis refers to the way these subparts (each of them a potential CAS) interact, as they are also part of a broader CAS. One of the consequences of technological advancements is that such subparts are much more interconnected than paradigms from the past. In the past scholars from different fields studying the dynamics of international finance approached the subject in a rather fragmentary way: capital markets, corporate governance, financial networks, and central banking were not considered adopting a holistic approach, and an easy explanation could probably be that there was no need to develop alternative approaches. However, nowadays disruptive technologies trigger interconnection and, ultimately, complexity. Here the word 'complexity' connects to a key feature of the new paradigm: that of enhanced multidimensionality in the architecture of international finance.

Such multidimensionality identifies a much stronger and intense relationship between the different elements that are part of the financial and economic ecosystem and the way such elements interact within the new emerging framework. This is also consistent with the way technological changes generate 'ambiguity in the definition of domain of businesses',[448] and such ambiguity contributes to multidimensionality because one highly technological entrepreneurial initiative in a specific field may be in a position to play a prominent role in different fields. This happened in the context of blockchain in particular with cryptocurrencies, which could be a tool for operating in a broad range of contexts (such as capital markets, shadow banking, and central banking). Here multidimensionality refers to the increased interactions between heterogeneous fields.

When reasoning in terms of complex adaptive systems, there are multiple consequences of such multidimensionality. Multidimensionality increases the size of the network: while such heterogeneous subparts were only accidentally in a relationship, they have become systematically interrelated in the new one, developing much stronger forms of interactions. Indeed, multidimensionality is a driver contributing to a significant increase in the intensity of such interactions, in particular when coupled with specific structural transformations triggered by technology, such as disintermediation and decentralization.

Decentralization and disintermediation *trigger* the further consequence of *multiplying* the interactions within the networks, and this is especially clear in the context of financial markets. Here decentralization and disintermediation *trigger* the *multiplication* of edges and nodes involved, and such new individual entities do not need to rely on centralized institution in charge of executing any action for them. In fact, decentralization increases peer-to-peer interactions, triggering greater interactions within the network. When decentralization and disintermediation couple with an enlarged multidimensional network, the consequences might be relevant.

---

[448] Kumiko Miyazaki and Kyoichi Kijima, 'Complexity in Technology Management: Theoretical Analysis and Case Study of Automobile Sector in Japan' (2000) 64 TechForec&SocChange 39, 39.

Therefore, multidimensionality, especially when coupled with decentralization and disintermediation, implies faster changes happening on a large scale within the network. Such changes affect a broader range of actors, now much more numerous (as an effect of decentralization and disintermediation) than in the past.

VI. The Structure of the Technological Implications and the Key Questions

A. An Ascending Climax

Focusing on the cryptoeconomy and the tokeneconomy, the best way to understand the substance of such economic paradigms is by looking at the different instruments and tools that are implemented in the new economic and financial environment, which are also likely to have an impact on the law. From this angle, the focus of this book is limited to specific key instruments and structures.

Taking into account the different subsections as identified in Section V.B., the emerging conceptual dimension of the book is built around the idea of an ascending climax (see Figure 1.4), a figure of speech characterized by the utilization of concepts in ascending order of importance and force. After the identification of what was defined as a precise Time Zero (i.e., the development of shadow banking) in Section IV, the technological reaction to the financial crisis triggered specific events that have gradually increased in complexity and dimension.

This increasing complexity can be identified with an 'infrastructural' technological transformation; its application to a fundamental notion of the law, the contract, and its multiple applications to a broad range of activities; and the creation of new

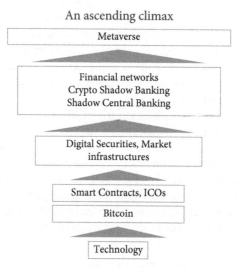

Fig. 1.4 An ascending climax

economic paradigms and financial networks. Technology proves to be a transformative force of capitalism and economy like never before. This unprecedented situation triggers important questions that go beyond the potential successful or unsuccessful establishment of the cryptoeconomy as a new paradigm. The cryptoeconomy affects commercial practices, finance, corporate governance, central banking, and shadow banking. This multiplicity of changes offers the opportunity to test the main institutions of the law and capitalism, and whether they are fit to react to innovations and shocks.

B. The Key Problems and the Two Dimensions

The emergence of a new economic and financial environment may be a structural consequence of a new infrastructural innovation. The epochal technology advancements may be characterized as an 'infrastructural' innovation, which is significantly different from other 'continuous' forms of innovation, such as financial innovation.[449] This kind of infrastructural transformation triggers many economic consequences, and by being a radical transformation raises two different problems that are the core underlying aspects of this book and represent the two components of the same research question. What is the role of the law in addressing the concerns emerging from the transformative phases of capitalism?

1. The Static Component of the Problem

The first problem is a 'static' one. It relates to the need to assess whether existing legal categories or—more generally—a specific regulatory framework can be safely extended to solve the challenges posed by the establishment of the new environment. This new environment has the key feature of coupling two layers of innovation, in particular 'traditional' financial innovation and, on top of that, a technical (technological) layer. This analysis requires a systematic assessment of the specific novelties in each context, putting them in a proper relationship with the existing categories of law. The historic debate between Frank Easterbrook and Lawrence Lessig exemplifies the two options that regulators have. When referring to cyberlaw, the two authors adopt opposite approaches. Frank Easterbrook concluded that this new field did not require the creation of *ad hoc* regulation,[450] whereas Lawrence Lessig strongly advocated the creation of a new framework.[451] This problem is clearly not a new one in law. It has important antecedents related to the way definitions adapt to new cases, in particular on the role and the effectiveness of hermeneutics, with two different alternatives. First, an adequate hermeneutical activity would not require the creation of new definitions to regulate new cases (the Latin *facti species*). The opposite alternative would be based on the intrinsic limits of this hermeneutical activity and would therefore justify the need

---

[449] Dell'Erba, '"Do No Harm" Approach in Initial Coin Offerings' (n 197).
[450] See generally Frank H. Easterbrook, 'Cyberspace and the Law of the Horse' (1996) UChiLF 207 (arguing for the adjustment of the existing legal framework to accommodate new technologies).
[451] See generally Lawrence Lessig, 'The Law of the Horse: What Cyberlaw Might Teach' (1999) 113 HarvLRev 501 (arguing for a new legal framework to address new technologies). See also Edmund Schuster, 'Cloud Crypto Land' (2021) 84 ModLRev 974.

to provide new regulations to regulate such new cases,[452] and such new regulations would serve as a tool for educating the interpreters of the law.

This book considers the existing regulatory framework, and questions whether it proves to be flexible enough to continue to adapt to the new emerging framework. The book applies these considerations not only at the level of single contractual or financial instruments, as in the context of smart contracts and ICOs—where the existing commercial rules and securities laws represent an important basis—but also at a higher level of complexity, in the context of infrastructures and networks involved.

Consistent with this approach, when dealing with the superior broader level of financial networks, the book emphasizes the analogies with other economic and financial networks. Therefore, even at this conceptual level technology should not be treated as 'special', and existing rules can still be adequate to respond to new technological developments, sometimes by enacting specific adaptations. In doing this, it proposes the possibility of developing some *ex ante* measures that are based on a better understanding and contextualization of some problems as previously emerged in traditional finance, when such technological developments were not in place yet. The book emphasizes the similarities between the starting point of the 'line of disruption' and the way the new crypto-financial network evolved. The beginning was the emergence of the shadow banking system, and the last step of this analysis is the possibility that the new financial networks recreate the same dynamics, leading to the establishment of 'shadow central banking' and 'crypto shadow banking.' In this context, specific economic analogies between the emerging paradigm and the existing framework can clearly be observed and would support the possibility of applying certain policy and regulatory measures adopted to regulate traditional finance.

2. The Dynamic Component of the Problem

A second problem is rather dynamic. A broad legal analysis is instrumental not only to clarify the way specific innovations propagate in different legal contexts and to identify a proper characterization of such rules, but it also serves another purpose. Unpacking and analysing each segment becomes necessary to assess the potential risks and to consider further regulatory options. In doing this, this book identifies the cross-sectorial multidimensionality underlying the 'line of disruption' (see Figure 1.5) as a key feature of disruption, and an issue to take into account when proposing new regulations.

This 'dynamic' dimension goes beyond the problem of solving individual issues related to technology and highlights the connections between events and concepts belonging to different contexts. For the purposes of the book, this chapter proposed

---

[452] On this topic the literature is vast. For a philosophical analysis of the role of hermeneutics, see generally Martin Heidegger, *Being and Time* (Joan Stambaugh tr, SUNY Press 2010); Hans Georg Gadamer, *Truth and Method* (3rd edn, Bloomsbury 2013); Friederich Daniel Ernst Schleiermaker, *Hermeneutics and Criticism* (Andrew Bowie ed, CUP 1998); Whilelm Dilthey, *Introduction to the Human Sciences* (Rudolf A. Makkreel ed, PUP 1991); Edmund Husserl, *Logical Investigations* (Dermot Morat ed, Routledge 2001). For an analysis of the role of hermeneutics in law, see Emilio Betti, *L'ermeneutica come metodica generale delle scienze dello spirito* (Tab Edizioni 2022); Emilio Betti, *La teoria generale dell'interpretazione* (Giuffre 1955). See also Luigi Mengoni, *Ermeneutica e dogmatica giuridica* (Giuffre 1996). See also Hans Kelsen, *Pure Theory of Law* (Max Knight tr, The Lawbook Exchange 2014).

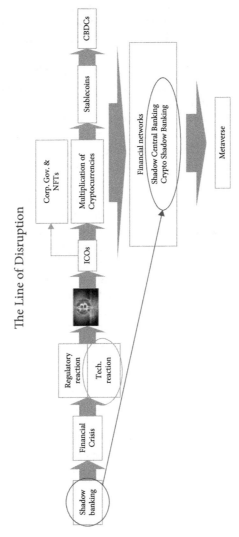

Fig. 1.5 The line of disruption

to identify the beginning of a new era of financial capitalism in the shadow banking system—a new era that partially imploded with the financial crisis of 2008. Starting from that point, the chapter proposed to identify Bitcoin as a response to the financial crisis. Starting from this new point, the 'line of disruption' intends to focus on the transformations that Bitcoin and the underlying blockchain technology induced at the level of commercial practices, capital markets, corporate governance, central banks, and shadow banking, also looking at the next point of disruption: the metaverse. The resulting analysis is an emphasized multidimensionality of the problems identified, in which all these underlying disciplines are intertwined as never before.

In its dynamic component, the line of disruption highlights the risk that the new economic paradigm might replicate similar dynamics to those emerged in the context of traditional finance. Section IV addressed the development of the shadow banking system, and the last two chapters of this book focus on disruption at the level of financial networks, in the dual dimension of central banks and shadow banking in the cryptoeconomy. This situation may generate a series of risks, which might be the ones identified as a starting point and are exactly those that Bitcoin, in principle, aimed to challenge and disrupt.

A further purpose of this 'dynamic component', and ultimately of the book, is to highlight the enhanced multidimensionality of the problems as a way to identify a methodology to make the law a useful tool to solve the criticalities emerging under the specific transformative phases of economic history which reshape capitalism.

Finally, the dynamic component should also serve to highlight the continuity in the way specific problems emerge through different eras of capitalism, always posing a threat. An example is the problem of rating, which underlies the need to quantify the value of any financial entity or its instrument, in order to cover risk. The financial crisis of 2008 highlighted the problems related to credit ratings, with credit rating agencies (CRAs) captured by financial institutions and their extremely complicated financially engineered products. Such a problem is also emerging in the context of technology, given the difficulty of understanding and rating many financial products, as well as of assessing the technological risks related to the market actors of the cryptoeconomy. Finally, it is emerging in the form of so-called environmental social governance (ESG) ratings in the context of sustainability, in which the lack of reliable ratings based on non-financial metrics may lead to unintended negative consequences at the level of liquidity of the investments, as well as of so-called green-washing, posing a threat to both the system (with new systemic risks) and investor protection (with new scams and bubbles).

Furthermore, the line of disruption is also useful to highlight specific traits of internationality that inexorably grow when technological trends are coupled with the cross-border dimension. The cross-border dimension and the lack of international harmonization as a threat to the financial system emerge in all chapters of this book, especially when addressing the prominent role of market infrastructures in any era of capitalism—including a supposed 'decentralized' one.

Finally, another constant element is the lack of an adequate public regulatory response, with regulators struggling in two different ways. First, they still cannot identify proper regulatory and enforcement strategies in the changed context. Second, they did not find adequate ways to cooperate with private self-regulators to solve important matters for which knowledge of the industry (financial trends plus technology) becomes essential.

Technological changes have become relevant at the level of the public sector, to discuss broad approaches to regulatory governance and new regulatory strategies. However, this book has opted to limit its scope to the 'private side' of technological disruption—although certain specific issues are considered in some of the analysis proposed in the following chapters. A systematic analysis of such topics and their relationship with the multidimensionality of the 'line of disruption' is the focus of a different project, outside the scope of the present book.

C. Limiting the Scope of the Analysis to Technology

In addition to technology, another force emerging in current capitalism, and of vital importance for its future developments, is sustainability. Sustainability and technology share specific characteristics. When referring to the political dimension, technology (and in particular blockchain technology) was generally associated with the concepts of financial inclusion and disintermediation to achieve more accountability and increase trust and confidence in societal governance. This dimension also exists in the context of sustainability, and when referring to the 'S' factor within the ESG indicators.

Consistent with the trend of technology permeating multiple activities at an increasing level, the trend of sustainability is experiencing similar exponential growth. Furthermore, sustainability is triggering important questions at the level of capital markets, corporate governance, central banks, and investment funds, exactly as technology has been doing in the past years. Awareness of this multidimensionality and applying the experience that technology generated may help not only to solve the definitional problems that sustainability triggers but also to address the possibility of developing appropriate regulatory approaches. Therefore, technology and the issues that it has raised, and continues to raise, may be approached as a 'case study' for dealing with any transformational phase in the economy and finance.

However, while technology and sustainability share important structural implications, they cannot be considered perfectly superimposable. Indeed, sustainability and technology are contributing to reshape corporate governance, financial markets, and central banking activities in different ways. This explains two main aspects of this book. First is the exclusive focus of the 'line of disruption' on technology. The way in which technology, and in particular blockchain technology, has permeated the different institutions and functions that are part of the current ecosystem is very special and requires a special focus. Second, the similarities observable in the ways in which technology (and now sustainability) is disrupting the economic and financial ecosystem and this substantial independence between these two 'determinants' in recent economic and financial history makes analysis of technology instrumental to analysis of sustainability.

If properly emphasized and understood by regulators, this conceptual instrumentality between technology and sustainability becomes a tool to interpret the facts in their much more complex and interconnected reality and effectively intervene with adequate policy responses, without underestimating the importance of a multijurisdictional and cross-border approach.

More broadly, a new approach to policy responses goes beyond technology and sustainability. Therefore, it may be helpful not only in reaction to pure financial and economic transformations but also in reaction to any sort of shock, including that represented by pandemics spreading in the globalized world. The contemporary events related to COVID-19 prove the need to put in place a coordinated plan based on cross-sectorial interventions (commercial practices, financial markets, corporate governance, and central bank policies), to safeguard the stability of the global economy and its recurring transformations.[453]

Conclusion

The line of disruption is a fairly simple concept referring to a succession of events happening in different contexts, and such line is leading to the development of a new paradigm characterized by a strong interconnected multidimensionality. In this new multidimensional environment, the contractual sphere, the financial dimension, and the central banking functions are significantly interconnected. Such significant interconnection provides the basis for understanding the way the line of disruption develops.

Multidimensionality is a way to address the problem of complexity in two different ways. First, multidimensionality necessarily requires referring to a significantly increased network, where each subpart contributes to enhanced interactions. Adopting a dynamic approach, complexity science provides an adequate conceptual tool for understanding the way each subpart independently develops, and at the same time how all the subparts collectively interact in the evolving system. From this angle, the individual subparts are complex adaptive systems, and the resulting transformations are relevant for understanding how the resulting CAS develops. Second, multidimensionality is a structural attribute instrumental to a better understanding of current and, likely, even future economic and financial networks.

A full comprehension of complexity requires multidisciplinary insights. Certainly, an important point is the need to deepen the legal dimension with the traditional tools of legal analysis, such as hermeneutics of law, a comparative approach, and an analysis of the policy dimension adopting the proper financial and corporate law categories.

Beyond this theoretical approach offered by the law, three core parts emerge as extremely important for navigating the complexity within the line of disruption. First, understanding the financial and economic dimension is fundamentally important to avoid any mistake in the sense of a systematic characterization of any transformation as radically new and innovative. To do this, it would be important to consider

---

[453] For a primer on the relationship between digital finance and the Covid crisis, see Douglas W. Arner, Janos N. Barberis, Julia Walker, Ross P. Buckley, Andrew M. Dahdal, and Dirk A. Zetzsche, 'Digital Finance & the COVID-19 Crisis' (2020) University of Hong Kong Faculty of Law Research Paper No. 2020/017 <https://ssrn.com/abstract=3558889> accessed 4 April 2022.

CONCLUSION

the potential similarities and affinities at the level of financial structures and the way regulators have approached them.

Second, understanding the way technologies (both disruptive and sustaining ones) enter the financial system is extremely important to identify two different layers of transformations that they trigger. One layer of transformation is the micro-economic dimension, understanding how each individual activity changes. Another layer of transformation is the macro-economic dimension, leading to a shift in the economic and financial paradigm.

Third, a clear view of the historical dimension justified by one of the characteristics of complex adaptive systems as informed by 'history dependency' is equally important. Such an approach would be complimentary to the abovementioned (legal, financial, and economic) angles, and helps to better contextualize the evolution against a complete revolution of the economic, financial, and legal system.

Emphasizing this historical angle, this chapter has contextualized the emergence of technology as an 'exogenous' reaction to the financial crisis, as opposed to the 'endogenous' and traditional one represented by the regulatory response emerging in both Europe and the United States. In identifying the structural conceptualization and key dimensions, the chapter proposes the adoption of an 'ascending climax' structure and a two-layer analysis. The first layer of analysis is static and consists of assessing the possibility of using the existing regulatory frameworks to regulate technology. The second layer is 'dynamic' and refers to the need to identify the key constituencies of the 'line of disruption.' All this starts from the contractual dimension of smart contracts and finishes with the creation of radically new financial networks emerging at the central banking (shadow central banking) and shadow banking (crypto shadow banking) levels as a way to emphasize a new multidimensionality and interconnectedness when considering the role of the law and enacting new regulations.

2
Starting from the Basics
Regulating Smart Contracts

Introduction

Over the past few years the financial sector and the commercial sector have undergone a structural change. As mentioned in Chapter 1, new providers who combine digital technologies with financial services and consumer finance in an innovative manner (so-called Fintechs[1]) have been increasingly entering financial markets and commercial transactions, taking over established financial intermediaries' economic functions or parts of their value chain. The Fintech sector comprises a vastly diverse group of providers of technology-driven financial and commercial innovations. Some of them open up new markets in the financial industry; others offer new solutions for existing products or services offered by banks, asset managers, or insurance companies. The entities and activities summarized under the 'Fintech' label are heterogeneous, as are the regulations to which they are subject. Some technological innovation may even give rise to new financial products and services that escape the current regulatory perimeter ('sector-transcending'[2] or 'regulatory disruptive' innovation[3]).

Within the ecosystem of Fintech, blockchain—a specific implementation of 'distributed ledger technology'—reshapes the financial industry as well as the general commercial practices, due to its promise of implementing a full disintermediation. As a distributed database capable of holding a secure and immutable record of past transactions, blockchain is easily optimized for a broad range of activities and objectives, and has the potential to apply to all existing manual processes where information needs to be communicated and stored.[4] For these reasons, this technology is often referred to as a 'disruptive innovation' or 'foundational innovation'. Further, blockchain has contributed to the diffusion of so-called smart contracts, as it is capable of revolutionizing the way contracts are drafted, concluded, and finally executed. As a result

---

[1] For bibliographical references to Fintech, please refer to Chapter 1.
[2] See Bob Weiler, 'How Digital Disruption Transcends Industry Borders' (*Forbes*, 23 March 2017) <https://www.forbes.com/sites/ciocentral/2017/03/23/how-digital-disruption-transcends-industry-borders/#5eeb4d7d4d00> accessed 12 April 2022 (exploring business and regulatory challenges posed by accelerating rates of technological change).
[3] See Chapter 1, Section III.C.
[4] See Charles Brennan and William Lunn, 'The Trust Disrupter' (*Finextra*, 3 August 2016) <https://www.finextra.com/finextra-downloads/newsdocs/document-1063851711.pdf> accessed 12 April 2022 (finding 'blockchain more easily optimizable to different objectives'); see also Marco Dell'Erba, 'Initial Coin Offerings: The Response of Regulatory Authorities' (2018) 14 NYUJL&Bus 1107, 1109 (hereafter Dell'Erba, 'Initial Coin Offerings') ('blockchain can easily be adapted to a broad range of activities and objectives').

of its multiple implementations and their complexities, blockchain poses significant challenges to regulators in different contexts, including securities laws[5] and monetary policy.[6]

However, this chapter aims to illustrate the issues and challenges posed by blockchain. In fact regulators and supervisors are constantly exposed to the problem of regulating and supervising new market practices which result from the entrepreneurial initiative of market actors, in particular within financial institutions. Therefore, despite the uniqueness of this historic moment, one should not make the mistake of believing that financial and technological innovation applied to a specific context (e.g. commercial transactions) is completely new and out of the ordinary.

Innovations in the financial sector provide useful examples to demonstrate the continuity between issues raised by blockchain technology and what came before it. In the past fifteen years, particularly in the aftermath of the financial crisis, there has been much legal (both regulatory and academic) debate about the role of financial innovation and the difficulties of systematization that it entails.[7] Such difficulties emerged in particular when regulators shifted from a substantially deregulated system to a more regulated environment, preferring 'public regulation' to 'private regulation' (self-regulation[8]).

The transition from a self-regulatory environment to a public-regulatory one has accelerated since the financial crisis of 2008, with policymakers supporting the view that stronger regulation would have been the correct tool to restore market confidence and integrity. Over time, there have been changes of direction, and the degree of integration (ratio) between self-regulation and government regulation has differed throughout history.[9] Self-regulation was often criticized on the assumption that self-regulatory organizations (SROs) operate in the interest of their members, coupled

---

[5] See generally Marco Dell'Erba, 'From Inactivity to Full Enforcement: The Implementation of the "Do No Harm" Approach in Initial Coin Offerings' (2020) 26 MichTechLRev 175 (hereafter Dell'Erba, '"Do No Harm" Approach in Initial Coin Offerings').

[6] See Marco Dell'Erba, 'Stablecoins in Cryptoeconomics: From Initial Coin Offerings (ICOs) to Central Bank Digital Currencies (CBDCs)' (2019) 22 NYUJL&PubPol'y 1 (describing the performance of stablecoins as currency). See generally Chapter 4.

[7] See generally Emilios Avgouleas, 'Regulating Financial Innovation' in Niamh Moloney, Eilís Ferran, and Jennifer Payne (eds), *The Oxford Handbook of Financial Regulation* (OUP 2015) (discussing the framework, costs, benefits, and risks of financial regulation in the aftermath of the financial crisis).

[8] See generally Julia Black, 'Constitutionalising Self-Regulation' (1996) 59 ModLRev 24 (hereafter Black, 'Constitutionalising Self-Regulation') (analysing the constitutional questions raised by self-regulatory associations); Julia Black, 'Decentring Regulation: Understanding the Role of Regulation and Self-Regulation in a "Post-Regulatory" World' (2001) 54 CLP 103 (defining self-regulation and decentring regulation and locating self-regulation in the analytic framework of decentred regulation).

[9] In the period from the eighteenth to the nineteenth century, in a very different context, regulatory issues were completely in the hands of so-called market organizations, such as the London Stock Exchange or the Lloyds Corporation. The situation changed after the First World War and especially after the Wall Street crash of 1929, after which the regulatory functions were reassigned by the states to the governmental apparatus. This is especially true in the United States: important Acts, such as Glass–Steagall, were enacted and played a key role in reordering market activities and the role of banks. New supervisory authorities were created, including the SEC, whose mandate was to monitor even the self-regulatory organizations, and the New York Stock Exchange. For an analysis of this topic, see generally (*ex multis*) John Braithwaite and Peter Drahos, *Global Business Regulation* (CUP 2000).

with concerns related to inadequate incentives for the enforcement of rules whose purpose may predominantly be an effective protection of the community interests.[10]

In general, post-crisis or post-scandal regulatory reactions implemented a 'rule-based' approach as opposed to a principle-based one. For the same reason of restoring market confidence and enhancing harmonization within market practices, regulators might opt for providing clear rules instead of principles.[11] Switzerland is an exception and it has never implemented any *revirement*, in the sense of renouncing its strong self-regulatory environment coupled with an equally strong principle-based approach.[12]

Financial innovation, coupled with financial engineering, challenged regulators in two different ways. First, defining and identifying the practices and related products that are newly implemented by heterogeneous institutions (including fully regulated financial institutions such as banks and private funds, in particular hedge funds and private equity funds) proved difficult. For example, the concept of 'shadow banking'[13] as well as the definition of 'hedge funds' raised many regulatory questions, mostly due to their hybrid nature and their engagement in a broad range of activities, both regulated and nonregulated.

Second, financial innovation often enhanced the problem of complexity: sophisticated institutions systematically employed complexity to capture supervisors, with the purpose of avoiding the applicability of the existing legal framework.[14] As mentioned in Chapter 1, complex financial products, such as derivative contracts, or complex functions, including highly sophisticated risk-management models, were a tool for market actors to capture regulators and supervisors, who were not in a position to effectively challenge them. Consequently, although financial innovation and financial engineering certainly have potential for positive ends—that is, reducing counterparty risks via derivatives, or decreasing operational costs and promoting economies of

---

[10] See generally Hedvah L. Shuchman, *Self-Regulation in the Professions: Accounting, Law, Medicine, Final Report* (Glastonbury 1981); David P. Mcaffrey and David W. Hart, *Wall Street Polices Itself: How Securities Firms Manage the Legal Hazards of Competitive Pressures* (OUP 1998).

[11] See Julia Black, 'Forms and Paradoxes of Principles Based Regulation' (2008) 3 CMLJ 425 (discussing the political rhetoric surrounding principles-based regulation); see also Dan Awrey, 'Regulating Financial Innovation: A More Principles-Based Proposal?' (2011) 5 BrookJCorpFin&CommL 273, 273 (examining 'the desirability of "more principles-based" financial regulation (or "'more principles-based' financial regulation" (MPBR)) as a potential response to the challenges stemming from the complexity and innovativeness of modern financial markets'); Julia Black, Martyn Hopper, and Christa Band, 'Making a Success of Principles-Based Regulation' (2007) 1 LFinMarRev 191, 191 (examining the fundamentals, benefits, opportunities, risks, and challenges associated with principles-based regulation in the United Kingdom); Julia Black, 'The Rise, Fall and Fate of Principles Based Regulation' in Alexander Kern and Niamh Maloney (eds), *Law Reform and Financial Markets* (Elgar 2011) (discussing the shift in principles-based regulation by the Financial Service Authority—now Financial Conduct Authority—after the financial crisis).

[12] For a deeper analysis, see Chapter 3, Section II.C.

[13] See Steven L. Schwarcz, 'Regulating Shadow Banking' (2012) 31 RevBank&FinL 619, 620–623 (contextualizing competing definitions of 'shadow banking' and proposing that 'shadow banking' ought 'to mean not only the provision of financial products and services by shadow banks, but also the financial markets used to provide those products and services'); see also Steven L. Schwarcz, 'Banking and Financial Regulation' in Francesco Parisi (ed), *The Oxford Handbook of Law & Economics: Volume 2: Private and Commercial Law* (OUP 2017) 424 (hereafter Parisi, *Law & Economics*) ('Shadow banking is a loose term that refers to [a] process of disintermediation' wherein 'non-banks have increasingly begun replacing ... traditional banks as the intermediaries of funds').

[14] See generally Dan Awrey, 'Complexity, Innovation, and the Regulation of Modern Financial Markets' (2012) 2 HarvBusLRev 235 (explaining the failure of conventional financial theory to adequately account for the complexity of modern financial markets).

scale—in particular starting from the 1970s,[15] new innovations led to increased opacity in the markets.

As extensively considered in Chapter 1, the emergence of shadow banking depended on different factors, and one of these factors was a light regulatory regime favouring the establishment of certain practices, including excessive risk taking, fraud, and scandals.[16] The deregulated environment was a catalyst for an uncontrolled development of financial markets and eventually resulted in the collapse of part of the financial system with the failure of Lehman Brothers in 2008.[17]

Both problems (definitional issues and complexity) exist in the context of Fintech and blockchain and challenge regulators in the same way. Similar to the complexity that characterized the 'more classic' financial innovations in the past decades, Fintech, and in particular blockchain, pose challenges to regulators and supervisors that appear to be even more difficult to solve. This could mostly depend on the higher level of technical complexity related to such phenomena. In addition to the sophistication associated with financial innovation, blockchain provides a further opportunity for creating structures and products that are difficult to regulate as well as supervise. In this way, market actors can perpetrate their 'capture' of regulators, leveraging their expertise in sophisticated technologies associated with complex financial techniques, which regulators and supervisors cannot adequately challenge.

Further, blockchain has significantly increased the divergence between the rates at which regulation and technology grow: while the first is linear, the second is exponential. As a consequence, the existing legal framework, specifically legal definitions, is perceived as obsolete, putting downward pressure on regulators, who may be systematically unprepared to adequately tackle innovation in general. Such difficulties are emblematic of the broader relationship between the market and the law, which seems to consistently reproduce the paradox of Achilles and the tortoise, with the law resigned to chase market actors but conscious that it will never reach them.[18] As a result, the temptation for regulators may be to consider technological innovation an exception and to provide new *ad hoc* regulation in order to fill this gap, instead of making efforts to characterize technological innovation by adopting the existing categories of law.

Contract law and commercial law highlight the nature of the problem that regulators and interpreters constantly face.[19] By adopting a purely legal perspective, lawyers may provide a significant contribution in the sense of demystifying the supposed inherent novelty of blockchain and its implementations. Blockchain and smart contracts represent a great case study for this purpose. While smart contracts provide new

---

[15] See generally Charles K. Whitehead, 'The Evolution of Debt: Covenants, the Credit Market, and Corporate Governance' (2009) 34 JCorpL 641.

[16] See Chapter 1, Section IV.A.

[17] On the financial crisis, see generally U.S. Financial Commission, *Final Report of the National Commission on the Causes of the Financial & Economic Crisis in the U.S.* (2011), which details widespread recklessness, fraud, and under-capitalization among financial institutions prior to the collapse of Lehman Brothers.

[18] See Guido Rossi, *Il Gioco delle Regole* (Adelphi 2006) 29.

[19] See Kevin Werbach and Nicolas Cornell, 'Contracts Ex Machina' (2017) 67 DukeLJ 313, 318 (hereafter Werbach and Cornell, 'Contracts Ex Machina') (exploring the potential and limitations of smart contracts to address problems in traditional contract law).

forms of escrows, self-help, and entire agreement,[20] regulators and judges should first consider applying the existing law.

Notwithstanding the clear structural and interpretative differences between common law and civil law countries, legal definitions (in particular in commercial transactions) are of normative significance in both the common law and civil law systems, specifically with respect to the creation of a *legal order*. The concept of 'order' implies the regularity and predictability of actions: those entering the market or, more specifically, engaging in a commercial transaction know that their actions and the actions of others are governed by rules, and therefore that behaviours are predictable within the perimeters of the rules. In this way, order reduces uncertainty and improves forecasting capacity, because people are confident in the likely and predictable actions of others.

Financial innovation may have the effect of reducing the predictability of market actors, at least at the conceptual level. Blockchain may pose similar concerns and a systematic analysis requires the consideration of whether new definitions, new categories of law, and more generally the enactment of *ad hoc* regulation may be the best regulatory option.

This chapter considers the specific problem of systematization that blockchain entails at the level of contracts, especially within commercial transactions, taking smart contracts as a case study. It intends to do that by looking at the formation of the agreement in the context of blockchain smart contracts, considering whether the rules provided in the commercial context for contracts concluded by two human counterparts may be a valuable tool to regulate smart contracts.

In doing this, this chapter considers the American system, where the Uniform Commercial Code (UCC) offers a unitary definition of 'contract', formulated adopting broad terms. Any systematic comparative analysis at this level would have the effect of being repetitive and redundant without adding further content to the specific point. However, this chapter opens to a comparative assessment with Europe, highlighting the way the European Union and some specific states, including Switzerland and the United Kingdom beyond the European Union, approached the regulation of smart contracts.

Furthermore, the American regulation relies on two further regulatory sources impacting on contracts, in particular an observable corpus of laws enacted after the internet revolution, as well as a new wave of regulations at the state level, which provide definitions of smart contracts and blockchain. Therefore, in the United States, a general definition coexists with trends of regulatory fragmentation and competition at state level. The UCC was adopted by the vast majority of states, generally in its entirety; therefore it is legally binding, and coexists with other state regulations. The resulting analysis can be compared to other contexts, such as the European Union or confederations of states as Switzerland is, while bearing in mind crucial structural differences. The European Union mostly regulates in this area via directives, therefore maintaining the existing differences at the national level in the area of contract law. In Switzerland, the competence to regulate in the area of contracts is on

---

[20] Ibid, 344–350 (describing the function of smart contracts in escrow, self-help, and entire agreements).

the federal level, with a much stronger degree of harmonization within the different cantons.

This chapter is structured as follows. Section I provides a description of particular smart contracts. Next, Section II briefly analyses smart contracts adopting a Law & Economics perspective and considers the application to smart contracts of some specific rules provided by the UCC, in particular Article 2, as well as the regulations enacted in the aftermath of the internet era. Furthermore, it considers the most relevant initiatives in Europe, both at the European Union and the member state levels, as well as in Switzerland and the United Kingdom, proceeding to the identification of two subgroups. Section III then analyses more broad aspects, in particular the reason why smart contracts are a matter of law, and tries to explain the problem of the formation of the agreement in the context of smart contracts. Furthermore, it considers the risk of regulatory fragmentation, and the need to establish common general principles, while at the same time advocating for stronger and more reliable self-regulatory activity.

I. A New Technical and Infrastructural Environment for Contracting: Smart Contracts

A. What Are Smart Contracts?

Due to the potential of blockchain as a disruptive technology, an impressive number of 'second generation' blockchain applications have flourished.[21] Among them are cryptocurrencies together with the phenomenon of initial coin offerings (ICOs),[22] which facilitate the distribution of 'cryptographic tokens that can represent property or ownership interest'[23] and 'smart contracts'. Blockchain technology offers the possibility to create and execute smart contracts through distributed ledger technology (DLT) platforms.[24] This is achieved through two different technologies—electronic contracting and cryptography[25]—combining consensus with tamper-proof and algorithmic executions.[26]

There is no consensus on what a 'smart contract' is, when a smart contract is 'smart',[27] and whether contracting through smart contracts means to some extent contracting

---

[21] Gareth Peters and Efstathios Panayi, 'Understanding Modern Banking Ledgers Through Blockchain Technologies: Future of Transaction Processing and Smart Contracts on the Internet of Money' in Paolo Tasca, Tomaso Aste, Loriana Pelizzon, and Nicolas Perony (eds), *Banking beyond Banks and Money* (Springer 2016) 239 (hereafter Peters and Panayi, 'Understanding Modern Banking Ledgers').
[22] For an analysis of Initial Coin Offerings, see generally Chapter 3.
[23] Aaron Wright and Primavera De Filippi, 'Decentralized Blockchain Technology and the Rise of Lex Cryptographia' (2017) SSRN 8 <https://www.ssrn.com/abstract=2580664> accessed 12 April 2022 (hereafter Wright and De Filippi, 'Decentralized Blockchain Technology').
[24] Andrew Zapotochnyi, 'What Are Smart Contracts' (*Blockgeeks*, last updated 19 October 2016) <https://blockgeeks.com/guides/smart-contracts/> accessed 12 April 2022.
[25] Werbach and Cornell, 'Contracts Ex Machina' (n 19) 320.
[26] Lin William Cong and Zhiguo He, 'Blockchain Disruption and Smart Contracts' (2019) 32 RevFinStud 1754, 1787.
[27] See David Adlerstein, 'Are Smart Contracts Smart? A Critical Look at Basic Blockchain Questions' (*CoinDesk*, 26 June 2017) <https://www.coindesk.com/tech/2017/06/26/are-smart-contracts-smart-a-critical-look-at-basic-blockchain-questions/> accessed 12 April 2022 (hereafter Adlerstein, 'Are Smart

out of contract law.[28] Therefore, '[t]he term "smart contract" is itself imperfect, and a smart contract is not necessarily a contract',[29] with differences emerging depending on each country.[30] In Switzerland, for example, the Swiss Federal Council reports an established doctrinal approach taking the view that a smart contract is not necessarily a contract in the sense of the Swiss Code of Obligations, and should more correctly be characterized as a computer 'technology' for contract execution.[31]

In addition, the term 'smart contract' does not necessarily refer to contracts executed through a DLT platform but may also encompass contracts executed outside the context of a blockchain platform,[32] as with the case of contracts made and executed

Contracts Smart?') (illustrating the wide disparity of understandings of the nature of smart contracts in the technology community).

[28] See Stephen McJohn and Ian McJohn, 'The Commercial Law of Bitcoin and Blockchain Transactions' (2016) 47 UniformComCodeLJ 187 (hereafter McJohn and McJohn, 'The Commercial Law of Bitcoin') (discussing whether smart contracts are legally binding and therefore governed by contract law). On the possibility to apply existing contract law, see Rolf H. Weber, 'Smart Contracts: Do We Need New Legal Rules?' (hereafter Weber, 'Smart Contracts') in Alberto De Franceschi and Reiner Schulze (eds), *Digital Revolution: New Challenges for the Law* (Verlag C. H. Beck 2019) (hereafter De Franceschi and Schulze, *Digital Revolution*) 308–311. See also Fransesco A. Schurr, 'Anbahnung, Abschluss un Durchfuhrung von Smart Contracts im Rechtsvergleich' (2019) 118 ZVRW 257. See also Mateja Durovic and Franciszek Lech, 'The Enforceability of Smart Contracts' (2019) 5 ItLJ 493. For the possibility of a case-by-case analysis, see Florian Moslein, 'Legal Boundaries of Blockchain Technologies: Smart Contracts as Self-Help?' in De Franceschi and Schulze, *Digital Revolution* (n 28) 313. On the possibility that smart contracts may characterize as term and conditions, see Mirjam Eggen, 'Smart Contracts und allgemeine Geschäftsbedingungen' in Susan Emmenegger, Stephanie Hrubesch-Millauer, Fréderic Krauskopf, and Stephan Wolf (eds), *Brücken bauen—Festschrift für Thomas Koller* (Stämpfli 2018) 155. For an analysis of smart contracts under English Law, see also Roger Brownsword, 'Regulatory Fitness: Fintech, Funny Money, and Smart Contracts' (2019) 20 EBOR 5. On the possibility that a smart contract characterizes as an implied offer and acceptance, see Christoph Müller, 'Art.1-18 OR mit allgemeiner Einleitung in das Schweizerische Obligationenrecht' in Regina E. Aebi-Müller and Christoph Müller (eds), *Berner Kommentar* (Stämpfli 2019); and Michael Kaulartz Michael and Jörn Heckmann, 'Smart Contracts—Anwendungen der Blockchain-Technologie' (2016) 9 CompRecht 618, 621. On the possibility to apply existing internet laws to smart contracts, see generally Ticho J. De Graaf, 'From Old to New: From Internet to Smart Contracts and from People to Smart Contracts' (2019) 35 CompL&SecRev 1.
[29] Amy Paul and Paul Brigner, 'Diving into Smart Contracts' (*Chamber of Digital Commerce*, 25 September 2018) <https://digitalchamber.org/smart-contracts-blog/> accessed 1 May 2023 (hereafter Paul and Brigner, 'Smart Contracts').
[30] See Sections II.B and II.C.
[31] Swiss Federal Council, *Report on the Legal Framework for Distributed Ledger Technology and Blockchain in Switzerland* (2018) 80 <https://www.newsd.admin.ch/newsd/message/attachments/55153.pdf> accessed 12 April 2022 (hereafter Swiss Council, *Report on the Legal Framework for DLT*). See Andreaas Furrer, 'Die Einbettung von Smart Contracts in das schweizerische Privatrecht' (2018) 3 Anwaltsrevue 103, 109 (hereafter Furrer, 'Die Einbettung von Smart Contracts'). See also Gabriel Jaccard, 'Smart Contracts and the Role of Law' (*Jusletter IT*, 2017) paras 8–9 <https://jusletter-it.weblaw.ch/en/issues/2017/23-November-2017/smart-contracts-and-_42155d7e26.html__ONCE&login=false> accessed 12 April 2022. See also Stephan D. Meyer and Benedikt Schluppi, '"Smart Contracts" und deren Einordnung in das schweizerische Vertragsrecht' (2017) 3 Recht 204, 208. See also Rolf H. Weber, 'Leistungsstörungen und Rechtsdurchsetzung bei Smart Contracts: Eine Auslegeordnung möglicher Problemstellungen' (*Jusletter IT*, 2017) para 2 <https://jusletter.weblaw.ch/juslissues/2017/917/leistungsstorungen-u_3e7a005a8f.html__ONCE&login=false> accessed 12 April 2022.
[32] In the sense of enlarging the definition of smart contracts to other agreements executed even outside DLT platforms, David Adlerstein notes that 'while blockchain promises to facilitate arrangements of this type[,] ... a smart contract can exist outside of the context of a blockchain ... and that a smart contract can have as its subject matter something other than the custody or transfer of an asset.' Adlerstein, 'Are Smart Contracts Smart?' (n 27).

between devices or electronic agents.[33] Indeed, smart contracts have existed for decades and often involved automated payments: the vending machine was introduced in 1883 in a subway in London.[34] Therefore, automatically associating smart contracts with blockchain technology is not necessarily accurate. In fact, as the example of the vending machine confirms, smart contracts do not require blockchain.[35]

At the same time, blockchain has the potential to open up much richer opportunities for implementing new ideas, with two main consequences: removing many intermediaries and the related strategic behaviour, and automating many commercial relationships not only on a business-to-business basis but even more interestingly in personal finance.

The term 'smart contract' was first introduced by the computer scientist and legal theorist Nick Szabo, who theorized this notion in a series of articles published between 1994 and 1997. Although 'smart contracts' have existed for decades,[36] blockchain technology made them more concrete and plausible.[37] Szabo defines smart contracts as 'a set of promises, specified in digital form, including protocols within which the parties perform on these promises',[38] and associates specific benefits with this coded form of contracting. These benefits include the fulfilment of contractual obligations, lowered bad-faith behaviours and good-faith mistakes, and decreased enforcement and general transaction costs.[39]

---

[33] McJohn and McJohn, 'The Commercial Law of Bitcoin' (n 28) 15 (noting the variety of kinds of smart contracts and the legal implications thereof). Regarding the legal regime of smart contracts executed outside the blockchain, see generally Stacy-Ann Elvy, 'Hybrid Transactions and the Internet of Things: Goods, Services, or Software?' (2017) 74 Wash&LeeLRev 77 (hereafter Elvy, 'Hybrid Transactions and the Internet of Things') (examining the applicability of the UCC to hybrid transactions involving the Internet of Things (IoT)).

[34] See Christian Catalini and Joshua S. Gans, 'Some Simple Economics of the Blockchain' (2019) 63 CommACM 80 <https://cacm.acm.org/magazines/2020/7/245703-some-simple-economics-of-the-blockchain/fulltext> accessed 12 April 2022; Nick Szabo, 'The Idea of Smart Contracts' (1997) <https://www.fon.hum.uva.nl/rob/Courses/InformationInSpeech/CDROM/Literature/LOTwinterschool2006/szabo.best.vwh.net/idea.html> accessed 12 April 2022 (hereafter Szabo, 'The Idea of Smart Contracts'); see also Nick Szabo, 'Smart Contracts: From Vending Machines to Global Finance Machines' (*Swiss Re*, 2016) <https://www.swissre.com/dam/jcr:e1775ba6-2ad5-4aac-a1c5-e35d584fb59b/Presentation_Nick_Szabo.pdf> accessed 12 April 2022.

[35] See Capgemini, 'Smart Contracts in Financial Services: Getting from Hype to Reality' (August 2018) 4 <https://www.capgemini.com/at-de/wp-content/uploads/sites/25/2017/08/smart_contracts_in_fs.pdf> accessed 12 April 2022 (hereafter Capgemini, 'Smart Contracts').

[36] For a discussion of the evolution of smart contracts, see Werbach and Cornell, 'Contracts Ex Machina' (n 19) 320–324 (explaining how smart contracts function and analysing their legal enforceability). The authors mention Electronic Data Interchange (EDI), i.e. automated digital communications between or within firms; the electronic (or data-oriented) contract; the 'computable' contract; and blockchain-based smart contracts.

[37] Norton Rose Fulbright and R3, 'Can Smart Contracts Be Legally Binding Contracts?' (White paper, 2016) 8 <https://www.nortonrosefulbright.com/-/media/files/nrf/nrfweb/imported/norton-rose-fulbright--r3-smart-contracts-white-paper-key-findings-nov-2016.pdf> accessed 12 April 2022 (hereafter Norton Rose Fulbright and R3, 'White Paper').

[38] Nick Szabo, 'Smart Contracts: Building Blocks for Digital Markets' (1996) <https://www.fon.hum.uva.nl/rob/Courses/InformationInSpeech/CDROM/Literature/LOTwinterschool2006/szabo.best.vwh.net/smart_contracts_2.html> accessed 12 April 2022 (hereafter Szabo, 'Smart Contracts: Building Blocks').

[39] Nick Szabo, 'Smart Contracts' (1994) <https://www.fon.hum.uva.nl/rob/Courses/InformationInSpeech/CDROM/Literature/LOTwinterschool2006/szabo.best.vwh.net/smart.contracts.html> accessed 12 April 2022; see also Nick Szabo, 'Formalizing and Securing Relationships on Public Networks' (*First Monday*, 1 September 1997) <https://firstmonday.org/ojs/index.php/fm/article/view/548/469> accessed 12 April 2022 (hereafter Szabo, 'Formalizing and Securing Relationships').

The combination of protocols with user interfaces is instrumental to formalizing and enhancing the security of the contractual relationships in the context of these networks.[40] When Szabo conceptualized smart contracts in these terms, although he considered the role of cryptography in securing agreements, he did not design the enforcement phase or the subsequent operations of transferring the value as part of the execution of the contract.[41] However, he clearly identified the relationship between implementing smart contracts and making a breach of contract more expensive.[42]

An analysis of Szabo's core definition ('a set of promises, specified in digital form, including protocols within which the parties perform on these promises'[43]) suggests four definitional elements.[44] First, it defines 'a set of promises': promises may be structured as contractual terms or assume the form of 'rules-based operations designed to carry out business logic'.[45] Second, such promises are 'specified in digital form': similarly to the common mantra that characterizes the core of the blockchain revolution—'code is law'[46]—smart contracts are designed as digital codes to be electronically executed.[47] A third element of Szabo's definition of smart contracts is 'protocols', consisting of a set of rules in the form of an algorithm.[48] Fourth is the locution 'within which the parties perform': as the white paper emphasizes, the possibility to implement automated

---

[40] Szabo, 'Formalizing and Securing Relationships' (n 39).
[41] Werbach and Cornell, 'Contracts Ex Machina' (n 19) 15. See David Z. Morris, 'Bitcoin Is Not Just Digital Currency. It's Napster for Finance' (*Fortune*, 21 January 2014) <https://fortune.com/2014/01/21/bitcoin-is-not-just-digital-currency-its-napster-for-finance/> accessed 12 April 2022 ('Szabo defines smart contracts as agreements enforced not by law, but by hardware or software ... ').
[42] See Szabo, 'The Idea of Smart Contracts' (n 34) (explaining that the basic idea behind smart contracts is that '[m]any kinds of contractual clauses (such as collateral, bonding, delineation of property rights, etc.) can be embedded in the hardware and software we deal with, in such a way as to make breach of contract expensive').
[43] Szabo, 'Smart Contracts: Building Blocks' (n 38).
[44] See Smart Contracts Alliance and Deloitte, 'Smart Contracts: 12 Use Cases for Business & Beyond' (December 2016) 8 <https://www.perkinscoie.com/images/content/1/6/v2/164979/Smart-Contracts-12-Use-Cases-for-Business-Beyond.pdf> accessed 12 April 2022 (hereafter Smart Contracts Alliance, '12 Use Cases') (detailing the elements of a smart contract); Norton Rose Fulbright and R3, 'White Paper' (n 37) 7.
[45] On the relationship between business process automation and smart contracts, see Julia Eggers, Andreas Hein, Jörg Weking, Markus Böhm, and Helmut Krcmar, 'Process Automation on the Blockchain: An Exploratory Case Study on Smart Contracts' (2021) Proceedings of the 54th Hawaii International Conference on System Sciences 2021 <https://scholarspace.manoa.hawaii.edu/server/api/core/bitstreams/fb7c4e3a-2fdc-4582-bbe3-07114765da77/content> accessed 12 April 2022.
[46] On the meaning of the expression 'code is law' and its extensive interpretation, see Lawrence Lessig, 'Code Is Law' (*Harvard Magazine*, 1 January 2000) <https://www.harvardmagazine.com/2000/01/code-is-law-html> accessed 12 April 2022 (describing how code is a new form of regulation of cyberspace). On the interpretation of 'code is law', see also Weber, 'Smart Contracts' (n 28) 302. The author considers that because of the characteristics of smart contracts, the sentence 'code is law' could potentially be reverted to 'law is code'. In a smart contract 'parties build legal rules as well as rights and obligations being expressed in a code'. As the author further notes, 'this change leads to a fundamental challenge for the legal system that is made in principle for relations between humans. The legislator is confronted with the question how the steering function of law in the society can be assumed if the execution of transactions is (solely) determined by private legal rules'. See also Rolf H. Weber, ' "Rose Is a Rose Is a Rose Is a Rose"—What about Code and Law?' (2018) 34 CompL&SecRev 704. See also Primavera De Filippi and Samer Hassan, 'Blockchain Technology as a Regulatory Technology: From Code Is Law to Law Is Code' (*First Monday*, 5 December 2016) <https://firstmonday.org/article/view/7113/5657> accessed 12 April 2022 (describing the history of the phrase 'code is law' and how it regulates internet interactions).
[47] Paul and Brigner, 'Smart Contracts' (n 29).
[48] See Ayushi Abrol, 'DeFi Protocols: A Complete Overview' (*Blockchain Council*, 22 March 2022) <https://www.blockchain-council.org/defi/defi-protocols/> accessed 1 May 2023.

performance is the core innovation in smart contracting.[49] Such automated performance is generally characterized as irrevocable and impossible to be stopped.[50] The only way to stop it is the possibility that the contractual 'outcome depends on an unmet condition'.[51]

This last element leads to a significant distinction between smart contracts and other forms of electronic agreements related to the enforcement of the contract. In the context of a data-oriented or computable contract, the performance is automatic and ensured by computers determining that the requisite state has been achieved, and humans can interrupt such performance.[52] Conversely, in the context of a smart contract, the execution of the contract is immutable, including any transfer of value, with the computers belonging to the blockchain network ensuring the performance, instead of any 'appendage of the state'.[53] The difficulty to modify the contractual terms of a blockchain smart contract with an impact on the certainty of the execution makes personal trust or confidence in the counterparty unnecessary or at least redundant.[54]

Immutability is also important to differentiate strong and weak smart contracts. Such differentiation is based on the costs of revocation and modification, with 'strong' smart contracts being prohibitively expensive in comparison with 'weak' smart contracts.[55]

A working definition of 'smart contract' developed by David Adlerstein is helpful to highlight two further important elements. Adlerstein defines smart contracts as 'a consensual arrangement between at least two parties for an automated, independent commercial result from the satisfaction or non-satisfaction, determined objectively through code, of a specific factual condition'.[56] From this definition, it can be inferred that a smart contract is the result of at least a bilateral consensus, and all non-consensual or single-party arrangements shall not be included within the definition of smart contract.[57][58]

Another key element is the 'independent commercial result', on the basis that computer binary code is based on 'deterministic "if–then" statements'.[59] Moreover, it is helpful to emphasize another nuance about the notion of code (or source code). The code may be qualified in two different ways: (a) as a language, with the consequence

---

[49] See Jenny Cieplak and Simon Leefatt, 'Smart Contracts: A Smart Way to Automate Performance' (2017) 1 GeoL&TechRev 418.

[50] Ibid, 425–426.

[51] Norton Rose Fulbright and R3, 'White Paper' (n 37) 7.

[52] Werbach and Cornell, 'Contracts Ex Machina' (n 19) 332.

[53] Ibid, 332.

[54] See Weber, 'Smart Contracts' (n 28) 302. See also Lukas Muller and Reto Seiler, 'Smart Contracts aus Sicht de Vertragsrechts' (2019) 3 AJP 317. The authors note that because smart contracts cannot hardly be altered, difficulties can arise in regard to the law concerning the breach of the contractual obligations.

[55] As Raskin explains, if a court is able to alter a contract after it has been executed with relative ease, then it will be defined as a weak smart contract. If there is some large cost to altering the contract in such a way that it would not make sense for a court to do so, then the contract will be defined as strong. Max Raskin, 'The Law and Legality of Smart Contracts' (2017) 1 GeoL&TechRev 305, 310 (hereafter Raskin, 'The Law and Legality of Smart Contracts').

[56] Adlerstein, 'Are Smart Contracts Smart?' (n 27).

[57] Ibid.

[58] See generally Furrer, 'Die Einbettung von Smart Contracts' (n 31). Furrer identifies three types of contracts involved: a contract between the parties, the platform contract, and the application contract, and he concludes that the smart contract mirrors the contractual intent of the parties. For a distinction between the conclusion of a contract in 'off chain' or 'on chain' modes see generally Christoph Müller, 'Die Smart Contracts aus Sicht des Schweizerischen Obligationenrechts' (2019) 5 ZBJV 330.

[59] Ibid.

of structuring the contractual relationship excluding the ambiguity of words in a self-executing manner;[60] or (b) more properly as a further contractual form.[61] Considering for a moment the option that the code is a contractual form, its characterization (as a contract) is an issue to be solved at the level of private law or even procedural law. This problem is not entirely new. In fact, when the advent of the internet caused many jurisdictions to consider the transition from a paper-based system to an electronic-based system for the notification of acts, in many European jurisdictions it was essential to characterize the electronic notification as equivalent to any other more traditional material or written notification.[62] The recognition of the legal validity of the electronic signature posed similar problems in the US, where regulators proposed the Uniform Electronic Transaction Act (UETA) in 1999.[63]

Blockchain-based smart contracts specifically refer to smart contracts executed through DLT platforms.[64] They are prewritten logic computer programs[65] that can be impartially 'executed by DLT itself'[66] (by DLT validating nodes).[67] All parties involved agree on the contractual terms, which are coded in the form of predefined terms and execution conditions. A specific event or a series of events initiates the transaction[68] without relying on a central authority.[69] A smart contract is executed by transferring the value between the contract signing parties[70] when the transaction is triggered and its settlement—'the settlement of both on-chain assets and off-chain assets'.[71] Two additional elements are typical in smart contracts: multi-signature (or multi-sig) and oracles. The former guarantees the approval of transactions by two or more parties 'before funds can be released or some other aspect of the contract can move forward'.[72] The latter serves to monitor and provide support regarding external input, including, inter alia, 'prices, performance, or some other aspect of the real world'.[73]

---

[60] Wright and De Filippi, 'Decentralized Blockchain Technology' (n 23) 11.

[61] For an overview of the form requirements, and the difficulties emerging from the 'programming language' of a smart contract, see Weber, 'Smart Contracts' (n 28) 304–306.

[62] For example, in Italy, the service of documents via certified email has become the primary method of simple serving, after the entry into force of Article 16(4) of Legislative Decree No. 179/2012 (*Decreto-Legge 18 ottobre 2012, n. 179*). Similar regulations were promulgated in the vast majority of European States. For an overview see generally 'Serving Documents—National information and online forms concerning Regulation No. 1393/2007' (*European E-Justice*) <https://e-justice.europa.eu/373/EN/serving_documents> accessed 12 April 2022.

[63] Uniform Law Commission, Uniform Electronic Transactions Act 1999, s 2(8) (hereafter UETA).

[64] See Section I.B. (noting the distinction between smart contracts executed through DLT and other automated mechanisms).

[65] IOSCO, *Research Report on Financial Technologies (Fintech)* (February 2017) 51 <https://www.iosco.org/library/pubdocs/pdf/IOSCOPD554.pdf> accessed 12 April 2022.

[66] Hong Kong Applied Science & Technology Research Institute, 'Whitepaper on Distributed Ledger Technology' (2016) 5 <https://www.hkma.gov.hk/media/eng/doc/key-functions/financial-infrastructure/Whitepaper_On_Distributed_Ledger_Technology.pdf> accessed 12 April 2022 (hereafter HKASTRI, 'Whitepaper on DLT').

[67] Ibid.

[68] Ibid.

[69] See Capgemini, 'Smart Contracts' (n 35) 5 (describing how smart contracts automatically make transactions without a central authority overseeing the process).

[70] Ibid ('Multisig allows two or more parties to the contract to approve the execution of a transaction independently—a key requirement for multi-party contracts').

[71] HKASTRI, 'Whitepaper on DLT' (n 66) 27.

[72] Houman Shadab, 'What Are Smart Contracts, and What Can We Do with Them?' (*Coincenter*, 15 December 2014) <https://www.coincenter.org/education/key-concepts/smart-contracts/> accessed 12 April 2022.

[73] Ibid. See also Capgemini, 'Smart Contracts' (n 35) 5, 13.

Finally, a characteristic of smart contracts may be their limitation to the digital world, as 'smart contracts allow to transfer digitally referenced goods and services, not a performance in the real world'.[74]

B. The Role of Blockchain Platforms for Popularizing Smart Contracts and Increasing Their Complexity

1. General Remarks

The creation of blockchain platforms has significantly increased the interest and popularity of smart contracts designed for a wide range of activities.[75] Ethereum, launched in July 2015, is certainly the most successful blockchain platform designed to implement smart contracts. Financed with an ICO, Ethereum is supported by Ether, the second most capitalized cryptocurrency.

Ethereum can be considered as a sort of infrastructure or platform to provide internet services built on smart contracts,[76] as inferred from the main page of the Ethereum website.[77] Ethereum was built with so-called Turing-completeness in mind,[78] and thus created to be a Turing-complete blockchain.[79] Ethereum differs from Bitcoin, which is supported by a blockchain that does not provide any mechanism other than the distribution of money. It allows the application of any contingency that can be coded upon a computer to a contract on Ethereum, therefore creating rules expressed by code, and enabling smart contracts.[80] In fact, as further explained by Vitalik Buterin, its founder, Ethereum is designed as an open-ended protocol, and this structural characteristic makes it especially suited for 'serving as a foundational layer' for a broad range of applications in the future.[81]

---

[74] Weber, 'Smart Contracts' (n 28) 302.
[75] See Primavera De Filippi and Aaron Wright, *Blockchain and the Law. The Rule of Code* (HUP 2018) 74 (hereafter De Filippi and Wright, *The Rule of Code*).
[76] Peters and Panayi, 'Understanding Modern Banking Ledgers' (n 21) 7.
[77] In the past, Ethereum's website has described smart contracts as follows:

> Ethereum is a decentralized platform that runs smart contracts: applications that run exactly as programmed without any possibility of downtime, censorship, fraud or third-party interference. These apps run on a custom built blockchain, an enormously powerful shared global infrastructure that can move value around and represent the ownership of property. This enables developers to create markets, store registries of debts or promises, move funds in accordance with instructions given long in the past (like a will or a futures contract) and many other things that have not been invented yet, all without a middleman or counterparty risk.

AscendEX, 'ETH (Ethereum)' (last update 6 May 2022) <https://ascendex.com/en/support/articles/36773-eth-ethereum> accessed 23 May 2022.
[78] Turing completeness refers to the English computer scientist Alan Turing, who created the eponymous Turing machine, an antecedent of modern computers, contributing to the Allied forces' victory in the Second World War.
[79] Kyle Wang, 'Ethereum: Turing-Completeness and Rich Statefulness Explained' (*Hackernoon*, 6 July 2017) <https://hackernoon.com/ethereum-turing-completeness-and-rich-statefulness-explained-e650d b7fc1fb> accessed 12 April 2022 (explaining the difference that Turing-completeness makes in contrasting Bitcoin and Ethereum).
[80] Ibid.
[81] Vitalik Buterin, 'A Next-Generation Smart Contract and Decentralized Application Platform' (*Ethereum*, 2018) <https://ethereum.org/669c9e2e2027310b6b3cdce6e1c52962/Ethereum_Whitepaper_-_Buterin_2014.pdf> accessed 12 April 2022 (providing a history and overview of the concept of decentralized currency and consensus).

In the context of Ethereum, the term 'contracts' does not precisely match the legal notion of 'contract', as it more closely refers to the concept of 'autonomous agents'. These 'autonomous agents' fulfil the tasks of 'executing a specific piece of code when "poked" by a message or transaction, and having direct control over their own ether balance and their own key/value store to keep track of persistent variables'.[82] A blockchain platform such as Ethereum offers the possibility to use the scripting language for determining the fulfilment of the contractual conditions related to the performance of a smart contract, and, in a second phase, to execute the contractual transaction while bypassing human interaction.[83] The digital currency is in 'a neutral account controlled by the smart contract'[84] (Werbach and Cornell refer to this as a 'suspended state on the blockchain') until the contractual conditions triggering the execution of the contract are met.[85] A further distributed ledger platform, R3 Corda (co-financed by the State of Illinois), was designed with the purpose to meet the need of regulated financial institutions, providing the possibility for a more advanced model of smart contracts.[86]

2. Increasingly Complex Smart Contracts, Distributed Autonomous Organizations (DAOs), and 'The DAO Case'

The advancement of DLT platforms supports the creation of smart contracts with enhanced complexity. In fact, smart contracts may be coded not only for the simple purchase of music through Apple's iTunes platform[87] or a daily insurance contract against the risk of flight delay,[88] but also to derivative contract[89] or the management of entire market infrastructures (e.g. to trade derivatives).[90]

---

[82] Ibid.
[83] Werbach and Cornell, 'Contracts Ex Machina' (n 19) 334.
[84] Jay Cassano, 'What Are Smart Contracts? Cryptocurrency's Killer App' (*FastCompany*, 17 September 2014) <http://www.fastcolabs.com/3035723/app-economy/smart-contracts-could-becryptocurrencys-killer-app> accessed 12 April 2022.
[85] Werbach and Cornell, 'Contracts Ex Machina' (n 19) 330.
[86] R3, 'Illinois Becomes First State Level Regulator to Join R3 Distributed Ledger Group' (16 March 2017) <https://r3.com/press-media/illinois-becomes-first-state-level-regulator-to-join-r3-distributed-ledger-group/> accessed 12 April 2022.
[87] See Thorsten Koeppl and Jeremy Kronick, 'Blockchain Technology—What's in Store for Canada's Economy and Financial Markets?' (2017) C. D. Howe Institute Commentary No. 468 <https://www.cdhowe.org/sites/default/files/2021-12/Commentary_468_0.pdf> accessed 12 April 2022 (pointing to Apple's enforcement of the terms and conditions of its iTunes store as an example of the successful use of smart contracts); Douglas Vaugh and Anna Outzen, 'Understanding How Block Chain Could Impact Legal Industry' (*Law360*, 11 January 2017) <https://www.law360.com/articles/879810/understanding-how-blockchain-could-impact-legal-industry> accessed 12 April 2022 (asserting that '[u]tilizing blockchain in smart contracts has the effect of automating enforcement of contracts without human action', as demonstrated by the Apple example, in which the iTunes platform simply blocks use of a song in any way that is not authorized under the user agreement).
[88] Stan Higgins, 'AXA Is Using Ethereum's Blockchain for a New Flight Insurance Product' (*CoinDesk*, 13 September 2017) <https://www.coindesk.com/axa-using-ethereums-blockchain-new-flight-insurance-product/> accessed 12 April 2012. The French insurance company AXA created a new flight delay insurance product (called Fizzy), implemented through Ethereum blockchain, to store and process pay-outs, allowing flyers to insure trips in case their flights are delayed by two hours or more. The self-executing piece of code triggers once specific conditions are met. Ibid.
[89] See generally Houman B. Shadab, 'Regulating Bitcoin and Block Chain Derivatives' (2014) SSRN <https://papers.ssrn.com/sol3/papers.cfm?abstract_id=2508707> accessed 12 April 2022 (discussing the potential use of blockchain protocol in automated derivatives contracts).
[90] As Del Castillo explains, DTCC reports that it has completed an early version of a blockchain that could one day support the trade of $11 trillion-worth of credit derivatives. The milestone signifies a major development for the financial infrastructure provider, one that also marks a continuation of the largest effort

An example of complex smart contracts is that of distributed autonomous organizations, where full automation substitutes the need to have humans in charge of implementing any action within the organization.

The DAO was one of the very first experiments in this area. As the SEC explained, '"The DAO" is the "first generation" implementation of the White Paper concept of a DAO Entity, and it began as an effort to create a "crowdfunding contract" to raise "funds to grow [a] company in the crypto space".'[91] Listed on the Ethereum platform, The DAO was different from any other smart contract previously coded on that platform. Before The DAO, all smart contracts were owned and executed by other accounts generally held by humans.[92] The DAO's white paper emphasized its characteristic as 'the first implementation of a [DAO entity] code to automate organizational governance and decision making'.[93] The white paper further explained that it 'can be used by individuals working together collaboratively outside of a traditional corporate form. It can also be used by a registered corporate entity to automate formal governance rules contained in corporate bylaws or imposed by law.'[94] As the SEC also contributed to clarifying in its report, The DAO relied on smart contracts to solve problems generally associated with traditional corporations, thereby substituting 'traditional mechanisms of corporate governance and management with a blockchain where contractual terms are "formalized, automated and enforced using software"'.[95]

As DAO expert Richard Brown further explains,

> contracts can create arbitrary actions ... can own tokens, participate in crowdsales and even be voting members of the contracts ... The organization has a central manager that decides who are the members and the voting rules [that can be changed] ... The way this particular democracy works is that it has an owner which works like an administrator, CEO or a President. The owner can add (or remove)

---

yet to adapt an existing financial infrastructure to a blockchain. Michael Del Castillo, 'DTCC Milestone: $11 Trillion in Derivatives Gets Closer to the Blockchain' (*CoinDesk*, 20 October 2017) <https://www.coindesk.com/dtcc-milestone-11-trillion-derivatives-gets-closer-blockchain/> accessed 12 April 2022. For an analysis of smart contracts applied to derivative contracts, see ISDA, 'Legal Guidelines For Smart Derivative Contracts—Introduction' (January 2019) <https://www.isda.org/a/MhgME/Legal-Guidelines-for-Smart-Derivatives-Contracts-Introduction.pdf> accessed 12 April 2022. See also ISDA and King & Wood Mallesons, 'Smart Derivatives Contracts: From Concept to Construction Whitepaper' (October 2018) <https://www.isda.org/a/cHvEE/Smart-Derivatives-Contracts-From-Concept-to-Construction-Oct-2018.pdf> accessed 12 April 2022.

[91] See SEC, *Report of Investigation Pursuant to Section 21(a) of the Securities Exchange Act of 1934: The DAO* (25 July 2017) 4 <https://www.sec.gov/litigation/investreport/34-81207.pdf> accessed 12 April 2022 (hereafter SEC, *The DAO Report*) citing Christoph Jentzsch, 'The History of the DAO and Lessons Learned' (*Slock.it*, 24 August 2016) <https://blog.slock.it/the-history-of-the-dao-and-lessons-learned-d06740f8cfa5?gi=19bb43e6d75f> accessed 12 April 2022

[92] Richard Brown, 'Decentralized Autonomous Organization' (*Ethereum*) <https://ethereum.org/en/dao/> accessed 12 April 2022

[93] Christoph Jentzsch, 'Decentralized Autonomous Organization to Automate Governance Final Draft—Under Review' (2017) <https://lawofthelevel.lexblogplatformthree.com/wp-content/uploads/sites/187/2017/07/WhitePaper-1.pdf> accessed 12 April 2022

[94] Ibid.

[95] SEC, *The DAO Report* (n 91) 3.

voting members to the organization. Any member can make a proposal, which is in the form of an Ethereum transaction to either send ether or execute some contract, and other members can vote in support or against the proposal. Once a predetermined amount of time and a certain number of members has voted, the proposal can be executed: the contract counts the votes and if there are enough votes it will execute the given transaction.[96]

The DAO epitomizes the difficulties that may be encountered in seeking to design a blockchain infrastructure. After the launch of the DAO on the Ethereum platform, on 17 June 2016 a hacker exploited a loophole in the coding structure, 'legitimately' draining funds for ETH 3.6 million (equal to $70 million at that time) from The DAO. The weakness was not on the Ethereum platform but was rather in the way The DAO was built (or coded) on top: for this reason the hacker could 'ask the smart contract (DAO) to give the Ether back multiple times before the smart contract could update its balance'.[97] Although the money was eventually refunded, this hacking attack proved how difficult and risky it could be to build (or code) an entirely autonomous governance structure on blockchain.

In The DAO example, cyberattacks and the security breach arose from a failure in designing the infrastructure, different from any other violations generally associated with hacking websites, portals, and systems that may be perfectly legitimate. In the same way, it would be easy to imagine frauds in corporate governance, especially if technology creates more opacity and vulnerabilities instead of simplifying extremely complex structures and making them more transparent.

II. Towards a Regulatory Framework for Smart Contracts

A. The Law and Economics of Smart Contracts

Buying a Coke from a vending machine instead of from a counter entails significant differences, such as no relationship with a human vendor, which implies no tips, no further questions about any other potential products, no additional time to be devoted to the simple action of buying a standardized product. Two main consequences of this negotiation lie in a higher certainty of the specific performance and in screening out moral hazard problems and strategic behaviours.[98] These two risks become relevant when considering more complex transactions in the context of specific markets, such as the insurance sector, that have the important characteristic of being almost entirely subject to the formalization of contingencies.[99] In such contexts, a machine may be advantageous to solve both problems.

---

[96] Ibid.
[97] See Samuel Falkon, 'The Story of the DAO—Its History and Consequences' (*Medium*, 24 December 2018) <https://medium.com/swlh/the-story-of-the-dao-its-history-and-consequences-71e6a8a551ee> accessed 12 April 2022.
[98] See David Yermack, 'Corporate Governance and Blockchains' (2017) 21 RevFin 7, 24–26 (discussing how the use of smart contracts may reduce agency costs).
[99] Ibid.

In the sphere of contracts related to consumer finance, auto loans serve as a more complex example. A classic car loan requires the payment of monthly instalments. Assume that one of the clauses of the contract provides that on the first of every month, the buyer has to pay the instalment. If other circumstances happen (e.g. if the buyer loses his job or any further personal debts unexpectedly arise), the buyer can ultimately choose to skip a payment, delaying it by two months. Eventually, the car dealer may get frustrated and decide to go to court in order to get a lien to repossess the car. The judge will ultimately grant this lien and plaintiffs would send the so-called repo man to return the vehicle to the car company. In this way, the car company ultimately regains possession of the vehicle (or in other circumstances the car may be held as collateral) and may then auction it off to another customer. But what if the car company could remotely shut down the car if the buyer fails to make the payment? Smart contracts may provide such an option. If the customer does not pay, the smart contract shuts off the car, programming this action in the form of a code.

This produces two main effects. First, it makes the process of obtaining restitution from a breach of contact much easier. The lawyer who argues the case and the so-called repo man are excluded from the process of repossession. Second, on the side of the buyer/borrower, there are more radical consequences. Up until this software was in place, the borrower may have taken the view that the car loan was a bill that could have been skipped or delayed. This may be due to the knowledge that the car company will act, for example, no earlier than after three months, and the borrower, who is aware of the cost of initiating a civil process, may opportunistically decide to consistently wait until the end of the three months to pay the loan. Instead, when executing the contract with a smart contract, the monthly deadline is a real one: the borrower will be unlikely to consider missing a payment or, even more radically, will likely decide not to buy the car, unless he is extremely confident that he can honour the obligations of the contract (i.e. pay the monthly instalments).

Applying these considerations to the credit industry, the fulfilment of these specific obligations assumes a more systemic relevance. There is a significant effect from deterring potential borrowers who do not intend to pay the credit back from borrowing the money, for the purpose of implementing 'strategic default' strategies, a very well-known problem in corporate finance.[100] Deterring this kind of borrower (excluding them ex ante from this market) could have beneficial consequences: increasing the quality of the borrower pool's average creditworthiness may lead to a drastic cut in interest rates. These examples clarify the kind of problems that smart contracts can solve.

Smart contracts improve the certainty of specific performance. Entering into an agreement with a counterparty and coding it up in such a way that the program will execute the contract without further intervention enhances certainty that everything that has been agreed upon will happen. From a broader, societal perspective, this would seem to be a positive development: encouraging the moral good of people

---

[100] Julia Kagan, 'Strategic Default' (*Investopedia*, updated 30 November 2021) <https://www.investopedia.com/terms/s/strategic-default.asp> accessed 12 April 2022.

keeping their promises. As such, this technology proves to be a better, that is, more effective, tool to make parties honour their contracts. However, this conclusion faces a challenge from the 'efficient breach' theory. This law and economics theory suggests that contractual flexibility (or mutability, as opposed to immutability) has its advantages. This view argues that there may be mutual agreements that parties are not willing to keep: when one of the parties does not keep a contractual promise but does something else instead, an alternative opportunity can compensate the person who suffered from the breach, while still generating a surplus for the breaching party.[101]

Further, smart contracts economize on contracting and enforcement costs. Keeping in mind the purchase of a Coke from a vendor at a counter, rather than the vending machine, the conclusion of this transaction requires further interactions with the effect of making the whole process longer and more complicated. In connection to this, smart contracts deter strategic behaviours, reducing moral hazard problems. Strategic behaviours and moral hazard characterize both the seller and the buyer: in the case of the sale of a Coke, the seller may have an interest in selling further products in addition to the Coke. In the case of the car loan, the buyer may have an interest in not honouring the payment of the bills and may implement the abovementioned 'strategic default' strategies.

Furthermore, smart contracts reduce the role of trust in the conclusion of a contract, since there is no need to trust the counterparty as a condition of concluding the contract. One of the major purposes of Bitcoin was to take trust out of the payment system.[102] Similar to Bitcoin, smart contracts take trust out of the contracts; parties do not need to know anything about the persons they are contracting with to rely on them and trust them, because the code will implement required action.

However, smart contracts may have significant inconveniences. They may execute specific performance even where, given external (and unforeseeable) conditions that have not been coded, it does not make sense to demand it. They may not work as all parties intended; there may be a bug in the code, or the parties may reconsider what they want. Also, if a smart contract cannot be stopped, there may be negative consequences, so-called cascading effects, that cannot be easily remedied. The only potential solution to stop the execution of a smart contract is a so-called hard fork (as opposed to a so-called soft fork). Commonly known in the context of cryptocurrencies, a 'hard fork' consists of 'a radical change to a network's protocol that makes previously invalid blocks and transactions valid, or vice-versa'.[103] However, this procedure may prove too complex to be applied in the context of a common commercial transaction, which may necessarily require a higher degree of flexibility.

Indeed, smart contracts are irrevocable and are meant to be impossible to interrupt. As already mentioned, the costs of revocation and modification may vary depending

---

[101] See generally Gregory Klass, 'Efficient Breach' in Gregory Klass, George Letsas, and Prince Saprai (eds), *Philosophical Foundations of Contract Law* (OUP 2014) 362–387. See also Daniel Markovits and Alan Schwartz, '(In)Efficient Breach of Contract' in Parisi, *Law & Economics* (n 13).

[102] On the role of trust in Bitcoin, see generally Kevin Werbach, *The Blockchain and the New Architecture of Trust* (MIT Press 2018).

[103] Jake Frankenfield, 'Hard Fork (Blockchain)' (*Investopedia*, updated 24 June 2021) <https://www.investopedia.com/terms/h/hard-fork.asp> accessed 12 April 2022.

on the type of smart contract.[104] 'Strong' smart contracts are prohibitively expensive, while 'weak' smart contracts are cheaper.[105] Generally speaking, smart contracts may continue to operate in future states unanticipated by either party (i.e. law may change in the middle of a smart contract, making its continuation illegal); specific performance may cause irreparable economic damages; smart contracts may take unseen actions, such as transmission of customer data without consent; smart contracts may prevent courts from intervening in the interest of justice (much of contract law deals with 'unforeseeable' circumstances that neither party would have envisioned).

This risk, to some extent highly theoretical, of unintended consequences was also raised by the Committee on Payment and Market Infrastructures of the Bank of International Settlements (BIS). The BIS considered that 'in a possible future configuration with many automated contract tools, macroeconomic conditions could automatically trigger margin calls across [financial market infrastructures], leading to severe liquidity demand across the financial system and creating a systemic event'.[106] Such a scenario, where smart contracts trigger coordinated, unstoppable, and potentially destructive contractual executions, does not greatly differ from the events of 'Black Monday' in 1987, when computers automatically executed coordinated 'sell' orders, causing one of the most spectacular stock crashes in history.[107]

B. The Legal Regime of Smart Contracts in the United States

1. Uniform Commercial Code

A smart contract does not always constitute a contract. This may depend on the ability of smart contracts to specify 'the programmatic *means* by which some or all of the terms of the legal contract are performed', and the underlying contractual terms and their legal effects have a great importance.[108]

Therefore, smart contracts shall be considered legal contracts when they 'represent the implementation of a contractual agreement',[109] characterized by legal provisions in the form of a code. In other circumstances, a smart contract may merely represent a digital instruction which is simply coded as part of a sequence of events without representing a contract.[110] In this case, although smart contracts enable the creation of new

---

[104] See Raskin, 'The Law and Legality of Smart Contracts' (n 55) 310 ('Strong smart contracts have prohibitive costs of revocation and modification, while weak smart contracts do not').
[105] Ibid.
[106] BIS Committee on Payments and Market Infrastructures, 'Distributed Ledger Technology in Payment, Clearing and Settlement' (February 2017) 19 <https://www.bis.org/cpmi/publ/d157.pdf> accessed 12 April 2022.
[107] See Barry Ritholtz, 'Black Monday Really Did Look Like 1929 Again' (*Bloomberg*, 19 October 2015) <https://www.bloomberg.com/opinion/articles/2015-10-19/1987-stock-market-crash-looked-like-1929-all-over-again> accessed 12 April 2022.
[108] Chamber of Digital Commerce, ' "Smart Contracts" Legal Primer' (January 2018) <https://bw-98d8a23fd60826a2a474c5b4f5811707-bwcore.s3.amazonaws.com/photos/SmartConPrimer.pdf> accessed 1 May 2023 (hereafter CDC, 'Legal Primer').
[109] Wright and De Filippi, 'Decentralized Blockchain Technology' (n 23) 11.
[110] Amy Davine Kim, 'State-by-State Smart Contract Laws? If It Ain't Broke, Don't Fix It' (*CoinDesk*, 26 February 2018) <https://www.coindesk.com/state-state-smart-contract-laws-aint-broke-dont-fix/> accessed 12 April 2022.

codified relationships defined and enforced by code, there is no relationship with an underlying contractual right or obligation,[111] and the chain of codified events does not turn on the creation of any new contractual relationship.

Therefore, both general contractual rules and commercial rules are triggered only by those smart contracts whose underlying relationship is a contractual one. All the others do not fall within the legal consideration. In addition, regarding both these frameworks, it must be noted that these rules were imagined governing the formation of agreements concluded by two or more human parties. These paradigms were gradually enlarged to encompass different types of negotiations: in a first stage, those that emerged in the internet era; in a second stage, those involving so-called electronic agents, which (similar to blockchain smart contracts) have a high degree of automation in the negotiation phase, without requiring human interaction.[112]

Before approaching the definition of smart contracts as contracts under the UCC, it is important to take into consideration the more general (and abstract) definition of 'contract' provided by the Restatement of Contracts. According to this standard definition, '[a] contract is a promise or a set of promises for the breach of which the law gives a remedy, or the performance of which the law in some way recognizes as a duty'.[113]

Werbach and Cornell provided an exhaustive analysis in this regard, which should be agreed with in its entirety. Leaving aside any issue affecting the qualification of 'contracts' for specific contractual relationships representing 'unconscionable', 'fraudulent', or 'illegal' contracts, an important preliminary question (although not probative of the characteristics of smart contracts of being contracts) refers to the legal enforceability of smart contracts, that is, whether smart contracts create 'promises or agreements that are *intended* to be legally enforceable'.[114] While traditional contracts necessarily require specific guarantees or actions to be legally recognizable and, consequently, legally enforceable in the context of a specific legal system, a crucial difference when referring to smart contracts lies in the fact that they are structured to bypass the legal traditional enforceability, simply because their structure does not require any form of legal enforceability. By qualifying a legal system as a platform, it can be argued that smart contracts do not require that specific platform since they bypass such rules and they implement other coded steps. The conclusion that, on this basis, smart

---

[111] Wright and De Filippi, 'Decentralized Blockchain Technology' (n 23) 11.

[112] For an analysis of electronic agents (including their characterization in different jurisdictions), see Norton Rose Fulbright and R3, 'White Paper' (n 37) 25.

[113] The Restatement (Second) of the Law of Contracts 1981, s 1 (hereafter Second Restatement of Contracts); see also Guenter H. Treitel, *The Law of Contract* (S&M 1995) (defining a contract as 'an agreement giving rise to obligations which are enforced or recognised by law. The factor which distinguishes contractual from other legal obligations is that they are based on the agreement of the contracting parties').

[114] Werbach and Cornell, 'Contracts Ex Machina' (n 19) 339. On the point of the enforceability, the law firm Norton Rose Fulbright has observed that where a smart contract has legally binding contractual effect, the technology within which it is deployed may sometimes give rise to problems in relation to legal enforceability (this is particularly so in the case of a so-called permissionless distributed ledger). This may be because, for example, there may be no central administering authority to decide a dispute, there may be no obvious defendant, or enforcement of a court judgment or arbitration award in respect of a transaction using particular distributed ledger technologies may be problematic. Norton Rose Fulbright and R3, 'White Paper' (n 37) 6.

contracts should not qualify in principle as contracts, and would, for example, qualify as 'gentlemen's agreements',[115] may be misleading.

Therefore, beyond any matter connected to legal enforceability, it is more relevant to a plausible definition of smart contracts as (legal) contracts to consider whether they may represent an exchange of concrete obligations and, if so, may qualify as contracts if they lead to a concrete alteration of the 'normative relation between the parties'.[116] A further problem is whether smart contracts involve promises or obligations: although at a first analysis it may seem that they do not involve any promise or obligation, the view that smart contracts in this regard are agreements has to be agreed.[117] This conclusion is strictly connected with the problem of bypassing legal enforceability: referring again to their structure, smart contracts are essentially the implementation of an automatic system that parties cannot subsequently prevent. However, smart contracts concretely 'alter the rights and the duties of the parties', and certainly lead to the conclusion of 'present agreements without further promises to perform'.[118]

Finally, a further element supporting the thesis that smart contracts may qualify as contracts under the definition of the Restatement is related to their characteristic of definitely being agreements. In fact, they clearly implement a mutual assent no matter the form of this mutual agreement, that is, a code executed through a blockchain platform.[119]

After clarifying this general view pertaining to smart contracts falling within the perimeter of the definition of 'contract' provided by the Restatement, a further step to consider the potential applicability of the existing framework to smart contracts is certainly the analysis of Article 2 (related issues) of the UCC. Although contracts can successfully be constituted implementing common law principles,[120] the UCC generally regulates commercial contracts for the sale of goods, integrated from time to time with common law principles.[121] The UCC provides a distinction between the notions of 'contract'[122] and 'agreement'.[123] The existence of an offer and acceptance, coupled

---

[115] Werbach and Cornell, 'Contracts Ex Machina' (n 19) 339–340.
[116] Ibid, 340.
[117] In the academic discourse of some civil law countries, in particular Italy (and indirectly in France), private and commercial law scholars have advanced the hypothesis that 'vending machine'-type contracts, or even those conducted on the internet, could represent 'exchanges with no agreement' ('*scambi senza accordo*') and therefore lead to the category of 'contracts with no agreement' ('*contratti senza accordo*'). See for example Natalino Irti, *Norma e Luoghi—Problemi di Geo-diritto* (Laterza 1990). This conclusion cannot be agreed to, and cannot be safely extended to smart contracts, where it may be assumed that the willingness of the parties is coded ex ante, without requiring an explicit willingness for each step leading to the conclusion of the contract.
[118] Werbach and Cornell, 'Contracts Ex Machina' (n 19) 341.
[119] Ibid, 342–343. The authors correctly note that smart contracts executed on Ethereum as well as on other platforms are by default unilateral, since only one party places them on the blockchain.
[120] For a historical analysis on the origins of contract law in common law, see generally Eric Alden, 'Promissory Estoppel and the Origins of Contract Law' (2017) 9 NEULJ 1 (exploring the development of contract law since the year 1350 through the lens of the doctrine of promissory estoppel).
[121] See Norton Rose Fulbright and R3, 'White Paper' (n 37) 27.
[122] See Uniform Commercial Code (UCC) s 1–201(b)(12) (noting that a '"[c]ontract", as distinguished from "agreement", means the total legal obligation that results from the parties' agreement as determined by [the Uniform Commercial Code] as supplemented by any other applicable laws').
[123] Ibid, s 1–201(b)(3) (explaining that an '"[a]greement", as distinguished from "contract," means the bargain of the parties in fact, as found in their language or inferred from other circumstances, including course of performance, course of dealing, or usage of trade as provided in Section 1–303').

with intent and consideration, generally lead to the creation of an enforceable contract.[124] Article 2 of the UCC is a clear example of the implementation of a common law principle, by providing that mutual assent of the parties via offer and acceptance is crucial to contract formation.[125]

Article 2 of the UCC does not provide a definition of offer, instead implicitly adopting the common law definition of an offer ('manifestation of willingness to enter into a bargain').[126] This is the expression of a general approach, which also emerges from Sections 2-204, 2-205, and 2-206 of the UCC. In fact, the UCC adopts a flexible approach when considering the conclusion of a deal, by recognizing the informality of the negotiations as well as the conclusion of the deal.[127] This leads to legal meaning being given to the resulting deal, even in a context of extreme informality.[128] When referring to smart contracts, such flexibility becomes crucial: if the UCC recognizes even extremely informal negotiations, it would not be difficult to extend these rules, and more generally the ones governing contracts on commercial goods, to smart contracts. Indeed, smart contracts are far from being informal in the negotiations phase, since the phase of the negotiation could be considered as standardized and formalized in the form of a code. Therefore, if the UCC gives legal relevance to informal situations leading to the conclusion of a transaction, it may be plausible to conclude that smart contracts could fall within the perimeter of such rules. The clear formality characterizing smart contracts reflects, among others, a precise intent and a precise consideration: as will be noted further in the following paragraph, cryptographic keys ensure that smart contracts are signed and acknowledged.

Regarding specifically Section 2-204, the conclusion of a contract for the sale of goods encompasses any manner that would be sufficient to show agreement.[129] Similarly, under the UCC acceptance is broadly defined, adopting a factual approach, since any manner in any medium may be legally valid, depending upon the specific circumstances.[130] Both the broad notions of offer and acceptance do not exclude a priori any extensive interpretation that would encompass smart contracts.

With the advent of the internet era, so-called shrinkwrap and clickwrap agreements raised the problem of showing agreement and consent. In that context, by clicking to accept the terms and conditions, US courts were satisfied that an agreement existed, without requiring a negotiation for each single term within the agreement.[131]

---

[124] See Norton Rose Fulbright and R3, 'White Paper' (n 37) 27.
[125] Stacy-Ann Elvy, 'Contracting in the Age of the Internet of Things: Article 2 of the UCC and Beyond' (2016) 44 HofLRev 839, 872 (hereafter Elvy, 'Contracting in the Age of the Internet of Things').
[126] Second Restatement of Contracts (n 113) s 24; see also Elvy, 'Contracting in the Age of the Internet of Things' (n 125) 872 (indicating that, because Article 2 does not define the term 'offer', the implied intent is that the common law definition—the same 'manifestation of willingness to enter into a bargain'—will be adopted).
[127] Douglas Whaley and Stephen McJohn, *Problems and Materials on Commercial Law* (11th edn, Wolters Kluwer 2016) 87 (hereafter Whaley and McJohn, *Problems and Materials on Commercial Law*).
[128] Ibid.
[129] UCC s 2-204(1).
[130] Ibid, s 2-206(1).
[131] See *Hill v Gateway* [2000] 105 F.3d 1147, 1149 (7th Cir. 1997) (finding that plaintiffs were bound by the terms of the arbitration clause included with computer packaging).

Notwithstanding this practical consideration, US courts continue to require 'notice of the existence of a term before agreement to it',[132] consistent with the caselaw elaborated for 'electronic agents'.[133] What seems to emerge is a sort of 'proceduralization' of the consensus, which mirrors the imaginary (and to some extent metaphysical) concept of 'meeting of the minds', as laid down in both common law and civil law private law doctrines. This is consistent with the idea of a computer system serving as a 'matching system': in this 'procedure' the computer facilitates the contract formation, that is, the meeting of the legal minds, without becoming a contractual part.[134] Contract law contributed to the liberalization of this requirement, by implementing rules and interpretations useful to 'determine when an offer is made and when a manifestation of assent is present'.[135] For this reason there should be careful consideration of the way parties agree on terms and conditions and what steps are relevant to ensure that parties have sufficient notice of the contract's terms.[136] This is useful to demonstrate the existence of a binding contract: the manifestation proves the intention of one party to accept the terms of the offer, taking place with an exchange of promises or alternatively performing the contractual obligations.[137]

A further issue is the problem of the form, exacerbated by the problem of defining the essence of smart contracts, that is, the code. Form is far from being homogeneously treated in contract law, since a different emphasis on this issue (sometimes one of the requirements of validity) depends on the nature of the consideration, as well as the jurisdiction, affecting the degree of formalism, particularly in the context of civil law jurisdictions.

Referring specifically to common law countries, and in particular to the United States, when approaching the form in the context of commercial contracts and commercial transactions, the so-called battle of forms is in some ways related to a broader concept of 'form'. The battle of forms commonly originates from two main problems: first, the business practices of either negotiating deals orally and then exchanging printed forms that no one reads until a dispute arises or dealing at arm's length with non-matching purchase orders and acknowledgments; second, the complexities of UCC Section 2-207 and its official comments. Smart contracts may be a useful tool in this regard, contributing to provide clarification to the negotiations,[138] on the one hand bypassing the informality of the negotiation deals and the following exchange

---

[132] See Norton Rose Fulbright and R3, 'White Paper' (n 37) 27.
[133] See McJohn and McJohn, 'The Commercial Law of Bitcoin' (n 28) 15. Regarding the legal regime of smart contracts executed outside the blockchain, see Elvy, 'Hybrid Transactions and the Internet of Things' (n 33) 77 (discussing their application in the context of IoT); see also Norton Rose Fulbright and R3, 'White Paper' (n 37) 28.
[134] See Rolf H. Weber, 'Smart Contracts: Vertrags-und verfügungsrechtlicher Regelungsbedarf?' (2018) 22 ZIIW 291, 291–294 (hereafter Weber, 'Smart Contracts: Vertrags'). For an analysis on contract formation in the context of smart contracts, see also generally Weber, 'Smart Contracts' (n 28).
[135] Donnie L. Kidd, Jr. and William H. Daughtrey, Jr., 'Adapting Contract Law to Accommodate Electronic Contracts: Overview and Suggestions' (2000) 26 RutgersComp&TechLJ 215, 240 (hereafter Kidd and Daughtrey, 'Adapting Contract Law').
[136] Ibid, 238, 240.
[137] Ibid, 240.
[138] See Section II.A.

of printed forms, and on the other hand bypassing the complexities emerging from Section 2-207 and its official comments.

The Uniform Law Commission, along with the American Law Institute Emerging Technology Committee, has drafted a proposal for amendments to the UCC which was approved on 13 July 2022, and to be enacted by each state.[139] The proposed amendments seek to establish regulations for transferring property rights in specific digital assets, including cryptocurrencies such as Bitcoin and Ether, stablecoins, and non-fungible tokens. The primary objective is to create a regulatory framework that enables the use of such digital assets as collateral in secured transactions. The proposed UCC amendments intend to establish a new set of regulations for the transfer of property rights in a novel category of digital assets known as controllable electronic records (CERs). These amendments seek to accomplish this by introducing a new Article 12 that governs the transfer of property rights in CERs. Additionally, the proposed UCC amendments modify Article 9 to provide clarity on the procedures for the attachment and perfection of security interests in CERs.[140]

2. The Regulation of Smart Contracts under the Uniform Electronic Transaction Act (UETA), the Electronic Signature in Global and National Commerce Act (ESIGN), and the Uniform Computer Information Transaction Act (UCITA)

Having taken into account the way classic contract law and commercial law (in particular from the angle of Section 2 of the UCC) may be useful sources to be applied to smart contracts (both blockchain and non-blockchain smart contracts), a subsequent step may consist in identifying further regulatory texts applicable to blockchain. A useful corpus of regulation may be the one that regulators developed when regulating the internet at the end of the 1990s. Internet technology shares significant characteristics with blockchain technology, as they are both disruptors and moving targets.[141]

At the beginning of the internet era, American regulators opted for the implementation of a 'do no harm approach' principle (together with four other key principles)[142] due to the potential role that regulation could have played in frustrating innovation: the Framework for Global Electronic Commerce adopted by the Clinton Administration in 1997 certainly implemented this view. It recognized that an increased share of transactions happened online and that the internet would revolutionize retail and

---

[139] For an analysis see Carla L. Reyes, 'Emerging Technology's Unfamiliarity with Commercial Law' (2023) SMU Dedman School of Law Legal Studies Research Paper No. 590 <https://papers.ssrn.com/sol3/papers.cfm?abstract_id=4388919> accessed 2 May 2023. See also Carla L. Reyes and Andrea Tosato, 'Crypto's Future Is at Stake in a Dispute Over Commercial Law's Definition of Money' (*Barron's*, 7 April 2023) <https://www.barrons.com/articles/crypto-commercial-laws-definition-of-money-5fbd8fe4> accessed 2 May 2023.

[140] For an analysis of the problems connected to the need for a reform of Article see Carla L. Reyes, 'Creating Cryptolaw for the Uniform Commercial Code' 78 Wash&LeeLRev 1521.

[141] See Dell'Erba, 'Initial Coin Offerings' (n 4) 1109 (endorsing the description of blockchain as a disruptive, foundational innovation because of its easy adaptability to a broad range of policies and objectives).

[142] For a critical analysis, see Adam Thierer, '15 Years On, President Clinton's 5 Principles for Internet Policy Remain the Perfect Paradigm' (*Forbes*, 12 February 2012) <https://www.forbes.com/sites/adamthierer/2012/02/12/15-years-on-president-clintons-5-principles-for-internet-policy-remain-the-perfect-paradigm/?sh=4425ecb57170> accessed 12 April 2022.

direct marketing.[143] At that time, the regulation of the internet required a balanced approach different from both 'laissez-faire' and 'knee-jerk' regulation: it was important not to make the mistake of applying an old economy policy framework or, at the other extreme, expecting the development of the internet without any guidance and framework, pursuing the importance of building market confidence (especially with regard to e-commerce) while not suffocating the potential exponential development of the internet.[144]

In that context regulators had to recognize the advancement of new technologies affecting market practices, pertaining in particular to the conclusion and the execution of electronic transactions, including the recognition of the digital signature.[145] Both regulators and courts proved to be flexible and open enough to accept electronic contracts[146] that were mostly developed in the context of financial services, in particular in so-called consumer finance. Therefore, the development and, in a way, the disruption determined by the advent of the internet led the Uniform Law Commissioners to adopt the UETA and the ESIGN, two key pillars in the development of the regulation of electronic commerce. The common purpose of the two acts consisted in ensuring that both physical and digital signatures had equivalent legal status and therefore could produce equivalent legal effects.[147] The two acts were designed to facilitate transactions, in particular those related to Article 2 and 2A of the UCC.[148]

The UETA was adopted in 1999 with the endorsement of the American Bar Association, and enacted in the majority of the states, excluding Illinois, New York, and Washington.[149] When describing the UETA, the Uniform Law Commission stated that it 'establishes the legal equivalence of electronic records and signatures with paper writings and manually-signed signatures, removing barriers to electronic

---

[143] See William J. Clinton and Albert Gore, 'The Framework for Global Electronic Commerce' (1997) <https://clintonwhitehouse4.archives.gov/WH/New/Commerce/read.html> accessed 12 April 2022 (describing how consumers will be able to shop from the comfort of their living rooms).

[144] See Adam Smith, 'E-Commerce in the New Century' (2002) 8 NewEngJIntl&CompL 1, 4 (warning of the dangers of failing to coordinate e-commerce regulation internationally).

[145] See Adam R. Smart, 'E-Sign versus State Electronic Signature Laws: The Electronic Statutory Battleground' (2001) 5 NCBankInst 485, 486 (explaining that '[t]he digital signature is an encrypted electronic signature... [that generally] incorporate[s] public key infrastructure technology (PKY)... enabl[ing] the parties to a transaction to verify that the sent document has not been altered and has been signed by the party purporting to sign document').

[146] See Smart Contracts Alliance, '12 Use Cases' (n 44) (mentioning the increasing comfort of regulators and courts toward electronic financial transactions).

[147] See Alan Cohn, Travis West, and Chelsea Parker, 'Smart After All: Blockchain, Smart Contracts, Parametric Insurance, and Smart Energy Grids' (2017) 1 GeoL&TechRev 273, 287 (hereafter Cohen et al., 'Smart After All') (emphasizing the consequences of common provisions guaranteeing that any electronic signature will not be held legally ineffective, clarifying that any law requiring a written record may be satisfied by an electronic record, and asserting that an electronic signature is the legal equivalent of a written signature for any law requiring a signature).

[148] Among the exclusions, the ESIGN and UETA listed wills, codicils, and testamentary trusts, as well as UCC transactions with exception of Article 2 and Article 2A transactions. DocuSign, 'Detailed Discussion of the Legal Issues Surrounding E-signature Deployment' <https://community.corporatecompliance.org/HigherLogic/System/DownloadDocumentFile.ashx?DocumentFileKey=40bffdbb-226a-4cef-b6f4-8843152a114a> accessed 12 April 2022 (hereafter DocuSign, 'E-signature Deployment').

[149] Uniform Law Commission, 'A Few Facts about the Uniform Electronic Transactions Act' <https://www.uniformlaws.org/HigherLogic/System/DownloadDocumentFile.ashx?DocumentFileKey=c5976d91-07e2-b3f8-9b1e-4450fe809c21&forceDialog=0> accessed 12 April 2022.

commerce'.[150] Notwithstanding the enactment of the UETA in the vast majority of states, many states amended several provisions with the consequence of inconsistent implementation.[151] Among them, California introduced many provisions aimed at protecting consumers.[152] The consequence was the impossible-to-solve problem of a fragmented and inconsistent regulation harmful for market actors, who promoted the adoption of a new legislative action that could establish equivalence between electronic signatures and other forms of signatures on a national level.[153]

For this reason, the ESIGN Act, adopted by Congress only one year after the UETA, extends the validity for electronic records and signatures for transactions in or affecting interstate or foreign commerce. Signed into law on 30 June 2000, the ESIGN Act allows the use of electronic records to satisfy any statute, regulation, or rule of law requiring that such information be provided in writing, if the consumer has affirmatively consented to such use and has not withdrawn their consent.[154]

Notwithstanding the adoption of the ESIGN, the Uniform Law Commission has affirmed the importance of the UETA, regarded as more comprehensive than ESIGN, and more effective in pursuing consumer protection, recordkeeping, recognizing the enforceability of automated transactions involving an agent in contract formation.[155]

However, the two acts share important features aimed at granting to signatures and records in electronic form the same legal authority as physical documents and signatures.[156] In fact, both the acts recognize the effectiveness of signatures and records in electronic form; they recognize that the electronic form satisfies the written requirements and similarly establish an equivalence between the electronic signature and the written signature.[157] Further rules in the statutes regulate consent, providing that parties have to agree 'to conduct transactions by electronic means',[158] as well as the retention, accessibility, and producibility of electronic records.[159]

The two acts may apply to smart contracts because cryptographic keys prove the actual intent of the parties to enter into the agreement, ensuring that smart contracts are effectively signed and their legal effects acknowledged by the parties.[160] This would make the notion of cryptographic keys consistent with the one of 'electronic signature'. Both the UETA and ESIGN define an electronic signature as 'an electronic sound, symbol, or process attached to or logically associated with a contract or other record and executed

---

[150] Stephen Mettling and David Cusic, *Principles of Real Estate Practice in North Carolina* (2nd edn, PPC 2020) 483.
[151] Cohen et al., 'Smart After All' (n 147) 286; see also Thomas J. Smedinghoff, 'The Legal Challenges of Implementing Electronic Transactions' (2008) 41 UniformComCodeLJ 1, 7–8
[152] Cohen et al., 'Smart After All' (n 147) 286 (n 63).
[153] Ibid, 286.
[154] Federal Deposit Insurance Corporation, *Consumer Compliance Examination Manual* (2020) x-3.1 <https://www.fdic.gov/resources/supervision-and-examinations/consumer-compliance-examination-manual/documents/compliance-examination-manual.pdf> accessed 2 May 2023.
[155] Patricia Brumfield Fry, 'Why Enact UETA? The Role of UETA after E-Sign' (2000) <https://www.uniformlaws.org/HigherLogic/System/DownloadDocumentFile.ashx?DocumentFileKey=97560e15-8b54-1237-70ca-683b36af5f43&forceDialog=0> accessed 12 April 2022.
[156] See Cohen et al., 'Smart After All' (n 147) 287.
[157] DocuSign, 'E-signature Deployment' (n 148) 7.
[158] UETA (n 63) s 5(b).
[159] 15 U.S. Code (USC), s 7001(e); UETA (n 63) s 5(b), s 12.
[160] See Cohen et al., 'Smart After All' (n 147) 287.

or adopted by a person with the intent to sign the record'.[161] Therefore, electronic signatures (and key cryptography) are characterized by the signature and the intent to sign as key features.[162] By providing a broad definition, regulators granted legal compliance to a multiplicity of technology and processes for the electronic signature.[163] This broad definition offers the possibility to include within the notion of 'electronic signature' the cryptographic key, a key feature in the context of blockchain smart contracts.

A further important source regulating the advent of the internet era and the new ways of contracting through the internet which were not covered by the UCC has been the UCITA, initially drafted with the intent to amend the UCC by adding a further Section 2-B.[164] Due to many issues during its drafting process and even after its approval, the UCITA was not successful.[165] However, in this context it is important to consider some specific rules in connection to smart contracts. The UCITA not only adopts a language similar to the provisions of the UCC (in particular Sections 2-204 and 2-206 regarding offer and acceptance), but also expressly provides that a contract may be formed through the use of electronic agents and recognizes acceptance through electronic means.[166] Although not expressly drafted for smart contracts, it would not be difficult to apply these rules to smart contracts.

3. The Regulation of Blockchain and Smart Contracts at the State Level

Different states have implemented specific projects and initiatives to regulate blockchain and smart contracts, among them the states of Arizona, California, Delaware, Nevada, New York, Tennessee, Vermont, and Wyoming. These states, in particular Delaware and Wyoming, tried to benefit from the advantages of being first movers, in a way replicating in this context the model of state competition that the United States already experienced in the development of corporate law,[167] where the state of Delaware emerged as the reference for the state of the art.[168]

---

[161] 15 USC (n 159), s 7006(5); UETA (n 63) s 2(8).

[162] DocuSign, 'E-signature Deployment' (n 148) 7.

[163] As DocuSign explains, this new legislation effectively solves the 'signed writing' problem, by providing provisions that make electronic communication and contracts equivalent to their paper cousins: 'Electronic Signature' is defined as an electronic sound, symbol or process attached to or logically associated with a record and executed or adopted by a person with the intent to sign the record. Ibid.

[164] See Jane K. Winn and Benjamin Wright, *Law of Electronic Commerce* (4th edn, Wolters Kluwer 2019) 50–56.

[165] See generally Brian D. McDonald, 'The Uniform Computer Information Transactions Act' (2001) 16 BerkeleyTechLJ 461.

[166] Uniform Computer Information Transactions Act 1999, ss 203(4), 206 (hereafter UCITA).

[167] See Lucian A. Bebchuk, 'Federalism and the Corporation: The Desirable Limits on State Competition in Corporate Law' (1992) 105 HarvLRev 1435, 1442–1443 (detailing the history and motivations of state charter competitions to become corporate domiciles); Marcel Kahan and Ehud Kamar, 'The Myth of State Competition in Corporate Law' (2002) 55 StanLRev 679, 684–685 (hereafter Kahan and Kamar, 'The Myth of State Competition') (explaining that Delaware has historically done so well in competing for incorporations of public companies that currently no other state challenges it).

[168] American scholars have analysed this topic for a long time. See generally William L. Cary, 'Federalism and Corporate Law: Reflections upon Delaware' 1974) 88 YaleLJ 663 (reflecting on Delaware's rise to prominence in corporate law); Ehud Kamar, 'A Regulatory Competition Theory of Indeterminacy in Corporate Law' (1998) 98 ColumLRev 1908 (discussing the unique characteristics of Delaware that prevent other states from competing effectively in corporate law); Roberta Romano, 'Law as a Product: Some Pieces of the Incorporation Puzzle' (1985) 1 JLEcon&Org 225 (giving an overview of state corporate competition and how Delaware has come to be so dominant).

The state of Arizona, passing the so-called Blockchain Bill into law, provided specific regulation for electronic signatures, blockchain, and smart contracts.[169] The law now expressly defines blockchain[170] and smart contracts.[171] It also recognizes 'a signature ... secured through blockchain technology' as equivalent to an electronic signature and 'a record or contract secured through blockchain' as equivalent to an electronic record in an electronic form, as well as the existence of smart contracts.[172]

Like Arizona, the state of Nevada passed a law defining blockchain[173] and including blockchain within the definition of electronic record for similar purposes.[174] Furthermore, the statute prescribes that local governments shall not:

> Impose any tax or fee on the use of a blockchain by any person or entity; (b) Require any person or entity to obtain from the board of county commissioners any certificate, license or permit to use a blockchain; or (c) Impose any other requirement relating to the use of a blockchain by any person or entity.[175]

The state of Vermont adopted a more prudent approach. Vermont's report *Blockchain Technology: Opportunities and Risk*[176] considered that 'at present, the costs and challenges associated with the use of blockchain technology for Vermont's public recordkeeping outweigh the identifiable benefits'.[177] The report also emphasized the relevance of recognizing blockchain technology, which would determine 'a "first mover" advantage with the potential to bring economic activity surrounding the development of blockchain technology to Vermont', but remarked that such potential was 'difficult to quantify and challenging to capture due to the nature of the technology'.[178] Vermont has recognized the possibility of using blockchain for state purposes in the context of a trial, under specific conditions, and finally adopted legislation S. 135 regulating blockchain technology and smart contracts.[179]

---

[169] Arizona Revised Statutes 2022, t 44, ch 26, s 7061.
[170] As the statute describes, 'blockchain technology' means distributed ledger technology that uses a distributed, decentralized, shared, and replicated ledger, which may be public or private, permissioned or permissionless, or driven by tokenized crypto economics or tokenless. The data on the ledger is protected with cryptography, is immutable and auditable, and provides an uncensored truth. Ibid.
[171] '"Smart contract" means an event-driven program, with state, that runs on a distributed, decentralized, shared and replicated ledger and that can take custody over and instruct transfer of assets on that ledger.' Ibid.
[172] See ibid (noting that 'a contract relating to a transaction may not be denied legal effect, validity or enforceability solely because that contract contains a smart contract term').
[173] See Statutes of Nevada 2017, ch 391, s 1 ('"Blockchain" means an electronic record of transactions or other data which is: 1. Uniformly ordered; 2. Redundantly maintained or processed by one or more computers or machines to guarantee the consistency or nonrepudiation of the recorded transactions or other data; and 3. Validated by the use of cryptography').
[174] Ibid, s 2 ('"Electronic record" means a record created, generated, sent, communicated, received or stored by electronic means. The term includes, without limitation, a blockchain').
[175] Ibid, s 4.
[176] James Condos, William Sorrell, and Susan Donegan, 'Blockchain Technology: Opportunities and Risks' (2016) <https://legislature.vermont.gov/assets/Legislative-Reports/blockchain-technology-report-final.pdf> accessed 12 April 2022.
[177] Ibid, 3.
[178] Ibid.
[179] See Vermont State General Assembly, Act No. 69 (S. 135) (6 October 2017). See also, The Vermont Statutes Annotated, t 12, ch 81, s 1913. The statute defines 'blockchain technology' as 'a mathematically

II. TOWARDS A REGULATORY FRAMEWORK FOR SMART CONTRACTS 103

The state of New York debated the introduction of four bills. Only one of them, Bill 8780, was enacted. Bill 8780 is 'an act to amend the state technology law, in relation to blockchain technology and smart contracts',[180] which introduces definitions of 'blockchain'[181] and 'smart contracts'[182] that recognize their commercial function. The other three bills that were not enacted had heterogeneous purposes, including: the evaluation of blockchain technology as a tool to 'protect voter records and election results';[183] the establishment of 'a task force to study and report on the potential implementation of blockchain technology in state record keeping, information storage, and service delivery';[184] and the creation of a digital currency task force 'to provide the governor and the legislature with information on the effects of the widespread use of cryptocurrencies and other forms of digital currencies and their ancillary systems in the state'.[185]

Delaware launched the Delaware Blockchain Initiative in 2016, developed in partnership with the private company Symbiont.[186] It was structured around three goals: first, the implementation of the blockchain technology at Delaware Public Archives; second, the implementation of 'smart UCC' filings, consisting of implementing smart contracts in the context of UCC filings; third, the creation of 'distributed ledger shares',[187] to maintain its leading role in the context of corporate governance.[188] Furthermore, Delaware is highly involved with leading service provider Broadridge to implement an infrastructure based on smart contracts to improve the proxy voting system for corporations.[189]

Similar to Delaware, the state of Illinois launched the Illinois Blockchain Initiative in November 2016, with the mandate 'to determine if this groundbreaking technology

---

secured, chronological, and decentralized consensus ledger or database, whether maintained via Internet interaction, peer-to-peer network, or otherwise'.

[180] Allowing Signatures Secured Through Blockchain Technology to be Considered an Electronic Signature, New York State Assembly Bill (2017–2018) [8780].

[181] The bill describes 'blockchain technology' as distributed ledger technology that uses a distributed, decentralized, shared, and replicated ledger, which may be public or private, permissioned or permissionless, or driven by tokenized crypto economics or tokenless. The data on the ledger is protected with cryptography, is immutable and auditable, and provides an uncensored truth. Ibid, s 1, sub-s 6.

[182] '"Smart contract" shall mean an event-driven program that runs on a distributed, decentralized, shared and replicated ledger and that can take custody over and instruct transfer of assets on that ledger.' Ibid, sub-s 7.

[183] Study of the Use of Blockchain Technology in Elections, New York State Assembly Bill (2017–2018) [8792].

[184] Establishing a Task Force to Study and Report on The Potential Implementation of Blockchain Technology in State Record Keeping, Information Storage, and Service Delivery, New York State Assembly Bill (2017–2018) [8793].

[185] Creation of the Digital Currency Task Force, New York State Assembly Bill (2017–2018) [8783B] s 1.

[186] See Andrea Tinianow and Caitlin Long, 'Delaware Blockchain Initiative: Transforming the Foundational Infrastructure of Corporate Finance' (*HLS Forum on Corporate Governance*, 16 March 2017) <https://corpgov.law.harvard.edu/2017/03/16/delaware-blockchain-initiative-transforming-the-foundational-infrastructure-of-corporate-finance/#more-80025> accessed 12 April 2022 (discussing Delaware's efforts to introduce blockchain into corporate law).

[187] Ibid.

[188] Ibid.

[189] See Lily Katz, 'Proxy Voting is the Latest Target for Blockchain Disruption' (*Bloomberg*, 10 May 2018) <https://www.bloomberg.com/news/articles/2018-05-10/broadridge-gets-blockchain-patent-to-make-proxy-voting-easier> accessed 12 April 2022 (announcing Broadridge has been awarded a patent that could use blockchain technology to improve proxy voting).

can be leveraged to create more efficient, integrated and trusted state services, while providing a welcoming environment for the Blockchain community'.[190] For this purpose, the Illinois General Assembly has adopted a resolution for the creation of a task force.[191] In addition, it has implemented a web-based eProcurement system (BidBuy) as part of the Illinois Blockchain Initiative. State agencies will use BidBuy for the advertisement of solicitation opportunities, evaluation of bids, and publication of contract awards, making it the state's primary solution for sourcing and placing orders from vendors for the Chief Procurement Office–General Services.[192] Furthermore, the Illinois Department of Financial and Professional Regulation has become the first regulator in the United States to join a blockchain consortium, the R3 consortium.[193] Led by the New York-based startup R3 CEV, the R3 consortium is supported by heterogeneous institutions, including banks, financial firms, professional associations, professional services firms, and technology companies, with the purpose to develop a specific blockchain technology for financial services (Corda).[194]

The state of Wyoming implemented a blockchain and crypto-assets-friendly environment aimed at attracting new entrepreneurs and companies and directly competing with Delaware to incorporate new companies. In February 2018 the Wyoming House of Representatives passed a bill on blockchain, defining the 'utility token bill' and the 'bitcoin bill'.[195] The newly issued legislation is relevant because it provides a definition of utility tokens (as opposed to security tokens). Utility tokens do not constitute securities (creating the basis for a potential conflict with the Securities and Exchange Commission). Furthermore, they are 'deemed property', although exempted from property tax,[196] and a further category, the one of 'payment tokens', exempted from money transmitter law.[197] Also, the creation of a new category, so-called digital property, would benefit from a different fiscal treatment compared to other forms of properties.[198] A further important advancement for commercial practices in Wyoming

---

[190] NASCIO, 'Digital Transformation in Government: The Illinois Blockchain Initiative' (1 June 2017) <https://www.nascio.org/resource-center/resources/digital-transformation-in-government-the-illinois-blockchain-initiative-webinar/> accessed 2 May 2023.
[191] Illinois General Assembly, House Joint Resolution No. 25 (12 December 2017).
[192] See Illinois BidBuy <https://www.bidbuy.illinois.gov/bso/> accessed 12 April 2022 (announcing the new BidBuy system to vendors).
[193] See Anna Irrera, 'Illinois Watchdog First U.S. Regulator to Join Blockchain Consortium R3' (*Reuters*, 16 March 2017) <https://www.reuters.com/article/us-blockchain-illinois-idUSKBN16N2FN> accessed 12 April 2022 (reporting on the entry of Illinois into the R3 consortium); Business Insider, 'One US Regulator Has Joined the R3 Blockchain Consortium' (20 March 2017) <https://www.businessinsider.com/one-us-regulator-has-joined-the-r3-blockchain-consortium-2017-3?r=US&IR=T> accessed 12 April 2022 (describing the entry of the Illinois Department of Financial and Professional Regulation into the R3 consortium).
[194] See R3, 'About us' <https://www.r3.com/about/> accessed 12 April 2022.
[195] Gary Miller, 'Blockchain Valley: Wyoming Is Poised to Become the Cryptocurrency Capital of America' (*Newsweek*, 2 March 2018) <http://www.newsweek.com/wyoming-cowboy-state-poised-today-become-blockchain-valley-828124> accessed 12 April 2022.
[196] See ibid (chronicling recent legislative efforts on blockchain in Wyoming).
[197] Ibid.
[198] Molly Jane Zuckerman, 'Wyoming Introduces New Bill to Exempt Crypto from Property Taxation' (*Cointelegraph*, 19 February 2018) <https://cointelegraph.com/news/wyoming-introduces-new-bill-to-exempt-crypto-from-property-taxation> accessed 12 April 2022.

state law would be (if approved) the creation of a blockchain-based commercial filing system.[199]

More recently, North Dakota has introduced blockchain-friendly laws aimed at tasking legislative management to explore use in cases in government operations.[200]

C. Europe

1. General Remarks

The European Union lacks the existence of a common body of directly binding principles and regulations for contract law comparable to the American UCC, which was adopted by the vast majority of states and is legally binding.[201] The Principles of European Contract Law (PECL) are a relevant source of lex mercatoria[202] (including, for example, the UNIDROIT Principles[203] and the United Nations Convention on Contracts for the International Sale of Goods (CISG)[204]). However, unlike the UCC, they are not legally binding; therefore, they will not be analysed in this context.[205] The PECL do not provide a general definition of 'contract', while still defining in very broad terms the conditions for the conclusion of a contract,[206] the intention,[207] and the sufficient agreement.[208]

Consistent with the lack of a general framework, there is no unitary definition of 'contract' common to all EU member states. This implies that it is not possible to replicate the same structure adopted for the US system, mostly focused on the unitary approach deriving from the Restatement of Contracts and the UCC. Thus, to determine whether a smart contract constitutes a contract, it will be necessary to refer to the regulatory approach peculiar to each specific EU member state that is relevant.[209]

---

[199] Commercial Filing System, Wyoming State HR Bill (2019) [70] (citing to a newly introduced bill in Wyoming that would create a commercial blockchain filing system through the Secretary of State).
[200] North Dakota Century Code, s 9-6-19.
[201] See Harry Flechtner, 'Comparing the General Good Faith Provisions of the PECL and the UCC: Appearance and Reality' (2001) 13 PaceIntlLRev 295, 297.
[202] See Section III.C.
[203] UNIDROIT Principles of International Commercial Contracts 2016 <https://www.unidroit.org/wp-content/uploads/2021/06/Unidroit-Principles-2016-English-i.pdf> accessed 12 April 2022.
[204] UN Convention on Contracts for the International Sale of Goods (opened for signature 11 April 1980, entered into force 1 January 1988) 1498 UNTS 3 <https://uncitral.un.org/sites/uncitral.un.org/files/media-documents/uncitral/en/19-09951_e_ebook.pdf> accessed 12 April 2022.
[205] See Ole Lando and Hugh Beale (eds), *Principles of European Contract Law Parts I And II Combined And Revised* (Kluwer Law 2000).
[206] Ibid, art 2:101.
[207] Ibid, art 2:102.
[208] Ibid, art 2:103.
[209] For the sake of completeness, it is worth mentioning in the context of the UNIDROIT Principles of International Commercial Contracts those referring to the definition of offer (2.1.2) and acceptance (2.1.6) and the principle of freedom of contractual form (1.2). However, considering the non-binding nature of such Principles and given the existence not only of formal requirements at the state level but also of specific signing requirements at the EU level, dwelling upon the above-mentioned common notions would most likely turn out to be a substantially useless exercise for the purpose of identifying the perimeter of applicable (binding) laws and analyse them.

2. The Debate on Smart Contracts within the European Union

Within the European Union, the European Parliament emphasized the importance of 'not regulat[ing] DLT *per se*' but acting 'to remove existing barriers to implementing blockchains', and highlighted the central role of the European Commission in exploring potential regulatory approaches to DLT.[210] Finally, it called on the European Commission and EU member states 'to foster convergence and harmonization of regulatory approaches'.[211]

In this context, the European Commission has taken an active role, and its initiatives are pushing toward the adoption of comprehensive pro-innovation policies in the areas of digital assets[212] and smart contracts.[213] Indeed, the European Commission recently showed its willingness to create a pan-European framework and establish a clear regulatory regime in areas concerning by the application of blockchain technologies. This action was not exclusively focused on crypto-assets (as in the case of the Regulation on Markets in Crypto-Assets,[214] which will be extensively analysed in the following chapters[215]) but also opened a significant debate on smart contracts.[216]

In this respect, the European Commission's Digital Innovation and Blockchain team in collaboration with the European Blockchain Partnership[217] announced the launch of a pan-European regulatory sandbox by 2022. The main purpose of this joint venture is to identify existing regulatory and technical barriers and test innovative solutions as to data portability, smart contracts, and digital identity in the environmental, energy, and health areas, starting from use cases.[218]

Consistent with the conclusions of the Chamber of Digital Commerce, the European Union Blockchain Observatory and Forum (a European Commission initiative to accelerate blockchain innovation and the development of the blockchain ecosystem within the European Union[219]) identifies two different categories of smart contracts

---

[210] European Parliament, Resolution of 3 October 2018 on distributed ledger technologies and blockchains: building trust with disintermediation [2018] OJ C 11/7, para 68 (hereafter EU Parliament, 'Resolution 3 October 2018').

[211] Ibid.

[212] See Chapters 3, 4, and 5.

[213] See generally European Commission, 'Shaping Europe's Digital Future—Blockchain Strategy' (last update 27 February 2023) <https://ec.europa.eu/digital-single-market/en/blockchain-technologies> accessed 1 May 2023.

[214] European Parliament, Resolution of 20 April 2023 on the proposal for a regulation of the European Parliament and of the Council on Markets in Crypto-assets and amending Directive (EU) 2019/1937 (COM(2020)0593, C9-0306/2020, 2020/0265(COD)) <https://www.europarl.europa.eu/doceo/document/TA-9-2023-0117_EN.pdf> accessed 2 May 2023.

[215] See in particular Chapter 4, Section II.B.3.c.ii.

[216] This is consistent with the call of the European Parliament. See EU Parliament, 'Resolution 3 October 2018' (n 210) para 38.

[217] Created on 10 April 2018, the European Blockchain Partnership (EBP) is a European initiative which involves thirty countries to date with the aim to develop an integrated infrastructure for the delivery of secure and interoperable cross-border digital public services (the so-called European Blockchain Services Infrastructure (EBSI)). See generally European Commission, 'European Countries Join Blockchain Partnership' (10 April 2018) <https://digital-strategy.ec.europa.eu/en/news/european-countries-join-blockchain-partnership> accessed 12 April 2022.

[218] European Commission, 'Legal and Regulatory Framework for Blockchain' (updated 23 February 2022) <https://digital-strategy.ec.europa.eu/en/policies/regulatory-framework-blockchain> accessed 12 April 2022.

[219] See The European Union Blockchain Observatory & Forum <https://www.eublockchainforum.eu/> accessed 12 April 2022.

based on the assumption that self-executing programs running on a blockchain can be used for purposes other than just entry into agreements between parties.[220]

On the one hand, the European Union Blockchain Observatory and Forum labels as 'smart legal contracts' those smart contracts representing—or aiming to represent—legally binding contracts, with all requirements and consequences that this entails.[221]

On the other hand, it recognizes that smart contracts in a broader sense can also include artefacts based on smart technology that have legal implications but cannot be defined as contracts *stricto sensu*. Such constructs are classified as 'smart contracts with legal implications' and comprise, for instance, smart contracts representing assets in digital form, smart contracts used to create decentralized autonomous organizations (DAOs), and smart contracts that become autonomous agents.[222]

As previously observed,[223] the interactions encompassed by the latter category of smart contracts do not generate any new contractual relationship. With respect to the abovementioned examples, the use of a code has different functions: respectively, to represent different assets online; to 'form an interconnected system of technically enforced relationships';[224] or to enable a software to automatically execute a function or even an agreement. These functionalities attributed to a code entail legal implications on different levels beyond the mere contractual sphere. Therefore, 'smart contracts with legal implications' may be included in a broad notion of smart contracts. However, consistent with the preceding analysis on the legal regime of smart contracts in the United States, an enquiry into smart contracts' legality in Europe should similarly focus on 'smart legal contracts'.

As mentioned at the beginning of this section, an analysis of the regulatory approach within each specific EU member state is an essential source for assessing whether a smart contract is characterized as a 'contract'. However, the European Union Blockchain Observatory and Forum identified certain issues generally arising in connection to a codified relationship and its characterization as a contract under the law of a member state. This analysis might be useful to establish an interpretative roadmap for identifying and conceptualizing the different legislative approaches adopted by European countries. Furthermore, it is also useful to identify specific challenges to the applicability of the European Parliament Regulation on electronic identification and trust services for electronic transactions in the internal market (eIDAS)[225] to smart contracts. This is also consistent with the previous analysis on UETA and UCITA in the United States.

First, smart contracts must meet the formal requirements for the conclusion of the relevant contract under the applicable law. In various European jurisdictions, the written form is necessary to validly conclude specific contracts related to certain

---

[220] The European Union Blockchain Observatory & Forum, 'Legal and Regulatory Framework of Blockchains and Smart Contracts' (27 September 2019) 25 <https://www.eublockchainforum.eu/sites/default/files/reports/report_legal_v1.0.pdf> accessed 12 April 2022 (hereafter EUBOF, 'Legal and Regulatory Framework').
[221] Ibid, 23.
[222] Ibid, 25.
[223] See Section II.B.
[224] EUBOF, 'Legal and Regulatory Framework' (n 220) 27.
[225] Regulation (EU) 910/2014 of 23 July 2014 on electronic identification and trust services for electronic transactions in the internal market [2014] OJ L 257/73.

categories of assets, as in the case of a contract for the sale and purchase of real estate. In addition to the written form, several state laws also require fulfilment of specific notarial perfection formalities for such contracts to be legally binding and/or actionable against third parties. Furthermore, certain jurisdictions might require the contract to be entered into in the national language or in such languages as to be understandable by each party thereunder. Thus, questions relating to the translation of the contract from code to natural language are likely to arise when considering the legality of smart contracts in Europe.[226] This also raises the issue of establishing which version shall prevail if a conflict occurs.[227]

Second, signing requirements are extremely important. In this regard eIDAS plays a pivotal role, especially when ascertaining whether a signature is valid and if it refers to an authorized signatory.[228] eIDAS introduced a definition of electronic signatures[229] and identified three distinct subcategories—simple, advanced, and qualified signatures—corresponding to different protection standards. Only the highest standard is satisfactory for the contract to be legally binding, and it requires the validation of a recognized Trust Service Provider (TSP).[230]

Therefore, in order to establish the legality of a smart contract under eIDAS, the digital signatures of the relevant parties must be verified by a TSP, with the consequence that DLT and blockchain technologies could prove to be intrinsically noncompliant with eIDAS itself.[231] This could raise doubts in the specific context of a member state adopting a technology-neutral approach with regard to smart contracts. In this situation the centralized trust system delineated under eIDAS could generate 'an infrastructural bias against the source of trust'—decentralized by nature—which would be necessarily involved when contracting using DLT or blockchain technologies.[232]

In this regard a possibility would be to amend eIDAS itself to acknowledge that the requirements laid down thereunder are associated with certain specific technologies rather than being generally applicable to all tools generating electronic signatures. If different technologies are involved (as in the case of DLT and blockchain), the compliance of the relevant electronic signatures with eIDAS shall be established by analysing the technical design and functionalities of the technology used to generate the signatures with the aims of eIDAS itself on an equivalence basis.[233]

---

[226] EUBOF, 'Legal and Regulatory Framework' (n 220) 23.
[227] Ibid.
[228] EU Parliament, 'Resolution 3 October 2018' (n 210) par 37, emphasizing 'that legal certainty surrounding the validity of a digital cryptographic signature is a critical step towards facilitating smart contracts'.
[229] eIDAS defines an 'electronic signature' as 'data in electronic form which is attached to or logically associated with other data in electronic form and which is used by the signatory to sign'. See art 3 para 10.
[230] EUBOF, 'Legal and Regulatory Framework' (n 220) 24.
[231] Ibid, 12, 23–24, observing that blockchain transactions meet the first two levels of eSignatures under the eIDAS Regulation, but not the third, making necessary the validation of the signature by a TSP.
[232] See generally Anne Veerpalu, Liisi Jürgen, Eduardo da Cruz e Silva, and Alex Norta, 'The Hybrid Smart Contract Agreement Challenge to European Electronic Signature Regulation' (2020) 28 IJLIT 39 (hereafter Veerpalu et al., 'The Hybrid Smart Contract Agreement').
[233] Ibid, 45, 66–67. For a more in-depth analysis of the so-called principle of functional equivalence, see Andreas Furrer and Luka Müller, '"Functional Equivalence" of Digital Legal Transactions. A Fundamental Principle for Assessing the Legal Validity of Legal Institutions and Legal Transactions under Swiss Law'

In this way a smart contract using signature technologies able to replace the layers of protection offered by eIDAS (i.e. offering a level of assurance functionally equivalent to the validation of a TSP) would be deemed legally binding under European law, and transactions concluded via smart contracts in member states adopting a technology-neutral approach would not be *per se* penalized.[234]

Third, the European Union Blockchain Observatory and Forum's report points out that each jurisdiction aiming to recognize the validity of smart contracts and integrate them within its legal system shall face the issue of their immutability.[235] As mentioned above,[236] smart contracts are differentiated into weak and strong, and such differentiation is based on the costs of revocation and modification, with 'strong' smart contracts being prohibitively expensive.[237] As such costs associated with strong smart contracts suggest, what is often perceived as one of the main advantages of contracting on a blockchain can actually be a cause of concern for contracting parties and regulators. The report highlights the issue of a smart contract becoming obsolete, under specific changing circumstances, as in the case of a change in the law or in the best practices regulating the business area relevant to the smart contract at stake.[238] Each jurisdiction shall determine which legal recourse parties may avail themselves of before it becomes impossible to amend the code according to the changes.[239]

Fourth, the possibility of a bug in the code representing the terms and conditions of the contract could raise a question as to whether a technical audit of the code should be a legal requirement, which would operate as a validity condition for such code to be qualified as a smart legal contract.[240] This might also be useful also in those situations where, rather than a bug in the code, the encoded contractual terms do not properly reflect the complexity of the agreement and cause negative consequences for the parties.[241]

A final key point that the report emphasizes is the importance of ensuring that the effects of smart contracts are recognized outside the digital dimension. Digital transactions concluded via smart contracts shall produce enforceable effects on the parties' rights involved in the agreement; otherwise, the utility of contracting on a blockchain would definitely be preempted and operators' confidence certainly blemished. Therefore, the European Union Blockchain Observatory and Forum concludes that the participants to a relevant digital platform should be those electing the law

---

(*MME*, 20 June 2018) 5 <https://www.unilu.ch/fileadmin/fakultaeten/rf/furrer/dok/180619_Funktionale_AEquivalenz_translation.pdf> accessed 12 April 2022. Importantly, the UNCITRAL Model Law on Electronic Signatures (see UNCITRAL Model Law on Electronic Signatures with Guide to Enactment 2001 <https://uncitral.un.org/sites/uncitral.un.org/files/media-documents/uncitral/en/ml-elecsig-e.pdf> accessed 12 April 2022) was also based on the principle of functional equivalence.

[234] As highlighted in Weber, 'Smart Contracts' (n 28), European regulation is an extremely 'cumbersome exercise not being practical in daily life. Therefore, it is highly unlikely that electronic signatures will be used by consumers when entering into a smart contract. Consequently, other means appear to be necessary in order to overcome the written form requirements.'
[235] EUBOF, 'Legal and Regulatory Framework' (n 220) 24.
[236] See Section I.A.
[237] See Raskin, 'The Law and Legality of Smart Contracts' (n 55) 310.
[238] EUBOF, 'Legal and Regulatory Framework' (n 220) 24.
[239] Ibid.
[240] Ibid.
[241] Ibid, 24–25.

applicable to the transactions closed on such a platform.[242] In this way it would be possible to avoid referring to the traditional international law connecting factors (other than the parties' choice, of course), as they would likely be unfeasible instruments for making a fair and practical choice of law in these circumstances.[243]

Another legislative source that will impact smart contracts is the European Data Act.[244] This regulation provides rules for the use of data. At the same time it mandates that smart contracts must contain a 'kill-switch'.[245] According to some critics, this would create an equivalence between smart contracts and smart legal contracts, and would be at the 'odds with the current functioning of smart contracts'.[246]

3. Mapping the Main Initiatives in Europe

In Europe two groups of states can be identified. A first group comprises those countries opting not to regulate smart contracts, opening the possibility of applying existing laws. These countries include the Netherlands, the United Kingdom, Switzerland, and to some extent Germany. A second, smaller group refers to those countries that drafted new laws explicitly referring to smart contracts, defining the essential elements that a smart contract must have for the purpose of being characterized as 'legal', that is, legally binding and with legal effects, under their national legislation. This second group includes Italy and Malta.

a. First group

Switzerland, the Netherlands, and the United Kingdom explicitly excluded the option of an *ad hoc* regulation for smart contracts. Germany has not issued a regulation for smart contracts yet, although the German government is still evaluating specific 'accredited certification procedures' and launched the new initiative 'Industry 4.0 Law Testbed', with a focus on legal questions regarding the negotiation and processing of contracts between machines via smart contracts.[247]

---

[242] Ibid. As the report notes, an important consideration is that different levels of decentralization and different kinds of crypto-assets would lead to different solutions as to how to select the law applicable to the 'proprietary effects' of transactions conducted via smart contracts on a case-by-case basis.

[243] Ibid, 25. See also Gisela Rühl, 'The Law Applicable to Smart Contracts, or Much Ado about Nothing?' (*OBLB*, 23 January 2019) <https://www.law.ox.ac.uk/business-law-blog/blog/2019/01/law-applicable-smart-contracts-or-much-ado-about-nothing> accessed 12 April 2022, making specific reference to Council Regulation 593/2008 [2008] OJ L177, 6 (generally referred to as 'Rome I').

[244] See Regulation (EU) on harmonised rules on fair access to and use of data [2023] (Data Act) <https://data.consilium.europa.eu/doc/document/PE-49-2023-INIT/en/pdf> accessed 1 December 2023.

[245] See Data Act (n 244) Art. 30 (b) including among the requirements for smart contracts: 'safe termination and interruption: ensure that a mechanism exists to terminate the continued execution of transactions: the smart contract shall include internal functions which can reset or instruct the contract to stop or interrupt the operation to avoid future (accidental) executions'. In this regard, the conditions under which a smart contract could be reset or instructed to stop or interrupted should be clearly and transparently defined. Especially, it should be assessed under which conditions non-consensual termination or interruption should be permissible.

[246] Alexandru Circiumaru, Federico Casolari, Mariarosaria Taddeo, Aina Turillazzi, and Lucino Floridi, 'How to Improve Smart Contracts in the European Union Data Act' (2023) 2 DISO 9.

[247] Bundesministerium für Wirtschaft und Energie, 'Blockchain Strategy of the Federal Government: We Set Out the Course for the Token Economy' (18 September 2019) 9 <https://www.bmwk.de/Redaktion/EN/Publikationen/Digitale-Welt/blockchain-strategy.pdf?__blob=publicationFile&v=3> accessed 12 April 2022.

II. TOWARDS A REGULATORY FRAMEWORK FOR SMART CONTRACTS 111

In Switzerland, the Federal Council issued its 'Legal Framework for Distributed Ledger Technology and Blockchain in Switzerland' (the Report) in 2018 and took the position that it is premature to legislate in the area of smart contracts, because of the embryonic stage of the technology.[248] The Report defined smart contracts as 'a computer protocol, usually based on a decentralised blockchain system, which allows automated contract execution between two or more parties with previously coded data'.[249] Furthermore, as mentioned above,[250] it reported the position of major academics taking the view that smart contracts do not necessarily qualify as contracts under the Swiss Code of Obligations (CO) but are rather a technology for executing contracts.[251]

The Report further identifies specific issues inherently related to smart contracts that could affect their qualification and legal effectiveness. Main concerns relate to the lack of human intervention, immutability, and their inherent limitation. With regard to the lack of human intervention, parties first define the contractual terms to subsequently convert them into a 'machine readable form', whereby the performance and conditions are programmed and automatically verified by the system.[252] In this context, the manifestation of the intent does not take place in the conventional way, with the system serving as an intermediary. Therefore, the prevailing doctrine has determined that a party cannot conclude the contracts solely with a computer system, due to the lack of legal personality within the meaning of the Swiss Code of Obligations.[253] With regard to immutability, the Report highlighted that smart contracts clearly embody the doctrine of *pacta sund servanda*, which is clearly part of the Swiss legal system (with some exceptions, i.e. *clausula rebus sic stantibus*, fraud, and termination of open-ended contracts for good cause without notice).[254] Finally, the Report considers the intrinsic limitation of smart contracts to the digital world.[255] This characteristic has two implications: first, this impacts the nature of the smart contracts' subjects, which can be exclusively electronic, as in the case of digital assets or money transfer. More importantly, this makes coding specific nuances or vague terms problematic.[256]

Reasons for concern also emerge when considering specific problems. An example is the manifestation of intent, which does not take place in the conventional way, with the system serving as an intermediary, or a 'matching system'.[257] With regard to the execution, problems could emerge in relation to the possibility of a poor execution, where a key question refers to who would be liable in case of programming errors or machine errors despite correct programming.[258] The Report

---

[248] Swiss Council, *Report on the Legal Framework for DLT* (n 31) 80.
[249] Ibid, 81.
[250] See Section II.C.3.a.
[251] Swiss Council, *Report on the Legal Framework for DLT* (n 31) 80.
[252] Ibid.
[253] Ibid, 81.
[254] Ibid, 80. See also Weber, 'Smart Contracts' (n 28) 308.
[255] Ibid. See also Weber, 'Smart Contracts' (n 28) 302.
[256] Ibid, 8.
[257] See Weber, 'Smart Contracts: Vertrags' (n 134) 291–294.
[258] Swiss Council, *Report on the Legal Framework for DLT* (n 31) 81.

takes the view that Articles 197 and 369 CO may apply in cases of technical program defects.[259]

The Netherlands and the United Kingdom followed a similar strategy, each issuing a statement clarifying their positions.

In the UK[260] the UK Jurisdictional Taskforce (the Taskforce) opted for not defining but rather describing smart contracts. The Taskforce highlighted the key characteristic of automaticity, in the sense that 'a smart contract is performed, at least in part, automatically and without the need for, and in some cases without the possibility of, human intervention'.[261] English law does not normally require contracts to fulfil specific formal requirements, and the only condition for enforcing any promise is respect of the common law requirements for formation (in addition to a lack of vitiating factors).[262] The Taskforce explains:

> Contract law is concerned with the enforcement of promises. It might be argued that the automaticity of smart contracts, and the mechanistic way in which computer code operates, means that there is strictly no need for a party either to promise performance or to resort to the law to enforce a promise by their counterparty: the code will simply do what it has been programmed to do. Even if that is right, however, we do not think it is a good reason for treating smart contracts as being different in principle from conventional contracts.[263]

In the Netherlands, the Research and Documentation Centre of the Dutch Ministry of Justice and Security published a report. Consistent with the UK, under Dutch law there are generally no specific formal requirements, and therefore a contract can be concluded in computer code. Accordingly, Dutch contract law, in principle, allows the creation of smart contracts, and would not require any specific regulation for ensuring their validity.[264]

Although Switzerland, the Netherlands, and the United Kingdom opted not to issue *ad hoc* regulations, it seems that the underlying reasons justifying the same choice

---

[259] Ibid.
[260] For a doctrinal analysis of the applicability of current law to smart contracts, see generally Roger Brownsword, 'Regulatory Fitness: Fintech, Funny Money, and Smart Contracts' (2019) 20 EBOR 5.
[261] UK Jurisdictional Taskforce, 'Legal Statement on the Status of Cryptoassets and Smart Contracts' (18 November 2019) 31 <https://35z8e83m1ih83drye28o09d1-wpengine.netdna-ssl.com/wp-content/uploads/2019/11/6.6056_JO_Cryptocurrencies_Statement_FINAL_WEB_111119-1.pdf> accessed 12 April 2022.
[262] As the Taskforce explains, the three 'requirements for formation of a contract are three-fold: first, that agreement has, objectively, been reached between the parties as to terms that are sufficiently certain; secondly, that the parties intended (again, objectively) that they would be legally bound by their agreement; thirdly that, unless the contract is made by deed, each party to it must give something of benefit, which is referred to as "consideration"—a gratuitous promise in return for nothing is not generally enforceable'. Ibid, 31.
[263] Ibid. See also the Law Commission, 'Smart Legal Contracts: Advice to the Government' (2020) <https://s3-eu-west-2.amazonaws.com/lawcom-prod-storage-11jsxou24uy7q/uploads/2021/11/Smart-legal-contracts-accessible.pdf> accessed 12 April 2022. In this report, the Law Commission confirmed the same position.
[264] See Stibbe, 'Blockchain and the Law—Regulation for Smart Contracts on the Way?' (30 October 2019) <https://www.stibbe.com/en/news/2019/october/blockchain-and-the-law---regulation-for-smart-contracts-on-the-way> accessed 12 April 2022.

are rather different, especially with respect to the United Kingdom and Switzerland. In this group the United Kingdom is the country that more explicitly opted for almost automatically extending existing contract law provisions to smart contracts. In Switzerland the majority of the legal scholars are inclined not to characterize smart contracts as contracts under the CO. At the same time, the Federal Council has also referred to the non-maturity of the technology as a reason for not regulating it, which might also be interpreted as a temporary decision subject to technical evolutions, implementing a traditional wait-and-see strategy.[265] Therefore, these two specific reasons might have led to this outcome. Different from the United Kingdom, Switzerland might opt for implementing reforms in the sense of a slight adaptation of existing contract law where necessary, as advocated by some scholars.[266] Compared to the United Kingdom and Switzerland, the Netherlands was slower in the process of analysing the legality of smart contracts; therefore, specific regulatory initiatives might emerge in the future.

b. Second group
A second group of countries (including Italy and Malta) has opted to issue *ad hoc* regulations, in the sense of defining smart contracts and attributing to them legal effects.

Italy was one of the first movers in Europe, providing a legal definition for DLT technology[267] and smart contracts. Italian law defines smart contracts as 'computer programs that operate on distributed registers-based technologies and whose execution automatically binds two or more parties according to the effects predefined by said parties'.[268] The Agenzia per l'Italia Digitale (AgID) issued the guidelines setting out the best practices for DLT and smart contracts, which define smart contracts as '*codici eseguibili*' (literally 'executable codes'),[269] opting against employing any lexical reference to the pure contractual sphere.

In addition to the definition of DLT and smart contracts, the new law has also introduced the digital identification ('*identificazione informatica*') of the parties. The digital identification coupled with the satisfaction of the AgID requirements as provided in the abovementioned guidelines would satisfy the requirement of the written form.[270]

---

[265] For further details on the wait-and-see strategy see Chapter 1, Section III.C.2.b.
[266] See Weber, 'Smart Contracts' (n 28) 307.
[267] See Law No. 12/2019 (12 February 2019). The law defines DLT technology as 'technologies and information protocols that use a shared, distributed, replicable, simultaneously accessible, architecturally decentralised registry on a cryptographic basis, such as to allow registration, validation, updating and archiving of data, both in clear and further protected by cryptography, that are verifiable by each participant, are not alterable and not modifiable'. Ibid, art 8-ter.
[268] Ibid, art 8-ter(2).
[269] AgID, 'Linee Guida per la Modellazione delle Minacce ed Individuazione delle Azioni di Mitigazione Conformi ai Principi del Secure/Privacy By Design' (7 May 2020) para 1.1.1.3 <https://www.agid.gov.it/sites/default/files/repository_files/allegato_4_-_linee_guida_per_la_modellazione_delle_minacce-dlt.pdf> accessed 12 April 2022.
[270] See Alessandro Tanno, 'Italy Affirms Legal Effectiveness of DLTs and Smart Contracts' (*Linklaters*, 2019) <https://www.linklaters.com/en/insights/blogs/fintechlinks/2019/fintech-italy-affirms-legal-effectiveness-of-distributed-ledger> accessed 12 April 2022. See also Veerpalu et al., 'The Hybrid Smart Contract Agreement' (n 232) 57. See also Gregorio Gitti and Marisaria Maugeri, 'Blockchain-Based Financial Services and Virtual Currencies in Italy' (2020) 9 JEuCML 43, 45.

In Malta, the Malta Digital Innovation Authority (MDIA) was set up to address key questions on blockchain, DLT, and smart contracts.[271] The Maltese Virtual Financial Assets Act (VFA) defines smart contracts as 'a form of technology arrangement consisting of: (a) a computer protocol; or (b) an agreement concluded wholly, or partly in an electronic form, which is automatable and enforceable by computer code, although some parts may require human input and control and which may be also enforceable by ordinary legal methods or by a mixture of both'.[272] As Veerpalu et al. have considered, this definition is not specific enough with regard to the smart contract form,[273] leaving open the possibility of a computer protocol or an electronic form. As a consequence, 'all requirements of electronic-form contract as provided by *ex-ante* regulation would apply to smart contracts under Maltese law, hence leaving the form to be qualified under existing requirements applicable to all contracts'.[274]

In addition to the VFA, the Innovative Technology Arrangements and Services Act (ITASA) provided a certification system for developers of new technologies, including DLT and smart contracts, by system auditors registered with the MDIA.[275] This certification has two benefits. For developers, it enhances trust in their innovations; therefore, they are more credible. From a broader systemic angle, this might be beneficial for the entire ecosystem, contributing to leverage the overall trust in these nascent markets.[276] At the moment, Maltese law does not require developers to have such a licence. It is, rather, a voluntary decision for those who seek to meet the standards of the law and obtain a public certification for this.[277]

A consequence of this certification is the possibility for the developer to appoint a technical administrator who has relevant powers, in case of an unexpected loss or a breach of law that had not been previously addressed as part of the governance structure of the arrangement.[278] On the one hand, this would be a way for managing the downsides related to the immutability of the code (and smart contracts). On the other hand, it could be a controversial solution, taking into account the importance that immutability has in the DLT sphere.

c. First group versus second group: what's the difference after all?
Beyond any classification, how do the two solutions (regulating versus not regulating) differ?

At the time of writing, Italy and Malta did not provide an *ad hoc* regulation for smart contracts, in the strictest sense. Furthermore, there are no planned initiatives to amend their existing contract laws. Rather, in these two countries regulators have opted for providing a definition of 'smart contract' and have identified (or will likely

---

[271] Joshua Ellul, Jonathan Galea, Max Ganado, Stephen McCarthy, and Gordon J. Pace, 'Regulating Blockchain, DLT and Smart Contracts: A Technology Regulator's Perspective' 21 ERA Forum 209, 216–217 (hereafter Ellul et al., 'Regulating Blockchain').
[272] Malta Virtual Financial Assets Act 2018, art 2(2).
[273] Veerpalu et al., 'The Hybrid Smart Contract Agreement' (n 232) 57.
[274] Ibid.
[275] Malta Digital Innovation Authority Act 2018, ch 591.
[276] Ellul et al., 'Regulating Blockchain' (n 271) 217.
[277] Ibid.
[278] Ibid.

do so in the future) specific requirements that smart contracts should have in order to be recognized as 'legal contracts' and be subject to traditional contract law. By doing so, regulators explicitly recognized the potential legality of smart contracts. This is also what the majority of states did in the United States, where the centrality of the UCC is not questioned, although multiple definitions of smart contracts were formalized.

After all, this approach does not substantially differ from the one adopted in the UK. In this legal system, regulators considered that an explicit recognition of smart contracts as contracts under British law was not necessary, with the consequence that existing contract law might apply without any further legislative (or interpretative) action. Indeed, both these approaches conclude that existing contract law is applicable, although the second group deemed it necessary to provide a further regulatory piece, explicitly defining smart contracts and connecting them to existing laws.

III. Critical Considerations

A. Why Smart Contracts Are a Matter of Law

Technological (infrastructural) innovation, as in the case of blockchain, may be distinguished from financial innovation. The difference between the two phenomena can be explained by taking into account the conceptual difference between 'stock' and 'flow' variables that apply to different contexts, from accounting to more strictly scientific subjects.[279] Financial innovation (more recently coupled with financial engineering) is 'flow', due to its characteristic of being a systematic and constant trend in finance. As mentioned in Chapter 1,[280] although financial innovation varies in its intensity, it has always existed. An example of its continuity in all époques is the development of the so-called Commenda in the Middle Ages, the antecedent of modern investment trusts and private funds, created with the purpose of diversifying risk, as well as for financing medieval maritime trades.[281]

Unlike the systematic financial innovation, the implementation of specific technologies can be associated with the notion of 'stock' variable.[282] Instead of a constant flow of financial innovation, the creation of specific technological innovations implies the specific implementation of totally new (and potentially disruptive) infrastructures, and this happens at a more recognizable and specific time 'zero'. For example, the so-called internet era emerged twenty-five years ago as a mass

---

[279] For an overview of the notions of 'stock' and 'flow', see J. Singh, 'Difference between Flow Variables and Stock Variables' (*Economic Discussion*) <https://www.economicsdiscussion.net/difference-between/difference-between-flow-variables-and-stock-variables/555> accessed 30 April 2023 (hereafter Singh, 'Flow and Stock Variables').

[280] See Chapter 1, Section III.A.1.

[281] See Henry Hansmann, Reinier Kraakman, and Richard Squire, 'Law and the Rise of the Firm' (2006) 119 HarvLRev 1335, 1372 (discussing the commenda as a form of financing medieval maritime trade). See also Robert Yee, 'Financial Innovation and Commenda Contracts in Medieval Europe' (*Vanderbilt Historical Review*, updated 21 December 2019) <https://www.vanderbilthistoricalreview.com/post/financial-innovation-and-commenda-contracts-in-medieval-europe> accessed 12 April 2022 (discussing commenda as a way to split labour and capital and diversify risk).

[282] For an overview of the notion of 'stock', see Singh, 'Flow and Stock Variables' (n 279).

phenomenon, when the European Center of Nuclear Research (known as CERN) made the world wide web free, renouncing any right over the software created by researcher Tim Berners-Lee.[283] The creation and implementation of the internet represented a disruptive event, resulting in rapid interconnection of the financial markets, coupled with significant economies of scale. Similar to the internet revolution, blockchain significantly reshapes financial markets, shifting them towards a more disintermediated model.

A crucial difference between the two innovations is that technological (infrastructural) innovations bring with them the development of specific rules and, under specific circumstances, the emergence of new social and commercial conventions. Both these conventions implement predictability through 'legal order', which is beneficial for the development of the society and more specifically for the market.[284] According to this conception, both the market and society are *loci artificiali*, as opposed to *loci naturali*, or an 'order which spontaneously forms itself', in the words of Friedrich von Hayek.[285]

Further, these conventions can be regarded as law in two ways. Theoretically, 'social conventions' represent (or are) a matter of law *per se*. Practically, new social conventions become relevant when they are in conflict with the established legal conventions and existing legal rules. Blockchain and smart contracts can be viewed this way. The new social and commercial conventions emerging in this specific context challenge the established existing legal conventions at different levels. They build a new concept of 'trust'; they provide a new concept of enforcement which is not structurally based on legal rules, since it does not require legal rules to function. Further, smart contracts change the basic paradigms of traditional negotiations as codified by the contractual and commercial regulation.

Regarding the last point, contractual and commercial rules were designed to be applied to contractual negotiation generally involving two humans. This paradigm has gradually changed with the advent of technology. As previously mentioned under Section I.B, smart contracts have existed for a long time, and their archetype is the vending machine, based on an elementary 'if–then' structure: if the buyer wants the product that the vending machine sells, the buyer will buy it. Deconstructing this contract and insulating each step, the formation of the agreement appears easily intelligible: a machine is placed in a public space and the potential buyer can see it (proposal); the potential buyer gets close to the machine, and decides to insert the coin to buy the product (acceptance); the product is provided to the buyer (execution). Similarly, with the advent of the internet era and the so-called shrinkwrap and clickwrap agreements, the conclusion of these contracts implied a mechanical operation of the (human) buyer who clicked on a box to express consent, instead of inserting the coin as in the case of the vending machine.

---

[283] CERN, 'Where the Web Was Born' <https://home.cern/science/computing/where-web-was-born> accessed 12 April 2022.
[284] See Natalino Irti, *L'Ordine Giuridico del Mercato* (Laterza 2003) (hereafter Irti, *Ordine Giuridico*).
[285] See for example Friedrich von Hayek, *The Confusion of Language in Political Thought* (The Inst. Of Econ. Aff. 1968) 29.

An extensive interpretation of the formation of the agreement was conducive to recognizing both the situations as legal contracts, where the traditional rules apply, such as the Second Restatement and Article 2 of the UCC. A further step in the evolution of traditional negotiations is represented by contracts implemented through so-called electronic agents. By significantly extending the 'if–then' binary structure, these contracts offer multiplied opportunities to conclude agreements, due to the broad range of practical implementations.

The 'Internet of Things' is a clear example of the potentials related to contracts between two nonhuman parties. The classic example is the Brita filter: once the filter is exhausted, the Brita pitcher will automatically order a new filter.[286] In relation to commercial contracts in general (as well as consumer contracts), the 'Internet of Things' raises issues very similar to smart contracts, executed through a blockchain-type infrastructure.[287] The next evolution will be the execution of smart contract related to the 'Internet of Things' on blockchain.[288] In cases such as the current 'Internet of Things' smart contracts, as well as blockchain smart contracts, the formation of the agreement is completely subject to automation.

From this evolution, new commercial uses (and therefore social conventions) have emerged, with the possibility of disrupting or challenging the existing ones exemplified in the current rules, and incorporating current social conventions. A relevant matter then becomes whether the law should take into consideration these new developments, that is, new social conventions.

The question should be affirmatively answered. Blockchain and smart contracts pose issues that go beyond specific concepts codified into the existing law, including the concept of enforcement. It may be argued that all of this system is and operates outside the law, because it builds and develops a system of rules that goes beyond the existing legal structure. However, this is still a problem triggering the law from inside. It is endogenous. Blockchain and smart contracts pose specific issues that certainly trigger specific questions to be solved within the parameters of the existing law. Similarly, lex mercatoria was the result of a parallel (transnational) environment but posed issues in relation to the current legal environment, in particular in the context of international finance and over-the-counter (OTC) derivatives.[289]

---

[286] Madeline Vuong, 'This Smart Water Pitcher Orders Its Own Filters: Amazon and Brita Unveil the "Infinity Pitcher"' (*GeekWire*, 29 February 2016) <https://www.geekwire.com/2016/amazon-dash-replenishment-powers-first-brita-smart-pitcher-that-orders-its-own-filters/> accessed 12 April 2022.

[287] See generally Chris O'Connor, 'What Blockchain Means for You, and the Internet of Things' (*IBM IoT Blog*, 10 February 2017) <https://www.ibm.com/blogs/internet-of-things/watson-iot-blockchain/> accessed 12 April 2022 (explaining how IBM plans to deploy its blockchain to enable IoT transactions).

[288] Bonpay notes that many companies are already working on implementation of blockchain technology to the IoT system. For example, IBM and Samsung have been developing a concept called ADEPT (Autonomous Decentralized Peer-to-Peer Telemetry) that is based on blockchain-type technology to form a foundation for a decentralized network of IoT devices. In this system blockchain will be a public ledger, eliminating the need of a central hub to maintain communication between them. Bonpay, 'Blockchain as a Perfect Solution for the Internet of Things' (*Medium*, 1 December 2017) <https://medium.com/@bonpay/blockchain-as-a-perfect-solution-for-the-internet-of-things-953ef5eef8b> accessed 12 April 2022.

[289] See Section III.C.

B. The Formation of the Agreement in the Context of Smart Contracts

A further, more specific question is whether the UCC provides a valid and useful basis to be applied to blockchain smart contracts. In this context, the traditional paradigm regulating the interaction of two human parties forming an agreement is completely subverted. Conversely, when the formation of the agreement depends on the autonomous interaction of two or more (generally defined) automated entities, it is the result of a process. Should this process be treated in the same way that human interactions leading to the formation of the agreement are regulated under the UCC, or do they require a new framework? After all, this is a more specific declination of the general problem highlighted by Easterbrook in relation to cyberlaw, which according to him did not require the creation of a new legal framework.[290] On the contrary, Lessig strongly advocated the creation of a new framework.[291]

When comparing smart contracts to traditional human negotiations and consequent formation of the agreements, the problem is mostly related to 'perception'. The phases leading to the formation of a smart contract are less clear when compared to traditional contracts, or to clickwrap agreements, or to those connected to electronic agents and the Internet of Things. In fact, even in the context of the 'Internet of Things', smart contracts are triggered after the purchase of an object: when buying a Brita, the buyer may also opt for automatic purchase of the filters. In all these situations there are material actions triggering the contract formation, making more explicit and recognizable the problem of consent and the consequent formation of the agreement.

When referring to smart contracts, this process of 'hidden' negotiations leading to the formation of the agreement is more difficult to understand, at least when applying the traditional standards existing in the context of traditional negotiations. However, this does not imply that there are no mechanics leading to the formation of the agreement that can be emphasized. For example, of great relevance is the phase when the parties define the 'if–then' conditions that trigger the execution of the contract. After formalizing such conditions, the rest of the process should not be relevant.

In general terms, the formation of smart contracts implies a specific process that is autonomous from the traditional concept of 'meeting of legal minds'.[292] The legal problem consists in qualifying this process as equivalent to a traditional contract and may be solved by considering whether consent has been reached by two counterparts. Whether these counterparts have power to decide or are autonomous structures should be irrelevant as long as the contract is fair (and not affected by unconscionability). Delegating the formation of an agreement to two autonomous counterparts (theoretically with less asymmetries) should not be an issue.

---

[290] See Frank H. Easterbrook, 'Cyberspace and the Law of the Horse' (1996) UchiLF 207, 207, 208, 210, 215 (arguing for the adjustment of the existing legal framework to accommodate new technologies).
[291] See Lawrence Lessig, 'The Law of the Horse: What Cyberlaw Might Teach' (1999) 113 HarvLRev 501, 502 (arguing for a new legal framework to address new technologies).
[292] On the challenges related to the code in relation to the 'meeting of the minds', see Weber, 'Smart Contracts' (n 28) 304–305.

III. CRITICAL CONSIDERATIONS

The current version of UCC 2-204 (as well as similar regulations in the major European jurisdictions, and in Switzerland) does not identify any subtype of contractual negotiation. This re-proposes the problem of determining whether the process of consensus leading to the formation of an agreement in the context of blockchain smart contracts is similar to or different from those concluded by two human parties. The decision whether to recognize an equivalence or to distinguish the two processes leading to the formation of the agreement can be made ex ante, adopting a reasonable framework of rules that could solve this problem, or ex post, with a hermeneutic analysis based on caselaw.

To consider the legislative option, a useful precedent is the proposed (but failed) 2003 reform of the UCC, to amend, among others, Section 2-204 with regard to electronic agents. In the proposed amendment, regulators opted for distinguishing different ways of forming an agreement.[293] The proposed amendments to the UCC concluded a revision process, which began in 1989 with the appointment of the Permanent Editorial Board Study Committee, by the National Conference of Commissioners on Uniform State Laws (NCCUSL) and the American Law Institute (ALI).[294] After troubled negotiations, a reform of the UCC Article 2 was proposed.[295] The amended Article 2 under the proposal provided: 'A contract for sale of goods may be made in any manner sufficient to show agreement, including offer and acceptance, conduct by both parties which recognizes the existence of a contract, the interaction of electronic agents, and the interaction of an electronic agent and an individual.'[296] The reform of Article 2 was not enacted by a sufficient number of states.[297]

Would this rule-based solution have proved an adequate solution for the purpose of recognizing the formation of an agreement as a result of the 'negotiations' of two entirely automated counterparts? It would have contributed to clearly identifying two different subcategories of negotiation (human negotiation and situations where electronic agents are involved) eventually applicable to blockchain smart contracts. By sharing the same legal regime, this solution had the advantage of not fragmenting the unity of Section 2-204 or any other related rules. This framework would have provided a stronger common basis for extending (through a hermeneutic process) the rules provided for the formation of an agreement concluded by two electronic agents to the formation of an agreement in the context of a smart contract executed on the blockchain. However, the overall processes and phases leading to the formation of the smart contract need to emerge and be more intelligible before opting for the creation of a new framework. For this reason, a rule-based option aimed at qualifying smart contract is still premature.

---

[293] See Kidd and Daughtrey, 'Adapting Contract Law' (n 135) 238–245.
[294] See generally Richard E. Speidel, 'Revising UCC Article 2: A View from the Trenches' (2001) 52 HastingsLJ 607 (detailing the revision process of Article 2).
[295] Linda J. Rusch, 'Summary of Amendments to UCC Article 2' (*Commercial Law Newsletter*, December 2003) 1 <https://www.americanbar.org/content/dam/aba/administrative/business_law/newsletters/CL190 000/full-issue-200312.pdf> accessed 12 April 2022.
[296] UCC s 2-204(1) ('A contract for sale of goods may be made in any manner sufficient to show agreement, including conduct by both parties which recognizes the existence of such a contract').
[297] On the difficulties of reforming the Article, see generally Robert K. Rasmussen, 'The Uneasy Case against the Uniform Commercial Code' (2002) 62 LaLRev 4.

A further option is an ex post analysis implemented by judges. If regulators opted for non-intervention, in the silence of the UCC, courts might build a caselaw by applying to smart contracts principles of equity. The advantage of an equity-based solution is its *in principle* flexibility, which would lead to the careful application of a case-by-case approach. An equity solution may be an efficient *transitory* solution or may lead to the creation of tests that may prove sufficiently flexible and adequate to be applied to a broad range of cases. The best example of an efficient test successfully applied in a context of high innovation such as the securities law is the 'Howey test', which was more recently criticized in the context of ICOs. The 'Howey test' is a four-prong test to verify whether a specific product is a security.[298] It proved to be a useful tool due to its characteristic of incorporating 'a flexible rather than a static principle, one that is capable of adaptation to meet the countless and variable schemes devised by those who seek the use of the money of others on the promise of profits'.[299]

A case-by-case analysis of the procedure leading to the formation of the agreement would also be useful for evaluating both substantial and procedural fairness of the smart contracts. This would lead to the theorization of unconscionability, good faith, and clearer boundaries between the role played by the machines and their owners (problems of representation). At the moment, all these issues are extremely unclear and cannot be solved by simply providing new regulations. Due to its inner vagueness and the possibility to integrate it with the equity principles, the UCC represents a great opportunity for regulators, who would not be forced to pass an entirely new regulation. It could be concluded that caselaw is by nature the best tool to implement the principle of 'technology neutrality' in the most comprehensible way.

C. The Problem of Regulatory Fragmentation and the Importance of Uniform Principles: Regulatory Fragmentation and Lex Cryptographia

An equity solution may also have the benefit of overcoming legislative and political barriers at the state level aimed at defining the specific concepts of 'blockchain' and 'smart contracts'. These initiatives are contributing to the emergence of clear regulatory competition in this field. Due to its regulatory framework, the federal system of the United States clearly favours regulatory competition, as demonstrated in the context of corporate law, with the emergence of Delaware as the most prominent state in that context.[300] However, the activities and the dynamics characterizing corporate law are significantly different when compared to commercial law. Commercial law is by nature more fragmented since it involves individuals who conclude specific

---

[298] For an analysis of the Howey Test in the context of Initial Coin Offerings and the extension of the securities law framework to new technologies, see Chapter 3. See also M. Todd Henderson and Max Raskin, 'A Regulatory Classification of Digital Assets: Toward an Operational Howey Test for Cryptocurrencies, ICOs, and Other Digital Assets' (2019) 2 ColumBusLRev 443.

[299] *SEC v W.J. Howey Co.* [1946] 328 U.S. 293, 299.

[300] According to Marcel Kahan and Ehud Kamar, Delaware has 'won' the competition. See Kahan and Kamar, 'The Myth of State Competition' (n 167) 684 (noting that only Delaware seriously attracts incorporation for public companies, and other states do not compete).

commercial transactions. Regulatory fragmentation may increase regulatory uncertainty,[301] leading to two unintended consequences: it would undermine the development of new commercial practices and would also be a threat to the attractiveness of the United States for potential foreign market actors.

Europe is by nature more fragmented and the process of harmonization in the context of contract law (implemented via directives) did not lead to the creation of truly established European categories of contract law and private law. Different from the United States, the emergence of smart contracts did not really trigger regulatory competition, and overall the process for identifying a regulatory solution in this field was rather slower. Although technology is a challenge for European private and contract law,[302] Europe maintained the pre-smart contract fragmentation characterizing contract law, and this might be surprising when confronting this approach with the one implemented in those areas more closely related to finance and cryptoeconomy. As will be explained in the following chapters, the European Union as an institution as well as some individual member states (in particular France, Estonia, Liechtenstein, and Malta) adopted successful approaches. Looking at Switzerland, it has confirmed its ability to maintain stability by taking important initiatives in any field of blockchain, including smart contracts. In this area, the Swiss Federal Council was especially receptive and concretely adopted much of the advice coming from academia, and more specifically its counsellors, opting for not redrafting laws in this sense of explicitly mentioning 'smart contracts'.[303]

The need for uniform principles has been a trend that characterized commercial practices since the very beginning of their development. For example, the lex cryptographia (also referred to as cryptographica)[304] emerged as a parallel system similar to the lex mercatoria, and the intermediate step of the lex informatica.[305] Any trend that does not contribute to the establishment of common practices may cause significant friction and obstacles to entrepreneurial initiatives in the commercial sphere. In addition, blockchain is strictly connected to the transnational dimension,

---

[301] See Iris H-Y Chiu, 'Transcending Regulatory Fragmentation and the Construction of an Economy-Society Discourse: Implications for Regulatory Policy Derived from a Functional Approach to Understanding Shadow Banking' (2016) 42 JcorpL 327, 354 (asserting that a functional approach to shadow banking is preferred to the current fragmented regulatory framework).

[302] See generally Stefan Grundmann and Philipp Hacker, 'The Digital Dimension as a Challenge to European Contract Law' in Stefan Grundmann (ed), *European Contract Law in the Digital Age* (Intersentia 2018) 3–45

[303] See for example Weber, 'Smart Contracts' (n 28) 307: 'In a nutshell, no need exists to re-write the whole contract law, even if traditional interpretation in law (e.g. the interpretation guidelines in respect of legal rules and of contractual provisions) cannot be applied in the context of smart contracts, in particular the grammatical and the historical interpretation method.' At the same time, the author notes that some specific changes in relation to the contract formation could require some amendment. Ibid, 307.

[304] Some works adopt the label 'lex cryptographia'. See Wright and De Filippi, 'Decentralized Blockchain Technology' (n 23). See also Thibault Schrepel, Blockchain and Human Rights: Utopia, or Dystopia, or Both? (*OBLB*, 4 December 2019) <https://www.law.ox.ac.uk/business-law-blog/blog/2019/12/blockchain-and-human-rights-utopia-or-dystopia-or-both> accessed 12 April 2022. Other works refer to 'lex cryptographica'. See De Filippi and Wright, *The Rule of Code* (n 75). See also Pietro Sirena and Francesco Paolo Patti, 'Smart Contracts and Automation of Private Relationships' in Hans-W Micklitz, Oreste Pollicino, Amnon Reichman, Andrea Simoncini, Giovanni Sartor and Giovanni De Gregorio (eds), *Constitutional Challenges in the Algorithmic Society* (CUP 2021) 315–330.

[305] See generally Wright and De Filippi, 'Decentralized Blockchain Technology' (n 23)

due to the geographical distribution of those who operate in the blockchain infrastructure. The decision to promote regulatory state competition as well as any passive approach with a similar outcome is highly risky in a context where there are no parameters, in terms of both regulation and caselaw. In such a context the competition among states may lead to a race to the bottom.

In a recent statement, Commodity Futures Trading Commission (CFTC) Chairman Cristopher Giancarlo, while emphasizing the potential role of regulation in frustrating blockchain innovation and advocating for the implementation of a 'do no harm' approach, suggested that regulators should opt for the provision of uniform principles, which are beneficial for investments in DLT and innovation.[306] In an effort to reduce state-level regulatory fragmentation in the context of cryptocurrency-related activities, the Uniform Law Commission drafted the Uniform Regulation of Virtual-Currency Business Act (URVCBA) in July 2017.[307] With the provision of this text, the Uniform Law Commission intended to 'regulate persons that issue virtual currencies or that provide services that allow others to transfer virtual currencies, provide 'virtual-currency' exchange services to the public, or offer to take custody of virtual currency for other persons'.[308] The URVCBA, adopted only by three states (Connecticut, Hawaii, and Nebraska),[309] confirms the need for common practices and principles in a new space. In the context of smart contracts, a similar approach was supported by the Chamber of Digital Commerce when criticizing the multiplication of national laws, providing autonomous definitions for blockchain and smart contracts.[310]

The need for uniform principles is certainly not new, especially in the context of commercial law. In the Middle Ages, many national laws were inadequate in granting a rapid solution to cases, in addition to creating significant problems connected to the transnationality of the commercial traffic. English courts at the time of the Middle Ages based their functioning on arcane rules which proved to be inadequate to grant justice in a reasonable time or could not grant justice at all.[311] Therefore, the merchants bypassed the application of national laws by creating the lex mercatoria, which, as mentioned above, incorporated a uniform and transnational system of laws. After all, even the dynamics that led to the creation of the UCC did not significantly differ from the 'merchant law': the UCC is the result of the initiative of two private bodies, the ALI and the NCCUSL, with the difference that the lex mercatoria is anational and has 'de jure autonomy'.[312]

---

[306] J. Christopher Giancarlo, 'Keynote Address' (*ISDA's Trade Execution Legal Forum*, 9 December 2016) <http://www.cftc.gov/PressRoom/SpeechesTestimony/opagiancarlo-18> accessed 12 April 2022.
[307] The Uniform Regulation of Virtual-Currency Businesses Act 2018.
[308] Ibid, s 103 cmt 1.
[309] Proskauer LLP, 'A Proposed Statutory Framework for State Regulation of Virtual Currency Businesses: The Uniform Law Commission's "Uniform Regulation of Virtual-Currency Businesses Act"' (*Blockchain & the Law*, 4 April 2018) <https://www.blockchainandthelaw.com/2018/04/a-proposed-statutory-framework-for-state-regulation-of-virtual-currency-businesses-the-uniform-law-commissions-uniform-regulation-of-virtual-currency-businesses-act/> accessed 12 April 2022.
[310] See generally CDC, 'Legal Primer' (n 108).
[311] Whaley and McJohn, *Problems and Materials on Commercial Law* (n 127) 1.
[312] Orsolya Toth, *The Lex Mercatoria in Theory and Practice* (OUP 2014) 174–175.

Consistent with the criticisms emerging from financial innovation and blockchain, further analogies can be identified in this specific context. The internationalization of commercial practices was a process of constant evolution starting from the Middle Ages and culminating in the emergence of blockchain. The different phases of such process (including the emergence of the internet, international finance, and blockchain) resulted in the creation of a parallel system of rule, favoured by the emergence of new paradigms and infrastructures, and detached from any specific jurisdiction. When referring to international finance, this is clear when taking into account the evolution of the derivatives market, where the peculiar market practices characterizing this market have led to a reviviscence of the lex mercatoria. Not only are derivatives transactions based on a marked transnationality, but also the specific methods of negotiation, on the basis of standard form contracts (e.g. the ISDA master agreement), are the expression of a transnational law,[313] which is de facto autonomous of any national regulation.[314]

Similarly, the globalization of the exchanges led by the internet revolution created a parallel world, where technology itself developed a parallel form of regulation,[315] and saw the emergence of the so-called lex informatica, considered as a natural extension of the lex mercatoria. Similar to the lex mercatoria, the lex informatica has a set of features distinguishing it from legal regulation. This clearly emerges when distinguishing lex informatica from common legal regulation, adopting specific parameters. According to Reidenberg, while in the context of a common legal regulation the framework is represented by the law, in the lex informatica what he calls 'architecture standards' are the relevant framework. 'Architecture standards' operate in a distinct jurisdiction (i.e. the 'network'), where the source of the law is not the state but technologists, and primary enforcement is granted not by courts but derives instead from automated self-execution.[316]

The creation and the development of the internet and cyberspace is helpful to understand the relevance of the development of a new and potentially disruptive infrastructure as a main source of a new parallel regulation. Both the internet and blockchain prove that the creation of entirely new technologies and infrastructures leads to the creation of new parallel regulations and that sometimes the technology itself is an example of regulation. If this was clear when taking into account common informatics, it is even clearer in the context of blockchain, due to its foundational characteristics. Blockchain is entirely based on codes representing at the same time the essence of the technology, as well as the basis and the proof of the transactions implemented through it. Codes are the basic element of the new parallel regulation that does not have any specific connection with any jurisdiction or legal system.

---

[313] On the emergence of transnational law as a new category, see Roger Cotterrell, 'What Is Transnational Law?' (2012) 37 L&SocInq 500, 501 (pointing to 'transnational law' as a term for 'new legal relations, influences, regimes, doctrines and systems that are not those of nation state (municipal) law, but equally, are not grasped by extended definitions of the scope of international law').
[314] Joanne P. Braithwaite, 'Standard Form Contracts as Transnational Law: Evidence from the Derivatives Markets' (2012) 75 ModLRev 779, 781, 783 (hereafter Braithwaite, 'Standard Form Contracts').
[315] Wright and De Filippi, 'Decentralized Blockchain Technology' (n 23) 46.
[316] Joel R. Reidenberg, 'Lex Informatica: The Formulation of Information Policy Rules through Technology' (1997) 76 TexLRev 553, 571–572.

In addition, smart contracts are self-executing. This characteristic is a key promise of the blockchain technology and leads to self-enforcement, bypassing any classic concept connected to legal enforcement. Therefore, the concept of a parallel regulation coupled with the possibility of complete self-enforcement developed in the context of self-regulation epitomizes the continuity of the lex mercatoria and the lex informatica in a new concept of regulation, specifically related to blockchain as a new technology and a new infrastructure at the same time: the lex cryptographia, identifiable with the brocade 'code is law'.

The emergence of lex cryptographia not only addresses the physiologic development of the regulation connected to the infrastructure, but also solves a practical need for those market operators involved in transnational commercial and financial activities (and intuitively nonjurisdictional) in the space of blockchain: lex cryptographia as a spontaneous corpus emerging from the technical needs of the infrastructure offers the advantage of being entirely separated from any formalistic and bureaucratic international regulation, which is *per se* difficult to achieve as well as concretely difficult to be enforced.

The vast majority of cross-border activities proved to be extremely difficult to regulate, due to many factors, in particular for significant political and economic interests, motivating the adoption of specific and fragmented regulation. An example is the regulation of hedge funds, a most debated regulatory issue emerging in the first decade of the twenty-first century and partially concluded after the last financial crisis. The regulatory process proved particularly difficult, both at global level (considering the different positions of European and American regulators) and at 'regional' level (e.g. taking into account the negotiations and the adoption of the European directive regulating private funds, the 'Alternative Investment Fund Manager Directive').[317]

The area of smart contracts applied to the sale of goods characterized by a context of high transnationality and the additional difficulty of dealing with a fragmented activity, where individuals conclude contracts. Therefore, the need for uniform principles and rules becomes relevant and should be the best way to implement an efficient system, due to the advantage of preventing regulatory arbitrage.

D. The Importance of Self-Regulatory Organizations

One of the consequences of innovation is the transformation that it may trigger not only at the level of market practices but also at the institutional level. This is clear when analysing the governance of federal agencies in the United States as well other national agencies in the world. The SEC created a task force devoted to blockchain in 2015 (the Working Group on Blockchain) and a Strategic Hub for Innovation and Financial Technology;[318] other securities agencies have created *ad hoc* Fintech departments

---

[317] See Marco Dell'Erba, 'The Regulation of Alternative Investment Funds in Europe: The Alternative Investment Fund Managers Directive' in Raphaël Douady, Clément Goulet, and Pierre-Charles Pradier (eds), *Financial Regulation in the EU: From Resilience to Growth* (Palgrave 2017) 321–354.

[318] SEC, 'SEC Launches New Strategic Hub for Innovation and Financial Technology' (18 October 2018) <https://www.sec.gov/news/press-release/2018-240> accessed 12 April 2022.

(among them, the French AMF, the Swiss FINMA, and the Singaporean MAS).[319] However, institutional transformations happen not only at the level of public institutions but also on the side of private actors. This may lead to the creation of new self-regulatory entities for the development of new standards, as well as to the emergence of new industry's representatives. These organizations are extremely relevant for the regulatory process and the success of regulatory initiatives, since their specific knowledge of the market is crucial for the creation of an efficient and adequate regulatory framework.

In the specific context of smart contracts and commercial transactions executed through the blockchain, a new industry representative was created in 2014: the Chamber of Digital Commerce, the largest trade association representing the blockchain industry.[320] Among its initiatives, the Chamber of Digital Commerce launched the Smart Contract Alliance in 2016, with the purpose of promoting the application of this technology,[321] and published one of the first white papers on smart contracts and their potential applications in today's commercial and financial world. Authoritative self-regulatory organizations are in the best position to cooperate with regulators and provide useful advice regarding how the blockchain facilitates commercial transactions, as well as to take a leading position in the debate about the benefits that blockchain-based smart contracts may generate for commercial transactions. This becomes particularly relevant when taking into consideration the different regulatory approaches that have characterized the adoption of the internet versus blockchain technology. In fact, in the context of the internet revolution, regulators adopted a more consistent (and in a way optimistic) view, but blockchain certainly raised more scepticism.

Two major issues caused such scepticism. A first major problem depended on the novelty of applying blockchain to quotidian application. In October 2016, the Federal Reserve emphasized the need for 'complex demonstrations in real-world situations before these technologies can be safely deployed in today's highly interconnected synchronized and far-reaching financial markets'.[322] Understandably, such scepticism was mostly due to uncertainty on the state of the art of the technological advancements connected to blockchain, and was not entirely without merit. An example in this sense is so-called wallets and exchanges for cryptocurrencies, which often prove to be unstable and unreliable, with the effect of producing 'downtime which can impact on the ability to trade', as stated in an email sent to all the customers of Coinbase, a major platform for investing in cryptocurrencies, on 8 December 2017.[323] In a context of

---

[319] See generally Dell'Erba, 'Initial Coin Offerings' (n 4); Dell'Erba, '"Do No Harm" Approach in Initial Coin Offerings' (n 5).

[320] Chamber of Digital Commerce, 'The Chamber Is Turning 4!' <https://digitalchamber.org/chamber-anniversary/> accessed 12 April 2022.

[321] Chamber of Digital Commerce, 'Chamber of Digital Commerce Launches Smart Contracts Alliance' (28 July 2016) <https://digitalchamber.org/chamber-of-digital-commerce-launches-smart-contracts-alliance/> accessed 12 April 2022.

[322] Lael Brainard, 'Distributed Ledger Technology: Implications for Payments, Clearing, and Settlement' (Speech at the Institute of International Finance Annual Meeting Panel on Blockchain, Washington DC, 7 October 2016) <https://www.bis.org/review/r161014a.pdf> accessed 12 April 2022.

[323] One of the most relevant paragraphs of the email stated: 'Despite the sizable and ongoing increases in our technical infrastructure and engineering staff, we wanted to remind customers that access to Coinbase services may become degraded or unavailable during times of significant volatility or volume. This could

high volatility, timely execution of orders is essential for investor protection, which should be the base of blockchain technology. When hypothetically extending this kind of problem to smart contract and the world of commercial transactions, smart contracts may not be regarded with favour due to the inadequacy of the technology, which has not reached a relevant level of maturity.

A second source of scepticism was connected to the speculative nature of specific activities implemented in the context of blockchain, such as cryptocurrencies and the phenomenon of ICOs (smart contract-based tools for capital formation[324]). These activities had a clear speculative intent and were characterized by a high number of scams, coupled with frequent theft of Bitcoin.[325] In this scenario, regulators and politicians struggled to identify any potential benefit of the blockchain technology as a revolutionary tool to support commerce and commercial transactions and to distinguish any such from any speculative spiral of uncertainty related to the most popular applications.[326] In addition, the regulatory uncertainty surrounding the most popular applications of the blockchain negatively affected the development of other blockchain applications, including smart contracts. In this regard, the Chamber of Digital Commerce is to make further efforts in clarifying the importance of this technology for commercial transactions, and the positive role it may play in the market.

Smart contracts should not necessarily imply the creation of a new contract law, because it would jeopardize the application of the existing legal framework.[327] Furthermore, the Chamber of Digital Commerce expressed strong dissent regarding the issuance of state-level regulation aimed at defining blockchain technology or smart contracts or ensuring the legal enforceability of smart contract. State regulation is harmful due to its redundancy, inconsistency, and federal preemption determined by the ESIGN (providing that any state law giving special effect to a specific technology is preempted).[328] Enlarging its analysis to the global trends, the Chamber of Digital Commerce has also advocated for global initiatives to pursue regulatory harmonization, emphasizing the role of the newly created Global Financial Innovation Network (GFIN).[329]

---

result in the inability to buy or sell for periods of time. Despite ongoing increases in our support capacity, our customer support response times may be delayed, especially for requests that do not involve immediate risks to customer account security.' E-mail from Coinbase to customers (9 December 2017, 01:07 AM EST) (on file with author).

[324] See generally Paul P. Momtaz, 'Initial Coin Offerings' (2020) 15 PLOS ONE 1 <https://journals.plos.org/plosone/article?id=10.1371/journal.pone.0233018> accessed 12 April 2022.

[325] See generally Dell'Erba, 'Initial Coin Offerings' (n 4); Dell'Erba, '"Do No Harm" Approach in Initial Coin Offerings' (n 5).

[326] Ibid.

[327] Paul and Brigner, 'Smart Contracts' (n 29).

[328] Chamber of Digital Commerce, 'Joint Statement in Response to State "Smart Contracts" Legislation' (April 2018) <https://d3h0qzni6h08fz.cloudfront.net/Smart-Contract-Signatories1.pdf> accessed 12 April 2022; see also Chamber of Digital Commerce, 'Smart Contracts: Is the Law Ready?' (September 2018) <https://digitalchamber.org/smart-contracts-paper-press/> accessed 12 April 2022.

[329] See Chamber of Digital Commerce, 'Chamber Supports Coordinated Approach among Industry and Regulators Globally' (2 November 2018) <https://digitalchamber.s3.amazonaws.com/Smart-Contracts-Whitepaper-WEB.pdf> accessed 12 April 2022 (asserting that the GFIN can be a mechanism to harmonize best regulatory practices); see also Global Financial Innovation Network (GFIN), 'Consultation Document' (2018) paras 4, 6, 9 <https://www.fca.org.uk/publication/consultation/gfin-consultation-document.pdf> accessed 12 April 2022 (observing that one of the primary benefits of the GFIN is the opportunity for

A further general issue is the importance of authoritative representatives who contribute to identification of the best regulatory approach and enhance reliable self-regulatory initiatives, to fix and/or raise the operational standards in a new context. A crucial achievement for both the industry and regulators would involve fostering cooperation between self-regulators and public regulators, which would lead to better regulatory solutions in a shorter period of time. This is particularly relevant in the context of sophisticated and innovative practices such as those connected to blockchain, where the regulatory response is characterized by unprecedented time sensitivity and need for highly sophisticated private competences.[330] Adequate self-regulation supporting public regulation would also have the functional advantage of bridging the gap between a purely 'private' regulation solution (such as the lex cryptographia) and 'public' regulation.

E. Smart Contracts and Complexity

From the angle of complexity as extensively approached in Chapter 1, smart contracts are an essential and indispensable starting point in the line of disruption.

The contractual dimension has been one of the main pillars (together with property[331]) in allowing stable development of ancient and modern societies, and more specifically to construe economic and financial paradigms throughout history.[332] As some recent studies have considered, the contractual dimension will likely become an uncontested pillar (even more than property) in today's society—and even more so in the future—offering the opportunity to create synthetic property rights through contracts.[333] In such an evolving context, smart contracts as a specific opportunity opened up by blockchain offer a unique infrastructural environment for supporting and enhancing such changes. They might actively promote the establishment of new paradigms, including cryptoeconomy and tokeneconomy, as well as enhanced forms of sharing economy, identifying a system based on 'renting' or 'borrowing' instead of 'owning'. Indeed, the emergence of the sharing economy might confirm the trend related to the growing importance of the contractual dimension over property.

Looking more closely at the relevance of smart contracts for the 'line of disruption' as identified and defined in Chapter 1, smart contracts are the element that made several (if not all) applications possible in the context of cryptoeconomy. This is the case of ICOs and further debates in the context of corporate governance[334] and market infrastructures, as well as in the area of 'programmable' money, payment systems, and

---

regulators to work collaboratively and create joint policy). The consultation focused on four main themes, i.e. regulatory cooperation, regulatory engagement, speed to international markets, governance. Ibid.

[330] The literature on self-regulation is vast. See *ex multis* Black, 'Constitutionalising Self-Regulation' (n 8) 25 (asserting that self-regulation has been written about in different disciplines).
[331] Eveline Ramaekers, 'What Is Property Law?' (2017) 37 OJLS 588, 591.
[332] See Irti, *Ordine Giuridico* (n 284).
[333] On the relationship between contract law and property law, see generally Lutz-Christian Wolff, 'The Relationship between Contract Law and Property Law' (2020) 1 CLWR 49.
[334] See for example Broadridge, 'How Blockchain Transforms Proxy Voting' (24 April 2018) <https://www.broadridge.com/video/how-blockchain-transforms-proxy-voting> accessed 12 April 2022.

financial networks. For example, as Chapter 4 will consider, a specific subcategory of stablecoins, notably algorithmic stablecoins, implements a smart contract-based solution for a dynamic supply of money, potentially replacing central banks in one of their traditional tasks.

Looking at complexity as multidimensionality in the new paradigms,[335] smart contracts are a technical and legal tool for establishing and strengthening multidimensionality in the new paradigms. Historically, this is consistent with two elements: the scope of contract law and more generally the role of contracts. First, the scope of contract law has always been broad and multidimensional by nature: contract law involves 'a number of other topics' beyond the problem of creating legally binding agreements, and answering 'the two questions of agreement and legal effects or enforceability'.[336]

Second, contracts as a specific expression of the law and the legality represented an 'ordinary' tool for building strong societies and more specifically to build markets and financial markets (*loci artificiali*).[337] At a more advanced stage, contracts provide a basis for the implementation of a transnational system, as with the establishment of lex mercatoria[338] in the past, as well as the more recent international networks, as derivative contracts exemplify.[339] Throughout history, contracts as an instrument and the continuous adaptation of contract law as a framework responded to the evolving needs of individuals. Starting with simple bilateral barters, individuals gradually became merchants, entrepreneurs, bankers, and financiers, operating in increasingly larger geographic areas and gradually establishing (or affecting) larger networks.[340]

In line with this evolving reality, smart contracts as part of the broader category of contracts and contract law confirm that the contractual dimension is a complex adaptive system in a continuous evolution itself, and its adaptations trigger other 'systemic' consequences beyond the contractual dimension. There are two implications. First, from an 'internal' perspective that looks within the categories of contracts and contract law, smart contracts incorporate a new form of contractual adaptation in the changing technical and infrastructural landscape, potentially leading to the establishment of new forms of contractual negotiations and contractual relationships, accommodating and at the same time triggering new adaptations.

Second, from a broader perspective looking beyond the boundaries of the contractual dimension and contract law, smart contracts confirm that such contractual dimension is the subpart of a more extensive complex adaptive system, international finance, as defined in Chapter 1.[341] Smart contracts are an essential tool for transforming some economic and financial structures within society. In particular, smart contracts make peer-to-peer contractual relationships not only faster and to a

---

[335] See Chapter 1, Section V.
[336] Edwin Peel, *Treitel—The Law of Contract* (15th edn, S&M 2015) 6–7.
[337] See Irti, *Ordine Giuridico* (n 284).
[338] See Section III.C.
[339] See generally Braithwaite, 'Standard Form Contracts' (n 314).
[340] Robert C. Clark, 'The Four Stages of Capitalism: Reflections on Investment Management Treaties' (1981) 94 HarvLRev 561, has identified four phases of American capitalism. The first one corresponds to the creation of corporations; the second coincides with the separation between ownership and control; the third is characterized by the role of financial intermediation; and the fourth is characterized by a stronger role of financial intermediation.
[341] See Chapter 1, Section V.

certain extent automatized but also potentially more certain, posing the basis for a truly decentralized and disintermediated 'legal' environment. As also mentioned in Chapter 1, when multidimensionality couples with decentralization and disintermediation it leads to more intense forms of interactions within a significantly more expanded network, with relevant consequences also in terms of evolutionary patterns.

Conclusion

The significant impact of technology on commercial practices will continue to revolutionize the way commercial contracts are formed and executed and will lead to the emergence of new market practices. Regulators should avoid the systematic adoption of new regulatory frameworks as a tool to systematize technology. They should consider this option as an '*extrema ratio*' (the last available option) instead of building a stable system based on uniform principles. They should be the result of a careful and extensive interpretation of the existing regulatory framework, when it proves to be flexible enough to be safely extended to new paradigms. In this phase, regulatory fragmentation at state level does not set a clear standard for blockchain and smart contracts and should therefore be discouraged.

By modifying the mechanics leading to the formation of agreements, smart contracts executed on the blockchain significantly change the way negotiations are practically conducted and lead to the emergence of new processes. While these processes may differ from the ways in which human counterparts interact, the applicability of the existing contractual and commercial regulations to this new form of negotiation should not be excluded. This corpus of regulation has the advantage of being flexible enough to be integrated with adequate tests elaborated by the courts. At the moment, caselaw is the most 'technology-neutral' tool to regulate and demystify technology.

Smart contracts are an essential tool for establishing the new multidimensional paradigm triggered by technological transformation. Smart contracts are at the core of such important structural transformations, as they emerged in capital markets, corporations, and financial networks. This confirms the centrality of smart contracts in the context of 'complexity' approaches to contracts and contract law as well as to international finance.

3
Enhancing Disruption
Smart Contracts in Capital Markets, or Initial Coin Offerings: Breached Promises and Relevant Consequences

Introduction

Chapter 1 highlighted the importance of multidimensionality in the new emerging cryptoeconomy. This new paradigm relies on a new infrastructural environment in which smart contracts greatly contributed to make many radical structural transformations possible. This chapter focuses on the way blockchain technology and smart contracts have entered into capital markets and how this has triggered (or will likely trigger) significant changes beyond capital markets.

Multidimensionality is useful here for two different purposes. Adopting a static approach, it refers to a structural characteristic that better explains how and why international finance could become increasingly complex under the pressure of technology. Taking a more dynamic approach, multidimensionality is a key element for understanding the way international finance evolves because of an enhanced interaction among its subparts. In this sense, the approach to complexity is much closer to the original meaning elaborated in the context of complexity science.[1]

With his white paper, Satoshi Nakamoto proposed a new payment system infrastructure, and with it a new concept of money. One of the main characteristics of this 'new' money is that it is 'mined' instead of being issued by central banks as traditional modern money is. Money has specific functions in an economic ecosystem, in particular serving as a medium of exchange, a unit of account, and a store of value. Bitcoin had, and still has, the ambition to serve as a form of money. When referring to Bitcoin, the 'monetary' component is the dominant one, and the association between Bitcoin and the 'monetary' dimension is the most appropriate.

However, the novelty of Bitcoin was not exclusively related to its monetary 'layer' as a form of money or the other 'layer' of the payment and technological infrastructure. In fact, in 2008 Bitcoin, relying on a specific technology, proposed a concept of money that other individuals could replicate. As mentioned in Chapter 1, just four years later, J.R. Willett advanced the possibility of creating new coins *on top* of Bitcoins,[2] opening a new era of 'cryptoeconomy'. Furthermore, Willett later launched the first initial coin offering (ICO), Mastercoin[3] (now

---

[1] See Chapter 1, Section I.
[2] J. R. Willett, 'The Second Bitcoin Whitepaper' (2012) <https://cryptochainuni.com/wp-content/uploads/Mastercoin-2nd-Bitcoin-Whitepaper.pdf> accessed 11 April 2022.
[3] See Marco Dell'Erba, 'Initial Coin Offerings: The Response of Regulatory Authorities' (2018) 14 NYUJL&Bus 1107, 1136 (hereafter Dell'Erba, 'Initial Coin Offerings').

Technology in Financial Markets. Marco Dell'Erba, Oxford University Press. © Marco Dell'Erba 2024.
DOI: 10.1093/oso/9780198873617.003.0003

Omni[4]), displaying the potential of smart contracts to disrupt the phase of capital formation.

Capital formation is an extremely sensitive topic in entrepreneurial finance. Two ways to raise capital are traditionally associated with established financial institutions as well as regulations and procedures. A first possibility is that of 'going public' with initial public offerings (IPOs), despite their attractiveness significantly declined after the financial crisis of 2008.[5] IPOs represent the most important segment within the so-called primary market. Different from the secondary market, the primary market is characterized by high information asymmetries. Therefore, in this context, the role of mandatory disclosure in the form of prospectuses required by securities regulators in all jurisdictions and, most of all, the presence of financial institutions acting as underwriters should serve to mitigate such information asymmetries.[6]

A second possibility for entrepreneurs to fund their new venture consists in obtaining funding from private funds, generally venture capital funds or private equity funds. In this case, entrepreneurs agree to renounce a relevant stake, and sometimes even control of their new venture, in favour of such funds.

ICOs attempted to disrupt both traditional IPOs in the primary market and private funds. In fact, ICOs represented a tool for reducing the regulatory pressure and the financial costs related to IPOs, as well as limit the necessity to leave the control and the associated economic interests to third parties such as private funds. Before ICOs, crowdfunding emerged as a practice based on peer-to-peer lending, with private individuals financing specific entrepreneurial initiatives via crowdfunding platforms.

Looking at their economic and legal essence, ICOs trigger questions related to multiple concepts and definitions, which justify the interest and the competence of regulatory agencies beyond those dealing with securities. Cryptocurrencies that are created and then sold through ICOs still share some conceptual similarities with traditional currencies. For this reason, a significant debate on the characterization of cryptocurrencies as falling within the category of 'commodity' was sparked in the United States. At the same time, digital tokens issued and sold via an ICO are something different because they are much closer to the concept of 'security', which has become the dominant trait in the vast majority of jurisdictions.

Beyond any legal categorization, this direct or indirect nexus between ICOs, digital tokens, and cryptocurrencies is a source of disruption in two different dimensions: pure 'monetary' and 'securities'. In both these contexts, ICOs contributed to

---

[4] See Laura Shin, 'Here's the Man Who Created ICOs and This Is the New Token He's Backing' (*Forbes*, 21 September 2017) <https://www.forbes.com/sites/laurashin/2017/09/21/heres-the-man-who-created-icos-and-this-is-the-new-token-hes-backing/#108e76ad1183> accessed 11 April 2022.

[5] See European Commission, 'An SME Strategy for a Sustainable and Digital Europe' (Communication to the European Parliament, the Council, the European Economic and Social Committee, and the Committee of the Regions, 10 March 2020) <https://eur-lex.europa.eu/legal-content/EN/TXT/PDF/?uri=CELEX:52020DC0103&from=EN> accessed 11 April 2022 (hereafter Commission, 'An SME Strategy').

[6] See generally, John Armour, Dan Awrey, Paul Davies, Luca Enriques, Jeffrey N. Gordon, Colin Mayer, and Jennifer Payne, *Principles of Financial Regulation* (OUP 2016) 162 (hereafter Armour et al., *Principles of Financial Regulation*). For an analysis of ICOs in the context of capital market dynamics (including IPOs), see generally Jacques Iffland and Alessandra Läser, 'Die Tokenisierung von Effekten—Ein neuer Weg an den Kapitalmarkt' (2018) 4 GesKR 416. See also Jacques Iffland and Marie-Hélène Spiess, 'Acceptation de dépôts du public, émission d'obligations et ICO' (2019) 3 GesKR 459.

important structural transformations. An important characteristic of these structural transformations is that while they developed and continue to develop along two different trajectories, these dimensions are nonetheless strictly related and intertwined. ICOs as 'securities' could have not emerged without the 'monetary' origin of the process, because digital tokens issued via an ICO are instrumental for the 'cryptocurrency' to be successful. At the same time, the creation of a cryptocurrency via ICO digital tokens clearly brought disruption in another context, beyond the pure monetary one, and this process opened up a very broad range of applications in financial markets.

A relevant aspect of ICOs for their emblematic relevance and potential for disruption is the possibility of being a tool for entrepreneurs[7] interested in successfully completing the phase of capital formation in a much faster way. This is the precise moment when cryptocurrencies and ICOs become closer to the 'security' world, and the resulting cryptocurrencies launched via ICOs reflected this new and somehow more dominant trait. Along this trajectory, ICOs highlighted the potential of the underlying DLT as a disruptor in the corporate context, with the possibility of issuing shares on a blockchain platform. This option might bring potential advantages in attempts to solve recurring problems affecting corporate governance, especially in public companies.

At the same time, the characteristic of ICOs to serve the purpose of financing new entrepreneurial activities, and the multiplication of cryptocurrencies induced, resulted in extremely high volatility for cryptocurrencies. Such volatility was consistent with proximity to the securities world rather than the monetary one. While volatility does not represent a problem in the context of securities, it is a problem in the monetary context. This is the nexus that makes ICOs crucial for understanding their role in the further 'monetary' evolution of cryptocurrencies. Therefore, ICOs highlight the nexus between monetary and securities instruments (shifting from the 'monetary' to the 'securities' dimensions), but they also highlight the same nexus in the opposite direction, contributing to shift the attention from pure 'securities' problems to new 'monetary' problems, as in the case of volatility.

Volatility is relevant in the monetary context because it impairs the possibility of a currency, even in the form of a cryptocurrency, to serve the traditional functions generally associated with money; that is, to serve as a unit of account, a medium of exchange, and a store of value. Although the main goal of the vast majority of entrepreneurs launching ICOs was not to create their own 'money', the expansion in the number of cryptocurrencies that resulted from all these ICOs highlighted the need to pursue stability in the context of cryptocurrencies.

After the speculative frenzy surrounding ICOs, the cryptoeconomy achieved a higher stage of maturity. At this point, stablecoins emerged as a tool to bring stability in the cryptoeconomy, and they captured the attention of important market actors, including tech giants (in particular Facebook) and credit institutions (such as J.P. Morgan and Wells Fargo). These prominent corporations started to develop or become involved in the development of global stablecoin projects, such as JPMCoin and

---

[7] Sabrina Howell, Marina Niessner, and David Yermack, 'Initial Coin Offerings: Financing Growth with Cryptocurrency Token Sales' (2018) European Corporate Governance Institute (ECGI)—Finance Working Paper No. 564, 2.

Libra Coin (rebranded as Diem), that triggered the attention of securities regulators and of central bankers around the world. At this point, the initial purpose of Bitcoin to disrupt established institutions, including central banks, became clearer and was perceived as more achievable on both private and public sides.

Beyond their effective capacity to be an efficient or even a 'revolutionary tool' for capital formation,[8] ICOs are extremely important because of their relevance in the different steps of the cryptoeconomy. They function to prove both the inner dynamism emerging in capital markets (specifically stemming from capital formation) and the way this is reflected in the other interconnected subparts, in the context of international finance.

This chapter focuses on the structure of ICOs and the way they adapted their structural pattern to something different. Furthermore, it analyses the regulatory debate on ICOs, focusing on the dual dimension of 'commodity' and 'security' and how the United States, Europe, and Switzerland developed the characterization of ICOs under the existing regulatory frameworks. The chapter then focuses on the unsolved issues emerging from ICOs, highlighting, in particular, the difficulties regulators face in identifying an 'ideal' regulatory approach and how these difficulties are reflected in other key instruments emerging in the cryptoeconomy, such as stablecoins. Furthermore, this chapter assesses some of the breached promises of ICOs, in particular their ineffectiveness as a tool to foster financial inclusion, their inability to disintermediate venture capital funds (and more generally private funds), and the difficulty of building a capital market with no market infrastructures implementing the function of exchanges. Finally, this chapter considers the consequences of ICOs at the level of digital securities and market structures, highlighting their importance in the evolution and the establishment of the cryptoeconomy.

I. Key Aspects of ICOs and How They Evolved

A. The Structural Pattern

ICOs became extremely successful because they responded to entrepreneurs' need to finance their new ventures, especially at a time when recent economic crisis, coupled with increasingly rigorous banking requirements,[9] made access to funding much harder. Furthermore, venture capital funds, which traditionally focus their activity on financing new ventures, struggled to innovate their business model at a time of great economic and societal change, and ICOs proved capable of outperforming venture capitalists at the peak of their popularity.[10]

---

[8] See generally Dell'Erba, 'Initial Coin Offerings' (n 3) 1131.

[9] In particular Basel III, by increasing capital requirements and risk weighted assets, has exercised a higher pressure on banks and their Return on Equity (RoE). See EBA, 'Overview of the Potential Implications of Regulatory Measures for Banks' Business Models' (9 February 2015) <https://www.eba.eur opa.eu/documents/10180/974844/Report++Overview+of+the+potential+implications+of+regulatory+ measures+for+business+models.pdf/fd839715ce6d-4f48-aa8d-0396ffc146b9> accessed 11 April 2022.

[10] See Dell'Erba, 'Initial Coin Offerings' (n 3) 1109.

Although defining ICOs is not an easy task because of the multiple variables existing within the market,[11] ICOs generally consist of the sale of a stake in a project with the aim to raise funds[12] at an early stage of development (even before the project has started) via blockchain technology.[13] They differ from both crowdfunding campaigns and IPOs.[14] In all developed capital markets, IPOs achieved a high level of standardization in terms of mandatory disclosure, market actors involved, trading venues (regulated markets), and securities offered (stocks). On the contrary, ICOs involve the sale of digital coupons, so-called software presale tokens, to early investors via non-regulated exchange platforms.[15] The indelible distributed ledger is fundamental for issuing tokens[16] in the form of an organization's cryptocurrency.[17] These private cryptocurrencies implement new protocols generally based on Ethereum. These tokens create the capital inflow required for project finance[18] and can be purchased online with fiat currency or another digital currency at a predetermined exchange rate.[19] Tokens generally confer a discount on a cryptocurrency before it is listed on exchanges,[20] plus a right to vote on future decisions.[21] No market practices at the level of ownership or voting rights have emerged at the moment; therefore, some ICOs may offer different categories of participation (or levels of membership), such as voting member, founding member, third party service provider member, and asset gateway member.[22] Common stocks available in an IPO assign ownership rights.

---

[11] See generally Dirk Zetzsche, Ross P. Buckley, Douglas W. Arner, and Linus Föhr, 'The ICO Gold Rush: It's a Scam, It's a Bubble, It's a Super Challenge for Regulators' (2019) 60 HarvIntlLJ 267 (hereafter Zetzsche et al., 'The ICO Gold Rush'). The authors propose a taxonomy of ICOs.
[12] Maria Fonseca, 'ICOs and Blockchain Token Funding' (*IntelligentHQ*, 5 May 2017) <https://www.intelligenthq.com/finance/icos-and-blockchain-token-funding/> accessed 11 April 2022 (hereafter Fonseca, 'Token Funding').
[13] *Ex multis*, see Carla L. Reyes, 'Moving beyond Bitcoin to an Endogenous Theory of Decentralized Ledger Technology Regulation: An Initial Proposal' (2016) 61 VillLRev 191. See also Trevor I. Kiviat, 'Beyond Bitcoin: Issues in Regulation Blockchain Transactions' (2015) 65 DukeLJ 569.
[14] See generally Dell'Erba, 'Initial Coin Offerings' (n 3) 1110.
[15] Ibid.
[16] See generally The Economist, 'The Market in Initial Coin Offerings Risks Becoming a Bubble' (25 April 2017) <http://www.economist.com/news/finance-and-economics/21721425-it-may-also-spawn-valuable-innovations-market-initial-coin-offerings> accessed 11 April 2022.
[17] Brandon Kostinuk, 'Too Many Crypto Coin Crowd Sales Could Crowd Out True Innovators' (*American Banker*, 2016) <https://www.americanbanker.com/opinion/too-many-crypto-coin-crowd-sales-could-crowd-out-true-innovators> accessed 11 April 2022.
[18] Ibid.
[19] Ibid.
[20] See Richard Kastelein, 'Initial Coin Offerings (ICOs) Can Disrupt Both Traditional VC and Equity Crowdfunding' (*Intelligent HQ*, 31 March 2017) <https://www.intelligenthq.com/finance/initial-coin-offerings-icos-can-disrupt-vc-and-equity-crowdfunding/> accessed 11 April 2022.
[21] Ben Dickson, 'Can You Trust Crypto-Token Crowdfunding?' (*TechCrunch*, 12 February 2017) <https://techcrunch.com/2017/02/12/can-you-trust-crypto-token-crowdfunding> accessed 11 April 2022 (hereafter Dickson, 'Crypto-Token Crowdfunding').
[22] For example, OpenANX, a cryptocurrency exchange, provides for the following types of investors:

> Membership provides the holder with access to the openANX platform, and may convey voting privileges and other benefits as outlined below. The memberships will work through a tiered structure that allow for simple access, voting privileges or commercial (read: business) solicitation of services on the platform (*i.e.* escrow, legal, exchange, credit, asset gateway) with the relative number of tokens required for redemption varying with the level of benefits." Clause 5.2 further defines Voting membership and Founding membership. With regard to the former, it states that "A voting member shall have the privilege to vote on decisions regarding the

As the enforcement activity of the Securities Exchange Committee (SEC) has proved, ICOs differ from crowdfunding campaigns because they involve an investment and not donations.[23] In this framework, investors acquire a financial stake in the company,[24] which sometimes may include the right to vote on future decisions,[25] as mentioned above. Characterizing ICOs as an investment leads to the identification of their speculative intent, involving a material value generated by cryptocurrencies and platforms.[26]

These multiple variations of ICOs have a common structure[27] and share some similarities with IPOs, in particular as they relate to the pre-IPO phase. ICO promoters generally announce their new entrepreneurial initiatives on cryptocurrency forums and present an executive summary to a selected group of investors, followed by an executive summary generally referred to as a 'white paper'.[28] There are no disclosure requirements providing the minimum mandatory information to be supplied in a white paper; therefore, white papers do not have standardized content and do not provide any standard information. However, white papers generally provide the key terms and investment approach, such as the investment strategy, criteria, restrictions, processes, and returns.[29] In addition to the white paper, a yellow paper specifically addresses the technical specificities of the project.[30]

Similar to IPOs, ICO promoters address a preliminary offer exclusively to selected investors,[31] and only after the offer is signed is the launch of the ICO announced.[32] At this point ICO promoters target a broader segment of investors, which also includes small investors, via public relations campaigns.[33] Next, the ICO is launched and the new venture sells its cryptocurrency to be used with its software, even before the software is written.[34] Sometimes the company has a proof of concept or alpha version

openANX platform. These votes shall be determined via the Foundation's terms and shall be communicated to the Membership through the Foundation's website (www.openanx.org) and via social media and online channels." With regard to latter, it provides that "a founding member shall have all the privileges of a voting member. In addition, a founding member shall have the right to suggest topics for upcoming discussions.

OpenANX, 'Real World Application of Decentralized Exchanges V2.3.8' (White paper, 2017) <https://cryptorating.eu/whitepapers/openANX/openANX_White_Paper_ENU.pdf> accessed 11 April 2022.

[23] See Smith and Crown, 'What Is a Token Sale (ICO)?' (21 June 2016) <https://smithandcrown.com/research/what-is-a-token-sale-ico/> accessed 11 April 2022.
[24] Ben Dickson, 'What Is an Initial Coin Offering (ICO)?' (*TechTalks*, 7 December 2016) <https://bdtechtalks.com/2016/12/07/what-is-an-initial-coin-offering-ico/> accessed 11 April 2022.
[25] Dickson, 'Crypto-Token Crowdfunding' (n 21).
[26] Dell'Erba, 'Initial Coin Offerings' (n 3) 1112.
[27] In the sense of the identification of four different phases, see Roger Aitken, 'Investment Guide to "Crypto" Coin Offerings Ratings Blockchain Startups' (*Forbes*, 6 January 2017) <https://www.forbes.com/sites/rogeraitken/2017/01/06/investment-guide-to-crypto-coin-offerings-rating-blockchain-startups/#614e6940121b> accessed 11 April 2022 (hereafter Aitken, 'Investment Guide').
[28] Ibid, and Fonseca, 'Token Funding' (n 12).
[29] Fonseca, 'Token Funding' (n 12).
[30] Dell'Erba, 'Initial Coin Offerings' (n 3) 1112.
[31] Aitken, 'Investment Guide' (n 27).
[32] Dell'Erba, 'Initial Coin Offerings' (n 3) 1112.
[33] Ibid.
[34] See Josh Finer, 'How Blockchain Startups Are Driving an Under-the-Radar Fundraising Boom' (*Venturebeat*, 13 November 2016) <https://venturebeat.com/2016/11/13/how-blockchain-startups-are-driving-an-under-the-radar-fundraising-boom/> accessed 11 April 2022.

before starting the token sale, and more rarely it has a beta version.[35] The latter was the case with Storj.[36]

The preferred way to collect funds, generally Bitcoin or Ether, is by employing a public address so that the participants can send Bitcoin from an address for which they control the private key.[37] An alternative option would consist of creating an account for each investor and assigning to each of them a (unique) non-replicable Bitcoin address.[38] In this specific context, a widely implemented best practice favours the creation of a public multi-sig address for segregation purposes, in order to hold all the collected funds.[39] A key characteristic distinguishing ICOs from any other tools for raising capital is the duration of the fundraising. This round of fundraising (usually only one) occurs before the start-up has launched its project; however, the duration of an ICO may vary. Depending on the success of the ICO, the fundraising that begins before the launch of the start-up's project may last only a few minutes.

The final step consists of listing digital tokens on cryptocurrency exchanges, where trading eventually begins. The new start-up's team of developers and entrepreneurs are in charge of determining the pre-ICO price.[40] The post-ICO prices follow the rules of market supply and demand. Although the market for crypto-exchanges grew in the past few years,[41] it still lacks an effective secondary market for cryptocurrencies and tokens—except for a limited group of tokens.

B. ICO Problems and Structural Adaptations

ICOs have undergone many structural transformations, which reflect the need to optimize a new model of fundraising in an attempt to pursue efficiency and correct specific issues.[42] At the same time, ICO developers adapted ICO structures as a reaction to different factors emerging in this ecosystem. Such factors include the need to increase the reputation of ICOs, the importance to correct specific market practices typical of the cryptoeconomy, and regulation.

---

[35] Dell'Erba, 'Initial Coin Offerings' (n 3) 1113.
[36] Trond Vidar Bjorøy, 'Blockchain Fundings Are Trendy, But We're Still in the Wild West Days' (*Venturebeat*, 14 May 2017) 3 <https://venturebeat.com/2017/05/14/blockchain-fundings-are-trendy-but-were-still-in-the-wild-west-days/> accessed 11 April 2022.
[37] Sid Kalla, 'A Framework for Valuing Crypto Tokens' (*CoinDesk*, 3 March 2017) <https://www.coindesk.com/framework-valuing-crypto-tokens> accessed 11 April 2022.
[38] Ibid.
[39] Ibid. See also Ben Davenport, 'What Is Multi-Sig, and What Can It Do?' (*Coincenter*, 1 January 2015) <https://coincenter.org/entry/what-is-multi-sig-and-what-can-it-do> accessed 11 April 2022.
[40] Concern emerged in relation to the arbitrary practices instrumental to fixing the pre-ICO price. Richard Kastelein, 'What Initial Coin Offerings Are, and Why VC Firms Care' (*Harvard Business Review*, 24 March 2017) <https://hbr.org/2017/03/what-initial-coin-offerings-are-and-why-vc-firms-care> accessed 11 April 2022.
[41] Tim Lea, 'Venture Capital 3.0: The Initial Coin Offering Explained' (*Financial Review*, 3 May 2017) <http://www.afr.com/technology/venture-capital-30-the-initial-coin-offering-explained-20170502-gvxhos> accessed 11 April 2022.
[42] Marco Dell'Erba, 'From Inactivity to Full Enforcement: The Implementation of the "Do No Harm" Approach in Initial Coin Offerings' (2020) 26 MichTechLRev 175, 184–190 (hereafter Dell'Erba, ' "Do No Harm" Approach in Initial Coin Offerings').

A first factor was the concern generated by the high number of scams and bad-faith entrepreneurs. Although not all ICOs were scams, the structural deficiencies of the first ICOs affected their credibility. The market reacted in different ways. An important first radical transformation was the adoption of a 'capped sale' model and then the so-called 'reverse Dutch auction' model.[43] ICOs were originally based on an 'uncapped sale' model. The problem with uncapped sales is that the quantity of tokens sold to the public is not predetermined (as in the case of the sale of Ethereum). The heavy criticism raised against uncapped sales is that they promote greed and uncertainty in the value;[44] this was the main reason forcing entrepreneurs and developers to adopt 'capped sales'.[45] The implementation of 'reversible ICOs' is an attempt to increase the credibility of issuers, by acting on their incentives to fulfil their obligations. In this structure, ICOs provide the key feature for investors to renounce the investment at any stage of the project by returning the tokens and obtaining a reimbursement.[46] In this way, issuers are aware of the possibility that investors may renounce taking part in the ICO; therefore, they have stronger incentives to fulfil their obligations.[47]

Initial exchange offerings (IEOs) are the last frontier in ICO structure. As their label suggests, in an IEO one or more exchanges act as a counter-party.[48] The enhanced role of crypto-exchanges should provide some guarantees for the project. In this sense there are some similarities with the role of underwriters in the context of IPOs, in terms of the way they should both correct informational asymmetries. An IEO generally adopts a capped contribution per investor in an attempt to avoid so-called whales and maintain an adequate level of dispersion and liquidity; an IEO also maintains a fixed price per token.[49] The crypto-exchange is much more involved from the very beginning of the transaction. In fact, on the 'issuers' side' entrepreneurs immediately send the tokens to the exchange, which will be the acting intermediary with individual investors providing Ether.[50] The position of the exchange acting as an intermediary is reflected also on the 'investors' side'. In order to take part in the IEO, investors need to create a personal account with the exchange that will send the Ether.[51]

Another way to strengthen the credibility of ICOs was by creating alternative and more regulated forms of ICOs, especially for the US market. A first attempt was the Simple Agreement for Tokens (SAFT), derived from the Simple Agreement for Equity.[52]

---

[43] Ibid.
[44] See Vitalik Buterin, 'Analyzing Token Sale Models' (*Vitalik Buterin's website*, 9 June 2017) <http://vitalik.ca/general/2017/06/09/sales.html> accessed 11 April 2022. The author explains that 'uncapped sales' were perceived as something like as an expression of 'greed' by their promoters, and that from an investor perspective, a major concern was related to their exposure to the 'high uncertainty about the valuation' of what they were buying.
[45] Ibid.
[46] Helen Partz, 'ERC-20 Co-Author Proposes New ICO Model to Protect Investors from Fraudulent Token Sales' (*Cointelegraph*, 31 October 2018) <https://cointelegraph.com/news/erc-20-co-author-proposes-new-ico-model-to-protect-investors-from-fraudulent-token-sales> accessed 11 April 2022.
[47] Ibid.
[48] Gene Yan Ooi, 'What Is an Initial Exchange Offering (IEO)?' (*Medium*, 13 March 2018) <https://medium.com/traceto-io/what-is-an-initial-exchange-offering-ieo-245a7cf72f28> accessed 11 April 2022.
[49] Ibid.
[50] Ibid.
[51] Ibid.
[52] Dell'Erba, '"Do No Harm" Approach in Initial Coin Offerings' (n 42) 187.

The SAFT was created as an international framework for token sales,[53] and it pursued the separation between 'the pre-functional sale and the underlying consumer token, new financing instruments'.[54]

Security token offerings (STOs) are an evolution of the SAFT. Not only were STOs much more successful than the SAFT, but they currently represent one of the most widely used structures (together with IEOs), *de facto* replacing traditional ICOs.

In the United States, STOs are structured in a way that complies with securities regulations such as Reg. D, Reg. S, and Reg. A+;[55] they are also fully compliant with Know Your Customer/Anti-Money Laundering requirements and any additional local securities laws, depending on the jurisdiction in which they are located.[56] An entrepreneur interested in an STO has to comply with the prerequisites required by Reg. A+, in particular the existence of two years of audited financials and bookkeeping.[57] Furthermore, consistent with a traditional IPO, STOs require an underwriter and a banker because of the risks of selling unregistered securities.[58] The increased standards of an STO make it more expensive compared to other ICO structures, and this partially explains the difficulties experienced in growing STOs' prevalence in the market.

In addition to reputation, specific trends characterizing the primary market of cryptocurrencies affected the ICO market. A dangerous and still unsolved phenomenon in the cryptoeconomy is the abovementioned presence of so-called whales. Whales implement an investment strategy based on the purchase of the vast majority of the tokens that entrepreneurs issue. The concentration of tokens in the hands of a few whales has many negative impacts, such as the risk of reducing the liquidity of the investments, as well as an increased possibility of artificially manipulating the price of the tokens or the underlying cryptocurrency. An attempt to solve this issue was interactive initial coin offerings (IICOs), which should make token sales more egalitarian for both large and small buyers, pursuing a higher degree of fairness[59] and preventing larger investors from forcing small investors to renounce the IICO.[60]

Another driving force leading to the development of alternative ICO structures has been the increasing activity of enforcement by regulators, in particular in the United States. So-called airdrops were an attempt to develop an alternative scheme that escapes the securities laws framework. In an airdrop, both start-ups and established blockchain-based enterprises distribute cryptocurrency tokens to the users on

---

[53] See Zetzsche et al., 'The ICO Gold Rush' (n 11) 282.

[54] David L. Concannon, Yvette D. Valdez, and Stephen P. Wink, 'The Yellow Brick Road for Consumer Tokens: The Path to SEC and CFTC Compliance' in Josias Dewey (ed), *Blockchain & Cryptocurrency Regulation 2019* (Global Legal Insights 2019) 100 <https://www.lw.com/thoughtLeadership/yellow-brick-road-for-consumer-tokens-path-to-sec-cftc-compliance> accessed 11 April 2022.

[55] Ibid.

[56] Polymath Network, 'What Is a Security Token Offering (STO)?' (12 March 2018) <https://blog.polymath.network/what-is-a-security-token-offering-sto-4e5a92bf6bca> accessed 11 April 2022.

[57] Ibid.

[58] Ibid.

[59] See Dell'Erba, '"Do No Harm" Approach in Initial Coin Offerings' (n 42) 185.

[60] Kai Sedgwick, 'Six Alternatives to an Initial Coin Offering' (*Bitcoin.com*, 18 June 2018) <https://news.bitcoin.com/six-alternatives-to-an-initial-coin-offering/> accessed 11 April 2022. The author refers to the example of Fantom: 'In Fantom's recent crowdsale, for example, one investor spent 580k gwei, or around $24,000, just to ensure their transaction reached the front of the queue.'

a gratuitous basis by adding such tokens to the users' wallets.[61] Those who typically benefit from airdrops are community members related to the ICO and those engaged with the development of the community itself.[62]

As mentioned above, in the current ICO market, the two structures more widely in use are STOs and IEOs. One of the reasons for the success of STOs is that they relate to an underlying asset, typically company stocks or bonds,[63] and therefore can potentially attract institutional investors. Also, data has proven that STOs are the best-performing fundraising model, with an average of funds raised per project equal to $85 million, compared to $17 million for IEOs and $10 million for traditional venture capital. The popularity of IEOs depends on other factors.[64] IEOs are cheaper than STOs and as cheap as traditional ICOs. However, IEOs benefit from the reputation of the exchanges on which they are listed, although their tokens are not backed by real assets, as in the case of STOs.

II. The Regulatory Debate on ICOs

Since their inception, ICOs have triggered significant regulatory debate, not only in relation to their characterization within the existing legal framework but also for the dangers related to this emerging market practice for both investors and the financial system.

From a structural standpoint, ICOs have a dual dimension—the 'token', more closely related to a security, and the 'currency', which leads to assimilation with the regulation of commodities. The two components underlying ICOs triggered a relevant debate and some conflict with the authorities involved. For example, institutional tensions arose in the United States, where two different regulators, the SEC and the Commodity Futures Trading Commission (CFTC), respectively supervise the market for securities and the market for commodities.

This section will consider the characterization of ICOs and cryptocurrencies as commodities and securities in the United States, as well as in the European Union and Switzerland, where the securities law framework is the dominant one. This analysis shares important analogies with the discussion of stablecoins, triggering similar considerations and demonstrating some similarities between the United States, the European Union, and Switzerland, notwithstanding important key differences under multiple respects.

However, this section will not develop an analysis of digital securities. In mapping the different consequences triggered by ICOs, this chapter will explicitly consider their impact on the development of digital securities, analysing some specific

---

[61] Katalyse.io, 'What Are "Airdrops" in Crypto World?' (*Medium*, 15 February 2018) <https://medium.com/the-mission/what-are-airdrops-in-crypto-world-a345725c75e0> accessed 11 April 2022.

[62] Dell'Erba, '"Do No Harm" Approach in Initial Coin Offerings' (n 42) 188.

[63] Deloitte, King & Wood Mallesons, KHbitEX, University of Hong Kong—Asian Institute of International Financial Law (AIIFL), 'Security Token Offerings: The Next Phase of Financial Market Evolution?' (2020) 4 <https://www2.deloitte.com/content/dam/Deloitte/cn/Documents/audit/deloitte-cn-audit-security-token-offering-en-201009.pdf> accessed 11 April 2022.

[64] Gregory S. Mathew, 'IEO Vs STO Vs ICO; A Comparison of Tokenized Fundraising. Which One Is Better?' (*Medium*, 9 June 2019) <https://medium.com/hackernoon/ieo-vs-sto-vs-ico-a-comparison-of-tokenized-fundraising-which-one-is-better-ab71b1c2a32b> accessed 11 April 2022.

regulatory developments, and consequences at the infrastructural level (both trading and post-trading) in Section IV.B.3. Furthermore, these developments at the level of digital securities will be contextualized as part of a broader transformation affecting corporate governance in Section IV.C.

A. United States

1. CFTC and SEC: Two Faces of the Same Coin

The architecture of American regulatory agencies supervising financial markets peculiarly divides the responsibilities of the SEC and the CFTC. While the SEC is in charge of protecting investors, maintaining fair, orderly, and efficient markets, and facilitating capital formation, with a clear focus on 'securities', the mission of the CFTC is to foster open, transparent, competitive, and financially sound markets, in the context of 'commodities'. By working to avoid systemic risk, the CFTC aims to protect market users and their funds, consumers, and the public from fraud, manipulation, and abusive practices related to derivatives and other products that are subject to the Commodity Exchange Act (CEA). Therefore, as the CFTC has clarified, its 'jurisdiction is implicated when a virtual currency is used in a derivatives contract, or if there is fraud or manipulation involving a virtual currency traded in interstate commerce'.[65] Recent cases, including Telegram[66] and Ripple, confirm the dual extended jurisdiction triggered by the two broad definitions of 'security' and 'commodity', both of which might be relevant in the context of ICOs' digital tokens and cryptocurrencies. The following subsections will consider this dual dimension.

a. CFTC

In 2014, former CFTC Chairman Timothy Massad decided that the agency could have jurisdiction over Bitcoin and more generally over virtual currencies, depending 'on the facts and circumstances pertaining to any particular activity in question', and stated that derivative contracts based on a virtual currency represented 'one area within our responsibility'.[67] *Coinflip*[68] introduced a new era of 'Bitcoin' as a commodity, with the CFTC order stating that the CEA covers 'all services, rights, and interests in which contracts for future delivery are presently or in the future dealt in', and further stated that the definition of '"commodity" is broad ... Bitcoin and other virtual currencies are encompassed in the definition and properly defined as commodities'.[69] Similar to

---

[65] LabCFTC, 'A CFTC Primer on Virtual Currencies' (17 October 2017) <https://www.cftc.gov/sites/default/files/idc/groups/public/documents/file/labcftc_primercurrencies100417.pdf> accessed 11 April 2022 (hereafter LabCFTC, 'A Primer on Virtual Currencies'). On the general problems of the SEC and CFTC jurisdiction in this context see Howell E. Jackson and Margaret E. Tahyar, *Fintech Law: The Case Studies* (*Harvard.edu*, 2020) 127–139 <https://projects.iq.harvard.edu/fintechlaw/home> accessed 11 April 2022.

[66] See Section III.A.2.b.

[67] Timothy Massad, 'Testimony before the U.S. Senate Committee on Agriculture, Nutrition & Forestry' (10 December 2014) <https://www.cftc.gov/PressRoom/SpeechesTestimony/opamassad-6> accessed 11 April 2022.

[68] *Re Coinflip Inc.* [2015] CFTC No. 15–29, WL 5535736 (hereafter *Coinflip*).

[69] Ibid.

the definition of 'security', the definition of 'commodity' is very broad, encompassing a wide range of products: physical commodities, such as agricultural products or natural resources, as well as currencies and interest rates.[70] Further, the definition of 'commodity' encompasses 'all services, rights, and interests ... in which contracts for future delivery are presently or in the future dealt in'.[71] The CFTC charged Coinflip with a violation of sections 4c(b)[72] and 5h(a)(l)[73] of the CEA by 'conducting activity related to commodity options contrary to Commission Regulations and by operating a facility for the trading or processing of swaps without being registered as a swap execution facility or designated contract market'.[74] Specifically, Coinflip 'operated an online facility named Derivabit, offering to connect buyers and sellers of Bitcoin option contracts'.[75]

In October 2017, the CFTC issued a report indicating it was open to the possibility that virtual currencies and virtual tokens may trigger different regulation. In its document the CFTC expressed the position that the potential categorization of ICO tokens as securities would not be inconsistent with the CFTC's 'determination that virtual currencies are commodities and that virtual tokens may be commodities or derivatives contracts depending on the particular facts and circumstances'.[76] Similar to the definition of 'security', the definition of 'commodity' is very broad, encompassing a wide range of products—physical commodities, such as agricultural products or natural resources, as well currencies or interest rates. Further, the definition of 'commodity' encompasses 'all services, rights, and interests ... in which contracts for future delivery are presently or in the future dealt in'.[77]

b. SEC

i. Securities laws Section 2(a)(1) of the Securities Act of 1933 covers a wide variety of financial instruments[78] and includes a circular definition of 'security'[79] as 'any

---

[70] Commodity Exchange Act 1936 [as amended in 2012] (hereafter CEA 2012); 7 U.S. Code (hereafter USC), s 1a(9).
[71] See ibid.
[72] CEA 2012 (n 70) s 4c(b) makes it unlawful for any person to 'offer to enter into, enter into or confirm the execution of any transaction involving any commodity ... which is of the character of, or is commonly known to the trade as, an "option" ... "bid", "offer", "put", [or] "call" ... contrary to any rule, regulation, or order of the Commission prohibiting any such transaction'.
[73] CEA 2012 (n 70) s 5h(a)(1) forbids any person from operating 'a facility for the trading or processing of swaps unless the facility is registered as a swap execution facility or as a designated contract market'.
[74] *Coinflip* (n 68) 2.
[75] Ibid.
[76] LabCFTC, 'A Primer on Virtual Currencies' (n 65).
[77] See CEA 2012 (n 70) s 1a(9). 'The term "commodity" means wheat, cotton, rice, corn, oats, barley, rye, flaxseed, grain sorghums, mill feeds, butter, eggs, Solanum tuberosum (Irish potatoes), wool, wool tops, fats and oils (including lard, tallow, cottonseed oil, peanut oil, soybean oil, and all other fats and oils), cottonseed meal, cottonseed, peanuts, soybeans, soybean meal, livestock, livestock products, and frozen concentrated orange juice, and all other goods and articles, except onions (as provided by section 13–1 of this title) and motion picture box office receipts (or any index, measure, value, or data related to such receipts), and all services, rights, and interests (except motion picture box office receipts, or any index, measure, value or data related to such receipts) in which contracts for future delivery are presently or in the future dealt in.'
[78] See James D. Cox, Robert W. Hillman, and Donald C. Langevoort, *Securities Regulation, Cases and Materials* (8th edn, Wolters Kluwer 2017) 29.
[79] See Giovanni Patti, 'Prodotti finanziari e contratti con i consumatori. Una recente pronuncia della Corte di giustizia a confronto con la securities law Americana' (2011) 5 GC 1015 (on file with author)

interest or instrument commonly known as a "security".[80] To clarify the definition of 'security', the Supreme Court intervened by explicitly providing the definition of 'investment contract', one of the financial instruments listed as a security pursuant to section 2(a)(1) of the Securities Act of 1933: 'an investment contract for purposes of the Securities Act means a contract, transaction or scheme whereby a person invests his money in a common enterprise and is led to expect profits solely from the efforts of the promoter or a third party.'[81] In addition, the Supreme Court clarified that the notions of 'investment contract' and 'any interest or instrument commonly known as a "security"' were equivalent, making the definition of 'investment contract' the general definition of 'security'.[82]

(hereafter Patti, 'Prodotti finanziari e contratti'). The author emphasizes the presence of the 'definiendum' within the 'definiens'.

[80] Securities Act 1933 s 2(a)(1) defines 'securities' in these terms:

> The term 'security' means any note, stock, treasury stock, security future, bond, debenture, evidence of indebtedness, certificate of interest or participation in any profit-sharing agreement, collateral-trust certificate, preorganization certificate or subscription, transferable share, investment contract, voting-trust certificate, certificate of deposit for a security, fractional undivided interest in oil, gas, or other mineral rights, any put, call, straddle, option, or privilege on any security, certificate of deposit, or group or index of securities (including any interest therein or based on the value thereof), or any put, call, straddle, option, or privilege entered into on a national securities exchange relating to foreign currency, or, in general, any interest or instrument commonly known as a 'security', or any certificate of interest or participation in, temporary or interim certificate for, receipt for, guarantee of, or warrant or right to subscribe to or purchase, any of the foregoing.

Securities Act 1933 [as amended in 2012] s 2(a)(1); 15 USC (n 70), s 77b(a)(1) (emphasis added). A slightly different definition of 'security' was provided by the Securities Exchange Act 1934, s 3(a)(10); 15 USC (n 70) ch 2B, s 78c(a)(10). The Supreme Court has often considered the two definitions identical. See *Marine Bank v Weaver* [1982] 455 U.S. 551; *Int'l Bhd of Teamsters v Daniel* [1979] 439 U.S. 551; *United Hous Found Inc v Forman* [1975] 421 U.S. 837 (hereafter *Forman*); *Tcherepnin v Knight* [1967] 389 U.S. 332. The Uniform Securities Act provides a definition of 'security' almost identical to the one provided by the Securities Act 1933. See Uniform Securities Act 1956 [as amended in 2002] s 102(28). American regulators opted for a definition of security 'in sufficiently broad and general terms so as to include within that definition the many types of instruments that in our commercial world fall within the ordinary concept of a security.' Securities Act 1933, ch III, s 2(1). The Supreme Court emphasized the approach of Congress in adopting a broad definition of security: 'In defining the scope of the market that it wished to regulate, Congress painted with a broad brush ... Congress enacted a definition of "security" sufficiently broad to encompass virtually any instrument that might be sold as investment.' *Reves v Ernst & Young* (1990) 494 U.S. 56, 60–61 (hereafter *Reves*). According to this interpretation of the Supreme Court, the definition 'embodies a flexible rather than a static principle, one that is capable of adaptation to meet the countless and variable schemes devised by those who seek the use of the money of others on the promise of profits'. *SEC v WJ Howey Co* [1946] 328 U.S. 293, 299 (hereafter *Howey*). 'Congress therefore did not attempt precisely to cabin the scope of the Securities Acts. Rather, it enacted a definition of "security" sufficiently broad to encompass virtually any instrument that might be sold as an investment.' *Reves*, 61. See also Miriam R. Albert, 'The Howey Test Turns 64: Are the Courts Grading This Test on a Curve?' (2011) 2 Wm&MaryBusLRev 1, 4. On the need to combine flexibility and clarity with regard to the definition of 'security', see Giuliano Castellano, 'Towards a General Framework for a Common Definition of "Securities": Financial Markets Regulation in Multilingual Contexts' (2012) 17 UnifLRev 449, 457 (2012) (hereafter Castellano, 'Common Definition of "Securities"').

[81] *Howey* (n 80) 298–299.

[82] The Supreme Court has stated that '[w]e perceive no distinction, for present purposes, between an "investment contract" and an "instrument commonly known as a "security."' *Forman* (n 80) 852. This is consistent with *SEC v C.M. Joiner Leasing Corporation*, where the Supreme Court provided a more general definition of security: 'many documents in which there is common trading for speculation or investment.' *SEC v C.M. Joiner Leasing Corporation* [1943] 320 U.S. 344, 351.

The SEC characterized ICO tokens as securities after assessing the constitutive elements of the investment contract, applying the so-called Howey test. The Howey test serves to ascertain the existence of the four main components of a security as established in US caselaw: (1) the investment of money; (2) a common enterprise; (3) expectation of profits; and (4) to come solely from the efforts of the promoter or a third party.[83] The Howey test is a useful tool due to its characteristic of incorporating 'a flexible rather than a static principle, one that is capable of adaptation to meet the countless and variable schemes devised by those who seek the use of the money of others on the promise of profits'.[84] In *Report of Investigation Pursuant to Section 21(a) of the Securities Exchange Act of 1934: The DAO*[85] (the 'DAO Report'), the SEC suggested the adoption of a case-by-case approach, considering that '[w]hether a particular investment transaction involves the offer or sale of a security—regardless of the terminology or technology used—will depend on the facts and circumstances, including the economic realities of the transaction'.

From here the SEC extended its intervention to many ICOs, going beyond the semantics provided in the offering documents, such as 'initial membership offer' and 'utility token', as evidenced in the Recoin and Munchee cases. In October 2017, the SEC brought an emergency action to charge Recoin and Diamond Reserve Club (DRC), two ICOs launched by Maksim Zaslavskiy.[86] This decision is particularly relevant because of the interpretation of the semantics that the SEC used—not formalistic but strictly connected to the economic reality of the underlying offer. In the white paper and on the website for Recoin, Maksim Zaslavskiy did not refer to the terms 'ICO' or 'securities', adopting instead the terms 'initial membership offering' and 'IMO'.[87] Consistent with this decision, the SEC confirmed its extensive interpretation of the notion of 'securities' in relation to ICO tokens on 11 December 2017, in the Munchee case. The SEC stated that the offering of digital tokens to investors by a blockchain-based food review services company (Munchee) constituted an illegal unregistered securities offering.[88] In particular, the SEC challenged

---

[83] *Howey* (n 80) 298–301; Ronald J. Coffey, 'The Economic Realities of a "Security": Is There a More Meaningful Formula?' (1966) 18 CaseWResLRev 367, 373. Federal courts have characterized this as a three-factor test, where the 'expectation of profits' is distinct from the 'efforts of the promoter or a third party'. See *SEC v Unique Fin Concepts Inc* [1999] 196 F.3d 1195, 1199 (11th Cir. 1999) ('This Court has divided the Howey test into the three elements: (1) an investment of money, (2) a common enterprise, and (3) the expectation of profits to be derived solely from the efforts of others') (quotations omitted); *Williamson v Tucker* [1981] 645 F.2d 404, 417 (5th Cir. 1981) (also describing this a three-element test).

[84] *Howey* (n 80) 299.

[85] SEC, *Report of Investigation Pursuant to Section 21(a) of the Securities Exchange Act of 1934: The DAO* (25 July 2017) 4 <https://www.sec.gov/litigation/investreport/34-81207.pdf> accessed 12 April 2022 (hereafter SEC, *The DAO Report*).

[86] Regarding Recoin, Zaslavskyiy did not hire any professional, contrary to what he stated, and in addition he misrepresented the effective amount he raised, declaring an amount between 2 and 4 million dollars, instead of approximately 300,000 dollars in reality. With regard to DRC, Zaslavskiy bragged about non-existent relationships with diamond wholesalers that, through an arbitrage process, should have provided significant gains for his investors.

[87] See SEC, Complaint against Coin Group Foundation LLC (29 September 2017) <https://www.sec.gov/litigation/complaints/2017/comp-pr2017-185.pdf> accessed 11 April 2022.

[88] SEC Order Instituting Cease-and-Desist Proceedings and Imposing a Cease-and-Desist Order *Re Munchee Inc* [2017] Release No. 10445, 118 SEC Docket 5, 36–38 (11 December 2017) <https://www.sec.gov/litigation/admin/2017/33-10445.pdf> accessed 11 April 2022.

the view proposed by Munchee that the ICO tokens were 'utility tokens' instead of 'securities tokens', arguing that although such tokens had a practical use at the time of the offering, this circumstance would not be preclusive of the tokens being a security,[89] and highlighting the relevance of 'the economic realities underlying a transaction'.[90] For this reason, it ordered Munchee to cease and desist pursuant to section 8A of the Securities Act.[91] The same day, SEC Chairman Jay Clayton issued a statement on the risks of fraud and manipulation connected to ICOs that are not registered with SEC, encouraging investors to actively obtain information before deciding to invest.[92]

Finally, the SEC enlarged the scope of its interventions, taking into account all the structures and entities involved in the ICOs, on the assumption that if ICOs are securities, all such entities—including investment advisors, trading platforms, and crypto-exchanges—need to comply with securities regulations and register such activities. A fundamental step in this phase was the enforcement action against EtherDelta in November 2018 for being an unregistered digital token exchange. EtherDelta was 'an online platform that allow[ed] buyers and sellers to trade certain digital assets—Ether and "ERC20 tokens"—in secondary market trading'.[93] As the SEC noted, '[f]rom July 12, 2016 to December 15, 2017 ... more than 3.6 million buy and sell orders in ERC20 tokens that included securities as defined by Section 3(a)(10) of the Exchange Act were traded on EtherDelta, of which approximately 92% (3.3 million) were traded during the period following the DAO Report'.[94] For this reason, the SEC determined that EtherDelta met the criteria of an 'exchange' as defined by section 3(a)(1)[95] of the Securities Exchange Act of 1934 and Rule 3b-16[96] and was not excluded under Rule 3b-16(b).[97]

---

[89] Ibid.
[90] Ibid.
[91] Ibid.
[92] Jay Clayton, 'Statement on Cryptocurrencies and Initial Coin Offerings' (*SEC*, 11 December 2017) <https://www.sec.gov/news/public-statement/statementclayton-2017-12-11> accessed 11 April 2022.
[93] See SEC Order Instituting Cease-and-Desist Proceedings, Making Findings and Imposing a Cease-and-Desist Order *Re Zachary Coburn* [2018] Release No. 84553 (8 November 2018) <https://www.sec.gov/litigation/admin/2018/34-84553.pdf> accessed 11 April 2022 (hereafter SEC Order *Re Zachary Coburn*).
[94] Ibid.
[95] 15 USC (n 70), ch 2B, s 78c(a)(1): ' "exchange" means any organization, association, or group of persons, whether incorporated or unincorporated, which constitutes, maintains, or provides a market place or facilities for bringing together purchasers and sellers of securities or for otherwise performing with respect to securities the functions commonly performed by a stock exchange as that term is generally understood, and includes the market place and the market facilities maintained by such exchange.'
[96] Rule 16-b3 provides that 'An organization, association, or group of persons shall be considered to constitute, maintain, or provide "a market place or facilities for bringing together purchasers and sellers of securities or for otherwise performing with respect to securities the functions commonly performed by a stock exchange," as those terms are used in section 3(a)(1) of the Act (15 USC (n 70), s 78c(a)(1)), if such organization, association, or group of persons: (1) Brings together the orders for securities of multiple buyers and sellers; and (2) Uses established, non-discretionary methods (whether by providing a trading facility or by setting rules) under which such orders interact with each other, and the buyers and sellers entering such orders agree to the terms of a trade'. As the SEC explains, this rule provides a functional test to assess whether a trading system meets the definition of exchange under Section 3(a)(1) of the Securities Exchange Act 1934. See SEC Order *Re Zachary Coburn* (n 93).
[97] Ibid.

ii. **The Problem of Decentralisation: Why Ether and Bitcoin Are Not Securities, and Ripple ...** Despite the SEC's massive enforcement actions, the SEC Director of the Division of Corporation Finance, William H. Hinman, excluded an automatic characterization of ICO digital tokens as 'securities' in a June 2018 speech.[98] In Hinman's view, Ether tokens at the launch of Ethereum did not necessarily fall under the notion of 'security' because of specific factual circumstances that are relevant when determining whether ICO tokens are securities.[99] In fact, the DAO Report lacked clarifications or indications around 'the facts and circumstances, including the economic realities of the transactions', relevant to ascertaining 'whether a particular transaction involves the offer and sale of a security—regardless of the terminology used'.[100]

Hinman's speech questions whether 'a digital asset offered as a security can, over time, become something other than a security', and provides an illustrative but not exhaustive list of elements, helpful to take into account as 'facts and circumstances', that are relevant in considering the applicability of the securities laws to ICO tokens.[101] This factual analysis is consistent with the Supreme Court's holding in Howey about the test's flexibility and adaptability to a broad range of schemes.[102]

At the same time, Hinman provides a complimentary analysis by referring to *Gary Plastic Packaging v Merr Lynch, Pierce, Fenner & Smith Inc*[103] (*Gary Plastics*) as a relevant precedent, in particular when taking into account the role of the third parties and the secondary market. In this case the court held that, although specific instruments (bank certificates of deposit) were not intrinsically a security (such as the oranges in Howey), such instruments may still be qualified as 'securities' and subject to the application of the securities law if such instruments 'animate a broader investment contract'.[104]

In Hinman's analysis, the role of a third party in driving the expectation of a return and the 'economic substance of the transaction' are two relevant elements,[105] and for both of these elements he provides a non-exhaustive list to illustrate possible parameters. In relation to the first element, Hinman considers whether there is a person or a group that sponsored and created the sale of the digital offers and retained a stake or other interest in the digital asset. Furthermore, he considers whether the 'promoter raised an amount of funds in excess of what may be needed to establish a functional network', and whether purchasers are 'investing ... [or] seeking a return'.[106] A legitimate parameter explicitly mentioned by Hinman is related to applications of the Securities Act protections and the specific function of securities laws in general to

---

[98] William Hinman, 'Digital Asset Transactions: When Howey Met Gary (Plastic)' (*SEC*, 14 June 2018) <https://www.sec.gov/news/speech/speech-hinman-061418> accessed 11 April 2022 (hereafter Hinman, 'Digital Asset Transactions').
[99] Ibid.
[100] Ibid.
[101] Ibid.
[102] See *Howey* (n 80) 299.
[103] Hinman, 'Digital Asset Transactions' (n 98) (citing *Gary Plastic Packaging Corp. v Merrill Lynch, Pierce, Fenner & Smith, Inc.* [1985] 756 F.2d 230, 241 (2nd Cir. 1985)).
[104] David L. Concannon, Yvette D. Valdez, and Stephen P. Win, 'The Yellow Brick Road for Consumer Tokens: The Path to SEC and CFTC Compliance' in Josias Dewey (ed), *Blockchain & Cryptocurrency Regulation 2019* (Global Legal Insights 2019) 1033.
[105] Hinman, 'Digital Asset Transactions' (n 98).
[106] Ibid.

correct potential informational asymmetries that may exist between the promoters and potential purchasers/investors in the digital asset.[107]

Regarding the second element, the 'economic substance of the transaction', Hinman further highlights the importance of specific parameters. Among them, Hinman considers whether the token creation relates to speculation and who sets the price (independent actor or secondary market influencing the trading), the clarity of the primary motivation related to purchasing digital assets for personal use or consumption, the distribution of the tokens meeting users' needs, and whether the application is fully functioning or in early stages of development.[108] On this basis, the Howey test is not the only relevant way to ascertain the characterization of ICO tokens as securities, but Gary Plastics' analysis also comes into play. As Hinman explains,

> If the network on which the token or coin is to function is sufficiently decentralized—where purchasers would no longer reasonably expect a person or group to carry out essential managerial or entrepreneurial efforts—the assets may not represent an investment contract. Moreover, when the efforts of the third party are no longer a key factor for determining the enterprise's success, material information asymmetries recede. As a network becomes truly decentralized [as in the case of Bitcoin and Ethereum], the ability to identify an issuer or promoter to make the requisite disclosures becomes difficult, and less meaningful.[109]

The problem of decentralization also emerged as a key issue in the highly debated Ripple and XRP case. The specific structural issues of XRP are important for understanding way the SEC is keen to characterize it as a security. On the one hand, the XRP Ledger 'operates as a peer-to-peer database, spread across a network of computers that records data about transactions, among other things'.[110] Furthermore, consensus is achieved in this manner:

> each server on the network evaluates proposed transactions from a subset of nodes it trusts not to defraud it. Those trusted nodes are known as the server's unique node list, or UNL. Although each server defines its own trusted nodes, the XRP Ledger requires a high degree of overlap between the trusted nodes chosen by each server. To facilitate this overlap, Ripple publishes a proposed UNL.[111]

However, Ripple's management conducted unusual strategies of centralization. The challenges related to effective centralization vs decentralization emerged after December 2012. At this point the XRP Ledger was completed, and the management created a fixed supply of 100 billion XRP, opting to transfer 80 billion to Ripple and 20 billion to the founders. As a consequence, the founders had full control of XRP. This

---

[107] Ibid.
[108] Ibid.
[109] Ibid.
[110] Carol Goforth, 'SEC vs. Ripple: A Predictable But Undesirable Development' (*Cointelegraph*, 27 December 2020) <https://cointelegraph.com/news/sec-vs-ripple-a-predictable-but-undesirable-development> accessed 11 April 2022.
[111] Ibid.

is a compromise between a fully decentralized network, implementing peer-to-peer exchanges, and a fully centralized intermediary, who has full control of the currency, opening space for the possibility that XRP was not a cryptocurrency.[112]

On 22 December 2020, the SEC announced it had brought action against Ripple and two of its executives, former CEO Christian Larsen and current CEO Bradley Garlinghouse, for engaging in:

> illegal securities offering from 2013 to the present [14.6 billion units of a digital asset security called 'XRP', in return for cash or other consideration worth over $1.38 billion U.S. Dollars], even though Ripple received legal advice as early as 2012 that under certain circumstances XRP could be considered an 'investment contract' and therefore a security under the federal securities laws. Ripple and Larsen ignored this advice and instead elected to assume the risk of initiating a large-scale distribution of XRP without registration ... Over a years-long unregistered offering of securities, Ripple was able to raise at least $1.38 billion by selling XRP without providing the type of financial and managerial information typically provided in registration statements and subsequent periodic and current filings. Ripple used this money to fund its operations without disclosing how it was doing so, or the full extent of its payments to others to assist in its efforts to develop a 'use' for XRP and maintain XRP secondary trading markets.[113]

This action has triggered many reactions. Subsection III.A.2.c will analyse and contextualize this debate.

2. Recent Initiatives

In the near future, the regulation of cryptocurrencies and digital tokens could drastically change, in particular with the enactment of the Executive Order on Ensuring Responsible Development of Digital Assets signed by US President Joe Biden.[114] The Executive Order emphasizes the relevance of the market for digital assets and the importance of protect consumers, investors, and business while preserving financial stability and mitigating systemic risk and illicit finance.[115] An important aspect of the order is the need to enhance coordination of the legislative process among the national agencies involved, including the SEC and the CFTC.[116]

Some other initiatives have been undertaken in the recent past. One is the bipartisan initiative promoted by Congressmen Warren Davidson and Darren Soto, the Token Taxonomy Act.[117] The Token Taxonomy Act intended to exclude digital tokens from the definition of 'security' and exempt 'transactions involving the development, offer, or sale of a digital unit' under specific conditions from the Securities Act.[118] In

---

[112] Darryn Pollock, 'Ripple Hate: Is Ripple a Wolf in Sheep's Clothing?' (*Cointelegraph*, 18 January 2020) <https://cointelegraph.com/news/ripple-hate-is-ripple-a-wolf-in-sheeps-clothing> accessed 11 April 2022.
[113] SEC, 'Complaint against Ripple Labs, Inc., Bradley Garlinghouse and Christian A. Larsen' (22 December 2020) 2 <https://www.sec.gov/litigation/complaints/2020/comp-pr2020-338.pdf> accessed 11 April 2022.
[114] President Biden's Executive Order on Ensuring Responsible Development of Digital Assets (9 March 2022).
[115] Ibid, Section 1 and 2.
[116] Ibid, Section 3.
[117] Token Taxonomy Act, U.S. HR Bill (2021–2022) [1628].
[118] Ibid.

this way, the Token Taxonomy Act implements the view that digital tokens represent an alternative asset class and provides a definition of 'digital token' based on four main elements. This could affect the definition of both 'traditional' cryptocurrencies and stablecoins under existing securities laws.

SEC Commissioner Hester Peirce emphasized the difficulties of applying the Howey test to ICOs. To address the uncertainty surrounding the application of securities laws to tokens, he proposed a safe harbour. This safe harbour would exempt network developers for a three-year grace period from '(1) the offer and sale of tokens from the provisions of the Securities Act of 1933, other than the antifraud provisions, (2) the tokens from registration under the Securities Exchange Act of 1934, and (3) persons engaged in certain token transactions from the definitions of "exchange", "broker", and "dealer" under the 1934 Act'.[119] In Commissioner Hester Peirce's view, the exemption from the registration requirements of federal securities laws would be a way to pursue 'the development of a functional or decentralised network', making sure that new technologies can flourish while preserving investor protection.[120] In a past statement, Commissioner Hester Peirce discussed the difficulties related to applying the scheme of securities offerings to token offerings, mostly because of the decentralized nature of token offerings;[121] this was consistent with some commentators urging reassessment of the *Howey* test.[122]

The Token Taxonomy Act was not the only initiative. In January 2019 and again in August 2021, Representative Tom Emmer proposed the Blockchain Regulatory Certainty Act that never passed the Committees at the House of Representative. Between September 2020 and April 2022 the same Representative twice proposed two further texts, the Securities Clarity Act (SCA) and the Digital Commodity Exchange Act (DCEA). The SCA, with a technology-neutral approach, aimed at introducing a new definition of 'investment contract asset' which refers to any asset, whether tangible or intangible, including assets in digital form, sold as part of an investment

---

[119] Hester M. Peirce, 'Running on Empty: A Proposal to Fill the Gap Between Regulation and Decentralization' (Speech at Chicago, IL, 6 February 2020) <https://www.sec.gov/news/speech/peirce-remarks-blockress-2020-02-06> accessed 11 April 2022 (hereafter Peirce, 'Running on Empty').

[120] Ibid. As Commissioner Peirce further explains, 'The initial development team would have to meet certain conditions, which I will lay out briefly before addressing several in more depth. First, the team must intend for the network on which the token functions to reach network maturity—defined as either decentralisation or token functionality—within three years of the date of the first token sale and undertake good faith and reasonable efforts to achieve that goal. Second, the team would have to disclose key information on a freely accessible public website. Third, the token must be offered and sold for the purpose of facilitating access to, participation on, or the development of the network. Fourth, the team would have to undertake good faith and reasonable efforts to create liquidity for users. Finally, the team would have to file a notice of reliance.'

[121] Hester M. Peirce, 'Regulation: A View from Inside the Machine' (Speech at University of Missouri School of Law, Columbia, MO, 8 February 2019) <https://www.sec.gov/news/speech/peirce-regulation-view-inside-machine> accessed 11 April 2022 (hereafter Peirce, 'Regulation').

[122] See generally Todd Henderson and Max Raskin, 'A Regulatory Classification of Digital Assets: Towards an Operational Howey Test for Cryptocurrencies, ICOs, and Other Digital Assets' (2019) ColumBusLRev 443. See also Yuliya Guseva, 'A Conceptual Framework for Digital-Asset Securities: Tokens and Coins as Debt and Equity' 80 MdLRev 166. See also Yuliya Guseva, 'The Leviathan of Securities Regulation in Crypto-Offerings: A Cost–Benefit Analysis' (2020) SSRN <https://ssrn.com/abstract=3694709> accessed 11 April 2022.

contract that would not be considered a 'security' but for its sale as part of an investment contract.

The DCEA sought to create a 'single, opt-in national regulatory framework for digital commodity trading platforms' that will be regulated by the US CFTC. Under the DCEA, 'digital commodity means any form of fungible intangible personal property that can be exclusively possessed and transferred person to person without necessary reliance on an intermediary', and which does not represent a financial interest in a company, partnership, or fund; a profit or revenue share derived solely from the managerial efforts of others; or an entitlement to any interest or dividend payment. Moreover, a digital commodity must be of the nature of a digital asset.[123]

The SCA and DCEA together would have contributed to better defining the line between SEC and CFTC jurisdiction: pre-sale agreements would have continued to be regulated by the SEC, but there would have been less need for continued SEC wariness once the tokens were delivered and the network went live because the CFTC would have been picking up the regulatory slack and supervising sales to the public upon network launch.

B. European Union

In the European Union, there was a similar debate. At the end of 2017, the European Securities and Markets Authority (ESMA) issued a statement[124] warning firms involved in ICOs of the need to meet relevant regulatory requirements, mentioning in particular the Prospectus Directive,[125] MiFID II, AIFMD, and the Fourth Anti-Money Laundering Directive.[126]

Leaving aside the other regulatory texts, it is useful to refer to the Prospectus Directive and MiFID II, which take into account two general concepts: 'transferrable security' and 'financial instrument'. MiFID II provides both the definitions of 'transferable security'[127] and 'financial instrument'. In addition, with regard to the latter, the definition provided by MiFID II encompasses, among other things, transferable securities and derivative contracts.[128]

---

[123] Digital Commodity Exchange Act, U.S. HR Bill (2021–2022) [7614].

[124] ESMA, 'ESMA Alerts Firms Involved in Initial Coin Offerings (ICOs) to the Need to Meet Relevant Regulatory Requirements' (13 November 2017) <https://www.esma.europa.eu/document/esma-alerts-firms-involved-in-initial-coin-offerings-icos-need-meet-relevant-regulatory> accessed 11 April 2022.

[125] Directive 2003/71/EC of 4 November 2003 on the prospectus to be published when securities are offered to the public or admitted to trading [2003] OJ L 345/64.

[126] Directive (EU) 2015/849 of 20 May 2015 on the prevention of the use of the financial system for the purposes of money laundering or terrorist financing [2015] OJ L 141/73.

[127] A transferable security is defined as 'any class of security negotiable on the capital market, with the exception of instruments of payment, such as: (a) shares in companies and other securities equivalent to shares in companies, partnerships or other entities, and depositary receipts in respect of shares; (b) bonds or other forms of securitised debt, including depositary receipts in respect of such securities; (c) any other securities giving the right to acquire or sell any such transferable securities or giving rise to a cash settlement determined by reference to transferable securities, currencies, interest rates or yields, commodities or other indices or measures'. Ibid, art 4(1)(44).

[128] See ibid, annex I, s C.

A further notion to take into account under European Union law is that of 'financial product'. European Union law does not explicitly define the term. However, recital 10 of Directive 2005/29 (the 'Unfair Commercial Practices Directive')[129] refers to financial products, which clarifies the scope of the directive.[130] Furthermore, the directive provides a broad definition for 'product' without explicitly referring to financial products, while at the same time not excluding them: '"product" means any goods or service including immovable property, rights and obligations.'[131] At the European Union level, the notion of 'financial product' is broader than that of 'financial instrument', since 'financial instrument' refers only to typical instruments (mainly shares and debt instruments) with the further characteristic that they are negotiable (on a regulated market).[132] This would mean that tokens could, in principle, be qualified as financial products under European Union law—which would result in the applicability of the consumer protection regulation for those who purchase tokens.

Although the purpose of establishing a notion of 'transferable security' and 'financial instrument' was clearly inspired by the need to increase harmonization among the European Union member states' securities laws, these notions have been transposed in the different European countries in different ways.[133] Resolving this difficulty would require further case-by-case analysis in order to ascertain the potential qualification of ICO tokens and stablecoins as securities or financial instruments and their treatment in each specific jurisdiction. In addition, apart from any consideration connected to the transposition of the notions of 'transferable security' or 'financial instrument', member states may provide specific categories of law triggering specific obligations under each legal system.

In relation to the notion of a 'financial instrument', the list contained in Annex C of MiFID II refers to commodities, which would allow one to refer to the rules governing commodities. The MiFID Organisational Regulation defines a 'commodity' as 'any goods of a fungible nature that are capable of being delivered, including metals and their ores and alloys, agricultural products, and energy such as electricity'.[134] Tokens may fall within this definition, but they would not fall within the regulation if they

---

[129] Directive 2005/29/EC of 11 May 2005 concerning unfair business-to-customer commercial practices in the internal market [2005] OJ L 149/22.

[130] Recital 10 states:

> This Directive accordingly applies only in so far as there are no specific Community law provisions regulating specific aspects of unfair commercial practices, such as information requirements and rules on the way the information is presented to the consumer. It provides protection for consumers where there is no specific sectoral legislation at Community level and prohibits traders from creating a false impression of the nature of products. This is particularly important for complex products with high levels of risk to consumers, such as certain financial services products. This Directive consequently complements the Community *acquis*, which is applicable to commercial practices harming consumers' economic interests.

[131] Ibid, art 2, 1 c.

[132] See Patti, 'Prodotti finanziari e contratti' (n 79).

[133] See Castellano, 'Common Definition of "Securities"' (n 80) (discussing the different meanings that securities terminology acquires in different languages).

[134] Commission Delegated Regulation (EU) 2017/565 of 25 April 2016 supplementing Directive 2014/65/EU as regards organisational requirements and operating conditions for investment firms [2017] OJ L 87/1.

were not derivatives. Therefore, 'the fact that a token is capable of being offered via an ICO has no bearing on its classification as a commodity and vice versa'.[135]

This regulatory scenario may be subject to significant changes, generally affecting cryptocurrencies and specifically stablecoins.

The European Parliament worked on an *ad hoc* regulation aimed at providing new rules for ICOs in the context of crowdfunding, and eventually opted to drop the project. The proposed draft stated that it is an opportunity for ICOs to 'take ... a much-needed step toward imposing standards and protections in place for what is an excellent funding stream for tech start-ups'.[136] Furthermore, the draft contained one of the first formal definitions of ICOs elaborated by regulators: ' "Initial Coin Offering or ICO" means raising funds from the public in a dematerialized way using coins or tokens that are put for sale for a limited time by a business or an individual in exchange for fiat or virtual currencies.'[137] Also, the draft opened space for the possibility that crowdfunding service providers may be 'permitted to raise capital through their platforms using certain cryptocurrencies' if they comply with specific additional requirements provided by the regulation.[138] Finally, the draft provided exemptions for private placements: ICOs raising an excess of €8,000,000 or ICOs not using a counterparty would not have fallen within the scope of those requirements.[139] The intention of the proposal was to create a standard for ICOs, allowing projects to raise funds and conduct business in all twenty-eight member states.[140]

Furthermore, the European Banking Authority (EBA)[141] and the ESMA[142] called for a common regulatory framework for cryptocurrencies. The EBA identifies payment/exchange/currency tokens as different from 'investment tokens' and 'utility tokens' and has noted the lack of a common taxonomy in use by international standard-setting bodies.[143]

In September 2020, the European Commission proposed a new regime for crypto-assets with the Regulation on Markets in Crypto-Assets (MiCAR),[144] as part of a

---

[135] See Andrew Henderson and James Burnie, 'United Kingdom' in Thomas A. Frick (ed), *The Financial Technology Law Review* (The Law Reviews 2018) 152.

[136] See European Parliament Economic and Monetary Affairs Committee (ECON), *Draft Report on the Proposal for a Regulation of the European Parliament. and of the Council on European Crowdfunding Service Providers (ECSP) for Business (COM (2018)0113—C8-0103/2018—2018/0048(COD))* (10 August 2018) 80 <https://www.europarl.europa.eu/doceo/document/ECON-PR-626662_EN.pdf?redirect> accessed 11 April 2022.

[137] Ibid, amend 43.

[138] Ibid, amend 6.

[139] Ibid.

[140] Nikhilesh De, 'EU Lawmakers Weigh "Standard" for ICOs under Crowdfunding Rules' (*CoinDesk*, 11 September 2018) <https://www.coindesk.com/the-european-parliament-wants-to-make-icos-more-accessible/> accessed 11 April 2022.

[141] EBA, *Report with advice for the European Commission on crypto-assets* (9 January 2019) 7 <https://eba.europa.eu/sites/default/documents/files/documents/10180/2545547/67493daa-85a8-4429-aa91-e9a5ed880684/EBA%20Report%20on%20crypto%20assets.pdf> accessed 11 April 2022 (hereafter EBA, *Report on crypto-assets*).

[142] ESMA, 'Advice on Initial Coin Offerings and Crypto-Assets' (9 January 2019) 5 <https://www.esma.europa.eu/document/advice-initial-coin-offerings-and-crypto-assets> accessed 11 April 2022.

[143] See EBA, *Report on crypto-assets* (n 141) 7.

[144] See European Parliament legislative resolution of 20 April 2023 on the proposal for a regulation of the European Parliament and of the Council on Markets in Crypto-assets and amending Directive (EU) 2019/1937 (COM(2020)0593, C9-0306/2020, 2020/0265(COD)) <https://www.europarl.europa.eu/doceo/document/TA-9-2023-0117_EN.pdf> accessed 2 May 2023 (hereafter MiCAR).

broader action, the Digital Finance Package.[145] Following a two-year negotiation, the European Council and the European Parliament Committee on Economic and Monetary Affairs adopted a revised version of MiCAR in October 2022, and the European Parliament finally approved it in April 2023. As will be explained in greater depth in Chapter 4, MiCAR is an attempt to respond to the Libra Project (now Diem), therefore likely motivated by some sort of political concern raised by this project,[146] and its main purpose is the creation of a proper regulation for crypto-assets, with an emphasis on stablecoins, and crypto-asset service providers (CASPs). MiCAR provides a broad definition of crypto-assets, and not only it does not apply to crypto-assets characterizing as financial instruments (in particular security tokens), but also excludes crypto-assets representing unique and non-fungible assets.[147] This exclusion is relevant to understand the approach towards the regulation of ICO tokens as securities, because it implicitly confirms the intention to regulate them by applying the existing securities regulatory framework.

C. Switzerland

Switzerland has traditionally adopted a principle-based approach combined with self-regulation in financial regulation. In this context, the Swiss Financial Market Supervisory Authority (FINMA) adopted an approach based on issuing guidelines instead of formal legal provisions as a tool for addressing the major concerns raised by Fintech. Consistent with the case-by-case approach adopted by the SEC in the DAO Report, FINMA concluded that there is a multiplicity of legal issues related to ICOs and issued its guidelines on the enquiries regarding the relevant regulatory framework (the 'Guidelines').[148] This, combined with a lack of case law and applicable legal doctrines, makes it impossible to generalize.[149] The Guidelines also state that 'Circumstances must be considered holistically in each individual case. The minimum

---

[145] See Commission's Directorate-General for Financial Stability, Financial Services and Capital Markets Union, 'Digital Finance Package' (24 September 2020) <https://ec.europa.eu/info/publications/200924-digital-finance-proposals_en> accessed 11 April 2022.

[146] See Wolf-Georg Ringe, 'Building a European Market for Crypto-Assets: Who's Afraid of Libra?' (*OBLB*, 27 October 2020) <https://www.law.ox.ac.uk/business-law-blog/blog/2020/10/building-european-market-crypto-assets-whos-afraid-libra> accessed 11 April 2022.

[147] MiCAR (n 144) art 3(1)(5) defines crypto-assets as 'a digital representation of *a* value or of *a right* that is able to be transferred and stored electronically using distributed ledger technology or similar technology'. This definition is substantially aligned with the one provided by the Financial Action Task Force (FATF). See FATF, 'Second 12-Month Review of the Revised Fatf Standards on Virtual Assets and Virtual Asset Service Providers' (July 2021) <https://www.fatf-gafi.org/content/dam/fatf-gafi/guidance/Second-12-Month-Review-Revised-FATF-Standards-Virtual-Assets-VASPS.pdf> accessed 12 April 2022 (hereafter FATF, 'Second Review'). See also MiCAR (n 144) recital 10. As Recital 10 explains, 'This Regulation should not apply to crypto-assets that are unique and not fungible with other crypto-assets, including digital art and collectibles. The value of such unique and non-fungible crypto-assets is attributable to each crypto-asset's unique characteristics and the utility it gives to the token holder. Nor should this Regulation apply to crypto-assets representing services or physical assets that are unique and non-fungible, such as product guarantees or real estate.'

[148] See FINMA, 'Guidelines for Enquiries Regarding the Regulatory Framework for Initial Coin Offerings (ICOs)' (2018) <https://www.finma.ch/~/media/finma/dokumente/dokumentencenter/myfinma/1bewilligung/fintech/wegleitung-ico.pdf> accessed 22 April 2022 (hereafter FINMA, 'Guidelines for ICOs').

[149] Ibid.

information requirements for organizers form the basis for these decisions'. In such a context, the basis for FINMA assessment relates to the 'underlying economic purpose of an ICO, most particularly when there are indications of an attempt to circumvent existing regulations'.[150]

This approach is consistent with the identification of three categories of tokens. The Guidelines are among the very few documents from regulatory authorities to attempt to categorize ICO tokens, and this is certainly remarkable. The Guidelines identify payment tokens, utility tokens, and asset tokens, which in practice may be intertwined.

The first category is that of payment tokens, which is substantially equivalent to the notion of cryptocurrencies. According to FINMA, these tokens 'are intended to be used, now or in the future, as a means of payment for acquiring food or services or as a means of money or value transfer' and do not generate any claim on the issuer side.[151] In principle, Bitcoin and Ether should fall within this category.

A second category is that of utility tokens, which serve the purpose of providing 'access digitally to an application or service by means of a blockchain-based infrastructure'.[152] Utility tokens were traditionally a heavily debated issue within the SEC, which did not think they should be treated differently; some European scholars recently advocated for extending the securities regulation to utility tokens as well.[153]

Finally, asset tokens vest the same function as some traditional securities such as equities, bonds, or derivatives, and are the tokens that should be subject to securities laws.[154]

Consistent with the lack of precedent and case law, FINMA adopts a flexible approach emerging from the remark that 'the individual token classifications are not mutually exclusive', where 'asset and utility tokens can also be classified as payment tokens (referred to as hybrid tokens)', and the requirements are cumulative, with tokens characterized both as securities and a means of payment.[155]

The basis for ascertaining the characterization of tokens as securities is the Financial Market Infrastructure Act (FMIA), which identifies standardized certificated[156] or uncertificated securities,[157] derivatives,[158] and intermediated securities.[159][160] In its

---

[150] Ibid.
[151] Ibid.
[152] Ibid.
[153] See generally Dmitri Boreiko, Guido Ferrarini, and Paolo Giudici, 'Blockchain Startups and Prospectus Regulation' (2019) 20 EBOR 665.
[154] See FINMA, 'Guidelines for ICOs' (n 148).
[155] Ibid.
[156] Swiss Code of Obligations 1912 (*Obligationenrecht*) (hereafter CO) art 965 ff.
[157] Ibid, art 973c.
[158] Financial Market Infrastructure Act 2015 (*Bundesgesetz über die Finanzmarktinfrastrukturen und das Marktverhalten im Effekten- und Derivatehandel*) (hereafter FMIA), art 2, 1 c.
[159] Federal Intermediated Securities Act 2008 (*Bundesgesetz über Bucheffekten*) (hereafter FISA) art 3.
[160] The notion of 'security' under Swiss law was recently amended. The previous version of the FMIA (n 1598) art 2, 1 b (see also Financial Services Act 2018, art 3, 1 b), defined securities as 'standardised certificated and uncertificated securities, derivatives and intermediated securities, which are suitable for mass trading'. Furthermore, the previous version of art 2, para 1, of the Financial Market Infrastructure Ordinance 2015 provided that 'securities suitable for mass organized trading encompass certificated and uncertificated securities, derivatives, and intermediated securities which are publicly offered for sale in the same structure and denomination or are placed with more than 20 clients, insofar as they have not been created especially for individual counterparties'. The Federal Act on the Adaptation of Federal Law to Developments in Distributed Ledger Technology approved in September 2020, contains an amendment of both definitions,

extensive report 'Legal framework for distributed ledger technology and blockchain in Switzerland', the Federal Council took the view that the existing legal framework related to securities and derivatives adequately supports the technological developments, and therefore no changes were deemed necessary.[161]

These approaches at the level of civil law and bankruptcy law, as well as the FMIA, seem to be in line with what was adopted in the recently passed Federal Act on the Adaptation of Federal Law to Developments in Distributed Ledger Technology (the 'DLT Law').[162] This epochal reform passed by the Swiss parliament in September 2020 adapts the existing definitions to the new technological landscape, in an attempt to minimize lexical and substantial changes.[163]

With regard to the definition of 'security', the Federal Council confirms the views expressed by FINMA on the different categories of tokens and in particular emphasizes that token classifications cannot be considered as mutually exclusive, recognizing the possibility of 'hybrid' tokens, subject to multiple regulations triggered by such a 'hybrid' nature.[164] Another element that may cause uncertainty is the 'time dimension' due to multiple changes to the tokens' legal status, which is affected by the 'fast-moving nature of the business model' with consequential changes at the level of their legal treatment.

With regard to tokens' classification as derivatives, the Federal Council considers this option to be rather rare but does consider the broad impact that this kind of instrument may display at both the primary and secondary levels. The position of the Federal Council in this regard is more cautious, and it concludes that even a 'thorough review' of the definition of derivatives under Swiss law would be 'one-sided' and 'incomplete' when applied to blockchain and tokens.[165]

---

perfectly aligning them: 'standardised certificated and uncertificated securities, in particular uncertificated securities in accordance with art 973c of the CO (n 156) and ledger-based securities in accordance with art 973d of the CO (n 156) as well as derivatives and intermediated securities, which are suitable for mass trading.' In addition, it introduced a new art 2, 1 b bis, to the FMIA (n 158) explicitly recognizing securities in a DLT form, in the following terms: 'DLT securities: securities in the form of: 1. Ledger-based securities (art 973d CO); or 2. Other uncertificated securities that are held in distributed electronic registers and use technological processes to give the creditors, but not the obligor, power of disposal over the uncertificated security.' See Federal Act on the Adaptation of Federal Law to Developments in Distributed Ledger Technology 2020 (*Bundesgesetz zur Anpassung des Bundesrechts an Entwicklungen der Technik verteilter elektronischer Register*) (hereafter DLT Law).

[161] Swiss Federal Council, *Report on the Legal Framework for Distributed Ledger Technology and Blockchain in Switzerland* (14 December 2018) 96 <https://www.newsd.admin.ch/newsd/message/attachments/55153.pdf> accessed 11 April 2022 (hereafter Swiss Council, *Report on the Legal Framework for DLT*).

[162] DLT Law (n 1610).

[163] In addition to the changes at the level of the Federal Act on Financial Services 2018 and FMIA (n 158), the DLT Law (n 160) passed important changes at the level of the CO (n 1576), Federal Act on Debt Enforcement and Bankruptcy 1889 (*Bundesgesetz über Schuldbetreibung und Konkurs*), Federal Act on Private International Law 1989 (*Bundesgesetz über das Internationale Privatrecht*), National Bank Act 2003 (*Bundesgesetz über die Schweizerische Nationalbank*), Banking Act 1934 (*Bundesgesetz über die Banken und Sparkassen*), Financial Institutions Act 2018 (*Bundesgesetz über die Finanzinstitute*), Anti-Money Laundering Act 1997 (*Bundesgesetz über die Bekämpfung der Geldwäscherei und der Terrorismusfinanzierung*), and FISA (n 159).

[164] Swiss Council, *Report on the Legal Framework for DLT* (n 161) 94.

[165] Ibid, 96.

The document takes the view that tokens do not fall under the definition of 'certificated securities', whereas they may trigger the current notions of 'securities', 'derivatives', or 'intermediated securities'.[166]

However, the securities framework is only one of the potential regulations applying to ICOs, which may trigger a broad range of hypotheses. The Guidelines explicitly identify the possibility of characterizing them as deposits under the Banking Act[167] and the Collective Investment Scheme Act,[168] and they must also meet the requirements of the Anti-Money Laundering Act (AMLA).[169]

Consistent with its established tradition of self-regulation coupled with effective principle-based regulation, FINMA successfully created an efficient self-regulatory framework.[170] Therefore Switzerland benefits from established organizations, even in the context of the new technological frontier. This regulatory approach contributed to the emergence of Zug's Crypto Valley as one of the global blockchain hubs, alongside Singapore and Hong Kong.

In the context of ICOs, the Blockchain Taskforce, the predecessor of the Swiss Blockchain Federation (SBF),[171] issued a position paper in 2018, anticipating many of the securities law and money-laundering issues that have become part of the Swiss regulatory agenda.[172] As the SBF's website explains, 'The objective of the association is to promote the attractiveness of Switzerland as a location for blockchain-based activities and encourage the development of a secure and competitive legal framework. The SBF is a public–private partnership, combining agents from the blockchain sector, the fields of politics and economics, the scientific community and the public sphere.'[173]

---

[166] Ibid, 94.
[167] Ibid. See also FINMA, 'Guidelines for ICOs' (n 148): here, FINMA explains that 'The issuing of tokens is not generally associated with claims for repayment on the ICO organizer and such tokens do not therefore fall within the definition of a deposit'. Therefore, an issuer would not need a banking licence; nevertheless, if liabilities with a debt capital character exist, the funds are to be treated as deposits and a licence is required.
[168] FINMA clarifies that 'The purpose of the Collective Investment Schemes Act is to protect investors in, and ensure the proper functioning of the market for investment fund products. The provisions of the Collective Investment Schemes Act are relevant only if the funds accepted in the context of an ICO are managed by third parties.' Ibid, 6.
[169] See FINMA, 'Guidelines for ICOs' (n 148): 'The issuing of payment tokens constitutes the issuing of a means of payment subject to this regulation as long as the tokens can be transferred technically on a blockchain infrastructure. This may be the case at the time of the ICO or only at a later date.' 'In the case of utility tokens, anti-money laundering regulation is not applicable as long as the main reason for issuing the tokens is to provide access rights to a non-financial application of blockchain technology (See art 2, para 2, 1 A, no. 3 AMLA, FINMA Circ. 11/1 "Financial intermediation under AMLA" margin no. 13 et seq.)'. Furthermore, FINMA explains that '[u]nder [then] FINMA practice, the exchange of a cryptocurrency for fiat money or a different cryptocurrency falls under art 2, para 3 AMLA. The same applies to the offering of services to transfer tokens if the service provider maintains the private key (custody wallet provider).' Ibid, 6.
[170] See FINMA, 'Self-Regulation in Swiss Financial Market Law' <https://www.finma.ch/en/documentation/self-regulation/> accessed 11 April 2022 (hereafter FINMA, 'Self-Regulation').
[171] See Finextra, 'Swiss Blockchain Federation Founded' (31 October 2018) <https://www.finextra.com/pressarticle/76191/swiss-blockchain-federation-founded> accessed 11 April 2022.
[172] See Mirjam Eggen, Andreas Glarner, Martin Hess, Salvatore Iacangelo, Cornelia Stangel, and Rolf H. Weber, 'Position Paper on the Legal Classification of ICOs' (*Blockchain Taskforce*, April 2018) <https://www.wengervieli.ch/WEVI/media/MediaLibrary/News%20und%20Events/Blockchain-Taskforce-Position-Paper-Legal.pdf> accessed 11 April 2022.
[173] See Blockchain Federation, 'About Us' (2018) <https://blockchainfederation.ch/about-us/?lang=en> accessed 11 April 2022.

III. Unsolved Issues Emerging from ICOs

A. The Best Regulatory Approach

1. Emerging Regulatory and Enforcement Patterns and the Difficulty to Effectively Compare Them

ICOs proved extremely challenging for regulators and epitomize the difficulties related to the general problem of regulating technology.[174] When dealing with ICOs, national regulatory authorities adopted divergent regulatory approaches. These strategies not only displayed specific legal effects, but also affected the attractiveness of the different jurisdictions involved, with observable differences in the numbers of developers and entrepreneurs and the overall volumes of investment that developed in the different areas.

For a long time, the United States has been the uncontested global leader in the capital market industry. However, technology has contributed to significant advancements in the European Union—which became an attractive hub for Fintech projects— as well as in other strategic financial hubs like Switzerland, Hong Kong, Singapore, and the European Malta and Estonia.

Some of these jurisdictions have become established, to some extent even leading, Fintech hubs. Singapore, Hong Kong, and Switzerland share specific characteristics, in particular an effective and established principle-based approach,[175] coupled with a successful combination of public regulation and delegated private (or self) regulation.[176]

Another example is France, which became a rather attractive environment for Fintech and especially for ICOs, although its regulatory style strongly differs from the abovementioned jurisdictions and, consistent with a traditional continental European approach, is based on rigorous rules coupled with strong public regulation. Within the European Union, France tried to pursue a strategy of positioning itself as the most technology-friendly jurisdiction. In doing this, France was a first comer in Europe, pursuing a different strategy based on designing new regulation for ICOs with gradual legislative intervention.[177]

To better understand the differences between the multiple regulatory styles and their consequences, three angles can be adopted: (a) the way securities authorities prioritize their institutional goals; (b) the choice between adopting a new versus an old regulatory framework; and (c) the reliance on a rule-based versus principle-based approach in formulating the norms.

---

[174] See Michèle Finck, *Blockchain Regulation and Governance in Europe* (CUP 2018) 145–153.

[175] Julia Black, Martyn Hopper, and Christa Band, 'Making a Success of Principles-Based Regulation' (2007) 1 L&FinMarRev 191: 'Principles-based regulation means moving away from reliance on detailed, prescriptive rules and relying more on high-level, broadly stated rules or Principles to set the standards by which regulated firms must conduct business.' Ibid, 191.

[176] The literature on self-regulation is vast. Above all, see Julia Black, 'Constitutionalising Self-Regulation' (1996) 59 ModLRev 24, 26–28.

[177] For an overview, see Autorité des Marchés financiers, *Annual Report 2018* (4 November 2019) 15–16 <https://www.amf-france.org/en/news-publications/publications/annual-reports-and-institutional-publications/amf-annual-report-2018> accessed 11 April 2022 (hereafter AMF, *Annual Report 2018*).

a. The goals of securities authorities: the case of the SEC
The SEC typically pursues three institutional objectives, which include investor protection, maintenance of fair and orderly markets, and facilitation of capital formation. A new market trend, such as the ICO, forces regulators to prioritize their regulatory objectives when these missions enter into conflict instead of being complementary, as they typically are.[178]

This was the case for capital formation and investor protection, which became two conflicting objectives. By opting for a rigorous implementation of securities laws, securities authorities would—in principle—achieve higher levels of investor protection but at the same time run the risk of stifling innovation. However, approaches implementing more flexible securities law enforcement would contribute to increasing capital formation, with more investors attracted by a friendlier environment. At the same time, there are significant risks with such a strategy, which could be detrimental under two scenarios. First, more flexible approaches could be a driver for regulatory uncertainty, which would affect investor protection and—in the long run—capital formation. Second, this strategy would make a jurisdiction attractive to scammers and low-quality entrepreneurial initiatives instead of good-faith entrepreneurs with more solid and high-profile projects. Bad-faith market actors would be a threat to market integrity, with potentially considerable reputational damage for the capital market industry in the long run.

These policy considerations are observable in practice, in particular when referring to two extremes: (1) the role of many non-regulated crypto-centres in Asia and their growing importance in the development of the cryptoeconomy, in particular in the context of market infrastructures (namely crypto-exchanges); and (2) the activity of the SEC in the United States. A main concern for the SEC was limiting the wave of speculative frenzy and the consequent massive presence of scammers in the North American capital market.

As an unintended consequence, the SEC's systematic and rigorous enforcement of the securities law framework—consistent with the interpretation of 'security' and 'investment contract' offered by the Supreme Court—negatively affected the competitiveness of the American jurisdiction in an attempt to prioritize the identification of a specific regulatory framework and foster investor protection. However, according to many critics, this enforcement strategy did not even contribute to strengthening the levels of legal certainty, and the overall attractiveness of the American regulatory framework sharply declined. In the Ripple case, XRP[179] investors filed an action in an attempt to stop the SEC action against Ripple, noting:

> Instead of protecting investors and sharing information to help investors make informed decisions, as required by the mission statement, the Respondent knowingly and intentionally caused multi-billion-dollar losses to innocent investors who have

---
[178] See generally Christopher Brummer and Yesha Yadav, 'Fintech and the Innovation Trilemma' (2019) 107 GeoLJ 235.
[179] See Section II.A.1.b.ii.

purchased, exchanged, received and/or acquired the Digital Asset XRP, including the named Petitioners, and all others similarly situated.[180]

In addition to the internal tensions arising within the United States, this approach had a clear geopolitical effect, resulting in the consolidation of the abovementioned emerging Fintech hubs, in which a more effective regulatory approach led to more satisfactory results.

b. The old dilemma: old versus new regulation

When referring to different regulatory strategies, the key question remains whether the existing regulatory framework[181] should be preferred to the new one.[182]

In the United States, the SEC and the CFTC opined that the existing regulatory framework of securities and commodities fits with the new technologies, and in particular with ICOs. This is what emerges strongly from the observable pattern of rigorous regulatory enforcement put in place by the two authorities, especially by the SEC. Furthermore, while even in the European Union the same traditional definitions certainly apply, European regulators have considered in the past to regulate ICOs by creating a new legal framework, as in the case of the crowdfunding regulation—an option which was later abandoned.[183] At the member state level, as mentioned above, France has pursued a regulatory strategy aimed at creating a new regulatory framework for ICOs and digital assets.[184]

Switzerland lies between these two extremes, having adopted an approach that seems to be a compromise. Different from the United States and the European Union,

---

[180] John Deaton et al. Petition for Writ of Mandamous against Elad Roisman as acting SEC Chairman (1 January 2021) 1–2 <https://www.tbstat.com/wp/uploads/2021/01/xrp_investors_sec.pdf> accessed 11 April 2022.

[181] See Frank H. Easterbrook, 'Cyberspace and the Law of the Horse' (1996) UchiLF 207, 207, 208, 210, 215 (arguing for the adjustment of the existing legal framework to accommodate new technologies).

[182] See Lawrence Lessig, 'The Law of the Horse: What Cyberlaw Might Teach' (1999) 113 HarvLRev 501 (arguing for a new legal framework to address new technologies).

[183] See Regulation (EU) 2020/1503 of 7 October 2020 on European Crowdfunding Service Providers for Business [2020] OJ L 347/1. Recital 15 excludes the applicability of the Regulation to ICOs, stating: 'Whilst initial coin offerings have the potential to fund SMEs, innovative start-ups and scale-ups, and can accelerate technology transfer, their characteristics differ considerably from crowdfunding services regulated under this Regulation.' However, Bird & Bird emphasizes that discrepancies can emerge on this point, noting:

> Both the German version ('*Ausgabe neuer virtueller Krypto-Token*') and the French version ('*offres initiales de jetons*') are somewhat unclear in their respective language versions. If we look at the English version, on the other hand, it does not speak of crypto tokens, but of the term '*initial coin offerings*', which is a common term in the market. Initial coin offerings, or ICOs for short, are not generally understood to mean the issuance of any tokens, but usually only those that qualify as utility tokens or currency tokens in general usage. The issuance of security tokens, on the other hand, is referred to as a Security Token Offering—STO. It therefore seems obvious that only ICOs should not fall under the ECSPR, whereas STOs can in principle fall under the ECSPR. This is also supported by the indication that the characteristics of ICOs differ too much from those of crowdfunding. This is because security tokens do have parallels to crowdfunding, as will be shown in the further course of this article. Therefore, investment instruments do not fall outside the scope of the Regulation solely because they are crypto token.

See Michael Jünemann, 'ECSPR—Crowdfunding Regulation and Crypto Tokens' (*Bird & Bird*, 26 October 2021) <https://www.twobirds.com/en/insights/2021/germany/ecspr-crowdfunding-regulation-and-crypto-tokens> accessed 11 April 2022.

[184] See AMF, *Annual Report 2018* (n 177) 15–16.

Switzerland did not enact any new regulation with regard to ICOs, highlighting the continuities with the existing regulatory framework. Beyond financial market law, Swiss regulators thoroughly debated the possibility of a harmonized reform of the key regulations such as the Code of Obligations and fundamental Federal Acts.[185] Even these discussions before the Swiss Federal Council for regulating blockchain represent a smooth adaptation to the evolving framework, rather than a complete revolution. At the same time, Switzerland actively combined this approach with the issuance of guidelines by FINMA and with systematic self-regulatory initiatives delegated to private actors. FINMA guidelines on ICOs (which were supplemented with the guidelines on stablecoins) addressed specific regulatory concerns by identifying different categories of tokens without really affecting the current regulatory framework. The guidelines contributed to the identification, with a certain clarity, of three categories of tokens (utility tokens, payment tokens, and asset tokens), and each category triggers specific consequences in terms of applicable regulation, with the possibility that there may be some overlaps, depending on the factual circumstances. No other regulatory authority provided such helpful and clear (while simple) support in the interpretation of the law, still adapting it with flexibility thanks to thorough implementation of an effective case-by-case approach.

These different regulatory approaches partially explain the different emerging enforcement strategies, in particular taking into account the United States and Switzerland.

c. *Rule-based versus principle-based approach and further interpretative issues*
Maintaining the focus on the United States and Switzerland, it is possible to compare two traditional approaches—a rule-based approach and a principle-based approach—differing in the way norms are structured and interpreted.

In the United States, a rigorous rule-based approach emerged in the context of securities regulation.[186] Consistent with its activity in the past decades, the SEC implemented a unique strategy of enforcement even in the context of ICOs. In principle, a rigorous enforcement strategy is a tool for securities agencies to pursue market integrity and investor protection while at the same time defining the scope and interpretation of the existing rules. This is instrumental to protect capital formation, which is a key component of the SEC's activity as well as that of other securities regulators. However, by implementing such a rigorous enforcement strategy, the SEC did not prove capable to combine these goals, and the specific characteristics of the securities regulation might be the main cause.

While in the context of smart contracts the existing rules at the level of private law and commercial law may prove to be efficient tools to regulate innovation because of

---

[185] See Swiss Council, *Report on the Legal Framework for DLT* (n 161).
[186] However, American securities laws contains specific cornerstone regulation implementing a principle-based approach. The clearest example is Rule 10b-5 of the Securities Exchange Act 1934 (17 Code of Federal Regulations, s 240.10b-5), providing a broad anti-fraud rule, which the Supreme Court interprets in equally broad terms for preserving its remedial function in the context of securities frauds. See Douglas C. Conroy, Michael L. Zuppone, and David J. Kaplan, 'SEC Anti-Fraud Rule 10b-5 Broadly Construed by Supreme Court' (*Paul Hastings*, 2002) <https://www.paulhastings.com/docs/default-source/PDFs/303.pdf> accessed 11 April 2022.

effective flexibility in the language of the law, the situation might be different for securities regulations and those tasked with interpreting them, due to their complexity.

In the United States, securities regulation and most of the caselaw are characterized by a high level of rigidity, significantly limiting the options for the interpreter. Even when the existing regulatory framework leaves some space for a more flexible interpretation, the additional interpretative activity offered by caselaw drastically affects the potential flexibility of the norms.

This is the counterintuitive contradiction of a situation in which securities laws are, in principle, an effective tool to regulate technology (and specifically ICOs), but the tests established in caselaw, such as the Howey test (defining 'investment contracts' and 'securities'), and more generally the hermeneutical activity of courts, may not be the most appropriate (or even an obstacle) in the context of ICOs. An anecdotal precedent in this sense is the situation of Franklin Delano Roosevelt when he wanted to obtain approval for the New Deal during the Great Depression. The existing regulatory framework did not represent an obstacle to his initiatives, but the major difficulties originated from Supreme Court justices and their interpretation of that specific regulatory framework.[187]

In normal times, American securities law relies on a system in which detailed regulations coupled with elaborate tests serve the purpose of achieving standardization in high volumes of complex transactions. In this way, the activity of enforcement pursues the classic goals associated with securities regulation.[188] However, in times of transition requiring more structural flexibility for the goal of more effective interpretative activity, the same detailed rules and the way they are applied and developed in caselaw may not work. SEC Commissioner Hester Peirce's proposal to create a safe harbour for ICOs depends on the structural difficulties of applying the Howey test (and more generally the securities laws) to ICOs.[189] While the notion of 'security' is mostly accurate in the majority of situations, the Howey test did not prove the best tool to address the problem of decentralization existing in ICOs, as Commissioner Hester Peirce emphasized in a past statement.[190]

A principle-based approach, such as the one developed by Switzerland, offers 'in principle' more flexibility, although even in this context FINMA provides specific guidelines (i.e., those on ICOs) as well as other more detailed official interpretations that may have the equivalent effect of limiting the activity of the interpreter. According to FINMA's Annual Report for 2019,[191] in that year FINMA investigated sixty ICOs, with thirty cases concluded and three enforcement proceedings. Comparing this activity of investigation with the one put in place by the SEC, it is clear how the two enforcement approaches differ. The SEC's enforcement in 2019 and at the beginning of 2020 was based on violations of securities laws in a very strict sense (violation of the securities law in relation to distribution of unregistered securities), but FINMA has investigated other types of violations. In more than ten cases, FINMA

---

[187] See generally Theresa A. Niedziela, 'Franklin D. Roosevelt and the Supreme Court' (1976) 6 PSQ 51.
[188] See Armour et al., *Principles of Financial Regulation* (n 6) 61–62.
[189] Peirce, 'Running on Empty' (n 119).
[190] Peirce, 'Regulation' (n 121).
[191] FINMA, *Annual Report 2019* (April 2020) <https://www.finma.ch/en/news/2020/04/20200402-mm-finma-gb-2019/> accessed 11 April 2022.

contested a violation of the AMLA or unlawful receipt of public deposits in violation of the Banking Act.[192] Consistent with this approach, FINMA has anticipated that stablecoins also raise questions in relation to the AMLA, the Banking Act, and the Collective Investment Schemes Act, emphasizing the importance of these sensitive issues.[193] Two of the most important enforcement actions have been those against E-Coin (2017) and Envion AG (concluded in 2019). E-Coin was a case of fraud, and FINMA successfully took action against E-Coin promoters, in relation to the creation of a fake cryptocurrency.[194] The case was successfully defended in the Federal Administrative Court of Switzerland. The second enforcement action by FINMA involved Envion AG, a company in liquidation that launched its ICO without the proper statutory licence, defrauding 37,000 investors.[195]

With regard to other European states, a closer look at their enforcement strategy is not useful for this analysis. Consistent with what emerged in Switzerland, there are no substantial observable patterns arising from the enforcement actions.[196] At the European level, member states are still interpreting the existing regulations.[197] The German BaFin[198] and Italian CONSOB[199] did not refer to any enforcement activity targeting ICOs in their most recent annual reports. With regard to potential regulatory advancements involving the European Union, it is impossible—at the moment—to predict its effects at the level of enforcement strategy.

At this stage, it is still hard to compare the different regulatory styles and their impact on enforcement actions implemented by regulatory agencies. Indeed, not all jurisdictions offer an observable pattern in relation to enforcement actions, as is the case in the United States. The SEC could gradually develop a consistent enforcement strategy, starting with the characterization of ICOs digital tokens as securities and extending the securities law framework to all the entities involved with this activity (such as broker-dealers, trading platforms, and private funds).[200]

---

[192] Ibid, 48.
[193] For a broader analysis of stablecoin regulation under Swiss law, see Chapter 4.
[194] FINMA, 'Finma Closes Down Coin Providers and Issues Warning about Fake Cryptocurrencies' (19 September 2017) <https://www.finma.ch/en/news/2017/09/20170919-mm-coin-anbieter/> accessed 11 April 2022.
[195] FINMA, 'Finma Ascertains Illegal Activity by Envion AG' (27 March 2019) <https://www.finma.ch/en/news/2019/03/20190327---mm---envion/> accessed 11 April 2022.
[196] For a first comparative overview see Yuliya Guseva and Douglas Eakeley, 'Crypto-Enforcement around the World' (2021) 94 SCaLLRev 99. For a comparative analysis, see also Wulf A. Kaal, 'Initial Coin Offerings: The Top 25 Jurisdictions and their Comparative Regulatory Responses (as of May 2018)' (2018) 1 StanJBlockchainL&Pol'y 41.
[197] See for example Bundesanstalt für Finanzdienstleistungsaufsicht (hereafter BaFin), 'Supervisory Classification of Tokens or Cryptocurrencies underlying 'Initial Coin Offerings' (ICOs) as Financial Instruments in the Field of Securities Supervision' (23 March 2018) <https://www.bafin.de/SharedDocs/Downloads/EN/Merkblatt/WA/dl_hinweisschreiben_einordnung_ICOs_en.html;jsessionid=4D49DEF70 4E4A19C2AD8163869933C9D.2_cid370?nn=8249098> accessed 11 April 2022.
[198] See BaFin, *Annual Report 2020* (24 August 2021) <https://www.bafin.de/SharedDocs/Downloads/EN/Jahresbericht/dl_jb_2020_en.pdf;jsessionid=2F90C3647A6AC1447FCDB914F10029EE.1_cid501?__blob=publicationFile&v=3> accessed 11 April 2022.
[199] See Commissione Nazionale per le Società e la Borsa, *Annual Report 2020* (31 March 2021) <https://www.consob.it/documents/46180/46181/ar2020.pdf/4235c99f-0540-4784-980e-13c0ed91da0c> accessed 11 April 2022.
[200] See generally, Dell'Erba, '"Do No Harm" Approach in Initial Coin Offerings' (n 42).

When more enforcement actions take place in different jurisdictions, it will also be possible to make further considerations on another relevant aspect, that is, the impact of specific initiatives aimed at fostering an environment of cooperation between the securities agencies and the market actors, as a factor capable of leading to increased or decreased enforcement activity. Although no data can support this analysis, even in this context two different strategies have clearly emerged. While FINMA proved to be capable of fostering a cooperative environment, other regulatory agencies did not. The SEC attempted to correct its approach by creating the Strategic Hub for Innovation and Financial Technology ('Finhub') as a way to provide support to Fintech issuers with regard to federal securities laws matters, and also in relation to blockchain-related issues.[201] Via this channel, ICO issuers have the opportunity to create compliant concepts before the launch of their projects.[202] Originally created as a sub-unit of the Division of Corporation Finance, the Finhub has become a stand-alone office.[203]

If these institutional initiatives are successful they might contribute to gradually and increasingly curbing the number of enforcement actions in the future, when technological developments will become (even) more mainstream.

2. Implications of the Securities Enforcement beyond the 'Securities Space': The Problem of Stablecoins

a. General remarks

The emergence of stablecoins (or stable cryptocurrencies) has further complicated the issue of securities enforcement in ICOs by adding extremely relevant implications beyond the pursuit of important—and more traditional—goals for securities regulators. These difficulties are common to all jurisdictions and are intertwined with the regulatory enforcement against ICOs. While the geopolitical implications related to stablecoins will be more broadly developed in Chapters 4 and 5, it is important to highlight the implications of securities enforcement in the ICO space, beyond the 'securities' space, and the way this becomes a tool capable of generating geopolitical consequences itself.

Stablecoins are cryptocurrencies that maintain a stable value against a target price, generally US dollars.[204] To achieve stability, stablecoins generally combine liquid collateral (such as gold or US dollars)[205] or algorithmic mechanisms of stabilization with the management of the supply 'to incentivize the market to trade the coin for no more or less than $1'.[206] A collateral of high quality (one that is extremely liquid, such as US

---

[201] See SEC, 'Request Form for Fintech Related Meetings and Other Assistance' https://www.sec.gov/finhub-form#no-back> accessed 11 April 2022.

[202] See Michael Del Castillo, 'SEC Launches Fintech Hub to Engage with Cryptocurrency Startups and More' (*Forbes*, 18 October 2018) <https://www.forbes.com/sites/michaeldelcastillo/2018/10/18/sec-launches-fintech-hub-to-engage-with-cryptocurrency-startups-and-more/amp/?__twitter_impression=true> accessed 11 April 2022.

[203] SEC, 'SEC Announces Office Focused on Innovation and Financial Technology' (3 December 2020) <https://www.sec.gov/news/press-release/2020-303> accessed 11 April 2022.

[204] Nathan Sexer, 'State of Stablecoins' (*Medium*, 24 July 2018) <https://media.consensys.net/the-state-of-stablecoins-2018-79ccb9988e63> accessed 11 April 2022.

[205] Sherman Lee, 'Explaining Stable Coins, the Holy Grail of Cryptocurrency' (*Forbes*, 12 March 2018) <https://www.forbes.com/sites/shermanlee/2018/03/12/explaining-stable-coins-the-holy-grail-of-crytpocurrency/#4db76f8f4fc6> accessed 11 April 2022.

[206] CryptoCurrency Facts, 'What Is a Stable Coin?' <https://cryptocurrencyfacts.com/what-is-a-stable-coin/> accessed 11 April 2022.

dollars or gold) should, in principle, lead to the dual effect of making the stablecoin both stable and liquid. A new wave of stablecoins implement models that use other digital assets as collateral or are not collateralized at all, opting for riskier algorithmic mechanisms of price stabilization.[207] Tech giants joined consortia interested in issuing global stablecoins, which raised the concerns of central bankers and securities regulators.

The regulation of ICOs has a dual implication for stablecoins, one related to the applicability of the securities law framework and a second of a 'geopolitical' nature.

b. Applicability of the Securities Law Framework
Although a more extensive analysis of the applicability of the securities law framework to stablecoins will be conducted in Chapter 4, this subsection specifically focuses on the relationship between ICOs and stablecoins from a regulatory standpoint.

First, the regulatory enforcement of ICOs is related to the enforcement of stablecoins, and the doubts emerging in the context of ICOs are reflected in stablecoins. In the United States, Europe, and Switzerland, the same regulatory considerations developed for traditional ICOs might also apply here, although with some slight differences. With regard to the United States, the current commodities and securities laws may apply to stablecoins as they were described with regard to ICOs, with no substantial differences in relation to the stabilizing mechanisms and collateral implemented.[208] In addition, another possibility of characterizing stablecoins under the definition of 'security' is the notion of 'demand notes',[209] whereas, under the commodities regulation, stablecoins may trigger the definition of 'swap',[210] which falls under the notion of a 'commodity'.

In Switzerland, FINMA issued additional information in the form of a 'Supplement to the guidelines'.[211] FINMA recognized the lack of any specific regulations existing at either the national or global level and emphasized the importance of 'substance over form' as an approach to establish the characterization of stablecoins under different applicable regulations, depending on their structure and the possibility that they are linked to currencies, commodities, real estate, or securities.[212] FINMA considers the possibility that stablecoins may also trigger the licensing requirements under the Financial Market Infrastructure Act if stablecoins imply the creation of a 'payment system of significant importance'.[213]

---

[207] See Kirill Bryanov, 'Breaking the Peg: Every Stablecoin Has Its Points of Failure' (*Cointelegraph*, 19 November 2018) <https://cointelegraph.com/news/breaking-the-peg-every-stablecoin-has-its-points-of-failure> accessed 11 April 2022.
[208] See Chapter 4, Section II.B.3.c.i.
[209] Demand notes are two-party loans with no fixed term or repayment schedule, with the debtor in the position to repay the creditor upon request. Demand notes are securities within the meaning of section 3(a)(10) of the Exchange Act.
[210] The CEA 2012 (n 70) defines swaps as an 'option of any kind that is for the purchase or sale, or based on the value, of 1 or more interest or other rates, currencies, commodities, or other financial or economic interests or property of any kind'.
[211] FINMA, 'Supplement to the Guidelines for Enquiries Regarding the Regulatory Framework for Initial Coin Offerings (ICOs)' (2019) 2 <https://www.finma.ch/en/~/media/finma/dokumente/dokumentencenter/myfinma/1bewilligung/fintech/wegleitung-stable-coins.pdf?la=en&hash=70408DDE78369718148808FD4784E742373A0140> accessed 22 April 2022.
[212] Ibid, 2.
[213] Ibid, 2.1.

In Europe, as mentioned earlier,[214] the main goal of MiCAR is the creation of proper regulation for crypto-assets, including stablecoins, and CASPs. The decision to exclude crypto-assets related to financial instruments (in particular security tokens) could lead to a regulatory framework where ICOs and stablecoins are clearly separate.

c. Geopolitical considerations

From the geopolitical perspective, the analysis raises important issues. Once again, the United States offers a great example of the relevance of securities laws in a broader context, including their impact on the monetary sphere and the geopolitical consequences related to such choices. The Telegram case is an emblematic example. The enforcement action against Telegram demonstrates the core problem of applying the two definitions of 'security' from the SEA and 'commodity' from the CEA to ICOs. Telegram launched the second biggest ICO ever,[215] and the SEC reacted by bringing an emergency action in October 2019 to stop Telegram's unregistered initial coin offering[216] based on the application of securities laws. In March 2020, the US District Court for the Southern District of New York prevented the distribution of so-called Gram tokens. The court considered the initial sale as part of a wider scheme to distribute those tokens into a secondary market, which resulted in an unregistered offering of securities. The court extended the Howey analysis to include the potential resale of tokens by the initial purchasers.[217]

In this case, the CFTC joined the case of the SEC and took the divergent position that the digital tokens offered by Telegram should not be characterized as securities but rather as commodities.[218] This is consistent with the view expressed by Judge Jack B. Weinstein of the US District Court for the Eastern District of New York, who stated, 'Federal agencies may have concurrent or overlapping jurisdiction over a particular issue.'[219]

From a legal standpoint, this is perfectly legitimate and understandable, and it is a direct consequence of the broad (while at the same time extremely detailed) formulations of 'security' and 'commodity', as previously analysed. However, this might explain two different problems. First, it might reveal uncertainties at the level of the characterization of specific products, and more broadly at the level of the characterization

---

[214] See Section II.B.

[215] For an overview of the case, see Joseph Birch, 'Telegram's Legal Battle with the SEC Heats Up over TON Bank Records' (*Cointelegraph*, 16 January 2020) <https://cointelegraph.com/news/telegrams-legal-battle-with-the-sec-heats-up-over-ton-bank-records> accessed 11 April 2022.

[216] See SEC, Complaint against Telegram Group Inc., DRC Wold Inc. a/k/a Diamond Reserve Club and Maksim Zaslavskiy (29 September 2017) <https://www.sec.gov/litigation/complaints/2017/comp-pr2017-185.pdf> accessed 11 April 2022; see also SEC, Complaint against Telegram Group Inc. and Ton Issuer Inc. (11 October 2019) <https://www.sec.gov/litigation/complaints/2019/comp-pr2019-212.pdf> accessed 11 April 2022.

[217] See Alex Fader, 'SEC v. Telegram: SDNY Weighs In on the Gram ICO' (*BusinessLawToday*, 1 May 2020) <https://www.americanbar.org/groups/business_law/publications/blt/2020/05/sec-v-telegram/>.

[218] Shiraz Jagati, 'CFTC Joins the Telegram vs. SEC Case, Shedding Light on Likely Verdict' (*Cointelegraph*, 21 February 2020) <https://cointelegraph.com/news/cftc-joins-the-telegram-vs-sec-case-shedding-light-on-likely-verdict> accessed 11 April 2022.

[219] See Morrison & Foerster LLP, 'Federal Judge Upholds CFTC's Determination that Virtual Currencies are Commodities' (*Lexology*, 9 March 2018) <https://www.lexology.com/library/detail.aspx?g=cf5d9eb6-7060-4aa4-bde2-81111e8d0ca6> accessed 11 April 2022.

of technology within the existing regulatory regime. Second, this overlap could demonstrate a lack of coordination at different levels, and could be a further detrimental element affecting the attractiveness of a specific jurisdiction, in this case the United States, as a leading jurisdiction for capital markets.

The two agencies have traditionally developed different views on blockchain technology and philosophy of enforcement as they emerged in the past. Former CFTC Chairman Christopher Giancarlo explicitly mentioned the importance of adopting a 'do-no harm approach' in the context of blockchain,[220] and explicitly recognized the similarities with the birth and the development of the internet. As he stated,

> Governments and regulators should avoid undue restrictions, support a predictable, consistent and simple legal environment and respect the 'bottom-up' nature of the technology and its development in a global marketplace. This model is well-recognized as the enlightened regulatory underpinning of the Internet that brought about profound changes to human society.[221]

Another important element in his speech was the risk that regulation could stifle innovation: 'innovators and investors should not have to seek government's permission, only its forbearance, to develop DLT so they can do the work necessary to address the increased operational complexity and capital consumption of modern financial market regulation.'[222]

Different from the CFTC, the SEC has never fully recognized the same approach, although it has long waited before implementing a rigorous enforcement strategy.[223] However, SEC Chairman Jay Clayton and CFTC Chairman Christopher Giancarlo agreed on the importance of cooperating in the field of blockchain, as the only way to 'to bring transparency and integrity to these markets and, importantly, to deter and prosecute fraud and abuse ... to be nimble and forward-looking; coordinated with our state, federal and international colleagues; and engaged with important stakeholders, including Congress'.[224]

Analysing the Telegram case, it can be seen that, consistent with the lack of cooperation that emerged in the past few years, this case represented a relevant step back that subverts the advancements towards a closer cooperation in regulating innovation.

In this scenario, the two regulatory agencies purportedly exercised their jurisdiction on the same case. Various reasons might support this strategic approach, especially taking into account the symbolic relevance of the Telegram case. First, the size of the ICO, equal to $2.9 billion plays a crucial role. Second, and more importantly, the Telegram case came at a crucial moment, contemporary with the issues posed by Libra (then rebranded as Diem). Although the new version of Libra was released in April

---

[220] J. Christopher Giancarlo, 'Keynote Address' (*ISDA's Trade Execution Legal Forum*, 9 December 2016) <http://www.cftc.gov/PressRoom/SpeechesTestimony/opagiancarlo-18> accessed 12 April 2022.
[221] Ibid.
[222] Ibid.
[223] See generally Dell'Erba, '"Do No Harm" Approach in Initial Coin Offerings' (n 42).
[224] Jay Clayton and J. Christopher Giancarlo, 'Regulators Are Looking at Cryptocurrency' (*WSJ*, 24 January 2018) <https://www.wsj.com/articles/regulators-are-looking-at-cryptocurrency-1516836363> accessed 11 April 2022.

2020, and Diem in November 2020, this was a significant step backwards compared to the project of a global currency as described in the first version of the Libra white paper announced in 2019. Despite the Diem project ceased in early 2022, the debate on the best regulatory position in this matter is still open.

As Chapter 4 will consider, the decision of the Libra consortium (rebranded as Diem) to launch a stablecoin raised concerns not only from securities regulators but also from central bankers. Looking more closely at this situation, important similarities between Telegram and Facebook emerge, beyond the different 'monetary' implications of the two projects. Both Telegram and Facebook are extremely popular social media platforms, with Telegram counting 1 billion users across the world. Consistent with the concerns raised by Diem and the fact that billions of social media users may have access to the digital tokens and the underlying infrastructure, the SEC might have been equally concerned that 2.9 billion Gram tokens (the ones issued in the Telegram ICO) could circulate among 1 billion of Telegram's users. If this is true, the Telegram case was instrumental to implementing a specific concerted strategy to limit digital currencies in the United States, with the goal of affecting more disruptive instruments, such as stablecoins, and more generally new payment systems. This is also the case for Ripple, which is one of the most capitalized cryptocurrencies in the world, notwithstanding the volatility it experienced as a consequence of the SEC action in December 2020.[225] The end of the Diem saga would confirm this interpretation.

Beyond the sensational disruption that may go alongside specific ICO cases, such as those involving new stablecoins or huge market actors, the SEC approach will likely display an impact on the regulatory strategies of other securities authorities from other jurisdictions. Two different trends may emerge. A first hypothetical scenario is that securities authorities will align their decisions to those of the SEC, with the same purpose of addressing other concerns beyond the securities law dimension. An alternative scenario is that foreign securities regulators may opt to implement a different approach, competing with the SEC and attracting new key market players of the future. This would offer the advantage of direct control and regulation of such new entities and their global instruments. Based on the divergences emerged in the initial phase of enforcement, such differences will likely persist, and increase in intensity. This emerging fragmentation is a reason of concern that will be developed in the next subsection.

3. Residual Concerns

A further element of concern is the persistent lack of international coordination, in a context where the investment activity is essentially cross-border. This problem emerged in the past years, with scholars advocating for an increased level of international cooperation to avoid regulatory arbitrage and to protect investors, on the basis of the task forces created to solve other cross-border topical issues after 2008, such as the regulation of hedge funds and derivatives.[226] Beyond ICOs, the regulation of the cryptoeconomy has become much more complex, for many reasons. Investments in technology continue to grow and with them the sophistication of the

---

[225] See Section II.A.1.b.ii.
[226] See Dell'Erba, 'Initial Coin Offerings' (n 3) 1132.

III. UNSOLVED ISSUES EMERGING FROM ICOS

financial products that new entities create and propose all over the world. These transformations are leading to the creation of new financial networks, which this book terms 'shadow central banking' and 'crypto shadow banking' and which are the subject of analysis in the following chapters.

Finally, a significant point of concern is the unsolved issue related to the lack of self-regulatory initiatives. Not even the further evolution of ICOs towards so-called IEOs[227] that involve crypto-exchanges seems to be fully promising. In the United States, some private organizations have emerged, including the Wall Street Blockchain Alliance, the Brooklyn Project by Consensys, Messari,[228] the Crypto Community Watch, and the Virtual Commodity Association (VCA). The VCA focuses on crypto-exchanges and custodians,[229] and is the industry's first self-regulatory organization.[230] Overall, these initiatives were not capable of generating high-level debate or effectively challenging the SEC and the CFTC on specific points while at the same time proposing reliable measures to support the nascent industries.

In Switzerland, FINMA traditionally favours self-regulation as a fundamental tool to build efficient and reliable capital markets,[231] and self-regulatory initiatives proliferated. The Crypto Valley Association developed independent policies,[232] contributing to the creation of Zug's Crypto Valley as one of the global blockchain hubs. The Crypto Valley Association proposed a self-regulatory framework identifying general 'Core Values' and a 'General Code of Conduct', coupled with a more specific 'Code of Conduct for the Creation of Decentralized Ecosystems'—also referred to as the 'ICO Code of Conduct'. The Crypto Valley Association created this self-regulatory framework as a way to 'protect the reputation of the CVA and to create lasting value'[233] and pursue the main mission of developing the leading ecosystem for blockchain and DLT to flourish.[234] The 'ICO Code of Conduct' focuses on specific key points. Rigorous information and disclosure are two key points. Information has to be 'credible, objective and timely' and should cover technical and financial details, as well as broad governance issues.[235] Furthermore, disclosure encompasses an assessment of the technological, market, and counterparty risks, focusing also on the mitigation measures. Another key point is the requirement of a comprehensive audit report,[236] which was traditionally a point of weakness in the context of ICOs.

---

[227] See Section V.
[228] Twobitldiot, 'Introducing Messari: An Open-Source EDGAR Database for Cryptoassets' (*Medium*, 26 October 2017) <https://medium.com/tbis-weekly-bits/introducing-messari-an-open-source-edgar-database-for-cryptoassets-46fec1b402f6> accessed 11 April 2022.
[229] See Aaron Stanley, 'Just In Time? Winklevoss-Backed Crypto Self-Regulatory Effort Picks Up Steam?' (*Forbes*, 20 August 2018) <https://www.forbes.com/sites/astanley/2018/08/20/just-in-time-winklevoss-backed-crypto-self-regulatory-group-has-liftoff/#4a2cc0902ea5> accessed 11 April 2022.
[230] Paul Vigna, 'Winklevoss Effort to Self-Regulate Cryptocurrency Gets Members' (*WSJ*, 20 August 2018) <https://www.wsj.com/articles/winklevoss-effort-to-self-regulate-cryptocurrency-gets-members-1534804308> accessed 11 April 2022.
[231] FINMA, 'Self-Regulation' (n 170).
[232] See Dell'Erba, '"Do No Harm" Approach in Initial Coin Offerings' (n 42) 220.
[233] Crypto Valley Association, 'Mission and Policy Framework' (*Cryptovalley*, 8 January 2018) <https://cryptovalley.swiss/codeofconduct/> accessed 11 April 2022.
[234] Ibid, 'Mission'.
[235] Ibid, 4A.
[236] Ibid, 4F.

In addition to the Swiss Crypto Valley Association, the best initiatives in the ICO space were the ones adopted by the Fintech Association of Hong Kong, which intends to identify the best practices for token sales since December 2017,[237] and a similar initiative in the United Kingdom with the establishment of CryptoUK.[238] Furthermore, the Japanese Financial Services Agency authorized the Japan Virtual Currency Exchange Association[239] as a self-regulatory body[240] in that country.

A further important step for the most valuable self-regulatory initiatives from the emerging Fintech hubs will be a real contribution towards fostering some level of international coordination. In this way, private regulators may be a reliable tool to fill the gaps as they emerged in the public sphere.

B. The Breached Promises of ICOs

1. Financial Inclusion

Consistent with part of the post-crisis ideological background underlying blockchain and a general critique of traditional institutions of capitalism, ICOs promised to be a tool capable of enhancing a certain level of democratization as well as financial inclusion within capital markets, unlocking the liquidity of small investors.[241] However, this did not happen. Due to regulatory needs (with the SEC strengthening its enforcement on ICOs) and a more mature market, the majority of ICOs were structured as private sales exclusively targeting institutional investors or accredited investors. This trend became even stronger with stablecoins, which captured the attention of venture capitalists and important financial institutions.[242]

The inclusion of new masses in the financial system is not a novelty of modern times and responds to very precise needs, which can be traced to important

---

[237] Fintech Association of Hong Kong, 'Updated FTAHK Best Practices for Token Sales—Version 2.0' (October 2018) <https://ftahk.org/publication/updated-ftahk-best-practices-token-sales-version-20-october-2018-document> accessed 11 April 2022.

[238] See Crypto UK, 'Code of Conduct' <https://cryptouk.io/codeofconduct/> accessed 11 April 2022.

[239] *See* Jeff Benson, 'Japan Virtual Currency Exchange Association Asks FSA to Make It Official' (*itsisue*, 6 August 2018) <https://itsisue.tistory.com/1302> accessed 11 April 2022.

[240] See Omar Faridi, 'Japan's Virtual Currency Exchange Association (JVCEA) Now Authorized as Self-Regulatory Body' (*Crypto Globe*, 24 October 2018) <https://www.cryptoglobe.com/latest/2018/10/japans-virtual-currency-exchange-association-jvcea-now-authorized-as-self-regulatory-body/> accessed 11 April 2022.

[241] See generally Jonathan Rohr and Aaron Wright, 'Blockchain-Based Token Sales, Initial Coin Offerings, and the Democratization of Public Capital Markets' (2019) 70 HastingsLJ 463. See also Dell'Erba, 'Initial Coin Offerings' (n 3) 1118. For an analysis of the problem of financial inclusion and Fintech, see Douglas W. Arner, Ross P. Buckley, and Dirk A. Zetzsche, 'Sustainability, FinTech and Financial Inclusion' (2019) European Banking Institute Working Paper Series 2019/41 <https://ssrn.com/abstract=3387359> accessed 22 April 2022. See also Douglas Arner, Ross P. Buckley, and Dirk Zetzsche, 'Fintech for Financial Inclusion: A Framework for Digital Financial Transformation' (2018) SSRN <https://ssrn.com/abstract=3245287> accessed 11 April 2022.

[242] See Steven Ehrlich, 'Two Explanations for Venture Capital's Inexplicable Interest in Stablecoins' (*Forbes*, 25 September 2018) <https://www.forbes.com/sites/stevenehrlich/2018/09/25/two-reasons-for-venturecapitals-inexplicable-interest-instablecoins/#7feef7321a57> accessed 11 April 2022. See also Ana Alexandre, 'Bitcoin Investor and Speculator Hold Their Position over the Summer' (*Cointelegraph*, 24 September 2018) <https://cointelegraph.com/news/study-bitcoin-investors-and-speculators-maintained-their-positions-over-summer> accessed 11 April 2022.

III. UNSOLVED ISSUES EMERGING FROM ICOS

precedents of finance, especially in transformative stages of capitalism. Thinking beyond financial markets and referring to commercial and market practices more generally, merchant organizations and entrepreneurs need loans and financing. As early as 1609, with the completion of the first Aktien of the East India Company, an attempt was made to channel money toward commercial activities, and investment trusts spread.[243] This was possible because two different needs had aligned. Entrepreneurs were keen to explore new sources of capital through new methods and channels of funding to maintain their industrial activity. This financial need corresponded with an ever-growing need for a more substantial class of persons who wanted to invest their savings profitably. These developments became so established in the market that investment trusts emerged as an institution capable of reshaping the industrial and economic systems, as well as corporate governance at a more advanced stage of their development.[244]

This did not happen in the context of the cryptoeconomy. Different causes may have determined this situation. The most obvious consideration is that ICOs mostly attracted scammers at the very beginning of their inception. In fact, a significant number of scams occurred during this time,[245] most of them on the Ethereum platform in the form of Ponzi schemes or phishing.[246]

A complementary explanation would be to consider this a classic regulatory failure. Regulators struggled with identifying appropriate regulatory approaches for technology to prosper, and neither national nor international regulators implemented coordinated actions to reduce the number of scammers and attract solid entrepreneurial ventures. At this stage, an example of regulatory failure comes from the SEC. As mentioned earlier, SEC Commissioner Hester Peirce highlighted the inadequacy of the way securities laws, in particular the notion of 'security', are interpreted as a reliable tool to address the issues posed by cryptocurrencies, and in particular the decentralized nature of the investment. Therefore, she proposed the enactment of a safe harbour to create the conditions for innovation to prosper at a faster pace.

A third possibility may be the inadequacy of ICOs to foster the creation of appropriate conditions for implementing important structural changes, such as attracting new masses of individuals who are inclined to invest even small amounts in some sorts of primary market products and mechanisms. This would prove the impossibility to create a new self-enforcing ecosystem at the level of ICOs without an appropriate regulatory framework based on public regulations.

---

[243] Berardino Libonati, 'La categoria del diritto commerciale' (2002) 47 RSD 1.

[244] The bibliography is extremely vast. See generally Harold J. Berman, *Law and Revolution: The Formation of the Western Legal Tradition* (HUP 1983).

[245] Sherwin Dowlat, 'Cryptoasset Market Coverage Initiation: Network Creation' (*Satis Group*, 11 July 2018) <https://research.bloomberg.com/pub/res/d28giW28tf6G7T_Wr77aU0gDgFQ> accessed 11 April 2022 (finding that 78 per cent of ICOs were scams); see also Hugo Benedetti and Leonard Kostovetsky, 'Digital Tulips? Returns to Investors in Initial Coin Offerings' (2021) 66 JCorpFin. See also Zetzsche et al., 'The ICO Gold Rush' (n 11) 269.

[246] Gareth Jenkinson, 'From Ponzi Schemes to ICO Exits, Ethereum's Blockchain Has Been the Platform of Choice for Scammers' (*Cointelegraph*, 4 February 2019) <https://cointelegraph.com/news/from-ponzi-schemes-to-ico-exits-ethereums-blockchain-has-been-the-platform-of-choice-for-scammers> accessed 11 April 2022.

Another, more optimistic approach would lead to the conclusion that the exclusion of unsophisticated investors from a risky market with no available information is not negative and is instrumental to enhance investor protection and market integrity. Indeed, the majority of investors who were actively engaged with cryptocurrencies did not benefit from adequate information that was necessary to make responsible investment choices and gatekeepers. However, this would confirm the inability of ICOs to be a reliable alternative for small investors to be part of broader globalized financial market transactions.

The experience of investment trusts is also helpful to highlight another flaw of ICOs and more generally cryptoeconomy, at least at this very stage, consisting of the inability of attracting institutional investors, which would indirectly confirm the inability of ICOs to include non-sophisticated investors. Indeed, financial inclusion did not take place because ICOs failed to attract individual investors and financial intermediaries. Financial intermediaries, in the form of institutional investors—in particular mutual funds—are generally a way to pursue some forms of financial inclusion, as the case of investment trusts confirms, involving non-sophisticated investors who invest their savings in such collective schemes. ICOs proved incapable of attracting this category of investors, because of the inherent risks and the lack of credibility. STOs tried to propose a more regulated framework, also related to the existence of actual ownership of an underlying asset, as a tool to attract more institutional investors.

As the SBF has highlighted, a more regulated framework bringing more transparency in this context might be especially important for small–medium enterprises (SMEs). Indeed, SMEs are the most exposed to the difficulties of traditional forms of offerings. Therefore, these new developments could be beneficial for them, potentially increasing their chances to attract new capital.[247] Consistent with this approach, an initiative by the European Commission aimed at fostering sustainability and digitalization for SMEs in Europe considered the possibility of blockchain as a tool to increase opportunities for investments. In particular, the European Commission highlighted that SMEs could 'issue crypto-assets and digital tokens for instance in the form of bonds'.[248] Furthermore, it emphasized the attractiveness of such instruments for both investors, because of their characteristic of being immediately tradable, and SMEs, benefiting from an increasingly rapid, efficient, and cost-effective process.[249]

2. Disintermediation of Venture Capitalists

In the financial industry, the concept of disintermediation is often associated with banking. Banking disintermediation occurs when financial institutions other than credit institutions provide financial resources to individuals and corporations. However, the term disintermediation is extremely common in the blockchain space

---

[247] See Swiss Blockchain Federation, 'Guidelines for Issuers of Equity and Related Tokens' (12 December 2019) <http://blockchainfederation.ch/wp-content/uploads/2019/12/SBF-Circular-2019-01-Tokenized-Equity-1.pdf> accessed 11 April 2022 (SBFed, 'Guidelines for Issuers').
[248] Commission, 'An SME Strategy' (n 5).
[249] Ibid.

because it is generally associated with decentralization. Because of decentralization, a network of intermediaries should disappear. Since ICOs were mostly marketed online with no intermediary acting between the investors and the entrepreneurs, they promised to disintermediate the venture capital market, as part of a more general trend of disintermediation in finance and capital markets.

At the beginning of the ICO era, some commentators emphasized the contradiction of the venture capital industry, in that, while traditionally invested in financing innovation, it always failed to incorporate some sort of innovation in its business model.[250] In this context, ICOs should have been a way to create a specific function by which venture capitalists invest in innovation and potentially substitute this asset class. This did not happen, and the venture capitalist industry co-opted the ICO world—or what remains of it—although in 2017 ICOs outperformed both angel and venture capital funding because of a more efficient and cheaper method of financing.[251] Venture capitalists became active in the space in many different ways, in particular by continuing to directly invest in blockchain start-ups, as well as creating investment vehicles to indirectly invest in other blockchain ventures, crypto-assets, and ICOs.[252] In this respect, ICOs did not represent an exception to the general trend of Fintechs active in the banking sector, where established financial institutions often proved capable of absorbing those attempting to compete with them.[253]

Stronger development of new forms of ICOs, in particular STOs and IEOs, did not lead to a decrease in the role of venture capitalists, although some studies suggested that STOs and IEOs outperformed venture capitalists in May 2019,[254] with venture capital firms generating almost 40 per cent of the investments in new ventures for the month of May 2019, and IEOs equally generating another 40 per cent and STOs 10 per cent.[255] This kind of study do not show the number of STO and IEO projects in which venture capitalists have directly invested, with the possibility that the role of venture capitalists is even more prominent than the results emerging from this analysis might show.[256]

---

[250] For an overview of venture capital funds, ICOs, and new forms of financing, see Maximilian Klein, Florian Neitzert, Thomas Hartmann-Wendels, and Sascha Kraus, 'Start-Up Financing in the Digital Age— A Systematic Review and Comparison of New Forms of Financing' (2020) 21 JEF 46.

[251] See Lin Lin and Dominika Nestarcova, 'Venture Capital in the Rise of Crypto Economy: Problems and Prospects' (2019) 16 BerkeleyBusLJ 533, 536.

[252] Ibid, 537. See also Richard Kastelein, 'What Initial Coin Offerings Are, and Why VC Firms Care' (*Harvard Business Review*, 24 March 2017) <https://hbr.org/2017/03/what-initial-coin-offerings-are-and-why-vc-firms-care> accessed 11 April 2022.

[253] Lionel Laurent, 'Want to Be a VC? Just Flip a Bitcoin' (*Bloomberg*, 18 April 2017) <https://www.bloomberg.com/opinion/articles/2017-04-18/beating-vc-funds-is-as-easy-as-flipping-a-bitcoin> accessed 11 April 2022.

[254] See Darpan Kumari, 'The Battle: ICOs vs IEOs vs STOs' (*Medium*, 26 June 2019) <https://medium.com/towardsblockchain/the-battle-icos-vs-ieos-vs-stos-9c9b0d851960> accessed 11 April 2022. The article mentions research conducted by Inwara.

[255] Ibid.

[256] Other data from Bitmex and other independent researchers suggested an increase in the market for IEOs and STOs, with a sharp decline in ICO numbers. See BitMEX, 'Initial Exchange Offerings' (13 May 2019) <https://blog.bitmex.com/initial-exchange-offerings/> accessed 11 April 2022. See also Andrey Sergeenkov, 'Number of STOs May Double while IEOs Will Almost Triple By Q4 2019' (*Hackernoon*, 15 May 2019) <https://hackernoon.com/number-of-stos-may-double-while-ieos-will-almost-triple-by-q4-2019-a90a957d7c3f> accessed 11 April 2022.

3. Disintermediation of Market Infrastructures

ICOs did not lead to the disappearance of market infrastructures. Rather, they favoured the creation of new categories of market infrastructures. This may appear surprising or even contradictory, taking into account full 'disintermediation' as one of the key promises of blockchain.

Crypto-exchanges and online trading platforms emerged with the growth of cryptocurrencies and ICOs and bolstered the popularity of ICOs, in particular because they have unlimited trading hours, twenty-four hours a day, seven days a week.[257] During the speculative frenzy characterizing ICOs and cryptocurrencies, these new market infrastructures in no way contributed to detect frauds. They lacked reliable self-regulations, best practices, and standards, as well as any procedure of control of those entities they were listing. Therefore, the market failure of ICOs confirms the importance of market infrastructures, and the need to strengthen their role.

The term 'crypto-exchange' encompasses different heterogeneous entities. One category of crypto-exchanges operates like traditional stock exchanges. They are run by third parties or so-called DEXs (decentralized exchanges autonomously run by smart contracts), in which buyers and sellers can trade either cryptocurrencies exclusively or cryptocurrencies and fiat currencies, with a remuneration system based on transaction fees.[258] A second category implements peer-to-peer trading in which individuals can trade directly with sellers independently fixing the exchange rate;[259] buyers either implement OTC exchanges with sellers through the platform or denote rates at which they are willing to buy, and the platform matches buyers and sellers.[260] A third category is website-based exchanges, in which customers buy and sell cryptocurrencies with a broker who sets the price instead of implementing an exchange between a buyer and a seller.[261] Cryptocurrency funds do not have the characteristics or the functions of an exchange, but they typically are intermediaries and represent a way to invest in cryptocurrencies, benefiting from professional management. Further differences between the various types of crypto-exchanges mentioned above emerge with respect to technical issues related to the segregation of accounts and custodial services.[262]

Online trading platforms are, in principle, not authorized to act as securities exchanges, and in jurisdictions such as the United States requiring registration with a securities authority, they generally do not do so—although they do not fall under any exemption, such as the one granted to so-called alternative trading systems.

Both crypto-exchanges and trading platforms have many issues to be solved. First, there is much regulatory uncertainty in the legal characterization of ICO tokens (and

---

[257] Andrew M. Hinkes, 'Throw Away the Key, or the Key Holder? Coercive Contempt for Lost or Forgotten Cryptocurrency Private Keys, or Obstinate Holders' (2019) 16 NwJTech&IntellProp 225, 233 (hereafter Hinkes, 'Throw Away the Key').

[258] Cryptocurrency Facts, 'What Is a Cryptocurrency Exchange?' <https://cryptocurrencyfacts.com/what-is-a-cryptocurrency-exchange/> accessed 11 April 2022 (hereafter Cryptocurrency Facts, 'What Is a Cryptocurrency Exchange?').

[259] Steemit, 'Where Can You Trade Cryptocurrency? List of Crypto Exchanges' (2017) <https://steemit.com/cryptocurrency/@dragonsteem/where-can-you-trade-cryptocurrency-list-of-crypto-exchanges> accessed 11 April 2022.

[260] Cryptocurrency Facts, 'What is a Cryptocurrency Exchange?' (n 258).

[261] Ibid.

[262] Hinkes, 'Throw Away the Key' (n 257) 233.

cryptocurrencies), which is reflected at the level of crypto-exchanges. If ICO tokens are classified as securities, crypto-exchanges must register with or be authorized by the securities authorities, depending on the regulatory regime in which they work. Second, multiple scandals have emerged with regard to market manipulation (with the implementation of so-called pump and dump schemes), such as the scandal involving Bitfinex and its stablecoin, Tether (the most popular stablecoin in the world). These issues have diminished the credibility of crypto-exchanges and demonstrated the need for stricter and more rigorous regulations.

Wallets for crypto-assets are also important for the cryptoeconomy since they serve to store crypto-assets in a secure manner. Wallets consist of software downloaded and installed on an internet-connected computer that allows users to control credentials to transfer assets created by that system to other users. The user accesses her crypto-assets by inputting her private key, or a password derived from that private key, into the wallet software.[263] Although wallets for crypto-assets are extremely heterogeneous, a vast majority of them are digital, externalized, third party-hosted, brainwallet/incorporeal, and multiple-signature.[264]

To understand the risks related to these new 'market infrastructures' in the cryptoeconomy, some examples may be helpful.

Trading platforms became so relevant that they induced specific transformations at the level of ICO structural patterns, contributing to the creation of IEOs, in which one or more exchanges act as a counterparty.[265] The SEC has warned investors about IEOs, in particular with regard to the role of trading platforms. As the SEC explains, trading platforms offer IEOs 'on behalf' of companies for a fee, and they are typically not registered with the SEC, although they 'improperly refer to themselves as "exchange", [and] may also claim to perform due diligence or other quality assessments of the IEOs'.[266]

In terms of the role and the predominance of market infrastructures in the cryptoeconomy, IEOs and STOs may lead to significant transformations. In 2019, Coinbase's head of institutional sales in Asia confirmed the appetite for entering this new market with the launch of *ad hoc* platforms for IEOs and STOs.[267] The transformations at the level of ICOs confirm the trend that market infrastructures will increase their power in this market, contrary to what one might have expected when thinking about a fully decentralized environment. However, this shift in the market structures is not counterbalanced by a tangible increase in the levels of standards and best practices. This might be the prelude to other future market failures if the new market infrastructures operating in the cryptoeconomy do not opt for rigorous governance, taking as a parameter the market infrastructures operating in traditional finance. One of the purposes of the new financial regulation in the aftermath of the financial crisis was to increase transparency in capital markets, also better regulating so-called dark pools.

---

[263] Ibid.
[264] Ibid.
[265] Gene Yan Ooi, 'What Is an Initial Exchange Offering (IEO)?' (*Medium*, 13 March 2018) <https://medium.com/traceto-io/what-is-an-initial-exchange-offering-ieo-245a7cf72f28> accessed 11 April 2022.
[266] SEC, 'Initial Exchange Offerings (IEOs)—Investor Alert' (14 January 2020) <https://www.sec.gov/oiea/investor-alerts-and-bulletins/ia_initialexchangeofferings> accessed 11 April 2022.
[267] Brave NewCoin, 'Coinbase Is Evaluating IEO and STO Platforms' (17 September 2019) <https://bravenewcoin.com/insights/coinbase-is-evaluating-ieo-and-sto-platforms> accessed 11 April 2022.

The FTX scandal in October 2022 revealed weaknesses in the company's corporate governance arrangements and highlighted the risks associated with a business model that engages in multiple activities, including proprietary trading with affiliated companies such as Alameda Research. These practices generated significant conflicts of interests that were not properly managed and regulated.

Another example comes from stablecoins, as a tool for investing in ICOs and cryptocurrencies. Due to their structural characteristics, stablecoins may greatly benefit crypto-exchanges because of the profits generated by transactions that might require the conversion of fiat to cryptocurrencies and vice versa, where stablecoins would play a key role.[268] In such a situation, crypto-exchanges may be in a position of significant conflict of interest when deciding to list stablecoins and may have incentives to increasingly add stablecoins to their platforms.[269] An extreme situation might also be the one of a crypto-exchange directly owning and listing its own cryptocurrency, as happened in the case of Bitfinex owning Tether, the most capitalized stablecoin in the market.[270]

Notwithstanding their increasing role in the cryptoeconomy, crypto-exchanges did not tangibly contribute to elaborate or enhance any self-regulatory initiatives in the context of ICOs, especially to strengthen the levels and quality of disclosure—a highly debated topic in ICOs.[271] Disclosure is extremely relevant for ICOs because of their structural characteristics.

Although they can be assimilated to a new segment of the primary market, ICOs do not benefit from any of the mechanisms generally associated with this market, in particular the publication of a prospectus and the existence of a network of gatekeepers. Adopting a broad definition, the term 'gatekeeper' identifies a broad range of market actors who protect investors in their capacity as certification or verification service providers.[272]

---

[268] See generally Marco Dell'Erba, 'Stablecoins in Cryptoeconomics: From Initial Coin Offerings (ICOs) to Central Bank Digital Currencies (CBDCs)' (2019) 22 NYUJL&PubPol'y 1 (hereafter Dell'Erba, 'Stablecoins in Cryptoeconomics').

[269] Ibid, 28. The New York Attorney General issued subpoenas in November 2018 against Tether, explaining: 'Bitfinex no longer has access to over $850 million dollars of comingled client and corporate funds that it handed over, without any written contract or assurance, to a Panamanian entity called "Crypto Capital Corp.," a loss Bitfinex never disclosed to investors. In order to fill the gap, executives of Bitfinex and Tether engaged in a series of conflicted corporate transactions whereby Bitfinex gave itself access to up to $900 million of Tether's cash reserves, which Tether for years repeatedly told investors fully backed the tether virtual currency "1-to-1... Bitfinex has already taken at least $700 million from Tether's reserves. Those transactions—which also have not been disclosed to investors—treat Tether's cash reserves as Bitfinex's corporate slush fund, and are being used to hide Bitfinex's massive, undisclosed losses and inability to handle customer withdrawals": NY Attorney General, 'Attorney General James Announces Court Order against "Crypto" Currency Company Under Investigation for Fraud' (25 April 2019) <https://ag.ny.gov/press-release/2019/attorney-general-james-announces-court-order-against-crypto-currency-company> accessed 11 April 2022.

[270] Dell'Erba, 'Stablecoins in Cryptoeconomics' (n 268) 6. See also Marco Dell'Erba, 'Crypto-Trading Platforms as Exchanges' (2023) MichStLRev (forthcoming) <https://papers.ssrn.com/sol3/papers.cfm?abstract_id=4405361> accessed 26 April 2023.

[271] See generally Christopher Brummer, Trevor Kiviat, and Jai Ruhi Massari, 'What Should Be Disclosed in an Initial Coin Offering?' in Christopher J. Brummer (ed), *Cryptoassets: Legal, Regulatory, and Monetary Perspectives* (OUP 2019).

[272] Jennifer Payne, 'The Role of Gatekeepers' in Niamh Moloney, Eilis Ferran, and Jennifer Payne (eds), *The Oxford Handbook of Financial Regulation* (OUP 2015) 256 (hereafter Payne, 'The Role of Gatekeepers'). See also John C. Coffee, Jr., *Gatekeepers: The Professions and Corporate Governance* (OUP 2006) ch II

III. UNSOLVED ISSUES EMERGING FROM ICOS   175

A first category of gatekeepers acting in the primary market is that of underwriters, generally investment banks.[273] In the primary market scenario, insiders are not in a position to be credible about their beliefs, and at the same time outsiders are not in a position to buy inside information.[274] In this situation, the risk is the so-called market for lemon problem, in which investors opt to discount the value of the information received from the issuer.[275] Underwriters can effectively mitigate this risk by representing its good-faith evaluation to capital markets, putting at risk their reputation for certifying the consistency of the issue price with the intrinsic value of the security based on inside information.[276] Other gatekeepers acting in the primary market are auditors, in charge of evaluating the credibility and accuracy of issuers' financial statements, and securities analysts, who conduct extensive research about the issuers, their securities, and the industrial sector.[277]

In the primary market, retail investors tend to be reticent about reading the prospectuses, and they systematically rely on established financial institutions acting as underwriters as well as on analysts and sophisticated buyers, in particular institutional investors.[278] The signals from this network of financial institutions counterbalance the weakness of prospectuses as tools to correct information asymmetries.[279] Information asymmetries existing in the primary market are much higher than those in the secondary market, where price signals incorporate the relevant information.

ICOs lack all the guarantees existing in the traditional primary market, and here retail investors are not in a position to effectively and legitimately free-ride on any network of financial institutions and professionals, in particular underwriters, acting as gatekeepers;[280] although retail investors are likely the vast majority—if not the totality—of investors in principle active in the sphere of ICO. These structural characteristics make this environment rather extreme for retail investors, particularly taking into account that—among all the gatekeepers operating in the capital markets—the possibility of regulating underwriters was never considered as an option because they did not generate any significant market failure.[281]

In such a scenario, minimal disclosure standards combined with support of cryptoexchanges, as the only class of intermediaries involved in the cryptoeconomy, would have contributed to mitigating the problems as they emerged in the industry, and would have supported regulators in identifying efficient disclosure strategies in an especially challenging environment. The traditional trade-off between high levels of disclosure and related costs here is particularly relevant because one of the reasons

---

(hereafter Coffee, *Gatekeepers*). For another definition of gatekeeper see Rainer Kraakman, 'Corporate Liability Strategies and the Costs of Legal Controls' (1984) 93 YaleLJ 868, where the author refers to gatekeepers as private actors contributing to 'remedy enforcement insufficiencies by conscripting deputies within the enterprise'.

[273] See Chapter 1.
[274] Payne, 'The Role of Gatekeepers' (n 272) 257.
[275] Ibid.
[276] Ibid.
[277] Ibid.
[278] See Armour et al., *Principles of Financial Regulation* (n 6) 162.
[279] Ibid.
[280] Ibid.
[281] See Payne, 'The Role of Gatekeepers' (n 272) 274–275.

leading to the development of ICOs relates to the high costs generally associated with traditional IPOs.

By addressing information asymmetries via *ad hoc* disclosure approaches or other mechanisms, crypto-exchanges could have contributed to achieve higher levels of investor protection and would have also benefitted from an increased reputation. The reputation of market infrastructures and intermediaries is an essential tool for the cryptoeconomy to compete with traditional finance or even be absorbed into traditional finance. In Switzerland, the DLT Law attempts to solve some of the issues related to new market infrastructures as DLT trading systems are subject to most of the requirements provided for traditional trading facilities. According to Article 73a of the FMIA, a DLT trading facility is a facility for multilateral trading of DLT securities, which aims to simultaneously exchange offers between multiple participants and conclude contracts implementing non-discretionary rules.[282]

The European Parliament passed a regulation on a pilot regime for market infrastructures based on DLT.[283] In this way, specific regulated institutions (such as investment firms, market operators, and central securities depositors) would be allowed to test DLT-based infrastructures (multilateral trading facilities) in the context of trading, custody and settlement, if specific requirements are met. Article 3 limits the eligible instruments to: '(a) shares, the issuer of which has a market capitalisation or a tentative market capitalisation of less than EUR 200 million; or (b) convertible bonds, covered bonds, corporate bonds, other public bonds and other bonds, with an issuance size of less than EUR 500 million.'[284] Furthermore, the proposal excludes sovereign bonds and identified a threshold equal to EUR 2.5 billion for DLT transferable securities that can be recorded by a CSD or, if applicable, investment firm or market operator.[285]

MiCAR also regulates CASPs, including trading platforms offering crypto-assets and broker dealers, and requires the fulfilment of specific technical and organizational requirements for these categories.[286]

IV. ICOs' Relevant Consequences

Beyond the breached promises, ICOs have had an important symbolic relevance for the acknowledgment and development of the cryptoeconomy. From a regulatory standpoint, ICOs triggered a significant debate, probably superior to the one related to

---

[282] DLT trading facilities shall meet at least one of the following requirements must be fulfilled: it admits 'legal entities other than supervised financial institutions or private clients as participants' in accordance with art 73c (1); provides services 'of central custody of DLT securities based on uniform rules and procedures'; or provides services 'of clearing and settlement for transactions in DLT securities based on uniform rules and procedures'. See Silvan Thoma, 'Switzerland Strengthens Fintech and Blockchain Sector' (*PwC*, 15 September 2020) <https://www.pwc.ch/en/insights/fs/amending-act-DLT-blockchain.html> accessed 11 April 2022 (hereafter Thoma, 'Switzerland Fintech and Blockchain').

[283] Regulation (EU) 2022/858 of 30 May 2022 on a pilot regime for market infrastructures based on distributed ledger technology [2022] OJ L 151/1 (hereafter EU Pilot Regime on DLT).

[284] Art 3, para 1.

[285] Ibid.

[286] MiCAR (n 144) arts 59–85.

Fig. 3.1 The ascending climax of ICOs

Bitcoin. In fact, ICOs were a channel for making the debate on technology a more topical and mainstream one, and emphasizing its intersections with finance and economy, as well as corporate governance.

This section will consider the way ICOs were (or might be) a catalyst for transformations happening at many levels. Consistent with the structure of an ascending climax proposed in Chapter 1 to read the transformations through the 'line of disruption', it is possible to identify a specific ascending climax for ICOs and their consequences (see Figure 3.1). This clarifies the role of ICOs as a legal and factual 'junction' in the development of international finance as a multidimensional complex adaptive system, as extensively considered in Chapter 1.[287]

A. Consequences for Capital Market Structures

The possibility of applying smart contracts to capital formation has furthered the number of applications in securities and capital markets law in an unprecedented way. Focusing only on capital markets and excluding for a moment the significant transformations in other related contexts, ICOs for the first time posed new questions and doubts at the level of the primary market as well as that of venture capital firms (and private equity funds).

The established financial institutions populating and dominating the primary market, such as investment banks and venture capital firms, were impermeable to the economic and technological transformations, because they were in a dominant position which allowed them to manage their own innovation.

Even if ICOs did not entirely disrupt such institutions, their emergence forced them to consider the possibility of innovating themselves. Such institutions may not be entirely disrupted until adequate alternatives emerge under the pressure of technology and the market, because the primary market dynamics necessarily require their role, in particular as a tool to correct informational asymmetries.

---

[287] See Chapter 1, Sections II and III.

However, the debate on ICOs and their increasing application in different forms may lead to cost-cutting that has long-term effects on the business models of implicated financial institutions. From this angle, ICOs may have the effect of reviving specific alternatives to this new tool for capital formation, which already exist in capital markets. It may not be circumstantial that the debate on potential alternatives to traditional IPOs became a topical issue on Wall Street. A trend emerging from Wall Street deals is the possibility of bypassing IPOs while still opting to be listed on traditional capital markets.

Private companies can achieve this result via direct listings. In 2018 and 2019, Spotify and Slack preferred direct listing instead of an IPO.[288] In 2020 and 2021, other start-ups—including Coinbase—chose the same option, reinforcing this trend.[289] Similar to ICOs, direct listing is, in principle, a more efficient way for a company to go public, avoiding the costs and inefficiencies of an IPO.[290] In a direct listing, existing shares typically belong to employees and early investors, while founders generally keep their participation and therefore are indifferent to the choice of a direct listing instead of an ICO.[291] The company itself may benefit from the reduced fees to be paid to banks. In an IPO, banks are heavily invested in marketing the deal to investors, whereas direct listing does not require similar efforts.[292] The similarities with some of the specific reasons favouring the emergence of ICOs are clear because direct listings for specific dynamics pursue the same goal of cost-cutting.

In addition to the identification of less expensive ways for companies to go public, another consequence of ICOs might have been at the level of corporate governance structures. Another most important trend emerging from Wall Street was the launch of IPOs proposing a dual-class shares model, as in the case of Snapchat,[293] Lyft,[294] and Pinterest.[295] In these three cases, CEOs had supermajority voting, associated with no rights for public shareholders.

Dual-class structures are a tool for founders to protect their strategic power within the company while still benefiting from the advantages associated with going public. Their inception raised significant critiques, in particular as a potential

---

[288] Anne Sraders, '4 Things Investors Need to Know about Slack's Direct Listing' (*Fortune*, 9 June 2019) <https://fortune.com/2019/06/19/slack-direct-listing-stock-ipo-investors/> accessed 11 April 2022.

[289] See Ary Levi, 'Tech IPOs Have Been a Bad Bet in 2021—All But One are in Bear Market Territory' (*CNBC*, 7 December 2021) <https://www.cnbc.com/2021/12/07/tech-ipos-a-bad-bet-in-2021-all-but-one-in-bear-market-territory.html> accessed 11 April 2022.

[290] Allana Akhtar and Jennifer Ortakales, 'Asana Just Said It's Doing a Direct Listing—Here's How They Work and Why More Companies Are Thinking outside the Box When It Comes to Going Public' (*Business Insider*, 4 February 2020) <https://www.businessinsider.com/the-difference-between-a-direct-listing-and-an-ipo-2019-6?r=US&IR=T> accessed 11 April 2022.

[291] Ibid.

[292] Ibid.

[293] Ken Bertsch, 'Snap and the Rise of No-Vote Common Shares' (*HLS Forum on Corporate Governance*, 26 May 2017) <https://corpgov.law.harvard.edu/2017/05/26/snap-and-the-rise-of-no-vote-common-shares/> accessed 11 April 2022.

[294] Shannon Bond and Nicole Bullock, 'Lyft IPO Revs Up Debate on Dual-Class Share Structures' (*Financial Times*, 25 February 2019) <https://www.ft.com/content/c7d323ba-36b0-11e9-bd3a-8b2a211d90d5> accessed 11 April 2022.

[295] Therese Poletti, 'Opinion: Pinterest's IPO Filing: 5 Things Investors Should Know' (*Market Watch*, 14 April 2019) <https://www.marketwatch.com/story/pinterests-ipo-filing-5-things-investors-should-know-2019-03-22> accessed 11 April 2022.

violation of the common 'one share–one vote' principle, guaranteeing shareholders equal treatment. Dual-class share structures are consistent with the model proposed by ICOs, especially at the beginning of their development. A common practice for entrepreneurs launching an ICO was to provide investors not with any voting rights associated with the digital token, but with only an economic interest in the new venture.[296] However, this has gradually changed, and IEOs and STOs have mitigated this problem since both structures often opt for providing full rights to dividends and voting rights.[297]

B. Consequences for the Creation of 'Mainstream' Digital Securities

In addition to the specific categorization of ICO digital tokens under the securities and commodities laws, ICOs contributed to the debate on new and more modern and efficient forms of securities, by enriching the traditional debate surrounding 'certificated' and 'uncertificated' securities. The developments in the market for STOs will further enhance new discussions in this context. The most important underlying debate on ICOs and STOs is the mass transformation of the securities market, leading to consequences for how traditional corporations will issue their securities.

Some countries are opting to amend such definitions in order to recognize digital securities. Among them, Switzerland (see Section IV.B.1.b.ii) has proposed important amendments to its securities regulation to reflect the possibility of issuing securities in blockchain form.[298] The Swiss reform contains amendments affecting a broad range of areas, including financial law.[299] The DLT Law made Switzerland a first comer, together with Liechtenstein (which already enacted similar regulatory reforms in 2019), France, and more recently Italy and Germany.

Tokenized securities are the result of a long transformation characterizing financial markets and corporate governance, which is an area structurally and functionally connected to securities. The word 'dematerialization' has been often used in the contexts of both securities and public administration. The concept of dematerialization differs from other key words, such as digitalization or scanning. Scanning consists in transferring a material element on an immaterial support, generally with a scanner. This process is gradually disappearing in favour of increasing 'dematerialization', consisting in the creation of documents that were originally digital. Digitalization has a broader meaning and is used to refer to entire processes involving the way to implement specific processes, including transforming a business model.

In addition to these key words identifying distinct operations, the popularization of blockchain has led to the emergence of a new word, tokenization, generally referring

---

[296] PwC, *5th ICO/STO Report* (2019) 5 <https://www.pwc.ch/en/publications/2019/ch-PwC-Strategy&-ICO-Report-Summer-2019.pdf> accessed 11 April 2022.
[297] Ibid.
[298] See generally DLT Law (n 160).
[299] Swiss Federal Council, 'Federal Council Wants to Further Improve Framework Conditions for DLT/Blockchain' (27 November 2019) <https://www.admin.ch/gov/en/start/documentation/media-releases.msg-id-77252.html> accessed 11 April 2022.

to the process of issuing a blockchain token that is a digital representation of real assets.[300] Digital tokens have grown in popularity due to the phenomenon of ICOs, where distribution of tokens is part of the process of coin issuance.[301] The tokenization of assets is a growing phenomenon in the global economy, and is one of the main reasons why established financial institutions such as Goldman Sachs and J.P. Morgan are increasingly interested in the blockchain ecosystem and its infrastructural implications. This is particularly clear when considering stablecoins.[302]

The process of tokenization of securities may be considered a further structural development of the system. Digital corporate stocks issued on a blockchain infrastructure certainly represent a good example. In the aftermath of the 'paper crunch', American policymakers opted to use the immobilization system, based on the depositary system.[303] Continental European regulators, meanwhile, designed a structure based on the dematerialization of shares (full book-entry system). The issuance of e-shares is an evolution of the book-entry system, marking a new infrastructural and conceptual system, opening space for the real 'tokenization' of shares, that is, shares issued on a blockchain which are therefore tokenized, as part of the gradual process of creating 'digital securities'.

'Digital securities' may be capable of concretely revolutionizing market practices in many contexts, at a private and public level as well as at the infrastructural one. Furthermore, digital securities could become an important vector of innovation in corporate governance, where blockchain was proposed as a reliable tool for increasing overall transparency in corporate governance and strengthening the efficiency of specific actions, including, among others, corporate voting.

While the corporate governance implications of digital securities and, more generally, blockchain technology will be the focus of Section IV.C, the following subsections analyse the impact of digital securities on corporate offerings (with an analysis of the salient regulatory initiatives) and government offerings, and finally draw potential infrastructural consequences at the two levels of trading (exchanges) and post-trading (clearing-houses and central securities depositors, or CSDs).

1. Impact of Digital Securities on Corporate Offerings

The issuance of digital securities certainly affects the traditional corporate equity and debt securities market and impacts corporate governance dynamics. This subsection focuses on the first offering of digital securities relying on a blockchain infrastructure in the United States, by Overstock.com. Furthermore, it considers the most relevant regulatory developments in the field. Some of the corporate governance consequences will be analysed in greater depth in Section IV.C.

---

[300] Patrick Laurent, Thibault Chollet, Michael Burke, and Tobias Seers, 'The Tokenization of Assets Is Disrupting the Financial Industry. Are You Ready?' (*Wyoleg*, 2018) <https://www.wyoleg.gov/InterimCommittee/2019/S3-20190506TokenizationArticle.pdf> accessed 11 April 2022 (hereafter Wyoleg, 'Tokenization of Assets').

[301] See generally Dell'Erba, 'Stablecoins in Cryptoeconomics' (n 268).

[302] Ibid.

[303] The paper crunch in the 1970s led to a re-design of the system, culminating in the DTC. See generally David C. Donald, 'Heart of Darkness: The Problem at the Core of the U.S. Proxy System and Its Solution' (2011) 6 VaL&BusRev 41 (hereafter Donald, 'Heart of Darkness').

a. The example of Overstock.com in the United States

The first public company offering digital securities was Overstock.com (Overstock). In June 2015 Overstock announced its crypto-security offering, a bond trading on 't 0' instead of typical 't + 3', in the form of a 'coloured coin'.[304] According to the plan, Overstock intended to offer 'up to an aggregate amount of $500,000,000',[305] to be issued on a private blockchain[306] and held in the purchaser's name directly.[307] The plan was approved by the SEC in December 2015 and launched in December 2016.[308] Overstock's decision to offer crypto-securities was the last of a number of decisions implemented by Overstock in the blockchain space. The company was the first retailer to accept payments in Bitcoin, doing so in January 2014; it installed a Bitcoin ATM at its headquarters in Salt Lake City, and held a stake in a broker-dealer operating an Alternative Trading System (ATS) to develop a crypto-securities trading platform.

According to its Form S-3, Overstock's digital securities are traded

> on a closed-system trading platform [alternative trading system, ATS] ... maintained by Pro Securities ... [and] a person wishing to engage in [Overstock's] digital securities will be required to open an online brokerage account with the sole broker dealer licensed to provide access to the Pro Securities ATS digital securities trading platform with respect to Overstock digital securities.[309]

Overstock's broker-dealer's interface should allow both institutional and retail investors 'to directly purchase and sell' digital securities that are held in the customer's name. There is no 'street name' option.[310] Furthermore, the broker-dealer shares the identity of its customers with Overstock and its transfer agent, trustee, or other similar agent for each series of digital securities issued by Overstock.[311]

Another structural characteristic of Overstock's design is the existence of a 'sole broker-dealer ... licensed to provide access to the Pro Securities ATS digital securities trading platform' for its digital securities.[312] Therefore, the underwriters of any offerings have to open brokerage accounts with the same (sole) broker-dealer.[313]

---

[304] See David Floyd, 'Overstock's t0: Reconciling Fiat Currency and the Bitcoin Blockchain' (*Nasdaq*, 16 December 2015) <https://www.nasdaq.com/article/overstocks-t0-reconciling-fiat-currency-and-the-bitcoin-blockchain-cm555617> accessed 11 April 2022.

[305] Overstock.com, Inc., Prospectus (Form 424B3) (9 December 2015) <https://www.sec.gov/Archives/edgar/data/1130713/000104746915009167/a2226837z424b3.htm> accessed 11 April 2022 (hereafter Overstock, 'Prospectus').

[306] David J. Berger, Steven Davidoff Solomon, and Aaron Jedidiah Benjamin, 'Tenure Voting and the U.S. Public Company' (*WSGR*, 2016) <https://www.wsgr.com/publications/PDFSearch/tenure-voting.pdf> accessed 11 April 2022 (hereafter Berger et al., 'Tenure Voting'). See also Michael Sherlock, 'Digital Securities: Overstock.com and Beyond' (*Law360*, 2016) <https://www.law360.com/articles/873790/overstock-issues-first-ever-blockchain-shares-in-11m-offer> accessed 11 April 2022.

[307] See Overstock, 'Prospectus' (n 305).

[308] See Tom Zanki, 'Overstock Issues First-Ever Blockchain Shares in $11M Offer' (*Law360*, 16 December 2016) <https://www.law360.com/articles/873790/overstock-issues-first-ever-blockchain-shares-in-11m-offer> accessed 11 April 2022.

[309] Overstock, 'Prospectus' (n 305).

[310] Ibid.

[311] Ibid.

[312] Ibid.

[313] Ibid. See Reade Ryan and Mayme Donohue, 'Securities on Blockchain' (2018) 73 BusLaw 85 (hereafter Ryan and Donohue, 'Securities on Blockchain').

Underwriters with appropriate brokerage accounts (with their broker-dealers) can utilize such broker-dealer's interface to directly purchase and sell Overstock's digital securities. Such digital securities are held directly in that customer's name, rather than in 'street name'.[314]

Pro Securities ATS is also responsible for maintaining an electronic database (a proprietary ledger) where all transactions are recorded. This is a definitive electronic publication of ownership, and copies of the ledger based on 'cryptographically-secured distributed ledger network technology' are publicly available.[315]

Overstock implements a book-entry system, where 'each series of digital securities comprises the proprietary ledger maintained by the Pro Securities ATS, together with a database containing the personal identity information of holders of the applicable digital securities'. Overstock's transfer agent satisfies their 'books and records obligations by combining the information received from the proprietary ledger with the personal identifying information received from the sole broker-dealer that will be licensed to provide access to the Pro Securities ATS digital securities trading platform with respect to its customers trading in such digital securities'. For both institutional and retail investors' transactions, trade data related to the transactions are automatically recorded electronically in the proprietary ledger, which is publicly available, while simultaneously recording 'a cryptographic hash function to the distributed ledger network for [Overstock's] digital securities for mathematical proof of the validity of the publicly available proprietary ledger'. With regard to any problems related to the unavailability of the distributed ledger network, Overstock stated that 'the proprietary ledger maintained by the Pro Securities ATS will not be impacted and will continue to reflect the current state of ownership of the relevant series of our digital securities innovation'.

The distributed ledger records the company's beneficial owners and their holdings at a predetermined record date, and efficiently conducts data management, precisely defining each shareholder's entitlements (i.e. voting rights, right to view proxy materials, or right to submit a shareholder proposal subject to ownership thresholds).[316] In the proximity of a shareholders' meeting, the gatekeeper uploads the company's proxy materials to the shareholders, who have instant and simultaneous access to the documents.[317] The platform allocates votes subject to the company's capital structure and voting rights; therefore shareholders know exactly how many votes they control before casting them.[318] Before the meeting, the individual shareholder or a designated proxy executing the votes is responsible for authenticating the voters' personal identity with the gatekeeper. Typically, this operation occurs off-chain, and the gatekeeper keeps records of the authentication and proceeds with the creation of a digital ID for each shareholder or proxy.[319] Then, shareholders and proxies execute voting instructions

---

[314] Ibid, 34.
[315] Ibid.
[316] Ken Bertsch, 'Remarks to the SEC Investor Advisory Committee' (*SEC*, 13 September 2018) 3 <https://www.sec.gov/spotlight/investor-advisory-committee-2012/iac091318-opening-remarks-ken-bertsch.pdf> accessed 11 April 2022 (hereafter Bertsch, 'Remarks to the Advisory Committee').
[317] Ibid.
[318] Ibid.
[319] Ibid.

(on-chain) over the blockchain and cast the allocated votes for each proposal. The blockchain automatically provides the voting instructions and the verification that the votes are counted back to each shareholder, an immediate and accurate end-to-end confirmation and tabulation. Furthermore, anonymity of the vote is safeguarded, because neither the company nor other shareholders have access to the identity of other shareholders, and the properties of blockchain (the 'consensus' mechanism leading to the immutability of the ledger) guarantee that votes cannot be removed or altered.[320]

Although Overstock's initiative raised some scepticism, it was successful and Overstock distributed dividends to its shareholders via the new platform in May 2020 for the first time.[321]

b. Relevant regulatory initiatives addressing digital securities
i. France and Liechtenstein France was the first EU member state to apply blockchain to 'certificates of deposit',[322] authorizing the government to amend its securities law to apply blockchain technology to specific categories of securities[323] with order no. 2017-1674 dated 8 December 2017.[324] Among the categories of securities, French regulators identified unlisted equity securities issued by joint stock companies (consistent with other initiatives, such as that of the Italian branch of the London Stock Exchange),[325] together with negotiable debt securities notes, commercial papers, and units or shares of collective investment undertakings.[326] The issuance of digital securities has proceeded and escalated, also involving major financial players such as Société Générale and Banque de France in 2020. Because this deal involved so-called wholesale Central Bank Digital Currencies (w-CBDCs), this experiment will be analysed in Chapter 4.[327]

In October 2019, Liechtenstein adopted the Token and Trustworthy Technology Service Providers Act (the 'Token Act'), pursuing important policy objectives in cryptoeconomy. In regulating digital securities, the Token Act has introduced the concept of 'uncertificated right' to refer to dematerialized securities where the physical certificate is replaced by an entry in the book-entry register.[328] This new law entered into force in January 2020 and will be further analysed in relation to the tokenization of real assets in Section IV.D and Chapter 5.

---

[320] Ibid.
[321] Overstock, 'Overstock.com Announces Key Dates and Provides Detailed Information Regarding its Digital Series A-1 Preferred Stock Dividend' (7 April 2020) <https://www.sec.gov/Archives/edgar/data/1130713/000113071320000019/a991pressreleasedatedapril.htm> accessed 11 April 2022.
[322] Loi n° 2016–1691 du 9 décembre 2016 relative à la transparence, à la lutte contre la corruption et à la modernisation de la vie économique.
[323] Ibid, art 120.
[324] Ordonnance n° 2017–1674 du 8 décembre 2017 relative à l'utilisation d'un dispositif d'enregistrement électronique partagé pour la représentation et la transmission de titres financiers.
[325] See Section IV.B.3.
[326] See Frédérick Lacroix, Sébastien Praicheux, and Pierre d'Ormesson, 'Clifford Chance on France's Pioneering Blockchain Legal Framework for Unlisted Securities' (*CLS Blue Sky Blog*, 29 January 2018) <http://clsbluesky.law.columbia.edu/2018/01/29/clifford-chance-on-frances-pioneering-blockchain-legal-framework-for-unlisted-securities/> accessed 11 April 2022.
[327] See Chapter 4, Section II.C.2.b.iv.
[328] See Lubomir Tassev, 'Liechtenstein Adopts Token Act to Attract Crypto Business' (*Bitcoin.com*, 6 October 2019) <https://news.bitcoin.com/liechtenstein-adopts-token-act-to-attract-crypto-business/> accessed 11 April 2022.

ii. **Switzerland** In 2018 the Swiss Federal Council issued a report in which it highlighted the problems that the definition of 'uncertificated security' could have triggered. Particularly relevant is the analysis of the mechanics related to uncertificated securities. As the report further explains quoting Swiss law, the creation of an uncertificated security takes place 'with an entry in an uncertificated securities register of the borrower', and such a register is generally 'maintained electronically and is not public'.[329]

Furthermore, the report noted that FINMA and the Blockchain Taskforce (today replaced by the Swiss Blockchain Federation, SBF) took the view that a vast majority of the tokens currently circulating in Switzerland may be characterized as uncertificated securities because, in this context, the blockchain 'performs the function of an uncertificated securities register'.[330] On this basis ICOs may be a tool to create uncertificated securities, and they fall within the definition of security if publicly offered to more than twenty clients.[331]

The SBF has issued an important document, 'Guidelines for Issuers of Equity and Related Tokens',[332] for the establishment of best practices for security tokens, with a specific view on equity. The SBF recognizes the relevance of tokenized securities as one of the most promising applications in the field.[333] For the purposes of this section, the most important elements of these guidelines are the ones under Article 2 and Article 3.

Article 2 recognizes the possibility of different structures related to the issuance of equity tokens, in particular shares and options to buy shares or intermediation, in which a nominee holds the shares on behalf of the token holders.[334] The guidelines highlight an important aspect related to personal data: under Swiss law, there might be separation of the securities registry from the shareholder registry providing the information regarding beneficiaries. Consequently, there might be an option to tokenize registered shares while keeping 'the personal data of shareholders off-chain.'[335]

Article 3 emphasizes that technology should not be detrimental for corporate information purposes. Therefore, issuers have a duty to 'ensure that all token holders are informed about their rights as token holders and that the basic information about the company is always available and up to date'.[336] The Guidelines confirm the obligations generally applicable to traditional shares, such as periodic company updates, transparency, and auditing of financial statements.[337] In this scenario, smart contracts may be helpful for achieving these information obligations.[338]

---

[329] See Swiss Council, *Report on the Legal Framework for DLT* (n 161) 58. See also CO (n 156) art 973c, para 3.
[330] Ibid.
[331] Ibid, 116.
[332] See SBFed, 'Guidelines for Issuers' (n 247).
[333] Ibid, art 1.
[334] Ibid, art 2.1.
[335] Ibid.
[336] Ibid, art 3.1.
[337] Ibid, art 3.2.
[338] Ibid, art 4.1. With regard to voting, the Guidelines emphasize the importance of 'encouraging shareholder participation and in particular the exercise of voting rights' and importantly consider the role of open technology, which must be transparent, must be based on open standards, and—in order to achieve these objectives—should also be audited by an independent third party. Ibid, art 3.3.2. and art 3.4. Earlier in 2018, the Federal Council Report Legal framework for distributed ledger technology and blockchain in

In recent years Switzerland has proposed important amendments to its securities regulations, which were ultimately adopted with the DLT Law in September 2020, to reflect the possibility of issuing uncertificated securities in blockchain form.[339] This important reform, impacting many different areas of law, adopts measures in financial law that are consistent with those adopted in Liechtenstein. The purpose is to favour the issuance of digital securities.

More specifically, the DLT Law introduces in Article 973d of the Code of Obligation (CO) a new type of uncertificated security, 'register uncertificated security'[340] (*Registerwertrecht*). The definition of 'uncertificated security' is offered by Article 973c (*Einfache Wertrecht*), and the new DLT Law has partially amended this notion. 'Uncertificated securities' identify instruments that do not have the same function as 'register uncertificated securities' under Article 973d, being a mere private instrument corresponding to an obligation.[341] As FINMA highlighted in the ICO Guidelines, '[u]ncertificated securities are ... rights which, based on a common legal basis (articles of association/issuance conditions), are issued or established in large numbers and are generally identical'.[342] Furthermore, the Federal Council also highlighted:

> According to the legal definition, uncertificated securities are rights with the same function as negotiable securities. This definition does not say much, however. The criterion of the 'same function as negotiable securities' is not very helpful, since the functions of negotiable securities (proof of entitlement, transfer, protection of transactions) depend significantly on securitisation, *i.e.*, the physical embodiment of a right in an instrument. The conditions under which rights can be structured as uncertificated securities are not explained in more detail in the law.[343]

The new Article 973d refers to *Registerwertrecht*. The English translation offered by the government is 'ledger based securities', while other commentaries employ the

---

Switzerland highlighted the advantages related to e-shares in corporate voting, in an effort to clarify the mechanics related to this new potential infrastructural framework. See Swiss Council, *Report on the Legal Framework for DLT* (n 161) 23, 27, 128.

[339] See generally DLT Law (n 160).

[340] Translation in accordance with: Thoma, 'Switzerland Fintech and Blockchain' (n 282); Andreas Glarner, Dominik Hofmann, and Nathalie Uhe, 'Swiss Parliament Approves New DLT Regulations' (*MME*, September 2020) <https://www.mme.ch/en/magazine/magazine-detail/url_magazine/swiss_parliament_approves_new_dlt_regulations/> accessed 11 April 2022 (hereafter Glarner et al., 'New DLT Regulations').

[341] Swiss Federal Council, 'Botschaft zum Bundesgesetz zur Anpassung des Bundesrechts an Entwicklungen der Technik verteilter elektronischer Register' (BBl 2020 233) (27 November 2019) 259 <https://www.fedlex.admin.ch/eli/fga/2020/16/de> accessed 11 April 2022 (hereafter Botschaft zum Bundesgesetz).

[342] See FINMA, 'Guidelines for ICOs' (n 148). Before the DLT Law was passed, FINMA also highlighted that 'Under the Code of Obligations (CO), the only formal requirement is to keep a book in which details of the number and denomination of the uncertificated securities issued and of the creditors are recorded (art 973c, para 3, CO). This can be accomplished digitally on a blockchain.'

[343] Swiss Council, *Report on the Legal Framework for DLT* (n 161) 57. As the Federal Council highlighted, 'Due to their contractual nature, uncertificated securities are in principle amenable to a contractual link with tokens. Both FINMA and the Blockchain Taskforce assume that a large number of tokens in circulation or planned can be classified as uncertificated securities. The blockchain then performs the function of an uncertificated securities register.' Ibid, 58.

locution 'register uncertificated securities'.[344] These instruments ensure the following functions of securities: (i) transfer: the rights can be portrayed and transferred in an electronic register that is resistant to manipulation; (ii) proof of entitlement: the parties can agree that the rights can only be claimed and transferred through the register, and the person stated in the register as the entitled person is generally to be held true; and (iii) protection of transaction: the parties should be able to rely on the register, and an acquisition in good faith should be protected.[345]

Furthermore, the new DLT Law has amended the FMIA. Article 2, 1 b encompasses a new definition of securities (identical to the one of the new Article 3, let b of the Federal Act on Financial Services (FinSA) and the one contained in the Financial Market Infrastructure Ordinance). Here securities are defined as 'standardised certificated and uncertificated securities, in particular uncertificated securities in accordance with Article 973c of the CO and ledger-based securities in accordance with Article 973d of the CO, as well as derivatives and intermediated securities, which are suitable for mass trading.' Also, Article 2, let b*bis* of FMIA defines DLT securities identifying ledger-based securities (as defined by Article 973d) or 'other uncertificated securities that are held in distributed electronic registers and use technological processes to give the creditors, but not the obligor, power of disposal over the uncertificated security'.[346]

Additionally, the Federal Intermediated Securities Act (FISA) refers to registering uncertificated securities within the meaning of the Code of Obligations.[347]

iii. **United States** In the United States, the state of Delaware has been a first comer in opening the debate on digital securities, with an emphasis on corporate stocks. As mentioned in Chapter 2, the Delaware Blockchain Initiative (DBI), launched by Jack Markell in 2016, was structured around three milestones, with the third one focused on the creation of 'distributed ledger shares'.[348] Markell described distributed ledger shares as capable of holding 'the promise of immediate clearance, immediate settlement, and bring[ing] about [a] dramatic increase in efficiency and an increase in commercial transactions of which Delaware is known'.[349]

Consistent with this plan, Delaware Governor John Carney, Jr signed Senate Bill No. 69[350] into law. The bill amended section 224 of the DGCL and explicitly opened the possibility of blockchain to corporations in the regular course of their business, providing that '[a]ny records administered by or on behalf of [a] corporation in the

---

[344] Thoma, 'Switzerland Fintech and Blockchain' (n 282) and Glarner et al., 'New DLT Regulations' (n 340).
[345] Botschaft zum Bundesgesetz (n 341) 275 f.
[346] Art 2, 1 b *bis* FMIA.
[347] FISA (n 159) art 4, para 2, 1 g.
[348] See Andrea Tinianow and Caitlin Long, 'Delaware Blockchain Initiative: Transforming the Foundational Infrastructure of Corporate Finance' (*HLS Forum on Corporate Governance*, 16 March 2017) <https://corpgov.law.harvard.edu/2017/03/16/delaware-blockchain-initiative-transforming-the-foundational-infrastructure-of-corporate-finance/#more-80025> accessed 11 April 2022.
[349] See Stan Higgins, 'Delaware to Seek Legal Classification for Blockchain Shares' (*CoinDesk*, 2 May 2016) <https://www.coindesk.com/delaware-government-blockchain-shares/> accessed 11 April 2022.
[350] An Act to Amend Title 8 of the Delaware Code Relating to the General Corporation Law, Delaware State Senate Bill (2017–2018) [69].

regular course of its business, including its stock ledger, books of account, and minute books, may be kept on, or by means of, or be in the form of, any information storage device, method, or 1 or more electronic networks or databases (including 1 or more distributed electronic networks or databases)'. The definition of 'stock ledger' contained at section 218 of the DGCL specifically refers to section 224 when mentioning the different recording means. Senate Bill No. 69 also amended sections 151 (Classes and series of stock; redemption; rights), 202 (Restrictions on transfer and ownership of securities), 232 (Notice by electronic transmission), and 364 (Stock certificates; notices regarding uncertificated stock), to facilitate the introduction of blockchain technology for Delaware corporations.[351]

In addition to Delaware, other federal states are attempting to adopt or have adopted new laws for facilitating the issuance of digital securities for corporate records and/or digital transactions, among them Arizona,[352] South Carolina,[353] California,[354] Texas,[355] Colorado,[356] Maryland,[357] Nevada,[358] Montana,[359] Massachusetts,[360] and Wyoming.[361]

2. Impact on Government Offerings

Another level of significant change could be that related to public finance, with a potential impact on the international governance of public investments and loans offered to emerging countries.

In recent times, the geopolitical debate over blockchain and cryptocurrencies has mainly focused on stablecoins and the possibility (as well as the opportunities) for national states to develop their own cryptocurrencies (central bank digital currencies, CBDCs) as part of broader reforms in the payment system. These developments depended on higher pressure exercised by tech giants' initiatives over such countries, mostly due to their plans to put in place global payment systems, and governments

---

[351] See Trevor Dodge, 'Delaware Authorizes Stocks on Blockchain' (*New Media and Technology Law Blog*, 2 August 2017) <https://newmedialaw.proskauer.com/2017/08/02/delaware-authorizes-stocks-on-blockchain/> accessed 11 April 2022.

[352] Corporations; blockchain technology, Arizona State HR Bill (2018) [2603].

[353] SC Blockchain Industry Empowerment Act, South Carolina State HR Bill (2019–2020) [4351].

[354] Corporate records: articles of incorporation: blockchain technology, California State Senate Bill (2017–2018) [838].

[355] Relating to business entities, Texas State HR Bill (2019–2020) [3608].

[356] Colorado Digital Token Act 2019. This law amends the Colorado Securities Act. See Herbert F. Kozlov and Arthur C. Surratt III, 'Wyoming and Colorado Emerging as Leading Digital Asset Venues in the U.S.' (*Lexology*, 29 October 2019) <https://www.lexology.com/library/detail.aspx?g=c322a3c2-0a55-4a79-98b2-89ec4e327791> accessed 11 April 2022.

[357] Corporations—Corporate Records and Electronic Transmission, Maryland State Senate Bill (2019) [136].

[358] Revises provisions relating to technology used by certain business entities, Nevada State Senate Bill (2019) [163].

[359] Generally revise laws relating to cryptocurrency, Montana State HR Bill (2019) [584].

[360] An Act relative to blockchain and cryptocurrencies, Massachusetts State Senate Bill (2019–2020) [200].

[361] Electronic corporate records, Wyoming State HR Bill (2018) [101]; Open blockchain tokens-exemptions, Wyoming State HR Bill (2018) [70], and Wyoming Money Transmitter Act-virtual currency exemption, Wyoming State HR Bill (2018) [19], amending the Wyoming Securities Act. For an overview of the Wyoming approach, see Lydia Beyoud, 'Wyoming Wants to Be "Delaware of the West" with Business Court' (*Bloomberg Law*, 9 January 2019) <https://news.bloomberglaw.com/banking-law/wyoming-wants-to-be-delaware-of-the-west-with-business-court> accessed 11 April 2022.

and central banks' intention to avoid a loss of control over the monetary system.[362] Although the connection between issuing national currency and geopolitics is clear, this is not the only way to connect these two dimensions, particularly taking into account the international governance of public finance and debt at the level of sovereign nations.

The aspect of ICOs as a model for public finance is still relatively unexplored. The February 2018 issuance of Petro by the Venezuelan government proved that ICOs may theoretically be applied not only to entrepreneurial finance but also to public finance. The ICO model could be beneficial for both established and reputed nations as well as emerging countries. Established nations enjoying higher credit ratings could leverage their reputation by placing safe debt instruments on the market, attracting even more institutional and private investors from different geographic areas with far greater ease. In this way, government bond auctions would benefit from higher demand. At the same time, this mechanism would also be beneficial for emerging countries, for two reasons. First, these countries would have the possibility to reach a broader audience of potential investors. If such emerging countries fulfilled their duties, they would build a stronger reputation in a much faster manner. Second, this would be a way to disintermediate global financial institutions, such as the International Monetary Fund and the World Bank, which at the moment constitute the main source for emerging countries to finance their development. In the past, many controversies had arisen and the international governance of such institutions and the way they operate were often criticized by those that were supposed to benefit from such international finance measures.[363]

3. Potential Infrastructural Consequence of Digital Securities at the Level of Traditional Exchanges and Other Market Infrastructures

Potential reforms recognizing digital securities may be the main source of disruption at another level. Indeed, they may contribute to a more consistent implementation of DLT at the infrastructural level, leading to substantial modernization in the context of market infrastructures, at the levels of listing and trading as well as in post-trading phases.

a. Exchanges

The adoption of new regulations fully recognizing digital securities could accelerate the penetration of new technology at the level of traditional exchanges. A consequence at the level of market structures could be potential convergence between the traditional listing process and the processes emerging in the cryptoeconomy, with established

---

[362] See Chapter 5.

[363] For some critiques in different times, see Bahram Nowazad, 'The IMF and Its Critics' (1981) Princeton Essays in International Finance No. 146; Devesh Kapur, 'The IMF: A Cure or a Carse' (1998) 111 ForPol'y 114; Brahima Sangafowa Coulibaly and Kemal Derviş, 'The Governance of the International Monetary Fund at Age 75' (*Brookings Institution*, 1 July 2019) <https://www.brookings.edu/blog/future-developm ent/2019/07/01/the-governance-of-the-international-monetary-fund-at-age-75/> accessed 11 April 2022; Patricia Cohen, 'Critics Say I.M.F. Loan Fees Are Hurting Nations in Desperate Need' (*NYT*, 22 January 2022) <https://www.nytimes.com/2022/01/14/business/economy/imf-surcharges.html> accessed 11 April 2022.

market infrastructures entering the sector of STOs and digital securities. In this way, established market infrastructures may contribute to the maturation of STOs, making them equally reliable and at the same time cheaper than more established procedures used to go public (such as IPOs). In this way, by relying on higher standards elaborated at the level of traditional finance in the contexts of listing and trading that are directly applied to these new structures, the cryptoeconomy may spread at a much higher level, with increased levels of transparency and potential liquidity.

Established stock exchanges, service providers, and central depositors have implemented or are in the process of implementing pilot projects designed around blockchain. Nasdaq, the second-largest stock exchange in the world by market cap, has made significant efforts in implementing blockchain technology for its own transactions, as well as in order to support external blockchain-based solutions by market places.[364] Nasdaq is one of the founders of the New York Interactive Advertising Exchange (NYIAX), built using Nasdaq's exchange technology and created to provide an electronic marketplace to buy and sell future advertising inventory dedicated to publishers, advertisers, and media buyers.[365] In addition, Nasdaq has taken steps to implement blockchain in the context of the market for shares for both private companies (in the US) and public companies in Estonia and South Africa. In Estonia, it used blockchain technology to run voting for companies listed on the Estonian Exchange.[366]

In South Africa, Nasdaq and Strate (Pty) Ltd, the South African Central Securities Depositor, implemented Nasdaq's Estonian proof of concept for developing digital securities and electronic voting in South African capital markets, to provide general meeting services and a 'user-friendly and secure tool for voting remotely'.[367] Due to the administrative intensity and consequent inefficiencies and risks, blockchain technology has been viewed as a solution because of its characteristic as an 'end-to-end solution', beneficial for all stakeholders, who in this way enjoy enhanced efficiency and transparency.[368]

The London Stock Exchange Group Plc (LSEG), in partnership with IBM, started to build a blockchain-based platform to digitally issue private shares of SMEs in Italy in 2017.[369] The Italian exchange operator of LSEG, Borsa Italiana, aimed to increase opportunities to track and exchange shareholder information of unlisted companies, generally maintained manually on spreadsheets or paper-based records, where each party holds its own version of the information.[370] In the view of the LSEG, its platform

---

[364] Jordan French, 'Nasdaq Exec: Exchange Is "All-In" on Using Blockchain Technology' (*The Street*, 23 April 2018) <https://www.thestreet.com/investing/nasdaq-all-in-on-blockchain-technology-14551134> accessed 11 April 2022.
[365] Anna Irrera and John McCrank, 'Nasdaq Provides Blockchain Tech to New Advertising Exchange' (*Reuters*, 14 March 2017) <https://www.reuters.com/article/us-nasdaq-nyiax-idUSKBN16L18N> accessed 11 April 2022.
[366] Ibid.
[367] Nasdaq, 'Nasdaq to Deliver Blockchain E-Voting Solution to Strate' (22 September 2017) <http://ir.nasdaq.com/news-releases/news-release-details/nasdaq-deliver-blockchain-e-voting-solution-strate> accessed 11 April 2022.
[368] Ibid.
[369] Anna Irrera and Jemima Kelly, 'London Stock Exchange Group Tests Blockchain for Private Company Shares' (*Reuters*, 19 July 2017) <https://www.reuters.com/article/us-lse-blockchain/london-stock-exchange-group-tests-blockchain-for-private-company-shares-idUSKBN1A40ME> accessed 11 April 2022.
[370] Ibid.

should have improved communication between the companies and their shareholders, as well as increase opportunities to access credit.[371] In recent years, SMEs have experienced significant difficulties in accessing credit, with banks suffering from increased pressure due to the enactment of more stringent capital ratios as a consequence of the enactment of Basel II and Basel III. Previously, another similar initiative was that of the Japan Exchange Group, partnering with IBM to test blockchain in low transaction markets.[372]

More recently, the Shanghai Stock Exchange (SSE) announced the launch of a pilot programme implementing a new blockchain-powered trading platform with the support of the regulatory China Securities Regulatory Commission (CSRC).[373] With this initiative, the CSRC aims to foster stock market innovation, contributing to standardize market behaviour and increase transparency.[374]

In Japan, private initiatives in the area of digital securities flourished. In July 2020, Tokai Tokyo Financial Holdings launched a pilot programme in which securitized real estates will be digitalized as security tokens and traded on iSTOX, a security token exchange backed by the Singapore Exchange (SGX).[375] Some of the most prominent Japanese private actors have been active in the field of digital securities. An example is the Mitsubishi UFJ Financial Group, in particular the Mitsubishi UFJ Trust and Banking Corporation, which developed a blockchain-based platform named 'progmat' for automatic management of digital securities transactions. Another example comes from Nomura, which announced the creation of a technical infrastructure for digital securities and issued 'Digital Asset Bonds' and 'Digital Bonds'.[376]

b. Post-trading phase

With regard to the post-trading phase, the mandate for enlarging the scope of clearing and settlement through clearing-houses was a significant change in the aftermath of the financial crisis, with many reforms seeking to strengthen the reliance of market infrastructures acting in the globalized world. Clearing-houses in charge of clearing and settlement for the securities and OTC derivative markets are now key market actors, and DLT was likely to disrupt their business model. However, although DLT applications were always considered extremely relevant at the level of post-trading phases, they were never fully adopted, with significant doubts that this technology could really contribute to increase rapidity, clarity, and security in this phase. A potential evolution

---

[371] Ibid.
[372] See IBM, 'IBM and Japan's Largest Stock Exchange to Test Blockchain for Trading Environments' (16 February 2016) <https://www-03.ibm.com/press/us/en/pressrelease/49088.wss> accessed 11 April 2022.
[373] Tim Alper, 'Shanghai Stock Exchange, Regulator to Begin Blockchain Trading Pilot' (*Cryptonews*, 30 September 2020) <https://cryptonews.com/news/shanghai-stock-exchange-regulator-to-begin-blockchain-tradin-7848.htm> accessed 11 April 2022.
[374] Ibid.
[375] See Rachel Mui, 'SGX-Backed iSTOX Lists Unicorn Fund with US$20,000 Minimum Investment' (*The Business Times*, 22 December 2020) <https://www.businesstimes.com.sg/garage/sgx-backed-istox-lists-unicorn-fund-with-us20000-minimum-investment> accessed 11 April 2022.
[376] See Ken Kawai, 'Japan: Digital Securities Business Is About To Bloom' (*Mondaq*, 6 November 2020) <https://www.mondaq.com/securities/1002066/digital-securities-business-is-about-to-bloom> accessed 11 April 2022.

IV. ICOS' RELEVANT CONSEQUENCES

favouring the issuance of securities in these new forms would likely contribute to the transformation of this industry.[377]

Central Securities Depositors (CSD) also contributed to the development of new projects for digital securities. The CSD Working Group on DLT, assembling many CSD depositories from all over the world, promoted the creation of an electronic proxy-voting system that is both transparent and secure.[378] This project is aligned with the ISO-20022 standard developed for financial messages, with a focus on 'international (cross-border) financial communication between financial institutions, their clients and the domestic or international "market infrastructures" involved in the processing of financial transactions'.[379]

Not surprisingly, the North American Depository Trust & Clearing Corp (DTCC) Trade Information Warehouse is transitioning to blockchain, specifically a customized digital ledger called AxCore.[380] The Trade Information Warehouse holds records for about 50,000 accounts, equal to $10 trillion credit derivatives.[381] Although at the moment an electronic record of specific events is already in place, it has proved insufficient to reduce inefficiencies and redundancies, since each participant in a derivatives transaction keeps its own records, which are subject to multiple reconciliations before the investment matures.[382]

In addition to post-trading, the provision of custody services may be a further level of development triggered by digital securities. The financial crisis of 2008 revealed the importance of custodians for capital markets, in particular in relation to private funds. A relevant reform favouring the emergence of digital securities would definitely impact the custodial business, too. At the moment, the list of those start-ups offering such services is limited to a few companies, including sector-established institutions such as Coinbase.[383] At the same time, this business may attract other established market actors, such as Goldman Sachs.[384] In the current market framework, these

---

[377] See generally Federico Panisi, Ross P. Buckley, and Douglas Arner, 'Blockchain and Public Companies: A Revolution in Share Ownership Transparency, Proxy Voting and Corporate Governance?' (2019) 4 StanJBlockchainL&Pol'y 189 (hereafter Panisi et al., 'Blockchain and Public Companies'). See also Jacques Iffland and Ariel Ben Hattar, 'Central Securities Depositaries in the Age of Tokenized Securities' (*CapLaw*, 31 March 2020) <https://www.caplaw.ch/2020/central-securities-depositaries-in-the-age-of-tokenized-securities/> accessed 11 April 2022.

[378] Michael del Castillo, 'The World's Largest CSDs Are Forming a New Blockchain Consortium' (*CoinDesk*, 5 June 2017) <https://www.coindesk.com/worlds-largest-csds-forming-new-blockchain-consortium/> accessed 11 April 2022.

[379] See ISO <https://www.iso.org/home.html> accessed 11 April 2022.

[380] Michael Del Castillo, 'Blockchain Goes to Work at Walmart, Amazon, JPMorgan, Cargill and 46 Other Enterprises' (*Forbes*, 16 April 2019) <https://www.forbes.com/sites/michaeldelcastillo/2019/04/16/blockchain-goes-to-work/#40831b582a40> accessed 11 April 2022.

[381] Ibid.

[382] Ibid.

[383] The Business of Crypto, 'List of Blockchain Custody Companies | Crypto Custody' <https://www.thebusinessofcrypto.com/company/markets/custody> accessed 11 April 2022. See also Bitcoin Exchange Guide, 'Best Cryptocurrency Custody Companies in 2019: Top Bitcoin and Blockchain Asset Custodian Services' (8 January 2019) <https://bitcoinexchangeguide.com/best-cryptocurrency-custody-companies-in-2019-top-bitcoin-and-blockchain-asset-custodian-services/> accessed 11 April 2022.

[384] Ian Alison, 'Goldman Sachs to Enter Crypto Market "Soon" with Custody Play: Source' (*CoinDesk*, 15 January 2021) <https://www.coindesk.com/business/2021/01/15/goldman-sachs-to-enter-crypto-market-soon-with-custody-play-source/> accessed 11 April 2022. See also Stephen Stapczynski, 'Goldman Sachs Explores Entering Crypto Market, CoinDesk Reports' (*Bloomberg*, 15 January 2021) <https://www.bloomb

services are mainly offered to institutional investors, such as private funds investing in the cryptoeconomy. However, the mass adoption of digital securities issued on a DLT ledger may contribute to the expansion of the number of service providers in this field to satisfy a broader audience beyond the niche currently engaged in the cryptoeconomy.

C. Broader Consequences for Corporate Governance

ICOs as a phenomenon have contributed to accelerate the debate on technology in corporate governance. The issuance of tokenized shares is the most tangible and, to date, concrete transformation that blockchain technology might trigger.

The current debate on corporate governance and technology focuses on the way disruptive technologies (in particular blockchain and AI) might penetrate the corporate structures, even in the context of more traditional enterprises.[385] The acronym 'CorpTech' epitomizes this evolution in corporate governance aspects.[386] CorpTech includes blockchain, artificial intelligence, and machine learning developments in a series of functions,[387] including fundamental roles in the boardroom.[388] However, this section will focus exclusively on blockchain-based transformations in corporate governance.

Financial regulatory issues of ICOs and corporate governance are intertwined. The debate on the characterization of ICO tokens as securities under US securities laws originated from one of the most ambitious projects for corporate governance designed on the Ethereum platform, The DAO.[389] As the name suggests, The DAO was a project for a venture capital fund fully designed as a distributed autonomous organization ('DAO'). At the same time, it was one of the most striking failures in blockchain, highlighting the risks and the difficulties related to coding.

As mentioned in Chapter 2,[390] The DAO was an experiment trying to bring disruption in the phase of capital formation, launching an ICO campaign which raised the attention of the SEC. According to the SEC, The DAO's ICO tokens were characterized as an investment contract or security under section 2(a)(1) of the Securities Act of 1933.[391] In addition, The DAO was one of the very first experiments attempting to disrupt corporate governance by substituting traditional key roles generally assigned to humans with a general self-executing framework fully relying on smart contracts.

---

erg.com/news/articles/2021-01-16/goldman-sachs-explores-entering-crypto-market-coindesk-reports> accessed 11 April 2022.

[385] See Carla L. Reyes, '(Un)Corporate Crypto-Governance' (2020) 88 FordhamLRev 1875.
[386] See generally Luca Enriques and Dirk A. Zetzsche, 'Corporate Technologies and the Tech Nirvana Fallacy' (2020) 72 HastingsLJ 55 (hereafter Enriques and Zetzsche, 'Corporate Technologies').
[387] See also Mark Fenwick and Erik P. M. Vermeulen, 'Technology and Corporate Governance: Blockchain, Crypto, and Artificial Intelligence' (2019) 48 TexJBusL 1, 2 (hereafter Fenwick and Vermeulen, 'Technology and Corporate Governance').
[388] See for example Sergio Alberto Grammitto Ricci, 'Artificial Agents in Corporate Boardrooms' (2020) 105 CornellLRev 869. See also Enriques and Zetzsche, 'Corporate Technologies' (n 386).
[389] See SEC, *The DAO Report* (n 85).
[390] See Chapter 2, Section I.B.2.
[391] See Section II.A.

In any DAO, an important starting point would be the issuance of corporate securities in a rather different (digital blockchain-based) form. Here, the possibility to create and issue digital securities plays a fundamental role as a catalyst in the transformations that blockchain could bring into organizations, contributing to revolutionize corporate governance. More precisely, digital securities, coupled with broader blockchain-based transformations, could potentially increase the overall transparency of the organizations under many respects.[392]

This new environment could trigger radical corporate governance consequences, and this technological penetration within corporate governance is an unusually new trait. Until the inception of new disruptive technologies, previous innovations led to minor improvements in terms of lowering the costs of communicating with shareholders,[393] and they did not trigger any major debate on fundamental corporate governance issues. As mentioned above, blockchain greatly contributed to this debate.[394]

1. Ownership Transparency

Referring to the possibility of developing fully 'traceable' shares relying on blockchain technology, Geis identified their 'defining feature ... [in] that every unit of stock will have a clear chain of title identifying all current and prior owners'.[395] Geis touched on a key flaw, that is, a lack of transparency characterizing the current framework, which causes significant issues at multiple levels, in particular the trading and ownership phases as well as in sensitive operations related to ownership, such as voting at general meetings.

Focusing on the first aspect, digital securities (in particular tokenized shares) as part of a broader blockchain-based infrastructure might increase trading and ownership transparency, in both the settings of public and of private blockchain models. A corporation relying on a public blockchain would provide shareholders and other constituencies with a clear view of the ownership on a real-time basis, and even a private blockchain would provide 'more current and complete information' when compared to today's stock markets.[396]

Such increased transparency would likely benefit certain categories of market actors within financial markets because of the inherent mechanisms related to information asymmetries that would definitely be altered. As David Yermack pointed out, '[n]ot all shareholders would be attracted to this arrangement; activists, raiders, or managers might wish to conceal their trades for exactly the same reasons that small shareholders or fund managers might wish to observe them'.[397] Indeed, transparency

---

[392] See David Yermack, 'Corporate Governance and Blockchains' (2017) 21 RevFin 17 (hereafter Yarmack, 'Corporate Governance and Blockchains').
[393] Ibid.
[394] See Fenwick and Vermeulen, 'Technology and Corporate Governance' (n 387) 2. See also Daniel Ferreira, Jin Li, and Radoslawa Nikolowa, 'Corporate Capture of Blockchain Governance' (2019) European Corporate Governance Institute (ECGI)—Finance Working Paper No. 593/2019 <https://ssrn.com/abstract=3320437> accessed 11 April 2022. See also Mark Fenwick, Joseph McCahery and Erik P. M. Vermeulen, 'The End of "Corporate" Governance: Hello "Platform" Governance' (2019) 20 EBOR 171.
[395] See George S. Geis, 'Traceable Shares and Corporate Law' (2018) 113 NwULRev 227, 267 (hereafter Geis, 'Traceable Shares').
[396] Ibid.
[397] Ibid, 17.

brought by digital securities would impact key strategies and go on to impact other strategies, such as empty voting,[398] the practice of voting without owning an underlying economic interest, and decoupling shareholder voting rights from shareholder economic interests.[399] A typical situation is that of borrowing shares or entering into complex derivatives, such as equity swaps, total return swaps, or cash-settled options. Such instruments have been widely used tools for accumulating secret stakes in listed companies (as in the famous Wendel/Saint-Gobain case in France) or circumventing stock market regulation (as in the very much debated Ifil/Exor case in Italy, and the Schaeffler/Continental case in Germany).[400]

Blockchain-driven increased ownership transparency would likely not only display effects in terms of ownership dynamics related to capital markets but also impact the way disclosure duties and disclosure regulations are intended and implemented.[401] 'In principle' fully transparent ownership would potentially make the existing disclosure framework redundant. If so, a technological solution might lead to consideration of possible reforms of disclosure regulations.[402]

2. Shareholder Voting

a. General remarks

In addition to ownership transparency, a blockchain-based infrastructure could contribute to increasing the efficiency of shareholding voting, both in European countries (generally adopting a full book-entry system) and in the United States (based on custodial ownership).[403] A blockchain-based solution has the potential to simplify the complex system currently in place, based on a long chain of intermediaries, with benefits in terms of speed and accuracy of the voting system. In Switzerland, the Swiss Federal Council highlighted the importance of developing DAOs and the possibility that '[t]he community of token holders (investors) can then decide by e-voting (voting procedure is predefined and fixed in the software code) how the pooled assets are to be used (activities defined in advance and programmed in the software code). Once this decision has been taken, a smart contract implements it.'[404]

---

[398] Ibid, 24.
[399] For an overview of empty voting and its role in corporate governance, see generally Henry T. C. Hu and Bernard Black, 'The New Vote Buying: Empty Voting and Hidden (Morphable) Ownership' (2006) 79 SCalLRev 811; 'Empty Voting and Hidden (Morphable) Ownership: Taxonomy, implications and Reforms' (2006) 61 BusLaw 1011; 'Hedge Funds, Insiders and the Decoupling of Economic and Voting Ownership: Empty Voting and Hidden (Morphable) Ownership' (2007) 13 JCorpFin 343; 'Equity and Debt Decoupling and Empty Voting II: Importance and Extensions' (2008) 156 UPaLRev 625.
[400] See Romain Dambre and Marco Dell'Erba, 'Transalpine Look at Equity Derivatives: Convergence and Divergence in Disclosure and Takeover Regulations in the EU' (2012) 3 RTDF 64, 64. For an analysis of the *Schaeffler v Continental* case, see Dirk Zetzsche, 'Hidden Ownership in Europe: BAFin's Decision in Schaeffler v. Continental' (2009) 10 EBOR 115.
[401] Yermack, 'Corporate Governance and Blockchains' (n 392) 17–18.
[402] Ibid.
[403] See generally Marcel Kahan and Edward B. Rock, 'The Hanging Chads of Corporate Voting' (2008) 96 GeoLJ 1227 (hereafter Kahan and Rock, 'Corporate Voting'). See also Geis, 'Traceable Shares' (n 395). See also Donald, 'Heart of Darkness' (n 303). See also Christoph Van der Elst and Anne Lafarre, 'Blockchain and Smart Contracting for the Shareholder Community' (2019) 20 EBOR 111 (hereafter Van der Elst and Lafarre, 'Blockchain and Smart Contracting').
[404] See Swiss Council, *Report on the Legal Framework for DLT* (n 161) 127–128.

Scholars, practitioners, and market actors have advocated the adoption of blockchain-based infrastructure to solve some of the corporate voting-related issues that have emerged in recent years.[405]

The United States and Europe both offer examples highlighting the difficulties related to the current voting system. In Delaware, *In re* Appraisal of Dell, Inc. exemplifies the complexity connected to the different 'layers' involved in the voting infrastructure.[406] It originated from significant errors, affecting dissident shareholders who were against the 'go-private merger' decided in February 2013 and filed a petition for their appraisal rights.[407]

In re Dole Food Co. proves the inadequacy of the current infrastructures in the context of extreme (but common) situations in the proximity of a specific transaction, such as an M&A deal.[408] In this situation speculative initiatives involving a massive sale of the stocks and short-selling associated with that transaction are frequent. *In re* Dole let emerge significant mistakes notably related to short-selling practices emerged. As the Delaware Vice Chancellor underlined, the uncertainties on the ownership of the shares would have required the analysis of all the recorded transactions and a 'forensic audit of herculean proportions' that would unveil additional disputes about the ownership of the property rights in order to claim the settlement consideration.[409] The court concluded that it is 'functionally impossible to resolve the share discrepancy in a practical or cost-effective manner. The resulting process would be lengthy, arduous, cumbersome, expensive, and fundamentally uncertain.'[410]

---

[405] See Eva Micheler, 'Custody Chains and Asset Values: Why Crypto-Securities Are Worth Contemplating' (2015) 74 CLJ 505; Wulf A. Kaal, 'Blockchain-Based Corporate Governance' (2021) 4 StanJBlockchainL&Pol'y 3. See also Panisi et al., 'Blockchain and Public Companies' (n 377). See also J. Travis Laster, 'The Block Chain Plunger: Using Technology to Clean Up Proxy Plumbing and Take Back the Vote' (*Cii*, 2016) <https://www.cii.org/files/09_29_16_laster_remarks.pdf> accessed 11 April 2022. See also Van der Elst and Lafarre, 'Blockchain and Smart Contracting' (n 403). See also David A. Katz, 'Opening Statement' (Meeting of the Securities and Exchange Commission Investor Advisory Committee, 13 September 2018) <https://www.sec.gov/spotlight/investor-advisory-committee-2012/iac091318-david-katz-opening-remarks.pdf> accessed 11 April 2022. See Matt Levine, 'P&G Could Use the Blockchain in Its Next Proxy Fight' (*Bloomberg*, 17 November 2017) <https://www.bloomberg.com/view/articles/2017-11-17/p-g-could-use-the-blockchain-in-its-next-proxy-fight> accessed 11 April 2022. See Cydney Posner, 'What Happened at the SEC's Proxy Process Roundtable?' (*HLS Forum on Corporate Governance*, 21 November 2018) <https://corpgov.law.harvard.edu/2018/11/21/what-happened-at-the-secs-proxy-process-roundtable/> accessed 11 April 2022. In Europe, Directive (EU) 828/2017 of 17 May 2017 as regards the encouragement of long-term shareholder engagement [2017] OJ L 132/1 (generally referred to as the Shareholders Rights Directive II) opened a space for technology as a possible way to challenge the complexity of chain intermediaries, also to increase shareholder engagement. It highlighted that shareholders' identification is 'a prerequisite to direct communication between the shareholders and the company and therefore essential to facilitating the exercise of shareholder rights and shareholder engagement': ibid, art 3a, paras 1–3. However, the Shareholder Rights Directive's Implementing Regulation (EU) 2018/1212, which entered into force in September 2020, has adopted a more restricted approach towards technology, while still mentioning it at recitals 3 and 4.

[406] Geis, 'Traceable Shares' (n 395) 271.

[407] See *Re Appraisal of Dell Inc.* [2015] No. 9322-VCL, WL 4313206. See also Wonnie Song, 'Bullish on Blockchain: Examining Delaware's Approach to Distributed Ledger Technology in Corporate Governance Law and Beyond' (*Harvard Business Law Review Online*, 2018) <http://www.hblr.org/2018/01/bullish-on-blockchain-examining-delawares-approach-to-distributed-ledger-technology-in-corporate-governance-law-and-beyond> accessed 11 April 2022.

[408] See *Re Dole Food Company, Inc.* [2017] No. CV 8703-VCL, WL 624843.

[409] Ibid, 4.

[410] Ibid.

Finally, the P&G proxy fight of 2017 for a board seat in P&G (the most expensive and likely the closest proxy contest ever)[411] exemplifies the length and the inconvenience for both the fighters and the shareholders that emerges from inaccurate voting operations. According to an independent firm's count, Nelson Peltz had a margin of 0.0016 per cent, equal to 42,780 of the 2 billion votes in total.[412] The difficulties of identifying the winning party were not unexpected, since in past situations even where adverse parties garnered 55 and 45 per cent of the votes respectively, it was hard to establish with certainty who had won.[413]

In Europe, the case of a British public limited company (plc), Dnick Holding, listed on the Deutsche Börse has highlighted similar weaknesses, mostly due to a long chain of intermediaries involved in the voting operations. Consistent with the Dole case, mistakes in the voting procedure led to the dismissal of the appraisal procedure proposed by the minority shareholders.[414]

Blockchain proved to be effective in simplifying and accelerating the voting operations. One of the first successful examples in the sense of strengthening the voting operations comes from Santander's annual meeting and the contextual annual elections in 2018. Broadridge, a leading service provider, partnered with Santander, J.P. Morgan, and Northern Trust to develop a first pilot project based on its patent to improve shareholder voting for Santander's general meeting and elections. At that meeting, the votes of institutional investors (who owned 60.7 per cent of Santander's capital) were counted and confirmed much more quickly than the average two-week process, which includes manual activity by different intermediaries.[415] Furthermore, the quorum at the annual general meeting achieved 64.55 per cent, which confirmed the underlying key promise of blockchain technology to improve corporate democracy and shareholder engagement.[416]

The possibility of revolutionizing not only the way corporate voting is implemented but also the way shareholder meetings are conducted, by relying on a blockchain infrastructure,[417] would be a tool for democratizing corporate governance.[418] In this way, shareholders (in particular those who would systematically be excluded from participation because of the costs they would incur) would be encouraged to participate in shareholder meetings. This would change the vote dynamics, strengthening the importance of retail investors and shareholders who might have some sort of incentive in implementing voice (instead of exit) strategies on a more systematic basis. These aspects will be further considered in the following subsection.

---

[411] See Brian L. Schorr, 'Remarks to the SEC Investor Advisory Committee' (*SEC*, 13 September 2018) <https://www.sec.gov/spotlight/investor-advisory-committee-2012/iac091318-brian-schorr-opening-remarks.pdf> accessed 11 April 2022.
[412] David Benoit and Sharon Terlep, 'Activist Peltz Narrowly Wins P&G Board Seat, New Count Shows' (*WSJ*, 15 November 2017) <https://www.wsj.com/articles/activist-nelson-peltz-elected-to-p-g-board-1510782775#_=_> accessed 11 April 2022.
[413] Kahan and Rock, 'Corporate Voting' (n 403) 1279.
[414] See Van der Elst and Lafarre, 'Blockchain and Smart Contracting' (n 403) 112.
[415] See Broadridge, 'Santander and Broadridge Complete a First Practical Use of Blockchain for Investor Voting at an Annual General Meeting' (17 May 2018) <https://www.broadridge.com/press-release/2018/santander-and-broadridge-completed-practical-use-of-blockchain > accessed 11 April 2022.
[416] Ibid.
[417] See Van der Elst and Lafarre, 'Blockchain and Smart Contracting' (n 403) 25.
[418] Ibid.

b. Potential consequences for corporate democracy
In the context of corporate governance, important trends have emerged in the past few years, including an increased role for institutional investors and shareholder activism, which contributes to a redesign of the contours and the meaning of shareholder democracy. Furthermore, financial techniques related to corporate voting (including high-frequency trading, short-selling, and equity derivatives) have proliferated. All these elements have stressed the infrastructural deficiencies underlying corporate voting, engendering increased concern. The technical problems of the voting infrastructure were a threat to the transparency of the voting process, with political consequences for corporations, including questions about the equal treatment of institutional and retail investors and the risk that this situation could be detrimental to shareholder engagement.

The increased transparency brought by blockchain might have multiple consequences for corporate democracy, contributing to a redistribution of power among shareholders in different ways.[419] A first major consequence would be a potential increase of shareholder activism and the number of proxy fights. If the time horizon of proxy fights was drastically reduced, and situations like the P&G proxy fight were virtually eliminated, activist investors may have more incentives to enter into proxy fights. These incentives originate from a reduced time horizon for concluding the proxy fight, while the pure financial costs of the operation would likely remain the same. Indeed, the process of proxy solicitation (reaching out to shareholders who could be potential allies in the proxy fights) would continue to be mostly manual, and therefore the amount of resources to implement these actions would continue to be the same. However, what would drastically change would be the time horizon in a proxy fight, depending on the reliability of the results, and this would be a reason to decide to be invested in activist initiatives. It is questionable whether a reduced time horizon could be sufficient to cause an increase in the number of proxy fights, which has become a trend in the US and is becoming a trend even in Europe.

A second major change could be a shift in the relationship between institutional investors and retail investors, and their relevance for corporate decisions. There are two underlying issues with the possibility of creating a new infrastructure: (i) the role of retail investors in corporate voting and the reasons why they generally do not exercise their voting rights; and (ii) the opportunity to provide retail investors and institutional investors with comparable technical (infrastructural) means, so that they may exercise their voting rights. An underlying question common to both problems would be whether a different technological platform would change the mechanics of the vote and contribute to an increase in retail shareholders' voices.

In a world where institutional investors own the majority of voting stock in publicly traded companies, retail investors may still be determined to change the outcome of tight contests, as the DuPont proxy fight in 2015 exemplifies: on that occasion Trian

---

[419] Van der Elst and Lafarre, 'Blockchain and Smart Contracting' (n 403), stress the concept of power redistribution within the corporation also with reference to the manager–shareholder relationship. On the potential impact of technology on shareholder activism, see generally Anne Lafarre and Christoph Van der Elst, 'Blockchain Technology for Corporate Governance and Shareholder Activism' (2018) European Corporate Governance Institute (ECGI)—Law Working Paper No. 390/2018 <https://ssrn.com/abstract=3135209> accessed 11 April 2022.

Fund Management lost the votes of retail shareholders.[420] According to Jill Fisch, the mechanics of the voting process negatively affect the voting rate among retail investors, with institutional investors in a position to vote their stock much more easily and inexpensively than retail investors, due to third party servicers providing voting platforms that automate the voting process.[421] This suggests that some degree of technology already exists and is in use in the context of proxy voting.

However, the current technology, instead of increasing corporate democracy, contributes to discrimination against retail investors, who do not dispose of the same infrastructural facilitations as institutional investors. This problem emerged in the Concept Release on the US Proxy System, where the SEC explicitly mentioned the disparity between institutional investors and retail investors, and the need to provide retail investors with the same treatment of institutional investors.[422] In this respect, blockchain could emerge as an alternative system capable of democratizing technology, therefore reducing the disparity in treatment between retail investors and institutional investors.

A further consequence of implementing technology would be increased development of loyalty shares. Loyalty shares are an alternative to dual-class shares: while dual-class shares identify two different classes of shares as of the creation of the corporation, loyalty shares assign multiple voting rights that vary depending on the holding period.[423]. The difficulty in identifying which shareholders are entitled to more voting power when their shares are held in street name poses a challenge for corporations that want to introduce loyalty shares, and it can be a barrier to their implementation.[424] Only record holders of corporate shares are statutorily entitled to cast their votes, and when a shareholder holds their stock through a bank or broker, the company encounters significant obstacles in identifying the beneficial owner and tracking the duration of its possession of the stocks. A practical solution for companies is to treat all shares held in street name as low vote stock, with a great disparity negatively affecting those stockholders owning shares held in street name. In the current framework, loyalty shares do represent a further source of confusion and complication,[425] with many companies opting to rescind their tenure voting schemes.[426] In the future,

---

[420] Michael Flaherty, 'P&G, Peltz Vie for Small Investor Votes in Biggest-Ever Proxy Fight' (*Reuters*, 25 September 2017) <https://www.reuters.com/article/us-procter-gamble-trian-investors/pg-peltz-vie-for-small-investor-votes-in-biggest-ever-proxy-fight-idUSKCN1C01CW> accessed 11 April 2022. For an overview of these problems in the American system, see Jill E. Fisch, 'Standing Voting Instructions' (2017) 102 MinnLRev 11. For a historical approach, see also Jill E. Fisch, 'From Legitimacy to Logic: Reconstructing Proxy Regulation' (1993) 46 VandLRev 1129.

[421] Ibid.

[422] See SEC, 'Concept Release on the U.S. Proxy System' (Release No. 34-62495, 14 July 2010) <https://www.sec.gov/rules/concept/2010/34-62495.pdf> accessed 1 May 2023.

[423] See Berger et al., 'Tenure Voting' (n 306). See also Marco Becht, Yuliya Kamisarenka, and Anete Pajuste, 'Loyalty Shares with Tenure Voting—A Coasian Bargain? Evidence from the Loi Florange Experiment' (2018) European Corporate Governance Institute (ECGI) —Law Working Paper No. 398/2018 <https://ssrn.com/abstract=3166494> accessed 11 April 2022.

[424] Paul Edelman, Wei Jiang, and Randall S. Thomas, 'Will Tenure Voting Give Corporate Managers Lifetime Tenure?' 97 TexLRev 991 (2019).

[425] See Church & Dwight Co., 'Preliminary Proxy Statement' (3 April 2003) <https://investor.churchdwight.com/static-files/09f6df43-ffc1-4c0b-9167-c2b4df8ce142> accessed 11 April 2022.

[426] Lynne L. Dallas and Jordan M. Barry, 'Long-Term Shareholders and Time-Phased Voting' (2016) 40 DelJCorpL 541, 614–615.

the adoption of a more efficient framework could lead to an increase in the use of loyalty shares, indirectly favouring long-term shareholders' ownership.

3. Real-Time Monitoring

Blockchain has the potential to bring significant transformations, beyond the transparency of ownership and the voting phase. It might potentially affect the role of gatekeepers within corporations, in particular allowing for real-time monitoring for shareholders, and also contributing to a change to disclosure regulations.

As mentioned in Chapter 1, the credibility of gatekeepers in corporate law was a major issue, especially for auditing companies and CRAs, as significant corporate scandals, including Worldcom, Enron, and Parmalat, and the financial crisis of 2008 demonstrated. These events proved that the independence of auditors was under attack.[427] Furthermore, doubts as to the competence of CRAs and their methodologies for assessing the credit risk of structured products spread in the financial community and among policymakers.[428]

From a traditional principal–agent angle, gatekeepers (auditors, lawyers, securities analysts, and CRAs) serve as watchdogs for the public,[429] contributing to mitigate information asymmetry. Gatekeepers are in a position that allows them 'to acquire more information than the investing public has about an issuer's prospects and that provides them an opportunity to warn the public when that information is different than the impression given by management in the issuer's disclosures'.[430] For example, not even normal shareholders are in a position to verify that corporate documents, such as the annual balance sheets, provide a 'true and fair view' of the company.[431] Therefore, hiring an auditing company is the easiest way to supervise the management of the corporation and solve organizational problems that would otherwise be insurmountable if not delegated to external entities.

Scholars have advocated blockchain technology solutions for mitigating information asymmetry and the structural dependence on gatekeepers.[432] Blockchain

---

[427] Guido Ferrarini and Paolo Giudici, 'Financial Scandals and the Role of Private Enforcement: The Parmalat Case' (2005) European Corporate Governance Institute (ECGI)—Law Working Paper No. 40, 1 <https://ssrn.com/abstract=730403> accessed 11 April 2022. See generally John C. Coffee Jr., 'Understanding Enron: "It's the Gatekeepers, Stupid"' (2002) 57 BusLaw 1403. See also John C. Coffee, Jr., 'Gatekeeper Failure and Reform: The Challenge of Fashioning Relevant Reforms' in Klaus J. Hopt, Eddy Wymeersch, Hideki Kanda, and Harald Baum (eds), *Corporate Governance in Context: Corporations, States, and Markets in Europe, Japan, and the US* (OUP 2005). See also Frank Partnoy, 'Barbarians at the Gatekeepers? A Proposal for a Modified Strict Liability Regime' (2001) 79 WashULQ 491.

[428] See Aline Darbellay, *Regulating Credit Rating Agencies* (Elgar 2013) 31. See also SEC, *Summary Report of Issues Identified in the Commission Staff's Examinations of Select Credit Rating Agencies* (July 2008) 12 <https://www.sec.gov/news/studies/2008/craexamination070808.pdf> accessed 11 April 2022.

[429] See generally Coffee, *Gatekeepers* (n 271).

[430] Merritt B. Fox, 'Gatekeeper Failures: Why Important, What to Do' (2008) 106 MichLRev 1089, 1089.

[431] A true and fair view of the state of the company is a rather dynamic concept. See Lord Leonard Hoffmann QC and Mary Harden, 'Legal Opinion Obtained By Accounting Standards Committee of True and Fair View, with Particular Reference to the Role of Accounting Standards' (13 September 1983) <https://www.frc.org.uk/getattachment/afba0aa1-04fa-492a-beab-35918af6d97e/T-F-Opinon-13-September-1983.pdf> accessed 11 April 2022.

[432] See generally Yermack, 'Corporate Governance and Blockchains' (n 392). See also Ryan Lazanis, 'How Technology behind Bitcoin Could Transform Accounting As We Know It' (*Brainstation*, 22 January 2015) <https://www.borndigital.com/2015/01/22/how-technology-behind-bitcoin-could-transform-accounting-as-we-know-it-2015-01-22> accessed 11 April 2022. See also Enriques and Zetzsche, 'Corporate Technologies' (n 386) 68–69.

technology could be a tool for implementing real-time accounting and potentially contribute to removing the obstacles that currently impede consumers and shareholders from reading the financial statements of a company. In this way shareholders (and more generally investors) would no longer need to rely on auditors and managers.[433]

This could be part of a more general trend emerging in the new CorpTech scenario, with shareholders empowered with appropriate tools to 'fend for themselves'. One of the key promises of technology, in particular blockchain technology, is eliminating the need of gatekeepers as the sole (or in principle most efficient) tool for mitigating information asymmetry and more generally the traditional risks related to the principal–agent model.

A profound consequence of CorpTech could be the obsolescence of the traditional idea that the board of directors is a monitoring and mediating board.[434] An 'in principle' fully transparent organization would no longer need to rely on a board of directors overseeing the managers.[435] The mediating function of the board reposes on the existence of multiple competing instances within the corporation. In this context, the board is empowered with the right to decide the way duties and benefits among such competing interests are allocated within the corporation.[436] However, Enriques and Zetzsche challenge the possibility that technology will effectively change the centrality of the board, highlighting the flaws characterizing a more technological solution, in particular because of the risks that technology will likely replicate some of the problems of the traditional 'non-tech' corporate governance.[437]

4. A Hypothetical Blockchain-Based Infrastructure for Corporate Governance

Corporate governance operations require the interaction of fully automated operations with other 'manual operations' for executing some specific tasks. An example comes from corporate voting, which requires the identity verification of those who are entitled to vote and compiling the proxy statement (which is discretionary). These two operations cannot be entirely executed on blockchain ('on-chain') and therefore they will remain external operations ('off-chain').

The interaction between on-chain and off-chain operations means that an intermediary must implement blockchain technology for corporate governance, and in the context of some specific tasks (including the abovementioned example of voting) such intermediary will also act as a gatekeeper of a private (or permissioned) blockchain (infrastructure) for the company, the shareholders and their proxies.[438] As already mentioned, the need for an external gatekeeper (off-chain), does not undermine the concept of 'full disintermediation', and it is a common feature characterizing any network.[439]

---

[433] Yermack, 'Corporate Governance and Blockchains' (n 392) 24: 'Anyone could aggregate the firm's transactions into the form of an income statement and balance sheet at any time, and they would no longer need to rely on quarterly financial statements prepared by the firm and its auditors.'

[434] See Enriques and Zetzsche, 'Corporate Technologies' (n 386) 68 ff, 77 ff.

[435] Ibid, 70 ff.

[436] Raghuram G. Rajan and Luigi Zingales, 'Power in a Theory of the Firm' (1998) 113 QJEcon 387. See also Margaret M. Blair, 'Boards of Directors as Mediating Hierarchs' (2015) 38 SeattleULRev 297.

[437] Enriques and Zetzsche, 'Corporate Technologies'. (n 386) 77 ff.

[438] Bertsch, 'Remarks to the Advisory Committee' (n 316) 3.

[439] See Kevin Werbach, 'The Centripetal Network: How the Internet Holds Itself Together, and the Forces Tearing It Apart' (2009) 42 UCDavisLRev 343 (hereafter Werbach, 'The Centripetal Network').

Private and public blockchain have advantages and disadvantages. A permissioned blockchain restricts ledger management to trusted participants (authorized nodes),[440] who keep distributed identical copies of ledgers.[441] This restriction to a closed circle of authorized actors has the advantage that the validation process does not require a computationally intensive mining process, detrimental for both energy and computing resources; on the contrary, the validating nodes have only to check the validity of any transaction with no mining tasks involved, resulting in a faster process where operating costs are lower.[442] Furthermore, permissioned blockchain has fewer risks of cyberattacks and security breaches.[443] Therefore, a permissioned blockchain would be particularly effective to keep track of asset ownership, confidential documents, post-trading, and settlement of transactions. Corda is an example of permissioned blockchain, where only legitimated parties share the individual ledger data in Corda.[444]

Issuing e-shares is the first step in executing corporate governance on a blockchain infrastructure. In 2015, Overstock was the first company that issued e-shares after the SEC authorized this operation. Overstock's Form S-3 filed with the SEC is extremely helpful to understand how digital securities (in particular e-shares) would work, and how more generally this would affect the overall corporate governance.

An external gatekeeper in charge of accomplishing off-chain tasks is essential in both the processes of issuing e-shares and voting. This external gatekeeper (and service provider) would be the developer and, at the current technological stage, the network operator of the blockchain. As already mentioned, although part of the process is necessarily executed off-chain, this does not undermine the concept of 'full decentralization' (generally associated with blockchain), as the existence of some centralized points is a common characteristic of any decentralized network.[445]

Overstock's external gatekeeper, Pro Securities, is in charge of many tasks. As mentioned above, Overstock's digital securities are traded on a closed-system trading platform [alternative trading system, ATS] ... maintained by Pro Securities ... [and] a person wishing to engage in [Overstock's] digital securities will be required to open an online brokerage account with the sole broker dealer licensed to provide access to the Pro Securities ATS digital securities trading platform with respect to Overstock digital securities.[446]

On Overstock's broker-dealer's interface investors 'directly purchase and sell' digital securities, that are held in the customer's name, with no 'street name' option.[447,448] Furthermore, Overstock's design includes a unique feature where a single broker-dealer is licensed to provide access to the Pro Securities ATS digital securities trading

---

[440] See Hong Kong Applied Science & Technology Research Institute, 'Whitepaper on Distributed Ledger Technology' (2016) 5 <https://www.hkma.gov.hk/media/eng/doc/key-functions/financial-infrastructure/Whitepaper_On_Distributed_Ledger_Technology.pdf> accessed 4 April 2022.
[441] Ibid, 11.
[442] Ibid.
[443] Ibid.
[444] Ibid.
[445] See Werbach, 'The Centripetal Network' (n 439).
[446] Overstock, 'Prospectus' (n 305).
[447] Ibid.
[448] Ibid.

platform for its digital securities.[449] As a result, underwriters of any offerings are required to open brokerage accounts with the same broker-dealer[450] to directly buy and sell Overstock's digital securities in their own name, not in street name.[451]

Furthermore, Pro Securities ATS maintains an electronic database using a proprietary ledger to record all transactions, providing a definitive electronic publication of ownership,[452] and allowing the implementation of a full book-entry system.

Overstock is also a good example with regard to the relationship between the blockchain technology and shareholder voting. The distributed ledger records the company's beneficial owners and their holdings at a predetermined record date, and efficiently conducts data management, precisely defining each shareholders entitlements (i.e. voting rights, right to view proxy materials, or right to submit a shareholder proposal subject to ownership thresholds).[453] In the proximity of a shareholders' meeting, the gatekeeper uploads the company's proxy materials to the shareholders, who have instant and simultaneous access to the documents.[454] The platform allocates votes subject to the company's capital structure and voting rights, therefore shareholders know exactly how many votes they control before casting them.[455] Before the meeting, the individual shareholder or a designated proxy executing the votes is responsible for authenticating the voters' personal identity with the gatekeeper. Typically, this operation occurs off-chain, and the gatekeeper keeps records of the authentication and proceeds with the creation of a digital ID for each shareholder or proxy.[456] Then, shareholders and proxies execute voting instructions (on-chain) over the blockchain and cast the allocated votes for each proposal. The blockchain automatically provides the voting instructions and verification that the votes are counted back to each shareholder, an immediate and accurate end-to-end confirmation and tabulation. Furthermore, anonymity of the vote is safeguarded, because neither the company nor other shareholders have access to the identity of other shareholders, and the properties of blockchain (the 'consensus' mechanism leading to the immutability of the ledger) guarantees that votes cannot be removed or altered.[457]

5. Potential Problems of a Blockchain Solution

Blockchain infrastructures for corporate governance present both technical and corporate governance problems. Two main technical issues are scalability and interoperability. These aspects will be treated in Subsection IV.C.5.a.

Furthermore, other major concerns could potentially be related to the governance of the blockchain infrastructure. There are many governance-related problems, including: (1) defining the rules and procedures necessary to initiating and managing blockchain infrastructure with regard to a broad and heterogeneous range of issues

---

[449] Ibid.
[450] Ibid. See also generally Ryan and Donohue, 'Securities on Blockchain' (n 313).
[451] Ibid, 34.
[452] Ibid.
[453] Bertsch, 'Remarks to the Advisory Committee' (n 316) 3.
[454] Ibid.
[455] Ibid.
[456] Ibid.
[457] Ibid.

(such as 'network membership, management of permissions, transaction validity, issuance of new assets and their tokenisation, dispute resolution, software updates, regulatory reporting, and protection against cyber risks');[458] (2) the ownership of the gatekeeper managing the platform in the context of private (permissioned) blockchain platforms; and (3) issues related to security and cyberattacks. Although pilot projects and private initiatives promise to develop reliable DLT infrastructures, there are no accepted standards and governance risks may still be significant. Subsections IV.C.5.ii and IV.C.5.iii will focus on points (2) and (3).

a. Technical issues: scalability and interoperability

Two main issues are scalability and interoperability. Scalability relates to the general characteristic of a process, network, software, or organization to grow and manage increased demand, and represents an advantage due to the adaptability to the changing needs or demands of its users or clients, and a sign of stability and competitiveness due to the ability to manage an influx of demand, increased productivity, trends, changing needs, and even the presence or introduction of new competitors.[459]

While scalability represents an advantage, it may generate problems for blockchain infrastructures, which require the constant expansion of ledger sizes and storage capacity. In particular, public (permissionless) blockchain requires that every user store an immutable copy of the ledger, as part of the integrity mechanism corresponding to full global verifiability.[460]

However, a blockchain infrastructure for corporate governance would be more easily structured as a private (permissioned) blockchain. Although a private blockchain would require less storage (because there is no need to store an immutable copy of the ledger for each user), constantly increasing the information to be stored would require ever-increased ledger sizes. It is uncertain whether existing technology would be capable of accommodating these needs or whether quantum computing will be required.

Another nuance of blockchain for corporate governance is the problem of the interoperability of different blockchain infrastructures, that is, coordination between different entities that are part of the infrastructural environment connected to corporate stocks, such as stock exchanges and institutions involved in the post-trading phase. The creation of a unique platform for all these entities is unlikely to happen. Although at the very beginning of the debate surrounding blockchain technology, the idea of 'one blockchain to rule them all' was considered an option, the gradual implementation of blockchain technology led to the emergence of a more fragmented scenario for both private and public blockchain. This fragmentation depended on the different designing options that each developer and entrepreneur decided to adopt in relation

---

[458] See OECD, 'Blockchain Technology and Corporate Governance' (6 June 2018) 21 <http://www.oecd.org/officialdocuments/publicdisplaydocumentpdf/?cote=DAF/CA/CG/RD(2018)1/REV1&docLanguage=En> accessed 11 April 2022 (hereafter OECD, 'Blockchain Technology').

[459] See Techopedia, 'What Does Scalability Mean?' (27 January 2017) <https://www.techopedia.com/definition/9269/scalability> accessed 11 April 2022.

[460] OECD, 'Blockchain Technology' (n 458).

to its needs for security, privacy, efficiency, flexibility, and platform complexity.[461] As a consequence, the problem of coordinating the different chains became real.

Interoperability between different blockchains is an opportunity for different technology infrastructures to be operationally integrated. To understand this concept, an example from cryptocurrencies can be helpful: 'Bitcoin can't speak the language of Ethereum and vice versa. This means we can't spend Bitcoin on the Ethereum network, nor can we make use of Ethereum's smart contracts on the Bitcoin network.'[462] Therefore, interoperability between different infrastructures is the precondition to effectively change the existing process, which would otherwise remain extremely fragmented. It is obvious that a proxy-voting system where each entity involved develops its own blockchain technology would not solve any existing problem and would be a 'blockchained' copy of the existing fragmented proxy-voting system.

There are different ways to implement interoperability between different blockchain infrastructures: centralized or multisignature (multisig) notary schemes,[463] employing a trusted federation to carry out an action on chain B when some event on chain A takes place; sidechains[464] in association to relays[465] where relays enable sidechains to validate events on another chain;[466] hash-locking, implementing a system where operations on different blockchains have the same trigger, generally the

---

[461] See Vitalik Buterin, 'Chain Interoperability' (9 September 2016) <https://allquantor.at/blockchainbib/pdf/vitalik2016chain.pdf> accessed 11 April 2022 (hereafter Buterin, 'Chain Interoperability').

[462] Aleks Larsen, 'A Primer on Blockchain Interoperability' (*Medium*, 20 December 2018) <https://medium.com/blockchain-capital-blog/a-primer-on-blockchain-interoperability-e132bab805b> accessed 11 April 2022 (hereafter Larsen, 'Blockchain Interoperability').

[463] For an explanation of the multi-sig structure, see Ben Davenport, 'What Is Multi-Sig, and What Can It Do?' (*Coincenter*, 15 January 2015) <https://www.coincenter.org/education/advanced-topics/multi-sig/> accessed 11 April 2022: 'Since early 2012, Bitcoin has had an alternative to single-key addresses. Around that time, a new type of address called pay-to-script-hash (P2SH) was defined and standardized. P2SH addresses can be recognized by the fact that they begin with a "3" instead of a "1." Among the functionality supported by P2SH addresses is the ability to require multiple private keys in order to transact, known as multi-signature, or more commonly, multi-sig. A P2SH address can support arbitrary sets of N keys, any M of which are required to transact—this is commonly referred to as 'M-of-N.' In practice, the blockchain does enforce some limits as to the size of N, and by far the most typical multi-sig implementations are of the form 2-of-2 or 2-of-3. (Note that using this terminology, a single-key address would be considered 1-of-1.) The easiest real-world analogy for explaining multi-sig is a safe deposit box with 2 keys, one held by the customer, the other held by the bank. In order to open the box, both keys are required, making a safe deposit box analogous to a 2-of-2 multi-sig address.'

[464] For an overview of sidechains, see Keerthi Nelaturu, 'Blockchain Interoperability—Sidechains' (*Medium*, 1 August 2018) <https://medium.com/coinmonks/blockchain-interoperability-sidechains-e8204b8c2a10> accessed 11 April 2022. As the author explains, 'sidechains are secondary blockchains, that steer alongside a main chain like Bitcoin, Ethereum etc. They are chains pegged to the main chain which enables reading data, interpreting data from main chain and also the exchange of asset from main chain to sidechain and back. Sidechains can have their own consensus algorithms and tokens. They have to be maintained by their own miners, miners on main chain are not responsible for the maintenance of sidechains.'

[465] O'Reilly defines relays as a 'more direct method for facilitating interoperability, where instead of relying on trusted intermediaries to provide information about one blockchain to another, the blockchains effectively take on the task of doing that themselves.' See O'Reilly, 'Sidechains or Relays' <https://www.oreilly.com/library/view/blockchain-for-enterprise/9781788479745/6326eb12-e7d6-4752-be7c-edb74cb66b3d.xhtml> accessed 11 April 2022. See also Martin Westerkamp and Jacob Eberhardt, 'zkRelay: Facilitating Sidechains using zkSNARK-based Chain-Relays' (2020) <https://eprint.iacr.org/2020/433.pdf> accessed 11 April 2022.

[466] As Westerkamp and Eberhardt explain, 'the target ledger replicates the consensus mechanism of the source blockchain in order to incorporate events that took place on the source ledger'. Ibid, 2.1.

revelation of the preimage of a particular hash.[467] However, they are limited to use in a public blockchain, whereas platforms developed for corporate voting should be private. Furthermore, the vast majority of applications based on these interoperability chains are in the field of payment systems.

An experiment conducted by Broadridge and ICJ Inc., a joint venture of Broadridge and the Tokyo Stock Exchange, Inc. (TSE), revealed that the problem of interoperability seemed successfully solved. The experiment created a first 'Proof of Concept' of an interoperable blockchain-based proxy voting in Japan, which is similar to the American system in that there are numerous players in the chain of custody.[468] Although these results seem encouraging, it will be important to consider the relevance of interoperability at a higher level in order to pursue a full integration between corporations, custodians, clearing-houses, and exchanges. A useful example in existing cryptoeconomy comes from the vast majority of decentralized exchange protocols that operate only with tokens sharing the same technical implementation and built on the same distributed ledger platform.[469]

Interoperability also refers to the possibility of coordinating on-chain and off-chain actions, since non-coordination can be a major problem in corporate voting.[470] In 2019 Google proposed an integrated system relying on Google Cloud and Ethereum to increase interoperability, facilitating 'bidirection interoperation'. One of the foundational characteristics of a business process designed as a smart contract is the 'on-chain' performance, where the access to off-chain inputs is essential to increasing its utility. As Google explains, 'To close the loop and allow bidirectional interoperation, we need to be not only making blockchain data programmatically available to cloud services, but also cloud services programmatically available on-chain to smart contracts'.[471]

While interoperability has generally triggered concerns in relation to antitrust law,[472] additional issues emerge when taking into account the relationship between interoperability and blockchain service providers as a main obligation for such service providers. In this ambit, interoperability is not yet characterized as an obligation for service providers. Therefore, at the time of writing there is a relevant inconsistency with previous regulation in other fields related to network services. For example, in Europe, Directive of 11 December 2018 establishing the European Electronic Communications Code[473] highlights the importance of interoperability for public

---

[467] See Buterin, 'Chain Interoperability' (n 461) and Larsen, 'Blockchain Interoperability' (n 462).

[468] Broadridge, 'ICJ and Broadridge Execute the First Blockchain-Based Interoperable Proxy Voting Process in Japan' (14 January 2019) <https://www.broadridge.com/intl/press-release/2019/icj-and-broadridge-execute-the-proxy-voting-process> accessed 11 April 2022.

[469] See Lindsay X. Lin, 'Deconstructing Decentralized Exchanges' (2019) 2 StanJBlockchainL&Pol'y 58.

[470] See Section I.A.

[471] See Google Cloud, 'Building Hybrid Blockchain/Cloud Applications with Ethereum and Google Cloud' (13 June 2019) <https://cloud.google.com/blog/products/data-analytics/building-hybrid-blockchain-cloud-applications-with-ethereum-and-google-cloud> accessed 11 April 2022.

[472] Dirk A. Zetzsche, Ross P. Buckley, and Douglas W. Arner, 'The Distributed Liability of Distributed Ledgers: Legal Risks of Blockchain' (2018) 4 IllinoisLRev 1361, 1401 (hereafter Zetzsche et al., 'Distributed Liability'). This is a common and established problem related to innovation. For example, for an analysis of artificial intelligence from the same perspective, see Ariel Ezrachi and Maurice E. Stucke, 'Artificial Intelligence & Collusion: When Computers Inhibit Competition' (2017) 2017 IllinoisLRev 1775.

[473] Directive (EU) 2018/1972 of 11 December 2018 establishing the European Electronic Communications Code (Recast) [2018] OJ L 321/36.

electronic communications networks in the context of post-trading. Here, much emphasis emerges in relation to interoperability, with member states in a position to encourage interoperability and, under specific circumstances, impose 'obligations on relevant providers of number-independent interpersonal communications services which reach a significant level of coverage and user uptake, to make their services interoperable'.[474] Another example comes from Regulation (EU) No. 909/2014 requiring that a CSD gives access to another CSD or to other market infrastructures.[475]

With regard to interoperability and blockchain, the European Commission has emphasized 'the importance of standards in promoting blockchain technology and the need of a global engagement to pursue this goal.[476] Furthermore, the EU Regulation on a Pilot Regime for Market Infrastructures Based on DLT[477] establishes that ESMA shall present a report to the European Commission on 'any issues relating to interoperability between DLT market infrastructures and other infrastructures using legacy systems'.[478] Importantly, recital 25 referring to interoperability in the context of CSD highlights that '[t]he access to a CSD operating a DLT SS ("settlement system") can be ... burdensome or difficult to achieve, as the interoperability of legacy systems with DLT has not been tested yet.'[479]

With regard to blockchain, excluding the possibility of characterizing it as a 'product' under European law, a better qualification is the one of a 'usable and accessible service for users that is achieved through decentralised platforms'.[480] Adhering to this second possibility, European law currently does not regulate such services at the supranational level. Therefore, in the current situation, end-users are exposed to interoperability and cybersecurity issues (as in the case of a cyberattack), although such very concrete threats should be more logically and fairly allocated to the blockchain service providers.[481]

---

[474] Ibid, art 63, para 2, 1 c.
[475] Regulation (EU) 909/2014 of 23 July 2014 on improving securities settlement in the European Union and on central securities depositories [2014] OJ L 257/1.
[476] European Commission, 'Shaping Digital Future—Blockchain Strategy' (last update 27 February 2023) <https://ec.europa.eu/digital-single-market/en/blockchain-technologies> accessed 1 May 2023.
[477] EU Pilot Regime on DLT (n 283).
[478] Ibid, art 14, 1 j.
[479] Ibid, recital 36.
[480] See Luigi Buonanno, 'Civil Liability in the Era of New Technology: The Influence of Blockchain Blockchain as the Backbone of a New Technology-based Civil Liability Regime' (2019) European Law Institute <https://www.europeanlawinstitute.eu/fileadmin/user_upload/p_eli/YLA_Award/Submission_ELI_Young_Lawyers_Award_Luigi_Buonanno_ELI_2019.pdf> accessed 11 April 2022 (hereafter Buonanno, 'Civil Liability'). Adhering to the conceptualization of a blockchain platform as 'a shared and synchronised digital database that is maintained by an algorithm and stored on multiple nodes'—as defined by Michelle Finck, *Blockchain Regulation and Governance In Europe* (CUP 2018) 6—the author considers that a possible characterization of a blockchain platform under European law might be that of 'a product or service made available to the community by some platforms or protocols', opening to the possibility to apply the regulation provided for product liability, that is, Directive 85/374/EEC of 25 July 1985 on the approximation of the laws, regulations and administrative provisions of the member states concerning liability for defective products [1985] OJ L210/29. However, this characterization shall be excluded, leaving blockchain platforms currently unregulated under European law.
[481] Buonanno, 'Civil Liability' (n 480) 11. Zetzsche et al., 'Distributed Liability' (n 472), identify five groups of DLT:

> (1) the core group that sets-up the code design and (*de facto*) governs the distributed ledger, for instance by having the technical ability and opinion leadership to prompt a 'hard fork' of the

Some authors proposed the creation of a strict liability regime, which would trigger the compensation of end-users suffering this kind of malfunction.[482] Such strict liability regime should be coupled with an obligation for the blockchain service provider to be insured against this kind of damage, because of the systematic relationship between such services and this kind of risk.[483] Other scholars have emphasized the importance of case law for shaping the standards, the scope and thresholds leading to a breach of service providers' duty of care with regard to tort law when breach of contract is not a viable solution, or contractual breaches where possible.[484] Such authors also agree with the existence of an operational risk, which would require the need to 'establish a DLT-related risk budget, enter into insurance, or limit DLT participation to very large and established counterparties'.[485]

b. Security and cyberattacks

As mentioned in Chapter 2,[486] the case of The DAO epitomizes the difficulties that designing a blockchain infrastructure may encounter, with the security breach arisen from a failure in designing the infrastructure.

Not only may security risks originate from a bug in the design of the code. Uncertainties related to the security of the platform still persist. The classic attacks on crypto-exchanges and other infrastructures confirm the difficulty of properly identifying and assessing potentially new risks in this area.

A new form of attack is the so-called Dark Dao, which attacks a currency or enforces an information asymmetry, with the DAO's creator unable to 'determine the DAO's number of participants, the total amount of money pledged to the attack, or the precise logic of the attack'.[487] While Dark Daos are generally associated with public (permissionless) blockchain, it is uncertain whether they may act in private (permissioned) blockchain as well.

With regard to the liability regime for the service provider in relation to security issues, similar concerns consistent with the previous analysis on interoperability apply.[488]

---

system (under certain conditions); (2) the owners of additional servers running the distributed ledger code for validation purposes (such as Bitcoin nodes = owners, Ripple validation nodes (3) 'qualified users' of the distributed ledger, such as exchanges, lending institutions, miners etc; and (4) 'simple users' of the system, such as owners of Bitcoin, Ether or investors in the DAO; (5) third parties affected by the system without directly relying on the technology, for instance counterparties of, and banks lending to 'simple users', clients of intermediaries that clear their financial assets via DLT, clients of brokers that hold virtual currency on behalf of clients, etc.

[482] Ibid.
[483] Ibid.
[484] See Zetzsche et al., 'Distributed Liability' (n 472) 1398.
[485] Ibid, 1404.
[486] See Chapter 2, Section I.B.
[487] Philip Daian, Tyler Kell, Ian Miers, and Ari Juels, 'On-Chain Vote Buying and the Rise of Dark DAOs' (*Hacking Distributed*, 2 July 2018), <http://hackingdistributed.com/2018/07/02/on-chain-vote-buying/> accessed 11 April 2022.
[488] For a comparative analysis under French civil law, Germanic civil law, and common law, see Zetzsche et al., 'Distributed Liability' (n 472) 1391–1403.

c. New gatekeepers?

Assuming that corporations would opt for permissioned (blockchain) infrastructures, in addition to security they pose a problem related to who should be responsible for developing and maintaining such infrastructures. A hypothesis could be the emergence of a new category of gatekeepers. Operating an entire infrastructure means having access to a significant amount of company-sensitive data (such as but not limited to ownership).

An important question is whether the gatekeeper should be internal to the company, or rather an external service provider. While this option may bring more guarantees about the neutrality of the platform, for example from any undue influence or pressure of the board of directors, an 'internal gatekeeper' would have the advantage of not sharing any company's sensitive information with any external entity, privileging the overall 'privacy' of the company. External vs internal gatekeepers and their liability is a topical issue in corporate law and financial law.

As mentioned earlier, a typical example of the role of gatekeepers in a corporation's life is that of hiring lawyers, accounting firms, and investment banks in the context of business transactions.[489] As opposed to the negotiation of a deal, involving an intermediary directly acting as a gatekeeper for managing the overall blockchain infrastructure of the corporation would mean involving such entity in all the operations of the company.

In this context, the external gatekeeper would be in charge of providing a technical service related to maintaining an infrastructure and its ledger. At the current stage, the external gatekeeper would develop the technology and serve as a network operator. In the future, the tasks of a network operator may be distinct from those of a developing entity.

The novelty of the blockchain environment and the lack of standards in this specific field does not allow the identification of any specific requirement, or a list of reputed actors. The properties of the blockchain ledger—in particular its immutability and the characteristic of being theoretically tamper-proof—are guarantees against any voluntary or involuntary act leading to the alteration of specific actions or information within the company. However, it is uncertain whether a gatekeeper may have any active or even an inactive role in designing, providing, and managing a blockchain infrastructure, and this might affect corporate democracy.

D. The Impulse to the Development of Tokenized Crypto-Assets

A major contribution of ICOs is their great impulse to the development of crypto-assets, beyond the securities world, and their process of tokenization.

---

[489] See Andrew F. Tuch, 'Multiple Gatekeepers' (2010) 96 VaLRev 1583, 1585. The literature on gatekeepers in corporate governance is vast. *Ex multis*, see Coffee, *Gatekeepers* (n 272). See also Stephen Choi, 'Market Lessons for Gatekeepers' (1998) 92 NwULRev 916, focusing on the accuracy of gatekeepers. See also Reinier H. Kraakman, 'Corporate Liability Strategies and the Costs of Legal Controls' (1984) 93 YaleLJ 857, 890.

1. Crypto-Assets

Crypto-assets refer to a heterogeneous class of assets, including, depending on the countries, different categories of tokens. As mentioned above,[490] FINMA identified three categories, including security tokens, utility tokens, and asset tokens, which represent assets, such as debt or equity claims on the issuer.[491] Additionally, in the amendments regarding the Federal Debt Collection and Bankruptcy Act (Banking Act), the DLT Law employs the term 'crypto-based assets'. According to the Federal Council, those crypto-based assets in Article 242a of the Banking Act include all assets where the power of disposal is exclusively conveyed through a crypto access procedure.[492] Furthermore, it clarifies that the term 'crypto-based assets' was employed to avoid issues in distinguishing between different token categories.[493]

Germany proposed a definition of crypto-assets that is broad enough to cover both cryptocurrencies and asset-backed digital assets, and most likely utility tokens and hybrid tokens.[494]

In France the Loi Pacte employs the locution '*actifs numeriques*' (digital assets) to refer to ICO tokens and virtual currencies and potentially extends to tokens related to other industries (retail, transportation, healthcare, media, etc). It includes: (i) tokens and virtual currencies within the meaning of European law, apart from those that can be assimilated to financial instruments; and (ii) any digital representation of a value that is not issued or guaranteed by a central bank or a public authority, is not necessarily attached to a currency being legal tender, and does not have the legal status of a currency, but which is accepted by natural or legal persons as a means of exchange and can be transferred, stored, or exchanged electronically. After the Loi Pacte, French regulators employed the term 'crypto-assets', consistent with the vast majority of European countries and the European Union.

The heterogeneity of crypto-assets emerges also when taking into account the definition proposed in MiCAR[495] and the American SEC. The latter employs (again) the term 'digital asset' to refer to an asset that is issued and transferred using distributed ledger or blockchain technology, including, but not limited to, so-called virtual currencies, coins, and tokens.[496]

The terms 'crypto-assets' and 'digital assets' are not legally and technically equivalent: crypto-assets are possibly a sub-category of the broader 'digital asset' category, which should encompass any digital representation of an asset, therefore not limited

---

[490] See Section II.C.
[491] FINMA, 'Guidelines for ICOs' (n 148).
[492] Botschaft zum Bundesgesetz (n 341) 245.
[493] Ibid.
[494] For the purposes of the German Banking Act, a crypto-asset 'is a digital representation of value which has neither been issued nor guaranteed by a central bank or public body; it does not have the legal status of currency or money but, on the basis of an agreement or actual practice, is accepted by natural or legal persons as a means of exchange or payment or serves investment purposes; it can be transferred, stored and traded by electronic means'. See BaFin, 'Guidance notice—guidelines concerning the statutory definition of crypto custody business (section 1 (1a) sentence 2 no. 6 of the German Banking Act (Kreditwesengesetz–KWG)' (2020) <https://www.bafin.de/SharedDocs/Veroeffentlichungen/EN/Merkblatt/mb_200302_kryptoverwahrgeschaeft_en.html> accessed 11 April 2022.
[495] See Section II.B.
[496] See SEC, 'Framework for 'Investment Contract' Analysis of Digital Assets' (3 April 2019) <https://www.sec.gov/files/dlt-framework.pdf> accessed 11 April 2022.

to the blockchain/tokenized ones. However, the industry employs the labels 'crypto-assets' and 'digital assets' as essentially equivalent, and they are both increasingly associated with the concept of 'tokenization'.

As mentioned above, the tokenization of assets is the process of issuing a blockchain token that is a digital representation of real assets.[497] The tokenization of assets provides greater liquidity for securities as well as other specific assets that are illiquid by nature, such as fine art, in an attempt to increase the liquidity in such markets as well as the tradability in secondary markets. Furthermore, it is a faster and cheaper framework for transactions, and it promises to be more transparent and inclusive since it increases the opportunities to invest reduced amounts in assets generally precluded to a wide audience.[498]

The Token and Trustworthy Technology Service Providers Act adopted in Liechtenstein is extremely important because it is one of the very first attempts to conceptualize and regulate the tokenization of real assets. A key pillar of the new law is the Token Container Model (TCM).[499] The definition of token offered by the new law is very broad, and it refers to 'a piece of information on a TT [Trustworthy Technology] System which: 1. can represent claims or rights of memberships against a person, rights to property or other absolute or relative rights; and 2. is assigned to one or more TT identifiers'.[500] This broad definition offers the opportunity to use the token as a container in the sense that it has 'the ability to hold rights of all kinds [and] can be loaded with a right that represents a real asset such as real estate, stocks, bonds, gold, access rights, money ... [as well as being] empty, as in the case of digital code'.[501]

The advantage of this approach is the ability to separate (i) the right and the asset from (ii) the token that is running on the blockchain, therefore differentiating law and technology.[502] Liechtenstein's conceptualization is extremely important for understanding where the fundamental changes happen. They do not affect the rights and assets (and their legal framework) but rather the way such rights and assets are represented in a token. This latter aspect is the one requiring major legal adaptations.

In Switzerland three major projects for the tokenization of 'digital assets' have taken place, under the impulse of SEBA,[503] Sygnum's Digital Asset Trading Facility,[504] and Six Digital Exchange (in partnership with SBI).[505]

---

[497] Wyoleg, 'Tokenization of Assets' (n 299300).
[498] Ibid.
[499] Philipp Sandner, 'Liechtenstein Blockchain Act: How Can Nearly Any Right and Therefore Any Asset Be Tokenized based on the Token Container Model?' (*Medium*, 9 October 2019) <https://philippsandner.medium.com/liechtenstein-blockchain-act-how-can-nearly-any-right-and-therefore-any-asset-be-tokenized-based-389fc9f039b1> accessed 11 April 2022 (hereafter Sandner, 'Liechtenstein Blockchain Act').
[500] Liechtenstein Law on Tokens and TT Service Providers 2019 (*Liechtensteinisches Gesetz über Token und VT-Dienstleister LGBl 2019 Nr. 301, LR 950.6*) art 2, 1 c.
[501] Sandner, 'Liechtenstein Blockchain Act' (n 499).
[502] Ibid.
[503] Christian Gundiuc, 'Swiss Digital Bank Tackles Asset Tokenization for Fully Compliant Institutions' (*Securities*, 16 July 2020) <https://www.securities.io/swiss-digital-bank-tackles-asset-tokenization-for-fully-compliant-institutions/> accessed 11 April 2022.
[504] Sygnum, 'Sygnum's Digital Asset Trading Facility (OTF) Gets Regulatory Clearance from FINMA' (1 September 2020) <https://www.insights.sygnum.com/post/sygnum-s-digital-asset-trading-facility-otf-gets-regulatory-clearance-from-finma> accessed 11 April 2022.
[505] SIX, 'SIX and SBI Digital Asset Holdings Announce Plans for Singapore-Based Joint Exchange Venture' (8 December 2020) <https://www.six-group.com/en/newsroom/media-releases/2020/20201208-six-sbi-jev.html> accessed 26 April 2023.

The developments in the context of crypto-assets and digital assets will be the subject of Chapters 4 and 5.

Chapter 4 will focus on the tokenization of money, focusing on both private initiatives (which are part of a network labelled as shadow central banking) and public initiatives on the side of central banks, keen to issue tokenized fiat currencies, commonly known as CBDCs, as a reaction to the developments in the private sector.

Crypto-assets will be further developed in Chapter 5, showing how they will likely be the basis for new implementation at the level of financial networks, in the context of crypto shadow banking. Crypto shadow banking is a new label referring to the way market actors are replicating in the cryptoeconomy some of the structures already existing in traditional shadow banking.[506] Crypto-assets share significant similarities and risks with those illiquid assets that are generally 'securitized' as part of securitizations (or, as some commentators argued, with high-yield bonds spreading in leveraged finance)[507] within the shadow banking system. Adopting this angle, Chapter 5 will explicitly consider the similarities between tokenization and securitization.

2. NFTs

Similar to the symbolic relevance that ICOs had for the development of cryptofinance and DeFi, NFTs could be the tool for popularizing the debate on future technological developments, including the metaverse. This paragraph sheds light on this new phenomenon, while highlighting the similarities with the problems surrounding the evolution of ICOs.

a. Key characteristics

Non-fungible tokens, NFTs, are driving the development of DeFi and will likely play a pivotal role in the construction and development of the metaverse. NFTs are crypto-assets with specific characteristics. Like any other crypto-asset, NFTs are programmable units of data recorded on a blockchain or any other distributed ledger, digitally tradable or transferable.[508] They act as a representation of value, rights, or assets (either digital or physical) and are often associated with a licence providing the purpose and length of time for which the asset can be used.[509]

In addition, NFTs have peculiar features distinguishing them from traditional crypto-assets. NFTs are non-fungible cryptographic tokens; they are unique in value and cannot be mutually interchangeable. 'Fungibility' identifies the characteristic of an asset to be easily exchangeable with something of equal value.[510] For example, one

---

[506] For an analysis of traditional shadow banking, see Chapter 1.

[507] See Constantin Kurbatov, 'Tokenized Assts vs. High-Yield Bonds: Which Is the New Way to Increase Trust While Decrease Costs?' (*yahoo!finance*, 4 January 2018) <https://uk.news.yahoo.com/tokenized-asstes-vs-high-yield-143510373.html> accessed 11 April 2022.

[508] See Chiomenti, Cuatrecasas, Gide Loyrette Nouel, Gleiss Lutz, 'NFT: Cross-Border Perspectives on Unprecedented Regulatory Challenges' (February 2022) <https://www.gide.com/sites/default/files/nft_-_european_network_3.pdf> accessed 11 April 2022 (hereafter Chiomenti et al., 'NFT: Cross-Border Perspectives').

[509] See Andres Guadamuz, 'The Treachery of Images: Non-Fungible Tokens and Copyright' (2021) 16 JIPLP 1367, 1368–1376.

[510] Cornell Law School—Legal Information Institute, 'Fungible Things' (July 2021) <https://www.law.cornell.edu/wex/fungible_things> accessed 11 April 2022.

dollar bill, one Bitcoin, or one Tesla stock is indistinguishable and can be replaced with another dollar bill, Bitcoin, or Tesla stock. On the other hand, Banksy's *balloon girl* or a tailor-made diamond suit would be virtually impossible to substitute with an asset that is identical in all respects. To achieve non-fungibility, NFTs rely on technical standards allowing their individual identification on the blockchain where they are registered; therefore their characteristic of being individually identifiable does not depend on their quantity, but rather on their design.[511] Non-fungibility is complemented by indivisibility and scarcity.

Significant legal and economic consequences descend from NFTs' intrinsic non-fungibility. Non-fungibility is functional to demonstrate the authenticity and the ownership of any underlying asset, and this is a source of their value. Certainly, NFTs derive their value from their intrinsic scarcity, with NFT creators able to limit the number of outstanding NFTs. However, the nexus with the 'property' in the NFT is a key driver for the market value of NFTs,[512] both for digital art and gaming artefacts as well as in real-world assets. In the two scenarios, NFTs generate value, and offer the possibility to transfer or even fractionalize them,[513] as the new class of so-called fractional non-fungible tokens (F-NFTs) proves. F-NFTs are created starting from a whole NFT, which is divided into a number of shares, sold for a fixed price, and sold on secondary markets for a fixed price, without affecting the value of the original NFT.[514] This possibility to fractionalize them likely affects their characterization under securities laws. For example, MiCAR does not recognize fractional parts of a unique and non-fungible crypto-asset as unique and not fungible themselves. This makes F-NFTs more likely than NFTs to qualify as financial instruments under EU law.[515]

The accessibility and modishness of the concept, paired with the benefits of blockchain traceability, led to a spiralling expansion of the NFT market, which encompasses digital collectibles (e.g., digital images, videos, audio samples, domain names), artworks, legal deeds, in-game items, and anything that can be developed within the nascent metaverse.[516] While the metaverse market is in its infancy, NFTs are emerging as a relevant component of its economy. Users can in fact showcase their assets in the metaverse and NFTs allow the establishment of a property system; therefore the value of the metaverse and the NFT market are reaching mutual dependency. Beyond avatar fashion and merchandise,[517] one of the most relevant use-cases of metaverse NFTs is

---

[511] Chiomenti et al., 'NFT: Cross-border Perspectives' (n 508) 2.
[512] Iris H-Y Chiu and Jason G. Allen, 'Exploring the Assetisation and Financialisation of Non-Fungible Tokens (NFTs): Opportunities and Regulatory Implications' (2022) 37 Bank&FinLRev 401.
[513] Ibid.
[514] Bybit, 'Explained: Fractional NFTs (F-NFTs) and How They Work' (9 February 2022) <https://learn.bybit.com/nft/what-are-fractional-nfts/> accessed 11 April 2022.
[515] MiCAR (n 144) recital 11.
[516] See Matthieu Nadini, Laura Alessandretti, Flavio Di Giacinto, Mauro Martino, Luca Maria Aiello, and Andrea Baronchelli, 'Mapping the NFT Revolution: Market Trends, Trade Networks, and Visual Features' (2021) 11 Scientific Reports 20902 <https://www.nature.com/articles/s41598-021-00053-8.pdf> accessed 11 April 2022 (hereafter Nadini et al., 'Mapping the NFT Revolution'); Qin Wang, Rujia Li, Qi Wang, and Shipping Chen, 'Non-Fungible Token (NFT): Overview, Evaluation, Opportunities and Challenges' (*arXiv*, 16 May 2021) <https://arxiv.org/abs/2105.07447> accessed 11 April 2022.
[517] Maghan McDowell, 'What Fashion Week Looks Like in the Metaverse' (*Vogue Business*, 1 February 2022) <https://www.voguebusiness.com/technology/what-fashion-week-looks-like-in-the-metaverse> accessed 11 April 2022; Joseph DeAcetis, 'The Rise of the Metaverse: Where Crypto, NFT and Luxury Brands

real estate. Users can buy and rent virtual plots of land, actual 'pieces' of the metaverse, based on NFT-powered propriety deeds.[518]

Furthermore, the metaverse is currently filling up with play-to-earn (P2E) games played by individual users. They allow players to earn in-game assets as a reward for gaming, including NFT items (e.g., weapons, skins) which can be later traded on an open market (e.g., OpenSea), and cryptocurrencies or play-to-earn tokens can be traded by players in-game. The business model of P2E games has largely contributed to an increase in ICOs focused on the gaming industry (initial game offerings, IGOs).[519] This could be the next bubble within the NFT market and similarities with the past ICO bubbles are staggering.[520] In March 2022, there existed 308 play-to-earn and 238 metaverse tokens, while on 1 January 2021 the market only included 19 play-to-earn and 28 metaverse tokens.[521]

b. Tech standards

Originally NFTs were generated exclusively employing the Ethereum (ETH) ecosystem. Although Ethereum remains the most dominant platform for this market, high transaction fees coupled with Ethereum's carbon footprint raised concerns among users, who opted for alternative blockchain infrastructures, such as Ronin and Solana.[522]

NFTs are originated ('minted') via a smart contract, typically running on the Ethereum (ETH) blockchain, and following a specific standard. Looking at the Ethereum ecosystem, as mentioned in Chapters 1 and 2, a smart contract is a collection of code and data that resides at a specific address on the ETH blockchain and is associated with an ETH account.[523] A smart contract has logic programmed into it in curly-bracket language (typically Solidity or Vyper), providing for the contract rules and their automatic enforcement. The smart contract is then deployed onto the ETH network by paying a so-called gas fee, thus qualifying as a transaction and becoming immutable in its own right.[524] Once a contract is deployed, it becomes public and other users, including other smart contracts, can interact with it as they would with an application programming interface (API).[525] This makes smart contracts 'composable'; therefore they can be combined into larger structures so as to be

---

Merge' (*Forbes*, 8 February 2022) <https://www.forbes.com/sites/josephdeacetis/2022/02/08/the-rise-of-the-metaverse-where-crypto-nft-and-luxury-brands-merge/?sh=3091c19d454d> accessed 11 April 2022.

[518] Decentraland (<https://decentraland.org/>) accessed 11 April 2022) or the Sandbox metaverse (<https://www.sandbox.game/en/> accessed 11 April 2022), for example, offer such possibility.

[519] Binance Academy, 'What Is an Initial Game Offering (IGO)?' (7 January 2022) <https://academy.binance.com/en/articles/what-is-an-initial-game-offering-igo> accessed 11 April 2022.

[520] See Paul P. Momtaz, 'The Pricing and Performance of Cryptocurrency' (2021) 27 EurJFin 367; David Vidal-Tomas, 'The Entry and Exit Dynamics of the Cryptocurrency Market' (2021) 58 ResIntlBus&Fin 1 (101504).

[521] Statistics are available at https://coinmarketcap.com.

[522] See Forkast, 'State of the NFT Market' (2022) <https://forkast.news/state-of-the-nft-market/> accessed 11 April 2022 (hereafter Forkast, 'State of the NFT Market').

[523] Ethereum, 'Introduction to Smart Contracts' (12 April 2022) <https://ethereum.org/en/developers/docs/smart-contracts/> accessed 11 April 2022.

[524] Ethereum, 'Gas and Fees' <https://ethereum.org/en/developers/docs/gas/> accessed 11 April 2022.

[525] Ibid.

reusable by the entire system without the need to rewrite contracts from scratch.[526] To leverage composability, the inputs and outputs defining the functions a smart contract must perform ('interface') must be standardized. The most widely used standard to track and transfer NFTs is ERC-721 (Ethereum Request for Comments 721).[527] In addition to basic functions used in association with fungible tokens (name, symbol, total supply, and token balance of an account[528]), the ERC-721 standard defines a set of ownership functions and events specifically aimed at addressing token non-fungibility, relevant for determining token ownership and establishing how it can be transferred.[529]

The NFT underlying asset (e.g., a digital picture) is inserted into the smart contract via a JSON file. A JSON (JavaScript Object Notation) file format stores simple data structures and objects, such as NFT metadata. Metadata is what brings an NFT to life, allowing it to assign specific properties, such as a name, a description, and an image.[530] After the smart contract is written (or imported from a library for simplicity[531]) it is deployed onto the ETH main network, where it will become available to other users or contracts. This is possible by sending an ETH transaction containing the compiled code of the smart contract without specifying any recipient. The successful deployment will return the smart contract address, namely the location of the token on the ETH blockchain.[532] Subsequently, the minting

---

[526] Aragon Blogspot, 'What Is Composability?' (9 December 2021) <https://blog.aragon.org/what-is-composability/> accessed 11 April 2022.

[527] Smith Cornwith, 'ERC-721 Non-Fungible Token Standard' (*Ethereum*, 9 March 2022) <https://ethereum.org/en/developers/docs/standards/tokens/erc-721/> accessed 11 April 2022. This is not the only standard adoptable, see also Smith Cornwith, 'ERC-1155 Multi Token Standard' (*Ethereum*, 9 March 2022) <https://ethereum.org/en/developers/docs/standards/tokens/erc-1155/> accessed 11 April 2022.

[528] The ERC-20 (i.e. Ethereum Request for Comments 20) is the standard used for fungible tokens. See Paul Wackerow, 'ERC-20 Token Standard' (*Ethereum*, 3 December 2021) <https://ethereum.org/en/developers/docs/standards/tokens/erc-20/> accessed 11 April 2022.

[529] The address of the owner of a token is returned by 'ownerOf'. As each ERC-721 token is unique, they are represented by an ID on the ETH blockchain. Other users or contracts can use this ID to determine the owner of the token. Permission to transfer tokens on the owner's behalf is granted or approved by 'approve'. The 'takeOwnership' function acts like a withdrawal function, since an outside party can call it to take tokens out of another user's account. Therefore, it can be used when a user has been approved to own a certain amount of tokens and wishes to withdraw said tokens from another user's balance. The 'transfer' function allows the owner to transfer the token to another user, just like other digital tokens/coins. Gerald Nash, 'The Anatomy of ERC721' (*Medium*, 23 December 2017) <https://medium.com/crypto-currently/the-anatomy-of-erc721-e9db77abfc24> accessed 11 April 2022. Furthermore, the ERC-721 standards also define two types of events (ibid):

> Transfer (capital T): this event refers to the ownership of the token changes from one individual to another. It emits the information on which account transferred the token, which account received the token, and which token (by ID) was transferred.
> Approve: this event goes off when a user approves another user to take ownership of the token [identifies the user's approval of another user]. It emits the information on which account currently owns the token, which account is approved to take ownership of the token in the future, and which token ID is approved to have its ownership transferred.

[530] See Sumi Mudgil, 'How to Write & Deploy an NFT (Part 1/3 of NFT Tutorial Series)' (*Ethereum*, 22 April 2021) <https://ethereum.org/en/developers/tutorials/how-to-write-and-deploy-an-nft/> accessed 11 April 2022.

[531] See *inter alia* OpenZeppelin library's 'ERC-721' <https://docs.openzeppelin.com/contracts/3.x/erc721> accessed 11 April 2022.

[532] The address that can be viewed using a blockchain scanner, such as Etherscan (<https://etherscan.io/> accessed 11 April 2022).

process of the NFT can be completed by transferring the smart contract to a specific receiver.[533]

The whole process can be largely streamlined on NFT platforms. For example, OpenSea allows to mint and put up for sale an image-based NFT by connecting a wallet and uploading a digital image.[534]

c. NFT market

The NFT market is growing at an incredibly fast pace,[535] although it can still be considered at an early stage of its development. Looking more closely at the NFT market, Nadini and others identify six categories of NFTs (Art, Collectible, Games, Metaverse, Other, and Utility), with each category containing some visually homogeneous objects.[536] In their analysis, they show that in terms of market volume, the Art category unequivocally dominated the NFT market until the end of 2018; from January 2019 other categories emerged, in particular Games and Metaverse.[537] Looking at the number of transactions, the most exchanged NFTs belong to the categories of Games and Collectibles, and although all assets went through a primary sale, only 20 per cent underwent secondary sales.[538]

The emergence of F-NFTs will likely impact the market structure of NFTs, as they might be a driver for increasing the volume and the number of exchanges in the NFT industry, which has significant implications at different levels. An increase in the volume and the number of exchanges would positively affect NFTs' price discovery, enhance liquidity in the market, and contribute to further democratization of a sector characterized by high prices that generally attracts selected social groups. F-NFTs would lose some of the key characteristics distinguishing NFTs from other digital tokens, becoming more exchangeable, less scarce (or in other terms, more available), and non-unique, with the consequence of a significantly higher potential for tradability.

From a legal perspective, increased exchangeability, non-uniqueness, and enhanced tradability would significantly alter the characterization of NFTs. In fact, as F-NFTs make the whole concept of NFT functionally and legally closer to the notion of a security, as differently elaborated in multiple jurisdictions,[539] NFTs could fall under the scope of securities laws under specific circumstances.[540]

---

[533] See Sumi Mudgil, 'How to Mint an NFT (Part 2/3 of NFT Tutorial Series)' (*Ethereum*, 22 April 2021) <https://ethereum.org/en/developers/tutorials/how-to-mint-an-nft/> accessed 11 April 2022.

[534] Erik Genc, 'Beginner's Guide to NFTs: How to Mint a Non-Fungible Token on Ethereum' (*Decrypt*, 28 October 2021) <https://decrypt.co/resources/beginners-guide-to-nfts-how-to-mint-a-non-fungible-token-on-ethereum> accessed 11 April 2022.

[535] According to Forkast, 'State of the NFT Market' (n 522), 'Global sales of NFTs reached US$18.5 billion in 2021, which was 570 times higher than the previous year', with Asia emerging as the primary market. See Forkast, 'Asia Primed For NFT Growth' (2022) <https://forkast.news/state-of-the-nft-market/asia-primed-for-nft-growth/> accessed 11 April 2022.

[536] Nadini et al., 'Mapping the NFT Revolution' (n 516).

[537] Ibid.

[538] Ibid.

[539] See analysis in Chapter 3 on ICOs.

[540] For a comparative approach in Europe, see Chiomenti et al., 'NFT: Cross-Border Perspectives' (n 508). In March 2022, SEC Commissioner Hester Peirce warned issuers and investors about the risk that F-NFTs

A growth in the NFT and F-NFT markets could lead to significant developments. One of these is the emergence of a more systematic recurrence to so-called NFT derivatives. Derivatives have become common instruments in the crypto industry, with many companies offering different products.[541] Consistent with those products, NFT derivatives are instruments for retail users and traders, allowing them to take short or long positions in NFTs, leading to the implementation of more robust trading strategies for speculative or hedging purposes.[542] The underlying asset would be the NFT, and the derived NFT would be a fungible crypto token—such as ERC20 or BEP20—representing the non-fungible NFT created using the Ethereum based ERC721 standard.[543] NFT derivatives would further contribute to increase liquidity in the NFT marketplace and avoid any liquidity crunch and favour NFT trading on crypto-exchanges with the possibility to generate new revenues relying on staking, lending and borrowing against NFT derivatives.[544]

A further development of NFTs is their employment as a collateral. Collateralized lending is a technique for leveraging investments, and allow users to remain invested in crypto-assets while maintaining fiat liquidity available.[545] The practice of using crypto-assets as collateral has developed in the past years,[546] and more recently NFTs were employed as a further crypto-asset to collateralize for loans and derivatives deals.[547] An increasing number of platforms offer the opportunity to connect independent lenders with NFT owners (who invested significant amounts in these assets) interested in borrowing money by using their NFTs as collateral.[548] In this way, collateralized NFTs generate cash without liquidating the investment, as well as mitigating the potential illiquidity of NFTs themselves, which might be difficult to sell for different reasons, including their high economic value. Consistent with other sectors in the cryptoeconomy, the market for NFT-backed loans is currently unregulated,

---

could be subject to securities laws. See Samuel Haig, 'SEC's "Crypto Mom" Warns Selling Fractionalized NFTs Could Break the Law' (*CoinDesk*, 26 March 2021) <https://cointelegraph.com/news/sec-s-crypto-mom-warns-selling-fractionalized-nfts-could-break-the-law> accessed 11 April 2022. See also Matt Robinson, 'SEC Scrutinizes NFT Market over Illegal Crypto Token Offerings' (*Bloomberg*, 2 March 2022) <https://www.bloomberg.com/news/articles/2022-03-02/sec-scrutinizes-nft-market-over-illegal-crypto-token-offerings> accessed 11 April 2022.

[541] See Chapter 5.
[542] @pramodAIML, 'NFT Derivatives for Absolute Beginners?' (*Medium*, 26 January 2022) <https://medium.com/crypto-wisdom/nft-derivatives-for-absolute-beginners-12b57e5dc425> accessed 11 April 2022.
[543] Ibid.
[544] Ibid.
[545] Marco Quiroz-Gutierrez, 'Someone Got a $1.25 Million Loan by Using NFTs as Collateral. Here's How You May Be Able to Do the Same Thing' (*Fortune*, 8 February 2022) <https://fortune.com/2022/02/07/nft-collateral-for-million-dollar-loans/> accessed 11 April 2022 (hereafter Quiroz-Gutierrez, 'Using NFTs as Collateral').
[546] See World Bank, 'Distributed Ledger Technology & Secured Transactions: Legal, Regulatory and Technological Perspectives—Guidance Notes Series' (May 2020) <https://openknowledge.worldbank.org/bitstream/handle/10986/34007/Collateral-Registry-Secured-Transactions-Law-and-Practice.pdf?sequence=5> accessed 11 April 2022.
[547] Quiroz-Gutierrez, 'Using NFTs as Collateral' (n 545). See also Eva Szalay, 'Crypto Lender Genesis Accepts NFTs as Collateral for Loans' (*Financial Times*, 28 January 2022) <https://www.ft.com/content/ce600e79-93cf-40c8-928c-e9bbd66072c7> accessed 11 April 2022.
[548] Ibid.

contributing to low levels of investor protection that are a cause of concern for regulators in Europe and the United States.[549]

d. Regulatory approaches
NFTs are not specifically regulated yet. However, consistent with the analysis provided for digital tokens in the context of an ICO, NFTs could plausibly be characterized as 'tokenized' securities, especially in the case of F-NFTs. F-NFTs in fact represent a fraction ('shard') of ownership in the underlying, such as an artwork or a music track, thus allowing a non-fungible token to be broken down into a number of fungible share-like assets.[550] The intergovernmental Financial Action Task Force (FATF) has pushed for more clarity. Its 2021 Guidance on Virtual Assets and Virtual Asset Service Providers emphasized that it is important 'to consider the nature of the NFT and its function in practice ... Some NFTs that on their face do not appear to constitute virtual assets may fall under the virtual asset definition if they are to be used for payment or investment purposes in practice.'[551]

In the United States, an NFT could fall under the jurisdiction of the SEC unless non-fungibility can be demonstrated.[552] President's Biden Executive Order on Ensuring Responsible Development of Digital Assets does not explicitly address NFTs, although it extensively addresses cryptocurrencies and other digital assets.

In the European Union, no legal definition or regulation specifically applies to NFTs. MiCAR explicitly excludes its application to NFTs and similar non-fungible crypto-assets, but does cover F-NFTs as they are not deemed unique or non-fungible. In turn, both NFTs and F-NFTs can be qualified as financial instruments and thus fall under MiFID II.[553] At the member state level, a similar approach led to consider the applicability of financial regulations to NFTs. For example, in May 2021, the German government declared that no changes to the legal framework were planned to include provisions on NFTs.[554]. However, if an NFT issued in Germany presents the characteristics of a crypto-asset according to the Banking Law (*Kreditwesengesetz*),[555] or if

---

[549] See Gary Gensler, 'Remarks before the Aspen Security Forum' (Speech at the Aspen Security Forum, Aspen, 3 August 2021) <https://www.sec.gov/news/public-statement/gensler-aspen-security-forum-2021-08-03> accessed 11 April 2022. See also ESMA, EBA and EIOPA, 'Warning Report on the Risks of Virtual Currencies' (17 March 2022) <https://www.esma.europa.eu/sites/default/files/library/esma50-164-1284_joint_esas_warning_on_virtual_currenciesl.pdf> accessed 11 April 2022.

[550] See Arben Kane, 'Fractionalized NFT (F-NFTs): All That You Need to Know' (*Medium*, 9 September 2021) <https://medium.com/@arbenk/fractionalized-nft-f-nfts-all-that-you-need-to-know-46bc06ea486d> accessed 11 April 2022. See also Brian Elzweig and Lawrence J. Trautman, 'When Does a Nonfungible Token (NFT) Become a Security?' (2023) 39 GaStULRev 295.

[551] FATF, 'Second Review' (n 147). Importantly, a 'virtual asset' is defined under the FTF framework as a 'digital representation of value that can be digitally traded, or transferred, and can be used for payment or investment purposes. Virtual assets do not include digital representations of fiat currencies, securities and other financial assets that are already covered elsewhere in the FATF Recommendations.' Ibid, 43.

[552] Matt Robinson, 'SEC Scrutinizes NFT Market over Illegal Crypto Token Offerings' (*Bloomberg*, 2 March 2022) <https://www.bloomberg.com/news/articles/2022-03-02/sec-scrutinizes-nft-market-over-illegal-crypto-token-offerings> accessed 11 April 2022.

[553] See MiCAR (n 144) recitals 10, 11.

[554] Deutscher Bundestag, 'Die Bundesregierung plant derzeit keine Änderung der gesetzlichen Rahmenbe dingungen von NFTs.' (26 May 2021) 4 <https://dserver.bundestag.de/btd/19/301/1930141.pdf> accessed 11 April 2022.

[555] See s 1 (11) (11).

it qualifies as an investment instrument pursuant to the Capital Investment Act (*Vermögensanlagengesetz*),[556] specific legal obligations would arise, including prospectus obligations.[557]

In the United Kingdom, the legal status of NFTs is still equally undefined. Depending on their characteristics, NFTs may be regarded to be either security tokens, e-money tokens, or unregulated tokens.[558] According to the Financial Conduct Authority (FCA) guidance, an NFT falls under the security token category when amounting to a 'Specified Investment' under the Regulated Activities Order (RAO),[559] or a transferable securities or other financial instrument under MiFID II. In these cases, tokens are expected to fall under the remit of the FCA. Alternatively, whenever NFTs meet the definition of e-money under the Electronic Money Regulations (EMRs)[560] they would fall within its purview. Absent any wider regulatory framework encompassing crypto-assets, NFTs could fall within the residual category of unregulated tokens.[561] Furthermore, NFTs could fall within the definition of 'crypto-asset' under the Money Laundering Regulations (MLRs);[562] therefore any business providing crypto-assets exchange or custody service could be subject to it.

E. ICOs and Complexity

ICOs brought significant novelty to capital markets, contributing to a radical rethinking of specific phases, in particular the way capital formation takes place, as well as the connected market structures, including the distribution of roles that such market structures imply. Consistent with the conclusions drawn at the end of Chapter 2 for smart contracts and their implications in terms of complexity, ICOs confirm the intrinsic evolutionary tensions animating capital markets as a subpart of the whole financial system. Furthermore, they confirm that such evolutionary patterns within a well-defined context imply a general reconsideration of the overall financial system.

---

[556] Pt 1, s 1(2).
[557] Ibid, pt 1, sub-s 1, s 6.
[558] FCA, 'Cryptoassets: Our Work' (4 April 2022) <https://www.fca.org.uk/firms/cryptoassets> accessed 11 April 2022 (hereafter FCA, 'Cryptoassets').
[559] These may provide rights such as ownership, repayment of a specific sum of money, or entitlement to a share in future profits. See the Financial Services and Markets Act 2000, pt 3 <https://www.legislation.gov.uk/uksi/2001/544/contents?view=plain> accessed 11 April 2022.
[560] '"[E]lectronic money" means electronically (including magnetically) stored monetary value as represented by a claim on the electronic money issuer which—(a) is issued on receipt of funds for the purpose of making payment transactions; (b) is accepted by a person other than the electronic money issuer': Electronic Money Regulations 2011 <https://www.legislation.gov.uk/uksi/2011/99/regulation/2> accessed 11 April 2022.
[561] FCA, 'Cryptoassets' (n 558). Unregulated tokens 'are usually decentralised and designed to be used primarily as a medium of exchange. We sometimes refer to them as exchange tokens and they do not provide the types of rights or access provided by security or utility tokens, but are used as a means of exchange or for investment.'
[562] The Money Laundering, Terrorist Financing and Transfer of Funds (Information on the Payer) Regulations 2017 <https://www.legislation.gov.uk/uksi/2017/692/made> accessed 11 April 2022. The definition of a crypto-asset is 'a cryptographically secured digital representation of value or contractual rights that uses a form of distributed ledger technology and can be transferred, stored or traded electronically.'

ICOs triggered a fundamental debate on the form of securities, exactly as smart contracts did in the context of contract law and contractual practices. First of all, digital securities pose a problem of form, which is a rather *technical* problem, in the same way that the written form is a *technical* problem for contracts. Beyond this aspect, the way digital securities spread affected (and even more will likely affect) many related entities and tasks. This is the case for all activities, entities, and infrastructures functionally related to trading, including both trading and post-trading market infrastructures. This is also the case for contexts less intrinsically connected to trading, such as corporate governance. Indeed, digital securities are a catalyst for new debates on the role of technology in corporate governance and for further structural transformations driven by technological advancements. Therefore, the dynamic evolutions internal to one subpart (capital markets) propagate to the others.

Beyond the capital markets–corporate governance context, tokenized securities opened up to a more general debate on the tokenization of any 'tangible' real asset, with a cascade of effects. If money can be tokenized, central bankers have to rethink their function: ICOs' dynamism and evolution at the level of capital markets invades the monetary realm, that is, the monetary subpart of the financial system. Even beyond money, if assets that are even more 'tangible' and more 'real' than money can be tokenized, this is an epochal change with two consequences. First, it opens up new forms of shadow banking based on new forms of tokenization replacing the traditional securitizations. Second, and related to this point, tokenization will create the basis for a much greater and more intense financialization of society, which would come with both opportunities and risks, requiring a proper consideration and adequate regulatory (possibly dynamic) approaches.

Complexity approaches highlighting evolutionary patterns within a subpart (a complex adaptive system itself), and the way they are reflected on other subparts on the basis of a strong interaction, confirm their centrality for navigating such multi-dimensional changes. The problems raised by future changes might benefit from the consideration that transformations are intrinsically based on 'historicity dependency'. Taking this aspect into account might be helpful for anticipating potentially dangerous developments, designing appropriate forms of dynamic regulation to avoid negative consequences, as in the past. This is the basis for a deep understanding of the ratio underlying the next chapters and the proposal of the two labels 'shadow central banking' and 'crypto shadow banking', echoing specific concerns that acknowledge historicity dependency, as well cyclicality in economy and finance.

Conclusion

Beyond any 'quantitative' attempt to explain whether ICOs represented a market failure or rather disrupted the existing market structures, market actors, and market infrastructures, it can be seen that they represented an extremely important step in the evolution of the cryptoeconomy. As this chapter has shown, ICOs triggered important transformations; further developments in shadow banking and central banking will be laid out in the following chapters of this book.

The United States, the European Union, and Switzerland may substantially converge at the level of ICO characterization under existing securities laws (with the United States also applying commodities laws to cryptocurrencies) and the governmental authorities involved in these countries reached consistent conclusions. However, the available level of consistency prior to the technology wave, coupled with the interpretation provided in these cases, was not a sufficient basis for the emergence of consistent regulatory approaches and enforcements in the different jurisdictions.

At the moment, it is difficult to observe any consistent patterns emerging from the enforcement action of the securities and commodities laws frameworks. While the SEC and CFTC adopted a rigorous approach with a relatively high number of cases concluded with an enforcement action, the same did not happen in the European Union or Switzerland. This may depend on a series of factors, such as an objectively smaller number of entrepreneurial initiatives. However, other factors may be at play, including a different role played by self-regulatory initiatives or lack of cooperation between the SEC and good-faith developers and entrepreneurs. Such a situation may lead to the conclusion that the SEC did not fully and effectively pursue its mission of preserving capital formation beyond protecting investors, and other regulatory approaches—in particular the ones pursued in Hong Kong, Singapore, Switzerland, and France—better adapted to this new trend in the cryptoeconomy.

The persistent lack of international harmonization and adequate self-regulatory initiatives (beyond Switzerland, Hong Kong, and the UK) is a major source of concern and may likely increase opportunistic strategies based on regulatory arbitrage.

In addition to the regulatory concerns, a more objective analysis of ICOs leads to the conclusion that they breached some key promises. First, they did not increase the trend of financial inclusion nor did they democratize capital markets. Second, they did not disintermediate venture capitalists, which on the contrary became increasingly active in the ICO space. Third, ICOs did not disrupt market infrastructures but contributed to the creation of new platforms, which raise significant concerns due to their increasing role in the cryptoeconomy, with no counterbalancing regulation.

However, ICOs proved important for advancing the debate in many fields, in particular at the level of capital market dynamics, triggering important considerations on the prominent role of underwriters and their expensive fees, as well as at the level of digital securities. Digital securities opened up to further potential chain reactions in different directions, including market infrastructures and corporate governance. Finally, ICOs have been a catalyst for developing crypto-assets and discussing more systematic tokenization beyond the securities world (including tokenized forms of money as they will be developed in Chapter 4, and real assets). All this ultimately led to the establishment of shadow central banking and shadow banking in the cryptoeconomy, which will be broadly discussed in Chapter 5.

This leaves intact the potential for disruption of ICOs beyond their basic function of being a revolutionary tool for capital formation. Therefore, ICOs proved to be a key step for the development of new thought on blockchain and its application in broader contexts, such as corporations and financial networks, as will be discussed in the following chapters of this book. Adopting a more theoretical angle, ICOs proved to be a fundamental node in the development of the new multidimensionality (as it was identified in Chapter 1) in the cryptoeconomy.

4
Disrupting Central Banking or Shadow Central Banking

Introduction

Technology is contributing to the redesign of key functions and roles, and the ways in which they are generally assigned to established institutions in the existing market structures. In this context, money presents a fascinating case study, as technology is inexorably reshaping it. This chapter analyses the relationship between money and central banks, and the role of significant innovations supporting private initiatives, which disrupt the traditional dichotomy of 'central bank money' versus 'commercial bank money'.

Following the line of disruption, initial coin offerings (ICOs) made clear the potential disruption of digital tokens. An obvious consequence of digital tokens was the possibility to apply this new conceptual and infrastructural framework to the context of securities. ICOs greatly contributed to the development of digital securities, which might impact private and public organizations. A second, equally important step triggered by ICOs and digital securities is the possibility to use digital tokens as a representation of other assets. The idea of tokenized forms of money is part of this revolution, which this chapter will represent as even broader and more intense than the creation of Bitcoin itself.

This is the way in which the establishment of the cryptoeconomy depends on multi-dimensional transformations, which have never before been so profound, and which also include the central banking sphere. Financial complexity both as a static structural characteristic and as a dynamic approach necessarily considers the layer of central banking, which is likely to become increasingly integrated with the other subparts of the new system, contributing to its day-to-day operations and evolution. Central banks are also a tool for emphasizing the historical dimension as an important trait of complex adaptive systems.

In February 2019, J.P. Morgan became the first bank to launch its own cryptocurrency—a USD-backed stablecoin, the 'JPM Coin', to increase the efficiency of settlement transactions involving clients within the same payment business network.[1] A few months later, the Libra Association (now rebranded as Diem), initially supported by twenty tech giants including Facebook, Visa, and Mastercard,[2]

---

[1] Jesse Damiani, 'JPMorgan Announces "JPM Coin", a USD-Pegged Cryptocoin for Cross-Border Payments, Security, and More' (*Forbes*, 14 February 2019) <https://www.forbes.com/sites/jessedamiani/2019/02/14/jpmorgan-announces-jpm-coin-usd-pegged-cryptocoin-for-cross-border-payments-security-and-more/> accessed 22 April 2022. See Onyx by J.P. Morgan <https://www.jpmorgan.com/global/news/digital-coin-payments> accessed 1 May 2023.

[2] The Libra Association counted up to twenty-seven members. See Anna Irrera and Tom Wilson, 'Facebook-Backed Digital Coin Libra Renamed Diem in Quest for Approval' (*Reuters*, 1 December

Technology in Financial Markets. Marco Dell'Erba, Oxford University Press. © Marco Dell'Erba 2024.
DOI: 10.1093/oso/9780198873617.003.0004

announced the anticipated launch of the Libra Coin[3] in the first half of 2020. In February 2020, Google joined the consortium Hedera Hashgraph, comprising global corporations operating in a broad spectrum of industries. This generated rumours that Google might also contribute to the creation of a new global cryptocurrency.[4]

Libra's announcement of a new global cryptocurrency triggered the concerns of national central bankers. Some of them argued that the Libra Coin might be unstoppable;[5] others, such as then-Governor of the Bank of England Mark Carney, advocated for a new global monetary system, based on a multiplicity of Libra-like global digital currencies replacing the dollar. At the moment, a growing number of central banks are engaged in researching central bank digital currencies (CBDCs) but only 10 per cent have actually implemented pilot projects, especially among emerging market economies.[6] Important initiatives include one by the People's Bank of China,[7] which announced the testing of a digital yuan, and a very recent one by a group of seven central banks, including the Bank of England and the European Central Bank (ECB) alongside the Bank for International Settlements (BIS), to study potential uses for CBDCs.[8] More recent discussions were announced individually by the ECB, for the first time evoking the possibility of a digital euro;[9] by the Swiss National Bank (SNB) regarding its Helvetia project, developed in partnership with the BIS and SIX to study the possibility of a wholesale CBDC;[10] by the Swedish Riksbank, pushing to accelerate the

---

2020) <https://www.reuters.com/article/uk-facebook-cryptocurrency-idUKKBN28B57O> accessed 22 April 2022.

[3] Libra's first white paper was released in June 2019. For the first version of the white paper, see The Libra Association, 'Libra White Paper' (June 2019) <https://web.archive.org/web/20190618094622/https://libra.org/en-US/white-paper/> accessed 22 April 2022 (hereafter 'Libra White Paper v1.0'). Libra's second version was released in April 2020. See The Libra Association, 'Libra White Paper v2.0' (April 2020) <https://web.archive.org/web/20221129004028/https://wp.diem.com/en-US/wp-content/uploads/sites/23/2020/04/Libra_WhitePaperV2_April2020.pdf> accessed 22 April 2022 (hereafter 'Libra White Paper v2.0').

[4] Reputaction, 'Google USD Stablecoin on Hedera Hashgraph sooner than Libra?' (*Medium*, 12 February 2020) <https://medium.com/@reputaction/google-usd-stablecoin-on-hedera-hashgraph-sooner-than-libra-572b652a2ec2> accessed 22 April 2022 (hereafter Reputaction, 'Google USD Stablecoin on Hedera').

[5] David Pan, 'China's Crypto Czar: Facebook-Led Libra "Might Be Unstoppable"' (*CoinDesk*, 19 September 2019), https://www.coindesk.com/chinese-crypto-czar-no-one-would-say-welcome-to-libra-but-it-might-be-unstoppable> accessed 22 April 2022.

[6] Brian Swint, 'Carney Urges Libra-Like Reserve Currency to End Dollar Dominance' (*Bloomberg*, 23 August 2019) <https://www.bloomberg.com/news/articles/2019-08-23/carney-urges-libra-like-reserve-currency-to-end-dollar-dominance> accessed 22 April 2022 (hereafter Swint, 'Libra-Like Reserve Currency').

[7] Reuters, 'China Says New Digital Currency Will Be Similar to Facebook's Libra' (6 September 2019) <https://www.reuters.com/article/us-china-cryptocurrency-cenbank/china-says-new-digital-currency-will-be-similar-to-facebooks-libra-idUSKCN1VR0NM> accessed 22 April 2022 (hereafter Reuters, 'China New Digital Currency').

[8] ECB, 'Central Bank Group to Assess Potential Cases for Central Bank Digital Currencies' (21 January 2020) <https://www.ecb.europa.eu/press/pr/date/2020/html/ecb.pr200121_1~e99d7946d6.en.html> accessed 22 April 2022.

[9] See ECB, *Report on a Digital Euro* (October 2020) <https://www.ecb.europa.eu/pub/pdf/other/Report_on_a_digital_euro~4d7268b458.en.pdf> accessed 22 April 2022 (hereafter ECB, *Report on a Digital Euro*).

[10] Swiss National Bank, 'Swiss National Bank and Six Announce Successful Wholesale CBDC Experiment' (3 December 2020) <https://www.snb.ch/en/mmr/reference/pre_20201203/source/pre_20201203.en.pdf> accessed 22 April 2022.

process of issuing an e-krona;[11] and by El Salvador, which adopted Bitcoin as legal tender in September 2021.

The growing interest of private actors in the area of stable cryptocurrencies (or stablecoins) contributed to the emergence of a network which attempted to erode the activities of central banks. The way this business is developing, coupled with the lack of regulation, shares some analogies with the emergence of the so-called shadow banking system, a network of financial institutions recurring to specific financial instruments.[12] The negative consequences of the shadow banking system dominated the academic and regulatory debates, before and especially after the financial crisis of 2008. The shadow banking system sparked the gradual erosion of traditional banking activities as new actors entered the credit business. Starting in the 1970s, under the pressure of heterogeneous forces such as demand for financial collateral, innovation, regulation, and competition, the shadow banking system led to a gradual transformation of the credit market.

As mentioned in Chapter 1, regulators considered shadow banking one of the main causes of the financial crisis. Therefore, rigorous scrutiny and significant regulatory initiatives were implemented. Such initiatives included the G20 resolution on credit derivatives,[13] the Dodd–Frank Act[14] in the United States, and a new regulatory framework in Europe, including the Alternative Investment Fund Manager Directive (AIFMD),[15] the Short Selling Regulation (SSR),[16] and the European Market Infrastructure Regulation (EMIR).[17]

In addition to the regulatory reaction, the explosion of the financial crisis coincided with the beginning of a new wave of innovations that led to further significant transformations. In the aftermath of the financial crisis, the seminal white paper on Bitcoin authored by Satoshi Nakamoto in 2008[18] produced significant debate on the role of distributed ledger technology (DLT). Now, DLT technology has permeated the entire financial system through its core functions, including capital formation, clearing and settlement, and corporate voting for public listed companies.

As also mentioned in Chapter 1, so-called Fintech[19] was a phenomenon that developed in three different sectors of capital markets and banking. Many of these financial technology startups sought to disrupt retail and commercial banking. Other Fintech

---

[11] Danny Nelson, 'E-Krona or Bust, Says Sweden's Chief Central Banker, Trying to Drag Swedish Govt into Digital Age' (*CoinDesk*, 16 October 2020) https://www.coindesk.com/riksbank-governor-calls-for-swedish-digital-currency> accessed 22 April 2022.

[12] See Chapter 1.

[13] Group of Twenty (G20), 'Declaration of the Summit on Financial Markets and the World Economy' (15 November 2008) <http://www.g20.utoronto.ca/2008/2008declaration1115.html> accessed 22 April 2022.

[14] Dodd–Frank Wall Street Reform and Consumer Protection Act 2010 (hereafter Dodd–Frank Act).

[15] Directive 2011/61/EU of 8 June 2011 on Alternative Investment Fund Managers [2011] OJ L 174/1.

[16] Regulation (EU) 236/2012 of 14 March 2012 on short selling and certain aspects of credit default swaps [2012] OJ L 86/1.

[17] Regulation (EU) 648/2012 of 4 July 2012 on OTC derivatives, central counterparties and trade repositories [2012] OJ L 201/1.

[18] Satoshi Nakamoto, 'Bitcoin: A Peer-to-Peer Electronic Cash System' (31 October 2008) <https://bitcoin.org/bitcoin.pdf> accessed 22 April 2022.

[19] For the bibliography on Fintech refer to Chapter 1.

innovations supported the growth of shadow banking. Finally, a third subcategory of Fintech developments contributed to the emergence of other initiatives, in the context of payments and currencies, as in the case of Bitcoin and subsequent developments. The new technological platforms offer private actors the possibility to compete with established public institutions, such as central banks. New entities such as investment banks and tech giants attempted to redesign the payment system, which is one of the core areas supervised by central banks.

Although these kinds of initiatives experienced exponential growth after the launch of Bitcoin, older technologies such as e-money and cryptographic experiments started to emerge at the onset of the internet era. A main characteristic of these initiatives is that the target of disruption is not the banking system alone, as has happened more systematically in the past. By adopting Minsky's pyramidal structure of the economic system, with central banks in an apical position,[20] one could say that this time the target is the superior layer, because it is the central banking system. Furthermore, a significant difference from entrepreneurial initiatives of the past is the intensity of the changes that these contemporary initiatives may bring. The involvement of big tech giants and Fintech companies competing with banks, credit card companies, and central banks,[21] as well as the technological advancements that make any change faster and easier, are the two main factors leading to an increased intensity of these structural changes.

This chapter focuses on these initiatives and proposes to denominate them as 'shadow central banking', to emphasize the structural and historical analogies existing with 'shadow banking'—although they serve two different purposes, with shadow banking contributing to liquidity and credit creation and shadow central banking contributing to specific functions generally associated with central banks. Shadow central banking encompasses a broad range of private initiatives that are eroding the power of central banks in many key activities, using new forms of money as the channel for disruption. To that end, this chapter briefly describes the role of central banks and their origins, and the way shadow central banking developed. Furthermore, it identifies some causes that stimulated the emergence of both shadow banking and the shadow central banking. This chapter also focuses on some governance implications; the different scenarios that shadow central banking may bring about in the economic system; and its risks, regulatory implications, and potential scenarios. The chapter contributes to a better contextualization of the most recent developments.

---

[20] See generally Hyman P. Minsky, *Stabilizing an Unstable Economy* (McGraw-Hill 1986) (hereafter Minsky, *Stabilizing an Unstable Economy*).

[21] See Gary Gensler, 'Examining Facebook's Proposed Cryptocurrency and Its Impact on Consumers, Investors, and the American Financial System Financial Services Committee United States House of Representatives' (Hearing before the Committee on Financial Services of the U.S. House of Representatives, 17 July 2019) 3 <https://financialservices.house.gov/uploadedfiles/hhrg-116-ba00-wstate-genslerg-20190717.pdf> accessed 22 April 2022 (hereafter Gensler, 'Examining Facebook's Proposed Cryptocurrency').

I. Central Banking

A. Goals and Mission of Central Banks

Central banks are in charge of monetary policy, pursuing stability in three different directions: the value of the money, the real economy, and financial stability.[22] Furthermore, central banks are essential for supervising and maintaining efficient market infrastructures, including the overall function of payment systems as well as clearing and settlement infrastructures. These functions are necessary in the pursuit of central banks' main goal: maintaining trust in currency and facilitating its circulation.[23] In order to accomplish this public interest, central banks rely on a system which combines different types of money: central bank money (central bank liabilities to be used as money) directly issued by central banks co-exists with commercial bank money (assets and liabilities, which include capital reserves, deposits, and borrowings).[24] This structure, coupled with a plurality of payment mechanisms, is a common feature to all developed economies. Typically, central banks have operated wholesale payment systems. At the same time, they delegate retail payments to commercial banks in charge of providing services such as cards, cheques, and internet-based payments, while still relying on the centralized structure of central banks to complete the processes.[25]

As part of their monetary authority, central banks also operate as liquidity providers by using the traditional tool of interest rates, as well as by adopting extraordinary measures such as quantitative easing. Quantitative easing consists in direct intervention by central banks purchasing government (as well as private) bonds, and has the effect of decreasing the interest rates applied to loans, because rates on government bonds directly impact the totality of the interest rates in the economy.[26] Quantitative easing was implemented on a massive scale in the aftermath of the financial crisis of 2008 by the major central bankers, in particular former ECB Chairman Mario Draghi,[27] and during the early stages of the COVID-19 pandemic at the beginning of

---

[22] Michael D. Bordo, 'A Brief History of Central Banks' (2007) Federal Reserve Bank of Cleveland Economic Commentary (12 December 2007) <https://www.clevelandfed.org/en/publications/economic-commentary/2007/ec-20071201-a-brief-history-of-central-banks> accessed 22 April 2022 (hereafter Bordo, 'Brief History of Central Banks'). For an analysis of the role of Fintech in financial stability, see generally Douglas W. Arner, Dirk A. Zetzsche, Ross P. Buckley, and Janos N. Barberis, 'FinTech and RegTech: Enabling Innovation while Preserving Financial Stability' (2017) 18 GeoJIntlAff 47.

[23] BIS Committee on Payment and Settlement Systems, 'The Role of Central Bank Money in Payment Systems' (August 2003) <https://www.bis.org/cpmi/publ/d55.pdf> accessed 22 April 2022 (hereafter BIS, 'The Role of Central Bank Money').

[24] Ibid, 1.

[25] Charles M. Kahn, Francisco Rivadeneyra, and Tsz-Nga Wong, 'Should the Central Bank Issue E-Money?' (2018) Bank of Canada Staff Working Paper 2018-58, 3 <https://www.bankofcanada.ca/wp-content/uploads/2018/12/swp2018-58.pdf> accessed 22 April 2022 (hereafter Kahn et al., 'Should the Central Bank Issue E-Money?').

[26] Bank of England, 'How Does Quantitative Easing Work?' (updated 21 April 2022) <https://www.bankofengland.co.uk/monetary-policy/quantitative-easing> accessed 22 April 2022 (hereafter Bank of England, 'Quantitative Easing').

[27] Lionel Barber and Clare Jones, 'Interview: Mario Draghi Declares Victory in Battle over the Euro' (*Financial Times*, 30 September 2019) <https://www.ft.com/content/b59a4a04-9b26-11e9-9c06-a4640c9feebb> accessed 12 April 2022.

2020, in the form of a €750 billion pandemic emergency purchase programme by the ECB[28] and unlimited bond purchase by the Federal Reserve.[29] The Bank of England has increasingly used quantitative easing in recent years, from a round of £200 billion in 2009 to the recent decision of March 2020 to invest £645 billion as a response to the financial crisis triggered by COVID-19.[30]

In the context of their role as liquidity providers, central banks also operate as lenders of last resort; that is, they are the bankers' bank. Banks' business and function consists in credit, liquidity, and maturity transformation. Banks convert depositors' short-term funds and wholesale funding in riskier loans and credit assets.[31] Therefore, this business may generate liquidity mismatches, and a consequent run on assets, that could potentially harm the bank, leading to its insolvency. In this emergency case, central banks may decide on a discretional bilateral basis to act as lenders of last resort, solving the liquidity mismatch by exchanging their liquid assets for the risky illiquid loans. In this way central banks can avoid the bankruptcy of such credit institutions, with potential benefits for the entire system through avoiding the costs of bankruptcy and the risk of contagion spreading to other banks. The role of central banks as lenders of last resort generated some concerns. Central banks could put at risk their resources as well as their reputation while favouring moral hazard on the side of bankers, who, systematically relying on central bank intervention, could be more inclined to take greater risks.[32]

Central banks may be liquidity providers not only at the national level but also at the international level, as in the case of swap lines. In a swap line contract, a central bank, for example the Federal Reserve, exchanges its own fiat currency—in the case of the Federal Reserve, dollars—for an equivalent amount of a foreign currency from another central bank, at the present spot exchange rate, agreeing to re-sell the respective currencies at the same rate after a fixed period of time.[33] The central bank receiving such foreign currency is in the position to lend it to financial institutions operating in its jurisdiction, at the same rate as that negotiated with the foreign central bank, for high-liquid collateral.[34] Swap lines are not a new instrument for central banks, but have a long history. The prominent role of the dollar as an international currency for the great majority of the financial transactions *de facto* made the Federal Reserve one of the most important actors in the context of swap lines.[35] The Federal Reserve

---

[28] ECB, 'ECB Announces €750 billion Pandemic Emergency Purchase Programme (PEPP)' (18 March 2020) <https://www.ecb.europa.eu/press/pr/date/2020/html/ecb.pr200318_1~3949d6f266.en.html> accessed 12 April 2022 (hereafter ECB, 'PEPP').

[29] See Heather Long, 'Fed Announces Unlimited Bond Purchases in Unprecedented Move Aimed at Preventing an Economic Depression' (*Washington Post*, 23 March 2020) <https://www.washingtonpost.com/business/2020/03/23/fed-unlimited-credit-coronavirus/> accessed 12 April 2022.

[30] Bank of England, 'Quantitative Easing' (n 26).

[31] See John Armour, Dan Awrey, Paul Davies, Luca Enriques, Jeffrey N. Gordon, Colin Mayer, and Jennifer Payne, *Principles of Financial Regulation* (OUP 2016) 316 (hereafter Armour et al., *Principles of Financial Regulation*).

[32] Ibid, 326–330.

[33] See Saleem Bahaj and Ricardo Reis, 'Central Bank Swap Lines: Evidence on the Effects of the Lender of Last Resort' (2022) 89 RevEconStud 1654, 1659.

[34] Ibid.

[35] For an analysis of swap lines under American law, see generally Colleen Baker, 'The Federal Reserve's Use of International Swap Lines' (2013) 55 ArizLRev 603.

has recurred to swap lines ever since the 1960s. At that time the price of gold in the London market experienced significant growth, beyond the US gold-export point equal to $35.20. As a consequence, central banks had an incentive to exchange unwanted dollar reserves with the US Treasury for gold.[36] As Bordo and others explain:

> In August 1960 total outstanding dollar liabilities began to exceed the U.S. gold stock, and by December 1965, outstanding dollar liabilities to official institutions, which could exchange them directly with the U.S. Treasury, exceeded the U.S. gold stock. The imbalance indicated that the United States could not fulfill its Bretton woods commitment to freely exchange dollars for gold at the existing official price of $ 35.20.[37]

From the 1960s up to the financial crisis of 2008 (and throughout the market turmoil following 9/11), swap lines served as a tool to provide central banks with cover for unwanted dollar positions. The market turmoil in the aftermath of 9/11 and the financial crisis of 2008 opened a new era of swap lines 'as a way to finance global lender-of-last-resort operations in U.S. dollars'.[38] The COVID-19 pandemic required a massive recurrence to swap lines. In addition to individual actions, the major central banks established strong cooperation[39] in the form of temporary six-month US dollar liquidity arrangements (swap lines) between the Federal Reserve, the Reserve Bank of Australia, Banco de Mexico, the Norges Bank (Norway), the Reserve Bank of New Zealand, the Monetary Authority of Singapore, and the Sverigies Riksbank of Sweden, in addition to those already in place with the Bank of Canada, Bank of England, Bank of Japan, ECB, and Swiss National Bank. These measures serve to support the provision of US dollar liquidity, thereby reducing the pressure on such US dollar funding markets.

More generally, another prerogative of central banks in the post-crisis framework is their role in macroprudential oversight, as complementary to micro-prudential supervision, to increase financial stability and better control systemic risk concerns. The Agreements of Basel III have implemented such complementarity with a view to better addressing the systemic risk emerging in the aftermath of the financial crisis. Micro-prudential supervision focuses on safeguarding the stability of individual financial institutions, with a view to minimizing their risks, while macroprudential supervision considers the risks generated by the interaction of such financial institutions.[40] Micro-prudential and macroprudential supervision rely on different tools

---

[36] See Michael D. Bordo, Owen Humpage, and Anna J. Schwartz, 'The Evolution of the Federal Reserve Swap Lines Since 1962' (2014) NBER Working Paper 20755, 2 <https://www.nber.org/system/files/working_papers/w20755/w20755.pdf> accessed 22 April 2022.
[37] Ibid, 2.
[38] Ibid, 1.
[39] Christopher G. Collins, Simon Potter, and Edwin M. Truman, 'Enhancing Central Bank Cooperation in the COVID-19 Pandemic' (*PIIE Blog*, 9 April 2020) <https://www.piie.com/blogs/realtime-economic-issues-watch/enhancing-central-bank-cooperation-covid-19-pandemic> accessed 22 April 2022.
[40] Frederic Boissay and Lorenzo Cappiello, 'Micro- versus Macro-prudential Supervision: Potential Differences, Tensions and Complementarities' (May 2014) ECB—Financial Stability Review 135 <https://www.ecb.europa.eu/pub/pdf/fsr/art/ecb.fsrart201405_03.en.pdf> accessed 22 April 2022.

(such as counter-cyclical capital buffers exclusively for micro-prudential purposes), and differ in their timing of intervention.[41]

Central banks contribute to or directly designate the systemically important financial institutions (SIFIs) that must comply with increased regulatory requirements, such as increased capital requirements. In the United States, the Federal Reserve is a member of the Financial Stability Oversight Committee (FSOC), in charge of designating SIFIs. The FSOC was created through the Dodd–Frank Act, to identify threats to financial stability, promote market discipline, and promptly react to unintended risks to the stability of the financial system.[42] In Europe, the ECB is a member of the European Systemic Risk Board, together with national central bankers, and designates systemically important banks.[43] In Switzerland, the SNB is directly in charge of this task.[44]

Consistent with an expansive trend in the prerogatives of central banks, a significant debate on the role of central banks in pursuing sustainability has emerged in recent years. Central banks will be increasingly prominent in the debate on climate change, because of its implications for key prerogatives of central banks such as monetary and financial stability.[45] The international initiatives to pursue coordination among central banks with a focus on sustainability have grown. An example is the creation of the Network of Central Banks and Supervisors for Greening the Financial System (NGFS) in December 2017 during the Paris 'One Planet Summit', to strengthen the global coordination for a full implementation of the 2016 Paris Agreement, as well as 'the role of the financial system to manage risks and to mobilize capital for green and low-carbon investments in the broader context of environmentally sustainable development'.[46]

B. Central Banks' Main Characteristics

Characteristics that are generally associated with modern central banks were not always a prerogative of these institutions, but they emerged with gradual transformations. First, central banks have not always been public institutions. At the beginning of their history, so-called public banks were private entities. This holds true for example for the Sveriges Riksbank, which the Swedish monarchy established as a publicly owned bank in 1668, after the crash of the Stockholms Banco. This entity belonged to a private citizen, Johan Palmstruch, who was granted a banking charter in return for

---

[41] Ibid.
[42] U.S. Department of the Treasury, 'Financial Stability Oversight Council' <https://home.treasury.gov/policy-issues/financial-markets-financial-institutions-and-fiscal-service/fsoc> accessed 22 April 2022.
[43] See Michal Adam, Paul Bochmann, Maciej Grodzicki, Luca Mingarelli, Mattia Montagna, Costanza Rodriguez d'Acri, and Martina Spaggiari, 'Assessing the Systemic Footprint of Euro Area Banks' (November 2019) ECB—Financial Stability Review <https://www.ecb.europa.eu/pub/financial-stability/fsr/special/html/ecb.fsrart201911_02~5fd45e4b5a.en.html#toc1> accessed 22 April 2022.
[44] See National Bank Act 2003, s 3.
[45] See Kern Alexander and Paul G. Fisher, 'Central Banking and Climate Change' in Paul G. Fisher (ed), *Making the Financial System Sustainable* (CUP 2020) 50.
[46] Banque de France, 'Network for Greening the Financial System' (8 January 2019) <https://www.banque-france.fr/en/financial-stability/international-role/network-greening-financial-system> accessed 22 April 2022.

a pledge to send half the bank's profits to the Crown.[47] Other important early central banks, such as the Bank of Amsterdam, Banco de España, and Bank of England, were all joint-stock companies with private shareholders.[48] Banco de España ceased to be a private company in 1962, and until that point its main objective had been profit maximization.[49] Early central banks operated in support of the governments as clearinghouses—they purchased government debt and issued private notes serving as currency. In addition to these 'public' transactions, early central banks were also engaged in private banking activities, such as serving as banks for bankers, facilitating transactions between banks or providing other banking services, and acting as repositories for most banks.

The shift from private to public institutions was gradual. Napoleon created the Banque de France to finance the country's wars, although the Banque maintained its operational independence from the government, as did its predecessors, including the entity created by the legendary John Law, who will be further discussed in Section III.C.1.a.[50] In England, the Bank of England (the sole joint-stock company authorized in the country) also had a role in financing the war against France. By the beginning of the nineteenth century, the Bank had significantly expanded its role and responsibilities for economic and historic expeditions and had become a key public actor.[51] The Bank's activities and its network favoured the emergence of its role as lender of last resort in emergency crises,[52] which was consolidated toward the end of the nineteenth century and the beginning of the twentieth century.[53] During this time, not only the Bank of England but also other early central banks began to systematically act as lenders of last resort.[54]

Nowadays, modern 'public' state-owned, or state-controlled, central banks pursue public interest functions, including the stabilization of the macroeconomy. This mandate requires maintaining price stability, which is often accomplished by stabilizing the business cycle and maintaining full employment. Importantly, since the financial crisis of 2008, central banks are now often also in charge of financial stability.[55]

Second, consistent with economic governance without a publicly state-owned or controlled central bank, even the monopoly on the issuance of bank notes was not a key characteristic of central banks. In the UK, until the mid-nineteenth century, commercial banks could issue their own banknotes, and notes issued by provincial

---

[47] William Roberds and François R. Velde, 'Early Public Banks I' (hereafter Roberds and Velde, 'Early Public Banks I') in David Fox and Wolfgang Ernst (eds), *Money in the Western Legal Tradition: Middle Ages to Bretton Woods* (OUP 2016) 321 (hereafter Fox and Ernst, *Money in the Western Legal Tradition*).
[48] See Rodney Edvinsson, Tor Jacobson, and Daniel Waldenstrom, 'Introduction' in Rodney Edvinsson, Tor Jacobson, and Daniel Waldenström (eds), *Sveriges Riksbank and the History of Central Banking* (CUP 2018) 18 (hereafter Edvinsson et al., 'Introduction').
[49] Michael D. Bordo and Pierre Siklos, 'Central Banks: Evolution and Innovation in Historical Perspective' in Rodney Edvinsson, Tor Jacobson, and Daniel Waldenström (eds), *Sveriges Riksbank and the History of Central Banking* (CUP 2018) 26 (hereafter Bordo and Siklos, 'Central Banks: Evolution').
[50] Edvinsson et al., 'Introduction' (n 48) 18.
[51] See Willam Roberds and François R. Velde, 'Early Public Banks II' in Fox and Ernst, *Money in the Western Legal Tradition* (n 47) 471–472.
[52] See Bordo, 'Brief History of Central Banks' (n 22).
[53] Bordo and Siklos, 'Central Banks: Evolution' (n 49) 3.
[54] Ibid.
[55] Ibid.

banking companies were commonly in circulation. In the United States, commercial banks long printed their own money. The First Bank of the United States and the Second Bank of the United States were the first failed attempts in the eighteenth century to create a proper central bank. After these failures, in the nineteenth century, during the so-called free banking era (from 1837 to 1863),[56] commercial banks were in a position to issue notes. The 1863 National Banking Act intended to create a system of National Banks, with more rigorous reserve standards. A fundamental measure was the creation of a national currency, with all banks forced to accept each other's currencies at par value, to mitigate any risk of loss related to a bank default. The Comptroller of the Currency was in charge of printing the notes, to avoid counterfeiting. This situation ended in 1913 with the adoption of the Federal Reserve Act, which 'centralized' banking activity and created the Federal Reserve system currently in place.

In contemporary times, central banks maintain specific protections against political influence. The ECB, for example, maintains this independence along institutional, functional, personal, and financial dimensions,[57] as provided by Article 130 of the Treaty on the Functioning of the European Union.[58] The Federal Reserve's independence stems from the Federal Reserve Act of 1913 and goes beyond the literal interpretation of it.[59] These debated mechanisms of independence serve to insulate central banks from the undue influence of other governmental powers and their short-term political agendas, and depend on the technicality of the task.[60] Central bank independence consequentially leaves central bankers with exclusive control of the monetary policy instruments.[61] The intended outcome is the central bank's resistance to any political pressure to pursue objectives other than price stability.[62] Central bank independence has often provoked significant debate, since politicians are capable

---

[56] See generally Ranajoy Ray Chaudhuri, 'The Free Banking Era', in Ranajoy Ray Chaudhuri, *The Changing Face of American Banking* (Palgrave 2014) 7–19.

[57] Yves Mersch, 'International Trends in Central Bank Independence: The ECB's Perspective' (Speech at the ECB Roundtable Discussion on Central Bank Independence, Frankfurt am Main, 12 November 2019) <https://www.ecb.europa.eu/press/key/date/2019/html/ecb.sp191112_1~f304b47e14.en.html> accessed 22 April 2022 (hereafter Mersch, 'Central Bank Independence'). See also Lorenzo Bini Smaghi, 'Central Bank Independence: From Theory to Practice' (Speech at the Good Governance and Effective Partnership Conference, Budapest, 19 April 2007) <https://www.ecb.europa.eu/press/key/date/2007/html/sp070419.en.html> accessed 22 April 2022.

[58] See Consolidated Version of the Treaty on the Functioning of the European Union [2010] OJ C 83/47, art 130.

[59] See generally Peter Conti-Brown, 'The Institution of Federal Reserve Independence' (2015) 32 YaleJonReg 257.

[60] See Tobias Adrian and Ashraf Khan, 'Central Bank Accountability, Independence, and Transparency' (*IMF Blog*, 25 November 2019) <https://www.imf.org/en/Blogs/Articles/2019/11/25/central-bank-accountability-independence-and-transparency> accessed 22 April 2022 (hereafter Adrian and Kahn, 'Central Bank Accountability'). On the relationship between accountability and liquidity, see BIS Committee on the Global Financial System, 'Designing Frameworks for Central Bank Liquidity Assistance: Addressing New Challenges' (April 2017) CGFS Papers n 58 <https://www.bis.org/publ/cgfs58.pdf> accessed 12 April 2022.

[61] See Mario Draghi, 'Central Bank Independence' (Lecture at the Banque Nationale de Belgique, Brussels, 26 October 2018) <https://www.ecb.europa.eu/press/key/date/2018/html/ecb.sp181026.en.html> accessed 22 April 2022. Alesina and Lawrence purported the view that independent central banks operate better than those under political control. See Alberto Alesina and Lawrence H. Summers, 'Central Bank Independence and Macroeconomic Performance: Some Comparative Evidence' (1993) 25 JMCB 151.

[62] Ibid.

of exercising influence over central bankers,[63] and was criticized (by, among others, Nobel Laureate Joseph Stiglitz) for reducing the capacity of central banks to be efficient in times of crisis.[64]

Central bank independence works in an efficient manner only if strong mechanisms of accountability and transparency are in place, contributing to mitigation of the risks related to it.[65] Although accountability and transparency are referred to as synonyms, they do not have the same meaning. As Tommaso Padoa Schioppa explains, accountability refers to a political duty and has an '*ex-post* character', serving as 'a counterweight of independence'.[66] It concretely translates into 'an *ex-post* explanation and justification' of independent or autonomous decision-making.[67] Central bankers are accountable to citizens for their institutional missions.[68] In addition, transparency is instrumental to reinforcing accountability and consists of a real-time, or even an advanced, communication of central banks' initiatives to the general public, contributing to a better understanding.[69] For example, the ECB regularly holds press conferences following Governing Council meetings and directly produces its own publications.[70]

C. Traditional Money and Payment Systems

1. Central Bank and Commercial Bank Money

Shadow central banking's chief channel of disruption is the basic concept of money, because its currency escapes the traditional dichotomy based on central bank money and commercial bank money. In the past, at certain points central banks were the exclusive money issuer; on the contrary, in the free banking era, for example, money creation was exclusively in the hands of commercial banks. Both these arrangements proved to be suboptimal and modern systems rely on central banks as well as a multiplicity of commercial banks, acting as money creators.

Central bank money and commercial bank money can be interchangeably used by the public in the context of the payment system, mostly because they are exchanged at par value.[71] Central bank money encompasses different forms, including banknotes and electronically stored accounts, that is, bank accounts at the central bank. While

---

[63] Christopher Condon, 'Central Bank Independence' (*Bloomberg*, 8 July 2019) <https://www.bloomberg.com/quicktake/central-bank-independence> accessed 22 April 2022.

[64] Lucas Kawa, 'Stiglitz: Central Bank Independence Is Unnecessary and Impossible' (*Business Insider*, 3 January 2013) <https://www.businessinsider.com/stiglitz-on-central-bank-independence-2013-1?r=US&IR=T> accessed 22 April 2022 (hereafter Kawa, 'Central Bank Independence').

[65] See Adrian and Kahn, 'Central Bank Accountability' (n 60).

[66] Tommaso Padoa-Schioppa, 'An Institutional Glossary of the Eurosystem' (*ECB*, 8 March 2000) <https://www.ecb.europa.eu/press/key/date/2000/html/sp000308_1.en.html> accessed 22 April 2022.

[67] Ibid. See also Mersch, 'Central Bank Independence' (n 57).

[68] Ibid.

[69] Ibid. For an analysis on the transparency in central banking policy, see generally Christine Kaufmann and Rolf H. Weber, 'Transparency of Central Banks' Policy' in Peter Conti-Brown and Rosa Lastra (eds), *Research Handbook on Central Banking* (Elgar 2018). For a broader analysis of the role of transparency in financial regulation, including the institutional dimension of decision making, see Christine Kaufmann and Rolf Weber, 'The Role of Transparency in Financial Regulation' (2010) 13 JIntlEconL 779.

[70] Ibid.

[71] See BIS, 'The Role of Central Bank Money' (n 23) 1.

banknotes are universally accessible and available to the public, only specific entities have access to a central bank account, generally if they are implicated with systemically important payment systems.[72] Central banks implement this choice because they do not intend to compete with commercial banks in the provision of banking services, but allow specific institutions to hold accounts only if public policy reasons justify this need.[73] Consistent with this view, banks (a heterogeneous definition among the different legal systems)[74] are traditionally central bank account holders, and their special status is mostly related to their role as payment service providers for the economy.[75]

Different from central bank money, commercial bank money refers to the creation of account balances and credit by commercial banks. As explained in Chapter 1, commercial banks transform short-term liabilities (short-term debt of retail depositors and money markets) into medium and long-term loans.[76] Maturity transformation is completed with liquidity transformations, taking liquid short-notice debt and transforming it into more illiquid loans, and credit transformation, consisting in transforming deposits in more risky loans, thereby accomplishing the function of money creation. The advantage of multiple regulated or licensed financial institutions such as commercial banks acting as money creators or issuers relates to increased competition in the provision of better payment systems and financial services.[77] Regulatory and licensing mechanisms for commercial banks serve to increase both their solvency and their liquidity, thus contributing to pursuit of the ultimate goal: preserving trust in the currency.[78]

2. The Functions of Money

Money is vested with specific functions in an economic ecosystem, specifically serving as a medium of exchange, a unit of account, and a store of value. The medium of exchange function was identified by classical and neoclassical economists, and refers to the role of fiat currency to facilitate trade, although it has no intrinsic value.[79] As Nobuhiro Kiyotaki and Randall Wright explain in their seminal article 'Money as a Medium of Exchange', a commodity may serve as a medium of exchange when it is 'accepted in trade not to be consumed or used in production, but to be used to further trade', and it is defined as 'commodity money'.[80] As they further explain, 'if an object with no intrinsic value becomes a medium of exchange, it is called fiat money'.[81]

---

[72] Ibid, 3.
[73] Ibid, 26.
[74] As mentioned in Chapter 1, the European and American regulations provide two different notions, though substantially coincident, of credit institution. European Regulation No. 575/2013, art 4.1 defines a credit institution as 'an undertaking the business of which is to take deposits or other repayable funds from the public and to grant credits for its own account'. In the United States, the Bank Holding Company Act 1956, para 2 defines a bank as an institution 'which both—(i) accepts demand deposits or deposits that the depositor may withdraw by check or similar means for payment to third parties or others; and (ii) is engaged in the business of making commercial loans'.
[75] See BIS, 'The Role of Central Bank Money' (n 23) 26.
[76] Armour et al., *Principles of Financial Regulation* (n 31) 290.
[77] See BIS, 'The Role of Central Bank Money' (n 23) 1–2.
[78] Ibid, 2.
[79] Nobuhiro Kiyotaki and Randall Wright, 'On Money as a Medium of Exchange' (1989) 97 JPolEcon 927, 928–929.
[80] Ibid, 929.
[81] Ibid.

The unit of account function of currency is strictly related to the medium of exchange function,[82] and refers to the unit used to keep credits and debts[83] as well as goods and services.[84] While in the past economies relied on common goods (such as staple food or farm animals) serving the unit of account function, modern economies have shifted to currencies.[85] Although modern currencies serve as medium of exchange and unit of account, some precedents in history show that the two functions were often separated. This was the case in the Middle Ages, where a 'circulating coin' used as a unit of account for contracts did not serve to settle such contracts.[86] Finally, money serves as a store of value, when referring to the expectation that it will maintain its value throughout time.[87]

The traditional concept of money relies on different approaches that justify its essence and function, in particular a state theory, a social theory, and an institutional theory.[88] The first approach emphasizes the role of the state and was elaborated by Georg Friedrich Knapp, who challenged the 'metalist' approach. According to Knapp, the metalist approach focuses on money as a medium of exchange deriving from its link with a precious metal, without taking into account the importance of the state and the fact that 'the money of a state' is that which is 'accepted at the public pay offices'.[89] This view emphasizes the link between money and the law of the state, whose prerogative is issuing notes and coins as well as playing a predominant role in monetary policy, consistent with a more heterodox 'chartalist' approach.[90] The social theory tends to emphasize the role of society in contributing to the establishment of money, buttressing the decision of a state to formally create money.[91] The institutional theory of money stresses the essential relationship between the concept of money and the 'institutional set-up of the central banks' as well as the normative global framework under which the financial institutions operate.[92]

---

[82] See generally Lawrence H. White, 'Competitive Payments Systems and the Unit of Account' (1984) 74 AmEconRev 699. See also Fischer Black, 'Banking and Interest Rates in a World Without Money: The Effects of Uncontrolled Banking' (1970) 1 JBankRes 8. See also Eugene F. Fama, 'Banking in the Theory of Finance' (1980) 6 JMonEcon 39.

[83] Eric Tymoigne and Randall L. Wray, 'Money: An Alternative Story' in Philip Arestis and Malcolm Sawyer (eds), *A Handbook of Alternative Monetary Economics* (Elgar 2007) 6.

[84] Michael McLeay, Amar Radia, and Ryland Thomas, 'Money in the Modern Economy: An Introduction' (2014) Bank of England—Quarterly Bulletin 2014 Q1 5 <https://www.bankofengland.co.uk/quarterly-bulletin/2014/q1/money-in-the-modern-economy-an-introduction> accessed 22 April 2022 (hereafter McLeay et al., 'Money in the Modern Economy').

[85] Ibid, 6.

[86] Matthias Doepke and Martin Schneider, 'Money as a Unit of Account' (2017) 85 Econometrica 1537, 1537.

[87] McLeay et al., 'Money in the Modern Economy' (n 84) 5.

[88] Claus D. Zimmermann, 'Monetary Policy in the Digital Age' in Ioannis Lianos, Philipp Hacker, Stefan Eich, and Georgios Dimitropoulos, *Regulating Blockchain: Techno-Social and Legal Challenges* (OUP 2019) 101–103 (hereafter Zimmermann, 'Monetary Policy in the Digital Age').

[89] See L. Randall Wray, 'From the State Theory of Money to Modern Money Theory: An Alternative to Economic Orthodoxy' in David Fox and Wolfgang Ernst (eds), *Money in the Western Legal Tradition: Middle Ages to Bretton Woods* (OUP 2016), citing Georg Friedrich Knapp, *The State Theory of Money* (H. M. Lucas tr, MFB 2013).

[90] Ibid. See also Zimmermann, 'Monetary Policy in the Digital Age' (n 88) 101.

[91] See ibid.

[92] See Antonio Sainz de Vicuna, 'An Institutional Theory of Money' in Mario Giovanoli and Diego Devos (eds), *International Monetary and Financial Law: The Global Crisis* (2010) 519.

In modern times, modern money (fiat currency) derives its value from the credibility of the government: so-called full faith and credit to the government. Therefore, irrespective of any theory that may justify its characteristics and its function, money is inextricably and functionally connected to the issuing sovereign state. However, shadow central banking initiatives challenge this association by proposing a novel model of money, coupled with its necessary infrastructures, and managing this system privately. By breaking this association, shadow central banking creates the possibility of private institutions in charge of monetary policy. The model that Bitcoin proposes, for example, substitutes the reputation of the state as a tool to maintain the value of money, with a broad concept of trust.[93]

The legal characterization of private money in the form of cryptocurrencies is also especially difficult today because it requires many references to multiple concepts belonging to heterogeneous fields, beyond the monetary context. Cryptocurrencies indirectly triggered securities regulation, because ICO tokens are securities in most cases;[94] furthermore, they triggered commodity laws. Recently the American CFTC considered Ether as a commodity,[95] consistent with previous analysis. New stablecoins may eventually trigger derivatives regulation in the future as well.[96]

II. Shadow Central Banking

A. What Is Shadow Central Banking

1. The Role of Technology

Technology played an important role in the development of payment systems. From the 1990s on, e-money and its benefits of speed, transparency, and efficiency began to draw attention,[97] and prompted policy questions and concerns regarding competition between private actors and central bankers in the development of technological infrastructures. At the same time, initiatives such as e-money raised real concern among regulators—in particular in the United States, where the US government chose to shut down many projects, citing risks related to money laundering.[98]

---

[93] See Section II.B.2.
[94] See Chapter 3. See generally Marco Dell'Erba, 'The Implementation of the "Do No Harm" Approach. From Inactivity to Full Enforcement: The Case of Initial Coin Offerings' (2020) 26 MichTechLRev 175 (hereafter Dell'Erba, ' "Do No Harm" Approach in Initial Coin Offerings').
[95] See Daniel Roberts, 'CFTC Says Cryptocurrency Ether Is a Commodity, and Ether Futures Are Next' (*yahoo!finance*, 10 October 2019) <https://finance.yahoo.com/news/cftc-says-cryptocurrency-ether-is-a-commodity-and-is-open-to-ether-derivatives-133455545.html> accessed 22 April 2022.
[96] See generally Marco Dell'Erba, 'Stablecoins in Cryptoeconomics: From Initial Coin Offerings (ICOs) to Central Bank Digital Currencies (CBDCs)' (2019) 22 NYUJL&PubPol'y 1 (hereafter Dell'Erba, 'Stablecoins in Cryptoeconomics').
[97] See Ruth Wandhöfer, 'The Future of Digital Retail Payments in Europe: A Role for Central Bank Issued Crypto Cash?' (1 October 2017) <https://www.ecb.europa.eu/pub/conferences/shared/pdf/20171130_ECB_BdI_conference/payments_conference_2017_academic_paper_wandhoefer.pdf> accessed 22 April 2022.
[98] FSBT.tech, 'What Is Electronic Money and Is It Real?' (*Medium*, 28 August 2018) <https://medium.com/fsbtapi/what-is-electronic-money-and-are-they-real-5277578bcbcd> accessed 22 April 2022 (hereafter FSBT.tech, 'What Is Electronic Money').

The role of technology became extremely relevant with the emergence of DLT technology and mobile computing, which created new opportunities for both private and public initiatives to develop new concepts and infrastructures. In fact, private entrepreneurs were able to implement payment systems independent from central banks for settlement, while at the same time central banks could consider new forms of retail payments media without relying on intermediaries.[99] Bitcoin was the first cryptocurrency that proposed a new concept for a secured payment system that could bypass traditional centralized authorities, including central banks. Based on the success of these technological advancements, new cryptocurrencies have proliferated, entering the sphere of the payment system.

Stablecoins are an evolution of traditional cryptocurrencies because they are backed by some sort of collateral. Stablecoins therefore became part of the debate in relation to central banks and their activities, and are a rather peculiar phenomenon in the ecosystem of Fintech initiatives. The idea underlying stablecoins is the creation of a perfect cryptocurrency, which is stable, thereby serving as a medium of exchange, store of value, and unit of account. Such a concept goes beyond the level of banking (and shadow banking) and raises questions at a higher level. This is particularly clear when tech giants, such as Facebook or Google, form coalitions with other companies to develop a new cryptocurrency.

This phenomenon raises a legitimate question about the nature of Diem, and more broadly about similar initiatives—whether past or future: should these coalitions be considered as part of a new wave of shadow banking or are they the manifestation of a different phenomenon, more directly related to central banking activity than to banking? The possibility that these initiatives refer to traditional shadow banking is unlikely because of their main function in the system, which does not directly refer to or affect credit functions. Indeed, there is an impact on the credit market, but it is indirect. However, given the broad implications of these initiatives, these activities should be categorized under the distinct phenomenon of 'shadow central banking'.[100]

2. Shadow Central Banking versus Private Central Banking

Shadow central banking differs from private central banking activities, which encompass a broad range of heterogeneous activities and instruments that are generally regulated. While some activities and instruments are held in the hands of the government (broadly speaking), others are delegated to private entities, and still others are equally divided between the private and the public spheres. As mentioned, fiat money is based on a dichotomous system: central banks rely on a system where central banking money (central bank liabilities to be used as money) co-exists with commercial bank money.[101] Traditionally, central banks solely maintained the money supply, which directly impacts interest rates (fixing the cost of capital) and inflation rates. At the same time, central banks generally delegate the creation and the management of payment

---

[99] Kahn et al., 'Should the Central Bank Issue E-Money?' (n 25) 3.
[100] Dan Awrey refers to peer-to-peer payment platforms and 'aspiring stablecoin issuers' as 'bad money' issuers and identifies their common key characteristic in the attempt to issue money outside the perimeter of conventional bank and MMF regulation. See Dan Awrey, 'Bad Money' (2020)106 CornellLRev 1, 7.
[101] BIS, 'The Role of Central Bank Money' (n 23) 1.

systems to private institutions, although such institutions still fall under the supervision of central banks, which are responsible for their efficiency. The same applies to other market infrastructures such as clearing houses, dealing with clearing and settlement in a broad range of activities, involving different levels of complexity, from basic payments to highly complex derivatives. Therefore, private central banking, which encompasses many regulated practices, is not a novelty and manages extremely important tasks in the existing framework.

Furthermore, 'private' central banking (clearing, settlement, commercial banks issuing other forms of money complementary to central bank money) differs from shadow central banking, which escapes the perimeter of regulated activities delegated to the private sector. Yet, shadow central banking often includes the central banking activities that are typically delegated by central bankers to private institutions.

Shadow central banking is a disruptor of both private and public central banking entities and activities. The activity of mining cryptocurrencies clearly escapes the dichotomy of private versus public money and puts the creation of money in the hands of a third category of entities, which includes simple individuals. The role of simple individuals in mining aligns the creation of money with other phenomena existing in the financial system, in the sense that they are all subject to a process of high fragmentation. Other initiatives, such as stablecoins, revolutionize payment systems by coupling the implementation of an infrastructure with the issuance of a private cryptocurrency. Some algorithmic stablecoins are based on smart contracts that can independently increase or decrease money supply. The parameters of these activities are different when compared to activities where central banks retain exclusive competence and those activities where central banks opt to delegate tasks to private authorized entities, with some supervision.

3. Shadow Central Banking versus Shadow Banking

Although the label 'shadow central banking' suggests some similarities with shadow banking, such similarities cannot be traced at the level of their economic function. As explained in Chapter 1, traditional shadow banking performs three main functions generally associated with traditional banks (credit, maturity, and liquidity transformation).[102] In contrast, shadow central banking performs economic functions that are the same as those performed by a central bank or by an entity that has been delegated a task by a central bank. Such similar functions include issuing a currency, managing a payment system and in very specific cases contributing to the dynamic supply of money, as in the case of algorithmic stablecoins. Similar to the shadow banking system, the shadow central banking system may be considered a network of financial and non-financial institutions, including Fintech companies, regulated credit institutions, and tech giants. This network connects individuals, allowing them to transact and exchange money on a peer-to-peer basis without relying on a traditional centralized authority.

Shadow central banking entities justify their disruptive model in the same ways that blockchain (and Fintech) entrepreneurs support their development, including increased

---

[102] See Chapter 1, Section IV.A.

transparency, increased possibility to enhance financial inclusion,[103] and a structural disintermediation which relies on the theoretical lack of a central validator. The purpose of this characterization is rather the opposite: to identify some analogies between different entrepreneurial and economic experiments that had similar goals in common. This label helps to simplify the current trends and aid in the understanding of shadow central banking from the legal and the economic perspectives. Furthermore, this would be instrumental to potentially apply some of the existing policy approaches regulating preexisting financial networks (such as shadow banking) to this new network, if they are pertinent.

B. New Forms of Money as the Main Source of Disruption

The payment system is based on two forms of money: central bank money and commercial bank money. The creation of new forms of money escaping this dichotomy is the main channel for disruption, and this is a key characteristic of e-money, Bitcoin and traditional cryptocurrencies, and, more recently, stablecoins.

1. E-Money and Pre-Bitcoin Digital Currencies

A first experiment was so-called e-money. E-money encompasses a very broad mix of entities. The ECB defines e-money as any 'electronic store of monetary value on a technical device that may be widely used for making payments to entities other than the e-money issuer. The device acts as a prepaid bearer instrument which does not necessarily involve bank accounts in transactions. E-money products can be hardware-based or software-based, depending on the technology used to store the monetary value.'[104] Widespread access to the internet contributed to the development of e-money, and to the emergence of 'network money' as a concrete and viable option. Smart cards and debit cards are both examples of e-money.

However, alternative forms of money that could be broadly defined as e-money emerged before the spread of the internet. In 1982, American researcher David Chaum created the first secure digital currency system.[105] It was based on a 'cryptographic blind signature', that is, a digital signature where the content of a message is disguised (blinded) before it is signed.[106] In 1990, Chaum applied this idea to DigiCash, an

---

[103] On the relation between Fintech and financial inclusion, see generally Alliance for Financial Inclusion, 'Fintech for Financial Inclusion: A Framework for Digital Financial Transformation' (Special Report 2018) <https://www.afi-global.org/wp-content/uploads/publications/2018-09/AFI_FinTech_Special%20Report_AW_digital.pdf> accessed 22 April 2022. For a broader analysis on the relation between sustainability, Fintech, and financial inclusion, see generally Douglas W. Arner, Ross P. Buckley, and Dirk A. Zetzsche, 'Sustainability, FinTech and Financial Inclusion' (2019) European Banking Institute Working Paper Series 2019/41 <https://ssrn.com/abstract=3387359> accessed 22 April 2022.

[104] ECB, 'Electronic Money' <https://www.ecb.europa.eu/stats/money_credit_banking/electronic_money/html/index.en.html> accessed 22 April 2022. Directive 2009/110/EC of 16 September 2009 as amended and supplemented provides a normative definition of 'electronic money' and 'electronic money institution' at art 2. The definition of 'electronic money institution' does not exclusively encompass credit institutions, but opens the possibility to issue e-money to financial and even non-financial institutions, if they are granted authorization to do so.

[105] See Kevin Werbach, *The Blockchain and the New Architecture of Trust* (MIT Press 2018) 41 (hereafter Werbach, *The New Architecture of Trust*).

[106] FSBT.tech, 'What Is Electronic Money' (n 98).

electronic cash company created with the purpose of preserving users' anonymity. Other initiatives, such as E-Gold (1996, backed by gold) and Liberty Reserve (2006),[107] had similar purposes. However, none of these projects succeeded due to the risk of illegality, which was a particularly strong concern among American regulators after the 9/11 attacks in 2001.[108]

Additionally, pre-Bitcoin experiments based on cryptography were developed by Timothy May and Jim Bell in 1992 and by famous cryptographic scientist Nick Szabo in 1997. Inspired by libertarian and anarchist ideas, May and Bell proposed a platform for executing payments without relying on traditional financial institutions. Nick Szabo's BitGold anticipated many of the features that will be replicated in Bitcoin. In referring to this experiment, Szabo emphasized that money value, including currency issued by private banks with notes, was based on the risk of relying on trust in a third party for its value.[109] Different from the abovementioned DigiCash, BitGold did not rely on a centralized bank for oversight and was designed as a 'standalone asset',[110] where its value depends on its role in solving cryptographic equations assigned by the system.[111]

All these developments were the consequence of so-called laissez-faire banking. Governments have developed a policy of laissez-faire with regard to the medium of exchange as well as the banking and financial systems. These initiatives promoted the idea of an alternative monetary system, based on competition.[112] Before the advent of blockchain technology and the debate on central banks developing 'public' cryptocurrencies, the dominant thought was that because electronic payments technology was well disbursed among private institutions, it would have been extremely hard for central banks to compete with private actors in providing electronic money.[113] The development of a public alternative infrastructure would have been expensive and unpopular among taxpayers, who already benefited from the ability to charge and recharge cards via private infrastructures.[114]

While the majority of the laissez-faire banking scholars have focused on the possibility that banks could issues traditional notes and coins, the 'new monetary economics' (NME) proposed a different idea. The NME suggested to separate the function of unit of account from the one of medium of exchange,[115] with the possibility of a unit of account to be abstract or in the form of a real commodities.[116] This approach led to a shift from a monetary exchange system to an accounting system of exchange.[117]

---

[107] Ibid.
[108] Werbach, *The New Architecture of Trust* (n 105) 41.
[109] Nick Szabo, 'BitGold' (*Unenumerated*, 27 December 2008) <http://unenumerated.blogspot.com/2005/12/bit-gold.html> accessed 22 April 2022.
[110] Samuel Elliott, 'Bitcoin: The First Self-Regulating Currency?' (2018) 3 LSELRev 57, 62.
[111] Morgen E. Peck, 'Bitcoin: The Cryptoanarchists' Answer to Cash' (*IEEE Spectrum*, 30 May 2012) <https://spectrum.ieee.org/computing/software/bitcoin-the-cryptoanarchists-answer-to-cash> accessed 22 April 2022.
[112] See F. X. Browne and David Cronin, 'Payment Technologies, Financial Innovation, and Laissez-Faire Banking' (1995) 15 CatoJ 101 (hereafter Browne and Cronin, 'Payment Technologies').
[113] Ibid.
[114] Ibid.
[115] See Tyler Cowen and Randall Kroszner, 'The Development of New Monetary Economics' (1987) 95 JPolEcon 567, 568 (hereafter Cowen and Kroszner, 'New Monetary Economics').
[116] Ibid, 569.
[117] Browne and Cronin, 'Payment Technologies' (n 112) 109.

Furthermore, the separation between the unit of account and the medium of exchange functions of the money had antecedents in history. Around the time of the French Revolution, this approach found support from numerous theorists, including Montesquieu; it remained popular in France until the 1930s.[118] More recently, important economists such as Ficher Black, Eugene Fama, and Robert Hall were credited with expanding the separation of functions through the 'BFH system'. In this system the established unit of account is not a unit of money, and the value of money is tied to that of the unit of account instead of the contrary.[119]

2. Bitcoin

As explained in Chapter 1, Bitcoin was a new experiment developing an alternative view of the trust theory of money. It is a mechanism where people make payments with confidence using a decentralized currency, and because they pay with it, money becomes the input of the system rather the output.[120] When Bitcoin was theorized in 2009, the main idea was to provide an alternative payment system that could bypass the existing centralized authorities, including existing central banks. In doing this, Bitcoin created a new form of trust based on a decentralized consensus and secured by cryptography. Bitcoin is the very first cryptocurrency and an example of virtual currency (or digital money).[121] Bitcoin, like the cryptocurrencies that followed, involves cryptocurrency or 'Bitcoin mining'. Cryptocurrency mining is the conceptual beginning of the fragmentation of money creation, a function that has always been the prerogative of monetary policy and central banking.

As also mentioned in Chapter 1, the establishment of Bitcoin in 2017–18 as a medium of exchange and unit of account alternative to existing fiat currency was slower than expected. A high degree of volatility impaired a clear establishment of cryptocurrencies as a reliable alternative to fiat currencies. Volatility depended not only on speculation, but also on specific structural characteristics of cryptocurrencies, in particular the lack of backing assets, coupled with rigid issuance rules.[122] Among these characteristics, cryptocurrencies' novelty in the economic landscape was a physiological cause of volatility.

Volatility has impaired the opportunity for Bitcoin and other cryptocurrencies to establish themselves as a unit of account and has limited their use as a means of exchange in business transactions. At the same time, volatility has impaired long-term

---

[118] Cowen and Kroszner, 'New Monetary Economics' (n 115) 576–584.
[119] Warren Coats, 'In Search of a Monetary Anchor: Commodity Standards Re-examined' in Tomas J. T. Baliño and Carlo Cottarelli (eds), *Frameworks for Monetary Stability. Policy Issues and Country Experiences* (IMF 1994) 249.
[120] See Werbach, *The New Architecture of Trust* (n 105) 41.
[121] See Dong He, Karl Habermeier, Ross Leckow, Vikram Haksar, Yasmin Almeida, Mikari Kashima, Nadim Kyriakos-Saad, Hiroko Oura, Tahsin Saadi Sedik, Natalia Stetsenko, and Concepcion Verdugo-Yepes, 'Virtual Currencies and Beyond: Initial Considerations' (2016) IMF Staff Discussion Note 16/03, 7 <https://www.imf.org/external/pubs/ft/sdn/2016/sdn1603.pdf> accessed 22 April 2022 (hereafter IMF, 'Virtual Currencies and Beyond').
[122] See Tommaso Mancini-Griffoli, Maria Soledad, Martinez Peria, Itai Agur, Anil Ari, John Kiff, Adina Popescu, and Celine Rochon, 'Casting Light on Central Bank Digital Currency' (2018) IMF Staff Discussion Note 18/08 <https://www.imf.org/-/media/Files/Publications/SDN/2018/SDN1808.ashx> accessed 22 April 2022 (hereafter IMF, 'Casting Light on Central Bank Digital Currency').

investors approaching cryptocurrencies as a long-term store of value.[123] Although the establishment of blockchain technology goes beyond the sole purpose of creating a currency, the overall instability of cryptocurrencies is traditionally regarded as a key obstacle to the development of blockchain as an ecosystem. High volatility affects the cryptoeconomic mechanisms, making costs and incentives highly unpredictable.[124] These were the main triggers for the idea of creating stable cryptocurrencies, commonly referred to as 'stablecoins'.

3. Stablecoins

This section focuses on what stablecoins are and their main categories. It then analyses three major global stablecoin projects (JPM Coin, Diem Coin, and the Hedera Hashgraph), and finally develops some regulatory considerations, with a focus on the United States, Europe, and Switzerland, in continuity with the regulatory analysis of ICOs in Chapter 1.

a. *What Are They and What Are the Main Categories?*

In an attempt to solve the problems of Bitcoin and other cryptocurrencies implanting similar structural patterns, the idea of a stable cryptocurrency, or stablecoin, emerged. Stablecoins are cryptocurrencies that maintain a stable value against a target price, generally in US dollars.[125] Stablecoins generally combine liquid collateral (such as gold or US dollar)[126] or algorithmic mechanisms of stabilization with management of the supply, incentivizing 'the market to trade the coin for no more or less than $1'.[127]

While the first stablecoin projects were created to serve as 'a bridge between crypto and fiat currencies', in particular to reduce the holder's exposure to volatility in the course of transaction execution and settlement, a second generation of projects aimed to leverage the potential applications of the DLT and smart contracts.[128] At this more advanced stage of development, stablecoins proved essential for operating in DeFi, an ecosystem which could in principle rely exclusively on stablecoins.

The majority of stablecoins currently in circulation are built on a 'public blockchain' network,[129] in particular the Ethereum blockchain protocol: the reason for this choice is the opportunity it provides to instantaneously improve the compatibility of the newly issued asset with the pre-existing infrastructure and therefore with 'second

---

[123] Kingsley Advani, 'The Top 6 Stablecoins in Crypto' (*Medium*, 23 February 2018) <https://medium.com/@kingsleyadvani/the-top-6-stable-coins-in-crypto-e6f53e9b03be> accessed 22 April 2022.

[124] Nathan Sexer, 'State of Stablecoins' (*Medium*, 24 July 2018) <https://media.consensys.net/the-state-of-stablecoins-2018-79ccb9988e63> accessed 22 April 2022.

[125] Ibid.

[126] Sherman Lee, 'Explaining Stable Coins, the Holy Grail of Cryptocurrency' (*Forbes*, 12 March 2018) <https://www.forbes.com/sites/shermanlee/2018/03/12/explaining-stable-coins-the-holy-grail-of-crytpocurrency/?sh=4af8af614fc6> accessed 22 April 2022.

[127] CryptoCurrency Facts, 'What Is a Stable Coin?' <https://cryptocurrencyfacts.com/what-is-a-stable-coin/> accessed 22 April 2022.

[128] See Dan Awrey, 'Unbundling Banking, Money & Payments' (2021) ECGI Law Working Paper No. 565/2021, 50.

[129] President's Working Group on Financial Markets, the Federal Deposit Insurance Corporation, and the Office of the Comptroller of the Currency, *Report on Stablecoins* (November 2021) 6 (hereafter President's Working Group on Financial Markets, *Report on Stablecoins*).

II. SHADOW CENTRAL BANKING

generation' applications similarly built on top of the same blockchain protocol.[130] This is very important for the way wallets operate, with potential benefits for e-commerce. Further advantages depend on the adoption of the so-called ERC20 standard[131] by the stablecoin, with the possibility of using such stablecoin in any other application similarly designed on that standard.

Three main categories of stablecoins have emerged in the market, each using a different model to stabilize their value. First, fiat-currency asset-backed stablecoins (so-called off-chain collateralized stablecoins) rely on fiat currencies as collateral and, therefore, cannot be fully decentralized. Tether (USDT) is an off-chain collateralized stablecoin, with a theoretical ratio of 1:1 between USDT and the US dollar.[132]

A second category of stablecoins, so-called on-chain collateralized stablecoins, is collateralized with digital assets, generally with either one cryptocurrency or a basket of them. This category of stablecoins is fully decentralized.

Finally, non-collateralized stablecoins are the third category. They implement algorithmic tools to maintain the stability of stablecoins. As Robert Sams explains in his seminal paper, Bitcoin-like cryptocurrencies 'govern the supply of coins through simple and deterministic coin growth rules'.[133] For this reason, any unanticipated changes in coin demand impact the coin price, with the consequence that significant volatility limits their utility as media of exchange. Therefore, Sams proposed an alternative method of stabilization based on an elastic supply rule capable of adjusting the quantity of coin supply as a reaction to changes in coin market value.[134] Non-collateralized stablecoins are not backed by any form of collateral and instead are based on 'self-sustaining models that incorporate additional layers of game-theoretic incentives to encourage self-interested user behaviour that would be instrumental in sustaining the peg'.[135] In this context, the role of a central bank managing the supply of fiat currencies is overtaken by smart contracts in charge of algorithmically expanding or contracting the supply of the stablecoins.[136] The crash of TerraUSD (TUSD) in May 2022, an algorithmic stablecoin connected to the Luna native token as part of the Terra network, generated a liquidity crunch in the cryptoeconomy with significant consequences for the entire ecosystem.[137] This event triggered a cascade of failures in the cryptoeconomy—including

---

[130] Joseph Young, 'Why New Generation Stablecoins Are Crucially Based on Ethereum' (*yahoo!finance*, 24 October 2018) <https://finance.yahoo.com/news/why-generation-stablecoins-crucially-based-152605 210.html> accessed 22 April 2022. The author notes that 'users of GUSD, PAX, and TUSD can utilize hardware wallets like Trezor and Ledger along with software wallets such as Metamask to send and receive stablecoins'.

[131] For a technical protocol describing such standard, see IndexUniverse, 'ERC20 Token Standard' <https://www.indexuniverse.eu/erc20-token-standard/> accessed 22 April 2022.

[132] For further details, see Dell'Erba, 'Stablecoins in Cryptoeconomics' (n 96) pt IIIB.

[133] Robert Sams, 'A Note on Cryptocurrency Stabilisation: Seigniorage Shares' (*BitMex blog*, 28 April 2015) <https://blog.bitmex.com/wp-content/uploads/2018/06/A-Note-on-Cryptocurrency-Stabilisation-Seigniorage-Shares.pdf> accessed 22 April 2022 (hereafter Sams, 'Cryptocurrency Stabilisation').

[134] Ibid.

[135] See Kirill Bryanov, 'Breaking the Peg: Every Stablecoin Has Its Points of Failure' (*Cointelegraph*, 19 November 2018) <https://cointelegraph.com/news/breaking-the-peg-every-stablecoin-has-its-points-of-failure> accessed 22 April 2022.

[136] Ibid.

[137] See Krisztian Sandor and Ekin Genç, 'Timeline of the Meteoric Rise and Crash of UST and LUNA' (*Coindesk*, 12 May 2022) <https://www.coindesk.com/learn/the-fall-of-terra-a-timeline-of-the-meteoric-rise-and-crash-of-ust-and-luna/> accessed 26 April 2023.

the collapse of Three Arrows Capital, one of the most prominent crypto hedge funds in the world[138]—and major concerns on algorithmic stablecoins.

After Bitcoin mining, the dynamic supply of money is a further step toward a potential full substitution of private actors in the context of central banking functions. The majority of non-collateralized coins are based on a 'seigniorage system' where two types of coin co-exist, one acting like money and one acting like shares. However, while the two coins share the same features, the two processes regulating their supply differ.[139] As Sams explains, in situations where the coin supply has to be increased, 'coinbase is distributed to shareholders in exchange for a certain percentage of shares, which are destroyed (coin supply increases, share supply decreases)'.[140] When there is an opposite need to decrease the coin supply, 'sharebase is distributed to coin holders in exchange for a certain percentage of coin, which are destroyed (coin supply decreases, share supply increases)'/[141] Such 'shares-for-coin' and 'coin-for-shares' swap mechanisms are voluntary, and are implemented through a decentralized auction as programmed in the protocol.[142]

Stablecoins are generally associated with broader ecosystems where they serve specific functions, in particular, as identified by the G7: '(a) issuance, redemption and stabilization of the value of the coins; (b) transfer of coins; and (c) interaction with coin users for storing and exchanging coins.'[143] Because of these functions, stablecoins may be assimilated to payment systems as well as to financial services or products, including deposit liabilities or securities, and may as a consequence expose the system to similar risks.[144]

Focusing on stablecoin redemption rights, as the President's Working Group on Stablecoins emphasized, they can vary in many respects. A first considerable difference relates to who is entitled to a stablecoin redemption upon the issuer and whether specific limits are placed on the quantity of coins that may be redeemed.[145] Some issuers are permitted under the terms of the arrangement to postpone redemption payments for seven days, or even to suspend redemptions at any time, causing uncertainty about the timing of redemptions.[146] Second, a significant heterogeneity emerges also when taking into account the nature of the claim provided to the user, with some stablecoin arrangements 'providing a claim on the issuer and others [not providing] direct redemption rights to users'.[147] Furthermore, other factors might affect users'

---

[138] See MacKenzie Sigalos, 'From $10 billion to zero: How a crypto hedge fund collapsed and dragged many investors down with it' (*CNBC*, 12 July 2022) <https://www.cnbc.com/2022/07/11/how-the-fall-of-three-arrows-or-3ac-dragged-down-crypto-investors.html> accessed 26 April 2023.

[139] See Sams, 'Cryptocurrency Stabilisation' (n 133).

[140] Ibid.

[141] Ibid.

[142] Ibid.

[143] G7 Working Group on Stablecoins, 'Investigating the Impact of Global Stablecoins' (October 2019) 2 <https://www.bis.org/cpmi/publ/d187.pdf> accessed 22 April 2022 (hereafter G7, 'Impact of Global Stablecoins').

[144] See Financial Stability Board, 'Addressing the Regulatory, Supervisory and Oversight Challenges Raised by "Global Stablecoin" Arrangements' (14 April 2020) 8 <https://www.fsb.org/wp-content/uploads/P140420-1.pdf> accessed 22 April 2022.

[145] President's Working Group on Financial Markets, *Report on Stablecoins* (n 129) 5.

[146] Ibid.

[147] Ibid.

ability to redeem their stablecoins, such as the 'ability to transfer the proceeds of any redemption into the banking system'.[148]

While the stabilization mechanisms and such core functions are a common characteristic of any stablecoin project, the geographical scope is a key extremely variable element. The geographic scope of such initiatives depends on different factors, including the technological infrastructures, coupled with a broad range of users located in multiple jurisdictions, contributing to an exponential growth of the user base.[149] Under such circumstances, stablecoin projects become truly global. The label 'global stablecoin', coined by the G7 and widely adopted by IOSCO[150] and the FSF, differentiates stablecoin projects such as the Libra Coin from narrower stablecoin projects.

When looking at the central bank vs commercial bank money dichotomy, the prevalent view, considering stablecoins equivalent to 'commercial bank money', would certainly be accurate. As mentioned above, the primary form of private money remains commercial bank money, which relies on deposits, and is created when commercial banks finance the real economy by making loans to households and companies.[151] This is consistent with the majority of stablecoin arrangements: 'stablecoin reserves are held as commercial bank deposits, and commercial banks engage in fractional reserve lending and maturity transformation as they normally would with traditional bank deposits'.[152] Furthermore, as noted by Eichengreen and Viswanath-Natraj, while in the vast majority of cases stablecoins act as digital money market funds (MMFs), 'in cases where they have only partial reserve backing, they raise the same issues as fractional reserve banks'.[153] Consistent with these views, the Bank of England highlighted the importance of reflecting the four key pillars of banking regulation when dealing with systemic stablecoins, including capital requirements, liquidity requirements, a legal claim, and a backstop protecting coinholders.[154] The different business models of stablecoins would likely make it hard to simply extend banking regulation to regulate them, although the principle 'same risk, same regulation' could apply, with appropriate levels of clarity, proportionality, and risk-based characteristics of potential approaches in this sense.[155]

An alternative approach to stablecoins compares them to financial market infrastructures. The CPMI–IOSCO consultative report highlighted that 'stablecoin

---

[148] Ibid. The President's Working Group has highlighted a significant difference with a demand deposit held at an insured depository.

[149] Ibid, 10.

[150] IOSCO, 'Global Stablecoins Initiatives' (March 2020) <https://www.iosco.org/library/pubdocs/pdf/IOSCOPD650.pdf> accessed 22 April 2022 (hereafter IOSCO, 'Global Stablecoins Initiatives').

[151] See Bank of England, 'Responses to the Bank of England's Discussion Paper on New Forms of Digital Money' (24 March 2022) Discussion Paper <https://www.bankofengland.co.uk/paper/2022/responses-to-the-bank-of-englands-discussion-paper-on-new-forms-of-digital-money> accessed 22 April 2022 (hereafter Bank of England, 'New Forms of Digital Money').

[152] Gordon Y. Liao and John Caramichael, 'Stablecoins: Growth Potential and Impact on Banking' (2022) International Finance Discussion Papers No. 1334, 1 <https://www.federalreserve.gov/econres/ifdp/files/ifdp1334.pdf> accessed 22 April 2022.

[153] See Barry Eichengreen and Ganesh Viswanath-Natraj, 'Stablecoins and Central Bank Digital Currencies: Policy and Regulatory Challenges' (2022) 21 AsianEconPap 29 <https://direct.mit.edu/asep/article/21/1/29/109037/Stablecoins-and-Central-Bank-Digital-Currencies> accessed 22 April 2022.

[154] Bank of England, 'New Forms of Digital Money' (n 151).

[155] Ibid.

arrangements' might be characterized as implementing a transfer function comparable to the one performed by other financial market infrastructures.[156] If this is the case, 'stablecoin arrangements' should be considered financial market infrastructures and be subject to the principles applicable to market infrastructure, the Principles for Financial Market Infrastructures (PFMI).[157] The CPMI–IOSCO report has further identified key characteristics of 'stablecoin arrangements' as market infrastructures,[158] and has considered the possibility that they might be systemically important on the basis of their size as well as their nature and risk profile.[159]

Analysis of stablecoins as money market mutual funds (MMFs) for the cryptoeconomy and DeFi will be developed in Chapter 5.

b. Salient private initiatives

i. The J.P. Morgan experiment: JPM Coin In February 2019, J.P. Morgan issued the JPM Coin, the very first experiment in this area by an established market actor, which caught the attention of regulators and central bankers. According to J.P. Morgan's definition, 'JPM Coin is a digital coin designed to make instantaneous payments using blockchain technology'.[160] Therefore, it is not a coin but a digital representation of US dollars, held in designated accounts at J.P. Morgan Chase, maintaining a value equivalent to one US dollar.[161] The main function of the JPM Coin consists of arranging the exchange of value 'between different parties', where the object of this exchange can be 'money' (but is not limited to money, according to the formulation adopted in the website) and a cryptocurrency is needed. As J.P. Morgan explains, 'when one client sends money to another over the blockchain, JPM Coins are transferred and instantaneously redeemed for the equivalent amount of U.S. dollars, reducing the typical settlement time'.[162] These transactions are executed on a private blockchain model, Quorum, built by J.P. Morgan and 'forked' from the Ethereum blockchain.

JPM Coin raised doubts regarding its characterization as a cryptocurrency because it escapes the traditional characteristics generally associated with cryptocurrencies. The main feature of traditional cryptocurrencies consists in their being decentralized and, thus, fully operative on a public blockchain. Therefore, encryption techniques serve to regulate the generation of units of currency as well as to verify the transfer of funds without the intervention of a central bank.[163]

---

[156] BIS Committee on Payments and Market Infrastructures and IOSCO, 'Application of the Principles for Financial Market Infrastructures to Stablecoin Arrangements' (October 2021) <https://www.bis.org/cpmi/publ/d198.htm> accessed 22 April 2022 (hereafter BIS-IOSCO, 'Principles for Financial Market Infrastructures').
[157] Ibid.
[158] Ibid. Such characteristics are: '(i) the potential use of settlement assets that are neither central bank money nor commercial bank money and carry additional financial risk; (ii) the interdependencies between multiple SA functions; (iii) the degree of decentralisation of operations and/or governance; and (iv) a potentially large-scale deployment of emerging technologies such as distributed ledger technology.'
[159] Ibid, 11–12.
[160] Jason Bloomberg, 'JPM Coin from JPMorgan Chase vs. Crypto Fans: Who's Missing the Point?' (*Forbes*, 22 February 2019) <https://www.forbes.com/sites/jasonbloomberg/2019/02/22/jpm-coin-from-jpmorgan-chase-vs-crypto-fans-whos-missing-the-point/> accessed 22 April 2022.
[161] Ibid.
[162] Ibid.
[163] See Eric Brown, 'Breaking Down JPM Coin' (*Hakernoon*, 17 February 2019) <https://hackernoon.com/breaking-down-jpm-coin-f31c41f3f325> accessed 22 April 2022.

ii. The Diem Association

The Libra Association experiment: Libra Libra was promoted by the Libra Foundation, based in Geneva, Switzerland. The mission was the creation of 'a simple global currency and financial infrastructure ... that empowers billions of people'.[164] The Libra Association initially grouped together a broad range of entrepreneurs and institutions operating in different sectors, including payment systems (Mastercard, Visa, PayPal, Mercado Pago, Pay U, Stripe), technology and online marketplaces (eBay, Spotify, Facebook, Farftech, Lift, Booking Holdings), telecommunications (Iliad, Vodafone), Blockchain (Anchorage, Bison Trails, Coinbase, Xapo) venture capitals, and non-profit organizations. However, during the months of September and October 2019, seven companies (including eBay, PayPal, Visa and Mastercard) left the project.

The Libra Association was described as 'an independent, not-for-profit membership organization' with the purpose of coordinating and providing 'a framework for governance for the network and reserve and lead social impact grant-making in support of financial inclusion'.[165] It was structured as an association, which is rather peculiar in terms of corporate governance schemes of accountability. Furthermore, this not-for-profit scheme at the corporate level is inconsistent with the for-profit goal of Libra in creating a global payment system.

On the technical side, Libra proposed a model built on top of the 'Libra Blockchain', an open source blockchain which is supposed to be the foundational infrastructure for 'an open, interoperable ecosystem of financial services ... for everyday use'.[166]

In its initial version, Libra was designed to be a global payment system, backed by a basket of national fiat currencies.[167] According to the first version of its white paper, Libra should have been a 'stable digital cryptocurrency ... fully backed by a reserve of real assets ... and supported by a competitive network of exchanges buying and selling Libra'.[168] This first version of Libra was not backed with gold, but instead by a basket of low-volatility assets, including bank deposits and short-term government securities in currencies from stable and reputable central banks.[169] Furthermore, it was not designed to be 'pegged' to one single digital currency.[170]

The heavy critique to which Libra was exposed, in particular in the United States,[171] led the Libra Association to develop a rather different scheme, abandoning the ambition to become a global payment system exclusively built on its own currency. In its new version, the Libra payment system opened to 'single-currency stablecoins (e.g., ≈USD, ≈EUR, ≈GBP, etc.)', and maintained a 'multi-currency-coin (≈LBR)', all together defined

---

[164] 'Libra White Paper v1.0' (n 3) s 01.
[165] Ibid, 3.
[166] Ibid.
[167] See Philipp Sandner, 'Understanding Libra 2.0: A Compliant Global Platform for the Digital Programmable EUR, USD, GBP & Co' (*Medium*, 17 April 2020) <https://medium.com/@philippsandner/libra-2-0-a-compliant-global-platform-for-the-digital-programmable-eur-usd-gbp-co-67e1b8a2c0cb> accessed 22 April 2022 (hereafter Sandner, 'Understanding Libra').
[168] 'Libra White Paper v1.0' (n 3) s 04.
[169] Ibid.
[170] Ibid.
[171] Hannah Murphy and Izabella Kaminska, 'Facebook's Libra Overhauls Core Parts of Its Digital Currency Vision' (*Financial Times*, 16 April 2020) <https://www.ft.com/content/23a33fcb-1342-4a18-be39-504e8507f752>.

as 'Libra Coins'.[172] According to the White Paper 2.0, each single-currency stablecoin should be fully backed by the reserves, consisting of liquid assets which included 'cash or cash equivalents and very short-term government securities denominated in the relevant currency'.[173] As a result, each ≈LBR would in principle benefit from the backing and stability of those stablecoins, because it would be 'a composite of 1:1-backed single-currency stablecoins supported by the Libra network'.[174] The multicurrency coin (≈LBR) was a residual tool for those countries 'that do not have a single-currency stablecoin on the Libra network'.[175] Different from the previous version, ≈LBR should have consisted of 'a digital composite of some of the single-currency stablecoins available on the Libra network' and 'be defined in terms of fixed nominal weights', consistent with the special drawing rights (SDR) of the International Money Fund (IMF).[176] In this situation, ≈LBR should have been 'a neutral and low-volatility alternative ensuring users in such regions to benefit from accessing the network and increased financial inclusion'. Its main function would have been to operate 'as a settlement coin in cross-border transactions', with the possibility to convert it into local currencies.[177]

In its new version, Libra was defined as a 'global value platform' compared to the initial 'global means of payment'.[178] Others compared it to PayPal, sharing with it the characteristic of being a 'regulated payment processor',[179] although it still raised concerns related to the reputation of Facebook as a prominent promoter, and the potential risks of a multi-currency coin.[180]

From Libra to Diem   On 1 December 2020 the Libra Association underwent a major transformation, both formally, because it was rebranded adopting the new label of Diem, and substantially, partially redesigning its governance and shifting toward a new concept of the proposed stablecoin project.

The Libra Association was severely hit by regulatory blowback, mostly due to the mistrust of many regulators and central bankers in Facebook and its significant influence on the whole Libra Association. As a collateral effect, some major partners (including Visa and PayPal) opted to leave the association.[181] Earlier in May 2020, Facebook had already rebranded its wallet from Calibra to Novi.[182]

---

[172] 'Libra White Paper v2.0' (n 3) 5.
[173] Ibid.
[174] Ibid.
[175] Ibid, 11.
[176] Ibid, 2.
[177] Ibid, 11.
[178] Sandner, 'Understanding Libra' (n 167).
[179] Kiran Stacey and Hannah Murphy, 'How Facebook's Libra Went from World Changer to Just Another PayPal' (*Financial Times*, 17 April 2020) <https://www.ft.com/content/79376464-72b5-41fa-8f14-9f308acaf83b> accessed 22 April 2022.
[180] Ibid.
[181] Jacob Kastrenakes, 'Libra Cryptocurrency Project Changes Name to Diem to Distance Itself from Facebook' (*The Verge*, 1 December 2020) https://www.theverge.com/2020/12/1/21755078/libra-diem-name-change-cryptocurrency-facebook> accessed 22 April 2022 (hereafter Kastrenakes, 'Libra Cryptocurrency Project').
[182] Anna Irrera and Tom Wilson, 'Facebook-Backed Digital Coin Libra Renamed Diem in Quest for Approval' (*Reuters*, 1 December 2020) <https://www.reuters.com/article/uk-facebook-cryptocurrency-idUKKBN28B57O> accessed 22 April 2022 (hereafter Irrera and Wilson, 'Facebook-Backed Digital Coin').

The rebranding of Libra was an effort to gain some sort of regulatory approval by stressing the project's independence and autonomy, especially from Facebook,[183] in an attempt to enter emerging markets,[184] where new payment systems could play an especially significant role.[185] As will be explained in greater depth in the following sections, regulators and central banks raised a variety of concerns regarding financial stability and control over monetary policy, privacy, and money laundering.[186]

Beyond the rebranding strategy, the Diem Association had some specific features differentiating it from the Libra Association. The Diem Association was still a Geneva-based association, but with twenty-seven participants (Facebook is not one of them), and had abandoned the 100-member goal while still attempting to increase the current number of participants.[187] In an attempt to reinforce internal corporate governance and strengthen operational preparedness, Diem recruited senior staff from the banking sector, including HSBC and Credit Suisse.[188][189]

An important aspect at the intersection of both corporate governance and technical aspects relates to the decision to abandon the transition towards a permissionless blockchain.[190] This is consistent with the intention to strengthen policies in relation to anti-money laundering, terrorist financing, and sanction compliance.[191] The network should have also complied with the so-called travel rule[192] (technically the Financial Action Task Force Travel Rule), requiring virtual asset service providers to ensure that certain customer data is disclosed and transferred between counterparties as a part of the cryptocurrency transaction.[193]

A major shift also involved the initial concept of the Libra Coin. As mentioned earlier, Libra had originally planned to create a cryptocurrency supported by a basket of government-issued fiat currencies and securities.[194] The Diem Association planned to issue a stablecoin pegged to the US dollar, the Diem Dollar, backed by 'outside

---

See also Kastrenakes, 'Libra Cryptocurrency Project' (n 181). See also Olga Kharif, 'Facebook-Backed Libra Association Changes Its Name to Diem' (*Bloomberg*, 1 December 2020) <https://www.bloomberg.com/news/articles/2020-12-01/facebook-backed-crypto-group-libra-changes-name-to-diem-network> accessed 22 April 2022 (hereafter Kharif, 'Libra Association Changes Its Name').

[183] Irrera and Wilson, 'Facebook-Backed Digital Coin' (n 182).
[184] Kharif, 'Libra Association Changes Its Name' (n 182).
[185] See Section III.
[186] Irrera and Wilson, 'Facebook-Backed Digital Coin' (n 182).
[187] Kharif, 'Libra Association Changes Its Name' (n 182).
[188] Finextra, 'Libra Rebrands as Diem in Effort to Distance Itself from Facebook' (1 December 2020) <https://www.finextra.com/newsarticle/37057/libra-rebrands-as-diem-in-effort-to-distance-itself-from-facebook> accessed 22 April 2022.
[189] Kharif, 'Libra Association Changes Its Name' (n 182).
[190] Ibid.
[191] Irrera and Wilson, 'Facebook-Backed Digital Coin' (n 182).
[192] Nikhilesh De, 'Libra Rebrands to "Diem" in Anticipation of 2021 Launch' (*CoinDesk*, 1 December 2020) <https://www.coindesk.com/libra-diem-rebrand> accessed 22 April 2022 (hereafter De, 'Libra Rebrands to Diem').
[193] Bitcoin Suisse, 'What Is the FATF Travel Rule?' <https://www.bitcoinsuisse.com/research/specials/what-is-the-fatf-travel-rule> accessed 22 April 2022.
[194] Kastrenakes, 'Libra Cryptocurrency Project' (n 181) and Kharif, 'Libra Association Changes Its Name' (n 182).

assets'.[195] Therefore, the Diem Dollar would have directly competed with Tether, which is still the most capitalized stablecoin in the world.

In addition to the Diem Dollar, the Diem Association might have opted to issue additional fiat-based cryptocurrencies, without excluding developments in the sense of a basket-backed stablecoin.[196] This would have essentially replicated the original model proposed by the Libra Association.

The potential launch date was indicated to be 2021—as early as January[197]—subject to the approval of the FINMA.[198] Although the project was ready to be launched, it underwent a phase of testing and improvement in terms of infrastructural design.[199]

In May 2021, Diem Networks GmbH withdrew its application for authorization as a payment system with the Swiss FINMA as it planned the launch of its payment system from the USA, justifying this decision with the focus of the project 'on the USA as its target market and because [Diem] is now based on the US currency'.[200] In the USA, Diem developed a close cooperation with state-chartered bank Silvergate (which shut down in March 2023 in the context of a significant market turmoil) to issue the Diem USD stablecoin.[201] However, the Federal Reserve contacted both Silvergate and Diem before the launch of a Diem currency pilot to communicate 'that the government was uncomfortable condoning any project until it had put a "comprehensive regulatory framework" for stablecoins in place, and expressed nervousness about a coin with the potential to "massively scale" as Diem might'.[202]

Following the Federal Reserve's rejection, Diem executives could only resort to a state-level regulated stablecoin issuer and in the late summer of 2021 Facebook partnered with NY-based crypto-exchange Gemini. The project never took off and most details were not disclosed.[203] In October 2021, Diem launched a pilot of its digital wallet, renamed Novi, allowing users to send and receive payments in the stablecoin USDP (Pax Dollar, a rival stablecoin) while awaiting advancements in regulatory approval of the Diem currency. Novi's terms of service allowed customers to redeem 1 USDP for 1 US dollar, according to 1:1 parity between the stablecoin and the US dollar.[204] Although the new product was promising, the launch was cancelled after a Treasury report urged regulation of stablecoins and soliciting 'restrictions that limit affiliation with commercial entities or on use of users' transaction data'.[205] As a consequence of

---

[195] Kharif, 'Libra Association Changes Its Name' (n 182).
[196] De, 'Libra Rebrands to Diem' (n 192).
[197] Ibid and Kastrenakes, 'Libra Cryptocurrency Project' (n 181).
[198] Kharif, 'Libra Association Changes Its Name' (n 182). As the interview specifies, 'Diem is also in talks with U.S. federal and state regulators, but isn't waiting for any specific licenses or approvals from them'.
[199] De, 'Libra Rebrands to Diem' (n 192).
[200] FINMA, 'Diem Withdraws Licence Application in Switzerland' (12 May 2021) <https://www.finma.ch/en/news/2021/05/20210512-mm-diem/> accessed 22 April 2022.
[201] The Diem Association, 'Diem Announces Partnership with Silvergate and Strategic Shift to the United States' (12 May 2021) <https://www.diem.com/en-us/updates/diem-silvergate-partnership/> accessed 22 April 2022.
[202] Ibid.
[203] Ibid.
[204] Arthur E. Wilmarth Jr., 'It's Time to Regulate Stablecoins as Deposits and Require Their Issuers to Be FDIC-Insured Banks' (2022) 41 Banking & Financial Services Policy Report No. 2, 6–7 <https://scholarship.law.gwu.edu/cgi/viewcontent.cgi?article=2834&context=faculty_publications> accessed 22 April 2022.
[205] President's Working Group on Financial Markets, *Report on Stablecoins* (n 129) 2, 17.

the substantial contrariety to the Diem project, it was eventually shut down. Diem sold its intellectual property and all its assets to Silverlake on 31 January 2022.[206]

c. Regulatory context
i. United States In the United States, the same regulatory uncertainties on the classification of ICOs and cryptocurrencies that existed in 2017–18[207] re-emerged in the context of stablecoins. The 2018 decision of Basis' developers to shut down operations exemplifies this regulatory uncertainty[208] and its potentially negative consequences. Consistent with what happened with ICOs, the Securities and Exchange Commission (SEC) may qualify stablecoins not as cryptocurrencies but rather as 'securities', due to the similarities they share with the concept of the 'security token': a security token being backed by something tangible, including assets, profits, or revenue of the company.[209]

As mentioned in Chapter 3, after a period of inactivity,[210] in July 2017 the SEC issued the 'Report of Investigation Pursuant to Section 21(a) of the Securities Exchange Act of 1934: The DAO'[211] (the 'DAO Report'). In that case, the SEC applied a classic tool elaborated by American courts, the so-called *Howey* test, to ICO tokens and concluded that DAO ICO tokens qualified as a 'security' under section 2(a)(1) of the Securities Act of 1933.[212] Since then, the SEC has gradually extended the securities regulation to ICOs and a vast majority of activities involving cryptocurrencies.[213] In the past, the SEC confirmed the possibility that stablecoins might trigger securities laws: 'Whether a particular digital asset, including one labeled a stablecoin, is a security under the federal securities laws is inherently a facts and circumstances determination. This determination requires a careful analysis of the nature of the instrument, including the rights it purports to convey, and how it is offered and sold.'[214]

---

[206] The Diem Association, 'Statement by Diem CEO Stuart Levey on the Sale of the Diem Group's Assets to Silvergate' (31 January 2022) https://www.diem.com/en-us/updates/stuart-levey-statement-diem-asset-sale/> accessed 22 April 2022.
[207] See Chapter 3.
[208] Michael del Castillo, 'Crypto's Top Funded Startup Shutters Operations Following SEC Concerns' (*Forbes*, 13 December 2018) <https://www.forbes.com/sites/michaeldelcastillo/2018/12/13/sec-rules-kill-cryptos-top-funded-startup/#485ac2f22918 [https://perma.cc/PSC7-9RW4> accessed 22 April 2022.
[209] Polymath Network, 'What Is a Security Token Offering (STO)?' (12 March 2018) <https://blog.polymath.network/what-is-a-security-token-offering-sto-4e5a92bf6bca> accessed 22 April 2022. In addition, if a crypto token derives its value from an external, tradable asset, it is classified as a security token and becomes subject to federal securities regulations. Failure to abide by these regulations could result in costly penalties and could threaten to derail a project. However, if a start-up meets all its regulatory obligations, the security token classification creates the potential for a wide variety of applications, the most promising of which is the ability to issue tokens that represent shares of company stock.
[210] See Marco Dell'Erba, 'Initial Coin Offerings: The Response of Regulatory Authorities' (2018) 14 NYUJL&Bus 1107, 1128 (hereafter Dell'Erba, 'Initial Coin Offerings').
[211] Report of Investigation Pursuant to Section 21(a) of the Securities Exchange Act of 1934: The DAO [2017] Release No. 81207, WL 7184670 https://www.sec.gov/litigation/investreport/34-81207.pdf accessed 22 April 2022 (hereafter The DAO Report).
[212] Ibid, 8.
[213] See Dell'Erba, 'Initial Coin Offerings' (n 210) 1128–1129.
[214] SEC, 'SEC FinHub Staff Statement on OCC Interpretation' (21 September 2020) <https://www.sec.gov/news/public-statement/sec-finhub-statement-occ-interpretation#_ftn3> accessed 22 April 2022. These concerns also emerged in February 2023 with the SEC planning an enforcement action against Paxos Ltd, the company issuing Binance stablecoins (BUSD), which could be a security in violation of securities

In the context of stablecoins, the different stabilizing mechanisms with different types of collateral are unlikely to lead to different classifications of stablecoins as 'securities'. After a careful analysis, stablecoins backed with fiat currencies or commodities and stablecoins backed with cryptocurrencies may both qualify as securities. In the case of an off-chain stablecoin, two different situations may exist: if a stablecoin is collateralized with fiat currency, the latter is generally held by a custodian, be it a bank or a trust company's escrow account, with the value of the stablecoin deriving from that of the fiat currency. If a stablecoin is collateralized with gold or any other commodity, such a commodity, stored in a vault, will determine the value of the coin.[215] Therefore it is likely that in both scenarios stablecoins may be deemed securities, due to their similarities with 'security tokens'. A similar conclusion may be reached for stablecoins backed by crypto-assets: they are similar to off-chain stablecoins and derive their value from other assets. Algorithmic stablecoins rely on a mechanism with features that explicitly evoke terms and concepts characteristic of a 'security': the issuance of shares and bonds coupled with the expectations that they generate in their shareholders and bondholders.[216]

Another possible way in which stablecoins might trigger securities laws and the definition of 'security' is through 'demand notes'. Demand notes are two-party loans with no fixed term or repayment schedule,[217] with the debtor in the position to repay the creditor upon request. Demand notes are securities within the meaning of section 3(a)(10) of the Exchange Act.[218] An analysis focusing on the way stablecoins are redeemed may trigger stablecoins' qualification as a 'security'. In most cases, stablecoin purchasers deposit fiat currency with a stablecoin issuer, who provides an equivalent amount in stablecoins. When the purchasers intend to liquidate their position, stablecoin holders send the stablecoin back to the issuer, who provides an equivalent value of fiat currency.[219]

Consistent with the regulatory debate on ICOs,[220] an extremely relevant set of laws to take into account when discussing stablecoins is the Commodity Exchange Act (CEA); the US Commodity Futures Trading Commission can also play a role in the context of stablecoins. Stablecoins may trigger two different characterizations, 'commodity' or 'swaps'. Similar to the definition of 'security', the definition of 'commodity' is very broad, encompassing a wide range of products: physical commodities, such as agricultural products or natural resources, as well as currencies or interest rates.[221]

---

laws. See Dave Michaels, 'Stablecoins Attract Scrutiny in SEC's Drive to Control Crypto' (*WSJ*, 22 February 2023) <https://www.wsj.com/articles/stablecoins-attract-scrutiny-in-secs-drive-to-control-crypto-12179e04> accessed 26 April 2023.

[215] Merav Ozair, 'Stablecoins, Are They Coins or Security Tokens?' (*Elev8*, 17 October 2018) <https://www.elev8con.com/stablecoins-are-they-coins-or-security-tokens/#_edn8> accessed 22 April 2022.
[216] Ibid.
[217] See Adam Hayes, 'Demand Note' (*Investopedia*, last update 30 November 2020) <https://www.investopedia.com/terms/d/demandnote.asp> accessed 22 April 2022.
[218] See *Reves v Ernst & Young* [1990] 494 U.S. 56, 58.
[219] Jake Chervinsky and Benjamin Sauter, 'Will Fiat-Backed Stablecoins Pass Legal Muster with the SEC and CFTC?' (*CoinDesk*, 2 March 2019) <https://www.coindesk.com/will-fiat-backed-stablecoins-pass-legal-muster-with-the-sec-and-cftc> accessed 22 April 2022 (hereafter Chervinsky and Sauter, 'Pass Legal Muster').
[220] See Chapter 3.
[221] Commodity Exchange Act 1936 [as amended in 2012]; 7 U.S. Code (hereafter USC) s 1a(9).

Further, the definition of 'commodity' encompasses 'all services, rights, and interests ... in which contracts for future delivery are presently or in the future dealt in'.[222]

As mentioned in Chapter 3, since 2014, former Commodity Futures Trading Commission (CFTC) Chairman Timothy Massad has repeatedly stated that the agency could have jurisdiction over Bitcoin and more generally over virtual currencies, depending 'on the facts and circumstances pertaining to any particular activity in question', and that derivative contracts based on a virtual currency represented 'one area within our responsibility'.[223] This was the approach adopted in the case *In re Coinflip*,[224] where the CFTC order stated that the CEA covers 'all services, rights, and interests in which contracts for future delivery are presently or in the future dealt in', and that 'commodity' has a broad definition: 'Bitcoin and other virtual currencies are encompassed in the definition and properly defined as commodities'.[225] On this basis, stablecoins might be characterized as commodities, falling within the jurisdiction of the CFTC. Not surprisingly, when Facebook considered issuing a global payment network potentially based on stablecoins (at that time called GlobalCoin, in the preliminary pre-Libra stage) it entered into discussions with the CFTC to assess the regulatory implications of this initiative.[226]

A second possibility is that stablecoins could be characterized as 'swaps' under the CEA. The CEA defines swaps as an 'option of any kind that is for the purchase or sale, or based on the value, of 1 or more interest or other rates, currencies, commodities, or other financial or economic interests or property of any kind'.[227] In this second scenario, the CFTC might opt to characterize stablecoins as 'options for the purchase of, or based on the value of, fiat currencies'.[228]

ii. Europe
Applicability of existing securities and commodities laws   In Europe, similar considerations on securities and commodities laws may lead to analogous conclusions for stablecoins.

Here, the regulatory debate mainly coincides with what was considered in Chapter 3 for ICO tokens. Directive 2014/65 (MiFID II)[229] provides both the definitions of 'transferable security' and 'financial instrument'. With regard to the latter, MiFID II's definition of financial instrument encompasses, among other things, transferable securities and derivative contracts. Consistent with the analysis in Chapter 3, stablecoins might trigger such characterizations.

In relation to the notion of 'financial instrument', the list contained in Annex I, section C of the MiFID II Directive refers to commodities, which would allow one to refer

---

[222] See ibid.
[223] Timothy Massad, 'Testimony before the U.S. Senate Committee on Agriculture, Nutrition & Forestry' (10 December 2014) <https://www.cftc.gov/PressRoom/SpeechesTestimony/opamassad-6> accessed 11 April 2022.
[224] *Re Coinflip Inc.* [2015] CFTC No. 15–29, WL 5535736 <https://www.cftc.gov/sites/default/files/idc/groups/public/@lrenforcementactions/documents/legalpleading/enfcoinfliprorder09172015.pdf> accessed 11 April 2022.
[225] Ibid, 2.
[226] See Laura Noonan and Hannah Murphy, 'Facebook in Talks with US Regulator over Digital Currency' (*Financial Times*, 2 June 2019) <https://www.ft.com/content/3b2084fe-83c6-11e9-b592-5fe435b57a3b> accessed 22 April 2022.
[227] 7 USC (n 221), s 1a(47)(A).
[228] Chervinsky and Sauter, 'Pass Legal Muster' (n 219).
[229] Directive 2014/65/EU of 15 May 2014 on markets in financial instruments [2014] OJ L 173/1.

to the rules governing commodities. The MiFID Organisational Regulation defines a 'commodity' as 'any goods of a fungible nature that are capable of being delivered, including metals and their ores and alloys, agricultural products, and energy such as electricity'.[230] Tokens may fall within this definition, but they do not fall within the regulation if they are not derivatives. Therefore, 'the fact that a token is capable of being offered via an ICO has no bearing on its classification as a commodity and vice versa'.[231]

The Regulation on Markets in Crypto-Assets (MiCAR)   The Regulation on Markets in Crypto-Assets (MiCAR)[232] is part of the broader action targeting crypto-assets, the Digital Finance Package.[233] MiCAR was an attempt to respond to the political concerns originating from Libra (and then Diem).[234] The main purpose of MiCAR is the creation of a proper regulatory framework for crypto-assets, including stablecoins, and crypto-asset service providers (CASPs). The European law-maker intended to enhance legal certainty for trading activities in this area, thereby creating the basis for fostering innovation and strengthening both consumer protection and financial stability in European markets.[235] MiCAR does not cover crypto-assets related to financial instruments (in particular security tokens) or NFTs, nor deposits, structured deposits, and securitizations.

For the purpose of stablecoins, MiCAR presents two important definitions, in particular 'asset-referenced token' and 'electronic money token'.[236] An asset-referenced token identifies a 'type of crypto-asset that purports to maintain a stable value by referencing to any other value or right or a combination thereof, including one or

---

[230] Commission Delegated Regulation (EU) 2017/565 of 25 April 2016 supplementing Directive 2014/65/EU as regards organizational requirements and operating conditions for investment firms [2017] OJ L 87/1, art 2.

[231] See Andrew Henderson and James Burnie, 'United Kingdom' in Thomas A. Frick (ed), *The Financial Technology Law Review* (The Law Reviews 2018). See also Dell'Erba, 'Stablecoins in Cryptoeconomics' (n 96) 37. As Dell'Erba further explains (ibid):

> To the extent that an issuer takes the view that a token is a commodity, which by the regulatory definition in the EU MiFID Organisational Regulation would require the tokens to be goods of a fungible nature that are capable of being delivered, such as metals and their ores and alloys, agricultural products and electricity, these would be outside the realm of regulation to the extent they are not derivatives. As above, the fact that a token is capable of being offered via an ICO has no bearing on its classification as a commodity and vice versa.

[232] European Parliament legislative resolution of 20 April 2023 on the proposal for a regulation of the European Parliament and of the Council on Markets in Crypto-assets and amending Directive (EU) 2019/1937 (COM(2020)0593, C9-0306/2020, 2020/0265(COD)) <https://www.europarl.europa.eu/doceo/document/TA-9-2023-0117_EN.pdf> accessed 2 May 2023 (hereafter MiCAR).

[233] Commission's Directorate-General for Financial Stability, Financial Services and Capital Markets Union, 'Digital Finance Package' (24 September 2020) <https://ec.europa.eu/info/publications/200924-digital-finance-proposals_en> accessed 11 April 2022.

[234] Wolf-Georg Ringe, 'Building a European Market for Crypto-Assets: Who's Afraid of Libra?' (*OBLB*, 27 October 2020) <https://www.law.ox.ac.uk/business-law-blog/blog/2020/10/building-european-market-crypto-assets-whos-afraid-libra> accessed 22 April 2022 (hereafter Ringe, 'Building a European Market for Crypto-Assets').

[235] Ibid.

[236] For a critical view on the formulation, see Bitkom, 'Bitkom Position Paper on the European Commission's Proposals on Markets in Crypto-Assets (MiCAR) and a Pilot Regime for Market Infrastructures based on Distributed Ledger Technology' (16 October 2020) <https://www.bitkom.org/EN/Position-Paper-on-the-European-Commissions-proposals-on-Markets-in-Crypto-Assets-MiCA> accessed 22 April 2022:

more official currencies'.[237] This category will likely include stablecoins backed by a basket of currencies, whereas algorithmic stablecoins should not be characterized as asset-referenced tokens but could be included within the residual category of 'other crypto-assets'.[238]

MiCAR provides specific requirements for asset-referenced tokens. Issuers shall be subject to prior authorization granted by national competent authorities (NCAs), and shall publish a white paper subject to the approval of an NCA. Furthermore, asset-referenced token issuers shall fulfil specific requirements in terms of financial solidity (including own fund requirements and an obligation to hold a reserve of assets also for implementing stabilization mechanisms)[239] and sound corporate governance (providing disclosure arrangements, conflict of interest, custody of the reserves,[240] and investment of the reserve assets).[241]

An electronic money token (or e-money token) refers to 'a type of crypto-asset that purports to maintain a stable value by referring to the value of one official currency'.[242] This category will likely encompass stablecoin projects such as USDC (issued by Circle and backed by US dollars) as well as the multiple single currency-pegged Libra Coin as they emerged in the second version of the Libra white paper.[243]

E-money token issuers might be duly authorized as a credit institution or an electronic money institution.[244] MiCAR requires that holders of e-money tokens shall have 'a claim on the issuer of such e-money tokens', and if such e-money tokens do not fulfil this condition, they shall be prohibited.[245] Issuers shall issue e-money tokens at par value and on the receipt of fund,[246] and if requested by the e-money token holder,

---

we suggest a more precise differentiation of the individual types of stablecoins (asset-referenced tokens and e-money tokens). The definitions of asset-referenced tokens and e-money tokens both provide the following formulation: '... that purports to maintain a stable value by referring to the value of ...' We do not consider the term 'referring' suitable to actually allow a delimitation of the two types of stablecoins, since there are crypto-currencies like e.g. the Dai from MakerDAO that refers to the dollar as currency 1:1. However, the asset reserve or collateral of Dai does not consist of US Dollars, since Dai are not issued against receipt of US Dollars, but of other Ethereum-based assets that are recognized by MKR (MakerDAO governance token) holders as eligible assets as collateral. In our interpretation, a Dai would be an asset-referenced token and not an e-money token, even if it refers to the value of a US dollar. However, recital 10 of the MiCAR draft could also suggest a different understanding, which would provide for an EMoney Token term 'as wide as possible'. At some points in the recitals, it seems that the term 'backed' is used alternatively, *i.e.*, 'secured' instead of 'referring'. We urge the commission to create clarity here for issuers and the application of the law.

[237] MiCAR (n 232) art 3(1)(6).
[238] See Debevoise & Plimpton, 'European Commission Introduces Draft Regulation for Markets in Crypto Assets (MiCA)' (3 November 2020) <https://www.debevoise.com/insights/publications/2020/11/european-commission-introduces-draft-regulation> accessed 22 April 2022 (hereafter Debevoise & Plimpton, 'MiCA').
[239] See MiCAR (n 232) art 32.
[240] Issuers shall keep the reserves into segregated custody at credit institutions as well as investment firms or CASPs. See MiCAR (n 232) art 33.
[241] Issuers shall invest the reserve assets in liquid financial instruments, to mitigate any market and financial risk, in particular liquidity risk. See MiCAR (n 232) art 34.
[242] MiCAR (n 232) art 3(1)(7).
[243] See Debevoise & Plimpton, 'MiCA' (n 238).
[244] MiCAR (n 232) art 43(1)(a).
[245] MiCAR (n 232) art 44(2).
[246] MiCAR (n 232) art 44(3).

the issuer has a duty to 'redeem, at any moment and at par value, the monetary value of the e-money tokens held to the holders of e-money tokens in funds other than e-money'.[247] Furthermore, issuers have to provide the conditions of redemption in the crypto-asset white paper, including the fee.[248]

In addition to the two abovementioned categories (asset-referenced tokens and e-money tokens), MiCAR introduces a residual category, 'other crypto-assets', encompassing crypto-assets other than asset-referenced tokens and e-money tokens. Bitcoin might fall within this category.[249]

Furthermore, not only does MiCAR identify asset-referenced tokens and e-money tokens, but it also establishes—for both types of tokens—two further corresponding categories of significant asset-referenced tokens (to capture global stablecoins)[250] and significant e-money tokens. This different status of 'significance' depends on the major concerns in terms of financial stability as well as monetary policy and sovereignty on the side of the European Union as well as European member states.[251] These concerns lead to strengthening specific regulatory requirements in an attempt to mitigate these systemic risks.[252] Specific parameters trigger the significance in both cases,[253] and the European Banking Authority (EBA) is in charge of evaluating the applicability of such parameters to specific cases.

For significant asset-referenced tokens it is worth mentioning that issuers have to 'adopt, implement and maintain a remuneration policy that promotes sound and effective risk management of such issuers and that does not create incentives to relax risk standards'.[254] Furthermore, they have specific obligations in relation to liquidity, because they shall 'assess and monitor the liquidity needs to meet redemption requests by holders' of such assets,[255] and have to establish, maintain, and implement a liquidity management policy and procedures, in order to meet liquidity concerns under normal and liquidity-stressed scenarios.[256] For significant e-money tokens, issuers shall fulfil additional requirements in relation to the custody of the reserves and their

---

[247] MiCAR (n 232) art 44(4).
[248] MiCAR (n 232) art 44(5).
[249] See Debevoise & Plimpton, 'MiCA' (n 238).
[250] See Dirk A. Zetzsche, Filippo Annunziata, Douglas W. Arner, and Ross P. Buckley, 'The Markets in Crypto-Assets Regulation (MiCA) and the EU Digital Finance Strategy' (2021) 16 CMLJ 203 (hereafter Zetzsche et al., 'MiCA and the EU Digital Finance Strategy').
[251] See Debevoise & Plimpton, 'MiCA' (n 238).
[252] See Zetzsche et al, 'MiCA and the EU Digital Finance Strategy' (n 250) 17.
[253] See MiCAR (n 232) art 39(1). Among such parameters, MiCAR identifies the following: '(a) the number of holders of the asset-referenced tokens is larger than 10 million; (b) the value of the asset-referenced tokens issued, where applicable, their market capitalisation or the size of the reserve of assets of the issuer of the asset-referenced token, is higher than EUR 5 billion; (c) the number and value of transactions in those asset-referenced tokens, is higher than 2 500 000 transactions and EUR 500 million respectively, per day ... (da) the issuer of the asset-referenced tokens is a provider of core platforms services designated as gatekeeper ... (e) the significance of the activities of the issuer of the asset-referenced tokens on an international scale, including the use of the asset-referenced tokens for payments and remittances; (f) the interconnectedness with the financial system; (g) the fact that the same legal person or other undertaking issues at least one additional asset-referenced token or e-money token, and provides at least one crypto-asset service.'
[254] MiCAR (n 232) art 41(1).
[255] MiCAR (n 232) art 41(3).
[256] Ibid.

investments,[257] as well as those provided for issuers of significant asset-referenced tokens.[258]

Issuers of significant asset-referenced tokens would fall under the supervision of the EBA,[259] whereas issuers of significant e-money tokens are subject to the supervision of both the EBA and NCAs.[260] In this model, EBA would oversee the compliance with the more stringent requirements applicable, while NCAs would continue to supervise the compliance with the general requirements to which all e-money token issuers are subject.

iii. Switzerland As mentioned in Chapter 3 with regard to ICOs, FINMA first identified three categories of ICO tokens in the ICO Guidelines[261] (February 2018) and then issued the Guidelines on Stablecoins (October 2019).[262]

The ICO Guidelines identify payment tokens, utility tokens, and asset tokens, which in practice may be intertwined. Stablecoins may be characterized as payment tokens. When defining their use, FINMA noted that these tokens 'are intended to be used, now or in the future, as a means of payment for acquiring food or services or as a means of money or value transfer' and do not generate any claim on the issuer side.[263]

The FINMA Supplement to the Guidelines explicitly focuses on stablecoins. Here FINMA highlighted that 'many but not all "stable coins" confer a contractual claim against the issuer on the underlying assets (so-called redemption claim) or confer direct ownership rights. Depending on the specific purpose and characteristics of "stable coins", different financial market laws can apply.'[264]

A decisive consideration for stablecoin categorization is the asset to which the token is linked. FINMA identified different possibilities. First, where the token is linked to a specific fiat currency with a fixed redemption claim, it would likely trigger banking regulation, as a consequence of its characterization as a deposit under banking law. Alternatively, where the redemption claim is not fixed but depends on specific price developments, the token may trigger a collective investment scheme, especially if 'the underlying assets are managed for the account and risk of the token holder'.[265]

A second possibility is that the token is linked to commodities. In this case, FINMA notes that 'the exact nature of the claim on the assets as well as the type of commodity (in particular whether 'bank precious metals' or other commodities are involved) are of particular significance'. Different scenarios can emerge. In the case of an ownership

---

[257] MiCAR (n 232) art 52.
[258] Ibid.
[259] MiCAR (n 232) art 39.
[260] MiCAR (n 232) art 50.
[261] See FINMA, 'Guidelines for Enquiries regarding the Regulatory Framework for Initial Coin Offerings (ICOs)' (2018) <https://www.finma.ch/~/media/finma/dokumente/dokumentencenter/myfinma/1bewilligung/fintech/wegleitung-ico.pdf> accessed 22 April 2022 (hereafter FINMA, 'Guidelines for ICOs').
[262] FINMA, 'Supplement to the Guidelines for Enquiries regarding the Regulatory Framework for Initial Coin Offerings (ICOs)' (2019) 2 <https://www.finma.ch/en/~/media/finma/dokumente/dokumentencenter/myfinma/1bewilligung/fintech/wegleitung-stable-coins.pdf?la=en&hash=70408DDE78369718148808FD4784E742373A0140> accessed 22 April 2022 (hereafter FINMA, 'Supplement to Guidelines for ICOs').
[263] FINMA, 'Guidelines for ICOs' (n 261).
[264] FINMA, 'Supplement to Guidelines for ICOs' (n 262) 2.
[265] Ibid.

right of the token holder associated with the stablecoin, FINMA would not consider this to be a security if specific conditions are met.[266] Alternatively, the possibility of a contractual claim against the issuer on (i) bank precious metals, (ii) other commodities, or (iii) a link to a basket of commodities (including precious metals) associated with a price-dependent claim leads to the characterization of the token as (i) a security, (ii) a security and more rarely a derivative, and (iii) a collective investment scheme, respectively.[267]

Other potential configurations might be a token linked to securities, in which case the tokens would be securities, or a token linked to real estate, where the regulation on collective investment schemes would also be triggered.[268]

In its ICOs Supplement Guidelines, FINMA also confirmed that Libra had enquired with the Swiss regulator about the legal treatment of its project under Swiss law. At that time, FINMA responded that the most likely solution would have been to 'require a payment system license from FINMA, on the basis of the Financial Market Infrastructure Act (FMIA)'.[269] This aspect will be further analysed in the course of this chapter in Section III.C.

The direct involvement of the Swiss government in the debate on stablecoins and publication of the documents 'Federal Council informed of current status of stablecoin debate'[270] in October 2019 and 'Federal Council takes note of current stablecoin developments'[271] in January 2020 highlight an unusual, though still positive, participation in the regulatory process.

4. Payments and DeFi

Beyond cryptocurrencies and stablecoins, DeFi could lead to further developments in payments, in particular in the direction of broadening the possibilities of using heterogeneous crypto-assets as a medium of exchange. This is the case of 'globally decentralised instant payment networks', such as Flexa.[272] Here, users can spend a variety of crypto-assets in stores and online, including conversion, at zero cost. As the European Commission explains, this model relies on multiple partnerships with

---

[266] As FINMA notes, 'This presupposes that (i) an ownership right and not merely a contractual claim to the underlying commodities exists, (ii) the transfer of the token results in the transfer of the respective ownership right and (iii) the commodities are not deposited pursuant to art 481 Code of Obligations (CO; SR 220). Questions of validity under property law lie outside financial market law and regulation and remain the responsibility of the parties involved.' Ibid, 3.
[267] Ibid.
[268] Ibid.
[269] See FINMA, 'Finma Publishes "Stable Coin" Guidelines' (11 September 2019) <https://www.finma.ch/en/news/2019/09/20190911-mm-stable-coins/> accessed 22 April 2022 (hereafter FINMA, 'Stable Coin Guidelines'). For a further analysis of the FMIA in this context, see generally Corinne Zellweger-Gutknecht and Rolf H. Weber, 'Private Zahlungsmittel und Zahlungssysteme' (*Jusletter IT*, 2021).
[270] Swiss Federal Council, 'Federal Council Informed of Current Status of Stablecoin Debate' (16 October 2019) <https://www.admin.ch/gov/en/start/documentation/media-releases.msg-id-76722.html> accessed 22 April 2022 (hereafter Swiss Council, 'Current Status of Stablecoin Debate').
[271] Swiss Federal Council, 'Federal Council Takes Note of Current Stablecoin Developments' (15 January 2020) <https://www.admin.ch/gov/en/start/documentation/media-releases.msg-id-77785.html> accessed 22 April 2022.
[272] European Commission, 'European Financial Stability and Integration Review 2022' (2022) <https://commission.europa.eu/system/files/2022-04/european-financial-stability-and-integration-review-2022_en.pdf> accessed 30 April 2023.

leading crypto-exchanges, achieving a high degree of flexibility, and the collateral in the form of a crypto-asset has the function to secure all payments in real time, with the transactions confirmed and settled on the blockchain: 'anyone can provide collateral and, in return, earn a reward in the form of a processing fee that Flexa charges to merchants.'[273]

C. Similarities in the Causes Leading to the Emergence of Shadow Banking and Shadow Central Banking

How are shadow banking and shadow central banking similar? The shadow banking system invaded activities that were exclusively performed by established and regulated credit institutions. Similarly, in the context of shadow central banking, new market actors, such as tech giants as well as new entrepreneurial Fintech activities, attempted to infiltrate the typical activity of established institutions, such as central banks. Furthermore, the two financial networks share their cross-border vocation.

The most important similarity, however, is how both networks initially emerged. In the case of shadow banking, a lack of regulation (as well as active deregulation), an increasing demand for a specific need in the financial system (financial collateral) filled with financial engineering and derivatives, increased competition with credit institutions, and innovation favoured the establishment of a new financial network.

In the context of shadow central banking, the first important element is the demand for a specific 'good'. The technological innovations and the increased cross-border activity involved not only highly sophisticated actors but also common individuals with regard to day-to-day payments. This broad involvement of different societal constituents created an increased demand for faster ways of transmitting money and payments. This is very similar to the role that subprime mortgages had in involving many individuals in the financial system, leading to an increased need for financial collateral. The potential for growth associated with tokenized assets has increased the demand for these alternative forms of money, including tokenized money, and may serve to further initiate a mass adoption of DLT technology and its products.

Consistent with the trends in shadow banking, non-invasive regulation—and indeed a complete lack of regulation—has been equally important for shadow central banking. Many of the phenomenon's activities and entities remained unregulated for a time, while others still operate in the shadow of uncertainty regarding relevant legal rules and enforcement. The lack of a regulatory framework in the United States as well as in other jurisdictions favours legal and digital arbitrage, and therefore requires the adoption of a case-by-case approach,[274] which lacks important systematic features. The political sensitivity of these issues resounds at the national and the international

---

[273] Ibid.
[274] Katharina Pistor, 'Written Statement of Proposed Testimony for the Hearing entitled "Examining Facebook's Proposed Cryptocurrency and Its Impact on Consumers, Investors, and the American Financial System" before the Committee on Financial Services, U.S. House of Representatives' (17 July 2019) 2 <https://financialservices.house.gov/uploadedfiles/hhrg-116-ba00-wstate-pistork-20190717.pdf> accessed 22 April 2022 (hereafter Pistor, 'Written Statement').

levels, and further complicates the achievement of much-needed harmonized regulation. For example, although stablecoins are often identified as a potential threat to financial stability, they are not regulated.[275]

Indeed, the first wave of cryptocurrencies emerging from ICOs is still not regulated at all. Focusing on monetary issues, although Bitcoin promised to disrupt central banks, with some academic studies confirming this risk, central bankers seemed to underestimate the consequences of Bitcoin. The result was prolonged inactivity. Governments and central bankers were distracted by the market trends, failing to anticipate future events and dictate a reaction. While budget constraints may have produced this lack of a systematic and timely approach, this does not fully explain the complete lack of preparation. Those who had the power to anticipate private initiatives and developments could only run after them. However, regulators formulated a more systematic reaction after the announcement of J.P. Morgan's issuance of JPM Coin. And this response gained even more momentum after the announcement that Libra would issue its own stablecoin.

Another important common factor of shadow banking and shadow central banking is competition. While the shadow banking system placed downward pressure on banks, the shadow central banking system placed downward pressure on both central banks and their currencies. Furthermore, shadow central banking may also be capable of indirectly exercising downward pressure on banks. National currencies have historically competed with private money (including commodities such as gold and silver) and foreign governments (in particular the dollar) and private digital currencies are an equivalent competitor with foreign currencies for national central banks.

In the context of shadow central banking, the competition between public and private initiatives can be extremely brutal. Consequently, the political implications of shadow central banking may be greater than the implications triggered by shadow banking. This is especially true because of its cross-border capacity. The specific characteristics of some technologies involved, such as DLT, which have a very weak nexus with a specific jurisdiction exacerbate and facilitate the cross-border dimension. Although shadow banking activities may have the effect of leaving foreign capitals with less control over their system, shadow central banking could be a direct threat to the sovereignty of a country by threatening its national currency. In a recent letter to Federal Reserve Chairman Jerome Powell, Representatives French Hill and Bill Foster explicitly addressed these concerns and highlighted the risk that digital fiat currencies may jeopardize the primacy of the US dollar in the long-term.[276] By mentioning the initiatives of other sovereign countries, as well as initiatives by Libra, J.P. Morgan, and Wells Fargo, the Representatives implied that competitors include not only sovereign countries but also private entities. Such private entities are potentially dangerous because they could have the effect of removing 'important aspects of financial governance outside of' a specific country jurisdiction, in particular the loss of control of

---

[275] See FINMA, 'Guidelines for ICOs' (n 261).
[276] Letter from French Hill and Bill Foster to Federal Reserve Chairman Jerome H. Powell (30 September 2019) <https://src.bna.com/LO7> accessed 22 April 2022. Consistent views were expressed by former FDIC chair Sheila Bair in 'The Fed Needs to Get Serious about Its Own Digital Currency' (*yahoo!finance*, 21 June 2018) <https://finance.yahoo.com/news/former-fdic-chair-fed-needs-get-serious-digital-currency-131756819.html> accessed 22 April 2022.

monetary policy, coupled with more difficult applicability of anti-money laundering and counter-terrorism financing measures.[277] As mentioned above, similar reasons pushed Zhou Xiaouchan to accelerate the debate on digital currencies in China, to avoid the risk of being forced to adopt a standard, such as Bitcoin, created and controlled by third parties.[278] The same approach led French Minister of Economy Bruno Le Maire to propose a ban on Libra in Europe.[279]

Finally, innovation is also an important similarity between the two phenomena. Innovation in financial markets was generally associated with financial engineering. Exotic financial instruments such as extremely complex derivatives, asset-backed securities, or even the simply inconsiderate use of leverage spread in the financial system promised to increase capital gains while simultaneously dispersing financial risks. Pure technological innovation came later with the creation of high-frequency trading, robo-advisers, and various forms of artificial intelligence in finance. While an essential feature of both phenomena, technology plays an even more important role in shadow central banking. Indeed, technology is the precondition for private entities to compete with public actors. As briefly mentioned, before the development of DLT technology, a well-developed technological framework in the private sector was the main way central banks issued e-money. Cryptocurrencies and the underlying technology are part of this technological evolution, and without the technological support of these new initiatives, private actors could not have invaded the central banking sphere. Payment systems as well as other market infrastructures will certainly continue to evolve with the implementation of these new technological tools.

D. The Reaction of Central Banks

1. Central Bank Digital Currencies
a. Historical antecedents
The idea of CBDCs as a governmental initiative to enter 'into the issuance of non-cash money for public usage'[280] is not new, and its emergence does not coincide with that of cryptocurrencies.[281]

---

[277] Ibid.

[278] See Reuters, 'China New Digital Currency' (n 7).

[279] See Bruno Le Maire, 'Facebook's Libra Is a Threat to National Sovereignty' (*Financial Times*, 17 October 2019) <https://www.ft.com/content/bf2f588e-ef63-11e9-a55a-30afa498db1b> accessed 22 April 2022 (hereafter Le Maire, 'Libra Is a Threat to National Sovereignty').

[280] John Paul Koning, 'Fedcoin: A Central-Bank Issued Cryptocurrency' (2016) <https://www.r3.com/wp-content/uploads/2018/04/Fedcoin_Central_Bank_R3.pdf> accessed 22 April 2022 (hereafter Koning, 'Fedcoin').

[281] Already in 1935, James Tobin created a deposited currency system, which he described as 'the delegation to the private sector [of] the "government's sovereign right to coin money"'. In Tobin's view, putting the Federal Reserve in the position to offer deposits directly to the public (deposited currency accounts transferable by wire, cheque, or giro-type payments to other accounts within the system) served as a remedy for the physical defects of central bank money. Furthermore, CBDCs would not be the first governmental initiatives aimed at issuing non-cash money; the postal savings banking systems put in place in the nineteenth and the twentieth centuries are an antecedent in this sense. See Koning, 'Fedcoin' (n 280). A further example is the so-called 1933 Chicago Plan (ibid, 10):

In the past, governments have considered the issuance of non-cash money, and more recently e-money, that raised similar debates and policy questions among central bankers.[282] The key question was whether central banks should have opted to issue e-money or rather delegate this new development to private institutions.[283] In the 1980s, regulators and monetary economists, in particular new monetary economists (NMEs), also considered the possibility of different forms of money, with the express purpose of separating the functions of the unit of account from the one of medium of exchange.[284]

Although the issue of different forms of money dates back to the twentieth century, the public debate on the potential disruption of the monetary system by the private sector revamped with cryptocurrencies, but not in their early stages. Notwithstanding the clear intent of Bitcoin to disrupt central banks, its potential effects were long underestimated. The first wave of relevant public initiatives in the context of cryptocurrencies started only in 2017, in the form of a preliminary regulatory response to ICOs, when the capitalization of cryptocurrencies and their benefits was already quite widespread.

The nature of these interventions was predominantly legal, and mainly focused on the analysis of ICOs from the commodities and securities law angles. Therefore, these interventions failed to investigate the strong monetary implications related to the activity of issuing new forms of money. This is surprising because Bitcoin was launched in 2009 and the first stablecoin projects, such as BitShares (BitUSD), were launched in 2014. The hypothesis of a CBDC appeared in 2015 (Fedcoin), and the Bank of England and the Swedish Riksbank considered issuance of CBDCs as early as 2017. However, central bankers had not anticipated these events and instead found themselves in the position of chasing private initiatives in these strategic fields.

b. Key characteristics of central bank digital currencies

The term 'central bank digital currencies' (CBDCs) refers to a digital form of central bank money that combines 'new and already existing forms of central bank money'.[285] CBDC is 'a central bank liability [a claim on the central bank, backed by the full faith and credit of the government], denominated in an existing unit of account, which serves both as a medium of exchange and a store of value'.[286]

The 1933 Chicago Plan, named after a group of University of Chicago economists who wanted to avoid a repeat of the Great Depression, proposed the creation of 'deposit banks'. These institutions would be required to keep a 100% reserve of dollars, ensuring that sudden redemption requests by depositors could always be met. As for the traditional practice of matching savers with lenders, the Chicago economists called for the establishment of 'investment trusts'.

[282] The BIS defines e-money in the following terms: '*E-money products* are defined here as "stored-value" or "prepaid" products in which a record of the funds or "value" available to a consumer is stored on an electronic device in the consumer's possession'. See BIS, 'Implications for Central Banks of the Development of Electronic Money' (October 1996) <https://www.bis.org/publ/bisp01.pdf> accessed 22 April 2022.

[283] Mohamad Al-Laham, Haroon Al-Tarawneh, and Najwan Abdallat, 'Development of Electronic Money and Its Impact on the Central Bank Role and Monetary Policy' (2009) 6 IISIT <http://iisit.org/Vol6/IISITv6p339-349Al-Laham589.pdf> accessed 22 April 2022.

[284] Browne and Cronin, 'Payment Technologies' (n 112) 109–112.

[285] BIS Committee on Payments and Market Infrastructures and BIS Markets Committee, 'Central Bank Digital Currencies' (2018) iii <https://www.bis.org/cpmi/publ/d174.pdf> accessed 22 April 2022 (hereafter BIS, 'Central Bank Digital Currencies').

[286] Ibid.

A CBDC does not necessarily require the implementation of a blockchain infrastructure, because it could be token-based (with payments involving the transfer of an object, namely a digital token) or simply account-based (implementing payments through the transfer of claims recorded on an account).[287] The first option would require simply using Ethereum's ERC20 or ERC223 token standards for implementing a smart contract[288] or with so-called coloured coins, or alternatively developing a new blockchain, to issue central bank cryptocurrency on a public blockchain.[289] By buying and selling any token at par, the central bank would 'ensure parity between a crypto fiat unit and central bank reserves', with the valuation strictly correlated to the central bank's credibility.[290] In the context of creating a blockchain infrastructure, there might be different design options. Saule Omarova proposed the creation of a general-purpose CBDC that would replace bank deposit accounts, in combination with changes in the Federal Reserve's balance sheet, at the level of its liabilities.[291] Robert Hockett considered the possibility to create a public peer-to-peer payment system enabling all legal residents of a jurisdiction to operate on an 'inclusive value' ledger, that would be managed by local, state, or governmental authorities.[292]

The second option, the account-based option, does not deem necessary the creation of and reliance on a blockchain infrastructure; central banks could simply allow citizens to open accounts with them for the purpose of making their payments with central bank electronic money instead of resorting to commercial bank deposits.[293] A major benefit of this choice would be the satisfaction of the population's need for virtual currency while eliminating counterparty risk.[294]

Specific traits characterize CBDCs as opposed to the system currently in place, distinguishing them from other forms of money issued by central banks.[295] For example,

---

[287] IMF, 'Casting Light on Central Bank Digital Currency' (n 122) 4. Token-based and account-based have different characteristics. As the IMF explains, token-based CBDCs 'could extend some of the cash to the digital world. CBDC could provide varying degrees of anonymity and immediate settlement. It could thus curtail the development of private forms of anonymous payment but could increase risks to financial integrity. Design features such as size limits on payments in, and holdings of, CBDC would reduce but not eliminate these concerns.' Account-based CBDCs 'could increase risks to financial intermediation. It would raise funding costs for deposit-taking institutions and facilitate bank runs during periods of distress. Again, careful design and accompanying policies should reduce, but not eliminate, these risks.'

[288] For a comparison of the two standards, see Michiel Mulders, 'Comparing ERC20, ERC223, and the new Ethereum ERC777 Token Standard' (*Cointelligence*, 19 February 2018) <https://www.cointelligence.com/content/comparison-erc20-erc223-new-ethereum-erc777-token-standard/> accessed 22 April 2022. See also IndexUniverse, 'ERC20 Token Standard' (n 131).

[289] See Aleksander Berentsen and Fabian Schär, 'The Case for Central Bank Electronic Money and the Non-Case for Central Bank Cryptocurrencies' (2018) 100 FedResBankStLRev 97. The authors explain 'coloured coins' as follows: 'one could attach additional value components to fractions of existing crypto-assets, such as Bitcoin. The additional value—in this case, fiat currency—would then be part of a specific fraction of a Bitcoin (or more precisely an unspent transaction output) and could be represented and traded on the Bitcoin blockchain.' Ibid, 103.

[290] Ibid.

[291] See generally Saule Omarova, 'The People's Ledger: How to Democratize Money and Finance the Economy' (2021) 74 VandLRev 1301.

[292] See generally Robert C. Hockett, 'The New York Inclusive Value Ledger: A Peer-to-Peer Savings & Payments Platform for an All-Embracing and Dynamic State Economy' (2019) Cornell Legal Studies Research Paper No. 19-39.

[293] Ibid, 101. For an analysis of this option in the US, see Morgan Ricks, John Crawford, and Lev Menand, 'FedAccounts: Digital Dollars' (2021) 89 GWashLRev 113.

[294] Ibid.

[295] BIS, 'Central Bank Digital Currencies' (n 285) 1.

the balances in traditional reserve or settlement accounts are distinct.[296] At the same time, CBDCs would be, in principle, stable and afford the advantages generally associated with cryptocurrencies, opening space to design choices that may lead to great benefits.

Furthermore, traditional reserves are available exclusively to institutional operators and generally settle wholesale interbank payments only.[297] Central banks could opt for designing wholesale and retail CBDCs. While the idea of a wholesale CBDC is much closer to the current framework, retail CBDCs would target retail payments and would be widely available in a form different from physical cash.[298] This is one of the most debated points among central bankers. As the survey of the most important initiatives will show,[299] major experiments encompass both these options. Switzerland would likely opt for wholesale CBDCs whereas China is developing a retail CBDC system.

Similar to cryptocurrencies, CBDCs would be available twenty-four hours a day, while traditional cash is limited to central bank operating hours.[300] By being widely available, CBDCs could be easily used by a country's residents, as well as foreign individuals and organizations situated abroad, for person-to-person, person-to-business, and business-to-business transactions of any amount.[301] Therefore, CBDCs have the potential to disintermediate the existing system, which is based on commercial banks acting as intermediaries. This would depend on the design options, since a CBDC could be transferred either on a peer-to-peer basis or through a designated intermediary, such as a central bank, a commercial bank, or even a third-party agent.[302]

These flexible design features would then bear on the degree of anonymity provided, with token-based CBDCs having the potential to be fully anonymous, like cash.[303] CBDCs thus have the potential to provide more anonymity than existing cryptocurrencies, which are not anonymous due to the necessary intermediation of individuals and organizations that leave a digital footprint by using cryptowallets.[304] Central banks should also take into account the risks of fraudulent activity associated with full anonymity and choose to only offer full anonymity with strict and low limits on CBDC holdings, or to render the currency not anonymous at all.[305] Similar to other digital central bank liabilities, CBDCs may also pay positive and negative interest, and this is relevant for them to serve as a store of value.[306]

---

[296] IMF, 'Casting Light on Central Bank Digital Currency' (n 122) 7.
[297] Ibid.
[298] BIS, 'Central Bank Digital Currencies' (n 285) 4; see also IMF, 'Casting Light on Central Bank Digital Currency' (n 122) 7.
[299] See Section II.C.2.b.
[300] BIS, 'Central Bank Digital Currencies' (n 285) 5.
[301] IMF, 'Casting Light on Central Bank Digital Currency' (n 122) 7.
[302] BIS, 'Central Bank Digital Currencies' (n 285) 6; see IMF, 'Casting Light on Central Bank Digital Currency' (n 122) 14.
[303] Ibid.
[304] Nouriel Roubini, 'Why Central Bank Digital Currencies Will Destroy Cryptocurrencies' (*Project Syndicate*, 19 November 2018) <https://www.project-syndicate.org/commentary/central-banks-take-over-digital-payments-no-cryptocurrencies-by-nouriel-roubini-2018-11> accessed 22 April 2022 (hereafter Roubini, 'Central Bank Digital Currencies').
[305] IMF, 'Casting Light on Central Bank Digital Currency' (n 122) 29; see BIS, 'Central Bank Digital Currencies' (n 285) 6.
[306] Roubini, 'Central Bank Digital Currencies' (n 304).

2. Public Debate and Experiments

There is a pre- and a post-Libra era. In the pre-Libra era, a few states and international organizations, such as the BIS and the IMF, chose to experiment in the context of CBDCs. The variety and the peculiar characteristics of such experiments require a specific analysis of the most prominent.

a. The pre-Libra era

Sweden was extremely proactive in the field of CBDCs. As part of its task to 'promote a safe and efficient payment system', the Sverige Riksbank was concerned about the disappearance of cash as a means of payment, and for this reason it started to consider the possibility of a CBDC as a complementary tool to fiat money in the form of cash.[307] The Sverige Riksbank proposed a very advanced project of e-krona,[308] although it opted for an account-based version due to concerns related to the maturity of the blockchain technology. In 2018, the Sverige Riksbank confirmed the concerns expressed in 2017 regarding the blockchain technology, although it did not exclude the possibility of successfully implementing a token-based e-krona in the future.[309] More recently, the Sverige Riksbank governor Stefan Ingves pushed for the issuance of a CDBC, arguing that this is the only way for the Riksbank to ensure people to pay 'in a safe and efficient way' and for the krona to maintain its value and attractiveness as a means of payment.[310] Ingves highlighted five key pillars of the project:

> There shall be enough cash in case the electronic systems break down. There shall be a national, state-issued ID card with e-identification. There shall be digital state money as legal tender, an E-Krona, issued by the Riksbank. It shall be possible to make instant payments in Swedish krona, using state money, 24/7. It shall be possible to make instant payments between currencies across borders 24/7.[311]

The Bank of Canada launched its own initiative to assess the possibility of a CBDC with Project Jasper, a multi-stage project initiated in 2016 with the cooperation of private and public actors including R3 Corda, Accenture, Payments Canada, and TMX Group.[312] Project Jasper served to understand the real impact of the blockchain technology on payment systems. It explored a broad range of aspects, including securities settlement,[313] and tested them with the private sector.[314] As stated at the end of

---

[307] Sveriges Riksbank, 'The Riksbank's E-Krona Project—Report 2' (October 2018) <https://www.riksbank.se/globalassets/media/rapporter/e-krona/2018/the-riksbanks-e-krona-project-report-2.pdf> accessed 22 April 2022 (hereafter Sveriges Riskbank, 'E-Krona Project').
[308] See PwC, 'Central Bank Digital Currency—Benefits and Drawbacks' (2019) 6 <https://www.pwc.ch/en/publications/2019/Central%20Bank%20Digital%20Currency_EN-web.pdf> accessed 22 April 2022.
[309] Sveriges Riskbank, 'E-Krona Project' (n 307) 36.
[310] Stefan Ingves, 'Future Money and Payments' (15 October 2020) Sveriges Riskbank Economic Commentaries No. 9, 7 <https://www.riksbank.se/globalassets/media/rapporter/ekonomiska-kommentarer/engelska/2020/future-money-and-payments.pdf> accessed 22 April 2022.
[311] Ibid.
[312] Payments Canada, 'Project Jasper—Outline' (January 2017) <https://payments.ca/sites/default/files/2022-09/project_jasper_primer_EN.pdf> accessed 22 April 2022.
[313] Ibid.
[314] Payments Canada, 'Payments Canada Bank of Canada and R3 Release Detailed Findings of Blockchain Experiment' (29 September 2017) <https://www.payments.ca/industry-info/our-research/payments-canada-bank-canada-and-r3-release-detailed-findings-blockchain> accessed 22 April 2022.

February 2020, the position of the Bank of Canada is to not issue a CBDC, and this option will be considered only if specific trends occur. According to the position of the Bank of Canada, the benefits of a CBDC become relevant only in a scenario where banknotes 'continue to decline to a point where Canadians no longer had the option of using them for a wide range of transactions' or, alternatively, other digital currencies achieve a high utilization rate, substituting the Canadian dollar in its main functions as a method of payment, store of value, and unit of account.[315]

In the last phase of Project Jasper, the Bank of Canada engaged in one of the most interesting collaborative experiments with other governmental authorities. This collaboration consisted of creating cross-border interbank payments and settlements based on CBDCs, developed with the Monetary Authority of Singapore (MAS) and the Bank of England. This project combined Project Jasper with Project Ubin, developed by the MAS, with the specific purpose of making cross-border payments faster and cheaper.[316] The Jasper–Ubin project includes two models referred to as 'tokenized form of a wholesale central bank digital currency (w-CBDC) issued on blockchains by the central bank for use by commercial banks'.[317]

In 2017, the Bank of England elaborated a proof of concept with Ripple, for the purpose of exploring 'the synchronised movement of two different currencies across two different real-time gross settlement systems linked using Ripple Connect and the Interledger protocol'.[318] It did so for the purpose of demonstrating the way such synchronization could lead to lowering settlement risk while improving the speed and efficiency of cross-border payments. As the next subsections will show, this experiment anticipated what Banque de France[319] and the SNB[320] did in 2020.

Other countries, such as Ecuador and Uruguay, explored the possibility of issuing their own CBDC. Ecuador announced the issuance of its own digital currency denominated in dollars in 2014, although the project was cancelled in 2017.[321] The e-peso project of the Central Bank of Uruguay was a pilot project, part of a broader vision aimed at enhancing financial inclusion.[322] The Central Bank of Uruguay started to issue e-pesos in November 2017, creating an 'e-note manager platform', which was

---

[315] Bank of Canada, 'Contingency Planning for a Central Bank Digital Currency' (25 February 2020) <https://www.bankofcanada.ca/2020/02/contingency-planning-central-bank-digital-currency/> accessed 22 April 2022.

[316] Bank of Canada, 'Digital Currencies and Fintech: Projects' <https://www.bankofcanada.ca/research/digital-currencies-and-fintech/projects/> accessed 22 April 2022.

[317] Bank of Canada and the Monetary Authority of Singapore, 'Enabling Cross-Border High Value Transfer Using Distributed Ledger Technologies—Jasper—Ubin Design Paper' (2019) <https://www.mas.gov.sg/-/media/Jasper-Ubin-Design-Paper.pdf?la=en&hash=EF5857437C4857373A9287CD86F56D0E7C46E7FF> accessed 22 April 2022.

[318] Bank of England, 'FinTech Accelerator Proof of Concept' (10 July 2017) <https://www.bankofengland.co.uk/-/media/boe/files/fintech/ripple.pdf?la=en&hash=75E5F445230B8A2B794C208D29619A3E33F1FFE7> accessed 22 April 2022.

[319] See Section II.C.2.b.iv.

[320] See Section II.C.2.b.iii.

[321] Larry White, 'The World's First Central Bank Electronic Money Has Come—And Gone: Ecuador, 2014-2018' (*Alt-M*, 29 March 2018) <https://www.alt-m.org/2018/03/29/the-worlds-first-central-bank-electronic-money-has-come-and-gone-ecuador-2014-2018/> accessed 22 April 2022.

[322] Christian Barontini and Harry Holden, 'Proceeding with Caution—A Survey on Central Bank Digital Currency' (January 2019) BIS Papers No. 101, 4 <https://www.bis.org/publ/bppdf/bispap101.pdf>.

not based on DLT.[323] The project was shut down in April 2018, and is currently under evaluation for future implementations.[324]

b. The post-Libra era
In the post-Libra era, the debate has exploded. At the international level, G7 members expressed concerns almost at the same time.[325] Notwithstanding increasing concern about the possibility of entities that are not fully regulated being able to take over monetary function, the vast majority of central bankers from established economies are cautious about the possibility of issuing CBDCs in the short term. More generally, although central banks are continuing to explore the possibility of CBDCs, a 2020 survey conducted by the Bank for International Settlement noted that there is no evidence showing 'a widespread or general move to expand [CBDCs] research into experimentation and pilot arrangements'.[326] A 2021 survey confirmed that the majority of central banks at that time did 'not take a firm decision on issuing a CBCD'.[327] However, the survey also noted the emergence of 'a tentative inclination towards allowing use of a future CBDC by tourists and other non-residents domestically', which is coherent with a cross-border interest to develop 'multi-CBDC arrangements'.

The following subsections focus on some specific initiatives developed in key jurisdictions by the respective central banks. This brief analysis highlights some of the key features emerging from each approach.

i. United Kingdom Bank of England former governor Mark Carney advocated for a new global monetary system, based on a multiplicity of Libra-like global digital currencies replacing the dollar.[328]

Despite initial scepticism expressed by the Economic Affairs Committee of the UK Parliament,[329] the Bank of England actively consulted on the development of a CBDC

---

[323] Ibid.
[324] Ibid.
[325] See Leigh Thomas and Michael Nienaber, 'G7 Finance Chiefs Pour Cold Water on Facebook's Digital Coin Plans' (*Reuters*, 17 July 2019) https://www.reuters.com/article/us-g7-economy/g7-finance-chiefs-pour-cold-water-on-facebooks-digital-coin-plans-idUSKCN1UC0IC> accessed 22 April 2022.
[326] Codruta Boar, Henry Holden, and Amber Wadsworth, 'Impending Arrival—A Sequel to the Survey on Central Bank Digital Currency' (January 2020) BIS Papers No. 107, 9 <https://www.bis.org/publ/bppdf/bispap107.pdf> accessed 22 April 2022.
[327] Raphael Auer, Codruta Boar, Giulio Cornelli, Jon Frost, Henry Holden and Andreas Wehrli, 'CBDCs Beyond Borders: Results from a Survey of Central Banks' (June 2021) BIS Papers No. 116 <https://www.bis.org/publ/bppdf/bispap116.pdf> accessed 22 April 2022. Notwithstanding an interest in developing multi-CBDC arrangements, the vast majority of CBDC investigations by central banks focus on domestic issues. See BIS Committee on Payments and Market Infrastructures, BIS Innovation Hub, IMF and the World Bank, 'Central Bank Digital Currencies for Cross-Border Payments—Report to the G20' (July 2021) <https://www.bis.org/publ/othp38.htm> accessed 22 April 2022. For an analysis of a prototype implementing 'multiple Central Bank Digital Currencies' (mCBDCs), see BIS Innovation Hub Hong Kong Centre, Hong Kong Monetary Authority, Bank of Thailand, Digital Currency Institute of the People's Bank of China and Central Bank of the United Arab Emirates, 'Inthanon-LionRock to mBridge—Building a Multi CBDC Platform for International Payments' (28 September 2021) <https://www.bis.org/publ/othp40.pdf> accessed 22 April 2022 (hereafter BISIH et al., 'Inthanon-LionRock to mBridge').
[328] Swint, 'Libra-Like Reserve Currency' (n 6).
[329] See Economic Affairs Committee of the House of Lords, 'Central Bank Digital Currencies: A Solution in Search of a Problem?' (13 January 2022) HL Paper 131 <https://publications.parliament.uk/pa/ld5802/ldselect/ldeconaf/131/131.pdf> accessed 22 April 2022.

in pound sterling and partnered with the MIT Media Lab's Digital Currency Initiative (DCI) to undertake technical research and experimentation.[330]

The Bank of England focuses its interest on CBDCs' effective role in macroeconomics and financial stability while questioning the possibility of their interaction with other policy objectives, their effectiveness as a new policy tool, and issues related to their technical implementation.[331] As will be considered further below,[332] the Bank of England is also engaged in a collaborative project with other central banks and the BIS.

ii. **United States of America** Significant discussions on the opportunity to issue a CBDC took place in the United States as well. Specifically, a hearing before the United States Senate Committee on Banking, Housing, and Urban Affairs was held in July 2019 to address the flaws of the Libra Project. At that time, Federal Reserve Chairman Jerome Powell stated that although the development of a digital currency available to businesses and households is an option, the Federal Reserve is not considering issuing a CBDC.[333] This was a response to the request by the Chair of the AI Task Force and Congressional Blockchain Caucus Co-Chair, Congressman Bill Foster, explicitly asking the Federal Reserve to consider the possibility of a CBDC.[334]

In 2020, the Federal Reserve confirmed it was conducting active research and experimentation in relation to the most up-to-date payment technologies, in particular through 'the Federal Reserve Board's Technology Lab (TechLab) engaged in expanding experimentation with the technologies relevant to digital currencies and other payment innovations'.[335] Furthermore, the Federal Reserve confirmed that the Federal Reserve Bank of Boston, in cooperation with the Massachusetts Institute of Technology (MIT), 'is designing a hypothetical digital currency oriented for central bank use'. The purpose of this project is to support the Board of Governors in assessing the safety and efficiency of CBDC systems, in particular in the sense of supporting 'an understanding of the capacities and limitations of the relevant technologies, rather than serving as a prototype for a Federal Reserve issued digital currency or addressing the wide-ranging policy issues associated with its potential issuance'.[336]

---

[330] Bank of England, 'Bank of England and Massachusetts Institute of Technology Joint Central Bank Digital Currency Collaboration' (25 March 2022) <https://www.bankofengland.co.uk/news/2022/march/boe-and-massachusetts-institute-of-technology-joint-cbdc-collaboration> accessed 22 April 2022.

[331] See John Barrdear and Michael Kumhof, 'The Macroeconomics of Central Bank Issued Digital Currencies' (July 2016) Bank of England—Staff Working Paper No. 605 <https://www.bankofengland.co.uk/-/media/boe/files/working-paper/2016/the-macroeconomics-of-central-bank-issued-digital-currencies> accessed 22 April 2022.

[332] See infra Section II.C.2.b.vii.

[333] Michael S. Derby, 'Powell Says Fed Has No Plans to Create Digital Currency' (*WSJ*, 21 November 2019) <https://www.wsj.com/articles/feds-powell-says-in-letter-to-congress-fed-not-creating-digital-currency-11574356188> accessed 22 April 2022.

[334] Jason Brett, 'As Congress Asks the Fed to Look into a Digital Dollar, Former FDIC Chair Sheila Bair Is Ahead of the Curve ... Again' (*Fortune*, 5 October 2019) <https://www.forbes.com/sites/jasonbrett/2019/10/05/as-congress-asks-the-fed-to-look-into-a-digital-dollar-former-fdic-chair-sheila-bair-is-ahead-of-the-curve--again/#3b69bb8e3c14> accessed 22 April 2022.

[335] Federal Reserve, 'Federal Reserve Highlights Research and Experimentation Undertaken to Enhance Its Understanding of the Opportunities and Risks Associated with Central Bank Digital Currencies' (13 August 2020) <https://www.federalreserve.gov/newsevents/pressreleases/other20200813a.htm> accessed 22 April 2022.

[336] Ibid.

The Federal Reserve Bank of Boston and MIT put in place a multi-phase project, named 'Project Hamilton', for a total duration of three years (from 2020 to 2023). In its early stages, the cooperation aimed at designing and possibly testing a hypothetical CBCD 'for wide-scale, general purpose use' with a view to determine 'how to architect a scalable, accessible cryptographic platform to meet the needs of a theoretical U.S. dollar CBDC, including stringent design requirements for speed, security, privacy and resiliency'.[337] Further developments looked at the advantages and disadvantages of the technology, coding and testing various architectures, and seeking to understand the way 'they impact the CBDC's design goals'.[338] The Federal Reserve emphasized the importance of a CBDC for different reasons. These goals include (i) extending public access to central bank money while supporting monetary policy; (ii) reducing friction and cost in payments, particularly for cross-border transactions; (iii) promoting financial inclusion; and (iv) preserving the role of the US dollar as the world's reserve currency.[339]

As mentioned in Chapter 3, on 9 March 2022, US President Joe Biden signed the Executive Order on Ensuring Responsible Development of Digital Assets (hereafter 'the Order'), which features a number of direct references to CBDCs. In fact, 'the Order directs the U.S. Government to assess the technological infrastructure and capacity needs for a potential U.S. CBDC in a manner that protects Americans' interests'.[340] Furthermore, it 'encourages the Federal Reserve to continue its research, development, and assessment efforts for a U.S. CBDC, including development of a plan for broader U.S. Government action in support of their work. This effort prioritizes US participation in multi-country experimentation, and ensures U.S. leadership internationally to promote CBDC development that is consistent with U.S. priorities and democratic values.'[341] A CBDC project should be based on assessment of risks and benefits for 'consumers, investors, and businesses; financial stability and systemic risk; payment systems; national security' as well as in terms of implementing a full 'ability to exercise human rights; financial inclusion and equity; and the actions required to launch a United States CBDC if doing so is deemed to be in the national interest'.[342] Furthermore, the Order explicitly mentions the importance of taking into consideration 'democratic values, including privacy protections, and [ensuring] the global financial system has appropriate transparency, connectivity, and platform and architecture interoperability or transferability'.[343] Finally, it considers the international

---

[337] Federal Reserve of Boston, 'The Federal Reserve Bank of Boston Announces Collaboration with MIT to Research Digital Currency' (13 August 2020) <https://www.bostonfed.org/news-and-events/press-releases/2020/the-federal-reserve-bank-of-boston-announces-collaboration-with-mit-to-research-digital-currency.aspx> accessed 22 April 2022.
[338] Ibid.
[339] Board of Governors of the Federal Reserve System, 'Money and Payments: The U.S. Dollar in the Age of Digital Transformation' (22 January 2022) 14–16 https://www.federalreserve.gov/publications/files/money-and-payments-20220120.pdf> accessed 22 April 2022.
[340] White House, 'FACT SHEET: President Biden to Sign Executive Order on Ensuring Responsible Development of Digital Assets' (9 March 2022) <https://www.whitehouse.gov/briefing-room/statements-releases/2022/03/09/fact-sheet-president-biden-to-sign-executive-order-on-ensuring-responsible-innovation-in-digital-assets/> accessed 22 April 2022.
[341] Ibid.
[342] Ibid, Section IV (a).
[343] Ibid.

dimension of CBDCs, mentioning the problem of illicit finance and the need to reduce terrorism financing, as well as contributing to the development of international cross-border activity.

iii. Switzerland In Switzerland, an important discussion took place among both securities regulators and central bankers. The FINMA was extremely proactive, as it has always been in the Fintech space, and provided some guidelines on stablecoins in addition to guidelines for ICOs. At the level of central banking discussion, the SNB noted that the existing cashless payment system currently in place is already 'reliable, secure and efficient'; therefore, the SNB does not see an opportunity for extending access to digital central bank money to all households and companies operating in Switzerland.[344] In the view of the SNB, the financial markets may be a different situation. State-issued digital currencies may be deemed necessary depending on the establishment of security tokens in the financial sector. If so, CBDCs may become an essential tool 'as a means of payment for the new financial market infrastructures'.[345]

Consistent with this strategic approach of privileging the development of wholesale CBDCs, the SNB partnered with the BIS Innovation Hub and SIX to explore the feasibility of wholesale CBDCs in a project called Helvetia (as mentioned at the beginning of this chapter).[346] The SNB contributed by defining the role and properties of central bank money in the experiment, and contributed to the analysis of the policy implications with the BIS, relying on the DLT platform developed by SDX.[347] Not surprisingly, this experiment positions Switzerland among the leading jurisdictions in the CBDC area. This comes after a period of uncertainty in the specific area of central banking which contrasted with an incredibly advanced policy debate in other areas.

The Helvetia project is a two-phase experiment. The purpose of Phase I was to test 'the feasibility of two proofs of concept, using near-live systems to settle digital assets on a distributed ledger with central bank money'.[348] The two proofs of concept were designed and investigated to test the pros and cons of a system based on a wholesale CBDC. Phase II aimed at demonstrating the end-to-end settlement of tokenized transactions in wCBDC, while contributing to 'identify[ing] realistic control and monitoring functions in order to fulfil operational, legal or regulatory requirements related to wCBDC on a platform operated and owned by a third party'.[349]

The first phase of the project was developed in the context of the traditional real-time gross settlement (RTGS) Swiss Interbank Clearing (SIC) system and the near-live SDX platform, testing two different frameworks for settling tokenized assets in central

---

[344] Thomas J. Jordan, 'Currencies, Money and Digital Tokens' (Speech at the University of Basel, Switzerland, 5 September 2019) <https://www.snb.ch/en/mmr/speeches/id/ref_20190905_tjn/source/ref_20190905_tjn.en.pdf> accessed 22 April 2022.
[345] Ibid, 6.
[346] See Swiss National Bank, BIS Innovation HUB and SIX, 'Project Helvetia—Settling Tokenised Assets in Central Bank Money' (December 2020) 13 <https://www.bis.org/publ/othp35.pdf> accessed 22 April 2022 (hereafter Project Helvetia, Phase I).
[347] Ibid.
[348] Ibid.
[349] Swiss National Bank, BIS Innovation HUB and SIX, 'Project Helvetia Phase II—Settling Tokenised Assets in Wholesale CBDC' (January 2022) 13 <https://www.bis.org/publ/othp45.pdf> accessed 22 April 2022 (hereafter Project Helvetia, Phase II).

II. SHADOW CENTRAL BANKING   269

bank money. The first proof of concept involved the creation of a new framework: the SNB issued Swiss franc wholesale CBDC on the SDX platform for the settlement of tokenized assets. The second proof of concept relied on the existing framework, where the SDX platform was linked to SIC, to allow for the settlement of tokenized assets against payments in SIC balances with the central bank. Notwithstanding these important structural differences, the two proofs of concept share the characteristic that settlement happens on a deliver-versus-payment basis.[350] Furthermore, both the proofs of concept are structurally independent from the SDX project to launch its own stablecoin, 'SDX coin',[351] because the SDX coin is not a claim on the SNB but on SDX, while still being funded through SIC balances.[352]

Both proofs of concept were structured on four steps,[353] but clearly differed at the level of use-cases and business cases. The locution 'use-cases' refers to the actions that have to be put in place for a system to meet its objective.[354] 'Business cases' refers to the characteristics of a specific system from the perspective of the system's manager (in the case of Helvetia, the SNB) or end user.[355] In the case of the first proof of concept, they mainly focus on the fundamental role of the central bank,[356] whereas in the second the central bank and the RTGS system were equally relevant.[357]

Helvetia Phase I has drawn two scenarios to settle tokenized assets, defining both as 'legally feasible and robust'. However, although the report notes that there are some

---

[350] See Project Helvetia, Phase I (n 346) 13.
[351] Ibid. As the document explains, '[t]o enable the settlement of tokenized assets on the distributed ledger, SDX will issue a Swiss franc stablecoin. The "SDX coin" will be funded one-to-one by participants' SIC balances but will be a liability of SDX.' Ibid, 3.
[352] Ibid, 13.
[353] As the document explains, these four steps are: 'i) deciding on the tasks that the SDX and SIC system need to perform to achieve Deliver versus Payment settlement against central bank money (use cases); (ii) establishing requirements that the SDX and SIC system had to fulfil when carrying out the tasks (business requirements); (iii) designing the processes within the SDX and SIC system that will capture the tasks and requirements (solution designs); and (iv) testing the implemented solution designs using the respective test environments'. Ibid, 14.
[354] Ibid. As the document explains, in the first proof-of concept (relying on CBCDs) the use cases are four in number and include: (i) the issuance of wholesale CDBC (with a one-to-one conversion of RTGS balances into wholesale CBDCs); (ii) the redemption of wholesale CBDCs (with a one-to-one conversion of wholesale CBDC into RTGSs balances); (iii) delivery versus payment settlement in wholesale CBDC (delivery of tokenized assets against wholesale CBDC on a DLT platform); and (iv) wholesale CBDC payment (a transfer of w-CBDC on DLT platform). The second proof of concept on the contrary involves only one use-case, that is, the delivery versus payment settlement in RTGS balances, corresponding to the delivery of tokenized assets on DLT platform against RTGS balances.
[355] Ibid.
[356] As the document clearly explains, in eight points: '1. The central bank is the sole issuer of w-CBDC. 2. The central bank's balance sheet size remains unaffected by issuance and redemption of w-CBDC. 3. The central bank's reserve balances and w-CBDC are convertible one-to-one. 4. The central bank controls access to w-CBDC. 5. The central bank's reserve balances and w-CBDC have the same value date. 6. The central bank retains control and monitoring of w-CBDC settlement. 7. The central bank's reserve balance remuneration also applies to w-CBDC. 8. Issuance of and settlement with w-CBDC must be robust and final under the applicable legal framework.'
[357] Ibid, 17. Here the report identifies the following six points: '1. Settlement of tokenised assets in RTGS balances occurs according to DvP model 1. 2. The central bank controls who is eligible for DvP settlement of tokenized assets in RTGS balances. 3. Settlement of tokenised assets in RTGS balances is possible only during RTGS opening hours. 4. Settlement of tokenised assets in RTGS balances will not require any changes to the RTGS system. 5. The central bank retains control and monitoring of settlement of tokenized assets in RTGS balances. 6. Settlement of tokenised assets in RTGS balances must be robust and final under the applicable legal framework.'

similarities between the structures ('linking a DLT-based securities settlement system to an RTGS resembles the current setup in many ways'), a relevant trait has emerged from this first experiment:

> Yet what an RTGS link provides in terms of simplicity, it lacks in terms of potential benefits. The wholesale CBDC proof of concept demonstrates that an integration of tokenised central bank money and securities could enable functionality not possible with a link. This is worth exploring further. That said, a w-CBDC raises both practical and policy issues for a central bank. Project Helvetia explores some, but not all of these, and work continues.[358]

Phase II expanded the scope of Phase I, by involving five commercial banks in the study and targeting three core objectives. Phase II tested six use-cases, both transactional and non-transactional, against a series of business requirements within an extended version of the solution design proposed in Phase I.[359] The business requirements included ensuring central bank control over access, issuance, settlement, and redemption of wCBDCs, one-to-one convertibility between the wCBDC and reserve balances, and legal effectiveness of delegating responsibilities to a third-party platform operator.[360] Project Helvetia Phase II confirmed the feasibility of end-to-end settlement of tokenized assets in wCBDC, both between commercial banks (resident and non-resident) and between commercial banks and the central bank. Furthermore, it demonstrated 'how an overnight wCBDC, issued on a tokenised asset platform, could be integrated into core banking systems of the central banks and commercial banks'.[361,362]

The SNB also clarified some legal aspects, in particular in relation to its ability to delegate certain tasks to a third-party platform operator, who 'acts as the mandated party in relation to wCBDC and performs delegated tasks on behalf of the central bank based on contractual agreements, including the operation of nodes on behalf of the central bank'.[363] The wCBDC as referred to in Project Helvetia would not represent a novel category of central bank money, but rather an alternative representation of traditional reserve funds. Therefore, the SNB would retain its monitoring and control capabilities over wCBDCs, including the power to suspend 'individual participants from sending or receiving wCBDC or implementing a global wCBDC settlement stop'.[364]

iv. **France** France and Banque de France provided an important contribution to the debate on CBDC. Indeed, the world's first wholesale CBDC issuance to settle a financial transaction was carried out in 2020 by Banque de France, in cooperation

---

[358] Ibid, 27.
[359] Project Helvetia, Phase I (n 346) 19–20.
[360] Project Helvetia, Phase II (n 349) 16.
[361] Ibid, 24.
[362] A potential further phase was expected to take the testing to a deeper level, so as to include technical aspects such as error handling and latency, but also full automation of transaction processing, statistical and regulatory reporting of wCBDC, and privacy and cybersecurity. Ibid, 15.
[363] Ibid, 29.
[364] Ibid.

with Société Générale and its subsidiary Société Générale–Forge.[365] On 14 May 2020, Société Générale SFH, a subsidiary of Société Générale, issued 40 million euros of covered bonds with a private placement on an electronic distributed ledger.[366] These financial instruments, issued under French law and rated Aaa by Moody's and AAA by Fitch, were fully subscribed by the parent company Société Générale and simultaneously paid to the issuer by means of a digital form of euros issued by the Bank of France on a distributed ledger.

This bond issuance settled by a CBDC was the first ever for a G7 central bank. From a technological point of view, two types of distributed register were used for this issuance—one public, for the securities leg (chosen by the bond issuer), and the other private, for the cash leg (chosen by Banque de France)—made interoperable thanks to the operating model developed by Société Générale–Forge.

For the tokenization of financial instruments, the teams of Société Générale and its subsidiary Société Générale–Forge[367] relied on the French regulatory framework, which explicitly provides the possibility of issuing and registering a financial instrument that is not registered with a central depository in a 'distributed electronic ledger device' ('*dispositif d'enregistrement électronique partagé*' or 'DEEP', a concept which in French law encompasses the different types of distributed ledgers, whether they are permitted or not).[368]

With the DEEP Ordinance No. 2017-1674 of 8 December 2017,[369] as completed by the decree of 24 December 2018,[370] it is possible to register, sell, and pledge financial securities issued under French law on a DEEP. Under Article L. 211-3 of the Monetary and Financial Code, the registration of financial instruments on a DEEP is equivalent to registration in a securities account. The financial securities covered by this ordinance, and which may be registered in a DEEP, are not admitted to the operations of a central depository.[371]

With regard to the tokenization of central bank money and the issuance of the CBDC, Banque de France cannot decide to proceed with monetary creation via CBDC without the express approval of the Board of Governors of the European Central Bank. Until the ECB has publicly taken a position in favour of issuing CBDCs, the national central banks (NCBs) of the Eurosystem will thus have to experiment with CBDCs,

---

[365] Société Générale, 'Société Générale réalise la première transaction financière réglée en Monnaie Digitale de Banque Centrale' (30 May 2020) <https://www.societegenerale.com/sites/default/files/200023_cp_societe_generale_realise_la_premiere_transaction_financiere_reglee_en_monnaie_digitale_de_banque_centrale.pdf> accessed 22 April 2022.

[366] French law adopts the locution 'dispositif d'enregistrement électronique partagé' or DEEP.

[367] Raphaël Bloch, 'Société Générale donne le départ à sa plateforme blockchain' (*Les Echos*, 23 April 2019) <https://www.lesechos.fr/finance-marches/banque-assurances/societe-generale-donne-le-depart-a-sa-plateforme-blockchain-1013500> accessed 22 April 2022.

[368] See Stephan Blemus and Claire Pion, 'Blockchain, minibons et titres financiers—Des règles ad hoc pour les chaînes de bloc' (2019) 1 RDBF 25.

[369] *Ordonnance n° 2017-1674 du 8 décembre 2017 relative à l'utilisation d'un dispositif d'enregistrement électronique partagé pour la représentation et la transmission de titres financiers.*

[370] *Décret d'application n° 2018-1226 du 24 décembre 2018.*

[371] Under French law (art L. 211-7 of the *Code monétaire et financier*, this category encompasses negotiable debt securities (*titres de créance négociables*, commonly referred to as 'TCN'), securities issued by joint stock companies and debt securities other than negotiable debt securities (unlisted securities), and units or shares of a collective investment undertaking.

being careful not to expressly proceed with the monetary creation. Thus, there is some degree of flexibility for the NCBs to be able to interpret the conditions for the representation of central money, in particular when the duration of the representation of central bank money is less than one accounting day (this is referred to as an 'intra-day'), in order to be able to issue CBDCs for experiments without realizing money creation strictly speaking. The 'intra-day' representation of central money in the form of CBDC can be structured in many ways depending on the use case envisaged (issuance in exchange for reserves, etc.).[372]

The first CBDC issuance experiment, carried out in May 2020 entirely on distributed ledgers by Banque de France, as issuer of CBDCs, and by Société Générale SFH, as issuer of financial instruments on DEEP, demonstrated the feasibility of a 'native' and almost real-time settlement delivery of financial securities in CBDC for interbank settlements ('wholesale' CBDC). For Société Générale–Forge, the challenge of this experiment was to identify how innovative technologies could improve the efficiency and fluidity of payment systems and financial infrastructures, for a better financial sector and for the good functioning of the economy.

As a result of this accomplishment by Banque de France and Société Générale, and in order to strengthen its analysis on CBDCs, in March 2020 Banque de France published a call for applications to identify concrete cases of integration of CBDCs in innovative procedures for the issuance, exchange, and delivery against payment of tokenized assets.

This call for experiments was carried out jointly between 2020 and 2021 by Banque de France teams and the private players whose projects have been selected. This initiative should make it possible for France to provide the ECB with informed conclusions on the economic, technological, and regulatory advantages and disadvantages of CBDCs by 2021, and thus to participate in the reflections on this subject currently under way within the Eurosystem.

Banque de France considered CBDC experiments relevant at least for three reasons. First, for technological neutrality purposes, it is important to demonstrate the possibility of issuing CBDCs using different technologies (public/private distributed registers, etc.). Banque de France has not imposed any technology on project holders, but the innovative nature of the technology has been indicated as a selection criterion. Second, Banque de France intended to identify concrete use-cases for CBDCs, analysing the impact triggered by a CBDC on the current ecosystem and on financial innovation, based on concrete cases co-developed with private actors. Third, this is a way to conduct an appropriate and thorough analysis of CBDCs emphasizing the consequences at the level of financial stability, monetary policy, and regulatory environment.

Generally, Banque de France wanted to open up the field to innovation for CBDCs, with a focus on use-cases for:

(i) Payment in central currency against delivery of listed or unlisted financial instruments ('Delivery versus Payment');

---

[372] Luke Clancy, 'SocGen's Digitised Bond Passes Settlement Test' (*Risk.net*, 6 July 2020) <https://www.risk.net/derivatives/7650991/socgens-digitised-bond-passes-settlement-test> accessed 22 April 2022.

(ii) Payment in central currency against digital currency of another central bank ('Payment versus Payment'); or for
(iii) Payment in central bank money against digital assets (as defined by the French Monetary and Financial Code, art L.54-10-1 2°).

Banque de France continued its expriments on CBDCs, maintaining the private–public cooperation model.[373]

v. **European Union (European Central Bank)** Through the European System of Central Banks (ESCB), the ECB has established a proof of concept for anonymity in digital cash. The goal of this project is not the creation and implementation of a CBDC but rather a contribution to the topic.[374] As the ECB emphasized, an important contribution of the prototype currently under discussion is the possibility of using DLT as a tool for balancing two conflicting aspects, in particular the need for an individual to protect his privacy and the public interest dimension related to enforcing anti-money laundering and CFT regulations.[375]

More recently the ECB has taken important steps towards considering the possibility of issuing a digital euro. It would be a central bank liability offered in digital form to be used by citizens and businesses for their retail payments, to complement the current offer of cash and wholesale central bank deposits.[376] The ECB has further expanded its analysis with the 'Report on a Digital Euro',[377] and it involved stakeholders in a consultation[378] which registered a record level of public feedback (highlighting privacy and security concerns).[379] The ECB finally launched its digital euro initiative in July 2021, focusing on functional design as well as on potential regulatory changes to the European legal framework.[380]

The debate on a digital euro should be considered a main pillar of the European strategy, alongside appropriate regulation of private global and non-global stablecoins. As explained in Section II.B.3.c.ii, the regulatory process started as early as September 2020 with the European Commission MiCAR proposal.

The project on a digital euro started in October 2021, structured as a two-year investigation phase followed by a three-year realization phase, to test and develop the

---

[373] Banque de France selected eight projects, including Accenture, Euroclear, HSBC, Iznes, LiquidShare, ProsperUS, Seba Bank, and Société Générale–Forge, out of fifty applications. See Banque de France, 'Liste des candidatures retenues pour les expérimentations de monnaie digitale de banque centrale (MDBC)' (20 July 2020) <https://www.banque-france.fr/communique-de-presse/liste-des-candidatures-retenues-pour-les-experimentations-de-monnaie-digitale-de-banque-centrale> accessed 22 April 2022.

[374] See ECB, 'Exploring Anonymity in Central Bank Digital Currencies' (December 2019) In Focus No. 4 <https://www.ecb.europa.eu/paym/intro/publications/pdf/ecb.mipinfocus191217.en.pdf> accessed 22 April 2022.

[375] Ibid.

[376] ECB, *Report on a Digital Euro* (n 9).

[377] Ibid.

[378] ECB, 'Your views on digital euro' <https://www.ecb.europa.eu/euro/shared/files/Questionnaire_on_a_digital_euro.pdf> accessed 22 April 2022.

[379] ECB, *Eurosystem Report on the Public Consultation on a Digital Euro* (April 2021) <https://www.ecb.europa.eu/pub/pdf/other/Eurosystem_report_on_the_public_consultation_on_a_digital_euro~539fa8cd8d.en.pdf> accessed 22 April 2022 (hereafter ECB, *Consultation on a Digital Euro*).

[380] ECB, 'Eurosystem Launches Digital Euro Project' (July 2021), <https://www.ecb.europa.eu/press/pr/date/2021/html/ecb.pr210714~d99198ea23.en.html> accessed 22 April 2022.

appropriate technical solutions and the potential implementation of the project in 2025.[381] The focus of the investigation is currently divided into five key areas: reasons to issue a digital euro;[382] potential effects of a digital euro;[383] legal considerations;[384] functional design;[385] and technical approach.[386]

Designing the necessary features of the digital euro in particular requires striking the right balance between a number of priorities. The ECB report on the digital euro has identified key functional requirements. Among them, the report considers the problem of access to the digital euro, and highlights that users could access the digital euro either directly or through supervised intermediaries.[387] If users have direct access, the central bank will need to provide end user-facing services, such as customer identification and support. This would not be necessary if users access the digital euro indirectly, namely through intermediaries providing such services. The report also emphasizes the need to limit large-scale use of the digital euro as an investment.[388]

The report also strengthens the role of the digital euro as a medium of exchange to avoid any interference with the functioning of the financial system. The ECB has considered quantitative caps on digital euro holdings and tiered remuneration that disincentivizes excessive holdings as two viable options for pursuing this objective.[389]

With reference to the remuneration, the report suggests that a digital euro may be remunerated for financial stability, to lower demand for investment purposes and to prevent the Eurosystem becoming a large investment intermediary.[390]

In terms of legal tender, the report further highlights that without the status of legal tender, the drivers of digital euro acceptance would lead prospective payees to decide whether or not to accept it as a means to discharge obligations, which may in turn imply onboarding requirements along with specific tools needed to accept an incoming payment.[391]

The EU legal basis for issuing a digital euro may slightly vary depending on its design.[392]

The first scenario could be that the digital euro is issued as an instrument of monetary policy, therefore accessible only to central bank monetary policy counterparties in accordance with the ECB General Documentation or as participants in TARGET2 (non-retail access). This option would rely on Article 127(2) of the TFEU in

---

[381] ECB, 'Central Bank Digital Currencies: Defining the Problems, Designing the Solutions' (18 February 2022) <https://www.ecb.europa.eu/press/key/date/2022/html/ecb.sp220218_1~938e881b13.en.html> accessed 22 April 2022.
[382] ECB, *Report on a Digital Euro* (n 9) s 2.
[383] Ibid, s 3.
[384] Ibid, s 4.
[385] Ibid, s 5.
[386] Ibid, s 6.
[387] ECB, *Report on a Digital Euro* (n 9) 17.
[388] Ibid, 28. This is further highlighted in Corinne Zellweger-Gutknecht, Benjamin Geva, and Seraina Neva Grünewald, 'Digital Euro, Monetary Objects, and Price Stability: A Legal Analysis' (2021) 7 JFinReg 284.
[389] ECB, *Report on a Digital Euro* (n 9) 17.
[390] Ibid, 32.
[391] Ibid, 33.
[392] Ibid, 24.

conjunction with the first sentence of Article 20 of the Statute of the European System of Central Banks (ESCB).[393]

The second scenario would be that the digital euro is made available to households and other private entities through accounts held with the Eurosystem (retail account-based access, or 'token-based' or 'value-based' digital euro). In this case, Article 127(2) of the TFEU in conjunction with Article 17 of the Statute of the ESCB would provide the legal basis.[394]

The third scenario is that the digital euro is issued as an instrument equivalent to a banknote (retail, legal tender). Article 128 of the TFEU in conjunction with the first sentence of Article 16 of the Statute of the ESCB would provide the legal justification for it. The right to issue 'euro banknotes' (Article 128) could be understood to include the right to determine their format and other functional features. If so, the ECB's exclusive competence to 'authorise the issue of euro banknotes within the Union' (Article 128(1)) would represent the fundamental legal basis for issuing a digital euro with the status of legal tender. Of importance here is that, while the ECB's exclusive competence is limited to banknotes, member states, subject to ECB approval, have the right to issue euro coins (Article 128(2)), supposedly regardless of their format or medium.[395]

Adopting a broader perspective, as the ECB highlighted in its report:

Overall, invoking Article 128(1) of the TFEU in conjunction with Article 16 of the Statute of the ESCB would afford the Eurosystem the amplest margin of discretion for the issuance of a digital euro with the status of legal tender. Reliance on Article 127(2) of the TFEU in conjunction with Articles 17, 20 or 22 of the Statute of the ESCB would be more consistent with the issuance of digital euro variants for limited uses, devoid of general legal tender status.[396]

The notion of legal tender emphasizes the 'law's role of money'[397] or a quality of money cast by the law. A detailed definition of legal tender does not exist within the EU law. However, the legal tender of euro banknotes is enshrined in Article 128(1) TFEU, according to which 'the banknotes issued by the European Central Bank and the national central banks shall be the only suchnotes to have the status of legal tender within the Union'. Moreover, Commission Recommendation of 22 March 2010 on the scope and effects of legal tender of euro banknotes and coins defines three core features for the legal tender: mandatory acceptance, acceptance at full face value and power to discharge from payment obligations.[398] Also, according to a recent ruling of the European Court of Justice (ECJ), 'the status of legal tender of those notes and coins implies, in principle, an obligation to accept those notes and coins and, on the other

---

[393] Ibid.
[394] Ibid.
[395] Ibid.
[396] Ibid.
[397] John J. Chung, 'Money as Simulacrum: The Legal Nature and Reality of Money' (2009) 5 HastingsBusLJ 109, 114 <https://repository.uchastings.edu/hastings_business_law_journal/vol5/iss1/3/> accessed 22 April 2022.
[398] OJ L 83/1, 70–71.

hand, that obligation may, in principle, be restricted by the Member States for reasons of public interest'.[399] The consultation on a digital euro is exploring the advantages of regulating legal tender in detail at the EU level, along with the implications of recognizing the legal tender status of the digital euro.[400]

Article 133 TFEU provides that 'the use' of the euro—and, it is expected, the use of the digital euro as well—is regulated through secondary law laid down by the European Parliament and Council acting on a proposal from the Commission (Article 289 TFEU) and upon consultation with the ECB. Article 133 represents the general legal basis for the enactment of necessary monetary provisions,[401] for example those aimed at protecting the legal 'use' of the euro, such as Regulation 1210/2010 obliging financial institutions to run authenticity checks on euro coins.[402] For a digital euro to complement cash, and therefore to be used concurrently with banknotes and coins, 'necessary' monetary law measures, including those directed at adjusting the existing EU legal framework, would be enacted following the ordinary legislative procedure.

vi. People's Bank of China In contrast to the general prudent view related to the imminent possibility of issuing CBDCs, the People's Bank of China (PBOC) opted for an opposite strategy. In China, both central bankers and governors expressed concerns related to the possibility of a Libra-like monetary instrument in the country. The PBOC announced its intention to launch a new digital currency, the renminbi (RMB) in digital form, called digital currency electronic payment (DCEP). Initially, the DCEP was supposed to be similar to the original Libra project.[403] However, China's government and central bank governors did not provide any official timeline, although pilot projects started in four major cities: Shenzhen, Suzhou, Xiong'an and Chengdu.[404]

According to a comprehensive report prepared by Goldman Sachs, China's digital currency and electronic payments will have some key features. The new digital currency should rely on a two-tier issuance, with the PBOC issuing and clearing digital currency for commercial banks, and commercial banks in the position of distributing digital currency to customers and interfacing directly with customers, maintaining the same financial structure.[405] This decision to implement a two-tier structure with commercial banks fully involved in the distribution of digital currencies brings some clear advantages. First, this system relies on commercial banks' solid organization (both technically and in terms of human resources) and is based on substantial freedom for commercial banks to choose and implement their preferred technology, thereby creating the basis for open competition which is instrumental to foster innovation in this key area. Furthermore, the presence of commercial banks reduces the risks of bank

---

[399] C-422/19 and C-423/19 *Johannes Dietrich and Norbert Häring v Hessischer Rundfunk* [2021] ERC I-0422.
[400] ECB, *Consultation on a Digital Euro* (n 379) 14, 20.
[401] Monetary law measures must fulfil the criteria of 'necessity'. See Helmut Siekmann (ed), *The European Monetary Union: A Commentary on the Legal Foundations* (Bloomsbury 2021) 482.
[402] Arts 3, 4.
[403] Reuters, 'China New Digital Currency' (n 7).
[404] Goldman Sachs, 'Digital Currency—Reinventing the Yuan for the Digital Age' (17 November 2020) 5 (on file with author).
[405] Ibid, 15.

disintermediation, because digital currencies would continue to circulate within the banking system and not remain inside bank accounts.[406]

The two-tier structure will likely have a limited impact on balance sheets. In this context, households could be in the position of exchanging digital currencies for deposits or cash from commercial banks, before commercial banks exchange digital currency with the PBOC.[407] Other specific measures will further mitigate the risk that the new digital currency will cause bank disintermediation. Among them is that the new digital currency will not pay interest.[408]

With regard to anonymity, the Chinese digital currency will be designed with the purpose of establishing controllable anonymity, with digital currency wallets structurally independent of bank accounts for smaller transactions. In this way the PBOC would be in the position of replicating the anonymity characterizing physical cash, relying on a structure defined as 'loosely coupled account links' as opposed to the 'tightly coupled account links' generally associated with traditional bank accounts.[409]

From a technical standpoint, the PBOC is not planning to issue a cryptocurrency, because instead of a distributed ledger there will be a centralized processing.[410] This decision of the PBOC could likely be justified by the concerns about DLT's processing speed: Bitcoin is able to process only seven transactions per second and Libra's proposal (likely replicated in Diem) consisted of a hybrid structure to reach one thousand transactions per second.[411] On the other hand, the PBOC could consider a DLT infrastructure for wholesale payments, which do not require the same processing speed as retail payments.[412]

vii. **Cooperation involving multiple central banks** An important emerging trait involving some of the most established central bankers is observable enhanced cooperation. A group of six central banks, including the Bank of Canada, the ECB, the Bank of Japan, the Bank of England, the Sveriges Riksbank, the SNB, the Board of Governors of the Federal Reserve System, and the BIS, established a group focusing on CBDCs and the possibility to adopt them in the respective jurisdictions. The cross-sectorial approach of the group encompasses economic, legal, and technical design options and is currently co-chaired by the Head of the BIS Innovation Hub, Benoît Cœuré, and the Deputy Governor of the Bank of England, Jon Cunliffe.[413]

The group has issued its first report identifying the core CBDC features, distinguishing instrument features, system features, and institutional features.[414] Among the instrument features, the report highlighted the importance of strong convertibility,

---

[406] Ibid.
[407] Ibid, 20.
[408] Ibid, 21.
[409] Ibid, 17.
[410] Ibid, 5.
[411] Ibid, 18.
[412] Ibid.
[413] Bank of Canada, ECB, Bank of Japan, Sveriges Riksbank, Swiss National Bank, Bank of England, Board of Governors Federal Reserve System, and BIS, 'Central Bank Digital Currencies: Foundational Principles and Core Features—Report No 1' (October 2020) 11 <https://www.bis.org/publ/othp33.pdf> accessed 22 April 2022.
[414] Ibid.

in the sense of exchanging at par with cash and private money for the purpose of maintaining singleness of the currency.[415] Another key feature for a CBDC is its low cost, with end users in the position of not incurring additional costs when using it.[416] The system should be secure, grant instant or near-instant final settlement and availability '24/7/365', as well as being interoperable, flexible, and adaptable.[417] As well as identifying the institutional features, the report draws attention to the need to rely on a robust legal framework, where a central bank has clear authority when issuing CBDCs, coupled with the conformity of a CBDC system to appropriate regulatory standards.[418] The second report issued by the group, in September 2021, stressed the importance of involving both public and private actors when designing an effective CBDC system, for two main reasons: implementing interoperability and co-existence with the broader payment system, and anticipating the needs of future users and incorporating related innovations.[419]

The mBridge project[420] is a cooperative project involving the BIS Innovation Hub, the Hong Kong Monetary Authority, the Bank of Thailand, the Bank of China, and the Central Bank of the United Arab Emirates. The scope of the project is the creation of the first prototype for multiple CBDCs (mCBDCs), to deliver real-time, cheaper, and safer cross-border payments and settlements.[421] The prototype platform completed international transfers and foreign exchange operations in seconds, promising to reduce costs by up to half.[422]

III. Critical Considerations

Shadow central banking raises issues of differing scales at various levels. Here, stablecoins serve as a powerful example. In a recent report, the BIS/G7 identified two categories of stablecoins—local stablecoins and global-scale stablecoins—based on the scale of their impact on the local or global financial economies. Based on the different scales of these two entities, the G7 has identified different risks.[423] All stablecoins pose problems in terms of legal certainty; governance; money laundering; terrorist financing and other forms of illicit finance; safety, efficiency, and integrity of payment systems; cyber security and operation resilience; market integrity; data privacy; protection and portability; consumer/investor protection; and tax compliance. In addition to this, global stablecoins pose risks to financial stability, monetary policy, the international monetary system, and fair competition.[424]

---

[415] Ibid.
[416] Ibid.
[417] Ibid.
[418] Ibid.
[419] Bank of Canada, ECB, Bank of Japan, Sveriges Riksbank, Swiss National Bank, Bank of England, Board of Governors Federal Reserve System, and BIS, 'Central bank digital currencies: executive summary' (September 2021) <https://www.bis.org/publ/othp42.htm> accessed 22 April 2022.
[420] BISIH et al., 'Inthanon-LionRock to mBridge' (n 327).
[421] Ibid.
[422] Ibid.
[423] G7, 'Impact of Global Stablecoins' (n 143).
[424] Ibid.

These specific concerns may also apply to shadow central banking as a broader category. This chapter tends to emphasize the global dimension of the phenomenon, especially when highlighting the similarities with the global—not local—shadow banking system. With regard to the risks, the purpose of this section (and more generally of this chapter) is not to provide an exhaustive analysis of all the problems that may emerge from shadow central banking, but rather to focus on issues more closely related to the economic dimension that trigger concerns for the legal system. Therefore, the focus here is one of governance and conflicts of shadow central banking interests, as well as systemic risks and issues of interoperability. Furthermore, the approach is often a historical one, trying to identify analogies with previous époques that pose similar issues.

A. An Old Paradigm?

1. Private Central Banks

In the shadow banking system, both the disruptors (shadow banks) and the disrupted (regulated credit institutions) are necessarily private institutions whose main purpose relates to private interests, in particular the creation of profit for shareholders or investors. In the context of shadow central banking the situation may be different because shadow central banks are private while central banks are public. But isn't this true of other historical époques? It is, but only if taking into account modern times. Historically, it should not be surprising that private entities were in charge of public functions related to monetary policy and payment systems. Indeed, similar to how private Fintech firms today are invested in developing e-money, and more recently DLT-based solutions, early central banks were private institutions operating as clearing houses in their local economies, issuing bills and notes and not regulated as modern central banks. More generally, free banking systems do not design any specific rule for banks that are in the position to freely issue their own currency. The shift from private to public status was the result of a gradual process of transformation involving central banks, with the majority of the countries not opting for a free banking system. This shift in their roles corresponds to a different interpretation of the main interests to be pursued. Therefore, although in modern times central banks are public institutions in charge of pursuing a public interest, in the past the situation was rather different and until the twentieth century private central banks operated in the interest of their shareholders.[425]

Bitcoin emerged as a radical critique of a specific framework, which failed; and this financial system imploded, in part, because of the role and the risks related to shadow banking. Now, one of the unintended consequences of Bitcoin is that it may lead to the establishment of a new network, shadow central banking, that will in the long term replicate similar mechanisms and similar risks, although serving different economic purposes (central banking rather than banking). One of the 'solutions' to the financial crisis, rooted in the concept of transparency and trust, contributed to the definitive emergence of a new shadow network.

---

[425] See Kern Alexander, *Principles of Banking Regulation* (CUP 2019) 52.

Indeed, by looking back to the past it emerges that shadow central banking pre-existed not only this era of technological transformations, but also the central banking era, where central banks were public entities. Therefore, the long-term effect of Bitcoin would be a sort of 'restoration', a return to the pre-existing paradigm based on private institutions operating as central banks. In this old paradigm, the private interest of shareholders investing in the shadow central banking entity would be stronger than the public interest. As Katharina Pistor emphasized at the House of Financial Services Hearing for Libra, the Libra Association intended to create a global payment system on a for-profit basis and build a governance structure that avoids any form of accountability.[426]

2. A Pre-'Full-Faith-and-Credit' Paradigm

With regard to stablecoins (on- and off-chain ones), including Libra-like projects, their values are based on an underlying asset. This is also a restoration of the old idea that the value of money depends on the value of the underlying assets. In the past, the value of currencies was based on the gold standard. In this system, a country decides the fixed price for gold and buys and sells gold at that fixed price, and the value of the currency depends on gold's fixed price. The gold standard was gradually abandoned by the majority of countries from the 1930s on, but it formally remained in place until 1968, when central banks agreed to stop buying gold on the open market.[427]

The new standard is that of fiat currency (the shift from gold standard to dollar standard), and its adoption led to a shift also at the level of policy objective for central banks, focusing on inflation performance in the modern framework.[428] Fiat money is not backed by any physical commodity. Instead, it is directly backed by the government (so-called full faith and credit) and its value is exclusively based on trust—a system in which central bank assets are backed by the 'immaterial' power of the state to tax its citizen.[429] Cyclically, this trust depends on the fact that money represents government debt, which is liquid because it can be converted into money.[430]

Stablecoin-like currencies propose a model of stability that is based on the underlying fiat currency or basket of fiat currencies, owned by the issuing private entity through its custodians. However, this could be an intermediate step toward a pure 'trust' model for private digital currencies, just as the gold standard was an intermediate step toward a pure 'trust' model. A potential scenario could be that in the future, private cryptocurrencies may be stable because of the trust they generate, rather than for their reserves. It is also worth noting that the many stablecoin projects backed by gold have failed.[431]

---

[426] Pistor, 'Written Statement' (n 274) 8.
[427] See Robert L. Hetzel, 'Launch of the Bretton Woods System' (*Federal Reserve History*, 22 November 2013) <https://www.federalreservehistory.org/essays/bretton_woods_launched> accessed 22 April 2022.
[428] See generally Bordo and Siklos, 'Central Banks: Evolution' (n 49).
[429] Roberds and Velde, 'Early Public Banks I' (n 47) 322.
[430] Ibid.
[431] Matthew Beedham, 'Two-Thirds of Failed Stablecoin Projects Were Backed by Gold' (*Hard Fork*, 27 June 2019) <https://thenextweb.com/hardfork/2019/06/27/stablecoin-projects-gold-failed/> accessed 22 April 2022.

In this respect, Bitcoin and stablecoins strongly differ, and Bitcoin does not propose a model based on reserves, substituting both the role of reserves and 'full faith and credit' with a different mechanism. As previously explained, Bitcoin relies on distributed consensus secured by cryptography.

B. Independence, Governance, and Corporate Governance in Shadow Central Banking

1. Private Central Banks and Separation between Ownership and Control

While in many fields private companies exercise public functions, it would be hard to imagine a complete shift in the context of central banking and monetary policy. For example, private actors would have to determine sensitive money-supply decisions as well as other related objectives, including building, managing, and supervising resilient market infrastructures without any interference or role of public central banks. This possibility would require revisiting the governance of central banks, since private currencies imply private management.

In many respects, central bank governance has evolved over time. Specifically, the relationship between central bankers and executive powers has changed over time, especially because central bank independence has not always been a prerogative and after the financial crisis, central banking activity seemed to be less independent from government power. With respect to internal governance in the twentieth century, governors of central banks were the prominent single decision-makers, making important decisions on their own.[432] On the contrary, nowadays a governing body's staff is composed more of academics and economists than of classic bureaucrats. Relatedly, in the past twenty to thirty years central banks have gradually increased their transparency, strengthening their communication with the public.[433] Notwithstanding these significant changes, a key area of central banking governance that was never revisited is the virtual elimination of private ownership because most of the central banks were nationalized, becoming part of their respective governments.[434] Some central banks (such as the Federal Reserve, the Central Bank of Japan, and the SNB) have some form of private sector shareholding, while others, such as Banca d'Italia, are fully owned by private shareholders.[435] Although these private entities may be partially or even fully owned by private shareholders, the principle of separation between ownership and control within the corporate context is maintained in modern central banks without exception.[436] However, tech giants and generally newly created (fin)tech companies may prove an exception to this principle because they tend to maintain control and ownership. Therefore, even this basic principle may be violated in a scenario where

---

[432] See for example Liaquat Ahamed, *Lords of Finance: The Bankers Who Broke the World* (Tantor 2010).
[433] Bordo and Siklos, 'Central Banks: Evolution' (n 49) 9.
[434] Ibid.
[435] See David Bholat and Karla Martinez Gutierrez, 'The Ownership of Central Banks' (*Bank Underground*, 18 October 2019) <https://bankunderground.co.uk/2019/10/18/the-ownership-of-central-banks/> accessed 22 April 2022.
[436] Ibid.

these new entities take the lead on monetary policy, and operate as shadow central bankers.

However, in this paradigm based on private organizations, separation between ownership and control is not the only aspect that would be affected. Other key principles would require a new contextualization. One of these is central banking and the need to conceive the relationship between 'private' and 'public' central banking activities, and with other governmental branches and powers. Furthermore, there might be the risk of perennial conflicts of interest dominating the entire scene.

2. Corporate Governance
a. *Different approaches in designing corporate governance mechanisms*
Private entities operating in the monetary system would require extraordinarily strong governance tools. Unlike past organizations, new entities entering the payment system not only operate an infrastructure, but also issue their own currencies. These entities, like any other entering the realm of central banking activity and affecting monetary policy, would be in a position to manage a public interest function, occupying a position within the economic system not even achieved by banks. Typically, banks are in charge of the very sensitive task of managing depositors' savings,[437] and are often referred to as 'special' institutions. Therefore, if banks are special,[438] central banks and any entity involved in any central banking activity with a direct effect on monetary policy are possibly more special then banks. In fact, their public interest is even more important because of the activity that they perform. As a consequence, even their corporate governance is distinctive.

A private institution engaged in issuing some digital currency would need to address specific concerns regarding potential weaknesses in its corporate governance. To that effect, any characterization of such entities as banks, market infrastructures, and so on would be deemed irrelevant in this respect. In the aftermath of the financial crisis, the European Union took some measures at the level of corporate governance for bank institutions and chose to apply similar rules to asset managers and alternative asset managers in the AIFMD.[439] One of the purposes of this regulatory framework was to control managers' risk appetite and strengthen the risk-management function, in order to limit leverage and risky investments. Therefore, this regulatory framework was applied to multiple heterogeneous categories of financial institutions. The kinds of measures affecting the way managers make investment decisions, especially in relation to reserves, should be considered in this new frontier of shadow central banking. The first version of the Libra white paper was unanimously criticized by many commentators because it provided only an overview and failed to clarify any corporate governance details and mechanism.[440] Notwithstanding the issuance of other versions, the project continued to raise doubt among regulators and commentators.

---

[437] See Jonathan Macey and Maureen O'Hara, 'The Corporate Governance of Banks' (2003) 9 FRBNY EconPolRev 91, 95 <https://www.newyorkfed.org/medialibrary/media/research/epr/03v09n1/0304mace.pdf> accessed 22 April 2022.
[438] See Kern Alexander, 'Corporate Governance and Banks: The Role of Regulation in Reducing the Principal-Agent Problem' (2006) 7 JBankReg 14, 18–19.
[439] See n 15.
[440] See Pistor, 'Written Statement' (n 274) 5–9. See also Christopher Brummer, '"99 Problems"—Written Testimony Before the United States House Committee on Financial Services Examining Facebook's

There may be alternative ways to imagine the relationship between shadow central banking and other institutions, which would impact the design of their corporate governance.

A first approach would be to emphasize some analogies between shadow central banking and existing market infrastructures. This would, consequentially, demystify and 'normalize' a debate on shadow central banking corporate governance given that many of their market infrastructures already exist and their corporate governance is efficient. After all, payment systems are market infrastructures, and are often private ones.[441] The same applies to clearing houses, engaged in processing a wide range of transactions, from payments to credit derivatives.

The Swiss FINMA Guidelines on Stablecoins also suggest this similarity with market infrastructures. Indeed, when referring to inquiries from the Libra Association, FINMA suggests that 'if a payment system of significant importance is launched in connection with the creation of a "stable coin", a licensing requirement under the Financial Market Infrastructure Act (FMIA; SR 958.1) as a payment system is probable'.[442] This is consistent with the developments related to the Libra Association's application to FINMA to be recognized as a licensed payment system under Swiss law.[443] In the past, private institutions that became central banks were in charge of clearing and settlement operations. More recently, market infrastructures, specifically clearing houses, were a hot topic in the aftermath of the financial crisis. They came under the scrutiny of regulators, especially because of their important role in the derivative market, where they contribute to reduce systemic risk and enhance financial stability. The post-crisis regulatory framework contributed to strengthen these objectives. An option would be to extend clearing house regulatory framework to payment systems within the context of the payment infrastructure.

However, there is a significant difference between the typical market infrastructure in the context of clearing and settlement systems and the infrastructures of the payment system. Not only would a 'Libra-like' institution operate as a market infrastructure, but it would also issue its own currencies, exactly as a central bank would. In fact, not even central banks are in charge of the money-supply function while directly operating market infrastructures because they delegate this function to private entities, which they supervise. The combination of these two functions differentiates the 'Libra-like' institution as a far more complex entity when compared to traditional market infrastructures. Traditional market systems build and manage an infrastructure, while central banks are in charge of the overall functioning or supervision of an infrastructure while exclusively managing the money supply. Indeed, the combination of the two layers within a private entity makes these new entities far more complex, impacting the necessary regulations and corporate governance arrangements.

Proposed Cryptocurrency and Its Impact on Consumers, Investors, and the American Financial System' (17 July 2019) 2 <https://financialservices.house.gov/uploadedfiles/hhrg-116-ba00-wstate-brummerc-20190717.pdf> accessed 22 April 2022 (hereafter Brummer, '99 Problems'). See also Gensler, 'Examining Facebook's Proposed Cryptocurrency' (n 21) 13–14.

[441] See generally Angela Walch, 'Bitcoin as a Market Infrastructure' (2015) 18 NYUJL&PubPol'y 837.
[442] See FINMA, 'Stable Coin Guidelines' (n 269).
[443] See FINMA, 'Libra Association: FINMA Licensing Process Initiated' (15 April 2020) <https://www.finma.ch/en/news/2020/04/20200416-mm-libra/> accessed 22 April 2022.

Instead of elevating shadow central banking entities to 'central banking' status, an alternative approach would be to lower the rank of central banks. This approach would be substantially similar to that of 'free banking'. Technology may justify this approach because it, in effect, normalizes the role of central banks. If central banks were considered more ordinary entities with a more ordinary role in the economic ecosystem, new technologies would be perfectly fungible to central banks. Again, similar to other considerations developed in the previous section, this alternative shares some similarities with the free banking era in the United States, when each bank was acting as a micro-central bank, and each system relied on multiple private currencies. At that time, these entities lacked special consideration, special status, and a special regulatory framework to safeguard their stability and their functions within the economic and financial system. However, this did not lead to beneficial results. Indeed, that system collapsed.[444] In response, American regulators passed the Banking Act, which gave the Federal Reserve a special status, assigning it special functions.

b. Accountability

Accountability is a crucial issue in any form of governance, especially for central banks. In the context of central banks, accountability mechanisms mitigate the risks emerging from central bank independence.[445] In financial regulation and government, precise advantages and disadvantages are generally associated with private versus public entities. Public entities and powers are historically perceived as more accountable than private institutions. An example is the difference between public and private regulators and the products (regulations) that they generate. While private self-regulation brings specific benefits (among them rapid adoption, flexibility, and competence of the industry), a downside is its diminished public accountability. The significant regulatory initiatives pursued in the aftermath of the financial crisis exemplify the public pioneering of a new regulatory framework, reducing the role of private self-regulation as much as possible. This choice pursued accountability, fostered transparency, and eliminated any potential conflicts of interest resulting from private regulators.

These dynamics underlying regulation and regulators can be extended to any form of power and cuntions, including those underlying the entities managing monetary policy. Public authorities may be subject to more rigorous control and scrutiny, whereas private entities may enjoy more freedom when managing sensitive tasks, as it is more difficult to hold them accountable for their decisions. To fill this potential deficit, private authorities require equally strong governance mechanisms that provide more guarantees in terms of accountability. In the context of traditional corporate governance mechanisms, managers are held accountable by shareholders and a broader audience, if hypothetical corporate social responsibility applies.[446] In the

---

[444] Katharina Pistor and Co-Pierre Georg, 'The Right Response to the Libra Threat' (*Project Syndicate*, 5 August 2019) <https://www.project-syndicate.org/commentary/regulating-private-money-facebook-libra-by-katharina-pistor-and-co-pierre-georg-2019-08> accessed 22 April 2022 (hereafter Pistor and Georg, 'Response to Libra Threat').

[445] See Section I.B.

[446] See Larry E. Ribstein, 'Accountability and Responsibility In Corporate Governance' (2006) 81 NotreDameLRev 1431, 1432.

context of a private entity managing broad central banking activities, the public sphere of interests still remains extremely relevant. Therefore, a potential issue is whether managers should be held accountable—in a more pervasive way—towards public powers and authorities, when compared to any listed corporation. In this case, if managers commit specific types of fraud, securities authorities may prosecute them for fraud, as with the SEC in the United States. At a lower level, could a sovereign state exercise any form of influence to obtain the resignation of a shadow central banking executive? A further issue could also be whether, in the case of a global shadow central banking entity, a specific government actually has the power to do so.

These issues are not theoretical. A nodal point in the governance of the original Libra project was its accountability, which clearly relates to governance issues. As Katharina Pistor emphasized at the hearing for Libra, many powers were concentrated in the Libra Association. They were in charge of many sensitive tasks: economic (such as the decision on which assets are eligible for reserve, and how to manage them), technical (Libra's architecture as a permissioned or a permissionless system), and organizational (including the admission of future members).[447] However, this concentration of power was not counterbalanced by significant mechanisms of accountability.[448] This also depended on the decision to adopt the legal form of an association, further insulating this entity from the economic and social context.[449]

c. Central bank independence

Accountability is strictly interconnected with central bank independence and private entities' engagement in monetary policy would require a reconsideration of the role of central bank independence in the overall structure. As mentioned above, central bank independence is a common feature to many central banks and a tool designed to guarantee a clear separation between monetary policy and executive powers in the hands of other branches of the government. Those who do not support central bank independence argue that the benefits for removing powerful institutions from democratic oversight are not proven, emphasizing the inutility of central bank independence[450] and referring to it as an 'integral part of the neoliberal catechism'.[451] Central bank independence in the context of a new paradigm with private entities leads to fundamental questions. In the extreme scenario of private actors taking over central banking functions (payment side and money supply), central bank independence would not make much sense, because in principle there would be a clear separation between the government and central banks.

However, is it important to address whether this separation would prevent any conflicts of interest. This question relates to accountability and independence. By conducting central banking activities, would a private institution inherently obscure the decision-making processes and the dynamics of monetary policy? The risk is that private actors would be able to support the activity of certain governments and, vice

---

[447] Pistor, 'Written Statement' (n 274) 2.
[448] Ibid.
[449] Ibid.
[450] See Kawa, 'Central Bank Independence' (n 64).
[451] Sheri Berman and Kathleen R. McNamara, 'Bank on Democracy: Why Central Banks Need Public Oversight' (1999) 78 ForeignAff 2, 2.

versa, condescending governors may build stronger ties with private actors for their private interests; in both scenarios, this may result in a less efficient monetary policy. The corollary problem of potential conflicts of interest between interconnected private institutions will be treated in the section covering potential risks.

C. Potential Problems

1. Systemic Risk

Shadow central banking initiatives may go from being 'too small to care' to 'too big to fail' in a very short time.[452] In 2016, the IMF did not consider virtual currency as a systemic risk to financial stability due to its small scale and insignificant connections to the financial system.[453] However, it did recognize some inherent financial risks for holders and users of virtual currency[454] and it understood that these risks could spread to the broader financial sector if the phenomenon increased in popularity and embedded itself in the global economy.[455] This is what is happening today. In fact, in his October 2019 letter addressed to G20 Finance Ministers and Central Bank Governors, Financial Stability Board Chair Randal K. Quarles highlighted the risks emerging from stablecoins.[456] Consistent with this position, the Swiss FINMA stressed the need for consistent monitoring of financial stability risks posed by these instruments.[457]

The relationship between crypto-assets and systemic risk emerged in work performed by different institutions. The CPMI–IOSCO report stressed the similarities between certain 'stablecoin arrangements' and financial market infrastructures, explicitly mentioning specific sources of systemic risk in this context.[458] The Basel Committee on Banking Supervision focused on the quantification of banks' exposure to crypto-assets and the importance of developing an internationally consistent prudential treatment for banks' exposure to crypto-assets.[459] IOSCO focused on applying its Principles, Standards, Recommendations, and Guidance to 'global stablecoin' initiatives and the way they might affect securities regulators.[460]

Any institution as big as the tech giants that are engaging in payment system development using their own cryptocurrencies should necessarily be treated as a SIFI. These are the consequences of creating (or counting on) a significant network, or implementing a significant data–network–activities ('DNA') loop.[461] Tech giants in

---

[452] Ibid.
[453] See IMF, 'Virtual Currencies and Beyond' (n 121) para 54.
[454] Ibid, 55.
[455] Ibid, 56. For an analysis of the systemic risks related to the payment system, see also Hilary J. Allen, 'Payments Failure' (2021) 62 BCLRev 453.
[456] Letter from the Financial Stability Board to G20 Finance Ministers and Central Bank Governors (13 October 2019) <https://www.fsb.org/wp-content/uploads/P131019.pdf> accessed 22 April 2022 (hereafter FSB, Letter to G20).
[457] Swiss Council, 'Current Status of Stablecoin Debate' (n 270).
[458] See BIS-IOSCO, 'Principles for Financial Market Infrastructures' (n 156).
[459] BIS Committee on Banking Supervision, 'Prudential Treatment of Cryptoasset Exposures' (June 2021) <https://www.bis.org/bcbs/publ/d519.pdf> accessed 22 April 2022.
[460] IOSCO, 'Global Stablecoin Initiatives' (n 150).
[461] BIS, *BIS Annual Economic Report 2019* (2019) 55 <https://www.bis.org/publ/arpdf/ar2019e3.pdf> accessed 22 April 2022.

the financial sector such as Alibaba, Amazon, Meta, Google, and Tencent certainly introduce new risks.[462] Any disruption not only at the level of their reserves (on the pure monetary and financial side) but also at the corporate level may pose a serious systemic threat to network participants as well as to the financial sector as a whole. In this context, there are various potential causes of such large systemic risk. This too constitutes a similarity with shadow banking.

a. Risks of interconnections, financial conglomerates, and systemic conflicts of interest
First, both shadow banking and shadow central banking share inherent and relevant risks regarding interconnections and the common tendency to favour the creation of significant too-big-to-fail financial conglomerates (SIFIs). The shadow banking system contributed to the increasing interconnection of financial systems with a chain of investments that transferred risks from one entity to another via complex financial instruments. The interconnection between the involved entities did not disperse risk, but instead increased the fragility of the system and resulted in a financial system incapable of absorbing shocks, and requiring selective public intervention in order to avoid far more catastrophic consequences.

Shadow central banking (as the labels 'stablecoin arrangements' and 'global stablecoins' also suggest) increases interconnection on multiple fronts, including the ways in which global shadow central banking entities invest their reserves, a long chain of custodians and other financial institutions, and excessive exposures that other SIFIs may have to these entities. Furthermore, risks stemming from this interconnection may be due to a broad range of shadow central banking activities.

In the previous sections, central bank independence was characterized as a tool that is potentially capable of reducing conflicts of interest between different powers. In particular, central bank independence pursues a strong insulation of central bankers from political power, to avoid any opportunistic use of the monetary policy tools available. The risk is that the governing party may be tempted to implement expansive monetary policies for short-term reasons to increase consensus, despite these being ultimately detrimental to the entire system, which is inevitably exposed to inflationary trends. Avoiding any influence or conflict of interest at the level of shadow central banking institutions derives from central bank independence in this specific context where private institutions act as central banks. Thus, any measure aimed at reducing conflicts of interest would also be consistent with rules aimed at reducing financial interconnection. Furthermore, this would help to mitigate risks of excessive power concentrations and persistent conflicts of interest among entities that regularly interact with central banking.

A famous antecedent in history is the legendary John Law, a financier operating in Europe during the first two decades of the eighteenth century. Commonly associated with the first practices of market manipulation and insider trading, John Law dominated the French economy with his Mississippi Company. The interests of the Mississippi Company included trading companies, the national debt, the national

---

[462] Ibid.

bank, and the French national debt.[463] All this eventually led to a catastrophic market crash for France.[464]

As the President's Working Group on Stablecoins highlighted, an individual stablecoin could pose significant risks because a stablecoin issuer or a prominent participant, such as a custodial wallet provider, could be a source of systemic risk.[465] Furthermore, the combination of a stablecoin issuer or wallet provider and a commercial firm could lead to an excessive concentration of economic power, with negative effects also in terms of competition.[466] In such a scenario, regulatory systems should imagine a sort of Glass–Steagall provision that is applicable to shadow central banking entities. This would be necessary to separate private entities engaged in developing the infrastructures and networks of central banking activities from other SIFIs.[467] This would also prevent simple conflicts of interest. In the aftermath of the 1929 financial crisis, the Glass–Steagall Act was a key pillar in the United States' Pecora Commission's regulatory response to the largest financial crisis the world had ever experienced at that time. The Clinton administration replaced this legislation with the Gramm–Leach–Bliley Act, in effect sanctioning the commingling of activities between commercial banks and shadow banking. One of the most important and controversial reforms proposed in the aftermath of the financial crisis of 2008 was the so-called Volker Rule, proposed by former Federal Reserve Chairman Paul Volker. The main purpose of this reform was to sever ties between banks and private funds and, more notably, to reduce the ties between shadow banking and credit institutions. Notably, Volker Rule introduced at Article 13 of the Banking Holding Act[468] specific restrictions on the ability of a banking entity or nonbank financial company supervised by the same institution to engage in short-term proprietary trading and have certain interests in, or relationships with, a hedge fund or private equity fund (covered funds).[469] In this way, the reform intended to reduce the possibility that conflicts of interest could emerge in managing credit institutions.

Consistent with these concerns, the President's Working Group on Stablecoins proposed to require stablecoin issuers to comply with activities restrictions that limit affiliation with commercial entities, and to create standards for custodial wallet providers, including 'limits on affiliation with commercial entities or on us of users' transaction data.'[470]

---

[463] See Nouriel Roubini and Stephen Mihm, *Crisis Economics: A Crash Course in the Future of Finance* (Penguin 2010) 21.
[464] Ibid.
[465] President's Working Group on Financial Markets, *Report on Stablecoins* (n 129) 14.
[466] Ibid.
[467] See Financial Stability Board, 'Policy Measures to Address Systemically Important Financial Institutions' (4 November 2011) <https://www.fsb.org/wp-content/uploads/r_111104bb.pdf?page_moved=1> accessed 22 April 2022.
[468] Banking Holding Company Act 1956, s 13.
[469] The Volker Rule was recently amended. See Office of the Comptroller of the Currency, Treasury; Board of Governors of the Federal Reserve System; Federal Deposit Insurance Corporation; SEC; and Commodity Futures Trading Commission, 'Prohibitions and Restrictions on Proprietary Trading and Certain Interests in, and Relationships With, Hedge Funds and Private Equity Funds' (SEC Release No. BHCA-9, 1 October 2020) <https://www.sec.gov/rules/final/2020/bhca-9.pdf> accessed 22 April 2022.
[470] President's Working Group on Financial Markets, *Report on Stablecoins* (n 129) 17.

b. Payment system risks in stablecoin arrangements

Referring to payment stablecoin arrangements, the President's Working Group Report highlighted the similarities between the risks of any traditional payment system, as identified by the Committee on Payment and Settlement System referring to credit risk, liquidity risk, operation risk, ineffective governance, and settlement risk.[471] Improper management of such risks would affect payment systems in different ways: they would be less available and less reliable for users and could be a source of financial shocks or contribute to the contagion of financial shocks.[472] A difference with traditional payment systems is the manifestation of such risks, depending on technologies, transaction processes, and governance arrangements.[473]

Stablecoin arrangements might be exposed to traditional operational risk, originating from structural problems in the information systems or internal processes, as well as human errors or management failures, disrupting the possibility to make payments.[474] As the President's Report highlights, stablecoins could be exposed to these risks as well as to new ones associated with 'validation and confirmation of stablecoin transactions and the management and integrity of the distributed ledger.'[475] Furthermore, these risks could be more difficult to manage or supervise, in particular when the supporting infrastructure cannot be directly controlled by anyone and there is no clear entity to regulate.[476]

Settlement risk in stablecoin arrangements could depend on unclear definitions of the settlement rules, creating uncertainty that translates into credit and liquidity pressure for arrangement participants.[477] Furthermore, in the context of open network access combined with consensus-based settlement mechanisms, 'technical settlement may be subject to uncertainty for longer periods, with no single party accountable for defining or ensuring legal settlement finality, creating questions about the reliability and finality of payments.'[478]

Finally, liquidity risk in the context of payment system operations could be associated with 'misalignment of the settlement timing and processes between stablecoin arrangements and other systems, with the consequence of temporary shortages in the quantity of stablecoins available to make payments.'[479]

The President's Working Group noted that such risks may not be adequately addressed in the context of stablecoins for specific reasons, in particular a lack of consistent risk-management standards among arrangements, the number of different key constituencies involved, and difficulties related to supervisory activities.[480]

---

[471] Ibid, 12. See also BIS, 'Principles for Financial Market Infrastructures' (April 2012) <https://www.bis.org/cpmi/publ/d101a.pdf> accessed 22 April 2022.
[472] Ibid.
[473] Ibid.
[474] Ibid.
[475] Ibid.
[476] Ibid.
[477] Ibid.
[478] Ibid.
[479] Ibid.
[480] Ibid.

c. *The problem of the reserves*

An important cause of systemic risk relates to the reserves, which raise issues at two different levels: liquidity and corporate governance. Central banks dispose of very liquid assets, which include central bank reserves, gifts, and treasury bills. In this way, central banks are in a position to exchange such liquid assets for more illiquid ones, belonging to credit institutions in a situation of liquidity shortage, but still solvent. The liquidity of such assets is a tool for central banks to act as lenders of last resort under specific circumstances, significantly reducing the risk of contagion in the financial system originating from a specific bank's run on assets. Furthermore, central bank reserves are essential for central banks to have control of the wholesale payment and settlement system, where such reserves are the ultimate settlement asset.

The role of reserves is relevant for shadow central banking institutions, which intend to disrupt central banks by building a parallel payment system. It is questionable whether such institutions may dispose of equally highly liquid reserves, and whether they may have the economic incentives to do so. As the President's Working Group Report on Stablecoins highlighted, although stablecoins are often 'advertised as being supported or backed by a variety of reserve assets ... there are no standards regarding the composition of stablecoin reserve assets, and the information made publicly available regarding the issuer's reserve assets is not consistent across stablecoin arrangements as to either its content or the frequency of release'.[481]

Differences in the stablecoins' stabilization mechanisms (on-chain, off-chain, or algorithmic) affect their riskiness and the methods through which they could be a source of systemic risk. Those holding their reserve assets in deposits at insured depository institutions or in US Treasury bills are in principle safer than those fully backed by Bitcoin or Ethereum and algorithmic stablecoins. Reserves could experience a significant fall in price or become extremely illiquid, or could not be properly safeguarded.[482]

Christian Catalini and Alonso de Gortari referred to these risks by identifying two main problems, that is, 'volatility of the reserve assets against the reference asset, which defines the risk profile of the stablecoin for coin holders' and 'the degree to which stablecoin is exposed to the risk of a death spiral'.[483] The different stabilization mechanisms are reflected on the tools to address such risks. In fact, fiat-backed stablecoins require high-quality and liquid assets, whereas decentralized stablecoins require an over-collateralization 'to account for the lack of an intermediary'.[484]

Other concerns on the reserves might be triggered by the uncertainty surrounding the redemption rights of stablecoin holders, as well as operation risks related to cybersecurity, in particular for 'collecting, storing and safeguarding data'.[485]

With regard to corporate governance, the cause of systemic risk may be endogenous to organizations and may depend on the way central shadow central banking institutions manage their reserves. The original Libra project is helpful to understand this

---

[481] President's Working Group on Financial Markets, *Report on Stablecoins* (n 129) 5.
[482] Ibid, 12.
[483] See Christian Catalani and Alonso de Gortari, 'On the Economic Design of Stablecoins' (2021) SSRN <https://papers.ssrn.com/sol3/papers.cfm?abstract_id=3899499> accessed 22 April 2022.
[484] Ibid.
[485] Ibid.

specific risk. There was no specific evidence regarding the way reserves are managed but portfolio managers might have had the incentive, or might have even been instructed by the Libra Association, to invest the reserves in more risky assets, for the purpose of higher returns.[486] This would be a mechanism of financial risk origination, somewhat similar to the way financial risk snowballed into systemic risk in 2008 in the US MMFs. Due to problems related to the liquidity of the collateral (i.e., more risky assets), the Reserve Primary Fund, valued at $65 billion dollars, almost caused a run on MMFs ('breaking the buck' or one dollar). This left the US Treasury Guarantee Program as the only safeguard in a position to prevent a potential financial disaster.[487] Sound corporate governance that limits the incentives of risky investing would reduce this kind of systemic threat.

d. Endogenous instability of the shadow central banking organizations
A third cause of potential systemic risk may be endogenous to organizations and, therefore, may depend on their instability. How would a reputational scandal within the organization impact the entity as well as the system? Examples may include situations such as that of Cambridge Analytica and Facebook, or Wells Fargo and the associated fraud. Any private entity, including the big tech giants and banks, has specific weaknesses that may generate significant risks.[488] Furthermore, these types of scandal may be so critical for companies and their projects that they may pose an obstacle to even starting these sorts of initiatives. In the case of Libra, notwithstanding an attempt to market it as a joint project, its strong ties with Facebook, at a moment when that company faces privacy antitrust issues in Europe and the United States, have certainly damaged this new venture and delayed its launch.[489] Although Diem has tried to nuance the close relationship with Facebook, doubts in this sense still persist.

Furthermore, although no tech giant such as Google or Amazon has yet failed, this does not mean that these corporations are immune to such risk. In particular, none of these tech giants have engaged in substantial financial activities, and they have thereby avoided financial risks or shocks that could threaten their survival. A scenario involving these kinds of activities would have unpredictable risks, where technological and financial risks are coupled, making these entities especially vulnerable.

e. Regulatory approaches to reduce systemic risk
Many of the regulatory approaches already identified for reducing systemic risk[490] can be extended to these scenarios. Disclosure of the risks related to these activities is an important issue[491] that also serves to guide investors and stakeholders. Given the broad impact of these kinds of activities and their cross-border nature, it is crucial to identify ways

---

[486] Brummer, '99 Problems' (n 440) 8.
[487] Gensler, 'Examining Facebook's Proposed Cryptocurrency' (n 21) 13.
[488] Brummer, '99 Problems' (n 440) 8.
[489] See Hanna Murphy and Kiran Stacey, 'Where It All Went Wrong for Facebook's Libra' (*The Irish Times*, 16 October 2019) <https://www.irishtimes.com/business/technology/where-it-all-went-wrong-for-facebook-s-libra-cryptocurrency-1.4055121> accessed 22 April 2022.
[490] See generally Steven L. Schwarcz, 'Systemic Risk' (2008) 97 GeoLJ 193.
[491] See Brummer, '99 Problems' (n 440) 2. The author emphasizes the lack of disclosure to Libra investors about the inherent risks of investing in it.

to coordinate disclosure in order to make it meaningful. For example, disclosure should begin with the topic of sensitive information. Full disclosure should apply to the ways in which reserves are managed, held by custodians, and invested; to redemption rights and the redemption process; and more broadly to the integrity of corporate governance.

The management and investment of reserves is a key point. Ensuring liquidity likely keeps capital markets functioning and prevents financial entities from defaulting.[492] This is a fundamental tool in the maintenance of high collateral liquidity levels, which is a key advance in the new regulatory framework and the most important safety net capital markets have to avoid systemic collapse. The liquidity of collateral is a key feature for derivatives and clearing houses, which require a high level of liquidity for cross-border activity. Consistent with the regulatory approach adopted for clearing houses, international coordination is extremely important even in the context of shadow central banking. This is the only way to avoid any race to the bottom in regulating the quality of reserves.

This also relates to another important tool to reduce systemic risk: limiting excessive financial exposure and reducing the use of leverage.

Maintaining the liquidity of reserves and limiting excessive financial exposure are two instruments that would contribute to the maintenance of adequate stability levels in shadow central banking, thereby benefitting the entire system. These measures are extremely important in times of economic uncertainty when interest rates decline, becoming low or even negative, leading to risky asset prices, and private and public debt levels increase.[493]

Market discipline would be an inefficient tool because it would not allow the pursuit of stability. Market discipline has not proven effective in more 'traditional' financial contexts, such as reducing excessive leverage and financial exposures before the financial crisis of 2008.[494] In the context of shadow central banking, it would be an even weaker tool because there are no established self-regulatory rules that may serve as specific market discipline rules. Most importantly, there are no established and reputed market actors that may contribute to developing this area. Market discipline alone is not sufficiently strong; it requires the support of public regulatory initiatives seeking to pursue a minimum level of international harmonization.

One way to safeguard liquidity is proper regulation of the redemption rights and the redemption process for global stablecoin arrangements. As the FSB emphasized, there is a significant heterogeneity across the different types of stablecoins operating in the market.[495] This also applies to some of the most capitalized stablecoins, including Tether (reserving 'the right to delay the redemption or withdrawal of coins if such delay is necessitated by the illiquidity or unavailability or loss of any reserves held by the issuer to back the coin') and USDC ('promise to always redeem the coin at a rate of one unit of fiat currency (USD)').[496]

---

[492] Ibid.
[493] FSB, Letter to G20 (n 456).
[494] Ibid.
[495] Financial Stability Board, 'Regulation, Supervision and Oversight of 'Global Stablecoin' Arrangements—Progress Report on the implementation of the FSB High-Level Recommendations' (7 October 2021) <https://www.fsb.org/wp-content/uploads/P071021.pdf> accessed 22 April 2022.
[496] Ibid, 5.

Looking at cybersecurity risks as systemic risks, governance mechanisms and monitoring tools at the level of cybersecurity might be effective in at least mitigating such major problems. The Digital Operational Resilience Act (DORA), proposed by the European Commission in September 2020 and finally adopted in November 2022, goes in this direction.[497] Complementary to the requirements of MiCAR from issuers in crypto-assets, DORA would provide requirements at the level of information and communication technology (ICT) governance, with emphasis on overall risk management and tools to monitor such risks. DORA applies to regulated financial institutions, including Fintechs and crypto-asset issuers.

2. Shadow Central Banking as Liquidity Provider and Lender of Last Resort: Structural Limits

Would a system based on shadow central banking be capable of absorbing financial shocks and acting as a lender of last resort?

The debate on the instability of cryptocurrencies as a source of systemic risk is not relevant for answering this question. Cryptocurrencies were subject to much criticism because of the intrinsic risks related to their volatility, waves of speculation, and frequent flash crashes that affected their value. In this context, the issue is rather different, and refers to the inherent risks of not having a 'central bank-centric' system.

Price stability is an interesting starting point. There is a significant difference between systemic stability and price stability.[498] While existing fiat currencies, as well as stablecoins—including Libra— were designed with price stability, Bitcoin was designed around the concept of systemic stability, which is derived from the security of its network.[499] Consequentially, central bankers create the price stability of fiat currencies and, in doing this, interfere with natural market processes, which generates systemic instability.[500] Therefore, when central banks pursue price stability, they answer short-term concerns without eradicating instability. In fact, a system cannot be price-stable and systemically stable at the same time. Therefore, current fiat currencies, as well as the stablecoins pegged to them, are defined as systemically unstable but price-stable. Accordingly, Bitcoin is systemically stable but price-unstable. This then leads to another property of Bitcoin: its supply is fixed, its price depends on demand fluctuation, and more resources invested in its mining (hash) do not translate into more Bitcoin being mined, as would happen with gold mining. Instead, it simply leads to increased network security.[501]

Although Bitcoin and similar digital currencies are systemically stable, their fixed supply may be a problem. In a situation where an economic shock would require an

---

[497] Regulation (EU) 2022/2554 of the European Parliament and of the Council of 14 December 2022 on digital operational resilience for the financial sector [2022] OJ L 333/1.
[498] See Caitlin Long, 'Bitcoin, the Dollar and Facebook's Cryptocurrency: Price Volatility versus Systemic Volatility' (*Forbes*, 29 June 2019) <https://www.forbes.com/sites/caitlinlong/2019/06/29/bitcoin-the-dollar-and-facebooks-cryptocurrency-price-volatility-versus-systemic-volatility/#51fc0d6d88b8> accessed 22 April 2022.
[499] Ibid.
[500] Ibid.
[501] Ibid.

increase in the money supply, current cryptocurrencies would not represent a viable solution,[502] and this would not differ from the gold standard.[503] In fact, in such a situation it would be impossible to mine new currency in real time in order to make it available to satisfy increased demand.[504] The IMF highlighted the similarities between this issue and that of heavily dollarized countries, such as the risk of recession and deflationary spirals, similar to the situation with the gold standard at the time of the Great Depression.[505] Furthermore, Bitcoin and other cryptocurrencies implement a structure that does not rely on a lender of last resort, and according to some critics, this is the reason why Bitcoin-like cryptocurrencies have no future.[506]

In an extreme situation where all the infrastructure and digital currencies are private, a public institution serving as a lender of last resort would not exist or would be much more marginal, and the hypothetical action of a central bank or a government to issue debt to finance the system may not be enough.[507]

In addition to structural problems related to Bitcoin-like cryptocurrencies, private cryptocurrencies pose a problem at the level of an interest of a private organization to act as a lender of last resort, and their adoption (and a consequential impact in the sense of private entities in charge of central banking) affects the current structures. The debate on central banks as lenders of last resort is controversial. Among the different approaches to the function of lender of last resort, the 'free banking' school advocates for abolishing lender of last resort because of the risks related to increasing moral hazard among bankers, as strongly advocated in modern times by Friedrich von Hayek.[508] According to this approach, bankers may more systematically rely on central banks to implement riskier strategies; or, in other words, without lenders of last resort they would have more incentives to adopt more prudent business decisions.[509] The traditional view, expressed by Walter Bagehot, favours free lending to solvent but temporarily illiquid firms against highly liquid collateral.[510] More generally, continuous injection of liquidity has raised concerns in the sense of increasing the fragility of the overall financial system.[511] Furthermore, powerful strategies in times of emergency may come with specific risks for central banks, in particular in terms of credibility

---

[502] See IMF, 'Virtual Currencies and Beyond' (n 121) para 62.
[503] See Grégory Claeys, Maria Demertzis, and Konstantinos Efstathiou, 'Cryptocurrencies and Monetary Policy' (*European Parliament—Monetary Dialogue*, July 2018) 16 <https://www.europarl.europa.eu/cmsdata/150000/BRUEGEL_FINAL%20publication.pdf> accessed 22 April 2022.
[504] Ibid.
[505] See IMF, 'Virtual Currencies and Beyond' (n 121) para 62.
[506] See Leon Pick, 'UBS Chairman: Bitcoin Currency Will Fail, Has No Lender of Last Resort' (*Finance Magnates*, 12 November 2015) <https://www.financemagnates.com/cryptocurrency/news/ubs-chairman-bitcoin-currency-will-fail-has-no-lender-of-last-resort/> accessed 22 April 2022.
[507] See Tony Yates, 'Bitcoin and the Lender of Last Resort Function' (*longandvariable*, 18 September 2017) <https://longandvariable.wordpress.com/2017/09/18/bitcoin-and-the-lender-of-last-resort-function/> accessed 22 April 2022.
[508] See generally Friedrich von Hayek, *The Denationalization of Money* (IOEA 1976).
[509] See Paul Tucker, 'The Lender of Last Resort and Modern Central Banking: Principles and Reconstruction' (2014) BIS Papers No. 79, 17 <https://www.bis.org/publ/bppdf/bispap79.pdf> accessed 22 April 2022.
[510] Ibid.
[511] See generally Kathryn Judge, 'The First Year: The Role of a Modern Lender of Last Resort' (2016) 116 ColumLRev 843.

and independence if these measures should not work.[512] For example, the idea of a private lender of last resort was a pillar of the shadow banking system. In theory, the mortgage-backed securitizations offering liquidity were supposed to be 'backstopped by private lender of last resort assurances from sponsoring banks'.[513] However, the financial crisis of 2008 showed the fragility of such a structure, because the assurances of such private lenders of last resort and private deposit insurances imploded, leading to an overall increased level of systemic risk.[514]

The adoption of private cryptocurrencies, in the form of Bitcoin or global stablecoins, would lead to an approach not far from the one advocated by those supporting free banking, with no guarantee from the superior layer (central banks) acting as a lender of last resort to avoid more systemic consequences and restore confidence in the market.

In such a scenario, a fundamental prerogative of modern capitalism would be absent. For example, in the course of the 2008 financial crisis, public intervention was essential to preventing an even worse spiral of events,[515] with the Federal Reserve and the Bank of England strongly engaged in rescuing not only banks but other financial institutions, in particular in the United States, where investment banks and broker dealers are the pillars of a strong market-based credit system.[516] The previous banking panics that began in 1930 highlighted the problems of not relying on a lender of last resort, with the Federal Reserve failing to adequately responding to this crisis.[517]

The recent COVID-19 crisis can be considered an event exogenous to financial markets and the economy that triggered significant market and economic disruptions. It is a classic example of an unavoidable situation for capital markets and the economy. In such a situation, a massive intervention of central bankers was necessary to contain more tragic consequences for the economy. The Federal Reserve adopted quantitative easing strategies and lowered interest rates to zero.[518] It also made a massive injection of short-term loans available to Wall Street.[519] The Bank of England invested £645 billion[520] and lowered interest rates by 0.1 per cent.[521] The ECB adopted a €750 billion

---

[512] Kathryn Judge, 'How the Fed Is Helping the Economy and How Its Efforts Could Backfire' (*Forbes*, 8 April 2020) <https://www.forbes.com/sites/kathrynjudge/2020/04/08/how-the-fed-is-helping-the-economy-and-how-its-efforts-could-backfire/#2801faf66887> accessed 22 April 2022.

[513] See Armour et al., *Principles of Financial Regulation* (n 31) 435.

[514] Ibid.

[515] Ibid.

[516] See Armour et al., *Principles of Financial Regulation* (n 31) 326–327.

[517] Gary Richardson, 'The Great Depression' (*Federal Reserve History*, 22 November 2013) <https://www.federalreservehistory.org/essays/great_depression> accessed 22 April 2022. See also Gary Richardson, 'Banking Crises and the Federal Reserve as a Lender of Last Resort during the Great Depression' (*The Reporter*, 2013) <https://www.nber.org/reporter/2013number3/banking-crises-and-federal-reserve-lender-last-resort-during-great-depression> accessed 22 April 2022. See also Gary Richardson, 'Bank Distress during the Great Depression: The Illiquidity–Insolvency Debate Revisited' (2006) NBER Working Paper Series No. 12717 <https://www.nber.org/papers/w12717> accessed 22 April 2022.

[518] Jeanna Smialek and Neil Irwin, 'Fed Slashes Rates to Near-Zero and Unveils Sweeping Program to Aid Economy' (*NYT*, 15 March 2020) <https://www.nytimes.com/2020/03/15/business/economy/federal-reserve-coronavirus.html> accessed 22 April 2022.

[519] See Nick Timiraos and Julia-Ambra Verlaine, 'Fed to Inject $1.5 Trillion in Bid to Prevent "Unusual Disruptions" in Markets' (*WSJ*, 12 March 2020) https://www.wsj.com/articles/fed-to-inject-1-5-trillion-in-bid-to-prevent-unusual-disruptions-in-markets-11584033537> accessed 22 April 2022.

[520] Bank of England, 'Our Response to Coronavirus (Covid)' <https://www.bankofengland.co.uk/coronavirus> accessed 22 April 2022.

[521] Ibid.

Pandemic Emergency Purchase Program[522] but opted not to cut interest rates.[523] A comparison of these initiatives with the ones implemented by the same giants—some of them engaged in the development of stablecoins—would allow the emergence of the importance of central banks as an indispensable tool for reacting to economic shocks. For example, Google proposed a $800 million crisis response to support a heterogeneous group of entities that includes 'small sized business (SMBs), health organizations and governments, and health workers on the frontline of this global pandemic'.[524] Facebook announced '$100 million in cash grants and ad credits'[525] available for up to 30,000 eligible SMBs located in more than thirty countries, equal to an average of $3,333 per business.[526]

All of these issues are relevant not only for countries that have strong institutions and strong currencies, but also for marginalized areas where shadow central banking initiatives may spread at a fast pace and affect democracy too. This is the case with poorer countries where the control of monetary policy is likely to shift from governments to private entities, as was the case with Libra.[527] Many of these countries lack a stable currency and have a high rate of citizens without access to a bank account—those 'unbanked' citizens that Libra has often mentioned in many contexts. Therefore, many of these people may choose to switch from their national currency to a private currency, thereby increasing the risk that private institutions take over monetary policy in such marginalized areas.[528] Similarly, in the case of shadow central banking, instruments such as Libra, especially in its first version of 2019, may pose threats to developed countries too. By changing the composition of the basket backing the stablecoin, private organizations are in the position to alter the value of the affected currency, cutting out the sovereign states.[529]

From an international perspective, another hypothetical major problem with a private global currency would be granting some sort of liquidity support under specific circumstances of scarcity related to the private global currency in certain countries. In a standard situation, central banks, in particular the Federal Reserve, are in a position to negotiate swap lines with foreign central banks to alleviate the lack of liquidity of a specific foreign currency.[530] Such is the case with the dollar, where 90 per cent of the

---

[522] ECB, 'PEPP' (n 28).

[523] Silvia Amaro, 'ECB Surprises Markets by Not Cutting Rates, But Announces Stimulus to Fight Coronavirus Impact' (*CNBC*, 12 March 2020) <https://www.cnbc.com/2020/03/12/european-central-bank-stimulus-package-amid-coronavirus.html> accessed 22 April 2022.

[524] Sundar Pichai, 'COVID-19: $800+ Million to Support Small Businesses and Crisis Response' (*The Keyword*, 27 March 2020) <https://blog.google/inside-google/company-announcements/commitment-support-small-businesses-and-crisis-response-covid-19> accessed 22 April 2022.

[525] Facebook, 'Find your customers and grow your small business' <https://www.facebook.com/business/boost/grants> accessed 22 April 2022.

[526] Lauren Feiner, 'Facebook Announces $100 Million Program for Small Businesses Impacted by Coronavirus' (*CNBC*, 17 March 2020) <https://www.cnbc.com/2020/03/17/facebook-announces-program-for-small-businesses-impacted-by-covid-19.html> accessed 22 April 2022.

[527] See Dirk Andreas Zetzsche, Ross P. Buckley and Douglas W. Arner, 'Regulating LIBRA: The Transformative Potential of Facebook's Cryptocurrency and Possible Regulatory Responses' (2021) 41 OJLS 80.

[528] See Le Maire, 'Libra Is a Threat to National Sovereignty' (n 279).

[529] Ibid.

[530] See Section I.A.

financial transactions in the world are denominated in dollars.[531] As many commentators argued, in the recent COVID-19 crisis, the Federal Reserve *de facto* assumed the role of the world's lender of last resort.[532] Others proposed rethinking the international financial architecture with the IMF as a global lender of last resort, to avoid major disruptions at the level of emerging market crises.[533] In a situation in which a private cryptocurrency becomes widely adopted as a medium of exchange, it is questionable how these systems would effectively work in order to provide liquidity under specific circumstances, such as the financial crisis of 2008 and the COVID-19 pandemic. Hypothetically, a widely adopted global currency would remove the problem of swap lines; however, this situation may be unlikely. In such a scenario, it may be highly likely that swap lines would not be a tool that private entities issuing global stablecoins or any other decentralized structure 'issuing' Bitcoin-like digital currencies would technically have the ability to rely on.

3. Fragmented Network and Interoperability

What are the risks of a fragmented framework where many private cryptocurrencies co-exist? The problem prompts two considerations. First, a system where many different private currencies co-exist may lead to increased transaction costs related to converting private currencies. Second, from a technical angle, this prompts an investigation of problems related to the interoperability of different systems that have not been entirely solved.

A second issue relates to the governance of blockchain infrastructures. The interoperability between different blockchain infrastructures demands the coordination of different entities. The creation of a unique platform containing all of these entities is unlikely—although at the very beginning of the blockchain debate, the idea of 'one blockchain to rule them all' was an option. The gradual implementation of blockchain technology led to the emergence of a more fragmented scenario for both private and public blockchain, due to the different designing options that each developer and entrepreneur decided to adopt based on its levels of security, privacy, efficiency, flexibility, platform complexity.[534] As a consequence, the need to coordinate the different chains was realized.

Fundamental interoperability between different blockchains is an opportunity for different technology infrastructures to operate in an integrated way. To understand this concept, an example from cryptocurrencies can be helpful: 'Bitcoin can't speak the language of Ethereum and vice versa. This means we can't spend Bitcoin on the Ethereum network, nor can we make use of Ethereum's smart contracts on the Bitcoin

---

[531] See Marc Auboin, 'Use of Currencies in International Trade: Any Changes in the Picture?' (May 2012) World Trade Organization Staff Working Paper ERSD-2012-10, 11 <https://www.wto.org/english/res_e/reser_e/ersd201210_e.pdf> accessed 22 April 2022.

[532] Mike Bird, 'The Fed Is Settling into Its Role as the World's Central Bank (*WSJ*, 1 April 2020) <https://www.wsj.com/articles/the-fed-is-settling-into-its-role-as-the-worlds-central-bank-11585732095> accessed 22 April 2022.

[533] See Eduardo Levy Yeyati, 'Covid, Fed Swaps and the IMF as Lender of Last Resort' (*Vox*, 31 March 2020) <https://voxeu.org/article/covid-fed-swaps-and-imf-lender-last-resort> accessed 22 April 2022.

[534] See Vitalik Buterin, 'Chain Interoperability' (9 September 2016) <https://www.r3.com/wp-content/uploads/2017/06/chain_interoperability_r3.pdf> accessed 22 April 2022 (hereafter Buterin, 'Chain Interoperability').

network.'[535] Therefore, interoperability between different infrastructures is the foundation to effectively changing the existing process, which would otherwise remain extremely fragmented.

There are different ways to implement interoperability between different blockchain infrastructures, such as centralized or multi-signatory schemes that employ a trusted federation to carry out an action on chain B when some event on chain A takes place; sidechains/relays, where relays allowing the chain to validate events on another chain substitute a trusted federation; and hash-locking, or implementing a system where operations on different blockchains have the same trigger, generally the revelation of the preimage of a particular hash.[536] However, there are usage limits in a public blockchain, whereas platforms developed for corporate voting would be private. Furthermore, the vast majority of applications based on these interoperability chains are in the field of payment systems.

The economic concerns related to high transaction costs coupled with the technical problems of interoperability may prompt consideration of a new infrastructure, capable of managing private currencies and co-existing with public currencies. When designing these infrastructures, an important starting point would be to treat both public and private monies as public goods which are 'accessible on a non-profit basis' and 'open to anyone looking to develop specific new products or services, subject to a simple registration requirement'.[537] The MAS developed, alongside state investment firm Temasek Holdings and J.P. Morgan (operating as an infrastructure provider), a multicurrency blockchain-based network.[538] This experiment was part of Ubin, a collaborative project to test the applicability of the blockchain technology for clearing and settlement of payments and securities.[539] Although this is a for-profit project, it would allow for cutting costs, and would be a step towards a new idea of infrastructure.

D. Broader Regulatory Implications

Cryptocurrencies are complex entities that trigger many different regulations, among them securities laws, commodities regulation directly related to their potential characterization as money (in the case of North American law),[540] and money transmission, anti-money laundering (AML), and 'know your customer' (KYC) rules.

---

[535] Aleks Larsen, 'A Primer on Blockchain Interoperability' (*Medium*, 20 December 2018) <https://medium.com/blockchain-capital-blog/a-primer-on-blockchain-interoperability-e132bab805b> accessed 22 April 2022.
[536] See Ibid. See also Buterin, 'Chain Interoperability' (n 534).
[537] Pistor and Georg, 'Response to Libra Threat' (n 444).
[538] See Marie Huillet, 'Singapore's MAS, JPMorgan Unveil Multi-Currency Blockchain Prototype' (*Cointelegraph*, 11 November 2019) <https://cointelegraph.com/news/singapores-mas-jpmorgan-unveil-multi-currency-blockchain-prototype> accessed 22 April 2022.
[539] Fiona Lam, 'MAS, Temasek, JPMorgan Develop Prototype Network for Multi-Currency Payments' (*The Business Times*, 11 November 2019) <https://www.businesstimes.com.sg/banking-finance/mas-temasek-jpmorgan-develop-prototype-network-for-multi-currency-payments> accessed 22 April 2022.
[540] See Section II.B.3.c.i.

A similar complexity emerges when trying to characterize the private entities involved with cryptocurrencies and when applying the existing regulatory framework.[541]

In the United States, a hypothetical entity on the model of the Diem Association-like entity may be characterized as an asset manager, as it is in charge of managing the Diem Reserve. Therefore, it could potentially fall under the Investment Advisers Act. Furthermore, it may be required to comply with the SEC rules for 'Custody of Funds or Securities of Clients by Investor Advisers'.[542] Also, transactions under US securities law may require such entity to register as a broker-dealer or as a bank, and therefore it may become subject to minimum capitalization and other requirements.[543] In Switzerland, FINMA would regulate this hypothetical entity as a market infrastructure,[544] but other regulations may apply. In Europe it would fall under the definition of CASP provided by MiCAR and regulated as such.

Now, if cryptocurrencies were subject to the regulations of each jurisdiction in which they were used, the consequences would be nightmarish and the risk of regulatory arbitrage would be high. The more divergent and complicated regulations are, the easier it would be to circumvent them, thereby increasing economic and financial risks.

This example is helpful to highlight two different problems. First, complex entities may trigger different regulations and pose issues in terms of regulatory strategy, thereby affecting how regulators approach this problem. This difficulty is common to all the schemes that can operate in many different contexts. How to regulate blockchain is a frequently asked question that doesn't make much sense, because blockchain is a technology that, like any technology and organizational scheme, can be applied to many different fields and activities. The same applies to cryptocurrencies, which can concurrently involve many different legal characterizations. Any technological tool, including DLT, artificial intelligence, and the Internet of Things, requires a 'contextual' regulation, that is, a regulation that takes into account the context where these tools are applied.[545]

New technologies are not the only asset raising this problem; these issues are in fact rather common in financial regulation. The shadow banking system, for example, triggered similar challenges specifically with regard to the regulation of hedge funds. Because of their engagement in heterogeneous activities and their underlying risks, hedge funds raised relevant definitional issues, specifically in Europe. Even MMFs raised questions regarding their activity and strategy that regulators had to investigate in order to mitigate the related risks. In this regard, Paul Volcker said that 'if money market funds are going to talk like a bank and squawk like a bank, they ought to be regulated like a bank'.[546] To solve the problem of these multiple characterizations, it

---

[541] See generally Dell'Erba, '"Do No Harm" Approach in Initial Coin Offerings' (n 94) and Dell'Erba, 'Stablecoins in Cryptoeconomics' (n 96).
[542] See Gensler, 'Examining Facebook's Proposed Cryptocurrency' (n 21) 16.
[543] See Brummer, '99 Problems' (n 440) 10.
[544] See FINMA, 'Stable Coin Guidelines' (n 269).
[545] Lee Schneider, 'Blockchaingers Legal Deep Dive: Keynote by Lee Schneider' (30 November 2017) <https://www.youtube.com/watch?v=82S6NDzebFQ> accessed 22 April 2022.
[546] 'Enhancing Investor Protection and the Regulation of Securities Markets' (Hearing Before the U.S. Senate Committee on Banking, Housing, and Urban Affairs, 10 March 2009) 14 <https://www.govinfo.gov/content/pkg/CHRG-111shrg51395/pdf/CHRG-111shrg51395.pdf> accessed 22 April 2022.

will be important to develop toolkits that help regulators to clarify the function that specific entities and their instruments have in the system and to try to identify strategies leading to non-discordant treatments.

This leads to the second problem: the coordination between international regulators and supervisors, an essential aspect of an efficient regulatory environment. When promoting sound regulation in the aftermath of the financial crisis, the G20 and the Financial Stability Board contributed to enhanced coordination in the derivatives market, imposing financial and disclosure requirements and in turn strengthening financial stability by reducing liquidity and counterparty risks and enhancing transparency. Clearing houses are more or less homogeneously regulated across the continents, with regulations putting a special emphasis on the liquidity of their collateral and their corporate governance. The ESMA created many equivalence agreements with non-continental market authorities accommodating the requirements provided by EMIR that regulate clearing houses. Notwithstanding its limits, this strategy was quite effective and can be a starting point to regulate these new systemic and global initiatives. Delaying the process towards the identification of common standards (at least in geographical macro-areas if not at global level) would mean delegating to each state the development of a case-by-case approach to regulate the complex nuances of these entities. If a fragmented regulatory response emerges and takes hold, it will be much harder to harmonize the responses at an international level. Despite its limits, MiCAR could emerge as a standard setter leading the transition towards more clear rules at the global level.

E. Potential Scenarios

There are three possible scenarios related to shadow central banking and its development: shadow central banks take over public central banks (unlikely); central banks and governments react in order to ban shadow central banking activities and provide CBDCs; or a hybrid system emerges where both private regulated (non-shadow) and private non-regulated (shadow) central banking co-exist with public central banking. In the context of all three scenarios, regulation is an essential leg, and the decision not to regulate, to ban, or to proactively design a system for regulating private initiatives leads to very different consequences.

1. Scenario 1: Shadow Central Banking Replacing the Current Central Banking System

The prospect of shadow central banking replacing the current central banking system is unlikely (at least in the short term). Furthermore, this solution would lead to a more fragile ecosystem. This chapter has repeatedly referenced instability in the past, due to a lack of 'public' and state-controlled central banks. As history shows, private initiatives are susceptible to failure, and although no tech giant of the size of Google or Amazon has failed yet, this does not mean that this category of corporation is immune to such risk. In the best-case scenario, tech giants may be the category of private actor that could develop a relatively stable ecosystem, but this is far from being a constant foundational parameter.

However, even this best scenario would be much less stable than a situation in which a traditional central bank continues to maintain its apical role in 'governing the money'. 'Governing the money' means governing the economy and the lending activity, since monetary policy is strictly interconnected with capital markets, finance, and the real economy. According to Hyman P. Minsky's conception of money, it is 'unique in that it is created in the act of financing by a bank and is destroyed as the commitments on debt instruments owned by banks are fulfilled. Because money is created and destroyed in the normal course of business, the amount outstanding is responsive to the demand for finance.'[547] Furthermore, central banks are in the apical position in the pyramid of lending finance. Changing this structure would lead to a change in the entire framework of lending finance.

A more tangible risk of private central bankers replacing the current central banks emerges in those countries where central banks are not as strong as in Europe, Switzerland, or the United States. An example comes from Kenya and the concerns expressed in October 2020 by Central Bank of Kenya governor Patrick Njoroge.[548] Since 2007, the Central Bank of Kenya had been extremely proactive in the design and launch of M-Pesa, to allow individuals to transfer money among themselves on a peer-to-peer basis via their mobiles. Consistent with this innovative path, the Central Bank of Kenya was also advancing in the debate on issuing CBDCs. However, the internal difficulties of implementing these new tools, coupled with the lack of international cooperation, might be a threat for Kenya, even if it is among the most proactive states in the field.[549] In this context, private initiatives could more easily exploit internal and international political weaknesses, and become established central banking actors.

El Salvador's decision of 7 September 2021 to officially adopt Bitcoin as legal tender[550] opened a new era for cryptocurrencies. El Salvador did not suffer from significant inflationary or economic and financial turmoil undermining its stability.[551] Therefore the decision of the country's authoritarian president, Nayib Bukele, raises questions at two levels. First, unsolved uncertainties as to the overall transparency of Bitcoin might be a particular preoccupation when associated with a lack of full democracy affecting a specific country or, more broadly, an entire geographic area. Second, the IMF highlighted a series of risks at multiple levels, focusing on macroeconomic stability, financial integrity, consumer protection, and the environment.[552] The downgrade of the country's debt undertaken by Moody's reflects these concerns.[553] A study by the National Bureau of Economic Research (NBER) has shown that effective usage

---

[547] See generally Minsky, *Stabilizing an Unstable Economy* (n 20).

[548] Christopher Brummer and Evan Campbell, 'How Mpesa Transformed the World of Fintech' (*Rollcall*, 20 October 2020) <https://rollcall.com/podcasts/fintech-beat/how-mpesa-transformed-the-world-of-fintech/> accessed 22 April 2022.

[549] Ibid.

[550] Financial Times, 'El Salvador Dangerous Bet on Bitcoin' (7 September 2021) <https://www.ft.com/content/c257a925-c864-4495-9149-d8956d786310> accessed 22 April 2022.

[551] Ibid.

[552] Tobias Adrian and Rhoda Weeks-Brown, 'Cryptoassets as National Currency? A Step too Far' (*IMF Blog*, 26 July 2021) <https://blogs.imf.org/2021/07/26/cryptoassets-as-national-currency-a-step-too-far/> accessed 22 April 2022.

[553] Moody's, 'Moody's Downgrades El Salvador's Rating to Caa1, Maintains Negative Outlook' (30 July 2021) <https://www.moodys.com/research/Moodys-downgrades-El-Salvadors-rating-to-Caa1-maintains-negative-outlook--PR_450956> accessed 22 April 2022.

of Bitcoin for everyday transactions is low and favours social exclusion, because a mostly banked, educated, young, and male population uses it as a medium of exchange.[554] Furthermore, Bitcoin as legal tender triggers fixed costs, and problems in designing 'strategic complementarities for users' and in assessing 'the elasticity of substitution between mobile payments'.[555]

The Central African Republic followed the same strategy as El Salvador, announcing the shift to Bitcoin as a legal tender in April 2022. Although 85 per cent of the citizens have no access to internet services or electricity, this option would be a tool for achieving monetary independence that the current system, based on the local franc pegged to the euro, would not grant.[556]

Looking specifically at DeFi, shadow central banking, in particular stablecoins, could in principle replace traditional central banks, even those issuing CBDCs. To be fully operational, DeFi does not need CBDCs, and even in the circumstance of CBDCs availability, stablecoins could still be the preferred method of operation on certain platforms which may not accept CBDCs.

Shadow central banking with no central banks and CBDCs is an extremely risky option for DeFi and creates risks of propagation to traditional finance, as the problems emerging in May 2022 in relation to Terra UST, a major algorithmic stablecoin, confirm. Terra's inability to maintain the peg to the dollar, plummeting to a minimum of $0.23,[557] brought significant instability in the cryptoeconomy. It affected the major cryptocurrencies, including Bitcoin and Ethereum, that experienced a significant loss in value, and opened a debate on the likelihood of a collapse affecting the entire DeFi, as a sort of Lehman Brothers case for the cryptoeconomy.[558] Furthermore, different from other crises happening in the cryptoeconomy and previous stablecoin crashes—such as Basis Cash in 2020[559] and Tether in different circumstances—Terra's meltdown concretely showed the potential of stablecoins to destabilize the financial system beyond the crypto ecosystem. Before Terra's problems could emerge, Fitch highlighted the risks that Tether's potential loss of the peg could have had for the short-term credit markets, mostly related to 'potential asset contagion risks linked to the liquidation of stablecoin reserve holdings'.[560]

---

[554] See generally Fernando E. Alvarez, David Argente, and Diana Van Patten, 'Are Cryptocurrencies Currencies? Bitcoin as Legal Tender in El Salvador' (2022) NBER Working Paper No. 29968 <https://www.nber.org/system/files/working_papers/w29968/w29968.pdf> accessed 1 May 2023.
[555] Ibid.
[556] See David Pilling, 'Central African Republic's Adoption of Bitcoin Is Mostly about Geopolitics' (*Financial Times*, 26 May 2022) <https://www.ft.com/content/8b68b0cd-230c-4e9b-aa66-84bdbe98c9e0> accessed 30 May 2022.
[557] Alexander Osipovich and Caitlin Ostroff, 'Crash of TerraUSD Shakes Crypto. "There Was a Run on the Bank"' (*WSJ*, 12 May 2022) <https://www.wsj.com/articles/crash-of-terrausd-shakes-crypto-there-was-a-run-on-the-bank-11652371839> accessed 22 April 2022.
[558] Alex Hern, 'Could Terra Fall Prove to Be Lehman Brothers Moment for Cryptocurrencies?' (*The Guardian*, 11 May 2022) <https://www.theguardian.com/technology/2022/may/11/terra-price-cryptocurrency-stablecoin> accessed 22 April 2022.
[559] Sam Kessler and Danny Nelson, 'UST's Do Know Was Behind Earlier Failed Stablecoin, Ex-Terra Colleagues Say' (*CoinDesk*, 11 May 2022) <https://www.coindesk.com/tech/2022/05/11/usts-do-kwon-was-behind-earlier-failed-stablecoin-ex-terra-colleagues-say/> accessed 22 April 2022.
[560] Katie Martin, 'What Happens in Crypto May Not Stay in Crypto This Time Around' (*Financial Times*, 13 May 2022) <https://www.ft.com/content/6dcd0263-f974-4833-97a9-93b05be74f6e> accessed 22 April 2022.

2. Scenario 2: Reducing or Eliminating Shadow Central Banking

The opposite scenario would be a reduction or the elimination of shadow central banking. This could be the result of different measures that governments and central bankers may decide to implement.

a. Sub-scenario 2.1: banning shadow central banking

A first measure would be to react by formally banning shadow central banking activities implementing restrictive regulations. The starting point of this strategy would consist in banning the channel for disruption, that is, private currencies, in particular cryptocurrencies. Banning private cryptocurrencies with a central banking function would be problematic. It would be difficult to create and enforce such a decision because of the hybrid characteristics of private cryptocurrencies. This solution would have to operate on a case-by-case basis, considering each private cryptocurrency's economic role. For the same reasons discussed above in Section III.D, a starting point would be to increase efforts to develop an internationally harmonized taxonomy for cryptocurrencies. Cryptocurrencies emerged for precise structural reasons—specific currencies that are helpful in the context of a tokenized economy may be very much needed. Therefore, the option to ban them cannot be considered as the best decision because it may have the unintended consequence of stifling innovation more broadly: private cryptocurrencies have been and will likely continue to be a driver for change in economy and finance.

An example of this second approach comes from China. As mentioned in the previous sections, the Chinese government and the PBOC are among the most proactive public actors in the sphere of CBDC. While China is proceeding with the launch of its own CBDC, the DCEP (that is, an RMB in digital form), it has also taken steps in the direction of banning any stablecoin pegged to the yuan. The Chinese government has proceeded with a revision of the 'People's Bank of China Law', starting with the launch of a public consultation which was open from 23 October 2020 to 23 November 2020.

The proposed 'People's Bank of China Law' contains important novelties. Article 19 states that 'The unit of Renminbi is yuan, and the unit of Renminbi currency is jiao and cent. Renminbi includes the physical form and the digital form'.[561] Furthermore, Article 22 adds that 'No unit or individual may produce or sell tokens, coupons and digital tokens to replace RMB in circulation in the market'.[562]

These two articles have important consequences. First, PBOC digital currency is legal tender, exactly like the currencies issued in physical form. Second, the approach of the Chinese government tends to exclude the existence and the circulation in the country of any stablecoin pegged to the RMB, because this would require RMBs to be moved from circulation to reserves.[563] This is a way to impede any private development

---

[561] See Vipin Bharathan, 'People's Bank of China Draft Law Provides a Legal Basis for Digital Currency Electronic Payments (DC/EP) and Bans All Stablecoins Backed by Renminbi Reserves' (*Forbes*, 24 October 2020) <https://www.forbes.com/sites/vipinbharathan/2020/10/24/peoples-bank-of-china-draft-law-provides-a-legal-basis-for-digital-currency-electronic-payments-dcep-and-bans-all-stablecoins-backed-by-renminbi-reserves/> accessed 22 April 2022.
[562] Ibid.
[563] Ibid.

in this sense, and in particular a strong regulatory and political response against the possibility of developing a Libra-like coin pegged to the RMB. An even broader effect might lead to banning from circulation any cryptocurrency token in China. The violation of Article 22 leads to civil and criminal liability for more serious offences, opening space for a range of sanctions which include confiscation of profits, destruction of tokens, and pecuniary fines, as well as jail for criminal offences.[564]

The possibility of even more restrictive regulations banning cryptocurrencies in China favoured the migration of many cryptocurrency holders, in particular of Tether (extremely popular in China), towards less restrictive jurisdictions. According to the blockchain forensics firm Chinalysis, $50 billion in cryptocurrency assets were moved outside of China, with Tether contributing $18 billion due to its prominent market share in the region, equal to 93 per cent of stablecoins present in China.[565] Consistent with the analysis under the previous paragraph, a ban would have relative effects on the presence of certain cryptocurrencies in the system. A national ban on specific activities involving DeFi would not be effective and would be difficult to enforce against users, who would continue to operate relying on stablecoins. This option would not be ideal because a system would lose the advantages of effective coexistence between private currencies, such as stablecoins, serving specific functions, and CBDCs bringing the advantages of fully backed instruments in the context of the cryptoeconomy.

b. Sub-scenario 2.2: issuing CBDC with the intent of marginalizing shadow central banking and cryptocurrencies

A second alternative would be to issue reliable CBDCs with the consequence of displacing private cryptocurrencies, without formally banning them. In fact, this option would reduce, or completely marginalize, the role played by private cryptocurrencies, in particular in their function as a medium of exchange in global payments, and the clout of their issuing entities.

The decision by sovereign states to directly intervene in the cryptoeconomy by issuing CBDCs would be a reasonable measure for various reasons. First, the dominant role of non-regulated private entities in sensitive tasks that impact central banking does not automatically create the basis for stability and efficiency. As already mentioned, even gigantic private entities such as Meta, Google, or Apple remain more unstable than 'public' central banks, and this weakness generates risks. Therefore, this is a rather fragile system and the complete replacement of private cryptocurrencies with CBDCs poses unpredictable consequences.

However, a scenario where CBDCs *de facto* provoke an implosion of private currencies is not necessarily ideal, because of the abovementioned role that private currencies have had and will likely continue to have in bringing innovation and competition within international finance.

---

[564] Ibid.
[565] Matthew Leising, '$50bn in Cryptoassets Moved out of China in the Past Year' (*Aljazeera*, 20 August 2020) <https://www.aljazeera.com/economy/2020/8/20/50bn-in-cryptoassets-moved-out-of-china-in-the-past-year> accessed 22 April 2022.

III. CRITICAL CONSIDERATIONS   305

3. Scenario 3: Effective Co-Existence between CBDCs Issued by Central Banks and Private Currencies

A third scenario would emerge consequently to the decision by governments and central bankers to intervene by issuing CBDCs in order to explicitly and unequivocally create a safe hybrid environment where private currencies co-exist with CBDCs. This would allow commercial banks to continue to provide their contribution to the wealth and the stability of the ecosystem. Central banks would continue to provide stability to the system and, in critical situations of monetary shocks, they could promptly react with monetary policies or act as liquidity providers and lenders of last resort. At the same time, private currencies would develop specific functions (such as Bitcoin becoming a store of value), while contributing to innovate in the realms of payment systems and critical market infrastructure, thereby leading to the establishment of a more efficient framework, in an increasingly globalized ecosystem. This is what former IMF Managing Director Christine Lagarde advocated.[566] Indeed, a potential model where public and private cryptocurrencies co-exist would not differ very much from the one currently in place: under the supervision of central banks, private cryptocurrencies would act as a pure payment system relying on a private infrastructure—in particular in the context of DeFi protocols—with central banks continuing to operate their fundamental functions. In this way, central banks would maintain intact their full monetary authority, thereby operating on interest rates and being liquidity providers, especially under critical economic circumstances.

However, another element to consider is how shadow central banking may react if both central banks and commercial banks either issue or fail to issue CBDCs. If private currencies are well developed, there may be a migration from bank deposits to private currencies. If governments and central bankers decide to issue CDBCs, there may be a massive migration towards this new instrument. In both cases, traditional banks may have to reconsider their business model and activities, which would be affected by a massive structural bank disintermediation.

Accordingly, the IMF identified two different solutions. First, it proposed a 'Risk of Disintermediation in Tranquil Times', whereby banks undertake certain remedial measures. Banks may need to replace deposits and instead shift to private currencies or CBDCs with other forms of funding, including commercial paper, bonds, and equity.[567] This may lead to several consequences. In particular, the increased costs of bank funding (higher lending rates for margin preservation)[568] may diminish market discipline and increase risks,[569] enhance instability of bank funding due to an higher levels of volatility, and force banks to hold more liquid assets for regulatory purposes or cut lending.[570]

The larger the role of shadow central banking and public central banks with the issuance digital currency will be, the more likely it might be that downward pressure will be placed on commercial banks, thereby affecting banking intermediation and, most of all,

---

[566] See Christine Lagarde, 'Winds of Change: The Case for New Digital Currency' (Speech at Singapore Fintech Festival, Singapore, 14 November 2018) <https://www.imf.org/-/media/Files/News/Speech/111418-md-sg-fintech-speech.ashx> accessed 22 April 2022.
[567] IMF, 'Casting Light on Central Bank Digital Currency' (n 122) 41.
[568] Ibid, 43.
[569] Ibid, 44.
[570] Ibid, 45.

lending activities. This, coupled with the further well-known source of pressure arising from the Basel Agreement capital requirements, could be especially difficult to challenge. Therefore, allowing shadow central banking to disrupt commercial banks would necessarily require identifying alternative sources of funding. A possibility might be to consolidate shadow banking as an increasingly important source of funding, even in those countries where it is traditionally not so established. For the same reason, those states relying on a much stronger and developed shadow banking system (as in the case of United States and the United Kingdom) could more adequately counterbalance potential structural inefficiencies emerging from such transformations. In this scenario, shadow central banking, current public central banking engaged in issuing CBDCs, and shadow banking would emerge as three complementary layers.

A potential example of future co-existence between private and public initiatives might come from the European Union, which is attempting to design a clearer regulatory structure for crypto-assets while advancing with the debate on a retail digital euro available to all citizens. The European acceleration was very timely and promising, especially taking into account on the one hand, the contextual fragmentation and inconsistency characterizing the United States, and, on the other hand, the excessively restrictive approach developed in Asian jurisdictions.[571] However, the negotiations on MiCAR left the possibility of an excessively restrictive approach towards DeFi stablecoin protocols. MiCAR excludes from its scope services provided 'in a fully decentralised manner without any intermediary'. Nevertheless, services provided as a part of a broader decentralized arrangement are fully covered by MiCAR.[572] A similar path might be developed in Switzerland, where an even stronger regulatory approach to private currencies may be coupled with the issuance of wholesale CBDCs. Taking into account the developments in DeFi, co-existence between stablecoins and CBDCs would contribute to enhancing the stability of the entire financial ecosystem. As mentioned above, DeFi is structurally independent from CBDCs, and therefore does not need to rely on CBDCs to be fully operational. Even in the case of CBDCs' availability, they may not be accepted by certain platforms; therefore users would continue to use stablecoins for most transactions. However, the problems emerging with algorithmic stablecoins, in particular Terra in May 2022, as well as more traditional stablecoins, including Tether, suggest that co-existence of CBDCs and stablecoins would bring significant advantages, especially in terms of collateral, because CBDCs would be fully backed by central banks. This might be beneficial not only for the development of DeFi, but also to avoid specific risks of contagion outside the DeFi ecosystem that could affect traditional finance.

F. Shadow Central Banking and Complexity

The disruption brought by private currencies and technology in the context of the central banking sphere shows how such initiatives are contributing to the

---

[571] Ringe, 'Building a European Market for Crypto-Assets' (n 234).
[572] MiCAR (n 232) recital 22.

expansion of the network of international finance. Multiple considerations descend from this. First, the intensity of the transformations involving indisputably established institutions, as central banks are, confirms the importance of approaching the study of any financial institution (and more generally any financial entity) by highlighting its intrinsic dynamic evolution. Second, the way central banking operations are becoming an integrated part within international finance significantly expands the network of involved actors. Third, in connection to the second point, this significant integration of central banking operations in the broader dynamics of international finance confirms the shift of the system toward a higher level of multidimensional interconnections. All this eventually confirms that multidimensionality is real and represents an almost unstoppable and irreversible trend with concrete implications.

More than other fields (identified as subparts) considered in this book, shadow central banking also emphasizes the importance of dynamic forms of regulation. Interpreting the ways in which certain changes happen in international finance, and more specifically in each subpart, is an increasingly important task to which regulators will be more systematically exposed in the future. In this scenario, central banks are not an exemption. On the contrary, this chapter has shown how intense transformations in this context might be. Indeed, Bitcoin originated as an alternative scheme to existing payment systems and established centralized financial institutions (including central banks), and the new wave of stablecoins consolidates specific evolutionary trends in this area.

A 'prompt' reaction may not be prompt enough, because structurally it would come after the events. In this context, the need to anticipate potential developments has emerged, highlighting the importance of creating a system capable of dealing with the potential problems arising from capital market practices. The relationship between shadow banking and shadow central banking offers a possible way of interpreting dynamic regulation in the context of evolutionary patterns. In such a context, the starting point would consist of understanding how existing structures and their traditional problems transform throughout new stages of capitalism, with the consequence of exposing the system to the same problems 'masked' under apparently new forms.

As a consequence of complexity and multidimensionality, central bankers will need a far larger presence of technologists, who will necessarily have to be fully integrated with financiers and economists. In this way, central banks could adequately and actively monitor market developments, more easily identifying the potential sources of transformation even when they fall outside their traditional spheres of competence. In addition, central bankers could also be in the position to gradually design effective structures for channelling data flows and to effectively interpret them to provide a basis for real and more pervasive forms of dynamic adaptive regulation.[573]

---

[573] In this sense see Stefano Battiston, Doyne J. Farmer, Andreas Flache, Diego Garlaschelli, Andrew G. Haldane, Hans Heesterbeek, Cars Hommes, Carlo Jaeger, Robert May, and Marten Scheffer, 'Complexity Theory and Financial Regulation' (2016) 351 Science 818, 818.

Conclusion

Fintech has led to the development of many activities within the economic system. One of the effects of such developments is the erosion of central banking activities. These initiatives should be characterized as part of the shadow central banking system. The shadow central banking system shares many commonalities with shadow banking, including the causes leading to their emergence and their major risks, such as financial interconnectedness and systemic risk. Furthermore, the shadow central banking system shares some characteristics with older forms of central banking systems and their private currencies, before the birth of 'modern' central banks.

The launch of JPM Coin in 2019, and even more the global projects—in particular Libra's first version and the further developments leading to Diem—demonstrate the potential impact of such Fintech innovations on the function of modern central banking. In this area, these initiatives will have disruptive effects on the financial system, the banking system, and the central banking system. Governments have options in order to address these threats to central banking and monetary policy. They may choose to ban private central banking initiatives, or to compress their role by launching their own CBDCs. Consequently, sovereign states would retain the option of playing a leading role in the transition toward the new economic phase of the cryptoeconomy, without formally or substantially relinquishing their domains to private parties. If sovereign states do not ban these shadow central banking activities, they should aggressively require compliance with specific corporate governance requirements, thereby mitigating the negative effects of the risk appetite and moral hazards, as they did with banks. This is the only way to avoid systemic risks related to poor governance. Finally, regulators should also consider regulations similar to the Volcker Rule for entities interested in conducting central banking activities. This would help to avoid unprecedented, interconnectedness, and systemic conflicts of interest.

5
Disrupting Shadow Banking or Crypto Shadow Banking

Introduction

Complexity is characterized as a static concept when referring to the structural dimension of international finance, and as a dynamic attribute of evolving ecosystems. The label 'crypto shadow banking' summarizes both these aspects. From the static approach, its underlying idea refers to the possibility that new entities may lead to new forms of 'structural' complexity, in substitution or in addition to the traditional ones. At the same time, in its dynamic dimension, crypto shadow banking refers to a new financial network, representing a direct evolution of what was identified as a potential Time Zero, that is, the emergence of shadow banking starting from the 1960s. Disruptive technology led to new forms of adaptation, and will likely contribute to the emergence of new interactions within the nascent networks, as in the case of DeFi.

When Satoshi Nakamoto published the white paper on Bitcoin, it was difficult to imagine that it would have led to the emergence of a new economic paradigm, commonly referred to as the cryptoeconomy. At the very beginning of this process, blockchain certainly brought a significant wave of speculation within financial markets. In the past, this was also the case with the internet and the following internet bubble that imploded in 2000–1, and it happened again with the advent of blockchain technology, with many ICOs that turned out to be frauds or hyper-valued projects (and therefore a bubble). Similarly, this trend of hypervaluation could happen again in the context of sustainable finance, with significant risks of excessive evaluation of projects marketed as 'green'—a process commonly known as 'green-washing.'

Beyond this common speculative trend, the cryptoeconomy has grown and led to the emergence of a new network of financial actors. The emergence of this new network is somehow consistent with previous transformations within the markets, and it is indeed part of an ongoing process of financial transformation which depends on historical, economic, and legal factors. DeFi is part of this transformation.

As mentioned in Chapter 1, the process of financial transformations leading to the establishment of new financial institutions beyond traditional credit institutions emerged in the 1960s, and since then it has not stopped.[1] These transformations are the result of multiple layers. The first layer was financial engineering, with a wave of structured products that started to spread in the market, and the second layer is technology, contributing to the evolution of the financial industry. The cryptoeconomy is the result of the pressure that technology currently exercises on the capital market industry

---

[1] See generally Charles K. Whitehead, 'The Evolution of Debt Covenants, the Credit Market, and Corporate Governance' (2009) 34 JCorpL 641.

and more generally on the financial networks. The cryptoeconomy is a new economic paradigm based on a technological revolution originating from cryptographic applications to different economic processes and functions. The tokeneconomy may be characterized as a subcategory of the cryptoeconomy, and specifically refers to digital tokens as the centre of a new ecosystem.[2] Specific structural characteristics are generally associated with DLT. This mostly depends on the way market actors, those who are invested in the cryptoeconomy, tend to emphasize specific properties of decentralization as a core characteristic of DLT. Although decentralization is indeed a key characteristic, it was not fully implemented yet. For example, cryptocurrency miners are concentrated in specific geographic areas and new intermediaries are still the key nodes in a decentralized ecosystem that, in principle, should not require them.

At this point, an important question is whether the new emerging financial ecosystem of the cryptoeconomy, and more specifically DeFi, proposes new dynamics or if it rather tends to reproduce (or to 'clone', as suggested by the IOSCO)[3] existing trends as in the more traditional environment. The cryptoeconomy not only replicates this kind of concentration and this system of intermediaries, but also tends to replicate other trends, such as those existing in shadow banking.

Adopting this angle, this chapter explores analogies between the cryptoeconomy, DeFi, and the shadow banking system, a network of financial institutions and financial instruments, as described at the beginning of this book. In doing so, it tries to identify the new financial instruments and techniques emerging in the nascent cryptoeconomy and techniques might correspond to pre-existing entities in the traditional shadow banking system and replicate the same functions and model of business. At the current stage of its development, this new ecosystem shares some recognizable similarities with the pre-existing one. The same functions and model of business could potentially imply the same risks, coupled with the new ones emerging from technology. Adopting a complexity approach, the developments at the level of crypto shadow banking confirm the continuous evolutionary patterns characterizing each subpart of the financial system, and the way such changes are also reflected on the overall financial system.

Specific data purport the possibility that crypto shadow banking is emerging as a new phenomenon in the context of DeFi. In the United States, the economy grew at a slower pace compared to previous years, with a gross domestic product (GDP) increase equal to 2.3 per cent in 2019 against 2.9 per cent for 2018.[4] As a consequence of the Covid-19 pandemic, GDP dropped by 3.4 per cent for 2020 but it again gained traction in 2021, with growth equal to 3 per cent.[5] At such an economic conjuncture, a relevant point is the difference in the pace of growth in the loan balances registered by a traditional investment bank and the leading crypto-lending firm.

---

[2] See Chapter 1.
[3] IOSCO, 'IOSCO explains how Decentralised Finance Is Cloning Financial Markets' (24 March 2022) <https://www.iosco.org/news/pdf/IOSCONEWS637.pdf> accessed 26 April 2022.
[4] U.S. Bureau of Economic Analysis, 'Gross Domestic Product, Fourth Quarter and Year 2019 (Advance Estimate)' (30 January 2020) <https://www.bea.gov/news/2020/gross-domestic-product-fourth-quarter-and-year-2019-advance-estimate> accessed 26 April 2022.
[5] U.S. Bureau of Economic Analysis, 'Gross Domestic Product, Fourth Quarter and Year 2021 (Advance Estimate)' (27 January 2022) <https://www.bea.gov/news/2022/gross-domestic-product-fourth-quarter-and-year-2021-advance-estimate> accessed 26 April 2022.

J.P. Morgan increased its loan balance at a level aligned with national growth, while Genesis Capital (owned by Digital Currency Group, which also owns CoinDesk) has grown at a much faster pace, equal to more than ten times.[6] According to Genesis Capital's Digital Asset Lending Snapshot, the firm experienced an increase in active loans outstanding of 21 per cent in the fourth quarter, notwithstanding a decline in the Bitcoin price.[7] The number of originations experienced an increase equal to 34.8 per cent, with a total origination of more than 4 billion since its launch in March 2018.[8]

This chapter is structured as follows. Section I identifies a specific network of activities and instruments emerging in the cryptoeconomy as crypto shadow banking and recognizes the correspondence between this network and the pre-existing shadow banking. This chapter then focuses on derivatives, money market funds (MMFs), private funds, prime brokers, and securitizations and identifies their homologues in the cryptoeconomy. Section II assesses the related risks of crypto shadow banking in the financial sector, specifically, excessive leverage, liquidity risks, a lack of metrics to assess and rate the emerging cryptoeconomy and its entities and instruments, and the possibility that new financial conglomerates can emerge. Section III proposes specific regulatory measures at the level of market infrastructures, crypto-financial products, crypto-financial conglomerates, and ratings.

I. Crypto Shadow Banking?

Blockchain promoters emphasized its potential to disrupt many activities at different levels. Satoshi Nakamoto's white paper proposed a basic concept, a 'purely peer-to-peer version of electronic cash', that would have enabled online payments which bypassed any centralized financial institution.[9] Bitcoin was a new framework in principle capable of disintermediating the financial ecosystem. Therefore, the underlying DLT technology was considered a foundational technology potentially applicable to a wide range of activities. As a consequence, there has been increasing interest among entrepreneurs and private funds, individual and institutional investors—including banks—all of which are eager to verify new financial opportunities while at the same time avoiding any form of disruption by newcomers.

At the more mature stage of the cryptoeconomy in which we find ourselves, a new network of institutions is growing, relying on the more sophisticated financial instruments that are increasingly available. Furthermore, there may be the potential for enhanced sophistication in the landscape of financial instruments related to

---

[6] Bradley Keoun, 'Compared to Traditional Banks, Crypto Lenders See Booming Growth' (*CoinDesk*, 30 January 2020) <https://www.coindesk.com/compared-to-traditional-banks-crypto-lenders-see-booming-growth?utm_source=&utm_medium=&utm_campaign=clid=> accessed 26 April 2022.

[7] Matt Ballensweig, Roshun Patel, and Leon Marshal, 'Genesis Capital Digital Asset Lending Snapshot 2019 | Q4 insights' (*Genesis Trading*, 2019) <https://genesiscap.co/insights/q4-insights-2019/> accessed 26 April 2022 (hereafter Genesis Trading, 'Digital Asset Lending').

[8] Ibid.

[9] Satoshi Nakamoto, 'Bitcoin: A Peer-to-Peer Electronic Cash System' (31 October 2008) <https://nakamotoinstitute.org/static/docs/bitcoin.pdf> accessed 26 April 2022.

the cryptoeconomy, with a more predominant role of financial engineering, even for this area. This is the core of the emerging DeFi as a form of financial intermediation based on crypto-assets.[10] In this context, an important question is whether DeFi is attempting to replicate the same environment, and may consequently present risks that are similar to the ones that shadow banking posed to the financial and economic systems. In the following sections, this chapter considers the significant development in crypto lending activities, leverage, the potential spreading adoption of collateralized debt positions (CDPs), the increasing number of private funds, leading to the development of service providers, and finally the role of stablecoins as the equivalent of MMFs.

The reference to stablecoins is relevant for both shadow central banking and crypto shadow banking and offers the opportunity to consider important intersections and differences between these two networks. Although the similarities in the labels adopted in this book may lead one to consider that the same is true of their functions, this is not the case. Shadow central banking aims to disrupt specific central banking functions; therefore, the reference to shadow banking does not reflect a coincidence between the two in terms of their economic function. As mentioned in Chapter 1, shadow banking enters into specific economic and financial functions generally reserved to banks, that is, maturity, liquidity, and credit transformation. Consistent with such functions and a similar framework in terms of entities and instruments, crypto shadow banking is rather similar to the traditional shadow banking, though with some differences that will soon be analysed. Therefore, this also explains how shadow central banking and crypto shadow banking are different in their economic and financial roles in the context of the cryptoeconomy.

However, shadow central banking and crypto shadow banking share some similarities (which will be analysed in Section I.B) as well as some entities and instruments. One of these instruments is stablecoins, which play an important role in both networks. Depending on their main economic function (as a payment system or an MMF), as well as the geographic scale of their adoption and operations, stablecoins may trigger different, or in some cases also similar, concerns. Therefore, unsurprisingly, such similarities may sometimes generate similar systemic and operational concerns and eventually suggest similar regulatory solutions, notwithstanding the underlying differences in their economic functions. These considerations justify the presence of several references to shadow central banking in this chapter, especially when analysing the risks as well as the potential regulatory measures to be adopted in this context, which will be critically assessed in Sections II and III of this chapter.

With regard to the relationship between shadow banking and crypto shadow banking, Figure 5.1 offers a visual comparison of the similarities in the overall mechanism and specific differences at the level of individual entities and instruments, which will be explored in greater depth in the following sections. As was shown in Chapter 1 of this book, the shadow banking system is a 'network of financial instruments and

---

[10] IMF, *Global Financial Stability Report—Shockwaves from the War in Ukraine Test the Financial System's Resilience* (April 2022) 65 <https://www.elibrary.imf.org/downloadpdf/book/9798400205293/9798400205293.xml> accessed 1 May 2023 (hereafter IMF, *Global Financial Stability Report 2022*).

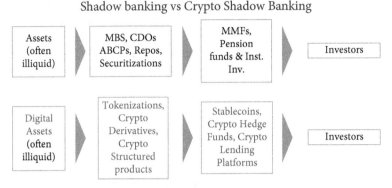

Fig. 5.1 Shadow banking vs crypto shadow banking

institutions' and serves to connect 'commercial and consumer borrowers indirectly to investors in capital markets'.[11]

Taking this definition into account, a starting point for the purposes of this chapter would be the possibility of characterizing the crypto shadow banking system as a network of financial instruments and institutions for the crypto space. Furthermore, looking at the functions of crypto shadow banking in comparison with traditional shadow banking, the function of indirectly connecting borrowers to investors in capital markets for the purpose of providing credit and liquidity transformation could also emerge in this context. This is one of the traits characterizing crypto shadow banking, especially when considering the new activities related to crypto-lending, as well as the possibility of developing specific types of derivatives and structured products. However, the current early stage of development suggests that crypto shadow banking is also a network for gaining access to highly speculative financial instruments populating the cryptoeconomy. This is especially the case when considering specific derivatives, such as perpetual swaps, which will be analysed in the following sections.

Crypto shadow banking is also important for confirming a salient trait of financial innovation to be continuous throughout time. Such continuity can be interpreted in two different ways. A first would be to consider that financial innovation continuously happened throughout time. As mentioned in Chapter 1, history has offered many examples of financial innovations since the Middle Ages.[12] A second approach would be to assess the way specific techniques are reiterated and trace such phenomenon in the context of the new paradigms emerging with disruptive technologies applied to finance. Omarova mentioned the importance of 'transaction meta-technologies' (pooling, layering, acceleration, and compression) and the way they continue to be implemented in the context of new technologies. Transaction meta-technologies encompass different ways of structuring financial assets and transactions, and all contribute

---

[11] Erik F. Gerding, 'The Shadow Banking System and Its Legal Origins' (2012) SSRN 3 <https://ssrn.com/abstract=1990816> accessed 26 April 2022.
[12] See Chapter 1, Section III.A.1.

to the 'constant growth and complexification of the financial market'.[13] Their common characteristic is that rather than identifying a specific product or transaction, they are 'system-level operational principles or core techniques that enable financial markets' continuous reproduction and expansion'.[14] The emergence of crypto shadow banking confirms Omarova's theory on meta-technologies, because this technique can also be traced in this financial network.

A. The Network of Crypto Shadow Banking

1. Crypto-Lending or DeFi Lending

The concept of shadow banking refers explicitly to banking, that is, the economic activity of generating credit activities, and more broadly to any activity related to 'maturity, credit and liquid transformation, without access to central bank liquidity or public sector credit guarantees'.[15] Crypto-lending or DeFi Lending and the activities of lending and borrowing in virtual currencies are emerging as new trends in the market, and are those more clearly related to shadow banking. DeFi lending experienced significant growth in particular since 2020, partly because of more systematic utilization of stablecoins.[16] More generally this connects to the opportunity offered by DeFi to crypto-asset holders 'to earn interest by depositing crypto and/or borrowing more crypto by posting collateral'.[17]

In the crypto-lending market, there are four categories of users: crypto lenders, cash lenders, crypto borrowers, and cash borrowers, and in addition the lending platforms acting as intermediaries. First, crypto-lenders are both individuals and investment funds who aim to make a profit on the crypto-assets that they hold by trading them.[18] Second, cash lenders are in the position of holding an excess of cash, and therefore can accept collateral in the form of crypto-assets.[19] Third, crypto borrowers can be either individuals or any kind of firm, such as OTC desks, interested in trading as well as making markets in the context of crypto-assets.[20] Fourth, cash borrowers are in the position of having significant amounts of crypto-assets but need to obtain additional cash.[21] Two reasons explain this situation. First, investment reasons for individuals interested in minimizing taxes or achieving a capital gain and second, business reasons, as in the case of ICO issuers.[22]

---

[13] See Saule T. Omarova, 'New Tech v. New Deal: Fintech as a Systemic Phenomenon' 36 YaleJonReg 735 (2019) (hereafter Omarova, 'New Tech v. New Deal').
[14] Ibid, 762.
[15] Zoltan Pozsar, Tobias Adrian, Adam Ashcraft, and Hayley Boesky, 'Shadow Banking' (July 2010) Federal Reserve Bank of New York Staff Reports—Staff Report No. 458 <https://www.newyorkfed.org/medialibrary/media/research/staff_reports/sr458_July_2010_version.pdf> accessed 26 April 2022.
[16] IMF, *Global Financial Stability Report 2022* (n 10) 75.
[17] Ibid.
[18] Noelle Acheson and Galen Moore, 'Crypto Lending 101' (*CoinDesk*, January 2020) 5 <https://downloads.coindesk.com/research/CryptoLending101_CoindeskResearch.pdf> accessed 26 April 2022 (hereafter Acheson and Moore, 'Crypto Lending 101').
[19] Ibid.
[20] Ibid.
[21] Ibid.
[22] Ibid.

2. (DeFi) Lending Platforms

The key actors in crypto-lending are DeFi lending platforms, which are different from traditional lending actors, in particular banks. DeFi lending platforms are experiencing extremely high growth, and the activity of crypto-lending is growing at a higher pace than traditional lending activities.[23] The scheme implemented by DeFi lending platforms is straightforward: lending platforms receive crypto-assets as deposits and lend them to borrowers, under the condition that they comply with certain collateral criteria.[24] Consistent with the vast majority of intermediaries currently active in the cryptoeconomy, both centralized and decentralized lending platforms operate within the current framework, and they differ in many respects. The core business of centralized platforms concentrates on specific clients, offering custodial services to those who need to exchange crypto-assets for cash or vice versa.[25] In addition to firms focusing on this business (such as Genesis Capital), other key actors in the space include OTC desks, exchanges, and other kinds of platforms interested in maximizing the management of their positions in crypto-assets, or offering the possibility of margin trading or margin lending (which will be further considered in the following sections). Decentralized platforms exclusively focus on crypto-assets; smart contracts manage the loan origination as well as the interest payments, and do not offer custodial services.[26]

Consistent with the general debate on centralization versus decentralization, this choice has an impact on the transparency of such platforms. Decentralized platforms are, in principle, more transparent because the full on-chain execution grants the traceability of each transaction, while centralization is inherently more opaque and requires more effort in order to fill this gap. Currently, the vast majority (if not the totality) of centralized platforms are not subject to any mandatory disclosure requirements, consequently, some uncertainty surrounds the activity. The leading crypto-lending platform, Genesis Capital, is one of the few market actors active in this space providing a quarterly report.[27]

The lack of a regulatory framework is not the only difference between traditional lending and crypto-lending. In fact, crypto-lending offers the possibility to transact on a much broader range of assets, including traditional securities, and should, in principle, be faster because of the lack of intermediaries, as opposed to transactions among traditional lending institutions.[28] Furthermore, crypto-lending transactions are fully or even over-collateralized,[29] with more liquid assets than the traditional lending institutions. Therefore, participants enjoy the benefit of the mitigation of high volatility.

DeFi crypto-lending platforms work in a specific manner, relying on deposits, borrowing, and collateral. Users have the opportunity to gain interest from their deposits in crypto-assets, which form part of a 'liquidity pool' corresponding to the specific type of crypto-assets.[30] After the deposit, the depositors obtain a certificate of deposit

---

[23] See Keoun, 'Compared to Traditional Banks, Crypto Lenders See Booming Growth' (n 6).
[24] IMF, *Global Financial Stability Report 2022* (n 10) 75.
[25] Acheson and Moore, 'Crypto Lending 101' (n 18) 6–7.
[26] Ibid, 7.
[27] See for example, Genesis Trading, 'Digital Asset Lending' (n 7).
[28] Ibid.
[29] See Acheson and Moore, 'Crypto Lending 101' (n 18) 4.
[30] See IMF, *Global Financial Stability Report 2022* (n 10) 75.

in the form of a 'platform-specific utility token', and its value is equal to the underlying asset deposited but bears interest.[31] A depositor would be in the position to withdraw the deposit at any time.[32] Furthermore, the depositor is also in the position to borrow a crypto-asset from a liquidity pool, by using the deposited asset as collateral, and the lending interest rate would vary on the basis of 'the level of utilization for the borrowing asset'.[33] Collateralization, and often over-collateralization, are required by lending platforms.[34] Borrowers can opt to repay their debt at any time, although they have to fulfil their collateral requirements.[35]

3. Towards Non-Collateralized Loans? The Case of Flash Loans

So-called flash loans are a new, fast, and disintermediated scheme of loan. Flash loans are uncollateralized loans, available on specific DeFi platforms offering these products.[36] The leading platform is Aave, which had executed $5 billion of flash loans as of December 2021.[37] Flash loans have some key characteristics. First, like any DeFi innovation, they are enabled by smart contracts, programmed as a single transaction, where both the borrower and the lender have to comply with the rules of the smart contract. The borrower must pay back the loan before the transaction ends, otherwise the smart contract reverses the transaction, like the loan never happened. Second, flash loans are unsecured loans and are instantaneously executed; therefore no collateral is required to enter into the transaction. While in a normal transaction the borrower offers the collateral, in a flash loan the borrower has to pay back the loan instantaneously; therefore, in order to fulfil the smart contract for the loan, the borrower has to call a separate smart contract to perform instant trades with the loaned capital before the end of the transaction.[38]

In principle, flash loans are an opportunity to borrow money for specific trades in the crypto markets,[39] in particular arbitrage investment strategies[40] and collateral swaps, and lead to a reduction of the transaction fees. Although they are designed

---

[31] Ibid.
[32] Ibid.
[33] Ibid.
[34] Ibid. As the Report explains, 'lending platforms often require overcollateralization by setting a discount factor (called a collateral factor) typically ranging from 0 to 0.8 across different types of assets. For example, when the collateral factor is 0.8, borrowers can borrow up to 80 percent of the collateral value posted; when a collateral factor is zero, however, as in the case of Tether (USDT) in some DeFi platforms, the user cannot borrow using the asset as collateral.'
[35] Ibid. Importantly, the Report explains that 'if at any time a borrower's collateral requirement falls below the required threshold as a result of adverse price movements, liquidation can be triggered by a liquidator who repays the debt and acquires the collateral in exchange for rewards (the liquidation bonus)'.
[36] See Alyssa Hertig, 'What Is a Flash Loan' (*CoinDesk*, 17 February 2021) <https://www.coindesk.com/learn/2021/02/17/what-is-a-flash-loan/> accessed 26 April 2022 (hereafter Hertig, 'What Is a Flash Loan').
[37] Samuel Becker, 'What Are Flash Loans & How Do They Work?' (*SoFi*, 28 December 2021) <https://www.sofi.com/learn/content/flash-loans/> accessed 26 April 2022 (hereafter Becker, 'What Are Flash Loans').
[38] Hertig, 'What Is a Flash Loan' (n 36).
[39] Becker, 'What Are Flash Loans' (n 37).
[40] Ibid. 'Traders can make money by looking for price discrepancies across a number of different exchanges. Say two markets are pricing pizzacoin differently. It's priced at $1 on Exchange A and $2 on Exchange B. A user can use a flash loan and call a separate smart contract to buy 100 pizzacoins for $100 at Exchange A, then sell them for $200 at Exchange B. The borrower then repays the loan and pockets the difference.'

to avoid default and increase security, severe attacks could take place through malicious actors gaming the loan mechanism by exploiting mistakes in the code of smart contracts.[41] One case involved Ethereum trading and lending protocol bZX. Here the borrower could fraud the lender by falsely making appear that the loan was repaid in full, 'by temporarily pushing up the price of the stablecoin used to repay the loan'.[42] In another case, BProtocol exploited flash loans to speed up a governance decision. As CoinDesk reported, 'BProtocol borrowed 13,000 MKR tokens worth some $7 million through a flash loan from derivatives platform dYdX swapped for MKR on lending platform Aave. Voting with the flash-loaned MKR tokens enabled BProtocol to speed up desired election results for its project built on MakerDAO.'[43]

4. Leverage in the Cryptoeconomy, Derivatives, and Other Instruments
a. Financial leverage
The post-crisis debate focused on the massive use of leverage by financial institutions, although the overall levels of leverage didn't diminish.[44] Leverage offers great speculative opportunities and its use is growing in the cryptoeconomy, relying on DeFi. A basic and general definition of leverage refers to the possibility of making an investment recurring to 'a small upfront monetary commitment using borrowed funds'.[45] It is generally associated with both OTC and exchange-traded derivatives, both offering great opportunities for leveraging.[46]

Speculative trends have characterized the emergence of the cryptoeconomy since the first wave of ICOs and cryptocurrencies, which contributed to make this market extremely volatile. After the speculative frenzy of ICOs and cryptocurrencies starting in 2017, a bear market, generally referred to as 'Crypto-Winter', emerged in the cryptoeconomy. During Crypto-Winter the vast majority of cryptocurrencies experienced a significant depreciation, and the general activities connected to ICOs slowing down significantly.[47] Different causes led to this market situation, in particular the number of frauds coupled with the increasing regulatory pressure. One of the consequences triggered by Crypto-Winter has been the sophistication of speculation in the cryptoeconomy. While leverage and more complex products may be a sign of increased maturity in the financial system, this may also be a sign of the speculative trait of investments in this ecosystem. Leverage and more sophisticated products may be an attempt to maintain high levels of returns that the sole investment in cryptocurrency cannot achieve anymore. Consistent with the trends in traditional finance, these

---

[41] Ibid.
[42] Ibid.
[43] William Foxley, '"Flash Loans" Have Made Their Way to Manipulating Protocol Elections' (*CoinDesk*, 29 October 2020) <https://www.coindesk.com/tech/2020/10/29/flash-loans-have-made-their-way-to-manipulating-protocol-elections/> accessed 26 April 2022.
[44] See John Authers and Lauren Leatherby, 'The Decade of Deleveraging Didn't Quite Turn Out That Way' (*Bloomberg*, 3 April 2019) <https://www.bloomberg.com/graphics/2019-decade-of-debt/> accessed 26 April 2022.
[45] See Alan N. Rechtschaffen, *Capital Markets, Derivatives, and the Law: Positivity and Preparation* (OUP 2019) 163 (hereafter Rechtschaffen, *Capital Markets*).
[46] Ibid.
[47] Max Yakubowski, 'What's Next for the Industry as "Crypto Winter" Thaws?' (*Cointelegraph*, 5 October 2019) <https://cointelegraph.com/news/whats-next-for-the-industry-as-crypto-winter-thaws> accessed 26 April 2022.

increased levels of sophistication and the use of leverage in the cryptoeconomy may exacerbate specific risks, such as liquidity and counterparty risks, thereby impacting overall levels of systemic risk.

Market infrastructures, in particular crypto-exchanges, played an important role in favouring an increase in the leverage in the cryptoeconomy and DeFi. In this process, a non-harmonized international regulation contributes to the emergence of new and potentially risky practices. While in the United States and Europe, crypto-exchanges are to some extent more regulated as a consequence of the enforcement activities of securities agencies and regulators, exchanges located in less regulated jurisdictions could benefit from different treatment, and for this reason they were defined as the 'biggest casino ever'.[48] Lighter regulations have favoured direct access to both retail and institutional investors to exchanges, and to the multiple possibilities to leverage their positions—up to 100 times.[49]

Multiple techniques and financial instruments led to increased financial leverage in the cryptoeconomy. New derivative contracts, short-selling,[50] and margin trading are all tools for leveraging financial investments and their use is increasing within the cryptoeconomy, thus enhancing their sophistication. These techniques and the way they developed in the cryptoeconomy will be analysed in the following subsections.

b. Derivatives

i. Traditional derivatives Traditional derivative contracts include futures, swaps, options, forwards, and contracts for difference (CFDs). Derivatives can be both OTC (privately negotiated) and exchange-traded (standardized).[51] OTC derivatives may have the advantage to allow counterparties to agree on specific clauses related to their specific needs, with the negative downside effect of increased liquidity and counterparty risks.[52] Exchange-traded derivatives are structured to 'virtually eliminate counterparty risk'.[53] Each type of derivative may have specific functions,[54] although derivatives contracts are generally used for hedging purposes or for speculation.[55]

In the rather unstable and volatile market surrounding the first developments in the cryptoeconomy, traders have suffered a significant decline in Bitcoin since late 2017, as they were limited by the thin liquidity of the Bitcoin market, controlled by Bitcoin

---

[48] Olga Kharif, 'Bitcoin Speculators Gain Upper Hand as Derivative Trading Surges' (*Bloomberg*, 22 October 2019) <https://www.bloomberg.com/news/articles/2019-10-22/bitcoin-speculators-gain-upper-hand-as-derivative-trading-surges> accessed 26 April 2022 (hereafter Kharif, 'Bitcoin Speculators Gain Upper Hand').

[49] Galen Moore, 'Crypto Derivatives—What to Expect in a Changing World' (*CoinDesk*, October 2019) 6 <https://downloads.coindesk.com/crypto-investing/crypto_derivatives.pdf> accessed 26 April 2022 (hereafter Moore, 'Crypto Derivatives').

[50] For an overview on short selling applied to cryptocurrencies, see Oliver Smith, 'How to Short Sell Bitcoin, and Why More People Aren't' (*Forbes*, 12 June 2018) <https://www.forbes.com/sites/oliversmith/2018/07/12/how-to-short-sell-cryptocurrencies-and-why-more-people-arent/#5c9ee2b14e63> accessed 26 April 2022.

[51] See Rechtschaffen, *Capital Markets* (n 45) 163.

[52] Ibid, 162.

[53] Ibid.

[54] Ibid, 165–172.

[55] See generally Lynn A. Stout, 'Risk, Speculation, and OTC Derivatives: An Inaugural Essay for Convivium' (2011) 1 AccountEconL: Conviv 1.

'whales' implementing buy-and-hold strategies.[56] In this context, speculation was a main reason for traders to push for the implementation of derivatives, thus increasing levels of exchanges.[57]

At the moment there are different options for investors interested in crypto-derivatives: exchange-traded products, custom derivatives OTC, futures and forwards, and perpetual swaps.[58] The Chicago Mercantile Exchange proposed a form of regulated Bitcoin futures in 2019. CME's Bitcoin futures contract is a USD cash-settled contract based on the CME CF Bitcoin Reference Rate (BRR), which serves as a once-a-day reference rate of the US dollar price of Bitcoin. The BRR aggregates the trade flow of major Bitcoin spot exchanges during a one-hour calculation window into the US dollar price of one Bitcoin as of 4pm Greenwich Mean Time (GMT).[59] A single BTC contract has a value of five times the value of the BRR Index and is quoted in US dollars per one Bitcoin. The tick increments are quoted in multiples of $5 per Bitcoin, meaning a one-tick move of the BTC future is equal to $25.[60] More recently, the CME Group completed its offer of derivatives with an option on its future contracts.[61]

Bitmex and Binance exchanges offer futures contracts for both Bitcoin and smaller coins that can be leveraged more than 100 times and often perpetually.[62] Bitmex created and now offers a new product, the perpetual swap. Different from futures, such perpetual swaps do not have a closing date. They settle to an index periodically (on Bitmex settlement occurs every eight hours) in cash, letting traders maintain their positions without rolling them over.[63]

Exchange-traded notes (ETN) existed in Europe since 2015. Although they may not be characterized as 'derivatives', they still serve the same economic function of providing exposure to Bitcoin and other crypto-assets via more regulated markets.[64] In Sweden, the Bitcoin ETN is consistently traded with all other listed instruments on the Nasdaq exchange. Investing in these instruments requires a bank account, perhaps one with an adviser or online broker. XTB Provider AB hedges all sales of the Bitcoin ETN by buying an equivalent value in the Bitcoin market.[65]

In the United States, exchange-traded funds (ETFs) were never granted approval by the SEC, because of concerns relating to market manipulation. This was the case of the Winklewoss' Gemini ETF application, as well as the other cases such as VanEck,

---

[56] Kharif, 'Bitcoin Speculators Gain Upper Hand' (n 48).
[57] Steven Zheng, 'Bakkt's Monthly Bitcoin Futures Hit All-Time-High of $15M' (*The Block Crypto*, 9 November 2019) <https://www.theblockcrypto.com/linked/46523/bakkts-monthly-bitcoin-futures-hit-all-time-high-of-15m> accessed 26 April 2022.
[58] Moore, 'Crypto Derivatives' (n 49) 6–7.
[59] CME Group, 'What Are Bitcoin Futures' <https://www.cmegroup.com/education/courses/introduction-to-bitcoin/what-are-bitcoin-futures.html> accessed 26 April 2022.
[60] Ibid.
[61] CME Group, 'Bitcoin Futures—Contract Specs' <https://www.cmegroup.com/cme-group-futures-exchange/options-bitcoin-futures.html> accessed 26 April 2022 (hereafter CME, 'Bitcoin Futures Specs').
[62] Kharif, 'Bitcoin Speculators Gain Upper Hand' (n 48).
[63] Moore, 'Crypto Derivatives' (n 49) 6. For an overview of the 'perpetual' contractual scheme, see also bitMEX, 'Perpetual Contracts Guide' <https://www.bitmex.com/app/perpetualContractsGuide> accessed 26 April 2022.
[64] Ibid, 7.
[65] Yessi Bello Perez, 'Sweden's Nasdaq Exchange Approves Bitcoin-Based ETN' (*CoinDesk*, 29 April 2019) <https://www.coindesk.com/swedens-nasdaq-exchange-approves-bitcoin-based-etn> accessed 26 April 2022.

Bitwise, and United States Bitcoin and Treasury Investment. In the Winkelwoss' rejection, the SEC highlighted the lack of a proper mechanism of price discovery underlying the Bitcoin market and the Gemini Exchange.[66]

The market for Bitcoin options offers 'put' and 'call' options. An investor pays a premium for the right—and not the obligation—to buy or sell specific amounts of Bitcoin on a specific date.[67] In addition to traditional put and call options, some offshore exchanges started to offer binary options. In this scenario, traders bet on a yes/no scenario.[68]

Cantor Futures Exchange, LP (Cantor Exchange) launched a Bitcoin Binary option on 1 December 2017: a cash-settled instrument with the structure of a swap.[69] The platform 'Nader' offers Bitcoin binary options to retail investors.[70] OKEx is a new Bitcoin/USD option trading that was launched on 9 January 2020.[71] Furthermore, the crypto-exchange FTX launched new Bitcoin options, generating a volume of $15 million in the first 24 hours,[72] and hit an all-time high on 22 April, reaching a $993 million trade.[73]

OTC trading is relevant for crypto-markets' activity and involves different market participants. Hedge funds, smaller asset managers, and family offices are buyers, while miners are the main sellers, with the involvement of regulated broker-dealers and crypto-exchange OTC desks.[74] Binance, Coinbase, and Circle all have their own OTC desks.[75] The vast majority of transactions involve actors in Asia and North America.[76] The fact that an asset management giant such as Fidelity entered the market of storing and trading crypto sourced from OTC markets for institutional investors[77] was a

---

[66] See generally SEC, 'Self-Regulatory Organizations; Bats BZX Exchange, Inc.; Order Setting Aside Action by Delegated Authority and Disapproving a Proposed Rule Change, as Modified by Amendments No. 1 and 2, to List and Trade Shares of the Winklevoss Bitcoin Trust' (Release No. 34-83723, 26 July 2018) <https://www.sec.gov/rules/other/2018/34-83723.pdf> accessed 26 April 2022.

[67] Aaron Hankin, 'Bitcoin Options Are Headed to the U.S.' (*Investopedia*, updated 5 November 2019) <https://www.investopedia.com/articles/investing/033115/it-possible-trade-bitcoin-options.asp> accessed 26 April 2022.

[68] Ibid.

[69] See Cantor Futures Exchange, 'New Contract Submission—Futures Exchange Bitcoin Swap Contract' (1 December 2017) 9 <https://www.cftc.gov/sites/default/files/filings/ptc/17/12/ptc120117cantordcm001.pdf> accessed 26 April 2022.

[70] Nadex, 'Products and Markets' <https://www.nadex.com/product-market/> accessed 26 April 2022.

[71] 'BTCUSD Options Now Available' (*OKX Support*, 9 January 2020) <https://okxsupport.zendesk.com/hc/en-us/articles/360038631171?utm_source=twitter.com&utm_medium=social&utm_campaign=okex options-the-much-awaited-btc-usd-o> accessed 26 April 2022.

[72] @SBF_FTX, 'FTX has 1,700 BTC of options traded in the last 24h—putting it squarely at the second highest volume crypto options exchange 1 day after launch!' (*Twitter*, 13 January 2020) <https://twitter.com/SBF_Alameda/status/1216797698113724416?utm_source=InstitutionalCrypto&utm_medium=Email&utm_campaign=2020-01-14clid=> accessed 26 April 2022.

[73] Jamie Crawley, 'FTX US Affiliate Sees Record Daily Trading Volume in First Half of 2021' (*CoinDesk*, 29 July 2021) <https://www.coindesk.com/markets/2021/07/29/ftx-us-affiliate-sees-record-daily-trading-volume-in-first-half-of-2021/> accessed 26 April 2022.

[74] Capco, 'The OTC Crypto Market: At a Glance' (4 February 2019) <https://www.capco.com/Intelligence/Capco-Intelligence/The-OTC-Market-At-A-Glance> accessed 26 April 2022.

[75] Joseph Birch, 'Major Crypto Exchanges Launch OTC Desks Despite the Crypto Winter' (*Cointelegraph*, 11 February 2019) <https://cointelegraph.com/news/major-crypto-exchanges-launch-otc-desks-despite-the-crypto-winter> accessed 26 April 2022.

[76] Ibid.

[77] See Anna Alexandre, 'Fidelity Investments Fully Rolls Out Crypto Custody Service, Exec Says' (*Cointelegraph*, 19 October 2019) <https://cointelegraph.com/news/fidelity-investments-fully-rolls-out-crypto-custody-service-exec-says> accessed 26 April 2022.

signal that more and more actors would have eventually entered this market. However, the wave of scandals and losses affecting the cryptoeconomy in 2022 has slowed down this process.

Institutional investors opting to enter the market of crypto-derivatives have limited options. An example is TeraExchange, LLC (TeraExchange), operating since 2014, provides support for institutional investors who want to be exposed to the Bitcoin market, offering a derivative contract falling under the supervision of the CFTC.[78] Second, LedgerX—the derivatives unit of the collapsed FTX crypto-exchange—also offers Bitcoin options: with the Long-Term Equity Anticipation Security, investors can have a right to buy or sell Bitcoins at the strike price before an expiration date (of one year or more).[79] Interestingly, an internal member of LedgerX alleged bad practices and financial mismanagement in a letter to the CFTC.[80] CME entered the space of options of Bitcoin futures, to respond to the growing interest of clients with hedging or trading purposes.[81] CME designed this option of Bitcoin futures consistently with the structure of Bitcoin futures: the contract unit consists of one CME's Bitcoin futures contract, representing five Bitcoins, and is quoted in US dollars per one Bitcoin, and a tick size of $25 or $5 in case of reduced tick size.[82] While not exclusively addressed to institutional investors, CME's reputation will likely attract the interest of institutional investors, too.

ii. **Collateralized debt instruments in the cryptoeconomy** CDOs and similar financial instruments played an important role in spreading financial risk and increasing opacity among investors during the financial crisis of 2008,[83] because commercial banks as well as hedge funds and investment banks took large positions in CDOs.[84] CDOs are a specific type of asset-backed security, where a portfolio of bonds, loans, and other assets backs the securities' value.[85]

What if CDOs start spreading in the cryptoeconomy? Currently, the majority of security tokens allow the representation of a single asset. The transition towards multi-asset representation will create new possibilities in the sense of collateralized debt positions (CDPs).[86] A security token CDP should be characterized as a debt token, the value of which is collateralized by an underlying pool of digital securities.[87] Consistent

---

[78] See Stan Higgins, 'CFTC Grants Full Registration to Bitcoin Swaps Trading Platform' (*CoinDesk*, 26 May 2016) <https://www.coindesk.com/us-swap-platform-registration-cftc> accessed 26 April 2022.
[79] See Giovanni Patti, 'The Regulation of Financial Product Innovation Typified by Bitcoin-Based Derivative Contracts' (2019) 38 RevBank&FinL 765, 783–784.
[80] Nikhilesh De, 'LedgerX Board Member Says Company in Disarray after Founders' Ouster' (*CoinDesk*, 10 January 2020) <https://www.coindesk.com/markets/2020/01/10/ledgerx-board-member-says-company-in-disarray-after-founders-ouster/> accessed 26 April 2022.
[81] Daniel Palmer, 'CME Says It Will Launch Bitcoin Options in January' (*CoinDesk*, 12 November 2019) <https://www.coindesk.com/markets/2019/11/12/cme-says-it-will-launch-bitcoin-options-in-january/> accessed 26 April 2022.
[82] See CME, 'Bitcoin Futures Specs' (n 62).
[83] See generally David Zaring, 'Litigating the Financial Crisis' (2014) 100 VaLRev 1405.
[84] See Stephen J. Choi and Adam C. Pritchard, *Securities Regulation, Cases and Analysis* (4th edn, Foundation Press 2015) 158 (hereafter Choi and Pritchard, *Securities Regulation*).
[85] Ibid.
[86] See Jesus Rodriguez, 'Collateralized Debt Positions for Security Tokens' (*Hackernoon*, 25 February 2019) <https://hackernoon.com/collateralized-debt-positions-for-security-tokens-28b7ec8f5522> accessed 26 April 2022.
[87] Ibid.

with CDOs, liquidity, value, and risk are also important in this context. The quality of the underlying assets is of extreme relevance in order to maintain high levels of liquidity, value and low risk. The opacity of existing digital assets may be a relevant source of risk that could be amplified with potential crypto-CDPs.

iii. Future developments: synthetic assets and on-chain derivatives? Further developments may come into play with the implementation of 'on-chain' derivatives and with the application of smart contracts and DLT to derivatives. However, it is uncertain whether these technologies will penetrate this market and to what extent.[88] A potential scenario would be that fully on-chain derivatives increase the opportunities for derivatives, facilitating the broad use of tokenized assets as underlying and collateral and increasing the ease of execution.

An emerging trend in DeFi is that of synthetic assets. Different from traditional derivatives, synthetic assets are tokenized derivatives that do not use contracts to create the chain between the underlying asset, but instead they tokenize it, mimicking the value of another asset.[89] Synthetic assets could bring specific advantages. Any user operating on open-source protocols can issue them and trade them on any crypto-exchange in the world, enhancing global liquidity.[90] Furthermore, synthetic assets do not require holding the underlying asset, enabling frictionless movement and borderless transfers implemented via cryptocurrency wallets.[91]

After analysing the legal framework of smart contracts,[92] the International Swaps and Derivatives Association (ISDA) explored potential opportunities for building smart derivatives contracts,[93] and defined four key principles for their development. The ISDA considered that: (i) smart derivatives contracts should be developed on the basis of existing standards; (ii) smart contracts should be developed only for 'those parts of a derivatives contract that are capable of being automated'; (iii) legal validation should be the basis for effective automation; and (iv) automation should be developed only for those parts of a derivatives contract bringing sufficient benefit.[94] Furthermore it developed an analysis of smart derivatives contracts in relation to the existing ISDA documentation architecture.[95]

The ISDA has considered specific problems, with an emphasis on the definition of disruption events and valuation issues for smart derivatives contracts. The ISDA defines disruptive events as those 'one-off or periodic events that could interrupt or

---

[88] ISDA, 'Legal Guidelines for Smart Derivative Contracts—Introduction' (January 2019) <https://www.isda.org/a/MhgME/Legal-Guidelines-for-Smart-Derivatives-Contracts-Introduction.pdf> accessed 26 April 2022 (hereafter ISDA, 'Legal Guidelines').

[89] Shrimpy, 'What Are Crypto Synths? Synthetic Assets Explained' (28 October 2021) <https://academy.shrimpy.io/post/what-are-crypto-synths-synthetic-assets-explained> accessed 26 April 2022.

[90] Ibid.

[91] Ibid.

[92] ISDA and Linklaters LLP, 'Smart Contracts and Distributed Ledger: A Legal perspective Whitepaper' (August 2017) <www.isda.org/a/6EKDE/smart-contractsand-distributed-ledger-a-legal-perspective.pdf> accessed 26 April 2022.

[93] ISDA and King & Wood Mallesons, 'Smart Derivatives Contracts: From Concept to Construction—Whitepaper' (October 2018) <https://www.isda.org/a/cHvEE/Smart-Derivatives-Contracts-From-Concept-to-Construction-Oct-2018.pdf> accessed 26 April 2022.

[94] ISDA, 'Legal Guidelines' (n 88) 10–12.

[95] Ibid, 13–19.

disrupt the functioning of a digital asset derivatives transaction'.[96] Such events include forks, airdrops, and cyberattacks as well as other technological disruptions affecting the underlying technology, changes in law or regulation, problems affecting the market infrastructures, and issues related to asset-referenced tokens becoming untethered with a consequent significant fall in value.[97] With regard to valuation, the ISDA identified the valuation sources (including trading venues, settlement prices, index prices, and decentralized activities) and valuation methodologies.[98]

c. Further tools for leveraging

In addition to credit derivatives, another way to leverage trading positions is so-called margin trading, a practice that involves purchasing a security with borrowed funds. In this case, borrowing the funds is a form of debt that generates leverage. AlphaPoint, Binance, Bakkt, PrimeXBT Leverage Trading, and Kraken introduced this mechanism of traditional finance into cryptoeconomics and offered the option of margin trading.[99]

Another trend involves the OTC lending market. SALT and Unchained Capital provide fiat in exchange for holding cryptocurrencies in a multi-sig wallet with the ability to liquidate it if the value of the collateral falls by a certain margin. Similarly to what happens in traditional markets, shorting and taking leveraged positions becomes easier.[100]

Finally, short-selling is another tool to increase leverage in investments. As is commonly known, short-selling is a specific trading technique that investors adopt to benefit from a fall in the price of a specific security.[101] Depending on whether the party wishing to short the security has borrowed such security or not, there are two different sub-species of short-selling: 'covered' and 'naked'.[102]

Crypto-lending platforms offer services that are functional to implementing short-selling strategies, by allowing investors with crypto-assets to borrow other crypto-assets.[103] Here, investors can create a leveraged long position, by borrowing stablecoins

---

[96] ISDA, 'Contractual Standards for Digital Assets' (December 2021) <https://www.isda.org/2021/12/14/contractual-standards-for-digital-asset-derivatives/> accessed 15 May 2022.

[97] Ibid, 10–12.

[98] Ibid, 14–17.

[99] Danny Nelson, 'AlphaPoint's White Label Tech Now Lets Crypto Exchanges Offer Margin Trading' (*CoinDesk*, 12 November 2019) <https://www.coindesk.com/alphapoint-to-support-margin-trading-at-its-crypto-exchange-clients> accessed 26 April 2022.

[100] Gary Basin, 'Crypto Derivatives, Lending, and a Touch of Stablecoin' (*Medium*, 12 July 2018) <https://medium.com/hackernoon/crypto-derivatives-lending-and-a-touch-of-stablecoin-59e727510024> accessed 26 April 2022.

[101] See John Armour, Dan Awrey, Paul Davies, Luca Enriques, Jeffrey N. Gordon, Colin Mayer, and Jennifer Payne, *Principles of Financial Regulation* (OUP 2016) 194 (hereafter Armour et al., *Principles of Financial Regulation*).

[102] Ibid. SEC, 'Key Points about Regulation SHO' <https://www.sec.gov/investor/pubs/regsho.htm#ftn1> accessed 26 April 2022, explains that 'In a "naked" short sale, the seller does not borrow or arrange to borrow the securities in time to make delivery to the buyer within the standard three-day settlement period'. Naked short sale posed systemic concerns in the aftermath of the financial crisis of 2008. See also Marco Dell'Erba and Giovanni Patti, 'The Monte dei Paschi di Siena Affaire. Distressed Banks and the European Regulation on Short Selling' (2017) 12 CMLJ 512, 512 (hereafter Dell'Erba and Patti, 'The Monte dei Paschi di Siena Affaire').

[103] IMF, *Global Financial Stability Report 2022* (n 10) 76.

in order to purchase riskier crypto-assets, or a short-sell position, by borrowing risky volatile crypto-assets and buying them back later.[104] Furthermore, there are different techniques to short cryptocurrencies, which include many derivatives mentioned earlier in this section. Among such techniques are margin trading, shorting contracts for difference (CFD), selling crypto futures and buying crypto put options, and selling binary options, or short-selling ETNs.[105] Each of these techniques involves different platforms, including crypto-exchanges, as in the case of margin trading; online brokerages for CFDs; or event crypto-asset derivative trading platforms.[106]

5. Money Market Funds (MMFs) and Stablecoins

MMFs are mutual funds, and they act as 'intermediaries between shareholders who desire liquid investments and borrowers who seek term funding'.[107] Typically, MMFs invest in highly liquid cash or cash-equivalent securities, with a short-term maturity of less than thirteen months and the possibility to redeem their shares at any time, at a stable value.[108] They provide credit to businesses, financial institutions, and governments, with significant investment in short-term funding markets.[109] In the context of the shadow banking system, money market liabilities have a role in financing long-term financial assets.[110]

Both the European Union and the United States passed laws to prevent runs on assets. The European Union adopted the MMF Regulation to reduce the risk of runs and cross-border contagions.[111] In 2016, the American SEC adopted a regulation, opting for so-called floating NAV. Under this new regime, MMFs are required to 'sell and redeem shares based on the current market-based value of the securities in their underlying portfolios, rounded to the fourth decimal place (e.g., $1.0000), i.e., transact at a "floating" net asset value per share ("NAV")'.[112] Furthermore, non-government MMF boards benefit from new tools—liquidity fees and redemption gates—to address runs.[113]

Due to their function as a payment infrastructure, stablecoins are relevant to an analysis with respect to central banking issues.[114] Their stability comes into play in their functional relevance in the cryptoeconomy, as a sort of MMF for the cryptoeconomy. In an attempt to solve the problems of volatility afflicting Bitcoin, and more generally

---

[104] Ibid.
[105] Alex Lielacher, '7 Ways to Short Crypto' (*Cryptonews*, 21 July 2019) <https://cryptonews.com/exclusives/7-ways-to-short-crypto-4282.htm> accessed 26 April 2022.
[106] Ibid.
[107] SEC, 'President's Working Group Report on Money Market Fund Reform' (Release No. IC-29497, October 2010) <https://www.sec.gov/rules/other/2010/ic-29497.pdf> accessed 26 April 2022.
[108] Troy Segal, 'Money Market Fund' (*Investopedia*, updated 7 April 2022) https://www.investopedia.com/terms/m/money-marketfund.asp> accessed 26 April 2022.
[109] Ibid.
[110] Morgan Ricks, 'Shadow Banking and Financial Regulation' (2010) Columbia Law and Economics Working Paper No. 370 <http://ssrn.com/abstract=1571290> accessed 26 April 2022.
[111] Regulation (EU) 1131/2017 of 14 June 2017 on money market funds [2017] OJ L 169/1 (hereafter MMF Regulation).
[112] SEC, 'Money Market Fund Reform; Amendments to Form PF' (Release No. 33-9616, 1 May 2014) <https://www.sec.gov/rules/final/2014/33-9616.pdf> accessed 26 April 2022.
[113] SEC, 'Money Market Funds' <https://www.sec.gov/spotlight/money-market.shtml> accessed 26 April 2022.
[114] See Chapter 4, Section II.B.3.

cryptocurrencies, the idea of a stable cryptocurrency, or stablecoin, emerged. As mentioned in Chapter 4, three main categories of stablecoins have emerged in the market, each using a different model to stabilize their value. First, fiat-currency asset-backed stablecoins (so-called off-chain collateralized stablecoins) rely on fiat currencies as collateral and, therefore, cannot be fully decentralized. The most capitalized off-chain collateralized stablecoin is Tether, with a theoretical ratio of 1:1 between USDT (Tether's stablecoin) and the US dollar.[115] A second category of stablecoins, so-called on-chain collateralized stablecoins, is collateralized with digital assets, generally with either one cryptocurrency or a basket of them. This category of stablecoins is fully decentralized. Finally, non-collateralized stablecoins are the third category, implementing algorithmic tools to maintain the stability of stablecoins.

Stablecoins work in a manner that can be compared to MMFs in the ecosystem of cryptocurrencies,[116] since, like MMFs, they should—in principle—invest their reserve in highly liquid financial instruments—although this is often not the case[117]—and guarantee nominal fixed returns. Particularly in DeFi, stablecoins act as 'enablers' similar to traditional deposits, where they have two basic functions. First, they serve as an 'entry and exit vehicle to the DeFi ecosystem' for market actors who do not want to be exposed to market risks related to other categories of tokens, avoiding the conversion of their crypto-assets into fiat currencies.[118] Second, stablecoins are a tool for enabling market actors who are exposed to volatile crypto-assets 'to retain their market exposure by pledging them as collateral for loans in stablecoins, which can be used for transactions in various DeFi applications'.[119]

For these reasons, the IMF considers that one possible approach to stablecoin regulation would be to extend the regulation for MMFs, especially in terms of sufficient liquidity and capital.[120] They may be a new form of money, notably investment-money (i-money).[121]

Stablecoins may also serve to foster the derivatives industry in the cryptoeconomy and DeFi. To date, the vast majority of derivatives used Bitcoin as an underlying asset; therefore, the procedures necessary to define the reference price are rather opaque.

---

[115] For further details, see Marco Dell'Erba, 'Stablecoins in Cryptoeconomics: From Initial Coin Offerings (ICOs) to Central Bank Digital Currencies (CBDCs)' (2019) 22 NYUJLPubPol'y 1, pt IIIB.

[116] Ibid, 8. Eichengreen and Viswanath-Natraj note that stablecoins 'are simply the digital equivalent of prime money market funds, which similarly invest in high-quality commercial paper, they raise the same financial stability', although 'The quality of the commercial paper held by stablecoins is uncertain; Tether for one provides no details'. Barry Eichengreen and Ganesh Viswanath-Natraj, 'Stablecoins and Central Bank Digital Currencies: Policy and Regulatory Challenges' (2022) 21 AsianEconPap 29, 38 <https://direct.mit.edu/asep/article/21/1/29/109037/Stablecoins-and-Central-Bank-Digital-Currencies> accessed 22 April 2022 (hereafter Eichengreen and Natraj, 'Stablecoins and CBDCs').

[117] Ibid.

[118] European Commission, 'European Financial Stability and Integration Review 2022' (2022) 47 <https://ec.europa.eu/info/sites/default/files/european-financial-stability-and-integration-review-2022_en.pdf> accessed 22 April 2022.

[119] Ibid.

[120] See Tobias Adrian and Tommaso Mancini-Griffoli, 'The Rise of Digital Money' (July 2019) IMF Fintech Notes, Note 19/01, 6–10 <https://www.imf.org/en/Publications/fintech-notes/Issues/2019/07/12/The-Rise-of-Digital-Money-47097> accessed 26 April 2022 (hereafter Adrian and Mancini-Griffoli, 'The Rise of Digital Money').

[121] Ibid, 5.

The supposed stability of stablecoins might favour their use as a reference in the context of derivatives given the need for stability.

6. Private Funds

Among the first entities investing and financing the cryptoeconomy, private funds played a major role. Private funds are engaged in two types of investment: direct investment in cryptocurrencies and investment in start-ups or scale-ups involved in cryptocurrency activities. Of a total market cap for all cryptocurrencies standing at around $230 billion,[122] crypto-hedge funds collectively manage $1 billion assets under management (AUM), excluding crypto index funds and crypto venture capital funds.[123] Although different research provides different numbers related to the industry,[124] a common finding is the growth of the sector.[125] As mentioned in the previous chapter on ICOs,[126] venture capital funds tried to enter the market of cryptocurrencies and ICOs to benefit from the explosion of ICOs used as a tool to make their business model more efficient. Venture capitalists are currently applying pressure to STOs and IEOs, which are emerging as the most reliable ICO structure in the market.[127]

In traditional finance, institutional investors' interest and investments in private funds grew through the years. In the context of hedge funds, for example, although individual wealthy investors were the initial target, a broad range of institutional investors, including mutual funds, pension funds, insurance companies, and university endowments, have become increasingly important to the industry.[128] Consistent with this precedent, crypto-private funds may increasingly attract the interest of institutional investors and, thus, cryptoeconomics will be positively affected. Specifically, the engagement of institutional investors in the cryptoeconomy may lead to further developments in terms of AUM, favouring the emergence of more established and transparent market practices. In 2018, investor Alan Howard launched a platform for designing portfolios of crypto funds for institutional investors, which attracted investments from Goldman Sachs and Barclays.[129]

---

[122] Coin360, 'Top 100 Cryptocurrency by Market Capitalization' (updated on a real-time basis) <https://coin360.com/table> accessed 26 April 2022.
[123] See PwC and Elwood Asset Management, *2019 Crypto Hedge Fund Report* (May 2019) <https://www.pwc.com/gx/en/financial-services/fintech/assets/pwc-elwood-2019-annual-crypto-hedge-fund-report.pdf> accessed 26 April 2022 (hereafter *Crypto Hedge Fund Report*).
[124] Crypto Fund Research estimates in around 800 cryptocurrency funds, half of them are crypto hedge funds and half crypto-venture capitalists. See Crypto Fund Research, 'Cryptocurrency Investment Fund Industry Graphs and Charts' <https://cryptofundresearch.com/cryptocurrency-funds-overview-infographic/> accessed 26 April 2022. However, *Crypto Hedge Fund Report* (n 123) estimates that there are 150 active crypto hedge funds.
[125] Constantin Kogan, 'The Story behind the Explosive Growth of Crypto Funds' (*Cointelegraph*, 28 September 2019) <https://cointelegraph.com/news/the-story-behind-the-explosive-growth-of-crypto-funds> accessed 26 April 2022.
[126] See Chapter 3.
[127] See Chapter 3.
[128] See for example IMF, 'World Economic Outlook—A Survey by the Staff of the International Monetary Fund' (May 1998) 4 <https://www.imf.org/~/media/Websites/IMF/imported-flagship-issues/external/pubs/ft/weo/weo0598/pdf/_0598ch1pdf.ashx> accessed 26 April 2022.
[129] Laurence Fletcher, 'Alan Howard-Backed Firm Plots $1bn Crypto Venture' (*Financial Times*, 30 August 2019) <https://www.ft.com/content/733e9b6c-ca68-11e9-af46-b09e8bfe60c0> accessed 26 April 2022. See also 'Goldman, Barclays Back Alan Howard's Crypto Platform' (*Bloomberg*, 22 May 2022)

Although the vast majority of private funds are relatively small portfolios, with average AUM of $10 million, some private funds established themselves as market leaders, demonstrating that even in this sector there may be relatively relevant concentrations of capital. Polychain Capital, with its $967 AUM in cryptocurrencies, is one of the largest crypto funds,[130] and continues to expand.[131] In addition to crypto-private funds that were born to exclusively invest in the cryptoeconomy, another market development is that established hedge funds, active in traditional finance, may gradually invest in this sector, creating significant consequences for the size and risks of the market. As an example, Andreesen Horowitz, a California-based venture capital firm managing $7 billion outside the crypto space, created a fund focusing on the cryptocurrency sector.[132]

7. Prime Brokers and Custodians

If the growth of private funds may be a prelude to increased interest in the cryptoeconomy among institutional investors, the development of necessary service providers for this industry would be a natural consequence. Just as in traditional finance, institutional investors in the cryptoeconomy need specific services, including liquidity, reliable platforms providing an advanced trading interface, sophisticated data analytics, high speed order execution, and a wide range of quantitative solutions, all provided for low rates and trading fees.[133]

Prime brokers, custodians, and depositories are extremely relevant in traditional finance, especially in the context of private funds. The three activities may be connected but refer to different contexts. The Alternative Investment Fund Manager Directive (AIFMD), regulating alternative investment fund managers in Europe, for example, defines prime brokers as 'a credit institution, a regulated investment firm or another entity subject to prudential regulation and ongoing supervision, offering services to professional investors primarily to finance or execute transactions in financial instruments as counterparty and which may also provide other services such as clearing and settlement of trades, custodial services, securities lending, customized technology and operational support facilities'.[134] This definition emphasizes the connection between the different phases, especially custody. At the same time, it provides the general principles underlying the appointment, role, and duties of depositories, with a view to avoiding conflicts of interests.[135]

<https://www.bloomberg.com/news/articles/2022-05-15/goldman-barclays-invest-in-alan-howard-crypto-trading-platform> accessed 27 May 2022.

[130] Simon Chandler, 'Biggest Crypto Hedge Funds and What They Tell about the Market' (*Cointelegraph*, 16 August 2019) <https://cointelegraph.com/news/biggest-crypto-hedge-funds-and-what-they-tell-about-the-market> accessed 26 April 2022.

[131] Ada Hui, 'Polychain Capital Targets $200M for Second Venture Fund, Slide Deck Reveals' (*CoinDesk*, 14 February 2020) <https://www.coindesk.com/polychain-capital-is-raising-a-200m-crypto-venture-fund-slide-deck-reveals> accessed 26 April 2022.

[132] Ibid.

[133] See Kai Sedgwick, 'How Prime Brokerage Will Affect Crypto Markets' (*Bitcoin.com*, 14 November 2019) <https://news.bitcoin.com/how-prime-brokerage-will-affect-crypto-markets/> accessed 26 April 2022 (hereafter Sedgwick, 'Prime Brokerage').

[134] See Directive 61/2011/EU of 8 June 2011 on Alternative Investment Fund Managers [2011] OJ L 174/1, art 4(af).

[135] Ibid, art 21.

The development of the prime broker industry began in the 1980s, to provide comprehensive investment services to financial institutions. Goldman Sachs, Morgan Stanley, and UBS are the market leaders, in particular linking hedge funds to their counterparties as well as providing complementary services, such as securities lending in exchange of collateral.[136] The activity of a custodian is limited to the physical or electronic safekeeping of their clients' securities, as well as to the post-trading phase (settlement) related to such securities.[137] Depositaries exclusively provide services to private funds and have a role in safeguarding the collective investment schemes' assets and the lawfulness of specific processes related to such assets.[138]

Many new ventures emerged in the business of prime brokerage in the cryptoeconomy. Troy Trade aspires to provide an all-in-one service for traditional investors, which includes margin and OTC, quant strategies and dynamic-data tools.[139] Altonomy, created in 2018 and acquired by a crypto-exchange Blockchain.com in 2022, focuses on specific services, in particular OTC derivatives, liquidity management, and institutional cloud mining, via AltMiner, a cloud-based mining product for institutions and accredited investors to 'rent' digital asset miners.[140]

In addition to newcomers, established investment banks may be in a position to enter this market and exploit their expertise in this new economic venue. Wall Street institutions reacted to Fintech by trying to absorb innovations in an attempt to avoid disruption. In an extremely lucrative business, such as prime brokerage, there are significant incentives for these institutions to do the same again.

With regard to the market of custodians, similar trends may be observed in the future. The custody of digital assets results in an increased level of complication compared to traditional assets. There are two chief concerns. First, there is a general problem of achieving an adequate level of security for both the private key and transaction addresses involved. Second, interaction with third parties, including regulators or even fund administrators, is necessary but represents a threat to the safety of the assets.

Even in this sector, fierce competition among newcomers emerged. According to a report by CoinDesk in July 2019, at that time there were '40 service providers offering stand-alone custody services' and Blockdata listed 135 service providers in 2023.[141] As

---

[136] Insider Monkey Staff, 'Prime Brokerage Services Are Coming to Crypto' (*yahoo!finance*, 16 September 2019) <https://finance.yahoo.com/news/prime-brokerage-services-coming-crypto-134018657.html> accessed 26 April 2022.

[137] Deloitte, 'The Evolution of a Core Financial Service Custodian & Depositary Banks' (2019) 7 <https://www2.deloitte.com/content/dam/Deloitte/lu/Documents/financial-services/lu-the-evolution-of-a-core-financial-service.pdf> accessed 26 April 2022. Under Investment Advisers Act 1940, rule 206(4)-2(c)(1), an adviser has custody of client assets, and therefore must comply with the rule, when it holds, 'directly or indirectly, client funds or securities or [has] any authority to obtain possession of them'. See SEC, 'Custody of Funds or Securities of Clients by Investment Advisers' (Release No. IA-2671, 5 November 2003) <https://www.sec.gov/rules/final/ia-2176.htm#P57_4850> accessed 26 April 2022.

[138] Ibid.

[139] Sedgwick, 'Prime Brokerage' (n 133).

[140] See Altonomy <https://www.altonomy.com/#/> accessed 26 April 2022.

[141] Galen Moore, 'Custody—Crypto Assets' Unique Challenge and Opportunity' (*CoinDesk*, 2019) 6 <https://downloads.coindesk.com/crypto-investing/custody-report.pdf> accessed 26 April 2022 (hereafter Moore, 'Custody Crypto Assets'). See also Blockdata, 'List of crypto custody providers' <https://www.blockdata.tech/markets/use-cases/custody-solutions> accessed 26 April 2023. This business has also attracted prominent financial institutions including Goldman Sachs and BNY Mellon. Sridhar Natarajan, 'Goldman Sachs Is Considering a Custody Offering for Crypto Funds' (*Bloomberg*, 6 August 2018) <https://

the report suggests, although the vast majority of such service providers market themselves as 'qualified custodians' under the US regulation,[142] it is unlikely that this corresponds to an effective qualification. Indeed, there are no US regulations providing specific requirements related to crypto-asset custody.

There are two different ways to ensure the custody of crypto-assets. The first is online storage, also referred to as 'hot storage', which is typically offered by major exchange platforms. The second is offline storage ('cold storage'), whereby the key and wallet are kept offline, though in a more expensive way.[143] The vast majority of crypto funds prefer offline storage because of the higher security it affords against hackers. In this market, three main providers have emerged: first, crypto-exchanges, such as BitGo and Gemini;[144] second, dedicated providers, such as Xapo and Swiss Crypto Vault, adopting physical offline protection (which also includes private police) of the master key and the related assets;[145] finally, specialist technology providers, such as Ledger and Trezor, which offer services based on a software and hardware combination, achieving adequate protection of the master key and crypto addresses.[146]

Currently, significant regulatory uncertainty exists. The relevant national authorities have failed to implement any regulatory measure addressing the specific concerns triggered by the custody of crypto-assets.

In the United States, custody service regulation affects investment companies and broker-dealers. Registered investment advisers and other SEC-regulated entities must hold their cryptocurrency with a qualified custodian, pursuant to Rule 206-4 of the Advisers Act (so-called 'Custody Rule').[147] Consistent with Custody Rule, the 'Customer Protection Rule' (Rule 15c3-3) requires broker-dealers to guarantee that client funds and securities are adequately protected from the potential failure of the broker-dealer.[148]

The SEC failed to address uncertainties related to what would be a 'qualified custodian' under US law and what conditions must be satisfied to achieve authorization in other jurisdictions. For example, there is no liability regime in the case of custodians losing the master keys due to problems in their security system, nor is there an insurance mechanism offering protection against the loss of crypto-assets, which is an essential requirement for crypto custody.[149] While in June 2019 the Financial Action Task Force issued important guidelines[150] on the applicability of anti-money

---

www.bloomberg.com/news/articles/2018-08-06/goldman-is-said-to-consider-custody-offering-for-crypto-funds> accessed 26 April 2022; Arnold Kirimi, 'BNY Mellon Plans to Launch Digital Asset Custody Platform Later This Year' (*Cointelegraph*, 25 February 2022) <https://cointelegraph.com/news/bny-mellon-plans-to-launch-digital-asset-custody-platform-later-this-year> accessed 26 April 2022.

[142] See Investment Advisers Act 1940, rule 206(4)-2(c)(3).

[143] See Tom Casteleyn and Lucien Foster, 'Cryptocurrencies, Custody and Third-Party Access' (*Post Trade 360*, May 2019) <https://posttrade360.com/news/technology/cryptocurrencies-custody-and-third-party-access/> accessed 26 April 2022.

[144] Ibid.

[145] Ibid.

[146] Ibid.

[147] 15 U.S. Code, s 80b-1–80b-21.

[148] See Amanda Gould, 'Crypto Custody' (*PennCareyLaw*) <https://www.law.upenn.edu/faculty/davidhoffman/crypto-custody.php> accessed 26 April 2022.

[149] See Moore, 'Custody Crypto Assets' (n 141) 10.

[150] FATF, 'Virtual Assets and Virtual Asset Service Providers' (June 2019) <https://www.fatf-gafi.org/media/fatf/documents/recommendations/RBA-VA-VASPs.pdf> accessed 26 April 2022. In the front page

laundering (AML) and know-your-customer (KYC) rules, there is still a lack of certainty regarding the implementation of such guidelines by the requisite financial institutions.[151] In February 2023 the SEC proposed to amend federal custody requirements, expanding the rules to include crypto-assets. According to the new regulations, for an institution to hold any client assets, which includes cryptocurrencies specifically, they must possess the necessary licenses or registrations, such as being a registered broker-dealer, futures commission merchant, or a certain type of trust or foreign financial institution.[152] This regime would be consistent with the high level of regulation that these custodians have to comply with in traditional finance.

In Europe, MiCAR regulates the custody and administration of crypto-assets, as 'crypto-asset services', and organizations providing such services are 'crypto-asset service providers'. MiCAR requires custody and administration service providers to be subject to specific obligations, such as the provision of a written agreement with the clients, the maintenance of a register of the positions opened, the creation of a custody policy, and a liability regime against any loss of crypto-assets as a consequence of technical malfunction or external hacks.[153]

In 2019, Germany approved the German Act Implementing the Amending Directive on the Fifth EU Anti-Money Laundering Directive,[154] which included the crypto custody business in the German Banking Act (Kreditwesengesetz—KWG) as a new financial service. Therefore, the German government has established licensing requirements for custody services, which also apply to crypto custody services.[155]

8. Securitization and Tokenization

Securitization is the process of issuing securities, creating a representation of real tradable assets. Securitization plays an important role in shadow banking, and although it proved a powerful financial tool, the risks associated with this practice were uncovered by the financial crisis. Home mortgages (including sub-prime loans), student loans, and credit card receivables are all common assets in a securitization transaction.[156] In a typical securitization, a financial institution (the originator) aggregates a pool of non-liquid assets and sells them to a special purpose vehicle (SPV).[157] The

---

of the document, the FATF defines itself as an 'independent inter-governmental body that develops and promotes policies to protect the global financial system against money laundering, terrorist financing and the financing of proliferation of weapons of mass destruction. The FATF Recommendations are recognised as the global anti-money laundering (AML) and counter-terrorist financing (CFT) standard'.

[151] See Moore, 'Custody Crypto Assets' (n 141) 10.

[152] Rohan Goswami and MacKenzie Sigalos, 'SEC proposes rules that would change which crypto firms can custody customer assets' (*CNBC*, 15 February 2023) <https://www.cnbc.com/2023/02/15/sec-chair-gensler-crypto-firms-need-to-register-to-custody-assets.html> accessed 26 April 2023.

[153] See European Parliament legislative resolution of 20 April 2023 on the proposal for a regulation of the European Parliament and of the Council on Markets in Crypto-assets and amending Directive (EU) 2019/1937 (COM(2020)0593, C9-0306/2020, 2020/0265(COD)) <https://www.europarl.europa.eu/doceo/document/TA-9-2023-0117_EN.pdf> accessed 2 May 2023 (hereafter MiCAR).

[154] Directive (EU) 2018/843 of 30 May 2018 on the prevention of the use of the financial system for the purposes of money laundering or terrorist financing [2018] OJ L 156/43.

[155] Caroline Herkströter and Michael Born, 'Crypto Assets: Germany Introduces New Regulatory Regime' (*Norton Rose Fulbright*, March 2020) <https://www.nortonrosefulbright.com/de-de/wissen/publications/5ee1e37e/new-regulatory-regime-for-crypto-assets-in-germany> accessed 26 April 2022.

[156] See Choi and Pritchard, *Securities Regulation* (n 84) 156.

[157] Ibid, 157.

SPV then sells interests in the stream of money from the pool and these interests may be structured as interests in the profits from the pool or as 'asset-backed securities' (ABS), namely debt secured by the assets in the pool.[158] The final stage consists in the SPV using the proceeds from the sale of interests in the pool to fund the initial purchase of the underlying pooled assets from the originator.[159] As an economic function, securitizations make illiquid assets more liquid and tradable. Subprime mortgages are an example of illiquid assets, partitioned and spread to investors, without achieving a higher level of liquidity and attractiveness simply because they are partitioned among multiple investors.

The tokenization of assets is the process of issuing a blockchain token that is a digital representation of real tradable assets, with the same function as a security in a securitization. Although tokens have different functions (as the case of utility and payment tokens shows), the ICO and its multiple transformations, in particular STOs,[160] illuminate the similarities between tokens and securities. Bitcoin, ICOs,[161] and NFTs are examples of asset synthetization with the digital representation or the tokenization of securities and assets, and DLT as infrastructural technology could potentially amplify the magnitude of the trading.[162] The exponential growth in the NFT market will increasingly contribute to the trends towards mass tokenization of assets.

The tokenization of assets provides greater liquidity in the context of private securities, or specific illiquid assets, such as fine art, and it strengthens their tradability in secondary markets. Furthermore, it is a faster and cheaper framework for transactions, and it promises to be more transparent and inclusive, since it increases the opportunities to invest reduced amounts in assets generally precluded from a wide audience.[163]

At the moment there are no rules equating the mechanisms of securitizations and of tokenization.

As mentioned in Chapter 3,[164] a major regulatory advancement which could facilitate the tokenization of assets is the Token and Trustworthy Technology Service Providers Act adopted in Liechtenstein. The broad definition of token (referred to as a Token Container Model)[165] includes 'a piece of information on a TT System which: 1. can represent claims or rights of memberships against a person, rights to property or other absolute or relative rights; and 2. is assigned to one or more TT identifiers'.[166]

---

[158] Ibid.
[159] Ibid.
[160] Patrick Laurent, Thibault Chollet, Michael Burke, and Tobias Seers, 'The Tokenization of Assets Is Disrupting the Financial Industry. Are You Ready?' (*Wyoleg*, 2018) <https://www.wyoleg.gov/InterimCommittee/2019/S3-20190506TokenizationArticle.pdf> accessed 26 April 2022.
[161] For a broad analysis of initial coin offerings and the way they contributed to market transformations at different levels, please refer to Chapter 3.
[162] Omarova, 'New Tech v. New Deal' (n 13) 771–782.
[163] Ibid.
[164] See Chapter 3, Section IV.D.
[165] Philipp Sandner, 'Liechtenstein Blockchain Act: How Can Nearly Any Right and Therefore Any Asset Be Tokenized based on the Token Container Model?' (*Medium*, 9 October 2019) <https://philippsandner.medium.com/liechtenstein-blockchain-act-how-can-nearly-any-right-and-therefore-any-asset-be-tokenized-based-389fc9f039b1> accessed 26 April 2022 (hereafter Sandner, 'Liechtenstein Blockchain Act').
[166] Liechtenstein Law on Tokens and TT Service Providers 2019 (*Liechtensteinisches Gesetz über Token und VT-Dienstleister LGBl 2019 Nr. 301, LR 950.6*) art 2, 1 c.

A major advantage is the possibility to use the token as a container, in the sense that it has 'the ability to hold rights of all kinds [and] can be loaded with a right that represents a real asset such as real estate, stocks, bonds, gold, access rights, money ... [as well as being] empty, as in the case of digital code'.[167] In this way, this approach offers the opportunity to clearly separate (i) the right and the asset from (ii) the token which is running on the blockchain, therefore differentiating law and technology.[168]

As also mentioned in Chapter 3, Switzerland is at the forefront of private projects in the area of tokenization. Three major initiatives for the tokenization of 'digital assets' have taken place, under the impulse of SEBA,[169] Sygnum's Digital Asset Trading Facility,[170] and Six Digital Exchange (in partnership with SBI).[171] The exponential development of NFTs showed the potential that tokenizations could have as well as the significant risks they could bring.

B. Similarities between Shadow Banking, Shadow Central Banking, and Crypto Shadow Banking

How are shadow banking and crypto shadow banking similar? The shadow banking system invaded activities that had been exclusively performed by established and regulated credit institutions. Similarly, in the context of crypto shadow banking, new market actors, such as tech giants, as well as new entrepreneurial Fintech activities attempted to infiltrate the typical activity of established institutions, operating in both the banking and the shadow banking industries. Furthermore, the two financial networks share a cross-border vocation.

The most important similarity, however, relates to the causes that led to the emergence of both shadow banking and crypto shadow banking. What Chapter 4 identified in relation to the emergence of shadow central banking can be extended also to crypto shadow banking. As explained earlier, in the case of shadow banking, lack of regulation (as well as active deregulation), increasing demand for a specific need in the financial system (financial collateral) to be fulfilled through financial engineering and derivatives, increased competition with credit institutions, and innovation favoured the establishment of a new financial network.

In the context of crypto shadow banking, as in the case of shadow central banking, the most important element is the demand for a specific 'good'. The technological innovations and increased cross-border activity involved broader societal constituents, which created an increased demand for faster (and more informal) means of

---

[167] Sandner, 'Liechtenstein Blockchain Act' (n 165).
[168] Ibid.
[169] Christian Gundiuc, 'Swiss Digital Bank Tackles Asset Tokenization for Fully Compliant Institutions' (*Securities*, 16 July 2020) <https://www.securities.io/swiss-digital-bank-tackles-asset-tokenization-for-fully-compliant-institutions/> accessed 26 April 2022.
[170] Sygnum, 'Sygnum's Digital Asset Trading Facility (OTF) Gets Regulatory Clearance from FINMA' (1 September 2020) <https://www.insights.sygnum.com/post/sygnum-s-digital-asset-trading-facility-otf-gets-regulatory-clearance-from-finma> accessed 26 April 2022.
[171] SIX, 'SIX and SBI Digital Asset Holdings Announce Plans for Singapore-Based Joint Exchange Venture to Drive Institutional Digital Asset Liquidity' (8 December 2020) <https://www.six-group.com/en/newsroom/media-releases/2020/20201208-six-sbi-jev.html> accessed 26 April 2023.

investment. The potential for growth associated with tokenized assets has increased the demand for these alternative forms of money, including tokenized money, and tokenized financial instruments and products. All these elements may serve to further unlock a mass adoption of DLT technology and its products.

Consistent with the trends in shadow banking and even more with shadow central banking, non-invasive regulations—and, arguably, complete lack of regulation—have been extremely important for crypto shadow banking as well. Many of the activities and entities of crypto shadow banking either remained unregulated for a time or still operate in the shadow of uncertainty regarding relevant legal rules and enforcement. The lack of a regulatory framework in the United States as well as in other jurisdictions favours legal and digital arbitrage, and therefore, requires the adoption of a case-by-case approach,[172] which lacks important systematic features. The political sensitivity of these issues resounds at the national and international level, and further complicates the achievement of much needed harmonized regulation.

Political sensitivity and a lack of harmonized regulation are key points not only for properly tackling shadow central banking initiatives, as in the case of global stablecoins aimed at implementing global payment systems.[173] They also affect stablecoins in their essential function as MMFs in cryptoeconomy. As mentioned above, MMFs play a crucial role in the context of shadow banking, and Tether-like stablecoins maintain their relevance for crypto shadow banking.

Therefore, a lack of regulation of stablecoins (although they are recognized as a potential threat to financial stability)[174] is relevant for both shadow central banking and crypto shadow banking, which may ultimately pose similar risks (as will be highlighted in Section II). The prolonged inactivity of central bankers in relation to Bitcoin and more recently global stablecoins has affected the entire cryptoeconomy, and in particular, importantly for the purposes of this chapter, the proper development of crypto shadow banking and its underlying financial and economic threats.

The more systematic debate following the announcement of Libra in 2019 will likely be beneficial not only for shadow central banking but also for crypto shadow banking. An example in this sense comes from the Regulation on Markets in Crypto-Assets (MiCAR).[175] Although the main priority of the European Commission was to provide a regulated framework for global stablecoins, MiCAR will likely contribute to advancing the debate on many activities (including service providers such as depositories and custodians), that are extremely relevant also for crypto shadow banking activities.

---

[172] Katharina Pistor, 'Written Statement of Proposed Testimony for the Hearing entitled "Examining Facebook's Proposed Cryptocurrency and Its Impact on Consumers, Investors, and the American Financial System" before the Committee on Financial Services, U.S. House of Representatives' (17 July 2019) 2 <https://financialservices.house.gov/uploadedfiles/hhrg-116-ba00-wstate-pistork-20190717.pdf> accessed 22 April 2022 (hereafter Pistor, 'Written Statement').
[173] See Chapter 4.
[174] See FINMA, 'Supplement to the Guidelines for Enquiries regarding the Regulatory Framework for Initial Coin Offerings (ICOs)' (2019) 2 <https://www.finma.ch/en/~/media/finma/dokumente/dokumentencenter/myfinma/1bewilligung/fintech/wegleitung-stable-coins.pdf?la=en&hash=70408DDE78369718148808FD4784E742373A0140> accessed 22 April 2022.
[175] See MiCAR (n 153).

The lightly regulated exchanges favoured exponential growth in the crypto-derivatives industry, with additional opportunities to increase leverage to potentially uncontrolled levels that would not be conceivable in a more traditional context. However, there was the further risk of allowing non-sophisticated retail investors to enter specific, extremely risky instruments. Similar to trends in traditional finance, lightly regulated investment vehicles such as private funds (in particular venture capital funds and hedge funds) entered the industry before any other established financial institution and started to emerge as important market actors.

Another common and important factor among shadow banking, shadow central banking, and crypto shadow banking is competition. While the shadow banking system places downward pressure on banks, and shadow central banking places pressure on both central banks and national currencies, crypto shadow banking enlarges the scope of its competition in other directions. In fact, crypto shadow banking may disrupt traditional banks, asset managers, as well as other service providers, such as prime brokers, due to the growing industry of derivatives. Although competition is always an important factor in capital markets, the risk of this new financial network is that the lack of regulation may lead to less-than-optimal benefits, at least in the short to medium term. At the international level, the cross-border capacity of crypto shadow banking may be even stronger than traditional shadow banking because of the specific characteristics associated with the technologies involved. As is very well known, the network of cryptoeconomic institutions relies on blockchain infrastructures and activities which, by definition, have a very weak legal nexus with specific jurisdictions, their regulations, and their enforcement mechanisms. This is a further way by which the cross-border dimension emerges and by which competition assumes an even more global dimension.

The same concerns applying to shadow central banking in relation to reduced controls on foreign capital entering the system also apply here. While concerns regarding the primacy of the national currency,[176] as in the case of shadow central banking, do not apply in the context of crypto shadow banking, specific problems may arise anyway, such as uncontrolled speculative actions aimed at disrupting or manipulating specific digital markets, with potential impacts on the real economy. Technological advancements may facilitate speculative initiatives similar to those undertaken by the legendary hedge fund manager Soros with the British pound, or the more recent initiative involving three American hedge funds, the Italian bank Monte dei Paschi di Siena, and the Italian government and speculative manoeuvres in the context of the more recent Italian banking crisis.[177]

Finally, innovation is also an important similarity between the three phenomena. Innovation in financial markets was generally associated with financial engineering. Exotic financial instruments such as complex derivatives, asset-backed securities, or simply inconsiderate use of leverage spread in the financial system, promised to

---

[176] Letter from French Hill and Bill Foster to Federal Reserve Chairman Jerome H. Powell (30 September 2019) <https://src.bna.com/LO7> accessed 22 April 2022. Consistent views were expressed by former FDIC Chair, Sheila Bair, 'The Fed Needs to Get Serious about Its Own Digital Currency' (*yahoo!finance*, 21 June 2018) <https://finance.yahoo.com/news/former-fdic-chair-fed-needs-get-serious-digital-currency-131756819.html> accessed 26 April 2022.

[177] See generally Dell'Erba and Patti, 'The Monte dei Paschi di Siena Affaire' (n 102).

increase capital gains while simultaneously dispersing financial risks. Pure technological innovation came later with the creation of high-frequency trading, robo-advisers, and various forms of artificial intelligence in finance. While an essential feature of both phenomena, technology plays an even more important role in crypto shadow banking. Indeed, technology is the precondition for newly established private entities to compete with the previous ones and with banks. In the context of crypto shadow banking there may be increased opportunities for coupling technological innovation with a new wave of pure financial engineering. The trend of digital asset tokenization may have many effects, including the exponential increase of possible goods to be used as collateral, leading to the creation of complex financial instruments that are difficult to understand and to regulate. Further, investors may be exposed to significant problems of adverse selection.

II. The Risks of Crypto Shadow Banking

Identifying this new network as crypto shadow banking would facilitate the identification of potential problems and regulatory solutions. The regulatory debate was mostly based on the need to characterize all the new entities under the existing regulatory framework. However, the overall problems related to the interactions generated within the new ecosystem (cryptoeconomics and tokeneconomics) were not really addressed from this perspective.

A. Excessive Leverage and Opacity

In the aftermath of the last financial crisis, the newly enhanced macroprudential approach in financial regulation intended to pursue an important objective: reducing systemic risk, by controlling the levels of leverage, while at the same time reducing the interconnectedness of financial institutions. Focusing on the containment of the leverage involved the implementation of a broad range of regulatory measures acting at different levels.[178] One of these levels included traditional corporate governance mechanisms, such as regulating executive compensation in the context of financial institutions. Such corporate governance mechanisms were combined with traditional bank deleveraging forces.[179]

Leverage in the cryptoeconomy is a new feature. As already mentioned with regard to financial derivatives, specific financial products have existed for the past two or three years. At the same time, traditional speculative actions such as short-selling and margin trading are commonly executed. However, a massive use of leverage is a novelty which emerged in 2020. While all the practices based on debt are by definition mechanisms aimed at exploiting a certain degree of leverage in financial markets, the new crypto-derivatives such as perpetual swaps are the main cause of increased

---

[178] See generally Steven L. Schwarcz, 'Systemic Risk' (2008) 97 GeoLJ 193.
[179] See ECB, Financial Stability Review (June 2012), IV A. <https://www.ecb.europa.eu/pub/pdf/fsr/financialstabilityreview201206en.pdf> accessed 26 April 2022.

leverage in the cryptoeconomy. Consistent with the analysis and conclusions reached with regard to the causes leading to the emergence of crypto shadow banking, the creation and diffusion of such financial instruments depend on regulatory arbitrage. Lightly regulated crypto-exchanges contributed to spreading highly speculative instruments with very high leverage ratios in the financial system, benefiting from a lack of regulation and supervision.

In the aftermath of the financial crisis of 2008, regulators put in place a new framework to regulate the market derivatives, including OTC derivatives. In key jurisdictions, the regulation of clearing houses was fundamental for increasing transparency, while strengthening risk management practices, monitoring transactions, and implementing netting by novation were functional to systemic risk mitigation.[180] For clearing houses to work efficiently, the quality of collateral for derivatives must correspond to the level of liquidity: the more liquid the collateral is, the higher its quality.[181] For example, cash, short-term monetary instruments, and bonds issued by reputable governments are all highly liquid.

In the context of the cryptoeconomy, the problem for crypto-derivatives is the lack of regulation involving the vast majority of the systems, at the financial product and market infrastructure levels. At the moment, the market for crypto-derivatives offers very few fully regulated possibilities. One such possibility is the CME futures (and a very few others mentioned under Section I.A) authorized by the Commodities Futures Trading Commission (CFTC). Other jurisdictions do not provide any restrictions or allow any category of individual investors, without distinguishing between sophisticated and unsophisticated investors, the possibility to invest in perpetual swaps and have access to leveraged instruments at up to 100 times the exposure. This is possible because there is no system of harmonized regulation to provide similar rules for market infrastructures, especially for crypto-exchanges. Furthermore, the level of involvement in this process for other market infrastructures, such as clearing houses, is highly uncertain. In the United States there are a few clearing houses operating in cryptocurrencies: Mint Exchange, Digital Asset Exchange,[182] and Apex Crypto, owned by SEC-registered and FINRA member Apex Clearing.[183] At this stage it is difficult to predict what kind of market practices exist in this new market, as well as what could predictably happen in the near future.

---

[180] See generally European Commission, 'Impact Assessment—Proposal for a Regulation of the European Parliament and of the Council amending Regulation (EU) No 1095/2010 establishing a European Supervisory Authority (European Securities and Markets Authority) and amending Regulation (EU) No 648/2012 as regards the procedures and authorities involved for the authorisation of CCPs and the requirements for the recognition of third-country CCPs' (Commission Staff Working Document, 13 June 2017) <https://eur-lex.europa.eu/legal-content/EN/TXT/HTML/?uri=CELEX:52017SC0246&rid=5> accessed 26 April 2022.
[181] See generally Yesha Yadav, 'The Problematic Case of Clearinghouses in Complex Markets' (2013) 101 GeoLJ 387. See also Jeremy C. Kress, 'Credit Default Swaps, Clearinghouses, and Systemic Risk: Why Centralized Counterparties Must Have Access to Central Bank Liquidity' (2011) 48 HarvJLegis 49.
[182] David Kariuki, 'Another Cryptocurrency Exchange Has Launched' (*Cryptomorrow*, 15 November 2018) <https://www.cryptomorrow.com/2018/11/15/another-cryptocurrency-clearinghouse-has-launched/> accessed 26 April 2022.
[183] See Marie Huillet, 'SEC-Registered Clearing House Brings Crypto Trading to 5 Million Clients' (*Cointelegraph*, 28 June 2019) <https://cointelegraph.com/news/sec-registered-clearing-house-brings-crypto-trading-to-5-million-clients> accessed 26 April 2022.

While cryptocurrencies and blockchain were often associated with transparency, the reality may be different and the current technological advances may be a step back rather than a step forward. An example of this opacity is the way exchanges in charge of offering derivatives on cryptocurrencies do not disclose the methodologies for fixing the target price.

A further source of opacity is the lending activity in the cryptospace. As mentioned in Section I.A.1, centralized crypto-lending platforms (which include the market leader, Genesis Capital) are less transparent than decentralized platforms, and make up the vast majority of platforms. The current regulatory framework does not address the activity of lending platforms and therefore does not require any prerequisites for involved entities; nor does it require any mandatory disclosure. The consequences of this particular opacity are likely multiplied. Individual investors are not in the position to assess the financial quality as well as the reputation of such platforms.

B. Liquidity Risks

The financial crisis of 2008 highlighted the significant risks related to liquidity. Subprime mortgages that backed both ABSs and CDOs issued by major credit institutions were not liquid. As mentioned at the beginning of this book, the emerging problem of liquidity coupled with market risk, counterparty risk, operational risk, and the interconnection of financial institutions set in motion a chain of events that ultimately led to catastrophic consequences for the entire financial network.[184]

Liquidity is a fundamental attribute in a financial ecosystem, especially in the context of a highly technological environment with extreme interconnections. As mentioned in this chapter, an important lesson after the financial crisis of 2008 is that illiquid assets do not necessarily become more liquid simply because they are sold directly to a multitude of investors.[185] Instead, their value is spread and partitioned among thousands of investors, potentially through the implementation of complex financial structures.

Consistent with any financial ecosystem, liquidity risk is extremely relevant in crypto shadow banking. There are many potential sources of liquidity risk in crypto shadow banking. First, the quality of tokenized assets is a major issue. In a context where speculative trends dominate the scene, issuers ('tokenizers', one could say) may be tempted to tokenize even the most illiquid assets, with the risk that the market presence of illiquid assets would be likely to grow. This practice could be much riskier than that of a traditional securitization. The tokenization of assets may be cheaper than a traditional securitization because it would drastically cut the number of entities and service providers involved. A negative downside would be the presence of less gatekeepers in the process, thus increasing the risk of toxic assets entering the market.

---

[184] Olufunmilayo B. Arewa, 'Financial Markets and Networks—Implications for Financial Market Regulation' (2009) 78 UCinLRev 613, 618 (hereafter Arewa, 'Financial Markets and Networks').

[185] For the issue of risk distribution in structured products and derivatives, see generally Robert F. Schwartz, 'Risk Distribution in the Capital Markets: Credit Default Swaps, Insurance and a Theory of Demarcation' (2007) 12 FordhamJCorp&FinL 167.

Furthermore, potential negative consequences of a tokenization in lieu of securitization to originate ABSs and CDOs may be even worse than the negative consequences experienced at the level of ICOs. Different from the first wave of ICOs, the origination of structured crypto-products may be much more systemic, exactly as in the case of subprime mortgages in the financial crisis of 2008.

Toxic assets are also extremely problematic in situations where they may be used as collateral, because of their illiquidity.[186] This is important in two contexts: crypto-derivatives and stablecoins. Collateral for derivatives is very important and assumes the form of an 'initial margin', the one that has to be posted initially, and the 'variation margin', the collateral that has to be posted on a daily basis, depending on the variations in the value of derivatives. This collateral has to be very liquid to reduce associated liquidity and counterparty risks, and the role and rules of clearing houses are extremely important to pursue this objective. There may be the risk that non-regulated market infrastructures accept highly illiquid collateral, contributing to increased systemic risk.

At the same time, the quality of collateral assets comes into play with regard to stablecoins. If stablecoins are characterized as MMFs operating in the cryptoeconomy, it is extremely important for them to maintain high levels of liquidity in the short term in order to pursue stability.[187] While regulators strengthened the regulation of MMFs in the aftermath of the financial crisis, stablecoins are currently not regulated; therefore, the reserves backing their value are extremely unstable.[188] This not only affects shadow central banking scenarios (as highlighted in Chapter 4)[189] but can also involve crypto shadow banking ones. Therefore, stablecoins operating as MMFs can 'break the buck' and freely invest their reserves as they prefer. This is a major concern, particularly in the context of the potential global schemes that big-tech giants may develop with the support of systemic banks. The significant problems experienced by Terra UST in May 2022, 'breaking the buck' and plummeting to $0.23, showed the danger of stablecoins as MMFs, and the risks for the whole cryptoeconomy.[190]

The IMF highlighted the liquidity risk in relation to the high concentration observable in the context of lending platforms and their liquidity providers.[191] Here, if demand for borrowing a crypto-asset increases, the utilization rate (measuring how much of the liquidity for a particular crypto-asset has been loaned out on each DeFi platform) for its liquidity pool increases accordingly.[192] In a scenario where the utilization rate is particularly high, there could be problems related to redemptions, in a

---

[186] On the role of toxic assets in the financial crisis of 2008, see William Poole, 'Causes and Consequences of the Financial Crisis of 2007–2009' (2010) 33 HarvJL&PubPol'y 421.

[187] See generally Hilary J. Allen, 'Money Market Fund Reform Viewed through a Systemic Risk Lens' (2010) 11 JBus&SecL 87. See also Charles K. Whitehead, 'Size Matters: Commercial Banks and the Capital Markets' (2015) 76 OhioStLJ 765.

[188] See Matt Levine, 'Put the Money Fund on the Blockchain' (*Bloomberg*, 4 September 2019) <https://www.bloomberg.com/opinion/articles/2019-09-04/put-the-money-fund-on-the-blockchain> accessed 26 April 2022.

[189] See Chapter 4, Section III.E.

[190] See Mark Gongloff, 'At Least There's a Bull Market in Death Spirals' (*Bloomberg*, 11 May 2022) <https://www.bloomberg.com/opinion/articles/2022-05-11/from-staglation-to-terra-ust-a-bull-market-in-death-spirals> accessed 14 May 2022.

[191] See IMF, *Global Financial Stability Report 2022* (n 10) 79.

[192] Ibid.

situation where multiple depositors withdraw their assets at the same time.[193] Because on average half of the deposits are provided by fewer than ten accounts, an idiosyncratic withdrawal of funds executed by any of those large depositors could significantly affect the platform's liquidity.[194]

C. Technology-Related Risks

The security of the networks and the reliability of smart contracts and more generally DLT technology are additional problems afflicting the technological space. This is particularly relevant for market infrastructures, such as crypto-exchanges, as well as clearing houses and financial institutions operating in the space, including lending platforms, and custodians. Any organization is exposed to the risks of bugs in the system or, for example, smart-contract failures. A further common problem is cybersecurity and inherent exposure to hacker attacks. In 2021, cyberattacks grew dramatically and generally involved compromised wallet keys, fallacies in computer code, and scams directly perpetrated by developers.[195]

Cyberattacks generate significant losses and could lead to the collapse of entire platforms.[196] Beyond the loss generated by the theft, cyberattacks affect the reputation of a platform, which will often suffer significant withdrawals by depositors who are concerned about their potential inability to redeem their deposits.[197] In light of this, cyberattacks are especially dangerous when the point of fragility is a financial conglomerate managing relevant amounts. In such a scenario, technological risks may become an especially strong cause of systemic risk when compared to the traditional systems, due to the sector's total reliance on technology.

In April 2019 the trading platform Bitmex, which specializes in trading Bitcoin-leveraged products, experienced a problem with its derivative contracts. A programming error led to automatic deleveraging as a consequence of the increase in the price of Bitcoin, causing significant losses for investors.[198] Similar problems have been seen in traditional finance, too. The 1987 Wall Street Crash, and later flash crashes, such as the one in May 2010, prove the fragility of the financial system when it is coupled with technology. To mitigate these risks, the SEC introduced the so-called circuit breakers, as a way to break market volatility and limit shocks.[199] In comparison with traditional

---

[193] Ibid.
[194] Ibid.
[195] Ibid.
[196] Ibid. In 2022, the losses related to cyberattacks amounted to $3.7 billion. See Chainanalysis, '2022 Biggest Year Ever for Crypto Hacking with $3.8 Billion Stolen, Primarily from DeFi Protocols and by North Korea-linked Attackers' (1 February 2023) <https://blog.chainalysis.com/reports/2022-biggest-year-ever-for-crypto-hacking/> accessed 26 April 2023.
[197] Ibid.
[198] William Suberg, 'BitMEX to Compensate Users Affected by Unforeseen Auto-Deleveraging after Bitcoin Bullrun' (*Cointelegraph*, 4 April 2019) <https://cointelegraph.com/news/bitmex-to-compensate-users-affected-by-unforeseen-auto-deleveraging-after-bitcoin-bullrun> accessed 26 April 2022.
[199] SEC, 'Investor Bulletin: Measures to Address Market Volatility' (1 July 2012) <https://www.sec.gov/oiea/investor-alerts-bulletins/investor-alerts-circuitbreakersbulletinhtm.html> accessed 26 April 2022. On the role of circuit breakers in capital markets, see also Dell'Erba and Patti, 'The Monte dei Paschi di Siena Affaire' (n 102) 516–517.

finance, it would be much harder in the context of the non-regulated cryptoeconomy to design similarly effective mechanisms.

Specific governance mechanisms may affect the way new financial institutions work and the risks (even the financial ones) to which they are exposed. An example comes from on-chain lending with fully decentralized platforms, based on Proof of stake (PoS) blockchain. A recent study has shown that in systems allowing on-chain lending, the security of the consensus is in danger even if all the agents are rational and do not want to purportedly boycott the consensus protocol.[200] Therefore, the lack of governance mechanisms that are able to react to such conditions may prevent the emergence of trust in such lending platforms.

D. Rating Crypto-Assets

1. Credit Rating and Environmental Social Governance Rating

The concept of 'rating' is generally associated with the notion of credit rating and the activity of CRAs. CRAs have traditionally played a crucial role in finance because of their ability to provide investors (especially institutional ones) with an indication of the quality of specific securities that are issued from heterogeneous institutions.

CRAs target individual securities issued by sovereign states (providing sovereign ratings), corporations (providing corporate ratings).[201] The resulting credit rating exclusively reflects the probability of default. Credit ratings are particularly relevant for regulated financial institutions, such as banks, pension funds, and insurance and reinsurance companies. They provide a simple way for the regulator to measure the credit risk on their balance sheets. Assuming that credit ratings are accurate and reliable, they are a tool to avoid excessive risk-taking and control systemic risk, thereby ensuring financial stability. The financial crisis of 2008 cast doubt on the accuracy of credit ratings as a measure of risk and resulted in regulatory scrutiny and action. In addition to self-regulatory initiatives, both the EU and the US strengthened the oversight of rating agencies.[202]

In recent years, the new market developments regarding sustainability and technology created new challenges when evaluating risks and quality. Therefore, new concepts of 'rating' have emerged and the automatic association between the words (and underlying concepts) of 'credit' and 'rating' has become more nuanced. This, however, creates more uncertainty about the actual meaning of the concept of 'rating' in the fields of technology and sustainability. Credit ratings and CRAs still play the most prominent role in the financial industry, but this hierarchy may rapidly change.

The environmental social governance (ESG) ratings offer a relevant example. Sustainability strategies were largely a niche field, until larger asset managers, such as BlackRock Inc. and Vanguard Group, started adding sustainability products to their offerings. Indeed, ESG assets under management have witnessed tremendous

---

[200] See Tarun Chitra, 'Competitive Equilibria between Staking and On-Chain Lending' (*arXiv*, 5 February 2020) <https://arxiv.org/abs/2001.00919> accessed 26 April 2022.
[201] See Aline Darbellay, *Regulating Credit Rating Agencies* (Elgar 2013) 31.
[202] Ibid, 68 ff.

growth in the past decade and it is by far the fastest growing smart-beta strategy,[203] with annual growth in excess of 70 per cent.[204] Global sustainable investments reached $35 trillion in 2021 and are set to rise to 50 trillion by 2025.[205] Beyond the private asset management industry, sustainability has taken a prominent role in sovereign wealth funds. In particular, the Government Pension Fund of Norway has invested more than $1 trillion in accordance with a responsible investment strategy,[206] owning more than 1 per cent of all the shares in the world.[207] However, the assessment is not just retrospective: several recent surveys suggest that millennials have a high interest in adding ESG assets to their portfolio. Based on upcoming demographic shifts, this means that sustainable investing may continue to attract large asset inflows.[208]

With the increasing relevance of sustainability and ESG investments, ESG ratings are becoming a fundamental tool to implement effective sustainable practices within the markets, requiring new regulatory intervention. ESG ratings represent an attempt to measure the impact of business activity on the environment and society and to assess the strength of the governance framework, emphasizing the importance of non-financial metrics.[209] Consistent with any other rating, ESG ratings respond to the need to provide an accurate measure of an increasingly important dimension in the financial industry. However, different from credit ratings, where a correlation of 99 per cent is found between Moody's and S&P, in the ESG space the study finds an average correlation of 61 per cent.[210] This highlights a lack of consensus when assessing the ESG quality of a company and its business, and the need to pursue a higher degree of harmonization.

ESG ratings significantly differ from credit ratings in many respects. First, they target entire companies because they assess overall business activities. Hence, all securities issued by the same entity, both equity and debt instruments, are identically treated for the purposes of ESG because both instruments are evaluated based on the sustainability of the company's business. The ESG quality measurement is a much

---

[203] A smart-beta strategy is an investment strategy aiming to capture specific investment factors or market inefficiencies in a rule-based manner: see iShares, 'What Is Smart Beta?' <https://www.ishares.com/us/education/smart-beta> accessed 26 April 2022.

[204] Bank of America, 'ESG from A to Z: Global Primer' (8 November 2019) (on file with author).

[205] See Bloomberg Intelligence, 'ESG Assets May Hit $53 Trillion by 2025, a Third of Global AUM' (23 February 2021) <https://www.bloomberg.com/professional/blog/esg-assets-may-hit-53-trillion-by-2025-a-third-of-global-aum/> accessed 26 April 2022.

[206] World Economic Forum, 'Norway's massive sovereign-wealth fund sets net-zero goals' (23 September 2022) <https://www.weforum.org/agenda/2022/09/norways-massive-sovereign-wealth-fund-sets-net-zero-goal/> accessed 26 April 2023.

[207] The Economist, 'Norway's Sovereign-Wealth Fund Passes the $1trn Mark' (23 September 2017) <https://www.economist.com/finance-and-economics/2017/09/23/norways-sovereign-wealth-fund-passes-the-1trn-mark> accessed 26 April 2022.

[208] See Alexander Gelfand, 'The ESG Generation Gap: Millennials and Boomers Split on Their Investing Goals (*Stanford GSB*, 10 November 2022) <https://www.gsb.stanford.edu/insights/esg-generation-gap-millennials-boomers-split-their-investing-goals> accessed 2 May 2023.

[209] For a general analysis see IOSCO, 'Environmental, Social and Governance (ESG) Ratings and Data Products Providers' (November 2021) <https://www.iosco.org/library/pubdocs/pdf/IOSCOPD690.pdf> accessed 29 April 2022.

[210] Florian Berg, Julian Fritz Kölbel, and Roberto Rigobon, 'Aggregate Confusion: The Divergence of ESG Ratings' (2019) MIT Sloan Research Paper No. 5822-19, 3 <https://papers.ssrn.com/sol3/papers.cfm?abstract_id=3438533> accessed 26 April 2022.

more multifaceted and complex task when compared to the estimation of credit risk. It represents a challenge for both market actors to develop a reliable and accurate methodology and for regulators to provide an adequate legal framework that is aligned with their mandate.

The problem of measuring in a reliable manner, coupled with the lack of standardization, underlies the risk of making significant misallocations of financial resources—ultimately contributing to increasing systemic risk—as well as the opportunity for unscrupulous bad-faith market actors to defraud investors. These two problems relate to different regulatory dimensions and competences, and ultimately to different regulatory mandates.

In the industry of ESG data providers, some market leaders have emerged. Among them, MSCI is considered the most prominent, as it leveraged its existing strong franchise in the indexing business. MSCI has been well known for producing the indexes MSCI World and ACWI and launched MSCI World ESG Leaders in October 2007[211] and MSCI ACWI ESG Leaders in June 2013.[212] MSCI is a spin-off of Morgan Stanley and has been in business since 1968.[213] Sustainalytics is a European-based research and rating firm founded in 1992[214] and exclusively focused on sustainability rating businesses, with a major stake held by Morningstar, which acquired 40 per cent of the company in 2016. Refinitiv is a London-based spin-off from Reuters, formerly the financial and risk business of Thomson Reuters. Previously controlled by Blackstone,[215] Refinitiv has been acquired by the London Stock Exchange Group (LSEG) with the purpose of creating leading market infrastructure for the future.[216] Its focus is on 'financial markets data and infrastructure, with a host of technology platforms, software and data and insights'.[217] Robeco Sam is a Swiss asset management company founded in 1995 and is devoted only to sustainable investments; S&P Global recently agreed to acquire Robeco Sam's ESG rating business.[218] Although the companies have different core businesses, they target the same customer base of institutional investors.

---

[211] Morgan Stanley Capital International, 'MSCI World ESG Leaders Index (USD)' (29 April 2022) <https://www.msci.com/documents/10199/db88cb95-3bf3-424c-b776-bfdcca67d460> accessed 29 April 2022.

[212] Morgan Stanley Capital International, 'MSCI ACWI ESG Leaders Index (USD)' (29 April 2022) <https://www.msci.com/documents/10199/9a760a3b-4dc0-4059-b33e-fe67eae92460> accessed 29 April 2022.

[213] Will Kenton, 'MSCI Inc.' (*Investopedia*, updated 29 March 2023) <https://www.investopedia.com/terms/m/msci.asp> accessed 26 April 2023.

[214] Sustainalytics, 'About us' <https://www.sustainalytics.com/about-us/#> accessed 29 April 2022.

[215] John Foley, 'Breakingviews—Thomson Reuters Beats Blackstone in Refinitiv Deal' (*Reuters*, 1 August 2019) <https://www.reuters.com/article/us-refinitiv-m-a-breakingviews/breakingviews-thomson-reuters-beats-blackstone-in-refinitiv-deal-idUSKCN1UR501> accessed 26 April 2022.

[216] Thomson Reuters, 'Thomson Reuters Announces Closing of Sale of Refinitiv to London Stock Exchange Group' (29 January 2021) <https://www.thomsonreuters.com/en/press-releases/2021/january/thomson-reuters-announces-closing-of-sale-of-refinitiv-to-london-stock-exchange-group.html> accessed 26 April 2022.

[217] Refinitiv, 'Meet Refinitiv' (1 October 2018) <https://www.refinitiv.com/perspectives/ai-digitalization/meet-refinitiv/> accessed 26 April 2022.

[218] Billy Nauman, 'S&P Acquires ESG Ratings Arm of RobecoSAM' (*Financial Times*, 21 November 2019) <https://www.ft.com/content/098258d6-0bc6-11ea-bb52-34c8d9dc6d84> accessed 26 April 2022.

2. Rating Analysis in the Cryptoeconomy

Overall, the rating analysis in the context of crypto-assets is much less developed than the sustainability analysis and, therefore, does not benefit from an equally established debate, at the financial metrics and non-financial metrics level, which are important in the context of ESG and sustainability. Expressing a rating of all the new financial instruments in this new technological ecosystem seems very arduous at the moment and established CRAs have not expressed an interest in developing an adequate level of expertise in this field, whether it be for a credit rating or any other form of rating.

Different initiatives aimed at rating ICOs or more broadly crypto-assets (such as Crypto Assets Ratings[219], Weiss Ratings, CryptoCompare, and Messari) emerged at the start-up level. Morningstar is the only established market actor showing a concrete plan to enter the business of credit rating for the cryptoeconomy. In October 2019, Morningstar announced its plan to develop an evaluation system for debt securities issued in the form of a token on blockchain infrastructures.[220]

When associated with the cryptoeconomy, the concept of rating becomes vague and inconsistent. Specific examples are helpful to clarify this emerging confusion. The Crypto Rating Council (CRC), for example, describes itself as a 'Leading crypto financial services firms committed to practical compliance with the U.S. securities laws'.[221] The CRC Securities Framework Assets Ratings assess the probability that a specific financial instrument may fall under the scope of American securities regulation.[222] Therefore, what CRC Securities Framework Assets Ratings calls a 'rating' does not relay the typical concepts of 'value' or 'risk'; rather, these ratings refer to a legal rating, that is, the likelihood that American securities laws apply to that specific financial instrument. Crypto Assets Ratings combines qualitative and quantitative factors to assess the 'risk and the potential performance' of a crypto-asset.[223] ICObench rates ICOs through a network of 'experts', and has developed its own methodology. According to its website, 'Rating is given in combination of: our assessment algorithm that uses more than 20 different criteria on which each ICO can earn more than 30 points and the rating the independent experts give to the ICO following our rating methodology suggestions'.[224] However, it is unclear what the ICObench rating indeed attempts to measure. Wise Crypto Ratings provides a rating which is the result of a score calculated on the basis of four main categories, including 'Technology', 'Security', 'Use Case & Product', and 'Core Team, Partnerships & Developers'.

An antecedent in finance is helpful to understand the importance of developing reliable rating measures. So-called Catastrophe Bonds (CAT) experienced significant

---

[219] See Crypto Assets Ratings <https://www.cryptoassetrating.com/> accessed 26 April 2022.

[220] See Michael Del Castillo, 'Morningstar Is Building a Blockchain Bridge to the $117 Trillion Debt Securities Industry' (*Forbes*, 1 October 2019) <https://www.forbes.com/sites/michaeldelcastillo/2019/10/01/morningstar-is-building-a-blockchain-bridge-to-the-117-trillion-debt-securities-industry/#3cee17703612> accessed 26 April 2022 (hereafter Del Castillo, 'Morningstar Is Building a Blockchain Bridge').

[221] Crypto Rating Council, '01–Who We Are' <https://www.cryptoratingcouncil.com/> accessed 26 April 2022.

[222] Crypto Rating Council, 'CRC Securities Framework Asset Ratings' <https://www.cryptoratingcouncil.com/asset-ratings> accessed 26 April 2022.

[223] See Crypto Rating Council, 'Rating Model' <https://www.cryptoassetrating.com/home/ratingmodel> accessed 26 April 2022.

[224] See ICObench <https://icobench.com/faq> accessed 26 April 2022.

growth after the development of more reliable credit rating methodologies.[225] Crypto-assets and the cryptoeconomy may experience a similar trend, benefiting from the development of reliable financial and non-financial metrics reflected in credit ratings as well as other categories of ratings. Not only would ratings unlock additional opportunities in a market that is quantified at more than $100 trillion,[226] but they would also provide more clarity and build expertise in a still underdeveloped field. There may be significant underdevelopment with respect to crypto-asset ratings, specifically their credit rating, notwithstanding the growth at the business level, in particular with the design of structured crypto-assets.

In such a scenario, there may be significant problems, mostly due to the impossibility of identifying those financial instruments which could be a significant source of risk in future economic paradigms and where technology could potentially play an increasingly relevant role.

The problem of measuring in a reliable manner, coupled with the lack of standardization, underlies the risk of significant misallocation of financial resources and the opportunity for unscrupulous bad-faith market actors to defraud investors. These two problems relate to different regulatory dimensions and competences (a macro- and a micro-prudential one), and ultimately to different regulatory mandates.[227]

E. From Speculation to the Creation of Financial Conglomerates

Speculation has been a dominant trait in these first years of the cryptoeconomy. However, the increasing interest in the cryptoeconomy gradually involved various societal constituencies, including established financial institutions and tech giants. In this process, private funds certainly played an essential part, especially at the very first stages of the cryptoeconomy. Private funds entering the market of the cryptoeconomy established two different strategies. Some of them intended to directly invest in cryptocurrencies, while others invested in start-ups. The significant losses experienced in cryptocurrencies led the funds to invest in stablecoins, for hedging purposes; namely, to cover losses due to significant cryptocurrency exposure. For the same reason of speculation, private fund—in particular hedge fund—investments may be the most important factor driving the development in crypto-derivatives.

Speculation was also a main driver for the major investment banks, including J.P. Morgan, Goldman Sachs, and Bank of America, to explore ways to enter the cryptoeconomy, due to increased bank demand for cryptocurrency and interest in blockchain networks and technology.[228]

---

[225] Szlvie Bouriaux and Richard MacMinn, 'Securitization of Catastrophe Risk: New Developments in Insurance-Linked Securities and Derivatives' (2009) 32 JInsurIssues 1, 2.
[226] Del Castillo, 'Morningstar Is Building a Blockchain Bridge' (n 220).
[227] See 'What's Next?' Section II.B.
[228] See Joseph Young, 'Big Banks Are Investing Heavily in Blockchain and Crypto: $364 Billion Investment Firm' (*CNN*, 12 May 2018) <https://www.ccn.com/big-banks-are-investing-heavily-in-blockchain-and-crypto-364-billion-investment-firm/> accessed 26 April 2022.

Finally, the most recent stage of the cryptoeconomy has attracted the interest of tech giants who entered the banking sphere.[229] As considered in Chapter 4, the Libra Association showed the potential of a consortium federating several giants belonging to heterogeneous economic sectors. This initiative, relevant for central banking, may be the prelude to new forms of alliances between tech giants and investment banks for mutual interests related to developing new entrepreneurial activities in crypto shadow banking as well as the traditional banking sector. And to some extent, this is already happening. In 2019, Google announced its intention to offer 'smart' checking accounts, with the support of Citigroup and Stanford Federal Credit Union, and Apple launched a credit card with Goldman Sachs.[230] Potential developments in a pure cryptoeconomy are likely to happen. Trends in open banking may accelerate this process.

The emergence of tech giants and their increasing prevalence in the cryptoeconomy, as well as the creation of such potential alliances both inside and outside the cryptoeconomy, necessarily leads to a reconsideration of the notion of a financial conglomerate, or systemically important financial institution (SIFI)—a notion introduced with the Dodd Frank Act—and 'too-big-to-fail' entities. In addition to 'too-big-to-fail', further problems have emerged in relation to the global nature of new entities, such as 'too-interconnected-to-regulate'/'too-interconnected-to-fail'[231] and 'too-big-to-regulate'.[232]

Technological developments may also increase the possibility that new financial conglomerates emerge, in three distinct ways. First, the number of new start-ups has grown and has become a dominant presence in the past few years. Ethereum became the major platform for programming smart contracts and may retain this economically dominant position in the future, although new competitors are gradually emerging. Another source of concern is the growth of multi-service crypto-trading and crypto-lending platforms, which are unregulated and lack insurance schemes related to custodial activities, thereby exposing the system to significantly increased counterparty risks.[233] This may also be the case for investment services in the cryptoeconomy, which may become as dominant as investment banks in traditional finance. Second, new dominant tech companies may create joint ventures with established systemically important financial institutions. Third, SIFIs (including corporations such as Google and Meta) may implement specific technologies to leverage their dominant networks.

---

[229] Maria Aspan, 'Why Every Company Wants to Look Like a Bank—Without Becoming One' (*Fortune*, 18 November 2019) <https://fortune.com/2019/11/18/big-tech-banking-regulation-apple-goldman-sachs-google-citigroup/> accessed 26 April 2022.

[230] David Z. Morris and Robert Hackett, 'Should "Fintech" Fear Big Tech's Push into Banking?' (*Fortune*, 20 November 2019) <https://fortune.com/2019/11/20/should-fintech-fear-big-techs-push-into-banking/> accessed 26 April 2022.

[231] See generally Anupam Chander and Randall Costa, 'Clearing Credit Default Swaps: A Case Study in Global Legal Convergence' (2010) 10 ChiJIntlL 639.

[232] See Peter Fox-Penner, 'Too Big to Regulate?' (*The Baseline Scenario*, 16 January 2010) <http://baselinescenario.com/2010/01/16/too-big-to-regulate> accessed 26 April 2022. See also Lawrence G. Baxter, 'Betting Big: Value, Caution and Accountability in an Era of Large Banks and Complex Finance' (2012) 31 RevBank&FinL 765.

[233] Acheson and Moore, 'Crypto Lending 101' (n 18) 10. See also Marco Dell'Erba, 'Crypto-Trading Platforms as Exchanges' (2023) MichStLRev (forthcoming) <https://papers.ssrn.com/sol3/papers.cfm?abstract_id=4405361> accessed 26 April 2023.

III. Regulatory Measures to Build a Sustainable Cryptoeconomic Ecosystem

The characterization of specific developments taking place in the cryptoeconomy as 'crypto shadow banking' is not a formal one, but it impacts how regulators should consider these changes. Specifically, regulators should address certain concerns with adequate *ex ante* measures. Regulators should reconsider past experiences and reassess their *ex post* reactions as a starting point from which to re-adapt existing strategies to this nascent paradigm.

A. Regulating Stablecoins as MMFs

Stablecoins acting as MMFs in the cryptoeconomy and DeFi, including Tether and Terra, experienced significant problems and 'broke the buck' multiple times. The 'death spiral' of Terra UST in 2022 was especially dramatic, highlighting the risks posed by stablecoins to the whole cryptoeconomy, and triggering major concerns among regulators.[234] This situation shares similarities with the financial crisis of 2008, when MMFs contributed to it in different ways.[235]

Consistent with the measures debated in Europe and United States for regulating MMFs at that time, regulators should act by extending MMF requirements to stablecoins, to mitigate liquidity risks and major systemic risks. In the aftermath of the financial crisis the European Union passed the European MMF Regulation,[236] which introduced stringent rules on the composition of MMFs' portfolios, for the purpose of making MMFs more resilient and limiting contagion. In particular, it provides rules on eligible assets, the maturities of assets, liquidity, diversification, and the credit quality of both issuers and money market instruments. Also, the MMF Regulation provides daily and weekly liquidity requirements that MMFs have to meet in order to strengthen their ability to deal with redemptions and mitigated procyclical sales.

In the United States, the reform of MMF regulation took place in two stages, which include: (i) a first series of reforms designed after the financial crisis of 2008 to make MMFs more resilient, looking at a reduction of the interest rate and credit and liquidity risks of their portfolio; and (ii) a second series of reforms adopted in June 2014 and entered into force in October 2016.[237] The rules identify three categories of MMFs, including retail, governmental, and institutional. Different from government and retail MMF, institutional MMFs are subject to the floating Net Asset Value (NAV) rule; therefore they don't have to maintain a fixed price of $1 per share, but their share

---

[234] Scott Chipolina, 'Terra Crisis Fans Regulatory Concerns over $180bn Stablecoin Market' (*Financial Times*, 11 May 2022) <https://www.ft.com/content/48d82c7a-495f-4d5e-a87a-a56bea58e760> accessed 30 May 2022.
[235] See Marcin Kacperczyk and Philipp Schnabl, 'How Safe Are Money Market Funds?' (2013) 128 QJEcon 1073.
[236] MMF Regulation (n 111).
[237] SEC, 'Money Market Funds' <https://www.sec.gov/spotlight/money-market.shtml> accessed 26 April 2022.

price depends on market fluctuations. Consistent with the European approach, the new rules enhanced portfolio diversification, disclosure, and stress-testing requirements, while also strengthening reporting requirements.

Regulators should consider adapting such requirements and extending them to stablecoin arrangements operating as MMFs in DeFi, where possible and relevant. This would drastically reduce liquidity and systemic risks, increasing the resilience of stablecoin arrangements.

In addition to MMFs, as mentioned in Chapter 4, it might be the case that some stablecoin arrangements trigger commercial bank-like concerns, especially in those cases where they have only partial reserve backing, leading to the same issues as fractional reserve banks.[238] In these cases, stablecoins could be subject to banking regulatory measures, which would include capital requirements, liquidity requirements, a legal claim, and a backstop protecting coin holders.[239] However, this approach to stablecoins adopting a banking angle should not consist in a simple extension of existing banking rules to stablecoins but rather in a smooth adaptation, that takes into account the different business models and implements appropriate levels of clarity, proportionality, and risk-based characteristics of potential approaches in this sense.[240]

B. Market Infrastructures

The regulation of market infrastructures remains an unsolved, key pillar. The levels of opacity surrounding market infrastructures in the cryptoeconomy are worse than those in traditional financial markets. In traditional financial markets, exchanges such as the New York Stock Exchange (NYSE), the London Stock Exchange (LSE), the Swiss Stock Exchange (SIX), and the Chicago Mercantile Exchange (CME), are reputed and established institutions. They are also self-regulatory organizations whose market practices are a successful example of 'private' self-regulation. In the post-crisis reforms, regulators intervened at the level of clearing houses to increase the levels of transparency in the post-trading phases, thereby reducing systemic risk.

In the context of the cryptoeconomy, the situation is more complex, because a lack of transparency affects both the trading and post-trading phases. For the specific purposes of this chapter, leaving aside the problem of the secondary market for cryptocurrencies as a form of tokenized equities, opacity in market infrastructures displays negative consequences at the derivative contracts level—the main source of leverage in the cryptoeconomy. While the CME offers a regulated framework for investing in crypto-derivatives, key exchanges remain rather opaque. The uncertainty surrounding the regulation of exchanges remains the main source of such uncertainty. The example of BitMex, its aggressive innovative strategies in creating and offering new products, and its leverage of up to 100 times makes clear the potential behind

---

[238] Eichengreen and Natraj, 'Stablecoins and CBDCs' (n 116).
[239] See Bank of England, 'Responses to the Bank of England's Discussion Paper on New Forms of Digital Money' (24 March 2022) Discussion Paper <https://www.bankofengland.co.uk/paper/2022/responses-to-the-bank-of-englands-discussion-paper-on-new-forms-of-digital-money> accessed 22 April 2022.
[240] Ibid.

these risks. Even more, the collapse of the crypto-exchange FTX in November 2022 was caused by the adoption of a risky business model implementing unscrupulous investment strategies, which included a conflict of interest arising from proprietary trading with its affiliate company Alameda Research, and the absence of proper corporate governance mechanisms. Under these circumstances the emergence of strong market discipline with some form of public intervention is necessary to address regulatory arbitrage and favour the establishment of reputed institutions.

A source of growing concern relates to crypto-lending activities. Regulators should take a position in order to extend the banking regulation to such entities and protect the whole system as well as individual investors. Adequate regulation would serve to bring much more clarity with regard to operational and financial risks, requiring the satisfaction of strict prerequisites in order to determine the reliability of the network's infrastructure. Further regulation should increase the overall transparency of their operations and ensure specific activities, such as custody, which at the moment are not ensured.

An emerging feature of market infrastructures (especially for crypto-exchanges) is their engagement in many different businesses, spanning from traditional crypto-exchanges, to custodial services, to the issuance of own financial products such as stablecoins. This situation is an unprecedented source of risk, with market infrastructure consisting of hybrid (and therefore) complex institutions that are leading many crucial businesses without clear regulation. The importance to the financial system of specific activities, such as custodial services, would require rigorous scrutiny in order to authorize, or qualify, such entities to perform such significant activities. New ventures as well as established financial institutions should comply with strict corporate governance requirements, aimed at minimizing conflicts of interest that may emerge, given the broad range of their operations. Furthermore, regulators should consider whether the engagement in many heterogeneous activities increases market risk, counterparty risk, operational risk and liquidity risk, thereby harming the entire financial system.[241]

American, European, and Swiss regulators are trying to bring more certainty to this context. As mentioned in Chapter 2, in Switzerland, the Federal Act on the Adaptation of Federal Law to Developments in Distributed Ledger Technology (DLT Law) attempts to solve some of the issues related to new market infrastructures. Under the DLT Law, DLT Trading systems are subject to most of the requirements provided for traditional trading facilities. According to Article 73a of the FMIA, a DLT trading facility is a facility for multilateral trading of DLT securities, which aims to simultaneously exchange offers between multiple participants and conclude contracts implementing non-discretionary rules.[242]

---

[241] See Arewa, 'Financial Markets and Networks' (n 184) 618.

[242] DLT trading facilities shall meet at least one of the following requirements must be fulfilled: it admits 'legal entities other than supervised financial institutions or private clients as participants' in accordance with art 73c (1); provides services 'of central custody of DLT securities based on uniform rules and procedures'; or provides services 'of clearing and settlement for transactions in DLT securities based on uniform rules and procedures'. See Silvan Thoma, 'Switzerland Strengthens Fintech and Blockchain Sector' (*PwC*, 15 September 2020) <https://www.pwc.ch/en/insights/fs/amending-act-DLT-blockchain.html> accessed 26 April 2022.

III. IMPLEMENTING A SUSTAINABLE CRYPTO-ECONOMY 349

Consistent with this initiative, the European Parliament passed a Regulation on a pilot regime for market infrastructures based on DLT.[243] In addition, the proposed MiCAR will bring more clarity, by imposing on trading platforms compliance with general obligations for crypto-service providers (which include a disclosure of potential conflicts of interests), as well as with specific obligations such as impossibility to deal on their own account in the platform that they operate, and to guarantee operational resilience.[244]

In the United States, the recently proposed Digital Commodity Exchange Act (DCEA) seeks to create a 'single, opt-in national regulatory framework for digital commodity trading platforms' that will be regulated by the US Commodity Futures Trading Commission (CFTC). Under the DCEA, 'digital commodity' means any form of fungible intangible personal property that can be exclusively possessed and transferred person-to-person without necessary reliance on an intermediary, and which does not represent a financial interest in a company, partnership, or investment vehicle.

Significant concerns emerged also in relation to custody, with an emphasis on broker-dealers.[245] After identifying different non-custodial broker-dealer models,[246] the SEC highlighted that in the case of a custodial broker-dealer model 'the same fundamental elements of the broker-dealer financial responsibility rules apply', while also acknowledging that 'market participants wishing to custody digital asset securities may find it challenging to comply with the broker-dealer financial responsibility rules without putting in place significant technological enhancements and solutions unique to digital asset securities'.[247] In December 2020, the SEC issued guidelines regarding the custody of digital asset securities by 'special purpose' broker-dealers in order to encourage innovation around the application of the Securities Exchange Act to digital asset securities. In this document, the SEC opened to the possibility that special purpose broker-dealer engages in custodial activities related to crypto-assets as long as it refrains from undertaking any activities pertaining to 'traditional' securities.[248] The

---

[243] Regulation (EU) 2022/858 of 30 May 2022 on a pilot regime for market infrastructures based on distributed ledger technology [2022] OJ L 151/1.
[244] See MiCAR (n 153) art 68.
[245] SEC, 'Joint Staff Statement on Broker-Dealer Custody of Digital Asset Securities' (8 July 2019) <https://www.sec.gov/news/public-statement/joint-staff-statement-broker-dealer-custody-digital-asset-securities> accessed 26 April 2022.
[246] Here, the SEC distinguishes three cases. First, 'the broker-dealer sends the trade-matching details (e.g., identity of the parties, price, and quantity) to the buyer and issuer of a digital asset security—similar to a traditional private placement—and the issuer settles the transaction bilaterally between the buyer and issuer, away from the broker-dealer. In this case, the broker-dealer instructs the customer to pay the issuer directly and instructs the issuer to issue the digital asset security to the customer directly (e.g., the customer's "digital wallet")'. Second, 'a broker-dealer facilitates "over-the counter" secondary market transactions in digital asset securities without taking custody of or exercising control over the digital asset securities. In this example, the buyer and seller complete the transaction directly and, therefore, the securities do not pass through the broker-dealer facilitating the transaction'. Third, 'a secondary market transaction involves a broker-dealer introducing a buyer to a seller of digital asset securities through a trading platform where the trade is settled directly between the buyer and seller'. Ibid.
[247] Ibid.
[248] SEC, 'Custody of Digital Asset Securities by Special Purpose Broker-Dealers' (Release No. 34-90788, 23 December 2020) <https://www.sec.gov/rules/policy/2020/34-90788.pdf> accessed 26 April 2022. For an overview of the approach developed by FINRA on these topics, see Nicholas J. Losurdo and Christopher Grobbel, 'FINRA Sheds Light on Path to Digital Asset Security Broker Registration' (21 November

abovementioned February SEC 2023 consultation will bring further clarity in the area of custodial activities.

Market infrastructures—and more generally market actors involved in the cryptoeconomy—should avoid to replicate a TBTF model that generates uncontrolled systemic risks. This problem will be further elaborated in section III.D.

C. Crypto-Financial Products

Offering a more regulated and internationally harmonized framework is fundamental to controlling unintended risks and establishing sustainable market practices that support the development of the cryptoeconomy. Achievement of this objective would require an increased ability to attract investors that are not exclusively interested in speculative manoeuvres, since they may need to recur to derivatives and leverage for hedging purposes. This is especially important in situations of extreme volatility, as well as in times of stable undervaluation of the crypto-assets. Where there is extreme volatility, speculative movements in crypto-derivatives amplify risks because of high financial leverage.

Uncertainty is also a problem for stablecoins. As mentioned earlier in this chapter, stablecoins (and their regulation) are relevant for both the shadow central banking and the crypto shadow banking dimensions. If stablecoins act exclusively or in part as crypto-MMFs, then they need to be treated as MMFs. Otherwise, they would be MMFs that can 'break the buck', acting as any other investment vehicle that does not have to maintain stable levels of liquidity.[249] To address these risks, stablecoins should be subject to strict policies related to the investment of their reserve in high-quality assets. Adrian and Mancini-Griffoli, of the IMF, suggest further important measures. Regarding the ratio between funds received by clients and issued money, the issued money should never exceed such funds.[250] Furthermore, issuers should not pledge assets as collateral for loans and they should maintain sufficient capital, ensuring full redemption of client funds, even in adverse market conditions.[251]

D. Financial Conglomerates

Another potential issue is the one of financial conglomerates. The problem of 'too-big-to-fail' (TBTF) and entities that are 'too interconnected' has emerged in the history of capitalism, in most cases strictly related to the shadow banking networks. TBTF entities typically encompass credit institutions that have adopted 'universal' banking in both the US and the EU, by providing a broad range of services.[252] They

---

2022) <https://www.goodwinlaw.com/en/insights/publications/2022/11/11_21-finra-sheds-light-on-path-to-digital-asset> accessed 26 April 2023.

[249] Adrian and Mancini-Griffoli, 'The Rise of Digital Money' (n 120) 6.
[250] Ibid.
[251] Ibid.
[252] See Yesha Yadav, 'Too-Big-to-Fail Shareholders' (2018) 103 MinnLRev 587, 604.

also maintain ties with investment funds as well as significant interests in their proprietary trading activities. However, the vast majority of TBTF entities encompass broker-dealers, insurance companies, government-sponsored enterprises, and hedge funds.[253] Credit and financial institutions were often interconnected, and in the aftermath of the financial crisis of 2008, measures such as the Volcker Rule intended to break this interconnection and halt any conflicts of interest among banks that invest in investment funds' proprietary trading.[254]

The way regulators reacted in the aftermath of the financial crisis of 2008 represents an *ex post* approach triggered by a shock in the financial system, and in particular by shadow banking. This happened in Europe and the United States. European regulators provided an entirely new regulatory framework, which included the Alternative Investment Fund Manager Directive (AIFMD), the Short Selling Regulation (SSR), the European Market Infrastructure Regulation (EMIR), and the creation of the European Systemic Risk Board (ESRB) and the Single Resolution Board (SRB). In the United States there were similar initiatives, the majority of them falling under the umbrella of the Dodd–Frank Act, which included the Private Fund Investment Advisers Registration Act of 2010 (PFIARA), and the recently amended Volker Rule. Even in the United States, an institutional redesign led to the creation of the Systemic Risk Council as well as the attribution of the resolution authority (with the Dodd–Frank Act) to the Federal Deposit Insurance Corporation (FDIC).

Although the concept of decentralization is often associated with DLT, specific trends prove that concentration affects the cryptoeconomy at various levels. For example, mining pools are geographically concentrated, and they are themselves intermediaries.[255] Up until now the cryptoeconomy has favoured the establishment of new intermediaries and market infrastructures. And on a par with this trend, even crypto shadow banking may lead to the faster creation of new financial conglomerates when compared to traditional finance. Tech giants became dominant in a very short time: Google and Facebook were created, respectively, in 1998 and in 2004. Foundational technologies such as the internet in the past and DLT now contribute to the accelerated key changes in the capitalist framework.

As mentioned under Section II.C, new financial conglomerates may be created in three different ways, each presenting specific problems that require attention. In the first scenario, where a start-up becomes a giant, different issues will likely manifest. Consider the example of Ethereum, a dominant 'service provider' serving as a platform for the vast majority of developers creating smart contract-based applications. Notwithstanding the properties of decentralization generally associated with DLT ecosystems, the extent to which a systemic shock (in particular one that is technological in nature) may affect the functioning of an entire network is unknown. In the same sphere, the possibility that specific service providers may become new giants in

---

[253] See Nouriel Roubini and Stephen Mihm, *Crisiseconomics: A Crash Course in the Future of Finance* (Penguin 2010) 223–230.

[254] See Charles K. Whitehead, 'The Volcker Rule and Evolving Financial Markets' (2011) 1 HarvBusLRev 39, 68.

[255] This theory is a work in progress. See Angela Walch, 'Intermediaries Who Must Not Be Named? A Legal & Policy Research Agenda for Crypto Miners' (21 November 2019) <https://www.youtube.com/watch?v=jywZcWoinVU> accessed 26 April 2022.

a naturally globalized cryptoeconomy poses different problems than the more classic 'too-big-to-fail' concerns. This may be the case of first movers investing in a broad range of activities in the context of the cryptoeconomy, who may enjoy the benefits of developing relevant activities on a global scale.

Tether, like other systemically important stablecoins, provides an example of potential conflicts of interest that would be difficult to understand in traditional finance. Tether shares common shareholders and management team with Bitfinex, one of the oldest and well-known crypto-exchanges in the industry. De facto, the same organization issued a stablecoin while also managing an exchange. It is not hard to imagine that similar conflicts of interest may easily develop in a lightly regulated environment, with the possibility that they might become systemic concerns in the near future. These potential conflicts of interest require an *ex ante* consideration and would require measures designed to prevent their formation and establishment, structuring a regulatory response that may adopt a 'Volcker Rule' style. This kind of regulatory intervention is part of what is commonly referred to as 'structural regulation', consisting of measures whose rationale is to preserve financial stability (especially in the banking sector) by limiting the range of activities that a credit institution can carry out.[256] Although institutions managing this kind of instruments are not banks (and Tether is not a bank), 'structural regulation' may still be an option, and would be beneficial in terms of limiting operational risks and conflicts of interest and increasing the overall stability of these organizations. As mentioned above, MiCAR aims to make it impossible for the provider of the trading platform to deal on its own account on the platform it operates. However, even more stringent regulations may be deemed necessary.

Market actors involved in artificial intelligence businesses as well as research and development provide a current example of tech giants developing strong cooperation with the established financial institutions. In the context of so-called open banking, as well as in other potential developments based on DLT, potential conflicts of interest in AI systemic institutions may become a systemic concern. For example, established financial institutions may be more fragile because of more direct exposure to technological risks. This would require the creation of methodologies created to anticipate the financial risks related to technology (a sort of 'technology stress-test'). Even in this area, the possibility of regulating the way in which tech giants, and more generally tech companies, operate with existing financial institutions may require more structured corporate governance measures, and some kinds of structural regulations. This would prevent the formation of conflicts of interest and would protect investors and shareholders, while preventing economic and systemic shocks.

Another possibility is that tech giants may enter the financial and banking industry, become systemically important financial institutions, and exploit loopholes because of the power of their existing networks. This would require a closer look at their corporate governance, more alert monitoring of the different types of financial operations and their implementation, and an extension of specific banking regulations, such as capital requirements and liquidity measures. The debate surrounding the issuance of the Libra Coin is a clear example of all these concerns. Libra exemplified the importance

---

[256] See Armour et al., *Principles of Financial Regulation* (n 101) 505–507.

of considerations from different spheres, where typical issues related to banking and financial regulation (the quality of the reserves, for example) co-exist with traditional corporate governance concerns such as mechanisms of accountability.[257]

E. The Discussion on Rating for Crypto-Assets

The problem of rating exists in any economic environment because it is related to the concept of value, which is relevant for two reasons. First, value comes into play at the level of risk. A reliable measure of risk is important to design adequate mechanisms of protection, such as risk dispersion in case of systemic shocks. So-called CAT Bonds are a clear example. They started to develop when reliable credit rating mechanisms were developed. Another example is financial collateral, representing an important measurement designed to control liquidity risks in day-to-day operations in many industries, such as credit derivatives. Second, value is relevant for setting precise strategies and goals in both the short and the long term.

Recent debates and developments on sustainability have made clear the relevance of such problems. The correct assessment of the risk, and the potential of a business in the long term, highlights the importance of both credit rating and other forms of rating, such as that in the ESG and sustainability contexts.

In the nascent cryptoeconomy, the lack of reliable rating systems may be detrimental to the effective implementation of this paradigm. The financial crisis of 2008 highlighted the difficulties CRAs face when rating ABSs and other complex financial instruments resulting from financial innovation and financial engineering, and now manifesting in the shadow banking system. As mentioned in Section II, these instruments played an important role in triggering the chain of events that severely affected the entire financial system. A report by the SEC highlighted that CRAs had been struggling with rating such products since 2006 because the complexity of these financial products posed significant difficulties for evaluating their credit risk.[258] The latest evolutions in finance pose ever greater difficulties, especially when compared to the difficulties faced in the era preceding the financial crisis of 2008.

In addition to financial engineering, new layers, such as technological developments and sustainability, have made the issuance of credit ratings much more complex. At the same time, developments in both sustainability and, in particular, technology demonstrate the difficulties of elaborating other categories of ratings when relying on non-financial metrics. It is currently extremely hard to predict how technological risks will be assessed, which kinds of measures should be taken into account, and how these categories relate to the creation of a credit rating. In fact, it is quite possible that new technological advances will present other forms of risks better captured by non-financial metrics, as in the context of sustainability.

---

[257] See Pistor, 'Written Statement' (n 172) 5–8. See Chapter 4, Section III.B.
[258] SEC, *Summary Report of Issues Identified in the Commission Staff's Examinations of Select Credit Rating Agencies* (July 2008) 12 <https://www.sec.gov/news/studies/2008/craexamination070808.pdf> accessed 26 April 2022.

To correct the lack of ratings, regulators should encourage the development of crypto-assets ratings and foster a debate, similar to what is happening in the context of sustainability. The developments in the ESG context may be helpful because of the analogies between the spheres of technological innovations and ESG, especially in terms of identifying appropriate measures functional to quantifying unpredictable risks in the context of the cryptoeconomy and DeFi.

A viable strategy for regulators would be the launch of public consultations. At relatively low cost, regulators could reach different societal constituencies, and involve private practices, or other parties with a significant lack of understanding and consensus. In this way, the contribution of heterogeneous stakeholders would serve to significantly advance the debate in this crucial area. Not only would public consultations promote the credibility of regulators in these new markets, but they would also be positive for stimulating the development of appropriate self-regulatory initiatives while promoting better public regulatory approaches. Previous instances have demonstrated the importance of relying on adequate self- and public regulation.

F. Facing Technological Risks in Crypto Shadow Banking

When approaching network security and cybersecurity, regulators have to take into account the emerging relevance of TechRisk, a new form of risk related to the great digitization of financial economy.[259] Regulators should approach TechRisk implications at different levels, from a corporate governance perspective and the broader angle of financial risks, and financial stability, especially when such risk is associated to SIFIs.[260] Consistent with the analysis in Chapter 4, the European DORA goes in the direction of strengthening the resilience of regulated financial institutions against cybersecurity risks.

To enhance the reliability of the technology and encourage its resilient development, another possibility would be to design new stress tests in order to create strategies that efficiently react to mistakes generated in the context of unstoppable smart contracts, or attacks of great relevance targeting systemic institutions.

Stress tests are a common practice when assessing the resilience of credit institutions and measuring their resistance to financial shocks. In the future, this framework will likely change under the pressure of new forces, such as climate change risks, which are, *per se*, extremely unpredictable.[261] Climate change risks pose an additional issue because the existing financial metrics do not anticipate future events. Although different in nature, technological risks are also highly unpredictable. The novelty of specific technologies, such as DLT and clouding, makes outcomes unpredictable. The crash of the DAO was one of the clearest signals of the fragility in the new technological ecosystem.

---

[259] See generally Ross P. Buckley, Douglas Arner, Dirk Zetzsche, and Eriks Selga, 'TECHRISK' (2020) SingJLS 35.
[260] Ibid, IIIA.
[261] Tobias Adrian, James Morsink, and Liliana Schumacher, 'Assessing Climate-Change Risk by Stress Testing for Financial Resilience' (*IMF Blog*, 5 February 2020) <https://blogs.imf.org/2020/02/05/assessing-climate-change-risk-by-stress-testing-for-financial-resilience/> accessed 26 April 2022.

Consistent with the famous theory of the black swan by Nassim Nicholas Taleb, stress testing would not be a way to predict what is by nature unpredictable, but it would contribute to achieving a higher level of systemic resilience.[262]

In the context of crypto shadow banking, the lack of regulation is an obstacle because there are no parameters guiding market participants. Therefore, at the moment there is no basis for concretely elaborating specific stress tests capable of assessing potential situations of emergency. After all, not only is the technology still unknown; so is the way the market is currently developing. In such a scenario, regulators should attempt to have a clearer picture of the characteristics and the volume of specific activities and to try to interact with the industry. To achieve stronger regulations, however, policy makers must first understand the interaction among specific actors, in particular trading platforms, crypto-lending platforms, and OTC desks. These institutions are not fully supervised, making it harder to understand the way the technological and financial practices are actually developing. These steps are fundamental to the identification of potential strategies to mitigate systemically risky future events and attempt to design new stress tests. The role of regulators in this field is essential because the private sector lacks adequate incentives.

G. Crypto Shadow Banking and Complexity

International finance was described as a complex adaptive system, in constant evolution under the pressure of the interactions happening at the level of its multiple subparts, which are also in constant evolution. In this context shadow central banking exemplifies how such evolutions lead to the transformation of existing financial networks (here shadow banking) and how this might impact the overall framework and functions within international finance.

Consistent with the conclusions on the relationship between shadow central banking and complexity provided in Chapter 4, crypto shadow banking raises questions relating to dynamic forms of regulation and the way central bankers and securities authorities—or more generally policy makers—should interpret specific changes happening in international finance and anticipate them.

From a structural perspective, crypto shadow banking highlights the importance of understanding the layers where transformation originates and propagates. Because of the strong functional nexus characterizing shadow banking and crypto shadow banking, the specific evolution of shadow banking in the sense of crypto shadow banking exemplifies the importance of identifying the source of changes and how these changes propagate. Although crypto shadow banking indisputably relies on a strong technological infrastructure, it is equally indisputable that many innovations are happening at the level of financial products (such as 'perpetual swaps' offered by certain crypto-exchanges) and at the level of financial processes or techniques (as in the case of tokenization and its conceptual relationship with securitization). Therefore, these innovations are originating at the level of traditional finance, which is still the

---

[262] See generally Nassim Nicholas Taleb, *The Black Swan* (2nd edn, Random House 2010).

conceptual centre for understanding the way certain changes happen. As mentioned at the beginning of this chapter, the technological layer operates on top of the 'traditional finance' layer.[263] The technological layer offers specific opportunities for testing and, in the best case scenario, developing and spreading new financial products and financial processes and techniques.

From a dynamic perspective, these transformations have the effect of significantly enlarging the network of market actors involved, potentially increasing the number and the intensity of the interactions. At a systemic level, increased interactions might lead to the further consequence of accelerating the evolutionary patterns emerging in international finance.

Conclusion

Technological innovations in financial markets are increasingly present and relevant. While technological advancements are generally a great opportunity for the economy and finance, they still bring specific risks. Such risks may depend on the intrinsic novelty of a new system and its reliance on different foundational infrastructures. At the same time, the way technological developments are absorbed and implemented by the financial system may raise concerns similar to those raised in the past.

The development of credit finance, as an alternative to banking credit, created a new paradigm that favours the establishment of shadow banking, or the network of financial institutions that systematically structure finance to generate new financial resources. The cryptoeconomy is increasingly permeating the financial system, with new instruments and processes, such as ICOs in entrepreneurial finance, as well as new market infrastructures and operations in the post-trading phase, such as clearing and settlement of financial instruments. At the same time, the overall ecosystem is developing schemes and practices that spread in traditional finance through long processes of market transformation under the pressure of law, economy, and finance. In particular, the new cryptoeconomy is replicating specific schemes that pre-existed shadow banking and are consistent with the market transformations experienced in traditional finance. This is leading to the establishment of a new network of financial institutions that systematically utilize specific financial instruments. This network, which this chapter termed 'crypto shadow banking', shares significant characteristics with traditional shadow banking. This new ecosystem is populated by new financial institutions that are implementing new technologies and new strategies in their business models, as well as established financial institutions and tech giants interested in entering these profitable markets.

The characterization of crypto shadow banking, while not a formal paradigm, should at least help regulators correctly understand the way this network will likely affect the cryptoeconomy and its future developments. Crypto shadow banking comes with old risks, allowing regulators to anticipate potential issues based on the problems that affected traditional finance in the decades up to the spectacular implosion

---

[263] See Introduction and Chapter 1, Section V.A.

of the financial crisis of 2008. Under the pressure of clear speculative trends, the cryptoeconomy favours the emergence of new financial institutions that create loans in the crypto space. New forms of derivatives and highly leveraged instruments are emerging in the market, favoured by the activity of crypto-private funds that are interested in higher returns in the current market conjuncture. This also leads to the emergence of new initiatives in response to the growing opportunities in the field of prime brokerage services, and the accompanying competition among market actors. All this comes with old problems, in particular the risk of new financial conglomerates, intensifying systemic risk levels. A further relevant problem is the lack of adequate tools to rate the cryptoeconomy and crypto-assets, similar to what is happening in the context of sustainable finance.

Identifying such analogies between the shadow banking system operating within the structures of traditional finance and the shadow banking system operating in this nascent economic paradigm presents an opportunity to consider specific regulatory strategies. In particular, regulators can assess the possibility that specific problems may yield similar negative consequences. If so, they might consider the possibility of *ex ante* regulatory measures based on the *ex post* reactions to the financial crisis of 2008. Therefore, regulators should identify ways to control a highly leveraged ecosystem by regulating financial institutions operating as banks. Furthermore, they have to consider the liquidity and counterparty risks that may result from leverage, from tokenizations (as equivalent to securitizations spreading in traditional finance), and from the possible emergence of new financial conglomerates. Finally, specific initiatives should lead to the development of new forms of rating in the cryptoeconomy and start the debate on specific stress tests for technology. These measures are instrumental to developing sustainable new market practices in the cryptoeconomy.

Concluding Remarks: What's Next?

Introduction

This book has highlighted a specific series of events, which started with the transformations happening at the banking and financial level that led to significant changes.

The book began by identifying a 'line of disruption'. Such line of disruption exemplifies a specific dynamic approach that relies on complexity theories (and complex adaptive systems) as an underlying theoretical foundation. Complexity theory was functional to emphasize the interconnections within the financial system and the multidimensionality of the changes. In this context, the book proposed both a starting and a finishing point, while recognizing the possibility to choose many different starting and finishing points, as a consequence of the continuity characterizing financial innovation. A plausible starting point was identified with the establishment of the shadow banking system, and a finishing one with the emergence of a new financial network, labelled as 'crypto shadow banking'. In proposing this succession of events, the book adopted an ascending climax by referring to increasingly broader dimensions and networks, that is, contractual networks, financial and corporate dynamics, and finally the interconnected institutions at the level of what Chapters 4 and 5 labelled 'shadow central banking' and 'crypto shadow banking' to refer to the nascent networks resulting from multiple consequential transformations. These broad dimensions also identify the different 'subparts' of international finance. Such subparts are complex adaptive systems in constant evolution, and such evolutions coupled with their interactions trigger equally constant evolutions at the systemic level, with international finance being characterized as a complex adaptive system.

Here the book posits some conclusions and addresses what would be the next step in the line of disruption. The emergence of disruptive technologies, in particular blockchain, poses questions as to their role beyond the pure financial and economic context. Specifically, disruptive technologies could play a major role in pursuing other goals beyond the traditional financial dimension, for example in the sense of sustainability.

At the beginning of this book, digital finance was identified as a broad category, which includes Fintech and comes with specific traits.[1] What if technology couples with sustainability? A potential, very short and sharp, answer could be 'sustainable digital finance'.

Although technology and sustainability are two rather different forces and each of them is contributing to reshape the financial system in pursuit of different dynamics, they also share specific characteristics. Not only is sustainability a transformative force for capitalism, just as technology is, but it is also characterized by its

---

[1] See Chapter 1, Section IV.C.2.c.

multidimensionality. Exactly as technology did, sustainability is permeating financial practices, corporate governance, central bank discourses, and financial networks.

A further fundamental question concerns the digitalization of finance in connection to the gradual digitalization of society. From this perspective, the potential implementation of the metaverse and the role of the cryptoeconomy and DeFi will be fundamental topics in future legal and societal discussions.

I. Answering the Key Questions

A. The Static Component

What the book identified as the 'static' dimension relates to the problem of characterizing technological transformations through hermeneutical and policy efforts to consider the existing theoretical legal and regulatory frameworks applicable to smart contracts, ICOs, and networks. In doing this the book proposed a specific structure that identified an ascending climax. In this ascending climax, the first structure was that of smart contracts, and the way the existing regulatory framework proves flexible enough to adapt to this new category. Chapter 2 looked at US law, in particular focusing on the rules of the Uniform Commercial Code (UCC), the law developed to respond to the internet revolution, and the regulations adopted at the state level. This regulatory environment presents a broad definition at the level of the UCC, which may be consistent with the broad definitions used in other regulatory environments, including the international ones. At the same time, this regulatory environment presented the characteristic of intense regulatory activity happening at the state level, with states engaged in providing their own inconsistent definitions of what blockchain and smart contracts are. This sort of regulatory competition replicates similar trends in US corporate law and risks increasing regulatory fragmentation, which would be detrimental to the development of commercial practices—especially considering the extraordinary cross-border use of blockchain. This situation that the United States is experiencing is similar to the regulatory dilemmas that other countries are facing, or will likely face soon. As Chapter 2 showed when referring to continental Europe and the United Kingdom, two different approaches are emerging. A first group of states is not regulating smart contracts, and it is rather opting to implicitly apply the existing regulatory framework to such new instruments. For example, this is the case with the United Kingdom and Switzerland. A second group of states, including Italy and Malta, implemented the different strategy of explicitly defining smart contracts and considered the possibility of applying the existing regulatory framework. Although the two choices are in principle different, they produce substantially similar effects.

A further step was to contextualize the application of smart contracts and blockchain to financial markets, where it was important to consider the problems of (i) regulating single financial 'instruments' (a term used here in a rather non-technical way) and (ii) the specific consequences of their implementation. Therefore, ICOs are relevant for two reasons.

First, they highlight the tensions emerging from the applicability of existing securities and commodities laws (in particular in the US) and offer the opportunity to evaluate the consequent enforcement activities as they emerged, or have yet to emerge, depending on the jurisdiction. In this context, different regulatory styles were implemented, with clear traditional problems related to the adoption of principle-based versus rule-based regulation, as well as in relation to public versus self-regulatory approaches. Although even in this context the existing categories of law proved in principle reasonable, securities regulators are still struggling to identify a regulatory framework that unequivocally protects investors while preserving capital formation. A further consequence is that the SEC's uncertainties have contributed to the establishment of other Fintech hubs, such as Hong Kong, Singapore, and Switzerland.

Second, considering additional effects triggered by the implementation of such financial 'instruments', ICOs offer a starting point to consider the broad transformation happening at the level of market infrastructures and corporate governance—and the cryptoeconomy more generally—while also demystifying some of the promises generally associated with the cryptoeconomy, such as financial inclusion and the concept of systematic disintermediation.

In the final two chapters, the book considered the emergence of two networks: 'shadow central banking' and 'crypto shadow banking'. Here, as these two labels imply, the characterization under the existing framework is more complex and refers to specific policy objectives that emerged in the aftermath of the last financial crisis. Shadow central banking and crypto shadow banking are expected transformations of the new economic environment and related ratings may take into account the existing regulations, pursuing the containment of too-big-to-fail entities, financial interconnection, conflicts of interest, and clarity, especially given the likelihood that new structured products will develop in this context. In these two chapters, the book intended to highlight the historic continuity of these problems and the need to approach these 'old new' phenomena by considering the possibility of applying some *ex ante* measures on the basis of what regulators have already formalized, with some adaptations.

B. The Dynamic Component

The dynamic component is the one that more clearly refers to the concept of the 'line', which—as stated in the preface—is a minimalistic and optimistic one. At the same time, this line is also *complex*, and it couldn't be different: international finance is a complex adaptive system, being a large network, where heterogeneous components (or subparts) interact among themselves without relying on a real central control. Financial regulation, corporate law, and other corpuses of law coupled with economic, financial, and monetary policies provide a perimeter for such activities, although the continuous and often unpredictable ('far-from equilibriums') developments escape the perimeter designed by policy-makers.

The line of disruption emerges at the end of this analysis involving different dimensions, and it is functional to acknowledge that complexity is not only a structural attribute but also refers to a dynamic evolutionary path, where each component is a complex adaptive system itself, all highly interconnected with one another. Transformations internal to each component trigger more general transformations at the systemic level of international finance, itself characterized as a complex adaptive system informed by 'historicity dependency'.

Shadow banking led to the emergence of a new paradigm, and with it, it brought new problems within the financial system. The uncontrolled risks of shadow banking greatly contributed to the financial crisis of 2008. In relation to this event, Chapter 1 identified an 'endogenous' regulatory reaction and an 'exogenous' and disruptive technological reaction, epitomized by the publication of the Bitcoin white paper in September 2008. Bitcoin's underlying technology, blockchain, was revolutionary because of the possibility of programming smart contracts. Smart contracts (like the blockchain technology) are extremely versatile and therefore can be applied to a broad range of activities, such as commercial transactions and financial transactions.

ICOs are an application of smart contracts in one of the most sensitive phases for entrepreneurs, capital formation. ICOs trigger two different concepts and regulatory dimensions, the 'securities' and, for the US, 'commodities' concepts, corresponding to the dual dimension of being a tool for investment with digital tokens (generally associated to the concept of 'security') while triggering some sort of monetary consequence, that is, the launch of a 'cryptocurrency'.

Although they did not disrupt the market as they promised, the symbolic relevance of ICOs is intact. ICOs highlighted the potential for issuing digital securities, in particular stocks and bonds, opening a space for broader applications in corporate governance. At the same time, ICOs had strong 'monetary' implications, contributing to the expansion of cryptocurrencies, which ultimately exacerbated the problem of instability (and volatility) of such alternative coins. These problems were consistent with those experienced by Bitcoin.

Among all the consequences at the level of the cryptoeconomy, a major problem driven by volatility was (and still is) the impossibility for cryptocurrencies to serve as a medium of exchange, unit of account, and store of value—these being the key economic functions of money. The quest for stability pushed private actors to develop a new concept of stable cryptocurrency or stablecoin. The great opportunities related to the development of a global payment system triggered the attention of tech and finance giants, such as Facebook, Google, and J.P. Morgan. The possibility of issuing a global stablecoin made clear the impact of private entities on central banking functions, showing the potential for technology to become a disruptor at the network level. Not surprisingly, these private initiatives ultimately triggered a debate on the role of public central bankers and the possibility for them to issue a public digital currency or central bank digital currency (CBDC). These are the tensions happening at the level of 'shadow central banking' with the underlying creation of a new financial network operating in this context. While the economic function of shadow banking is clearly related to that of traditional banks, in particular credit creation and transformation and liquidity transformation, shadow central banking initiatives invade the realm of specific central banking activities, starting from the payment system and escalating to other key functions related to monetary policies. Notwithstanding these differences, the two networks share specific similarities regarding the reasons for their establishment, the level of the risks involved, and the policy measures to mitigate such risks.

Some of the key instruments that were identified as part of the shadow central banking initiatives are also part of a contiguous financial network, labelled as crypto shadow banking, sharing the same characteristics of the shadow banking system. This is the case for stablecoins, which served the purpose of a payment system while acting as a *de facto*' money market fund in the cryptoeconomy. Crypto shadow banking is the 'new old' paradigm, in which new entities replace the old ones although they still perform the same functions and replicate the same dynamics, presenting similar risks for the financial system.

The line of disruption as a dynamic concept is relevant under three respects. First, if the last step of the evolution is an old paradigm applied to a new economic environment, what should policy-makers learn? With incorrect regulatory approaches, the 'line of disruption' naturally tends to replicate the same risks and mistakes, as demonstrated by past events. A compelling risk is that the evolutionary line becomes a vicious cycle. In this scenario, although the initial idea behind Bitcoin was to disrupt the existing framework of both private and public financial institutions, its creation may lead the system back to the same starting point. In this case, blockchain technology applied to finance would not lead to any systemic improvement and could be considered a failure in many respects.

Consistent with what was stated in the previous section, in this scenario, regulators should make efforts to adopt specific *ex ante* policies coupled with more dynamic (adaptive) forms of rule-making to avoid specific risks, such as systemic risk in its different forms, in the nascent economic paradigm. These regulatory interventions would not stifle innovation but would serve to address certain concerns and create the basis for a more stable and transparent financial system. This would likely be beneficial for the networks, and, in a sort of bottom-down process, would lead to beneficial consequences at the level of digital securities, corporate governance, and primary and secondary crypto markets.

Second, if the cryptoeconomy and DeFi are replicating themselves, this affects the way potential regulatory reactions are conceived. Potential regulatory reactions should look at the way similar problems were approached—and sometimes solved—in the past, in order to anticipate them.

Third, and in connection to the last point, this dynamic component also highlights the interconnectedness of these transformations happening at the commercial, financial, corporate, and monetary levels. Technology, in particular blockchain technology, has proven that any policy approach must be multidimensional. The line of disruption emphasized a rather abstract and conceptual interconnectedness. However, this interconnectedness becomes concrete because specific transformations that started at the securities level proved capable of impacting the different dimensions or layers of finance in an integrated manner. This strengthened interconnectedness is the precondition for the emergence of a new paradigm and emphasizes the meaning of the 'transformative stage' (or, in terms of complexity science, 'transition phase') of capitalism and, more generally, the economy. A transformative force implies significant changes at many different levels.

Continuing to consider and treat the dimensions of financial regulation, corporate governance and practices, and central banks as distinct and separate fields would be a mistake. The technological wave disrupting (even at the simple conceptual level) all these areas requires the existence of multiple heterogeneous competencies and backgrounds that need to act together in an unprecedented way. Regulators have to be aware of the impact that certain regulations, or even enforcement actions regarding specific financial instruments, may have on distant and uncorrelated sectors; they may have geopolitical consequences as well. The enhanced role of technology in the economy emphasizes the unitary conceptuality of different levels being part of the same environment; in other words, the same complex adaptive system.

C. Complexity, Dynamic Regulation, and the Problem of Managing Disruption

An unsolved problem is that of appropriately managing exponential—and multidimensional—changes as a result of technological disruption. Technological disruption is the new normal not only in finance but in society more broadly, and it will continue to reshape its fundamental entities, structures, and business models.

As mentioned in Chapter 1, one of the consequences of applying complexity theories to regulation would be to reconsider the traditional approach of financial regulators to provide new laws and policies on an *ex post* basis. So far, policy-makers have systematically elaborated *ex post* rules as a reaction to financial and economic crises and financial and corporate scandals. Indeed, stable and presumptively optimal rules designed as a reaction to preceding events have been considered the best approaches for policy-making activities, and reflected the liberal approach of the invisible hand to the regulation of financial markets.

Applying complexity theories to regulation would imply consideration of more dynamic forms of regulation, emphasizing the interconnection with preceding and succeeding events and the importance of feedback effects to provide *ex ante* forms of regulation. Here, dynamism, which is a proper attribute of complexity theories, becomes a fundamental trait of the regulatory response.

However, managing technological disruption relying on *ex ante* forms of regulation would be especially difficult. Disruptive innovations might be unpredictable, therefore by definition extremely difficult to anticipate, even if relying on data and predictive tools. Furthermore, general problems related to the legal certainty of *ex ante* regulations could be an additional issue, with both regulators and regulated market actors experiencing difficulties in designing, enforcing, and complying with this kind of regulation. The scope of anticipatory rule-making could be especially tricky to define.

At the same time, data and predictive tools could be limited to specific areas of law, such as systemic risk, where certain financial and liquidity risks could be more directly monitored and interpreted relying on new forms of information, including data. Furthermore, *ex ante* regulations could still be an option, under very limited circumstances, to challenge imminent risks to the financial system, which could realistically be detected by relying on datasets and predictive analytical tools, in combination with the identification of similar historic patterns of development, as in the case of crypto shadow banking.

Nonetheless, more dynamic forms of regulation do not necessarily imply a radical shift towards a systematic *ex ante* approach. Innovation hubs and regulatory sandboxes implement some forms of dynamism without formally leading to the creation of new laws. More realistically, these tools are leveraged on enhancing more sophisticated forms of interaction between the regulators and the regulated actors. In this framework, dynamism does not radically subvert an *ex post* approach to regulation but contributes to redesigning the timing of the regulatory activity, as well as the way regulators should act before enacting new laws.

Innovation hubs are helpful for providing points of contact for firms needing to solve specific regulatory uncertainties with competent authorities with regard to Fintech issues and to obtain non-binding guidance on licensing, registration, regulatory, and supervisory requirements of new financial products and services or even business models.[2] Furthermore, innovation hubs play an essential role in educating the regulators, because they institutionalize knowledge exchange between market actors and public authorities. Regulatory sandboxes complement the role of innovation hubs. They enable a selected group of highly innovative firms to test their new financial products, financial services, or business models in accordance with a specific testing plan agreed to and monitored by a dedicated function of competent authorities.[3] Sandboxes may also imply the use of legally provided discretions by the relevant supervisors,[4] including temporary exemptions from specific regulations.[5]

From the same perspective, regulators should more critically assess the possibility to combine rule-based and principle-based regulations and favour the emergence of strong self-regulatory initiatives as a complimentary pillar to public regulations. Although principle-based regulation comes with some risks, it could create a more flexible basis for regulating technological changes. Favouring self-regulatory approaches would bring important advantages, in particular in the sense of enhancing the dialogue between regulators and market actors, and including the best expertise from the industry in the regulatory process. Furthermore, self-regulation could be faster and easier to approve, therefore timelier, and would be useful for regulators, who would be in the position to elaborate more appropriate policy responses. There are two connected challenges. At this stage, it is difficult to identify reputable and stable institutions that are in a position to take the lead on self-regulatory developments. The second challenge connected to stability is their willingness and actual incentives to enforce self-regulation.

D. Technological Disruption as a Case Study? The Case of Sustainability

Beyond more 'traditional' events such as financial shocks and financial crises, other heterogeneous events prove that technology is not unique in the sense of leading to

---

[2] Radostina Parenti, 'FinTech: Regulatory Sandboxes and Innovation Hubs' (2020) <https://www.europarl.europa.eu/RegData/etudes/STUD/2020/652752/IPOL_STU(2020)652752_EN.pdf> accessed 22 April 2022.
[3] EBA, EIOPA, and ESMA, 'On the Use of Big Data by Financial Institutions' (2016) EBA Joint Committee Discussion Paper JC 2016/86 <https://www.esma.europa.eu/press-news/consultations/joint-committee-discussion-paper-use-big-data-financial-institutions> accessed 22 April 2022.
[4] Ibid, 4.
[5] Michele Finck, *Blockchain Regulation and Governance in Europe* (CUP 2018) 158.

radical transformation at different levels in different contexts. Therefore, regulators should capitalize on the experience of technology and use it to be ready to approach new significant changes in a different and more integrated way.

The aftermath of the financial crisis of 2008 has been an era of unprecedented disruption. Technology certainly contributed to this situation, experiencing exponential growth. In addition to technology, and almost simultaneously, sustainability has become a hot topic on the agendas of policy-makers and private actors (including investment funds, corporations, and financial institutions), who approach this issue from different angles and with different purposes. On the side of the international policy agenda, the adoption of the 2030 Agenda for Sustainable Development by all UN members in 2015, providing seventeen Sustainable Development Goals (SDGs),[6] is a cornerstone of international reform.

Sustainability and technology share specific characteristics. Consistent with the problems posed by technology, sustainability brings classic legal dilemmas related to the need to define or redefine specific notions (such as the 'corporate purpose' or 'rating' when applied to so-called ESG ratings) in multiple areas (including corporate governance, financial regulation, and central banking policies).

Furthermore, sustainability and technology share the characteristic of being transformative forces of capitalism and, more generally, of the economy. Exactly like technology, sustainability is multidimensional as it is permeating key areas of the economy, disrupting corporate governance, financial markets, and central banks. Therefore, disruption can be identified as the ability to simultaneously permeate many different aspects of the financial system in which such transformative (or disruptive) forces intervene and are therefore capable of generating a radical shift toward a new paradigm.

Among the most representative initiatives, the Business Roundtable declaration in 2019[7] and Blackrock Chairman Larry Fink's letter to investors in 2020[8] announcing the centrality of sustainability for future investment choices have had a symbolic relevance and have contributed to re-opening the traditional debate on the role of corporations within society ('stakeholderism' vs 'shareholderism') as part of the general role of private actors in building a new paradigm.[9] The debate on the corporate purpose, the increasing importance of the ESG dimensions, and the consequences at the central banking level are definitely interconnected, and such interconnection is posing similar political, legal, and financial problems consistent with those emerging in the context of disruptive technologies.

---

[6] UN Res 70/1 'Transforming Our World: The 2030 Agenda for Sustainable Development' (25 September 2015) UN A/RES/70/1 <https://sustainabledevelopment.un.org/post2015/transformingourworld> accessed 22 April 2022.

[7] Business Roundtable, 'Statement on the Purpose of a Corporation' (19 August 2019) <https://s3.amazonaws.com/brt.org/BRT-StatementonthePurposeofaCorporationOctober2020.pdf> accessed 22 April 2022.

[8] Letter from Larry Fink to Shareholders (14 January 2020) <https://www.blackrock.com/corporate/investor-relations/larry-fink-ceo-letter> accessed 22 April 2022.

[9] See Edward B. Rock, 'For Whom Is the Corporation Managed in 2020? The Debate over Corporate Purpose' (2021) 76 BusLaw 363. See also Jill E. Fisch and Steven Davidoff Solomon, 'Should Corporations Have a Purpose?' (2021) 99 TexLRev 1309. See also Lucian A. Bebchuk and Roberto Tallarita, 'The Illusory Promise of Stakeholder Governance' (2021) 106 CornellLRev 91.

Also, similar to the course of the events characterizing technology and its development, in particular referring to an emerging economic paradigm, sustainability has also led to the emergence of its own labelled economic paradigm, that is, 'sustainable economy' and 'sustainable finance', as well as green economy and green finance, which more explicitly focus on the environmental aspects. On the one hand, the approach of sustainable finance is broadly oriented towards a long-term investment horizon and refers to 'investment decisions in the financial sector, leading to increased longer-term investments into sustainable economic activities and projects', on the basis of the ESG dimensions. On the other hand, green finance identifies 'financing of investments that provide environmental benefits in the broader context of environmentally sustainable development'.[10]

Beyond the need to regulate the cryptoeconomy, academics and policy-makers should look at technology in finance and economy as a case study for developing an appropriate general theory of disruption. This would imply developing a methodological approach for regulating disruption, which would include the creation of reasonable mechanisms of dynamic regulation, functional to mitigate the emergence of specific risks, without stifling innovation or harming legal certainty. In this way, policy-makers could leverage the challenges posed by disruptive technological transformation. They would mitigate the risk of duplicating mistakes in terms of regulatory strategy and would facilitate a transition towards new paradigms.

E. The Intersection of Sustainability and Technology: Sustainable Digital Finance

As mentioned earlier, technology and sustainability individually and independently led to the emergence of new economic and financial paradigms. However, when considering the intersection of these two driving forces, a new paradigm is also emerging: so-called sustainable digital finance.

Sustainable digital finance identifies a financial paradigm implementing a 'technological ecosystem', to pursue sustainability, to be intended as 'a strong, sustainable, balanced and inclusive growth, by directly and indirectly supporting the targets set in the Sustainable Development Goals'.[11] Therefore, Sustainable Digital Finance is also strictly connected to 'aspirations captured in the business community', including not only sustainability but also 'corporate social responsibility', 'multicapital or shared value', and the ESG agenda.[12]

---

[10] G20 Green Finance Study Group, *G20 Green Finance Synthesis Report* (2016) 3 <http://unepinquiry.org/wp-content/uploads/2016/09/Synthesis_Report_Full_EN.pdf> accessed 22 April 2022.
[11] Ryan K. Merrill, Simon JD Schillebeeckx, and Sofie Blakstad, DBS, and Sustainable Digital Finance Alliance, 'Sustainable Digital Finance in Asia: Creating Environmental Impact through Bank Transformation' (2019) <https://greendigitalfinancealliance.org/wp-content/uploads/2019/11/SustainableDigitalFinanceinAsia.pdf> accessed 22 April 2022 (hereafter Merrill et al., 'Sustainable Digital Finance in Asia').
[12] UN Environment Inquiry, 'Green Digital Finance: Mapping Current Practice and Potential in Switzerland and Beyond' (September 2018) <https://www.greengrowthknowledge.org/sites/default/files/downloads/resource/Green_Digital_Finance_Mapping_in_Switzerland_and_Beyond.pdf> accessed 22 April 2022.

Similar to digital finance, sustainable digital finance relies on a technological ecosystem, where disruptive technologies including mobile payments platforms, crowdfunding, peer-to-peer lending, finance-related big data, artificial intelligence, machine learning, blockchain, digital tokens, and the Internet of Things operate with a high degree of complementarity.[13] Sustainable digital finance could definitely leverage technologies and contribute significantly towards environmental sustainability, as well as social and governance goals.

As the denomination suggests, the label 'sustainable digital finance' explicitly refers to sustainability and technology, via the utilization of the word 'digital'. Notwithstanding the ability of technology and, to some more limited extent, sustainability to independently develop and spread as market-driven trends, the role of regulation and policy is still a key pillar to contribute to the creation of a stronger and more sustainable 'sustainable digital finance'.

In their current stage, neither the formalization of an adequate policy approach nor the regulation of disruptive technologies in finance and sustainability have achieved satisfactory levels. The regulation of disruptive technologies is far from perfect and complete. There is no consensus as to the most appropriate regulatory approach in relation to innovation, with significant differences between countries on the role of new regulations, and at a broader level the design of a more complex 'smart solution' based on regulatory sandboxes and Fintech hubs. Not only do challenges emerge when designing more general policy approaches; significant friction also characterizes the debate on the regulation of more specific instruments.

Multiple examples of the difficulties encountered by regulators in recent years are observable and still unsolved. Among the regulation of disruptive technologies, this book has shown that blockchain and its multiple applications has caused major concern, and the reason could be the immediate economic and financial impacts of its applications on market structure and distribution of powers among markets, posing a threat to established private corporations as well as governmental institutions. The problems emerging at the level of ICOs and their developments (STOs, IEOs) as well as NFTs and stablecoins make clear that appropriate regulations are important for supporting the development of new markets. In all these cases, the lack of strong international cooperation was a burdensome obstacle to the development of a strong regulatory environment capable of supporting a specific type of innovation.

The regulation of sustainability is also imperfect. Consistent with the differences experienced in the regulation of Fintech and disruptive technologies, the regulation of sustainability in general and sustainable finance in particular is extremely fragmented. The European Union has taken important steps to regulate sustainability and sustainable finance, although other key international players did not implement a similar rule-based strategy. The different political views on the role of sustainability in economy and finance, as well as certain approaches seeking to question the existence of climate change as a threat to humanity, do not facilitate the adoption of a common policy approach to strengthen environmental sustainability.

---

[13] Merrill et al., 'Sustainable Digital Finance in Asia' (n 11).

When considering sustainability, an example of the current unsolved criticalities arises from the debate on ESG ratings. As mentioned in Chapter 5, currently there is no agreement on the classification of ESG indicators and the ESG ratings elaborated by the major ESG data providers make clear a strong inconsistency when compared to other more established measures of economy, such as credit ratings.

This kind of uncertainty and inconsistency at the level of technology and sustainability could negatively impact sustainable digital finance, and regulators will need to solve these issues if they intend to drive the change in environmental sustainability, by effectively leveraging the tool of 'sustainable digital finance'. When approaching sustainable digital finance, regulators should consider it the last step in the regulation of capital markets, the first two necessarily being sustainability and technology.

To advance the development of new entrepreneurial projects it will be crucial to reconsider the role of collaborative platforms, following the model of the Green Digital Financial Alliance, a partnership created at the World Economic Forum in Davos in 2017. The Green Digital Financial Alliance pursues the objective of leveraging digital technologies and innovations to enhance sustainable development, by providing a platform for public and private actors to cooperate.[14] Not only does this 'infrastructure' favour the development of new initiatives and projects in the private sphere, but it might also contribute to strengthening private–public partnerships, with both established financial institutions and newcomers.

The role of public actors might have two positive effects. First, public actors could engage with new projects, and therefore be in a position to directly inject financial resources into specific projects or programmes tailored with the purpose of making

---

[14] UN Environment Programme (UNEP), 'Revolutionary digital platform to boost green finance' (20 January 2017) <https://www.unep.org/news-and-stories/press-release/revolutionary-digital-platform-boost-green-finance> accessed 22 April 2022. The two main partners are UNEP and Ant Financial. Ant Financial is a technology company with a focus on developing 'inclusive financial services to the world', pursuing the creation of a 'technology-driven open ecosystem'. 'UNEP is in charge of setting the global environment agenda, and promoting the environmental dimension of sustainable development within the United Nations system, with a longtime engagement in sustainable finance. An important step designed and implemented by the UNEP was the Inquiry into the Design of a Sustainable Financial System in 2014, to support the activity of policy makers, as well as market actors and other stakeholders for the creation of sustainable financial system. Following this first initiative, other important initiatives took place in recent years, at the level of the G20, OECD and World Bank. The United Nations launched in 2018 the Task Force on Digital Finance for the SDGs, where private and public sectors co-exist. The OECD partnered with the UN Environment, the World Bank considered the possibility that digital finance could play in financing climate-smart infrastructures futures. Complementary to these initiatives, sixteen major financial centres engaged in exploring ways to strengthen the role of green and sustainable finance, with the establishment of the Financial Centres for Sustainability (FC4S).' Marco Dell'Erba, 'Sustainable Digital Finance and the Pursuit of Environmental Sustainability' in Danny Busch, Guido Ferrarini, and Seraina Grünewald (eds), *Sustainable Finance in Europe: Corporate Governance, Financial Stability and Financial Markets* (Palgrave 2021). At the national level, countries such as Switzerland and Singapore rely on strong regulatory platform capable of attracting fintech players, favouring a strong development of sustainable digital finance. In addition, France is one of the countries that implemented clear steps in order to become a leading actor in sustainable digital finance, and its strategic plans explicitly mention technology and environmental sustainability. See State Secretariat for International Finance, 'SIF launches Green Fintech Network' (5 November 2020) <https://www.sif.admin.ch/sif/en/home/dokumentation/fokus/fintech-network.html> accessed 22 April 2022. See also Sylvie Lemmet and Pierre Ducret, 'Executive Summary French Strategy for Green Finance' (December 2017) <https://2017.climatefinanceday.com/wp-content/uploads/2017/12/EXECUTIVE-SUMMARY-finance-verte-sircom-v3.pdf> accessed 22 April 2022.

the shift towards environmental sustainability faster and more concrete. Such projects should have an infrastructural aim, intended to create partnerships between public and private actors as well as favour new partnerships among private actors, with a view to involve the highest possible number of stakeholders. Second, direct investments could be a strategy for regulators to drive the change towards new paradigms (sustainable digital finance), as a complementary tool to formal regulation, or even as a substitute for formal regulation. Irrespective of the view related to providing a new regulatory framework as a tool for developing sustainable digital finance, this might be a way to counterbalance a key characteristic of sustainable digital finance—that of being largely market-driven—and contribute to the development of stronger best practices within the market. Although the characteristic of being essentially market-driven is not negative *per se*, an active role for public actors could increase the understanding of specific trends within the market and would increase monitoring activity. Where unintended consequences arise, the state would also be in a position to act faster to counter them by implementing better policy responses in case of non-satisfactory developments, effectively mitigating financial and non-financial risks emerging from such developments.

II. What's Next? The Metaverse as a Synthetic Universe

After the revolution brought about by blockchain, the problem posed by the broader digitalization of the society, where technological innovation is an essential enabler, is the societal transformative stage. In this sense, the emergence of the metaverse and its regulatory and policy implications is the next challenge in finance, economy, and society more broadly. The emergence of the metaverse is in continuity with the transformations triggered by the internet and blockchain. In this context DeFi will likely play a major role for the development of the metaverse and could be considered the 'finance of the metaverse'.

Adopting this perspective, the key regulatory aspects of the metaverse ecosystem involve: (a) securities law issues, in relation to financial instruments (in particular for security tokens and NFTs) and the way such product innovation is reflected in the market infrastructures of the metaverse; (b) corporate law, and automation in corporate governance; (c) central banking issues, understanding the monetary dynamics within the metaverse in relation to exchange value and therefore further rethinking payment systems, as well as the role of CBDCs and governing potential sources of crisis; (d) the relationship between financial law, property law, and intellectual property law to build an effective synthetic universe, focusing on the nature of property rights.

A. What Is the Metaverse?

The term 'metaverse' has become extremely popular in financial markets, although it originally emerged as a literary creation. Neal Stephenson's novel *Snow Crash* identified the metaverse as a three-dimensional virtual world that was a real place to its users, who interacted through avatars; the real world thus became a metaphor.[15] Today, the concept of the metaverse refers to a new generation of computing developing an 'immersive digital world', with specific structural and technical characteristics. Here, consistent with Stephenson's idea, people could interact via avatars, without any real-world physical constraints, and relying on various interconnected devices and multiple versions of interoperable virtual realities part of the same platform instead of switching between discrete apps.[16]

The metaverse does not exist yet, mostly because an underdeveloped technical infrastructure has so far impeded its creation.[17] Also, it does not identify a unique product, technology, or service, and so the key question is rather 'what could the metaverse become?'[18] The gaming industry, in particular online games such as Fortnite, Roblex, and Second Life, anticipated some of the key features currently discussed in the context of the metaverse, as a historical analysis would confirm.[19] At the time of writing, gaming continues to be an essential catalyst for channelling strategic investments in the metaverse and its development.

The shift in the technical infrastructure will not only make possible the creation of the metaverse, but could also lead to its exponential evolution from a set of discrete virtual environments into a limitless, borderless digital world. Consistent with the concept of decentralized finance and its multi-layer structure, the metaverse will be built on multiple layers too. In particular, DLT and further technical developments provide the technological basis for implementing a fully synthetic and dematerialized universe. On top of these coordinated technologies, the metaverse offers unprecedented opportunities to develop new forms of interaction, relying on new instruments (including new forms of property) and new applications. In this context, decentralized finance is especially important for the creation of the metaverse and its expansion beyond pure financial activities.

---

[15] Cory Ondrejka, 'Escaping the Gilded Cage: User Created Content and Building the Metaverse' (2005) 49 NYLSchLRev 81. See also Jelena Zec, 'The Metaverse Mall: From Science Fiction to Retail Reality' (*citiVentures*, 22 November 2021) <https://www.citi.com/ventures/perspectives/opinion/metaverse-mall.html> accessed 22 April 2022.

[16] Kevin Stankiewicz, 'Jim Cramer Says These 4 Companies Are the Best Ways to Invest in the Metaverse' (*CNBC*, 11 November 2021) <https://www.cnbc.com/2021/11/10/jim-cramer-says-these-4-companies-are-the-best-ways-to-invest-in-the-metaverse.html> accessed 22 April 2022 (hereafter, Stankiewicz, 'Best Ways to Invest in the Metaverse').

[17] World Economic Forum, 'What Is the Metaverse? And Why Should We Care?' (29 October 2021) <https://www.weforum.org/agenda/2021/10/facebook-meta-what-is-the-metaverse/> accessed 22 April 2022.

[18] Ibid.

[19] Developments in the gaming industry started in the 1970s and clear innovations emerged over the course of the next decades. For a historical analysis, see Jessica Mulligan and Bridgette Patrovsky, *Developing Online Games: An Insider's Guide* (New Riders 2003); see also John David Dionisio, William G. Burns III, and Richard Gilbert, '3D Virtual Worlds and the Metaverse: Current Status and Future Possibilities' (2013) ACM Computing Surveys 45, 3, Article 34. Fundamental developments in the gaming industry include text-based virtual worlds (late 1970s); 2D graphical interfaces (1980s); 3D graphics, user-created content, and audio (1990s); advanced virtual economy (early 2000s); and decentralized development (2007). The metaverse developments leveraging decentralization are part of this development.

B. The Key Elements of the Metaverse

Developments in DLT technology proved fundamental for providing a common platform where pre-existing technologies can be leveraged in an unprecedented way, such as virtual and augmented reality, coupled with the foundational tools emerging in the context of DeFi. Some of these concepts are essential for understanding the metaverse. The virtual world is a computer-based simulated environment intended for its users to inhabit and interact via avatars, whereas virtual reality uses software to generate realistic images, sounds, and other sensations to create a virtual environment. A complementary notion is that of ubiquitous/pervasive computing, referring to the computer devices spreading throughout the environment, embedded within the objects of our everyday life (such as the smartphone). The broader category of cyberspace indicates a global domain with the purpose of disrupting physical resources. It is made of data, but also network and computer systems.

The metaverse differs from internet technology but is complementary to it, especially with so-called Web 3.0, the future evolution of Web 2.0. The current version of the Web, Web 2.0, relies on a centralized structure, where companies operate owning the content and the control of the platform, as in the case of social media as well as online games.[20] On the contrary, Web 3.0 would allow users not only to create content, but also to own, control, and monetize it. The decentralized nature of the blockchain technology, as well as its application, including cryptocurrencies and so-called non-fungible tokens (NFTs), would be an essential driver for developing all this.

In this context, the metaverse is a digital space that in its most ambitious form is capable of transforming 2D internet into a 3D experience. This new digital space represents an emerging dimension, where different constituencies operate on the same platform, which is capable of 'mirroring' real-world activities in a rather unprecedented way when considered alongside more traditional online experiences.[21] Web 3.0 could favour the emergence of a decentralized web, which would be the basis for connectivity in the metaverse. Here the metaverse could enhance the creation of a whole new financial world, implementing fully decentralized solutions.[22]

As mentioned above, DeFi and its layers, in particular infrastructure, smart contracts, and crypto-assets, are extremely important for building and developing the metaverse. So far, Ethereum has emerged as the most popular infrastructure for designing smart contracts, and although new competitors have emerged, Ethereum is still the dominant platform. Smart contracts are functional to implementing applications and crypto-assets, and ultimately creating an interconnected unique platform. The concepts of virtual venues, virtual properties, and virtual cities[23] and the ways

---

[20] Henrique Centieiro, 'The Insane Future of Web 3.0 and the Metaverse' (*Medium*, 23 January 2022) <https://medium.datadriveninvestor.com/the-insane-future-of-web-3-0-and-the-metaverse-4cec3f138 95a> accessed 22 April 2022.
[21] Ibid.
[22] Ibid.
[23] See Jacqui Palumbo, 'Ambitious Plans Unveiled for a Libertarian City in the Metaverse' (*CNN style*, 24 March 2022) <https://edition.cnn.com/style/article/liberland-metaverse-city-zaha-hadid-architects/index.html> accessed 22 April 2022.

in which individuals interact in the metaverse in the form of avatars all rely on smart contracts; these will be the only means for concluding virtual transactions in the synthetic world, and more broadly interacting on a unique platform. In this context, the importance and the penetration of smart contracts in daily life would drastically increase, compared to the more traditional cryptoeconomy.

Consistent with their importance for DeFi, crypto-assets are equally relevant to the metaverse. Indeed, cryptocurrencies, CBDCs, and digital tokens are functional to the transition towards new paradigms, even beyond DeFi. NFTs are especially functional to the development of the metaverse, and at the same time they are important for understanding the pivotal role of financial law within the metaverse.

Although NFTs are not the most recent development in the cryptoeconomy (the first NFT dates back to 2014), they have become increasingly central and are further contributing to the mainstream adoption of new technologies and techniques.[24] NFTs show the potential for tokenizing any physical or digital asset, thereby transforming them into a valuable, tradable, and fractional (as in the case of so-called fractional non-fungible tokens, F-NFTs) crypto-asset. NFTs are the nexus between the previous advancements in cryptofinance and future potential developments in the metaverse, as they are the result of significant but gradual transformations happening in cryptofinance. ICOs showed for the very first time the disruptive potential of digital tokens and the possibility to create organizational cryptocurrencies. At the current stage of development, NFTs' proliferation is also possible because of the previous wave of ICOs, digital tokens, and cryptocurrencies and the infrastructural development that they triggered. Indeed, crypto-exchanges have become an essential catalyst for NFTs' success, and an increasing number of crypto-exchanges offer NFTs on their platforms.

Another essential part of the cryptoeconomy and decentralized finance is represented by cryptocurrencies. They will become especially important in the metaverse as a tool for rapidly exchanging value in the synthetic universe. Not surprisingly, the centrality of the cryptocurrencies to the whole synthetic universe re-proposes the same problem for central banks that was raised in relation to the opportunity to develop CBDCs. However, this option could have become an even more pressing matter. As this book has shown, central banks reacted strongly to developments in the cryptoeconomy in particular after the presentation of the Libra project. At that time, Libra, as a global stablecoin, raised concerns about the risk that existing fiat currencies, and consequently central banks, could lose their centrality in the financial system. Consistent with these developments, tech giants engaged in designing their metaverse could create and encourage the adoption of organizational—and potentially global—cryptocurrencies, on the basis of the Libra model, implementing so-called in-metaverse currencies or alternatively private cryptocurrencies. While the former would be accepted only within individual metaverses, the latter would be universally accepted within the metaverse.[25]

---

[24] See Victor dMdb and Victor Alexiev, 'NFTs and the Dawn of the Metaverse' (*citiVentures*, 6 April 2021) <https://www.citi.com/ventures/perspectives/opinion/nfts-metaverse.html> accessed 22 April 2022.

[25] Claire Harrop and Cyrus Pocha, 'Does the Metaverse Provide a Use Case for Central Bank Digital Currency?' (*Freshfields Technology Quotient*, 16 December 2021) <https://technologyquotient.freshfields.

C. Market Developments in the Metaverse

Some technological activities are still niche matters in the face of the traditional economy and finance. This is true of cryptoeconomy—although it has achieved a certain degree of 'mainstreaming'—and decentralized finance, and even more so of the metaverse, that is at an embryonic stage. However, central banks and financial regulators should not wait to explore this new ecosystem, as technology has demonstrated the ability to grow at an exponential pace. As a consequence, future developments might not be remote.

Although the metaverse is still in its infancy, the possibility of new technical and economic development is attracting the interest of multiple companies, operating in different business areas. Facebook's parent company was recently rebranded as Meta Platforms Inc (Meta), explicitly recalling the concept of the metaverse and further contributing to an increased popularization of the term. In October 2021 Meta launched a new division in charge of exploring the metaverse,[26] providing significant investment, that culminated with the creation of a $1.1 billion data centre functional for building a metaverse.[27] Microsoft invested in the metaverse by recently purchasing Activision Blizzard Inc. for $68 billion, thus becoming the third-largest gaming company in the world.[28] Online gaming platforms, such as Roblox, and companies connected to gaming—such as Unity Software Inc, owner of one of the two main 3D video game engines—understandably continue to invest in the sector. Other prominent investors in the metaverse include semiconductor companies—in particular Nvidia and Taiwan Semiconductor (TSM)[29]—and fast cloud computing solutions companies. Not surprisingly, the virtual world market is expected to grow by up to $75.57 billion, reaching 55.3 per cent CAGR between 2020 and 2025.[30]

The size of these investments, coupled with the exponential growth of financial activities exposed to technological developments, suggests that even the embryonic metaverse could become a source of social, economic, and financial interactions, as well as systemic risks that the financial system will need to monitor, control, and regulate.

---

com/post/102hefa/does-the-metaverse-provide-a-usecase-for-central-bank-digital-currency> accessed 22 April 2022.

[26] Andrew Bosworth and Nick Clegg, 'Building the Metaverse Responsibly' (*Meta*, 27 September 2021) <https://about.fb.com/news/2021/09/building-the-metaverse-responsibly/> accessed 22 April 2022.

[27] See Mark Haranas, 'Facebook's Meta to Build $1B Data Center for Metaverse' (*CRN*, 17 March 2022) <https://www.crn.com/news/data-center/facebook-s-meta-to-build-1b-data-center-for-metaverse> accessed 22 April 2022.

[28] Sarah Frier and Dina Bass, 'Microsoft Makes a $69 Billion Down Payment on the Metaverse' (*Bloomberg*, 19 January 2022) <https://www.bloomberg.com/news/articles/2022-01-19/microsoft-msft-activision-blizzard-atvi-deal-shows-big-tech-metaverse-push> accessed 22 April 2022.

[29] Stankiewicz, 'Best Ways to Invest in the Metaverse' (n 16).

[30] Investing, '4 Stocks to Buy as the Metaverse Takes Flight' (2 November 2021) <https://www.investing.com/news/stock-market-news/4-stocks-to-buy-as-the-metaverse-takes-flight-2664623> accessed 22 April 2022.

D. Key Questions

By leveraging technological advances coupled with financial transformations, the metaverse would realize the utopia of a fully synthetic universe. In this context, DeFi is a fundamental component. DeFi entities and instruments enable the full functions of the metaverse; therefore financial laws are essential for regulating this new environment.

Assessing the centrality of financial law in the metaverse is not only relevant as a theoretical issue. In fact, adopting a policy angle, it would require re-design of the relationship between financial law and other areas of law, including, but not limited to, property law, intellectual property law, and contract law. Therefore, new adaptations of existing laws might be required. At the beginning of their inception, the cryptoeconomy and cryptofinance systematically raised new questions related to the possibility to apply existing laws to new products, entities, and strategies. In addition to similar concerns, the metaverse will urgently pose a more sophisticated problem of coordination among the different areas of law, where financial law will likely play a prominent role. This depends on the characteristics of the products emerging in the metaverse and the related activities of trading—both on the primary and the secondary market. From a legal standpoint, these products will often be characterized as securities in the context of the metaverse. Consequently, an expansive trend in this sense will contribute to increasing and further expanding the importance of financial law beyond the traditional boundaries, as they emerge in the real physical world.

An example comes from an important debate in the metaverse in relation to land and property, and their market for sale. Compared to land and property in real life and the real economy, these entities are fully dematerialized. The purchase of virtual land concretely involves the purchase of a so-called land NFT, often a security, incorporating an exclusive ownership right on a digital asset, to be negotiated on crypto-exchanges. The purchase of a virtual construction is a 3D work, commissioned to a professional and designed with specific software. Therefore, intellectual property laws and industrial laws with an emphasis on architecture and design could apply. Even in this case, the resulting NFT can be purchased, exchanged, and fractionalized, like traditional securities. In these cases, the role of property law and proprietary rights is compressed in comparison to the physical world, with increased prominence of securities law.

In the area of contract law, the role of smart contracts in the metaverse is even more important due to an enhanced nexus with the key instruments and entities within the metaverse—in particular NFTs, DAOs, cryptocurrencies and CBDCs, and cryptoexchanges—and the possibility to develop further DApps (decentralized applications) and new use-cases. At the corporate law level, the emergence of the metaverse could lead to the multiplication of Distributed Autonomous Organizations (DAOs), and a key question is whether the creation of the DAO becomes a necessary precondition for companies and corporations to operate in the metaverse.

Looking at the central banking dimension, the metaverse could be a more urgent proposition of the same problems emerging in the cryptoeconomy—especially the need to rely on different tools for exchanging value in a decentralized environment—and of the same dilemma for central banks—whether to issue central banking money in alternative forms—in a context that would be in principle self-sufficient, relying on private stablecoins.

Similar to the risks seen in the aftermath of Libra, CBDCs could be an even more important tool in this situation, where one or multiple CBDCs could be adopted as a medium of exchange, avoiding the risks emerging from in-metaverse cryptocurrencies and universally accepted currencies. CBDCs would help central bankers preserve the centrality of fiat currencies in the context of a universe where private cryptocurrencies could potentially prosper and become even more prominent than was experienced in the early stages of decentralized finance. Furthermore, in an extreme-case scenario where the metaverse absorbs a vast majority of real-life activities (becoming a sort of 'new normal'), unbanked or even underbanked individuals might no longer be able to use cash, as a consequence being excluded from a significant number of activities.[31]

The problems, or the questions, for central banks might go even beyond the opportunity to conceive an appropriate alternative form for their fiat currencies. A further specific problem for the metaverse is the possibility that 'meta-financial crises' propagate to other segments of finance, including traditional finance and the real economy. This issue is directly connected to central banks' primary goal to pursue stable economic growth by maintaining price and financial stability, and indirectly contributing to investor protection. To continue to play a pivotal role in the changing ecosystem, central banks will have to assess the potential risks emerging within the metaverse and the likelihood that such risks could propagate beyond the metaverse and affect traditional societal structures, generating, for example, inflationary or deflationary trends, as well as financial stability concerns, emerging from speculative trends and relevant crashes happening in the metaverse. The metaverse could replicate certain speculative trends on a global scale.

Finally, a further question is whether the metaverse has the potential to become socially inclusive and environmentally sustainable. Technical problems—mostly related to availability of the infrastructure—design issues characterizing technology and potentially leading to different bias, and the economic and financial obstacles as they emerged in the cryptoeconomy could all be significant obstacles. Looking at the environmental risks, energy consumption in the context of platforms, cryptocurrencies, and smart contracts could be major problems. Strong self-regulatory initiatives will be necessary to mitigate these problems.

Conclusion

Characterizing technology as an exogenous response to the financial crisis and diving into the 'line of disruption' has led to the development of a static and a dynamic dimension, which responded to two different needs. The first serves to understand how to systematize the current legal trends in different contexts, while the second is a useful tool to consider the way the cryptoeconomy has developed in different ambits and how these ambits result in a strong interrelation. The new paradigms emerging

---

[31] Ibid.

from a systematic application of disruptive technologies to the economy and finance, characterized by their unusual multidimensionality, work to show the nature of international finance as a complex adaptive system, where several subparts interact among themselves in a continuous evolutionary pattern.

The line of disruption is used not only to clarify the nature of the process related to technology and the way regulators should react, but also to characterize technology itself as a transformative force operating within the economic system and to use it as a case study for future challenges reshaping the economy. The most important challenge is sustainability, as this book has highlighted; it will result in radical transformations affecting the financial industry, corporate governance, and central banks. Therefore, the same two dimensions are in play: (1) a static one related to the appropriateness of applying existing regulations or developing new rules on the basis of historic continuity (such as the constant need to provide reliable measures); and (2) a dynamic one to fully control (and benefit from) the way each sector, or layer, of the economy is disrupted and contributes to creating new risks and opportunities. Furthermore, sustainability will necessarily interact with technology, requiring an adequate policy approach for appropriately tackling the emergence of sustainable digital finance.

Finally, the next challenge for regulators is the emergence of a synthetic universe, as part of a gradual digitalization of the society and its fundamental structures. This poses new problems in terms of coordination among different areas of law. The central role of DeFi in the metaverse could lead to a prominence of financial law mechanisms over other areas of law.

References

@pramodAIML, 'NFT Derivatives for Absolute Beginners?' (*Medium*, 26 January 2022) <https://medium.com/crypto-wisdom/nft-derivatives-for-absolute-beginners-12b57e5dc425>

@SBF_FTX, "FTX has 1,700 BTC of options traded in the last 24h—putting it squarely at the second highest volume crypto options exchange 1 day after launch! (*Twitter*, 13 January 2020) <https://twitter.com/SBF_Alameda/status/1216797698113724416?utm_source=InstitutionalCrypto&utm_medium=Email&utm_campaign=2020-01-14clid=>

Abad, Jorge, Marco D'Errico, Neill Killeen, Vera Luz, Tuomas Peltonen, Richard Portes, and Teresa Urbano, 'Mapping The Interconnectedness Between EU Banks and Shadow Banking Entities' (2017) European Systemic Risk Board Working Paper Series No. 40 <https://eba.europa.eu/sites/default/documents/files/documents/10180/1431348/5a5b092b-dc8b-4816-89e0-9673bd75d304/Mapping%20the%20interconnectedness%20between%20EU%20banks%20and%20shadow%20banking%20entities_paper.pdf?retry=1>

Abrol, Ayushi, 'DeFi Protocols: A Complete Overwiew' (Blockchain Council, 22 March 2022) <https://www.blockchain-council.org/defi/defi-protocols/>

Acheson, Noelle and Galen Moore, 'Crypto Lending 101' (*CoinDesk*, January 2020) <https://downloads.coindesk.com/research/CryptoLending101_CoindeskResearch.pdf>

Adam, Michal, Paul Bochmann, Maciej Grodzicki, Luca Mingarelli, Mattia Montagna, Costanza Rodriguez d'Acri, and Martina Spaggiari, 'Assessing the Systemic Footprint of Euro Area Banks' (November 2019) ECB—Financial Stability Review <https://www.ecb.europa.eu/pub/financial-stability/fsr/special/html/ecb.fsrart201911_02~5fd45e4b5a.en.html#toc1>

Adlerstein, David, 'Are Smart Contracts Smart? A Critical Look at Basic Blockchain Questions' (*CoinDesk*, 26 June 2017) <https://www.coindesk.com/tech/2017/06/26/are-smart-contracts-smart-a-critical-look-at-basic-blockchain-questions/>

Adrian, Tobias and Ashraf Khan, 'Central Bank Accountability, Independence, and Transparency' (*IMF Blog*, 25 November 2019) <https://www.imf.org/en/Blogs/Articles/2019/11/25/central-bank-accountability-independence-and-transparency>

Adrian, Tobias and Rhoda Weeks-Brown, 'Cryptoassets as National Currency? A Step Too Far' (*IMF Blog*, 26 July 2021) <https://blogs.imf.org/2021/07/26/cryptoassets-as-national-currency-a-step-too-far/>

Adrian, Tobias and Tommaso Mancini-Griffoli, 'The Rise of Digital Money' (July 2019) IMF Fintech Notes, Note 19/01 <https://www.imf.org/en/Publications/fintech-notes/Issues/2019/07/12/The-Rise-of-Digital-Money-47097>

Adrian, Tobias, James Morsink, and Liliana Schumacher, 'Assessing Climate-Change Risk by Stress Testing for Financial Resilience' (*IMFBlog*, 5 February 2020) <https://blogs.imf.org/2020/02/05/assessing-climate-change-risk-by-stress-testing-for-financial-resilience/>

Advani, Kingsley, 'The Top 6 Stablecoins in Crypto' (*Medium*, 23 February 2018) <https://medium.com/@kingsleyadvani/the-top-6-stable-coins-in-crypto-e6f53e9b03be>

AgID, 'Linee Guida per la Modellazione delle Minacce ed Individuazione delle Azioni di Mitigazione Conformi ai Principi del Secure/Privacy By Design' (7 May 2020) <https://www.agid.gov.it/sites/default/files/repository_files/allegato_4_-_linee_guida_per_la_modellazione_delle_minacce-dlt.pdf>

Ahamed, Liaquat, *Lords of Finance: The Bankers Who Broke the World* (Tantor 2010)
Aitken, Roger, 'Investment Guide To "Crypto" Coin Offerings Ratings Blockchain Startups' (*Forbes*, 6 January 2017) <https://www.forbes.com/sites/rogeraitken/2017/01/06/investment-guide-to-crypto-coin-offerings-rating-blockchain-startups/#614e6940121b>
Akhtar, Allana and Jennifer Ortakales, 'Asana Just Said It's Doing a Direct Listing—Here's How they Work and Why More Companies Are Thinking Outside the Box When It Comes to Going Public' (*Business Insider*, 4 February 2020) <https://www.businessinsider.com/the-difference-between-a-direct-listing-and-an-ipo-2019-6?r=US&IR=T>
Albert, Miriam R., 'The Howey Test Turns 64: Are the Courts Grading this Test on a Curve?' (2011) 2 Wm&MaryBusLRev 1
Alden, Eric, 'Promissory Estoppel and the Origins of Contract Law' (2017) 9 NEULJ 1
Alesina, Alberto and Lawrence H. Summers, 'Central Bank Independence and Macroeconomic Performance: Some Comparative Evidence' (1993) 25 JMCB 151
Alexander, Kern, 'Corporate Governance and Banks: The Role of Regulation in Reducing the Principal-Agent Problem' (2006) 7 JBankReg 14
Alexander, Kern, *Principles of Banking Regulation* (CUP 2019)
Alexander, Kern and Paul G. Fisher, 'Central Banking and Climate Change' in Paul G. Fisher (ed), *Making the Financial System Sustainable* (CUP 2020) 49–74
Alexandre, Ana, 'Bitcoin Investor and Speculator Hold Their Position over the Summer' (*Cointelegraph*, 24 September 2018) <https://cointelegraph.com/news/study-bitcoin-investors-and-speculators-maintained-their-positions-over-summer>
Alexandre, Ana, 'Fidelity Investments Fully Rolls Out Crypto Custody Service, Exec Says' (*Cointelegraph*, 19 October 2019) <https://cointelegraph.com/news/fidelity-investments-fully-rolls-out-crypto-custody-service-exec-says>
Alison, Ian, 'Goldman Sachs to Enter Crypto Market "Soon" with Custody Play: Source' (*CoinDesk,* 15 January 2021) <https://www.coindesk.com/business/2021/01/15/goldman-sachs-to-enter-crypto-market-soon-with-custody-play-source/>
Al-Laham, Mohamad, Haroon Al-Tarawneh, and Najwan Abdallat, 'Development of Electronic Money and Its Impact on the Central Bank Role and Monetary Policy' (2009) 6 IISIT <http://iisit.org/Vol6/IISITv6p339-349Al-Laham589.pdf>
Allen, Darcy, 'Discovering and Developing the Blockchain Cryptoeconomy' (2017) <https://ssrn.com/abstract=2815255>
Allen, Hilary J., 'Money Market Fund Reform Viewed through a Systemic Risk Lens' (2010) 11 JBus&SecL 87
Allen, Hilary J., 'Driverless Finance' (2020) 10 HarvBusLRev 157
Allen, Hilary J., 'Payments Failure' (2021) 62 BCLRev 453
Allen, Hilary J., *Driverless Finance: Fintech's Impact on Financial Stability* (OUP 2022)
Alliance for Financial Inclusion, 'Fintech for Financial Inclusion: A Framework for Digital Financial Transformation' (Special Report 2018) <https://www.afi-global.org/wp-content/uploads/publications/2018-09/AFI_FinTech_Special%20Report_AW_digital.pdf>
Alpaydin, Ethem, *Machine Learning: The New AI* (MIT Press 2016)
Alper, Tim, 'Shanghai Stock Exchange, Regulator to Begin Blockchain Trading Pilot' (*Cryptonews*, 30 September 2020) <https://cryptonews.com/news/shanghai-stock-exchange-regulator-to-begin-blockchain-tradin-7848.htm>
Altonomy <https://www.altonomy.com/#/>
Alvarez, Fernando E., David Argente, and Diana Van Patten, 'Are Cryptocurrencies Currencies? Bitcoin as Legal Tender in El Salvador' (2022) NBER Working Paper No. 29968 <https://www.nber.org/system/files/working_papers/w29968/w29968.pdf>
Amaro, Silvia, 'ECB Surprises Markets by Not Cutting Rates, but Announces Stimulus to Fight Coronavirus Impact' (*CNBC*, 12 March 2020) https://www.cnbc.com/2020/03/12/european-central-bank-stimulus-package-amid-coronavirus.html

Aragon blogspot, 'What Is Composability?' (9 December 2021) <https://blog.aragon.org/what-is-composability/>

Arewa, Olufunmilayo B., 'Financial Markets and Networks—Implications for Financial Market Regulation' (2009) 78 UCinLRev 613

Armour, John, Dan Awrey, Paul Davies, Luca Enriques, Jeffrey N. Gordon, Colin Mayer, and Jennifer Payne, *Principles of Financial Regulation* (OUP 2016)

Armstrong, Patrick, 'Financial Technology: ESMA's Approach, 4th Luxembourg FinTech Conference' (Speech at the 4th Luxembourg FinTech Conference, Luxembourg, 10 October 2018) <https://www.esma.europa.eu/sites/default/files/library/esma71-99-1051_speech_on_cryptoassets_-_pa.pdf>

Arner, Douglas W., Janos N. Barberis, and Ross P. Buckley, 'The Evolution of Fintech: A New Post-Crisis Paradigm?' (2015) University of Hong Kong Faculty of Law, Research Paper No. 2015/047

Arner, Douglas W., Janos Barberis, and Ross P. Buckley, 'Fintech and Regtech in a Nutshell and the Future in a Sandbox' (2017) CFA Research Foundations Brief 2017, Vol. 3 <https://www.cfainstitute.org/en/research/foundation/2017/fintech-and-regtech-in-a-nutshell-and-the-future-in-a-sandbox>

Arner, Douglas W., Janos N. Barberis, and Ross P. Buckley, 'FinTech, RegTech and the Reconceptualization of Financial Regulation' (2017) 37 NWJIntlL&Bus 371

Arner, Douglas W., Dirk A. Zetzsche, Ross P. Buckley, and Janos N. Barberis, 'FinTech and RegTech: Enabling Innovation while Preserving Financial Stability' (2017) 18 GeoJIntlAff 47

Arner, Douglas, Ross P. Buckley and Dirk Zetzsche, 'Fintech for Financial Inclusion: A Framework for Digital Financial Transformation' (2018) <https://ssrn.com/abstract=3245287>

Arner, Douglas W., Ross P. Buckley, and Dirk A. Zetzsche, 'Sustainability, FinTech and Financial Inclusion' (2019) European Banking Institute Working Paper Series 2019/41 <https://ssrn.com/abstract=3387359>

Arner, Douglas W., Janos N. Barberis, Julia Walker, Ross P. Buckley, Andrew M. Dahdal and Dirk A. Zetzsche, 'Digital Finance & the COVID-19 Crisis' (2020) University of Hong Kong Faculty of Law Research Paper No. 2020/017 <https://ssrn.com/abstract=3558889>

AscendEX, 'ETH (Ethereum)' (last update 6 May 2022) <https://ascendex.com/en/support/articles/36773-eth-ethereum>

Aspan, Maria, 'Why Every Company Wants to Look Like a Bank—Without Becoming One' (*Fortune*, 18 November 2019) <https://fortune.com/2019/11/18/big-tech-banking-regulation-apple-goldman-sachs-google-citigroup/>

Atzori, Marcella, 'Blockchain Technology and Decentralized Governance: Is the State Still Necessary?' (2017) 6 JGov&Reg 1

Auboin, Marc, 'Use of Currencies in International Trade: Any Changes in the Picture?' (May 2012) World Trade Organization Staff Working Paper ERSD-2012-10 <https://www.wto.org/english/res_e/reser_e/ersd201210_e.pdf>

Auer, Raphael, Codruta Boar, Giulio Cornelli, Jon Frost, Henry Holden, and Andreas Wehrli, 'CBDCs Beyond Borders: Results from a Survey of Central Banks' (June 2021) BIS Papers No. 116 <https://www.bis.org/publ/bppdf/bispap116.pdf>

Auray, Stephane, Thomas Mariotti, and Fabien Moizeau, 'Dynamic Regulation of Quality' (2011) 42 RANDJEcon 246

Authers, John and Lauren Leatherby, 'The Decade of Deleveraging Didn't Quite Turn Out That Way' (*Bloomberg*, 3 April 2019) <https://www.bloomberg.com/graphics/2019-decade-of-debt/>

Autorité des Marchés financiers, *Annual Report 2018* (4 November 2019) <https://www.amf-france.org/en/news-publications/publications/annual-reports-and-institutional-publications/amf-annual-report-2018>

Avgouleas, Emilios, 'Regulating Financial Innovation' in Niamh Moloney, Eilís Ferran, and Jennifer Payne (eds), *The Oxford Handbook of Financial Regulation* (OUP 2015) 659–692

Awrey, Dan, 'Regulating Financial Innovation: A More Principles-Based Proposal?' (2011) 5 BrookJCorpFin&CommL 273

Awrey, Dan, 'Complexity, Innovation and the Dynamics of OTC Derivatives Regulation' (DPhil thesis, Oxford University of Oxford, 17 September 2012) <https://ora.ox.ac.uk/objects/uuid:340dff47-0a78-43a8-85eb-c39b950e5153/download_file?file_format=pdf&safe_filename=THESIS01&type_of_work=The>

Awrey, Dan, 'Complexity, Innovation and the Regulation of Modern Financial Markets' (2012) 2 HarvBusLRev 235

Awrey, Dan, 'Bad Money' (2020) 106 CornellLRev 1

Awrey, Dan, 'Unbundling Banking, Money & Payments' (2021) ECGI Law Working Paper No. 565/2021

Awrey, Dan and Kathryn Judge, 'Why Financial Regulation Keeps Falling Short' (2020) 61 BCLRev 2295

Bahaj, Saleem and Ricardo Reis, 'Central Bank Swap Lines: Evidence on the Effects of the Lender of Last Resort' (2022) 89 RevEconStud 1654

Bain, Read, 'The Concept of Complexity in Sociology' (1929) 8 SocForces 222

Bair, Sheila, 'The Fed Needs to Get Serious about Its Own Digital Currency' (*yahoo!finance*, 21 June 2018) <https://finance.yahoo.com/news/former-fdic-chair-fed-needs-get-serious-digital-currency-131756819.html>

Baker, Colleen, 'The Federal Reserve's Use of International Swap Lines' (2013) 55 ArizLRev 603

Baldwin, William L., 'The Feedback Effect of Business Conduct on Industry Structure' (1969) 12 JL&Econ 123

Ballensweig, Matt, Roshun Patel, and Leon Marshal, 'Genesis Capital Digital Asset Lending Snapshot 2019 | Q4 insights' (*Genesis Trading*, 2019) <https://genesiscap.co/insights/q4-insights-2019/>

Bank of America, 'ESG from A to Z: Global Primer' (8 November 2019) (on file with author)

Bank of Canada and the Monetary Authority of Singapore, 'Enabling Cross-Border High Value Transfer Using Distributed Ledger Technologies' (2019) <https://www.mas.gov.sg/-/media/Jasper-Ubin-Design-Paper.pdf?la=en&hash=EF5857437C4857373A9287CD86F56D0E7C46E7FF>

Bank of Canada, 'Contingency Planning for a Central Bank Digital Currency' (25 February 2020) <https://www.bankofcanada.ca/2020/02/contingency-planning-central-bank-digital-currency/>

Bank of Canada, 'Digital Currencies and Fintech: Projects' <https://www.bankofcanada.ca/research/digital-currencies-and-fintech/projects/>

Bank of Canada, ECB, Bank of Japan, Sveriges Riksbank, Swiss National Bank, Bank of England, Board of Governors Federal Reserve System and BIS, 'Central Bank Digital Currencies: Foundational Principles and Core Features—Report no 1' (October 2020) <https://www.bis.org/publ/othp33.pdf>

Bank of Canada, ECB, Bank of Japan, Sveriges Riksbank, Swiss National Bank, Bank of England, Board of Governors Federal Reserve System, and BIS, 'Central Bank Digital Currencies: Executive Summary' (September 2021) <https://www.bis.org/publ/othp42.htm>

Bank of England, 'FinTech Accelerator Proof of Concept' (10 July 2017) <https://www.bankofengland.co.uk/-/media/boe/files/fintech/ripple.pdf?la=en&hash=75E5F445230B8A2B794C208D29619A3E33F1FFE7>

Bank of England, 'Responses to the Bank of England's Discussion Paper on New Forms of Digital Money' (24 March 2022) Discussion Paper <https://www.bankofengland.co.uk/paper/2022/responses-to-the-bank-of-englands-discussion-paper-on-new-forms-of-digital-money>

Bank of England, 'Bank of England and Massachusetts Institute of Technology Joint Central Bank Digital Currency Collaboration' (25 March 2022) <https://www.bankofengland.co.uk/news/2022/march/boe-and-massachusetts-institute-of-technology-joint-cbdc-collaboration>

Bank of England, 'How Does Quantitative Easing Work?' (updated 21 April 2022) <https://www.bankofengland.co.uk/monetary-policy/quantitative-easing>

Bank of England, 'Our Response to Coronavirus (Covid)' <https://www.bankofengland.co.uk/coronavirus>

Banque de France, 'Network for Greening the Financial System' (8 January 2019) <https://www.banque-france.fr/en/financial-stability/international-role/network-greening-financial-system>

Banque de France, 'Liste des candidatures retenues pour les expérimentations de monnaie digitale de banque centrale (MDBC)' (20 July 2020) <https://www.banque-france.fr/communique-de-presse/liste-des-candidatures-retenues-pour-les-experimentations-de-monnaie-digitale-de-banque-centrale>

Barabasi, Albert-László, *Linked: The New Science of Networks* (Perseus 2002)

Barber, Lionel and Clare Jones, 'Interview: Mario Draghi Declares Victory in Battle over the Euro' (*Financial Times*, 30 September 2019) <https://www.ft.com/content/b59a4a04-9b26-11e9-9c06-a4640c9feebb>

Baron, David P., 'Commitment and Fairness in a Dynamic Regulatory Relationship' (1987) 54 RevEconStud 413

Baron, David P. and David Besanko, 'Regulation and Information in a Continuing Relationship' (1984) 1 InfEconPol'y 267

Barontini, Christian and Harry Holden, 'Proceeding with Caution—A Survey on Central Bank Digital Currency' (January 2019) BIS Papers No. 101 <https://www.bis.org/publ/bppdf/bispap101.pdf>

Barrdear, John and Michael Kumhof, 'The Macroeconomics of Central Bank Issued Digital Currencies' (July 2016) Bank of England—Staff Working Paper No. 605 <https://www.bankofengland.co.uk/-/media/boe/files/working-paper/2016/the-macroeconomics-of-central-bank-issued-digital-currencies>

Basel Committee on Banking Supervision, 'Basel III: The Liquidity Coverage Ratio and Liquidity Risk Monitoring Tools' (January 2013) <https://www.bis.org/publ/bcbs238.pdf>

Basel Committee on Banking Supervision, 'Basel III: The Net Stable Funding Ratio' (October 2014) <https://www.bis.org/bcbs/publ/d295.pdf>

Basin, Gary, 'Crypto Derivatives, Lending, and a Touch of Stablecoin' (*Medium*, 12 July 2018) <https://medium.com/hackernoon/crypto-derivatives-lending-and-a-touch-of-stablecoin-59e727510024>

Battiston, Stefano, Doyne J. Farmer, Andreas Flache, Diego Garlaschelli, Andrew G. Haldane, Hans Heesterbeek, Cars Hommes, Carlo Jaeger, Robert May, and Marten Scheffer, 'Complexity Theory and Financial Regulation' (2016) 351 Science 818

Baxter, Lawrence G., 'Adaptive Regulation in the Amoral Bazaar' (2011) 128 SALJ 253

Baxter, Lawrence G., 'Capture in Financial Regulation: Can We Channel It toward the Common Good' (2011) 21 CornellJL&PubPol'y 175

Baxter, Lawrence G., 'Betting Big: Value, Caution and Accountability in an Era of Large Banks and Complex Finance' (2012) 31 RevBank&FinL 765

BBVA, 'What Is the Difference Between Blockchain and DLT' (3 May 2018) <https://www.bbva.com/en/difference-dlt-blockchain/>

Bebchuk, Lucian A., 'Federalism and the Corporation: The Desirable Limits on State Competition in Corporate Law' (1992) 105 HarvLRev 1435

Bebchuk, Lucian, 'Executive Pay and the Financial Crisis' (*World Bank Blogs*, 31 January 2012) <https://blogs.worldbank.org/allaboutfinance/executive-pay-and-the-financial-crisis>

Bebchuk, Lucian A. and Roberto Tallarita, 'The Illusory Promise of Stakeholder Governance' (2021) 106 CornellLRev 91

Becht, Marco, Yuliya Kamisarenka, and Anete Pajuste, 'Loyalty Shares with Tenure Voting—A Coasian Bargain? Evidence from the Loi Florange Experiment' (2018) European Corporate Governance Institute (ECGI) —Law Working Paper No. 398/2018 <https://ssrn.com/abstract=3166494>

Becker, Samuel, 'What Are Flash Loans & How Do They Work?' (*SoFi*, 28 December 2021) <https://www.sofi.com/learn/content/flash-loans/>

Beedham, Matthew, 'Two-Thirds of Failed Stablecoin Projects Were Backed by Gold' (*Hard Fork*, 27 June 2019) <https://thenextweb.com/hardfork/2019/06/27/stablecoin-projects-gold-failed/>

Benedetti, Hugo and Leonard Kostovetsky, 'Digital Tulips? Returns to Investors in Initial Coin Offerings' (2021) 66 JCorpFin

Benoit, David and Sharon Terlep, 'Activist Peltz Narrowly Wins P&G Board Seat, New Count Shows' (*WSJ*, 15 November 2017) <https://www.wsj.com/articles/activist-nelson-peltz-elected-to-p-g-board-1510782775#_=_>

Benson, Jeff, 'Japan Virtual Currency Exchange Association Asks FSA to Make It Official' (*itsisue*, 6 August 2018) <https://itsisue.tistory.com/1302>

Berentsen, Aleksander and Fabian Schar, 'The Case for Central Bank Electronic Money and the Non-Case for Central Bank Cryptocurrencies' (2018) 100 FedResBankStLRev 97

Berg, Florian, Julian Fritz Kölbel, and Roberto Rigobon, 'Aggregate Confusion: The Divergence of ESG Ratings' (2019) MIT Sloan Research Paper No. 5822-19 <https://papers.ssrn.com/sol3/papers.cfm?abstract_id=3438533>

Berger, David J., Steven Davidoff Solomon, and Aaron Jedidiah Benjamin, 'Tenure Voting and the U.S. Public Company' (*WSGR*, 2016) <https://www.wsgr.com/publications/PDFSearch/tenure-voting.pdf>

Berman, Harold J., *Law and Revolution: The Formation of the Western Legal Tradition* (HUP 1983)

Berman, Sheri and Kathleen R. McNamara, 'Bank on Democracy: Why Central Banks Need Public Oversight' (1999) 78 ForeignAff 2, 2

Bertsch, Ken, 'Snap and the Rise of No-Vote Common Shares' (*HLS Forum on Corporate Governance*, 26 May 2017) <https://corpgov.law.harvard.edu/2017/05/26/snap-and-the-rise-of-no-vote-common-shares/>

Bertsch, Ken, 'Remarks to the SEC Investor Advisory Committee' (*SEC*, 13 September 2018) <https://www.sec.gov/spotlight/investor-advisory-committee-2012/iac091318-opening-remarks-ken-bertsch.pdf>

Betti, Emilio, *La teoria generale dell'interpretazione* (Giuffre 1955)

Betti, Emilio, *L'ermeneutica come metodica generale delle scienze dello spirito* (first published 1962, Tab Edizioni 2022)

Beyoud, Lydia, 'Wyoming Wants to Be "Delaware of the West" with Business Court' (*Bloomberg Law*, 9 January 2019) <https://news.bloomberglaw.com/banking-law/wyoming-wants-to-be-delaware-of-the-west-with-business-court>

Bharathan, Vipin, 'People's Bank of China Draft Law Provides a Legal Basis for Digital Currency Electronic Payments (DC/EP) and Bans All Stablecoins Backed by Renminbi Reserves' (*Forbes*, 24 October 2020) <https://www.forbes.com/sites/vipinbharathan/2020/10/24/peoples-bank-of-china-draft-law-provides-a-legal-basis-for-digital-currency-electronic-payments-dcep-and-bans-all-stablecoins-backed-by-renminbi-reserves/>

Bholat, David and Karla Martinez Gutierrez, 'The Ownership of Central Banks' (*Bank Underground*, 18 October 2019) <https://bankunderground.co.uk/2019/10/18/the-ownership-of-central-banks/>

Binance Academy, 'What Is an Initial Game Offering (IGO)?' (7 January 2022) <https://academy.binance.com/en/articles/what-is-an-initial-game-offering-igo>

Bini Smaghi, Lorenzo, 'Central Bank Independence: From Theory to Practice' (Speech at the Good Governance and Effective Partnership Conference, Budapest, 19 April 2007) <https://www.ecb.europa.eu/press/key/date/2007/html/sp070419.en.html>

Birch, Joseph, 'Major Crypto Exchanges Launch OTC Desks Despite the Crypto Winter' (*Cointelegraph*, 11 February 2019) <https://cointelegraph.com/news/major-crypto-exchanges-launch-otc-desks-despite-the-crypto-winter>

Birch, Joseph, 'Telegram's Legal Battle with the SEC Heats Up over TON Bank Records' (*Cointelegraph*, 16 January 2020) <https://cointelegraph.com/news/telegrams-legal-battle-with-the-sec-heats-up-over-ton-bank-records>

Bird, Mike, 'The Fed Is Settling into Its Role as the World's Central Bank' (*WSJ*, 1 April 2020) <https://www.wsj.com/articles/the-fed-is-settling-into-its-role-as-the-worlds-central-bank-11585732095>

BIS, 'Implications for Central Banks of the Development of Electronic Money' (1996) <https://www.bis.org/publ/bisp01.pdf>

BIS, 'Principles for Financial Market Infrastructures' (April 2012) <https://www.bis.org/cpmi/publ/d101a.pdf>

BIS, *BIS Annual Economic Report 2019* (2019) <https://www.bis.org/publ/arpdf/ar2019e3.pdf>

BIS Committee on Banking Supervision, 'Prudential Treatment of Cryptoasset Exposures' (June 2021) <https://www.bis.org/bcbs/publ/d519.pdf>

BIS Committee on Payment and Settlement Systems, 'The Role of Central Bank Money in Payment Systems' (August 2003) <https://www.bis.org/cpmi/publ/d55.pdf>

BIS Committee on Payments and Market Infrastructures and BIS Markets Committee, 'Central Bank Digital Currencies' (2018) <https://www.bis.org/cpmi/publ/d174.pdf>

BIS Committee on Payments and Market Infrastructures and IOSCO, 'Application of the Principles for Financial Market Infrastructures to Stablecoin Arrangements' (October 2021) <https://www.bis.org/cpmi/publ/d198.htm>

BIS Committee on Payments and Market Infrastructures, 'Distributed Ledger Technology in Payment, Clearing and Settlement' (February 2017) <https://www.bis.org/cpmi/publ/d157.pdf>

BIS Committee on the Global Financial System, 'Designing Frameworks for Central Bank Liquidity Assistance: Addressing New Challenges' (April 2017) CGFS Papers n 58 <https://www.bis.org/publ/cgfs58.pdf>

BIS Innovation Hub Hong Kong Centre, Hong Kong Monetary Authority, Bank of Thailand, Digital Currency Institute of the People's Bank of China and Central Bank of the United Arab Emirates, 'Inthanon-LionRock to mBridge—Building a Multi CBDC Platform for International Payments' (28 September 2021) <https://www.bis.org/publ/othp40.pdf>

BIS Monetary and Economic Department, 'CBDCs in emerging market economies' (April 2022) BIS Papers No. 123 <https://www.bis.org/publ/bppdf/bispap123.pdf>

Bitcoin Exchange Guide, 'Best Cryptocurrency Custody Companies in 2019: Top Bitcoin and Blockchain Asset Custodian Services' (8 January 2019) <https://bitcoinexchangeguide.com/best-cryptocurrency-custody-companies-in-2019-top-bitcoin-and-blockchain-asset-custodian-services/>

Bitcoin Suisse, 'What Is the FATF Travel Rule?' <https://www.bitcoinsuisse.com/research/specials/what-is-the-fatf-travel-rule>

Bitkom, 'Bitkom Position Paper on the European Commission's Proposals on Markets in Crypto-Assets (MiCAR) and a Pilot Regime for Market Infrastructures based on Distributed Ledger Technology' (16 October 2020) <https://www.bitkom.org/EN/Position-Paper-on-the-European-Commissions-proposals-on-Markets-in-Crypto-Assets-MiCA>

BitMEX, 'Initial Exchange Offerings' (13 May 2019) <https://blog.bitmex.com/initial-excha nge-offerings/>
bitMEX, 'Perpetual Contracts Guide' <https://www.bitmex.com/app/perpetualContractsGuide>
Bjorøy, Trond Vidar, 'Blockchain Fundings Are Trendy, but We're Still in the Wild West Days' (*Venturebeat*, 14 May 2017) <https://venturebeat.com/2017/05/14/blockchain-fundings-are-trendy-but-were-still-in-the-wild-west-days/>
Black, Fischer, 'Banking and Interest Rates in a World Without Money: The Effects of Uncontrolled Banking' (1970) 1 JBankRes 8
Black, Fischer and Myron Scholes, 'The Pricing of Options and Corporate Liabilities' (1973) 81 JPolEcon 637
Black, Julia, 'Constitutionalising Self-Regulation' (1996) 59 ModLRev 24
Black, Julia, 'Decentring Regulation: Understanding the Role of Regulation and Self-Regulation in a "Post-Regulatory" World' (2001) 54 CLP 103
Black, Julia, 'Forms and Paradoxes of Principles Based Regulation' (2008) 3 CMLJ 425
Black, Julia, 'The Rise, Fall and Fate of Principles Based Regulation' in Alexander Kern and Niamh Maloney (eds), *Law Reform and Financial Markets* (Elgar 2011) 3–34
Black, Julia, Martyn Hopper, and Christa Band, 'Making a Success of Principles-Based Regulation' (2007) 1 L&FinMarRev 191
Blair, Margaret M., 'Boards of Directors as Mediating Hierarchs' (2015) 38 SeattleULRev 297
Blemus, Stephan and Claire Pion, 'Blockchain, minibons et titres financiers—Des règles ad hoc pour les chaînes de bloc' (2019) 1 RDBF 25
Bloch, Raphaël, 'Société Générale donne le départ à sa plateforme blockchain' (*Les Echos*, 23 April 2019) <https://www.lesechos.fr/finance-marches/banque-assurances/societe-gener ale-donne-le-depart-a-sa-plateforme-blockchain-1013500>
Blockdata, 'List of crypto custody providers' <https://www.blockdata.tech/markets/use-cases/ custody-solutions>
Bloomberg, 'Goldman, Barclays Back Alan Howard's Crypto Platform' (22 May 2022) <https:// www.bloomberg.com/news/articles/2022-05-15/goldman-barclays-invest-in-alan-howard-crypto-trading-platform>
Bloomberg, Jason, 'JPM Coin From JPMorgan Chase Vs. Crypto Fans: Who's Missing the Point?' (*Forbes*, 22 February 2019) <https://www.forbes.com/sites/jasonbloomberg/2019/ 02/22/jpm-coin-from-jpmorgan-chase-vs-crypto-fans-whos-missing-the-point/>
Bloomberg Intelligence, 'ESG Assets May Hit $53 Trillion by 2025, a Third of Global AUM' (23 February 2021) <https://www.bloomberg.com/professional/blog/esg-assets-may-hit-53-trillion-by-2025-a-third-of-global-aum/>
Boar, Codruta, Henry Holden, and Amber Wadsworth, 'Impending Arrival—A Sequel to the Survey on Central Bank Digital Currency' (January 2020) BIS Papers No. 107 <https://www. bis.org/publ/bppdf/bispap107.pdf>
Board of Governors of the Federal Reserve System, 'Money and Payments: The U.S. Dollar in the Age of Digital Transformation' (22 January 2022) https://www.federalreserve.gov/publi cations/files/money-and-payments-20220120.pdf>
Boissay, Frederic and Lorenzo Cappiello, 'Micro- versus Macro-Prudential Supervision: Potential Differences, Tensions and Complementarities' (May 2014) ECB—Financial Stability Review 135 <https://www.ecb.europa.eu/pub/pdf/fsr/art/ecb.fsrart201405_03.en.pdf>
Bond, Shannon and Nicole Bullock, 'Lyft IPO Revs Up debate on Dual-Class Share Structures' (*Financial Times*, 25 February 2019) <https://www.ft.com/content/c7d323ba-36b0-11e9-bd3a-8b2a211d90d5>
Bonpay, 'Blockchain as a Perfect Solution for the Internet of Things' (*Medium*, 1 December 2017) <https://medium.com/@bonpay/blockchain-as-a-perfect-solution-for-the-internet-of-things-953ef5eef8b>

Bordo, Michael D., 'A Brief History of Central Banks' (2007) Federal Reserve Bank of Cleveland Economic Commentary (12 December 2007) <https://www.clevelandfed.org/en/publicati ons/economic-commentary/2007/ec-20071201-a-brief-history-of-central-banks >

Bordo, Michael D. and Pierre Siklos, 'Central Banks: Evolution and Innovation in Historical Perspective' in Rodney Edvinsson, Tor Jacobson, and Daniel Waldenström (eds), *Sveriges Riksbank and the History of Central Banking* (CUP 2018) 26–89

Bordo, Michael D., Owen Humpage, and Anna J. Schwartz, 'The Evolution of the Federal Reserve Swap Lines since 1962' (2014) NBER Working Paper 20755 <https://www.nber.org/system/files/working_papers/w20755/w20755.pdf>

Boreiko, Dmitri, Guido Ferrarini, and Paolo Giudici, 'Blockchain Startups and Prospectus Regulation' (2019) 20 EBOR 665

Bosworth, Andrew and Nick Clegg, 'Building the Metaverse Responsibly' (*Meta*, 27 September 2021) <https://about.fb.com/news/2021/09/building-the-metaverse-responsibly/>

Boudon, Raymond, 'Weber and Durkheim: Beyond The Differences A Common Important Paradigm?' (1995) 49 RIntlPh 22

Bouriaux, Szlvie and Richard MacMinn, 'Securitization of Catastrophe Risk: New Developments in Insurance-Linked Securities and Derivatives' (2009) 32 JInsurIssues 1

Brainard, Lael, 'Distributed Ledger Technology: Implications for Payments, Clearing, and Settlement' (Speech at the Institute of International Finance Annual Meeting Panel on Blockchain, Washington DC, 7 October 2016) <https://www.bis.org/review/r1610 14a.pdf>

Braithwaite, Joanne P., 'Standard Form Contracts as Transnational Law: Evidence from the Derivatives Markets' (2012) 75 ModLRev 779

Braithwaite, John and Peter Drahos, *Global Business Regulation* (CUP 2000)

Bratton, William and Adam J. Levitin, 'A Transactional Genealogy of Scandal: From Michael Milken to Enron to Goldman Sachs' (2013) 86 SCalLRev 783

Brave NewCoin, 'Coinbase Is Evaluating IEO and STO Platforms' (17 September 2019) <https://bravenewcoin.com/insights/coinbase-is-evaluating-ieo-and-sto-platforms>

Brennan, Charles and William Lunn, 'The Trust Disrupter' (*Finextra*, 3 August 2016) <https://www.finextra.com/finextra-downloads/newsdocs/document-1063851711.pdf>

Brett, Jason, 'As Congress Asks the Fed to Look into a Digital Dollar, Former FDIC Chair Sheila Bair Is Ahead of the Curve … Again' (*Fortune*, 5 October 2019) <https://www.forbes.com/sites/jasonbrett/2019/10/05/as-congress-asks-the-fed-to-look-into-a-digital-dollar-former-fdic-chair-sheila-bair-is-ahead-of-the-curve--again/#3b69bb8e3c14>

Broadridge, 'How Blockchain Transforms Proxy Voting' (24 April 2018) <https://www.broadri dge.com/video/how-blockchain-transforms-proxy-voting>

Broadridge, 'Santander and Broadridge Complete a First Practical Use of Blockchain for Investor Voting at an Annual General Meeting' (17 May 2018) <https://www.broadridge.com/press-release/2018/santander-and-broadridge-completed-practical-use-of-blockchain>

Broadridge, 'ICJ and Broadridge Execute the First Blockchain-Based Interoperable Proxy Voting Process in Japan' (14 January 2019) <https://www.broadridge.com/intl/press-release/2019/icj-and-broadridge-execute-the-proxy-voting-process>

Brown, Eric, 'Breaking Down JPM Coin' (*Hakernoon*, 17 February 2019) <https://hackernoon.com/breaking-down-jpm-coin-f31c41f3f325>

Brown, Richard, 'Decentralized Autonomous Organization' (*Ethereum*) <https://ethereum.org/en/dao/>

Browne, F. X. and David Cronin, 'Payment Technologies, Financial Innovation, and Laissez-Faire Banking' (1995) 15 CatoJ 101

Brownsword, Roger, 'Regulatory Fitness: Fintech, Funny Money, and Smart Contracts' (2019) 20 EBOR 5

Brumfield Fry, Patricia, 'Why Enact UETA? The Role of UETA after E-Sign' (2000) <https://www.uniformlaws.org/HigherLogic/System/DownloadDocumentFile.ashx?DocumentFileKey=97560e15-8b54-1237-70ca-683b36af5f43&forceDialog=0>

Brummer, Christopher, '"99 Problems"—Written Testimony Before the United States House Committee on Financial Services Examining Facebook's Proposed Cryptocurrency and Its Impact on Consumers, Investors, and the American Financial System' (17 July 2019) <https://financialservices.house.gov/uploadedfiles/hhrg-116-ba00-wstate-brummerc-20190717.pdf>

Brummer, Christopher, 'Prologue to Daniel Gorfine, FinTech Innovation: Building a 21st Century Regulator' (November 2017) Georgetown University IIEL Issue Brief 11/2017 <https://www.law.georgetown.edu/iiel/wp-content/uploads/sites/8/2018/01/LabCFTC-Chris-Brummer-Dan-Gorfine-IIEL-Issue-Brief-November-2017-Accessible.pdf>

Brummer, Christopher and Yesha Yadav, 'Fintech and the Innovation Trilemma' (2019) 107 GeoLJ 235

Brummer, Christopher and Evan Campbell, 'How Mpesa Transformed the World of Fintech' (*Rollcall*, 20 October 2020) <https://rollcall.com/podcasts/fintech-beat/how-mpesa-transformed-the-world-of-fintech/>

Brummer, Christopher, Trevor Kiviat, and Jai Ruhi Massari, 'What Should Be Disclosed in an Initial Coin Offering?' in Christopher J. Brummer (ed), *Cryptoassets: Legal, Regulatory, and Monetary Perspectives* (OUP 2019) 157–202

Brunnermeier, Markus K. and Martin Oehmke, 'Complexity in Financial Markets' (10 September 2009) <https://scholar.princeton.edu/sites/default/files/complexity_0.pdf>

Bryanov, Kirill, 'Breaking the Peg: Every Stablecoin Has Its Points of Failure' (*Cointelegraph*, 19 November 2018) <https://cointelegraph.com/news/breaking-the-peg-every-stablecoin-has-its-points-of-failure>

Buckley, Ross P., Douglas Arner, Dirk Zetzsche, and Eriks Selga, 'TECHRISK' (2020) SingJLS 35

Bundesanstalt für Finanzdienstleistungsaufsicht, 'Supervisory Classification of Tokens or Cryptocurrencies Underlying "Initial Coin Offerings" (ICOs) as Financial Instruments in the Field of Securities Supervision' (23 March 2018) <https://www.bafin.de/SharedDocs/Downloads/EN/Merkblatt/WA/dl_hinweisschreiben_einordnung_ICOs_en.html;jsessionid=4D49DEF704E4A19C2AD8163869933C9D.2_cid370?nn=8249098>

Bundesanstalt für Finanzdienstleistungsaufsicht, 'Guidance Notice—Guidelines Concerning the Statutory Definition of Crypto Custody Business (section 1 (1a) sentence 2 no. 6 of the German Banking Act (Kreditwesengesetz—KWG)' (3 February 2020) <https://www.bafin.de/SharedDocs/Veroeffentlichungen/EN/Merkblatt/mb_200302_kryptoverwahrgeschaeft_en.html>

Bundesanstalt für Finanzdienstleistungsaufsicht, *Annual Report 2020* (24 August 2021) <https://www.bafin.de/SharedDocs/Downloads/EN/Jahresbericht/dl_jb_2020_en.pdf;jsessionid=2F90C3647A6AC1447FCDB914F10029EE.1_cid501?__blob=publicationFile&v=3>

Bundesministerium für Wirtschaft und Energie, 'Blockchain Strategy of the Federal Government: We Set Out the Course for the Token Economy' (18 September 2019) <https://www.bmwk.de/Redaktion/EN/Publikationen/Digitale-Welt/blockchain-strategy.pdf?__blob=publicationFile&v=3>

Buonanno, Luigi, 'Civil Liability in the Era of New Technology: The Influence of Blockchain Blockchain as the Backbone of a New Technology-based Civil Liability Regime' (2019) European Law Institute <https://www.europeanlawinstitute.eu/fileadmin/user_upload/p_eli/YLA_Award/Submission_ELI_Young_Lawyers_Award_Luigi_Buonanno_ELI_2019.pdf>

Burgess, Matt, 'What Is the Internet of Things? WIRED Explains' (*Wired*, 16 February 2018) <https://www.wired.co.uk/article/internet-of-things-what-is-explained-iot>

Business Insider, 'One US Regulator Has Joined the R3 Blockchain Consortium' (20 March 2017) <https://www.businessinsider.com/one-us-regulator-has-joined-the-r3-blockchain-consortium-2017-3?r=US&IR=T>

Business Roundtable, 'Statement on the Purpose of a Corporation' (19 August 2019) <https://s3.amazonaws.com/brt.org/BRT-StatementonthePurposeofaCorporationOctober2020.pdf>

Buterin, Vitalik, 'Chain Interoperability' (9 September 2016) <https://allquantor.at/blockchainbib/pdf/vitalik2016chain.pdf>

Buterin, Vitalik, 'Analyzing Token Sale Models' (*Vitalik Buterin's website*, 9 June 2017) <http://vitalik.ca/general/2017/06/09/sales.html>

Buterin, Vitalik, 'A Next-Generation Smart Contract and Decentralized Application Platform' (*Ethereum*, 2018) <https://ethereum.org/669c9e2e2027310b6b3cdce6e1c52962/Ethereum_Whitepaper_-_Buterin_2014.pdf>

Bybit, 'Explained: Fractional NFTs (F-NFTs) and How They Work' (9 February 2022) <https://learn.bybit.com/nft/what-are-fractional-nfts/>

Cantor Futures Exchange, 'New Contract Submission—Futures Exchange Bitcoin Swap Contract' (1 December 2017) <https://www.cftc.gov/sites/default/files/filings/ptc/17/12/ptc120117cantordcm001.pdf>

Capco, 'The OTC Crypto Market: At a Glance' (4 February 2019) <https://www.capco.com/Intelligence/Capco-Intelligence/The-OTC-Market-At-A-Glance>

Capgemini, 'Smart Contracts in Financial Services: Getting from Hype to Reality' (August 2018) <https://www.capgemini.com/at-de/wp-content/uploads/sites/25/2017/08/smart_contracts_in_fs.pdf>

Cary, William L., 'Federalism and Corporate Law: Reflections upon Delaware' 1974) 88 YaleLJ 663

Cassano, Jay, 'What Are Smart Contracts? Cryptocurrency's Killer App' (*FastCompany*, 17 September 2014) <http://www.fastcolabs.com/3035723/app-economy/smart-contracts-could-becryptocurrencys-killer-app>

Casteleyn, Tom and Lucien Foster, 'Cryptocurrencies, Custody and Third-Party Access' (*Post Trade 360*, May 2019) <https://posttrade360.com/news/technology/cryptocurrencies-custody-and-third-party-access/>

Castellano, Giuliano, 'Towards a General Framework for a Common Definition of "Securities": Financial Markets Regulation in Multilingual Contexts' (2012) 17 UnifLRev 449

Catalini, Christian and Joshua S. Gans, 'Some Simple Economics of the Blockchain' (2019) 63 CommACM 80 <https://cacm.acm.org/magazines/2020/7/245703-some-simple-economics-of-the-blockchain/fulltext>

Catalani, Christian and Alonso de Gortari, 'On the Economic Design of Stablecoins' (2021) <https://papers.ssrn.com/sol3/papers.cfm?abstract_id=3899499>

Celerier, Claire and Boris Vallee, 'What Drives Financial Complexity? A Look into the Retail Market for Structured Products' (2013) Les Cahiers de Recherche—1013 HEC Paris

Centeno, Miguel A., Manish Nag, Thayer S. Patterson, Andrew Shaver, and A. Jason Windawi, 'The Emergence of Global Systematic Risk' (2015) 41 AnnRS 65

Centieiro, Henrique, 'The Insane Future of Web 3.0 and the Metaverse' (*Medium*, 23 January 2022) <https://medium.datadriveninvestor.com/the-insane-future-of-web-3-0-and-the-metaverse-4cec3f13895a>

CERN, 'Where the Web Was Born' <https://home.cern/science/computing/where-web-was-born>

Chainanalysis, '2022 Biggest Year Ever For Crypto Hacking with $3.8 Billion Stolen, Primarily from DeFi Protocols and by North Korea-linked Attackers' (1 February 2023) <https://blog.chainalysis.com/reports/2022-biggest-year-ever-for-crypto-hacking>

Chamber of Digital Commerce, 'Chamber of Digital Commerce Launches Smart Contracts Alliance' (28 July 2016) <https://digitalchamber.org/chamber-of-digital-commerce-launches-smart-contracts-alliance/>

Chamber of Digital Commerce, '"Smart Contracts" Legal Primer' (January 2018) <https://bw-98d8a23fd60826a2a474c5b4f5811707-bwcore.s3.amazonaws.com/photos/SmartConPrimer.pdf>

Chamber of Digital Commerce, 'Joint Statement in Response to State "Smart Contracts" Legislation' (April 2018) <https://d3h0qzni6h08fz.cloudfront.net/Smart-Contract-Signatories1.pdf>

Chamber of Digital Commerce, 'Smart Contracts: Is the Law Ready?' (September 2018) <https://digitalchamber.org/smart-contracts-paper-press/>

Chamber of Digital Commerce, 'Chamber Supports Coordinated Approach among Industry and Regulators Globally' (2 November 2018) <https://digitalchamber.s3.amazonaws.com/Smart-Contracts-Whitepaper-WEB.pdf>

Chamber of Digital Commerce, 'The Chamber Is Turning 4!' <https://digitalchamber.org/chamber-anniversary/>

Chander, Anupam and Randall Costa, 'Clearing Credit Default Swaps: A Case Study in Global Legal Convergence' (2010) 10 ChiJIntlL 639

Chandler, Simon, 'Biggest Crypto Hedge Funds and What They Tell about the Market' (*Cointelegraph*, 16 August 2019) <https://cointelegraph.com/news/biggest-crypto-hedge-funds-and-what-they-tell-about-the-market>

Chaudhuri, Ranajoy Ray, 'The Free Banking Era', in Ranajoy Ray Chaudhuri, *The Changing Face of American Banking* (Palgrave 2014) 7–19

Chervinsky, Jake and Benjamin Sauter, 'Will Fiat-Backed Stablecoins Pass Legal Muster with the SEC and CFTC?' (*CoinDesk*, 2 March 2019) <https://www.coindesk.com/will-fiat-backed-stablecoins-pass-legal-muster-with-the-sec-and-cftc>

Chick, Victoria and Sheila Dow, 'The Meaning of Open Systems' (2005) 12 JEconMeth 363

Chiomenti, Cuatrecasas, Gide Loyrette Nouel, and Gleiss Lutz, 'NFT: Cross-Border Perspectives on Unprecedented Regulatory Challenges' (February 2022) <https://www.gide.com/sites/default/files/nft_-_european_network_3.pdf>

Chipolina, Scott, 'Terra Crisis Fans Regulatory Concerns over $180bn Stablecoin Market' (*Financial Times*, 11 May 2022) <https://www.ft.com/content/48d82c7a-495f-4d5e-a87a-a56bea58e760>

Chitra, Tarun, 'Competitive Equilibria Between Staking and On-Chain Lending' (*Cornell University arXiv*, 5 February 2020) <https://arxiv.org/abs/2001.00919>

Chiu, Iris H-Y, 'Transcending Regulatory Fragmentation and the Construction of an Economy-Society Discourse: Implications for Regulatory Policy Derived from a Functional Approach to Understanding Shadow Banking' (2016) 42 JCorpL 327

Chiu, Iris H-Y and Jason G. Allen, 'Exploring the Assetisation and Financialisation of Non-Fungible Tokens (NFTs): Opportunities and Regulatory Implications' (2022) 37 Bank&FinLRev 401

Choi, Stephen, 'Market Lessons for Gatekeepers' (1998) 92 NwULRev 916

Choi, Stephen J. and Adam C. Pritchard, *Securities Regulation, Cases and Analysis* (4th edn, Foundation Press 2015)

Christensen, Clayton M., *The Innovator's Dilemma: When New Technologies Cause Great Firms to Fail* (HBSP 2016)

Christensen, Clayton M., Michael E. Raynor, and Rory McDonald, 'What Is Disruptive Innovation?' (*Harvard Business Review*, December 2015) <https://hbr.org/2015/12/what-is-disruptive-innovation>

Chung, John J., 'Money as Simulacrum: The Legal Nature and Reality of Money' (2009) 5 HastingsBusLJ 109 <https://repository.uchastings.edu/hastings_business_law_journal/vol5/iss1/3/>

Church & Dwight Co., 'Preliminary Proxy Statement' (3 April 2003) <https://investor.churchdwight.com/static-files/09f6df43-ffc1-4c0b-9167-c2b4df8ce142>

Cieplak, Jenny and Simon Leefatt, 'Smart Contracts: A Smart Way to Automate Performance' (2017) 1 GeoL&TechRev 418

Circiumaru, Alexandru, Federico Casolari, Mariarosaria Taddeo, Aina Turillazzi, and Lucino Floridi, 'How to Improve Smart Contracts in the European Union Data Act' (2023) 2 DISO 9

Claeys, Grégory, Maria Demertzis, and Konstantinos Efstathiou, 'Cryptocurrencies and Monetary Policy' (*European Parliament—Monetary Dialogue*, July 2018) <https://www.europarl.europa.eu/cmsdata/150000/BRUEGEL_FINAL%20publication.pdf>

Clancy, Luke, 'SocGen's Digitised Bond Passes Settlement Test' (*Risk.net*, 6 July 2020) <https://www.risk.net/derivatives/7650991/socgens-digitised-bond-passes-settlement-test>

Clark, Jen, 'What Is the Internet of Things (IoT)?' (*IBM Business Operations Blog*, 17 November 2016) <https://www.ibm.com/blogs/internet-of-things/what-is-the-iot/>

Clark, Robert C., 'The Four Stages of Capitalism: Reflections on Investment Management Treaties' (1981) 94 HarvLRev 561

Clayton, Jay, 'Statement on Cryptocurrencies and Initial Coin Offerings' (*SEC*, 11 December 2017) <https://www.sec.gov/news/public-statement/statementclayton-2017-12-11>

Clayton, Jay and J. Christopher Giancarlo, 'Regulators Are Looking at Cryptocurrency' (*WSJ*, 24 January 2018) <https://www.wsj.com/articles/regulators-are-looking-at-cryptocurrency-1516836363>

Clinton, William J. and Albert Gore, 'A Framework for Global Electronic Commerce' (1997) <https://clintonwhitehouse4.archives.gov/WH/New/Commerce/read.html>

CME Group, 'Bitcoin Futures—Contract Specs' <https://www.cmegroup.com/cme-group-futures-exchange/options-bitcoin-futures.html>

CME Group, 'What Are Bitcoin Futures?' <https://www.cmegroup.com/education/courses/introduction-to-bitcoin/what-are-bitcoin-futures.html>

Coats, Warren, 'In Search of a Monetary Anchor, Commodity Standards Re-examined' in Tomas J. T. Baliño and Carlo Cottarelli (eds), *Frameworks for Monetary Stability: Policy Issues and Country Experiences* (IMF 1994) 247–273

Coffee, Jr., John C., 'Understanding Enron: "It's the Gatekeepers, Stupid" ' (2002) 57 BusLaw 1403

Coffee, Jr., John C., 'Gatekeeper Failure and Reform: The Challenge of Fashioning Relevant Reforms' in Klaus J. Hopt, Eddy Wymeersch, Hideki Kanda, and Harald Baum (eds), *Corporate Governance in Context: Corporations, States, and Markets in Europe, Japan, and the US* (OUP 2005) 599–662

Coffee, Jr., John C., *Gatekeepers: The Professions and Corporate Governance* (OUP 2006)

Coffee, Jr., John C., et al., 'Enhancing Investor Protection and the Regulation of Securities Markets' (Hearing Before the U.S. Senate Committee on Banking, Housing, and Urban Affairs, 10 March 2009) <https://www.govinfo.gov/content/pkg/CHRG-111shrg51395/pdf/CHRG-111shrg51395.pdf>

Coffee, Jr., John C., 'Systemic Risk after Dodd–Frank: Contingent Capital and the Need for Regulatory Strategies beyond Oversight' (2011) 111 ColumLRev 795

Coffey, Ronald J., 'The Economic Realities of a "Security": Is There a More Meaningful Formula?' (1966) 18 CaseWResLRev 367

Cohen, Patricia, 'Critics Say I.M.F. Loan Fees Are Hurting Nations in Desperate Need' (*NYT*, 22 January 2022) <https://www.nytimes.com/2022/01/14/business/economy/imf-surcharges.html>

Cohn, Alan, Travis West, and Chelsea Parker, 'Smart After All: Blockchain, Smart Contracts, Parametric Insurance, and Smart Energy Grids' (2017) 1 GeoL&TechRev 273

Coin360, 'Top 100 Cryptocurrency by Market Capitalization' <https://coin360.com/table>

Coin Marketcap <https://coinmarketcap.com>

Collins, Christopher G., Simon Potter, and Edwin M. Truman, 'Enhancing Central Bank Cooperation in the COVID-19 Pandemic' (*PIIE Blog*, 9 April 2020) <https://www.piie.com/blogs/realtime-economic-issues-watch/enhancing-central-bank-cooperation-covid-19-pandemic>

Commission Recommendation of 22 March 2010 on the scope and effects of legal tender of euro banknotes and coins [2010] OJ L 83/1

Commission's Directorate-General for Financial Stability, Financial Services and Capital Markets Union, 'Digital Finance Package' (24 September 2020) <https://ec.europa.eu/info/publications/200924-digital-finance-proposals_en>

Commissione Nazionale per le Società e la Borsa, *Annual Report 2020* (31 March 2021) <https://www.consob.it/documents/46180/46181/ar2020.pdf/4235c99f-0540-4784-980e-13c0ed91da0c>

Committee on Payments and Market Infrastructures, BIS Innovation Hub, International Monetary Fund (IMF) and the World Bank, 'Central Bank Digital Currencies for Cross-Border Payments—Report to the G20' (July 2021) <https://www.bis.org/publ/othp38.htm>

Concannon, David L., Yvette D. Valdez, and Stephen P. Win, 'The Yellow Brick Road for Consumer Tokens: The Path to SEC and CFTC Compliance' in Josias Dewey (ed), *Blockchain & Cryptocurrency Regulation 2019* (Global Legal Insights 2019) 100–113

Condon, Christopher, 'Central Bank Independence' (*Bloomberg*, 8 July 2019) <https://www.bloomberg.com/quicktake/central-bank-independence>

Condos, James, William Sorrell and Susan Donegan, 'Blockchain Technology: Opportunities and Risks' (2016) <https://legislature.vermont.gov/assets/Legislative-Reports/blockchain-technology-report-final.pdf>

Cong, Lin William and Zhiguo He, 'Blockchain Disruption and Smart Contracts' (2019) 32 RevFinStud 1754

Conroy, Douglas C., Michael L. Zuppone, and David J. Kaplan, 'SEC Anti-Fraud Rule 10b-5 Broadly Construed by Supreme Court' (*Paul Hastings*, 2002) <https://www.paulhastings.com/docs/default-source/PDFs/303.pdf>

Conti-Brown, Peter, 'The Institution of Federal Reserve Independence' (2015) 32 YaleJonReg 257

Cornell Law School—Legal Information Institute, 'Fungible Things' (July 2021) <https://www.law.cornell.edu/wex/fungible_things>

Cornwith, Smith, 'ERC-1155 Multi Token Standard' (*Ethereum*, 9 March 2022) <https://ethereum.org/en/developers/docs/standards/tokens/erc-1155/>

Cortez, Nathan, 'Regulating Disruptive Innovation' (2014) 29 BerkeleyTechLJ 175

Cotterrell, Roger, 'What Is Transnational Law?' (2012) 37 L&SocInq 500

Coulibaly, Brahima Sangafowa and Kemal Derviş, 'The Governance of the International Monetary Fund at Age 75' (*Brookings Institution*, 1 July 2019) <https://www.brookings.edu/blog/future-development/2019/07/01/the-governance-of-the-international-monetary-fund-at-age-75/>

Council of the EU, 'Data Act: Member States Agree Common Position on Fair Access to and Use of Data' (24 March 2023) <https://www.consilium.europa.eu/en/press/press-releases/2023/03/24/data-act-member-states-agree-common-position-on-fair-access-to-and-use-of-data/>

Cowen, Tyler and Randall Kroszner, 'The Development of New Monetary Economics' (1987) 95 JPolEcon 567

Cox, James D., Robert W. Hillman, and Donald C. Langevoort, *Securities Regulation, Cases and Materials* (8th edn, Wolters Kluwer 2017)

Cox, Jeff, 'Shadow Banking Is Now a $52 Trillion Industry, Posing a Big Risk to the Financial System' (*CNBC*, 11 April 2019) <https://www.cnbc.com/2019/04/11/shadow-banking-is-now-a-52-trillion-industry-and-posing-risks.html>

Crawley, Jamie, 'FTX US Affiliate Sees Record Daily Trading Volume in First Half of 2021' (*CoinDesk*, 29 July 2021) <https://www.coindesk.com/markets/2021/07/29/ftx-us-affiliate-sees-record-daily-trading-volume-in-first-half-of-2021/>

Crypto Assets Ratings <https://www.cryptoassetrating.com/>

Crypto Assets Ratings, 'Rating Model' <https://www.cryptoassetrating.com/home/ratingmodel>

Crypto Fund Research, 'Cryptocurrency Investment Fund Industry Graphs and Charts' <https://cryptofundresearch.com/cryptocurrency-funds-overview-infographic/>

Crypto Rating Council, '01–Who We Are' <https://www.cryptoratingcouncil.com/>

Crypto Rating Council, 'CRC Securities Framework Asset Ratings' <https://www.cryptoratingcouncil.com/asset-ratings>

Crypto UK, 'Code of Conduct' <https://www.cryptocurrenciesuk.info/code-of-conducts/>

Crypto Valley Association, 'Mission and Policy Framework' (*Cryptovalley*, 8 January 2018) <https://cryptovalley.swiss/codeofconduct/>

Cryptocurrency Facts, 'What Is a Cryptocurrency Exchange?' <https://cryptocurrencyfacts.com/what-is-a-cryptocurrency-exchange/>

Cryptocurrency Facts, 'What Is a Stable Coin?' <https://cryptocurrencyfacts.com/what-is-a-stable-coin/>

Daian, Philip, Tyler Kell, Ian Miers, and Ari Juels, 'On-Chain Vote Buying and the Rise of Dark DAOs' (*Hacking Distributed*, 2 July 2018) <http://hackingdistributed.com/2018/07/02/on-chain-vote-buying/>

Dallas, Lynne L. and Jordan M. Barry, 'Long-Term Shareholders and Time-Phased Voting' (2016) 40 DelJCorpL 541

Dambre, Romain and Marco Dell'Erba, 'Transalpine Look at Equity Derivatives: Convergence and Divergence in Disclosure and Takeover Regulations in the EU' (2012) 3 RTDF 64

Damiani, Jesse, 'JPMorgan Announces "JPM Coin," a USD-Pegged Cryptocoin for Cross-Border Payments, Security, and More' (*Forbes*, 14 February 2019) <https://www.forbes.com/sites/jessedamiani/2019/02/14/jpmorgan-announces-jpm-coin-usd-pegged-cryptocoin-for-cross-border-payments-security-and-more/>

Darbellay, Aline, *Regulating Credit Rating Agencies* (Elgar 2013)

Davenport, Ben, 'What is Multi-Sig, and What Can It Do?' (*Coincenter*, 1 January 2015) <https://coincenter.org/entry/what-is-multi-sig-and-what-can-it-do>

Davenport, Thomas H., Erik Brynjolfsson, Andrew McAfee, and H. James Wilson, *Artificial Intelligence* (HBR 2019)

Davis, Kevin, 'Regulatory Responses to the Financial Sector Crisis' (2010) 19 GriffithLRev 117

De Filippi, Primavera and Samer Hassan, 'Blockchain Technology as a Regulatory Technology: From Code Is Law to Law Is Code' (*First Monday*, 5 December 2016) <https://firstmonday.org/article/view/7113/5657>

De Filippi, Primavera and Aaron Wright, *Blockchain and the Law: The Rule of Code* (HUP 2018)

De Filippi, Primavera, Morshed Mannanc, and Wessel Reijersd, 'Blockchain as a Confidence Machine: The Problem of Trust & Challenges of Governance' (2010) 62 TechSoc 1

De Graaf, Ticho J., 'From Old to New: From Internet to Smart Contracts and from People to Smart Contracts' (2019) 35 CompL&SecRev 1

De, Nikhilesh, 'EU Lawmakers Weigh "Standard" for ICOs under Crowdfunding Rules' (*CoinDesk*, 11 September 2018) <https://www.coindesk.com/the-european-parliament-wants-to-make-icos-more-accessible/>

De, Nikhilesh, 'LedgerX Board Member Says Company in Disarray After Founders' Ouster' (*CoinDesk*, 10 January 2020) <https://www.coindesk.com/markets/2020/01/10/ledgerx-board-member-says-company-in-disarray-after-founders-ouster/>

De, Nikhilesh, 'Libra Rebrands to "Diem" in Anticipation of 2021 Launch' (*CoinDesk*, 1 December 2020) <https://www.coindesk.com/libra-diem-rebrand>

DeAcetis, Joseph, 'The Rise of the Metaverse: Where Crypto, NFT and Luxury Brands Merge' (*Forbes*, 8 February 2022) <https://www.forbes.com/sites/josephdeacetis/2022/02/08/the-rise-of-the-metaverse-where-crypto-nft-and-luxury-brands-merge/?sh=3091c19d454d>

Debevoise & Plimpton, 'European Commission Introduces Draft Regulation for Markets in Crypto Assets (MiCA)' (3 November 2020) <https://www.debevoise.com/insights/publications/2020/11/european-commission-introduces-draft-regulation>

Decentraland <https://decentraland.org/>

Del Castillo, Michael, 'The World's Largest CSDs Are Forming a New Blockchain Consortium' (*CoinDesk*, 5 June 2017) <https://www.coindesk.com/worlds-largest-csds-forming-new-blockchain-consortium/>

Del Castillo, Michael, 'DTCC Milestone: $11 Trillion in Derivatives Gets Closer to the Blockchain' (*CoinDesk*, 20 October 2017) <https://www.coindesk.com/dtcc-milestone-11-trillion-derivatives-gets-closer-blockchain/>

Del Castillo, Michael, 'SEC Launches Fintech Hub To Engage With Cryptocurrency Startups And More' (*Forbes*, 18 October 2018) <https://www.forbes.com/sites/michaeldelcastillo/2018/10/18/sec-launches-fintech-hub-to-engage-with-cryptocurrency-startups-and-more/amp/?__twitter_impression=true>

Del Castillo, Michael, 'Crypto's Top Funded Startup Shutters Operations Following SEC Concerns' (*Forbes*, 13 December 2018) <https://www.forbes.com/sites/michaeldelcastillo/2018/12/13/sec-rules-kill-cryptos-top-funded-startup/#485ac2f22918 [https://perma.cc/PSC7-9RW4>

Del Castillo, Michael, 'Blockchain Goes to Work at Walmart, Amazon, JPMorgan, Cargill and 46 Other Enterprises' (*Forbes*, 16 April 2019) <https://www.forbes.com/sites/michaeldelcastillo/2019/04/16/blockchain-goes-to-work/#40831b582a40>

Del Castillo, Michael, 'Morningstar Is Building A Blockchain Bridge To The $117 Trillion Debt Securities Industry' (*Forbes*, 1 October 2019) <https://www.forbes.com/sites/michaeldelcastillo/2019/10/01/morningstar-is-building-a-blockchain-bridge-to-the-117-trillion-debt-securities-industry/#3cee17703612>

Dell'Ariccia, Giovanni and Robert Marquez, 'Competition among Regulators and Credit Market Integration' in Franklin Allen, Elena Carletti, Jan Pieter Krahnen, and Marcel Tyrell (eds), *Liquidity and Crises* (OUP 2011) 320–345

Dell'Erba, Marco, 'The Regulation of Alternative Investment Funds in Europe: The Alternative Investment Fund Managers Directive' in Raphaël Douady, Clément Goulet, and Pierre-Charles Pradier (eds), *Financial Regulation in the EU: From Resilience to Growth* (Palgrave 2017) 321–353

Dell'Erba, Marco, 'Initial Coin Offerings: The Response of Regulatory Authorities' (2018) 14 NYUJL&Bus 1107

Dell'Erba, Marco, 'Stablecoins in Cryptoeconomics: From Initial Coin Offerings (ICOs) to Central Bank Digital Currencies (CBDCs)' (2019) 22 NYUJL&PubPol'y 1

Dell'Erba, Marco, 'From Inactivity to Full Enforcement: The Implementation of the "Do No Harm" Approach in Initial Coin Offerings' (2020) 26 MichTechLRev 175

Dell'Erba, Marco, 'Sustainable Digital Finance and the Pursuit of Environmental Sustainability' in Danny Busch, Guido Ferrarini, and Seraina Grünewald (eds), *Sustainable Finance in Europe: Corporate Governance, Financial Stability and Financial Markets* (Palgrave 2021) 61–81

Dell'Erba, Marco, 'Crypto-Trading Platforms as Exchanges' (2023) MichStLRev (forthcoming)

Dell'Erba, Marco and Giovanni Patti, 'The Monte dei Paschi di Siena Affaire. Distressed Banks ant the European Regulation on Short Selling' (2017) 12 CMLJ 512

Deloitte, 'The Evolution of a Core Financial Service Custodian & Depositary Banks' (2019) <https://www2.deloitte.com/content/dam/Deloitte/lu/Documents/financial-services/lu-the-evolution-of-a-core-financial-service.pdf>

Deloitte, King & Wood Mallesons, KHbitEX, University of Hong Kong—Asian Institute of International Financial Law (AIIFL), 'Security Token Offerings: The Next Phase of Financial Market Evolution?' (2020) https://www2.deloitte.com/content/dam/Deloitte/cn/Documents/audit/deloitte-cn-audit-security-token-offering-en-201009.pdf

Depoorter, Ben, 'Law in the Shadow of Bargaining: The Feedback Effect of Civil Settlements' (2010) 95 CornellLRev 957

Derby, Michael S., 'Powell Says Fed Has No Plans to Create Digital Currency' (*WSJ*, 21 November 2019) <https://www.wsj.com/articles/feds-powell-says-in-letter-to-congress-fed-not-creating-digital-currency-11574356188>

Derry, Alexander, Martin Krzywinski, and Naomi Altman, 'Neural Networks Primer' (2023) 20 Nature Methods 165

Desjardins, Eric, 'Historicity and Experimental Evolution' (2011) 26 Bio&Phil 339

Deutscher Bundestag, 'Die Bundesregierung plant derzeit keine Änderung der gesetzlichen Rahmenbe dingungen von NFTs' (26 May 2021) <https://dserver.bundestag.de/btd/19/301/1930141.pdf>

Di Lorenzo, Vincent, 'Legislative Chaos: An Exploratory Study' (1994) 12 YLPR 425

Dickson, Ben, 'Can You Trust Crypto-Token Crowdfunding?' (*TechCrunch*, 12 February 2017) <https://techcrunch.com/2017/02/12/can-you-trust-crypto-token-

Dickson, Ben, 'What Is an Initial Coin Offering (ICO)?' (*TechTalks*, 7 December 2016) <https://bdtechtalks.com/2016/12/07/what-is-an-initial-coin-offering-ico/>

Digital Finance Institute, 'Innovation: Innovation Matters' (2015) <http://digifin.org/digital-finance-innovation/>

Digital Watch Observatory, 'Article 29 Working Party' https://dig.watch/actor/article-29-working-party

Dilthey, Whilelm, *Introduction to the Human Sciences* (Rudolf A. Makkreel ed, PUP 1991)

Dionisio, John David, William G. Burns III, and Richard Gilbert, '3D Virtual Worlds and the Metaverse: Current Status and Future Possibilities' (2013) ACM Computing Surveys 45

'Distributed Ledger Technology' (2016) In Focus 1 <https://www.ecb.europa.eu/paym/pdf/infocus/20160422_infocus_dlt.pdf>

dMdb, Victor and Victor Alexiev, 'NFTs and the Dawn of the Metaverse' (*citiVentures*, 6 April 2021) https://www.citi.com/ventures/perspectives/opinion/nfts-metaverse.html

DocuSign, 'Detailed Discussion of the Legal Issues Surrounding E-Signature Deployment' <https://community.corporatecompliance.org/HigherLogic/System/DownloadDocumentFile.ashx?DocumentFileKey=40bffdbb-226a-4cef-b6f4-8843152a114a>

Dodge, Trevor, 'Delaware Authorizes Stocks on Blockchain' (*New Media and Technology Law Blog*, 2 August 2017) <https://newmedialaw.proskauer.com/2017/08/02/delaware-authorizes-stocks-on-blockchain/>

Doepke, Matthias and Martin Schneider, 'Money as a Unit of Account' (2017) 85 Econometrica 1537

Donald, David C., 'Heart of Darkness: The Problem at the Core of the U.S. Proxy System and Its Solution' (2011) 6 VaL&BusRev 41

Dowlat, Sherwin, 'Cryptoasset Market Coverage Initiation: Network Creation' (*Satis Group*, 11 July 2018) <https://research.bloomberg.com/pub/res/d28giW28tf6G7T_Wr77aU0gDgFQ>

Draghi, Mario, 'Central Bank Independence' (Lecture at the Banque Nationale de Belgique, Brussels, 26 October 2018) <https://www.ecb.europa.eu/press/key/date/2018/html/ecb.sp181026.en.html>

Drake, Gordon W. F., 'Entropy', *Britannica* <https://www.britannica.com/science/entropy-physics>

DTCC, 'DTCC & Digital Asset Move to Next Phase after Successful Proof-of-Concept for Repo Transactions Using Distributed Ledger Technology' (27 February 2017) <https://www.dtcc.com/news/2017/february/27/dtcc-and-digital-asset-move-to-next-phase>

Durovic, Mateja and Franciszek Lech, 'The Enforceability of Smart Contracts' (2019) 5 ItLJ 493

Easterbrook, Frank H., 'Cyberspace and the Law of the Horse' (1996) 1996 UchiLF 207

Easton, David, *A Systems Analysis of Political Life* (UCP 1979)

ECB, Financial Stability Review (June 2012) <https://www.ecb.europa.eu/pub/pdf/fsr/financialstabilityreview201206en.pdf>

EBA, 'Overview of the Potential Implications of Regulatory Measures for Banks' Business Models' (9 February 2015) <https://www.eba.europa.eu/documents/10180/974844/Report++Overview+of+the+potential+implications+of+regulatory+measures+for+business+models.pdf/fd839715ce6d-4f48-aa8d-0396ffc146b9>

EBA, *Report with advice for the European Commission on crypto-assets* (9 January 2019) <https://eba.europa.eu/sites/default/documents/files/documents/10180/2545547/67493daa-85a8-4429-aa91-e9a5ed880684/EBA%20Report%20on%20crypto%20assets.pdf>

ECB, 'Exploring Anonymity in Central Bank Digital Currencies' (December 2019) In Focus No. 4 <https://www.ecb.europa.eu/paym/intro/publications/pdf/ecb.mipinfocus191217.en.pdf>

ECB, 'Central Bank Group to Assess Potential Cases for Central Bank Digital Currencies' (21 January 2020) <https://www.ecb.europa.eu/press/pr/date/2020/html/ecb.pr200121_1~e99d7946d6.en.html>

ECB, 'ECB Announces €750 billion Pandemic Emergency Purchase Programme (PEPP)' (18 March 2020) <https://www.ecb.europa.eu/press/pr/date/2020/html/ecb.pr200318_1~3949d6f266.en.html>

ECB, *Report on a Digital Euro* (October 2020) <https://www.ecb.europa.eu/pub/pdf/other/Report_on_a_digital_euro~4d7268b458.en.pdf>

ECB, *Eurosystem Report on the Public Consultation on a Digital Euro* (April 2021) <https://www.ecb.europa.eu/pub/pdf/other/Eurosystem_report_on_the_public_consultation_on_a_digital_euro~539fa8cd8d.en.pdf>

ECB, 'Eurosystem Launches Digital Euro Project' (July 2021) <https://www.ecb.europa.eu/press/pr/date/2021/html/ecb.pr210714~d99198ea23.en.html>

ECB, 'Central Bank Digital Currencies: Defining the Problems, Designing the Solutions' (18 February 2022) <https://www.ecb.europa.eu/press/key/date/2022/html/ecb.sp220218_1~938e881b13.en.html>

ECB, 'Electronic Money' <https://www.ecb.europa.eu/stats/money_credit_banking/electronic_money/html/index.en.html>

ECB, 'Your views on digital euro' <https://www.ecb.europa.eu/euro/shared/files/Questionnaire_on_a_digital_euro.pdf>

EBA, EIOPA, and ESMA, 'On the Use of Big Data by Financial Institutions' (2016) EBA Joint Committee Discussion Paper JC 2016/86 <https://www.esma.europa.eu/press-news/consultations/joint-committee-discussion-paper-use-big-data-financial-institutions>

Economic Affairs Committee of the House of Lords, 'Central Bank Digital Currencies: A Solution in Search of a Problem?' (17 January 2022) HL Paper 131 <https://publications.parliament.uk/pa/ld5802/ldselect/ldeconaf/131/13108.htm>

Edelman, Paul, Wei Jiang, and Randall S. Thomas, 'Will Tenure Voting Give Corporate Managers Lifetime Tenure?' (2019) 97 TexLRev 991

Edvinsson, Rodney, Tor Jacobson, and Daniel Waldenstrom, 'Introduction' in Rodney Edvinsson, Tor Jacobson, and Daniel Waldenström (eds), *Sveriges Riksbank and the History of Central Banking* (CUP 2018) 1–25

Eggen, Mirjam, 'Smart Contracts und allgemeine Geschäftsbedingungen' in Susan Emmenegger, Stephanie Hrubesch-Millauer, Fréderic Krauskopf, and Stephan Wolf (eds), *Brücken bauen—Festschrift für Thomas Koller* (Stämpfli 2018) 155–175

Eggen, Mirjam, Andreas Glarner, Martin Hess, Salvatore Iacangelo, Cornelia Stangel, and Rolf H. Weber, 'Position Paper on the Legal Classification of ICOs' (*Blockchain Taskforce*, April 2018) <https://www.wengervieli.ch/WEVI/media/MediaLibrary/News%20und%20Events/Blockchain-Taskforce-Position-Paper-Legal.pdf>

Eggers, Julia, Andreas Hein, Jörg Weking, Markus Böhm, and Helmut Krcmar, 'Process Automation on the Blockchain: An Exploratory Case Study on Smart Contracts' (2021) Proceedings of the 54th Hawaii International Conference on System Sciences 2021

Ehrlich, Steven, 'Two Explanations for Venture Capital's Inexplicable Interest in Stablecoins' (*Forbes*, 25 September 2018) <https://www.forbes.com/sites/stevenehrlich/2018/09/25/two-reasons-for-venturecapitals-inexplicable-interest-instablecoins/#7feef7321a57>

Eichengreen, Barry and Ganesh Viswanath-Natraj, 'Stablecoins and Central Bank Digital Currencies: Policy and Regulatory Challenges' (2022) 21 AsianEconPap 29 <https://direct.mit.edu/asep/article/21/1/29/109037/Stablecoins-and-Central-Bank-Digital-Currencies>

Elliott, Samuel, 'Bitcoin: The First Self-Regulating Currency?' (2018) 3 LSELRev 57

Ellul, Joshua, Jonathan Galea, Max Ganado, Stephen McCarthy, and Gordon J. Pace, 'Regulating Blockchain, DLT and Smart Contracts: A Technology Regulator's Perspective' 21 ERA Forum 209

Elvy, Stacy-Ann, 'Contracting in the Age of the Internet of Things: Article 2 of the UCC and Beyond' (2016) 44 HofLRev 839

Elvy, Stacy-Ann, 'Hybrid Transactions and the Internet of Things: Goods, Services, or Software?' (2017) 74 Wash&LeeLRev 77

Elzweig, Brian and Lawrence J. Trautman, 'When Does a Nonfungible Token (NFT) Become a Security?' (2023) 39 GaStULRev 295

E-mail from Coinbase to customers (9 December 2017, 01:07 AM EST) (on file with author)

Enriques, Luca and Alessandro Romano, 'Institutional Investor Voting Behavior: A Network Theory Perspective' (2019) 1 UillinoisLRev 223

Enriques, Luca and Dirk A. Zetzsche, 'Corporate Technologies and the Tech Nirvana Fallacy' (2020) 72 HastingsLJ 55

Enriques, Luca, Alessandro Romano, and Thom Wetzer, 'Network-Sensitive Financial Regulation' (2020) 45 JcorpL 351

Ereshefsky, Marc, 'Species, Historicity, and Path Dependency' (2014) 81 PoS 714

Erl, Thomas, Wajid Khattak, and Paul Buhler, *Big Data Fundamentals: Concepts, Drivers & Techniques* (Pearson 2016)

ESMA, *Report—The Distributed Ledger Technology Applied to Securities Markets* (2016) <https://www.esma.europa.eu/sites/default/files/library/dlt_report_-_esma50-1121423017-285.pdf

ESMA, 'ESMA Alerts Firms Involved in Initial Coin Offerings (ICOs) to the Need to Meet Relevant Regulatory Requirements' (13 November 2017) <https://www.esma.europa.eu/document/esma-alerts-firms-involved-in-initial-coin-offerings-icos-need-meet-relevant-regulatory>

ESMA, 'Advice on Initial Coin Offerings and Crypto-Assets' (9 January 2019) <https://www.esma.europa.eu/document/advice-initial-coin-offerings-and-crypto-assets>

ESMA, EBA, and EIOPA, 'Warning Report on the risks of Virtual Currencies' (17 March 2022) <https://www.esma.europa.eu/sites/default/files/library/esma50-164-1284_joint_esas_warning_on_virtual_currenciesl.pdf>

Ethereum, 'Gas and Fees' <https://ethereum.org/en/developers/docs/gas/>
Ethereum, 'Introduction to Smart Contracts' (12 April 2022) <https://ethereum.org/en/developers/docs/smart-contracts/>
European Commission, 'Impact Assessment—Proposal for a Regulation of the European Parliament and of the Council amending Regulation (EU) No 1095/2010 establishing a European Supervisory Authority (European Securities and Markets Authority) and amending Regulation (EU) No 648/2012 as regards the procedures and authorities involved for the authorisation of CCPs and the requirements for the recognition of third-country CCPs' (Commission Staff Working Document, 13 June 2017) <https://eur-lex.europa.eu/legal-content/EN/TXT/HTML/?uri=CELEX:52017SC0246&rid=5>
European Commission, 'European Countries Join Blockchain Partnership' (10 April 2018) <https://digital-strategy.ec.europa.eu/en/news/european-countries-join-blockchain-partnership>
European Commission, 'An SME Strategy for a Sustainable and Digital Europe' (Communication to the European Parliament, the Council, the European Economic And Social Committee and the Committee of the Regions, 10 March 2020) <https://eur-lex.europa.eu/legal-content/EN/TXT/PDF/?uri=CELEX:52020DC0103&from=EN>
European Commission, 'European Financial Stability and Integration Review 2022' (2022) <https://ec.europa.eu/info/sites/default/files/european-financial-stability-and-integration-review-2022_en.pdf>
European Commission, 'Legal and Regulatory Framework for Blockchain' (updated 23 February 2022) <https://digital-strategy.ec.europa.eu/en/policies/regulatory-framework-blockchain>
European Commission, 'Proposal for a Regulation of the European Parliament and of the Council on Harmonised Rules on Fair Access to and Use of Data' COM (2022) 68 final
European Commission, 'Shaping Digital Future—Blockchain Strategy' (last update 27 February 2023) <https://ec.europa.eu/digital-single-market/en/blockchain-technologies>
European Data Protection Supervisor, 'Opinion 7/2015—Meeting the challenges of big data' (19 November 2015) <https://edps.europa.eu/sites/edp/files/publication/15-11-19_big_data_en.pdf>
European Parliament Economic and Monetary Affairs Committee (ECON), *Draft Report on the Proposal for a Regulation of the European Parliament. and of the Council on European Crowdfunding Service Providers (ECSP) for Business (COM (2018)0113—C8-0103/2018—2018/0048(COD))* (10 August 2018) <https://www.europarl.europa.eu/doceo/document/ECON-PR-626662_EN.pdf?redirect>
Ezrachi, Ariel and Maurice E. Stucke, 'Artificial Intelligence & Collusion: When Computers Inhibit Competition' (2017) 2017 IllinoisLRev 1775
Falkon, Samuel, 'The Story of the DAO—Its History and Consequences' (*Medium*, 24 December 2018) <https://medium.com/swlh/the-story-of-the-dao-its-history-and-consequences-71e6a8a551ee>
Fama, Eugene F., 'Banking in the Theory of Finance' (1980) 6 JMonEcon 39
Farber, Daniel A., 'Probabilities Behaving Badly: Complexity Theory and Environmental Uncertainty' (2003) 37 UCalDLRev 145
Faridi, Omar, 'Japan's Virtual Currency Exchange Association (JVCEA) Now Authorized as Self-Regulatory Body' (*Crypto Globe*, 24 October 2018) <https://www.cryptoglobe.com/latest/2018/10/japan-s-virtual-currency-exchange-association-jvcea-now-authorized-as-self-regulatory-body/>
FATF, 'Virtual Assets And Virtual Asset Service Providers' (June 2019) <https://www.fatf-gafi.org/media/fatf/documents/recommendations/RBA-VA-VASPs.pdf>

FATF, 'Second 12-Month Review of the Revised Fatf Standards on Virtual Assets and Virtual Asset Service Providers' (July 2021) <https://www.fatf-gafi.org/content/dam/fatf-gafi/guidance/Second-12-Month-Review-Revised-FATF-Standards-Virtual-Assets-VASPS.pdf>

FCA, 'Cryptoassets: Our Work' (4 April 2022) <https://www.fca.org.uk/firms/cryptoassets>

Federal Deposit Insurance Corporation, *Consumer Compliance Examination Manual* (2020) X-3.1 <https://www.fdic.gov/resources/supervision-and-examinations/consumer-compliance-examination-manual/documents/compliance-examination-manual.pdf>

Federal Reserve, 'Federal Reserve Highlights Research and Experimentation Undertaken to Enhance Its Understanding of the Opportunities and Risks Associated with Central Bank Digital Currencies' (13 August 2020) <https://www.federalreserve.gov/newsevents/pressreleases/other20200813a.htm>

Federal Reserve Bank of Boston, 'The Federal Reserve Bank of Boston Announces Collaboration with MIT to Research Digital Currency' (13 August 2020) <https://www.bostonfed.org/news-and-events/press-releases/2020/the-federal-reserve-bank-of-boston-announces-collaboration-with-mit-to-research-digital-currency.aspx>

Feiner, Lauren, 'Facebook Announces $100 Million Program for Small Businesses Impacted by Coronavirus' (*CNBC*, 17 March 2020) <https://www.cnbc.com/2020/03/17/facebook-announces-program-for-small-businesses-impacted-by-covid-19.html>

Fenwick, Mark and Erik P. M. Vermeulen, 'Technology and Corporate Governance: Blockchain, Crypto, and Artificial Intelligence' (2019) 48 TexJBusL 1

Fenwick, Mark, Joseph McCahery, and Erik P. M. Vermeulen, 'The End of "Corporate" Governance: Hello "Platform" Governance' (2019) 20 EBOLR 171

Ferrarini, Guido and Paolo Giudici, 'Financial Scandals and the Role of Private Enforcement: The Parmalat Case' (2005) European Corporate Governance Institute (ECGI)—Law Working Paper 40/2005 <https://ssrn.com/abstract=730403>

Ferrarini, Guido and Maria Cristina Ungureanu, 'Executive Pay at Ailing Banks and Beyond: A European Perspective' (2010) 5 CMLJ 2

Ferreira, Daniel, Jin Li, and Radoslawa Nikolowa, 'Corporate Capture of Blockchain Governance' (2019) European Corporate Governance Institute (ECGI) —Finance Working Paper No. 593/2019 <https://ssrn.com/abstract=3320437>

Financial Crisis Inquiry Commission, *Final Report of the National Commission on the Causes of the Financial & Economic Crisis in the U.S.—The Financial Crisis Inquiry Report* (2011) (Inquiry Commission, *Financial Crisis Inquiry Report*) <https://www.govinfo.gov/content/pkg/GPO-FCIC/pdf/GPO-FCIC.pdf>

Financial Stability Board, 'Policy Measures to Address Systemically Important Financial Institutions' (4 November 2011) <https://www.fsb.org/wp-content/uploads/r_111104bb.pdf?page_moved=1>

[Letter from the] Financial Stability Board to G20 Finance Ministers and Central Bank Governors (13 October 2019) <https://www.fsb.org/wp-content/uploads/P131019.pdf>

Financial Stability Board, 'Addressing the Regulatory, Supervisory and Oversight Challenges Raised by "Global Stablecoin" Arrangements' (14 April 2020) <https://www.fsb.org/wp-content/uploads/P140420-1.pdf>

Financial Stability Board, 'Regulation, Supervision and Oversight of 'Global Stablecoin' Arrangements—Progress Report on the implementation of the FSB High-Level Recommendations' (7 October 2021) <https://www.fsb.org/wp-content/uploads/P071021.pdf>

Financial Times, 'El Salvador Dangerous Bet on Bitcoin' (7 September 2021) <https://www.ft.com/content/c257a925-c864-4495-9149-d8956d786310>

Finck, Michèle, *Blockchain Regulation and Governance in Europe* (CUP 2018)

Finer, Josh, 'How Blockchain Startups Are Driving an Under-the-Radar Fundraising Boom' (*Venturebeat*, 13 November 2016) <https://venturebeat.com/2016/11/13/how-blockchain-startups-are-driving-an-under-the-radar-fundraising-boom/>

Finextra, 'Swiss Blockchain Federation Founded' (31 October 2018) <https://www.finextra.com/pressarticle/76191/swiss-blockchain-federation-founded>

Finextra, 'Libra Rebrands as Diem in Effort to Distance Itself from Facebook' (1 December 2020) <https://www.finextra.com/newsarticle/37057/libra-rebrands-as-diem-in-effort-to-distance-itself-from-facebook>

FINMA, *Annual Report 2016* (December 2016) <https://www.finma.ch/en/~/media/finma/dokumente/dokumentencenter/myfinma/finma-publikationen/geschaeftsbericht/20170404_fin_jb16.pdf?la=en>

FINMA, 'Finma Closes Down Coin Providers and Issues Warning about Fake Cryptocurrencies' (19 September 2017) <https://www.finma.ch/en/news/2017/09/20170919-mm-coin-anbieter/>

FINMA, 'Guidelines for Enquiries regarding the Regulatory Framework for Initial Coin Offerings (ICOs)' (2018) <https://www.finma.ch/~/media/finma/dokumente/dokumentencenter/myfinma/1bewilligung/fintech/wegleitung-ico.pdf>

FINMA, 'FinTech License and Sandbox: Adjustments to FINMA Circulars' (15 March 2019) <https://www.finma.ch/en/news/2019/03/20190315-mm-fintech/>

FINMA, 'Finma Ascertains Illegal Activity by Envion AG' (27 March 2019) <https://www.finma.ch/en/news/2019/03/20190327---mm---envion/>

FINMA, 'Finma Publishes "Stable Coin" Guidelines' (11 September 2019) <https://www.finma.ch/en/news/2019/09/20190911-mm-stable-coins/>

FINMA, 'Supplement to the Guidelines for Enquiries regarding the Regulatory Framework for Initial Coin Offerings (ICOs)' (2019) <https://www.finma.ch/en/~/media/finma/dokumente/dokumentencenter/myfinma/1bewilligung/fintech/wegleitung-stable-coins.pdf?la=en&hash=70408DDE78369718148808FD4784E742373A0140>

FINMA, *Annual Report 2019* (April 2020) <https://www.finma.ch/en/news/2020/04/20200402-mm-finma-gb-2019/>

FINMA, 'Libra Association: FINMA Licensing Process Initiated' (15 April 2020), <https://www.finma.ch/en/news/2020/04/20200416-mm-libra/>

FINMA, 'Diem Withdraws Licence Application in Switzerland' (May 2021) <https://www.finma.ch/en/news/2021/05/20210512-mm-diem/>

FINMA, 'Self-Regulation in Swiss Financial Market Law' <https://www.finma.ch/en/documentation/self-regulation/>

Fintech Association of Hong Kong, 'Updated FTAHK Best Practices for Token Sales—Version 2.0' (October 2018) <https://ftahk.org/publication/updated-ftahk-best-practices-token-sales-version-20-october-2018-document>

Fisch, Jill E., 'From Legitimacy to Logic: Reconstructing Proxy Regulation' (1993) 46 VandLRev 1129

Fisch, Jill E., 'Standing Voting Instructions' (2017) 102 MinnLRev 11

Fisch, Jill E. and Steven Davidoff Solomon, 'Should Corporations Have a Purpose?' (2021) 99 TexLRev 1309

Flaherty, Michael, 'P&G, Peltz Vie for Small Investor Votes in Biggest-Ever Proxy Fight' (*Reuters*, 25 September 2017) <https://www.reuters.com/article/us-procter-gamble-trian-investors/pg-peltz-vie-for-small-investor-votes-in-biggest-ever-proxy-fight-idUSKCN1C01CW>

Flaiano, Ennio, *La solitudine del satiro* (Rizzoli 1973)

Flechtner, Harry, 'Comparing the General Good Faith Provisions of the PECL and the UCC: Appearance and Reality' (2001) 13 PaceIntlLRev 295

Fletecher, Laurence, 'Alan Howard-backed firm plots $1bn crypto venture' (*Financial Times*, 30 August 2019) <https://www.ft.com/content/733e9b6c-ca68-11e9-af46-b09e8bfe60c0>

Floyd, David, 'Overstock's t0: Reconciling Fiat Currency and the Bitcoin Blockchain' (*Nasdaq*, 16 December 2015) <https://www.nasdaq.com/article/overstocks-t0-reconciling-fiat-currency-and-the-bitcoin-blockchain-cm555617>

Foley, John, 'Breakingviews—Thomson Reuters Beats Blackstone in Refinitiv Deal' (*Reuters*, 1 August 2019) <https://www.reuters.com/article/us-refinitiv-m-a-breakingviews/breakingviews-thomson-reuters-beats-blackstone-in-refinitiv-deal-idUSKCN1UR501>

Fonseca, Maria, 'ICOs and Blockchain Token Funding' (*IntelligentHQ*, 5 May 2017) <https://www.intelligenthq.com/finance/icos-and-blockchain-token-funding/>

Forkast, 'Asia Primed for NFT Growth' (2022) <https://forkast.news/state-of-the-nft-market/asia-primed-for-nft-growth/>

Forkast, 'State of the NFT Market' (2022) <https://forkast.news/state-of-the-nft-market/>

Fox, Merritt B., 'Gatekeeper Failures: Why Important, What to Do' (2008) 106 MichLRev 1089, 1089

Foxley, William, '"Flash Loans" Have Made Their Way to Manipulating Protocol Elections' (*CoinDesk*, 29 October 2020) <https://www.coindesk.com/tech/2020/10/29/flash-loans-have-made-their-way-to-manipulating-protocol-elections/>

Fox-Penner, Peter, 'Too Big to Regulate?' (*The Baseline Scenario*, 16 January 2010) <http://baselinescenario.com/2010/01/16/too-big-to-regulate>

Frankenfield, Jake, 'Hard Fork (Blockchain)' (*Investopedia*, updated 24 June 2021) <https://www.investopedia.com/terms/h/hard-fork.asp>

French, Jordan, 'Nasdaq Exec: Exchange Is "All-In" on Using Blockchain Technology' (*The Street*, 23 April 2018) <https://www.thestreet.com/investing/nasdaq-all-in-on-blockchain-technology-14551134>

[Letter from] French Hill and Bill Foster to Federal Reserve Chairman Jerome H. Powell (30 September 2019) <https://src.bna.com/LO7>

Frier, Sarah and Dina Bass, 'Microsoft Makes a $69 Billion Down Payment on the Metaverse' (*Bloomberg*, 19 January 2022) <https://www.bloomberg.com/news/articles/2022-01-19/microsoft-msft-activision-blizzard-atvi-deal-shows-big-tech-metaverse-push>

FSBT.tech, 'What Is Electronic Money and Is It Real?' (*Medium*, 28 August 2018) <https://medium.com/fsbtapi/what-is-electronic-money-and-are-they-real-5277578bcbcd>

Fullerton, Elijah Journey and Peter J. Morgan, 'The People's Republic Of China's Digital Yuan: Its Environment, Design, And Implications' (February 2022) ADBI Discussion Paper 1306 <https://www.adb.org/sites/default/files/publication/772316/adb-wp1306.pdf>

Furrer, Andreaas, 'Die Einbettung von Smart Contracts in das schweizerische Privatrecht' (2018) 3 Anwaltsrevue 103

Furrer, Andreas and Luka Müller, '"Functional Equivalence" of Digital Legal Transactions: A Fundamental Principle for Assessing the Legal Validity of Legal Institutions and Legal Transactions under Swiss Law' (*MME*, 20 June 2018) <https://www.unilu.ch/fileadmin/fakultaeten/rf/furrer/dok/180619_Funktionale_AEquivalenz_translation.pdf>

G20 Green Finance Study Group, *G20 Green Finance Synthesis Report* (2016) <http://unepinquiry.org/wp-content/uploads/2016/09/Synthesis_Report_Full_EN.pdf>

G7 Working Group on Stablecoins, 'Investigating the Impact of Global Stablecoins' (October 2019) <https://www.bis.org/cpmi/publ/d187.pdf>

Gadamer, Hans Georg, *Truth and Method* (3rd edn, Bloombury 2013)

Gallagher, Daniel M., 'Complexities of Capital Markets Regulation' (*HLS Forum on Corporate Governance*, 7 March 2013) <https://corpgov.law.harvard.edu/2013/03/07/complexities-of-capital-markets-regulation/>

Geis, George S., 'Traceable Shares and Corporate Law' (2018) 113 NwULRev 227

Gelfand, Alexander, 'The ESG Generation Gap: Millennials and Boomers Split on Their Investing Goals (*Stanford GSB*, 10 November 2022) <https://www.gsb.stanford.edu/insights/esg-generation-gap-millennials-boomers-split-their-investing-goals>

Genc, Erik, 'Beginner's Guide to NFTs: How To Mint a Non-Fungible Token on Ethereum' (*Decrypt*, 28 October 2021) <https://decrypt.co/resources/beginners-guide-to-nfts-how-to-mint-a-non-fungible-token-on-ethereum>

Gensler, Gary, 'Examining Facebook's Proposed Cryptocurrency and Its Impact on Consumers, Investors, and the American Financial System Financial Services Committee United States House of Representatives' (Hearing before the Committee on Financial Services of the U.S. House of Representatives, 17 July 2019) <https://financialservices.house.gov/uploadedfiles/hhrg-116-ba00-wstate-genslerg-20190717.pdf>

Gensler, Gary, 'Remarks Before the Aspen Security Forum' (Speech at the Aspen Security Forum, Aspen, 3 August 2021) <https://www.sec.gov/news/public-statement/gensler-aspen-security-forum-2021-08-03>

Georgevici, Adrian Iustin, and Marius Terblanche, 'Neural Networks and Deep Learning: A Brief Introduction' (2019) 45 IntensiveCareMed 712

Gerding, Erik F., 'The Shadow Banking System and Its Legal Origins' (2012) <https://ssrn.com/abstract=1990816>

Giancarlo, Christopher J., 'Keynote Address' (ISDA's Trade Execution Legal Forum, 9 December 2016) <http://www.cftc.gov/PressRoom/SpeechesTestimony/opagiancarlo-18>

Gitti, Gregorio and Marisaria Maugeri, 'Blockchain-Based Financial Services and Virtual Currencies in Italy' (2020) 9 JEuCML 43

Glarner, Andreas, Dominik Hofmann, and Nathalie Uhe, 'Swiss Parliament Approves New DLT Regulations' (*MME*, September 2020) <https://www.mme.ch/en/magazine/magazine-detail/url_magazine/swiss_parliament_approves_new_dlt_regulations/>

Global Financial Innovation Network (GFIN), 'Consultation Document' (2018) <https://www.fca.org.uk/publication/consultation/gfin-consultation-document.pdf>

Goforth, Carol, 'SEC vs. Ripple: A Predictable But Undesirable Development' (*Cointelegraph*, 27 December 2020) <https://cointelegraph.com/news/sec-vs-ripple-a-predictable-but-undesirable-development>

Goldman Sachs, 'Digital Currency—Reinventing the Yuan for the Digital Age' (17 November 2020) (on file with author)

Goldstein, Itay, 'The Feedback Effect: How the Financial Markets Affect Decisions in the 'Real Economy'' (*Knowledge At Wharton*, 24 October 2012) <https://knowledge.wharton.upenn.edu/article/the-feedback-effect-how-the-financial-markets-affect-decisions-in-the-real-economy/>

Gomber, Peter, Jascha-Alexander Koch, and Michael Siering, 'Digital Finance and FinTech: Current Research and Future Research Directions' (2017) 87 JbusEcon 537

Gongloff, Mark, 'At Least There's a Bull Market in Death Spirals' (*Bloomberg*, 11 May 2022) <https://www.bloomberg.com/opinion/articles/2022-05-11/from-staglation-to-terra-ust-a-bull-market-in-death-spirals>

Goodfellow, Ian, Yoshua Bengio, and Aaron Courville, *Deep Learning* (MIT Press 2016)

Google Cloud, 'Building Hybrid Blockchain/Cloud Applications with Ethereum and Google Cloud' (13 June 2019) <https://cloud.google.com/blog/products/data-analytics/building-hybrid-blockchain-cloud-applications-with-ethereum-and-google-cloud>

Gorton, Gary and Andrew Metrick, 'Regulating the Shadow Banking System' (2010) Brookings Papers on Economic Activity 2010, No. 2 <https://www.brookings.edu/wp-content/uploads/2010/09/2010b_bpea_gorton.pdf>

Goswami, Rohan and MacKenzie Sigalos, 'SEC proposes rules that would change which crypto firms can custody customer assets' (*CNBC*, 15 February 2023) <https://www.cnbc.com/2023/02/15/sec-chair-gensler-crypto-firms-need-to-register-to-custody-assets.html>

Gould, Amanda, 'Crypto Custody' (*PennLaw*) https://www.law.upenn.edu/faculty/david-hoffman/crypto-custody.php

Gramitto Ricci, Sergio Alberto, 'Artificial Agents In Corporate Boardrooms' (2020) 105 CornellLRev 869

Greeninvest, 'Fintech, Green Finance And Developing Countries' (May 2017) <http://unepinquiry.org/wp-content/uploads/2017/06/Fintech_Green_Finance_and_Developing_Countries-input-paper.pdf>

Group of Twenty (G20), 'Declaration of the Summit on Financial Markets and the World Economy' (15 November 2008) <http://www.g20.utoronto.ca/2008/2008declaration1115.html>

Grundmann, Stefan and Philipp Hacker, 'The Digital Dimension as a Challenge to European Contract Law' in Stefan Grundmann (ed), *European Contract Law in the Digital Age* (Intersentia 2018) 3–46

Guadamuz, Andres, 'The Treachery of Images: Non-Fungible Tokens and Copyright' (2021) 16 JIPLP 1367

Gundiuc, Christian, 'Swiss Digital Bank Tackles Asset Tokenization for Fully Compliant Institutions' (*Securities*, 16 July 2020) <https://www.securities.io/swiss-digital-bank-tackles-asset-tokenization-for-fully-compliant-institutions/>

Guseva, Yuliya, 'The Leviathan of Securities Regulation in Crypto-Offerings: A Cost-Benefit Analysis' (2020) <https://ssrn.com/abstract=3694709>

Guseva, Yuliya, 'A Conceptual Framework for Digital-Asset Securities: Tokens and Coins as Debt And Equity' (2021) 80 MdLRev 166

Guseva, Yuliya and Douglas Eakeley, 'Crypto-Enforcement around the World' (2021) SCalLRev 99

Haenlein, Michael and Andreas Kaplan, 'A Brief History of Artificial Intelligence: On the Past, Present, and Future of Artificial Intelligence' (2019) 61 CalManagRev 5

Haig, Samuel, 'SEC's "Crypto Mom" Warns Selling Fractionalized NFTs Could Break the Law' (*CoinDesk*, 26 March 2021) <https://cointelegraph.com/news/sec-s-crypto-mom-warns-selling-fractionalized-nfts-could-break-the-law>

Hankin, Aaron, 'Bitcoin Options Are Headed to the U.S.' (*Investopedia*, updated 5 November 2019) <https://www.investopedia.com/articles/investing/033115/it-possible-trade-bitcoin-options.asp>

Hansmann, Henry, Reinier Kraakman, and Richard Squire, 'Law and the Rise of the Firm' (2006) 119 HarvLRev 1333

Haranas, Mark, 'Facebook's Meta to Build $1B Data Center for Metaverse' (*CRN*, 17 March 2022) <https://www.crn.com/news/data-center/facebook-s-meta-to-build-1b-data-center-for-metaverse>

Hardy, Daniel C., 'Regulatory Capture in Banking' (2006) IMF Working Paper WP/06/34

Harrop, Claire and Cyrus Pocha, 'Does the Metaverse Provide a Use Case for Central Bank Digital Currency?' (*Freshfields Technology Quotient*, 16 December 2021) <https://technologyquotient.freshfields.com/post/102hefa/does-the-metaverse-provide-a-usecase-for-central-bank-digital-currency>

Havelmo, Trygve, 'Econometrics and the Welfare State' (1997) 87 AmEconRev 13

Hayek, Friedrich von, *The Confusion of Language in Political Thought* (The Inst. Of Econ. Aff. 1968)

Hayek, Friedrich von, *The Denationalization of Money* (IOEA 1976)

Hayes, Adam, 'Demand Note' (*Investopedia*, last update 30 November 2020) <https://www.investopedia.com/terms/d/demandnote.asp>

He, Dong, Karl Habermeier, Ross Leckow, Vikram Haksar, Yasmin Almeida, Mikari Kashima, Nadim Kyriakos-Saad, Hiroko Oura, Tahsin Saadi Sedik, Natalia Stetsenko, and Concepcion Verdugo-Yepes, 'Virtual Currencies and Beyond: Initial Considerations' (2016) IMF Staff Discussion Note 16/03 <https://www.imf.org/external/pubs/ft/sdn/2016/sdn1603.pdf>

He, Laura 'China makes major push in its ambitious digital yuan project' (*CNN Business*, 24 April 2023) <https://edition.cnn.com/2023/04/24/economy/china-digital-yuan-government-salary-intl-hnk/index.html>

Hegel, Georg Wilhelm Friedrich, *The Phenomenology of Spirit* (Terry Pinkyard and Michael Baur eds, CUP 2018)

Heidegger, Martin, *Being and Time* (Joan Stambaugh tr, SUNY Press 2010)

Henderson, Andrew and James Burnie, 'United Kingdom' in Thomas A. Frick (ed), *The Financial Technology Law Review* (The Law Reviews 2018) 303–314

Henderson, Todd and Max Raskin, 'A Regulatory Classification of Digital Assets: Toward an Operational Howey Test for Cryptocurrencies, ICOs, and Other Digital Assets' (2019) 2 ColumBusLRev 443

Herkströter, Caroline and Michael Born, 'Crypto Assets: Germany Introduces New Regulatory Regime' (*Norton Rose Fulbright*, March 2020) <https://www.nortonrosefulbright.com/de-de/wissen/publications/5ee1e37e/new-regulatory-regime-for-crypto-assets-in-germany>

Hern, Alex, 'Could Terra Fall Prove to be Lehman Brothers Moment for Cryptocurrencies?' (*The Guardian*, 11 May 2022) <https://www.theguardian.com/technology/2022/may/11/terra-price-cryptocurrency-stablecoin>

Hertig, Alyssa, 'What Is a Flash Loan' (*CoinDesk*, 17 February 2021) <https://www.coindesk.com/learn/2021/02/17/what-is-a-flash-loan/>

Hetzel, Robert L., 'Launch of the Bretton Woods System' (*Federal Reserve History*, 22 November 2013) <https://www.federalreservehistory.org/essays/bretton_woods_launched>

Hezhao, 'Proof-of-Stake (POS)' (*Ethereum.org*, 20 April 2022) <https://ethereum.org/en/developers/docs/consensus-mechanisms/pos/>

Higgins, Stan, 'Delaware to Seek Legal Classification for Blockchain Shares' (*CoinDesk*, 2 May 2016) <https://www.coindesk.com/delaware-government-blockchain-shares/>

Higgins, Stan, 'CFTC Grants Full Registration to Bitcoin Swaps Trading Platform' (*CoinDesk*, 26 May 2016) <https://www.coindesk.com/us-swap-platform-registration-cftc>

Higgins, Stan, 'AXA Is Using Ethereum's Blockchain for a New Flight Insurance Product' (*CoinDesk*, 13 September 2017) <https://www.coindesk.com/axa-using-ethereums-blockchain-new-flight-insurance-product/>

Hinkes, Andrew M., 'Throw Away the Key, or the Key Holder? Coercive Contempt for Lost or Forgotten Cryptocurrency Private Keys, or Obstinate Holders' (2019) 16 NwJTech&IntellProp 225

Hinman, William, 'Digital Asset Transactions: When Howey Met Gary (Plastic)' (*SEC*, 14 June 2018) <https://www.sec.gov/news/speech/speech-hinman-061418>

Ho, Thomas S. Y. and Sang Bin Lee, *The Oxford Guide to Financial Modeling: Institutions* (OUP 2004)

Hochstein, Marc, 'Fintech (the Word, That Is) Evolves' (*American Banker*, 5 October 2015) <http://www.americanbanker.com/bankthink/fintech-the-word-that-is-evolves-1077098-1.html>

Hockett, Robert C., 'The New York Inclusive Value Ledger: A Peer-to-Peer Savings & Payments Platform for an All-Embracing and Dynamic State Economy' (2019) Cornell Legal Studies Research Paper No. 19-39

Hoffmann, Lord Leonard and Mary Harden, 'Legal Opinion Obtained By Accounting Standards Committee of True and Fair View, with Particular Reference to the Role of Accounting Standards' (13 September 1983) <https://www.frc.org.uk/getattachment/afba0aa1-04fa-492a-beab-35918af6d97e/T-F-Opinon-13-September-1983.pdf>
Hong Kong Applied Science & Technology Research Institute, 'Whitepaper on Distributed Ledger Technology' (2016) <https://www.hkma.gov.hk/media/eng/doc/key-functions/financial-infrastructure/Whitepaper_On_Distributed_Ledger_Technology.pdf>
Hornstein, Donald T., 'Complexity Theory, Adaptation, and Administrative Law' (2005) 54 DukeLJ 913
Howell, Sabrina, Marina Niessner, and David Yermack, 'Initial Coin Offerings: Financing Growth with Cryptocurrency Token Sales' (2018) European Corporate Governance Institute (ECGI) —Finance Working Paper No. 564
Hu, Henry T. C., 'Misunderstood Derivatives: The Causes of Informational Failure and the Promise of Regulatory Incrementalism' (1993) 102 YaleLJ 1457
Hu, Henry T. C., 'Empty Voting and Hidden (Morphable) ownership: Taxonomy, implications and Reforms' (2006) 61 BusLaw 1011
Hu, Henry T. C., 'Hedge Funds, Insiders and the Decoupling of Economic and Voting Ownership: Empty Voting and Hidden (Morphable) Ownership' (2007) 13 JCorpFin 343
Hu, Henry T. C., 'Equity and Debt Decoupling and Empty Voting II: Importance and Extensions' (2008) 156 UPaLRev 625
Hu, Henry T. C. and Bernard Black, 'The New Vote Buying: Empty Voting and Hidden (Morphable) Ownership' (2006) 79 SCalLRev 811
Hui, Ada, 'Polychain Capital Targets $200M for Second Venture Fund, Slide Deck Reveals' (*CoinDesk*, 14 February 2020) <https://www.coindesk.com/polychain-capital-is-raising-a-200m-crypto-venture-fund-slide-deck-reveals>
Huillet, Marie, 'SEC-Registered Clearing House Brings Crypto Trading to 5 Million Clients' (*Cointelegraph*, 28 June 2019) <https://cointelegraph.com/news/sec-registered-clearing-house-brings-crypto-trading-to-5-million-clients>
Huillet, Marie, 'Singapore's MAS, JPMorgan Unveil Multi-Currency Blockchain Prototype' (*Cointelegraph*, 11 November 2019) <https://cointelegraph.com/news/singapores-mas-jpmorgan-unveil-multi-currency-blockchain-prototype>
Huld, Arandse, 'China Launches Digital Yuan App—All You Need to Know' (*China Briefing*, 22 September 2022) <https://www.china-briefing.com/news/china-launches-digital-yuan-app-what-you-need-to-know/>
Husserl, Edmund, *Logical Investigations* (Dermot Morat, ed Routledge 2001)
IBM, 'IBM and Japan's Largest Stock Exchange to Test Blockchain For Trading Environments' (16 February 2016) <https://www-03.ibm.com/press/us/en/pressrelease/49088.wss>
IBM, 'Message Digests and Digital Signatures' (31 March 2022) <https://www.ibm.com/docs/en/ibm-mq/7.5?topic=concepts-message-digests10510_.html>
IBM, 'What Is Mobile Technology?' <https://www.ibm.com/topics/mobile-technology>
ICObench <https://icobench.com/faq>
ICObench <https://icobench.com/faq>
Iffland, Jacques and Alessandra Läser, 'Die Tokenisierung von Effekten—Ein neuer Weg an den Kapitalmarkt' (2018) 4 GesKR 416
Iffland, Jacques and Marie-Hélène Spiess, 'Acceptation de dépôts du public, émission d'obligations et ICO' (2019) 3 GesKR 459
Iffland, Jacques and Ariel Ben Hattar, 'Central Securities Depositaries in the Age of Tokenized Securities' (*CapLaw*, 31 March 2020) <https://www.caplaw.ch/2020/central-securities-depositaries-in-the-age-of-tokenized-securities/>

Illinois BidBuy <https://www.bidbuy.illinois.gov/bso/>
IMF, 'World Economic Outlook—A Survey by the Staff of the International Monetary Fund' (May 1998) <https://www.imf.org/~/media/Websites/IMF/imported-flagship-issues/external/pubs/ft/weo/weo0598/pdf/_0598ch1pdf.ashx>
IMF, *Global Financial Stability Report— Shockwaves from the War in Ukraine Test the Financial System's Resilience* (April 2022) <https://www.elibrary.imf.org/downloadpdf/book/9798400205293/9798400205293.xml>
IndexUniverse, 'ERC20 Token Standard' <https://www.indexuniverse.eu/erc20-token-standard/>
Ingves, Stefan, 'Future Money and Payments' (15 October 2020) Sveriges Riskbank Economic Commentaries No. 9 2020 <https://www.riksbank.se/globalassets/media/rapporter/ekonomiska-kommentarer/engelska/2020/future-money-and-payments.pdf>
Insider Monkey Staff, 'Prime Brokerage Services Are Coming to Crypto' (*yahoo!finance*, 16 September 2019) <https://finance.yahoo.com/news/prime-brokerage-services-coming-crypto-134018657.html>
Investing, '4 Stocks to Buy as the Metaverse Takes Flight' (2 November 2021) <https://www.investing.com/news/stock-market-news/4-stocks-to-buy-as-the-metaverse-takes-flight-2664623>
IOSCO, *Research Report on Financial Technologies (Fintech)* (February 2017) <https://www.iosco.org/library/pubdocs/pdf/IOSCOPD554.pdf>
IOSCO, 'Global Stablecoins Initiatives' (March 2020) <https://www.iosco.org/library/pubdocs/pdf/IOSCOPD650.pdf>
IOSCO, 'Environmental, Social and Governance (ESG) Ratings and Data Products Providers' (November 2021) <https://www.iosco.org/library/pubdocs/pdf/IOSCOPD690.pdf>
IOSCO, *Decentralized Finance Report* (March 2022) <https://www.iosco.org/library/pubdocs/pdf/IOSCOPD699.pdf>
IOSCO, 'IOSCO Explains How Decentralised Finance Is Cloning Financial Markets' (24 March 2022) <https://www.iosco.org/news/pdf/IOSCONEWS637.pdf>
Irrera, Anna, 'DTCC Completes Blockchain Repo Test' (*Reuters*, 27 February 2017) <https://www.reuters.com/article/us-dtcc-blockchain-repos/dtcc-completes-blockchain-repo-test-idUSKBN1661L9>
Irrera, Anna, 'Illinois Watchdog First U.S. Regulator to Join Blockchain Consortium R3' (*Reuters*, 16 March 2017) <https://www.reuters.com/article/us-blockchain-illinois-idUSKBN16N2FN>
Irrera, Anna and John McCrank, 'Nasdaq Provides Blockchain Tech to New Advertising Exchange' (*Reuters*, 14 March 2017) <https://www.reuters.com/article/us-nasdaq-nyiax-idUSKBN16L18N>
Irrera, Anna and Jemima Kelly, 'London Stock Exchange Group Tests Blockchain for Private Company Shares' (*Reuters*, 19 July 2017) <https://www.reuters.com/article/us-lse-blockchain/london-stock-exchange-group-tests-blockchain-for-private-company-shares-idUSKBN1A40ME>
Irrera, Anna and Tom Wilson, 'Facebook-Backed Digital Coin Libra Renamed Diem in Quest for Approval' (*Reuters*, 1 December 2020) <https://www.reuters.com/article/uk-facebook-cryptocurrency-idUKKBN28B57O>
Irti, Natalino, *Norma e Luoghi—Problemi di Geo-diritto* (Laterza 1990)
Irti, Natalino, *L'Ordine Giuridico del Mercato* (Laterza 2003)
ISDA, 'Legal Guidelines For Smart Derivative Contracts—Introduction' (January 2019) <https://www.isda.org/a/MhgME/Legal-Guidelines-for-Smart-Derivatives-Contracts->
ISDA, 'Contractual Standards for Digital Assets' (December 2021) <https://www.isda.org/2021/12/14/contractual-standards-for-digital-asset-derivatives/>
ISDA and King & Wood Mallesons, 'Smart Derivatives Contracts: From Concept to Construction—Whitepaper' (October 2018) <https://www.isda.org/a/cHvEE/Smart-Derivatives-Contracts-From-Concept-to-Construction-Oct-2018.pdf>

ISDA and Linklaters LLP, 'Smart Contracts and Distributed Ledger: A Legal perspective Whitepaper' (August 2017) <www.isda.org/a/6EKDE/smart-contractsand-distributed-ledger-a-legal-perspective.pdf>

Iseli, Thomas, Alexander F. Wagner, and Rolf H. Weber, 'Legal and Economic Aspects of Best Execution in the Context of the Markets in Financial Instruments Directive (MiFID)' (2007) 1 L&FinMktRev 313

iShares, 'What Is Smart Beta?' <https://www.ishares.com/us/education/smart-beta>

ISO <https://www.iso.org/home.html>

Jaccard, Gabriel, 'Smart Contracts and the Role of Law' (*Jusletter IT*, 2017) <https://jusletter-it.weblaw.ch/en/issues/2017/23-November-2017/smart-contracts-and-_42155d7e26.html__ONCE&login=false>

Jackson, Howell E. and Margaret E. Tahyar, *Fintech Law: The Case Studies* (*Harvard.edu*, 2020) <https://projects.iq.harvard.edu/fintechlaw/home>

Jagati, Shiraz, 'CFTC Joins the Telegram vs. SEC Case, Shedding Light on Likely Verdict' (*Cointelegraph*, 21 February 2020) <https://cointelegraph.com/news/cftc-joins-the-telegram-vs-sec-case-shedding-light-on-likely-verdict>

Jenkinson, Gareth, 'From Ponzi Schemes to ICO Exits, Ethereum's Blockchain Has Been the Platform of Choice for Scammers' (*Cointelegraph*, 4 February 2019) <https://cointelegraph.com/news/from-ponzi-schemes-to-ico-exits-ethereums-blockchain-has-been-the-platform-of-choice-for-scammers>

Jentzsch, Christoph, 'The History of the DAO and Lessons Learned' (*Slock.it*, 24 August 2016) <https://blog.slock.it/the-history-of-the-dao-and-lessons-learned-d06740f8cfa5?gi=19bb43e6d75f>

Jentzsch, Christoph, 'Decentralized Autonomous Organization to Automate Governance Final Draft—Under Review' (2017) <https://lawofthelevel.lexblogplatformthree.com/wp-content/uploads/sites/187/2017/07/WhitePaper-1.pdf>

Jiang, Jiaying and Karman Lucero, 'Background and Implications of China's E-CNY' (2023) UFlaJL&PubPol'y (forthcoming) <https://scholarship.law.ufl.edu/cgi/viewcontent.cgi?article=2238&context=facultypub>

Joint Committee of the Supervisory Authorities, 'On the Use of Big Data by Financial Institutions' (2016) Joint Committee Discussion Paper 2016/86 <https://www.esma.europa.eu/sites/default/files/library/jc-2016-86_discussion_paper_big_data.pdf>

Jordan, Thomas J., 'Currencies, Money and Digital Tokens' (Speech at the University of Basel, Switzerland, 5 September 2019) <https://www.snb.ch/en/mmr/speeches/id/ref_20190905_tjn/source/ref_20190905_tjn.en.pdf>

Judge, Kathryn, 'Fragmentation Nodes: A Study in Financial Innovation, Complexity, and Systemic Risk' (2012) 64 StanLRev 657

Judge, Kathryn, 'The First Year: The Role of a Modern Lender of Last Resort' (2016) 116 ColumLRev 843

Judge, Kathryn, 'How the Fed Is Helping the Economy and How Its Efforts Could Backfire' (*Forbes*, 8 April 2020) <https://www.forbes.com/sites/kathrynjudge/2020/04/08/how-the-fed-is-helping-the-economy-and-how-its-efforts-could-backfire/#2801faf66887>

Jünemann, Michael, 'ECSPR—Crowdfunding Regulation and Crypto Tokens' (*Bird & Bird*, 26 October 2021) <https://www.twobirds.com/en/insights/2021/germany/ecspr-crowdfunding-regulation-and-crypto-tokens>

Kaal, Wulf A., 'Evolution of Law: Dynamic Regulation in a New Institutional Economics Framework' in Wulf A. Kaal, Andreas Schwartze, and Matthias Schmidt (eds), *Festschrift Zu Ehren Von Christian Kirchner* (Mohr Siebeck 2014) 1211–1228

Kaal, Wulf A., 'Initial Coin Offerings: The Top 25 Jurisdictions and their Comparative Regulatory Responses (as of May 2018)' (2018) 1 StanJBlockchainL&Pol'y 41

Kaal, Wulf A., 'Decentralization—A Primer on the New Economy' (2019) <https://ssrn.com/abstract=3406323>

Kaal, Wulf A., 'Blockchain-Based Corporate Governance' (2021) 4 StanJBlockchainL&Pol'y 3

Kaal, Wulf A. and Erik P. M. Vermeulen, 'How to Regulate Disruptive Innovation—From Facts to Data' (2017) 57 Jurimetrics 169

Kacperczyk, Marcin and Philipp Schnabl, 'How Safe Are Money Market Funds?' (2013) 128 QJEcon 1073

Kades, Eric, 'The Laws of Complexity and the Complexity of Laws: The Implications of Computational Complexity Theory for the Law' (1997) 49 RutgLRev 403

Kagan, Julia, 'Strategic Default' (*Investopedia*, updated 30 November 2021) <https://www.investopedia.com/terms/s/strategic-default.asp>

Kahan, Marcel and Ehud Kamar, 'The Myth of State Competition in Corporate Law' (2002) 55 StanLRev 679

Kahan, Marcel and Edward B. Rock, 'The Hanging Chads of Corporate Voting' (2008) 96 GeoLJ 1227

Kahn, Charles M., Francisco Rivadeneyra, and Tsz-Nga Wong, 'Should the Central Bank Issue E-Money?' (2018) Bank of Canada Staff Working Paper 2018-58 <https://www.bankofcanada.ca/wp-content/uploads/2018/12/swp2018-58.pdf>

Kalla, Sid, 'A Framework for Valuing Crypto Tokens' (*CoinDesk*, 3 March 2017) <https://www.coindesk.com/framework-valuing-crypto-tokens>

Kamar, Ehud, 'A Regulatory Competition Theory of Indeterminacy in Corporate Law' (1998) 98 ColumLRev 1908

Kane, Arben, 'Fractionalized NFT (F-NFTs): All That You Need To Know' (*Medium*, 9 September 2021) <https://medium.com/@arbenk/fractionalized-nft-f-nfts-all-that-you-need-to-know-46bc06ea486d>

Kane, Edward J., 'Interaction of Financial and Regulatory Innovation' (1988) 78 AmEconRev 328

Kapur, Devesh, 'The IMF: A Cure or a Curse' (1998) 111 ForPol'y 114 <https://www.jstor.org/stable/1149382>

Kariuki, David, 'Another Cryptocurrency Exchange Has Launched' (*Cryptomorrow*, 15 November 2018) <https://www.cryptomorrow.com/2018/11/15/another-cryptocurrency-clearinghouse-has-launched/>

Kastelein, Richard, 'What Initial Coin Offerings Are, and Why VC Firms Care' (*Harvard Business Review Online*, 24 March 2017) <https://hbr.org/2017/03/what-initial-coin-offerings-are-and-why-vc-firms-care>

Kastelein, Richard, 'Initial Coin Offerings (ICOs) Can Disrupt Both Traditional VC and Equity Crowdfunding' (*Intelligent HQ*, 31 March 2017) <https://www.intelligenthq.com/finance/initial-coin-offerings-icos-can-disrupt-vc-and-equity-crowdfunding/>

Kastrenakes, Jacob, 'Libra Cryptocurrency Project Changes Name to Diem to Distance Itself from Facebook' (*The Verge*, 1 December 2020) https://www.theverge.com/2020/12/1/21755078/libra-diem-name-change-cryptocurrency-facebook>

Katalyse.io, 'What Are "Airdrops" in Crypto World?' (*Medium*, 15 February 2018) <https://medium.com/the-mission/what-are-airdrops-in-crypto-world-a345725c75e0>

Katz, David A., 'Opening Statement' (Meeting of the Securities and Exchange Commission Investor Advisory Committee, 13 September 2018) <https://www.sec.gov/spotlight/investor-advisory-committee-2012/iac091318-david-katz-opening-remarks.pdf>

Katz, Lily, 'Proxy Voting Is the Latest Target for Blockchain Disruption' (*Bloomberg*, 10 May 2018) <https://www.bloomberg.com/news/articles/2018-05-10/broadridge-gets-blockchain-patent-to-make-proxy-voting-easier>

Kaufmann, Christine and Rolf H. Weber, 'The Role of Transparency in Financial Regulation' (2010) 13 JIntlEconL 779

Kaufmann, Christine and Rolf H. Weber, 'Transparency of Central Banks' Policy' in Peter Conti-Brown and Rosa Lastra (eds), *Research Handbook on Central Banking* (Elgar 2018) 518–533

Kaulartz, Michael and Jörn Heckmann, 'Smart Contracts—Anwendungen der Blockchain-Technologie' (2016) 9 CompRecht 618

Kawai, Ken, 'Japan: Digital Securities Business Is About To Bloom' (*Mondaq*, 6 November 2020) <https://www.mondaq.com/securities/1002066/digital-securities-business-is-about-to-bloom>

Kelsen, Hans, *Pure Theory of Law* (Max Knight tr, The Lawbook Exchange 2014)

Kenton, Will, 'MSCI Inc.' (*Investopedia*, updated 29 March 2023) <https://www.investopedia.com/terms/m/msci.asp>

Keoun, Bradley, 'Compared to Traditional Banks, Crypto Lenders See Booming Growth' (*CoinDesk*, 30 January 2020) <https://www.coindesk.com/compared-to-traditional-banks-crypto-lenders-see-booming-growth?utm_source=&utm_medium=&utm_campaign=clid=>

Kessler, Sam and Danny Nelson, 'UST's Do Know Was Behind Earlier Failed Stablecoin, Ex-Terra Colleagues Say' (*CoinDesk*, 11 May 2022) <https://www.coindesk.com/tech/2022/05/11/usts-do-kwon-was-behind-earlier-failed-stablecoin-ex-terra-colleagues-say/>

Khan, Faisal, 'Fintech Startups Are Disrupting the Banking Industry around the World' (*Medium*, 20 October 2018) <https://medium.com/datadriveninvestor/fintech-startups-are-disrupting-the-banking-industry-around-the-world-7d5ca5bb3cb8>

Kharif, Olga, 'Bitcoin Speculators Gain Upper Hand as Derivative Trading Surges' (*Bloomberg*, 22 October 2019) <https://www.bloomberg.com/news/articles/2019-10-22/bitcoin-speculators-gain-upper-hand-as-derivative-trading-surges>

Kharif, Olga, 'Facebook-Backed Libra Association Changes Its Name to Diem' (*Bloomberg*, 1 December 2020) <https://www.bloomberg.com/news/articles/2020-12-01/facebook-backed-crypto-group-libra-changes-name-to-diem-network>

Khatri, Yogita, '4 Banks Complete €100K Commercial Paper Transaction on R3's Corda' (*CoinDesk*, 6 December 2018) <https://www.coindesk.com/4-banks-complete-e100k-commercial-paper-transaction-on-r3s-corda>

Kidd, Jr. Donnie L., and William H. Daughtrey, Jr., 'Adapting Contract Law to Accommodate Electronic Contracts: Overview and Suggestions' (2000) 26 RutgersComp&TechLJ 215

Kim, Amy and Paul Brigner, 'Diving into Smart Contracts' (*Chamber of Digital Commerce*, 25 September 2018) <https://digitalchamber.org/smart-contracts-blog/>

Kim, Amy Davine, 'State-by-State Smart Contract Laws? If It Ain't Broke, Don't Fix It' (*CoinDesk*, 26 February 2018) <https://www.coindesk.com/state-state-smart-contract-laws-aint-broke-dont-fix/>

Kim, Brian, 'Sarbanes-Oxley Act' (2003) 40 HarvJLegis 235

King, Amy, 'Fintech: Throwing Down the Gauntlet to Financial Services' (*Unquote*, 17 January 2014) <https://www.unquote.com/unquote/analysis/74596/fintech-throwing-down-the-gauntlet-to-financial-services>

Kirimi, Arnold, 'BNY Mellon Plans to Launch Digital Asset Custody Platform Later this Year' (*Cointelegraph*, 25 February 2022) <https://cointelegraph.com/news/bny-mellon-plans-to-launch-digital-asset-custody-platform-later-this-year>

Kirkpatrick, Grant, 'The Corporate Governance Lessons from the Financial Crisis' (2008) 1 OECD Financial Market Trends 1 <https://www.oecd.org/finance/financial-markets/42229620.pdf>

Kiviat, Trevor I., 'Beyond Bitcoin: Issues in Regulation Blockchain Transactions' (2015-16) 65 DukeLJ 569

Kiyotaki, Nobuhiro and Randall Wright, 'On Money as a Medium of Exchange' (1989) 97 JPolEcon 927

Klass, Gregory, 'Efficient Breach' in Gregory Klass, George Letsas, and Prince Saprai (eds), *Philosophical Foundations of Contract Law* (OUP 2014) 362–388

Klein, Maximilian, Florian Neitzert, Thomas Hartmann-Wendels, and Sascha Kraus, 'Start-Up Financing in the Digital Age—A Systematic Review and Comparison of New Forms of Financing' (2020) 21 JEF 46

Knapp, Georg Friedrich, *The State Theory of Money* (H. M. Lucas tr, Martino Fine Books 2013)

Koeppl, Thorsten and Jeremy Kronick, 'Blockchain Technology—What's in Store for Canada's Economy and Financial Markets?' (2017) C. D. Hower Institute Commentary No. 468 <https://www.cdhowe.org/sites/default/files/2021-12/Commentary_468_0.pdf>

Kogan, Constantin, 'The Story Behind the Explosive Growth of Crypto Funds' (*Cointelegraph*, 28 September 2019) <https://cointelegraph.com/news/the-story-behind-the-explosive-growth-of-crypto-funds>

Kolakowski, Marc, 'Stock and Flow Variables Explained: A Closer Look at Apple' (*Investopedia*, updated 19 January 2016) <https://www.investopedia.com.cach3.com/articles/investing/011916/stock-and-flow-variables-explained-closer-look-apple.asp.html>

Koning, John Paul, 'Fedcoin: A Central-Bank Issued Cryptocurrency' (2016) <https://www.r3.com/wp-content/uploads/2018/04/Fedcoin_Central_Bank_R3.pdf>

Kostinuk, Brandon, 'Too Many Crypto Coin Crowd Sales Could Crowd Out True Innovators' (*American Banker*, 2016) <https://www.americanbanker.com/opinion/too-many-crypto-coin-crowd-sales-could-crowd-out-true-innovators>

Kozlov, Herbert F. and Arthur C. Surratt III, 'Wyoming and Colorado Emerging as Leading Digital Asset Venues in the U.S.' (*Lexology*, 29 October 2019) <https://www.lexology.com/library/detail.aspx?g=c322a3c2-0a55-4a79-98b2-89ec4e327791>

Kraakman, Rainer, 'Corporate Liability Strategies and the Costs of Legal Controls' (1984) 93 YaleLJ 868

Kress, Jeremy C., 'Credit Default Swaps, Clearinghouses, and Systemic Risk: Why Centralized Counterparties Must Have Access to Central Bank Liquidity' (2011) 48 HarvJLegis 49

Kumari, Darpan, 'The Battle: ICOs vs IEOs vs STOs' (*Medium*, 26 June 2019) <https://medium.com/towardsblockchain/the-battle-icos-vs-ieos-vs-stos-9c9b0d851960>

Kurbatov, Constantin, 'Tokenized Asstes vs. High-Yield Bonds: Which is the New Way to Increase Trust While Decrease Costs?' (*yahoo!finance*, 4 January 2018) <https://uk.news.yahoo.com/tokenized-asstes-vs-high-yield-143510373.html>

LabCFTC, 'A CFTC Primer on Virtual Currencies' (17 October 2017) <https://www.cftc.gov/sites/default/files/idc/groups/public/documents/file/labcftc_primercurrencies100417.pdf>

Lacroix, Frédérick, Sébastien Praicheux, and Pierre d'Ormesson, 'Clifford Chance on France's Pioneering Blockchain Legal Framework for Unlisted Securities' (*CLS Blue Sky Blog*, 29 January 2018) <http://clsbluesky.law.columbia.edu/2018/01/29/clifford-chance-on-frances-pioneering-blockchain-legal-framework-for-unlisted-securities/>

Lafarre, Anne and Christoph Van der Elst, 'Blockchain Technology for Corporate Governance and Shareholder Activism' (2018) European Corporate Governance Institute (ECGI)—Law Working Paper No. 390/2018 <https://ssrn.com/abstract=3135209>

Lagarde, Christine, 'Winds of Change: The Case for New Digital Currency' (14 November 2018) <https://www.imf.org/-/media/Files/News/Speech/111418-md-sg-fintech-speech.ashx>

Lam, Fiona, 'MAS, Temasek, JPMorgan Develop Prototype Network for Multi-Currency Payments' (*The Business Times*, 11 November 2019) <https://www.businesstimes.com.sg/banking-finance/mas-temasek-jpmorgan-develop-prototype-network-for-multi-currency-payments>

Lando, Ole and Hugh Beale (eds), *Principles of European Contract Law Parts I and II Combined and Revised* (Kluwer Law 2000)

Langenbucher, Katja, 'Wirecard and Lessons Learnt' (Public Hearing before the European Parliament Economic and Monetary Affairs (ECON) and Legal Affairs (JURI) Committees, 23 March 2021)

[Letter from] Larry Fink to Shareholders (14 January 2020) <https://www.blackrock.com/corporate/investor-relations/larry-fink-ceo-letter>

Larsen, Aleks, 'A Primer on Blockchain Interoperability' (*Medium*, 20 December 2018) <https://medium.com/blockchain-capital-blog/a-primer-on-blockchain-interoperability-e132bab805b>

Lastra, Rosa María and Jason Grant Allen, 'Virtual Currencies in the Eurosystem: Challenges Ahead' (2022) 52 IntlLaw 177 <http://www.europarl.europa.eu/cmsdata/150541/DIW_FINAL%20publication.pdf>

Laurent, Lionel, 'Want to Be a VC? Just Flip a Bitcoin' (*Bloomberg*, 18 April 2017) <https://www.bloomberg.com/opinion/articles/2017-04-18/beating-vc-funds-is-as-easy-as-flipping-a-bitcoin>

Laurent, Patrick, Thibault Chollet, Michael Burke, and Tobias Seers, 'The Tokenization of Assets Is Disrupting the Financial Industry. Are You Ready?' (*Wyoleg*, 2018) <https://www.wyoleg.gov/InterimCommittee/2019/S3-20190506TokenizationArticle.pdf>

Law Commission, 'Smart Legal Contracts: Advice to the Government' (2020) <https://s3-eu-west-2.amazonaws.com/lawcom-prod-storage-11jsxou24uy7q/uploads/2021/11/Smart-legal-contracts-accessible.pdf>

Lazanis, Ryan, 'How Technology Behind Bitcoin Could Transform Accounting as We Know It' (*Brainstation*, 22 January 2015) <https://www.borndigital.com/2015/01/22/how-technology-behind-bitcoin-could-transform-accounting-as-we-know-it-2015-01-22>

Le Goff, Jacques, 'Church Time and Merchant Time in the Middle Ages' (1970) 9(4) SSI 151

Le Goff, Jacques, *Your Money or Your Life: Economy and Religion in the Middle Ages* (PUP 1988)

Le Maire, Bruno, 'Facebook's Libra Is a Threat to National Sovereignty' (*Financial Times*, 17 October 2019) <https://www.ft.com/content/bf2f588e-ef63-11e9-a55a-30afa498db1b>

Lea, Tim, 'Venture Capital 3.0: The Initial Coin Offering Explained' (*Financial Review*, 2 May 2017) <http://www.afr.com/technology/venture-capital-30-the-initial-coin-offering-explained-20170502-gvxhos>

LeCun, Yann, Yoshua Bengio, and Geoffrey Hinton, 'Deep Learning' (2015) 521 Nature 436

Lee, Peter, 'The Fintech Entrepreneurs Aiming to Reinvent Finance' (2015) 46 Euromoney 42

Lee, Sherman, 'Explaining Stable Coins, the Holy Grail of Cryptocurrency' (*Forbes*, 12 March 2018) <https://www.forbes.com/sites/shermanlee/2018/03/12/explaining-stable-coins-the-holy-grail-of-crytpocurrency/?sh=4af8af614fc6>

Leising, Matthew, '$50bn in Cryptoassets Moved Out of China in the Past Year' (*Aljazeera*, 20 August 2020) <https://www.aljazeera.com/economy/2020/8/20/50bn-in-cryptoassets-moved-out-of-china-in-the-past-year>

Lemmet, Sylvie and Pierre Ducret, 'Executive Summary French Strategy For Green Finance' (December 2017) <https://2017.climatefinanceday.com/wp-content/uploads/2017/12/EXECUTIVE-SUMMARY-finance-verte-sircom-v3.pdf>

Lessig, Lawrence, 'The Law of the Horse: What Cyberlaw Might Teach' (1999) 113 HarvLRev 501

Lessig, Lawrence, 'Code Is Law' (*Harvard Magazine*, 1 January 2000) <https://www.harvardmagazine.com/2000/01/code-is-law-html> (describing how code is a new form of regulation of cyberspace)

Levi, Ary, 'Tech IPOs Have Been a Bad Bet in 2021—All but One are in Bear Market Territory' (*CNBC*, 7 December 2021) <https://www.cnbc.com/2021/12/07/tech-ipos-a-bad-bet-in-2021-all-but-one-in-bear-market-territory.html>

Levine, Matt, 'P&G Could Use the Blockchain in Its Next Proxy Fight' (*Bloomberg*, 17 November 2017) <https://www.bloomberg.com/view/articles/2017-11-17/p-g-could-use-the-blockchain-in-its-next-proxy-fight>

Levine, Matt, 'Put the Money Fund on the Blockchain' (*Bloomberg*, 4 September 2019) <https://www.bloomberg.com/opinion/articles/2019-09-04/put-the-money-fund-on-the-blockchain>

Lewis, Tracy R. and Huseyin Yildirim, 'Learning by Doing and Dynamic Regulation' (2002) 33 RANDJEcon 22

Liao, Gordon Y. and John Caramichael, 'Stablecoins: Growth Potential and Impact on Banking' (2022) International Finance Discussion Papers No. 1334 <https://www.federalreserve.gov/econres/ifdp/files/ifdp1334.pdf>

Libonati, Berardino, 'La categoria del diritto commerciale' (2002) 47 RSD 1

Liechtensteinisches Gesetz über Token und VT-Dienstleister LGBl 2019 Nr. 301, LR 950.6

Lielacher, Alex, '7 Ways to Short Crypto' (*Cryptonews*, 21 July 2019) <https://cryptonews.com/exclusives/7-ways-to-short-crypto-4282.htm>

Lin, Lin and Dominika Nestarcova, 'Venture Capital in the Rise of Crypto Economy: Problems and Prospects' (2019) 16 BerkeleyBusLJ 533

Lin, Lindsay X., 'Deconstructing Decentralized Exchanges' (2019) 2 StanJBlockchainL&Pol'y 58

Lior, Anat, 'The AI Accident Network: Artificial Intelligence Liability Meets Network Theory' (2020) 95 TulLRev 1103

Long, Caitlin, 'Bitcoin, the Dollar and Facebook's Cryptocurrency: Price Volatility Versus Systemic Volatility' (*Forbes*, 29 June 2019) <https://www.forbes.com/sites/caitlinlong/2019/06/29/bitcoin-the-dollar-and-facebooks-cryptocurrency-price-volatility-versus-systemic-volatility/#51fc0d6d88b8>

Long, Heather, 'Fed Announces Unlimited Bond Purchases in Unprecedented Move Aimed at Preventing an Economic Depression' (*Washington Post*, 23 March 2020) <https://www.washingtonpost.com/business/2020/03/23/fed-unlimited-credit-coronavirus/>

Losurdo, Nicholas J. and Christopher Grobbel, 'FINRA Sheds Light on Path to Digital Asset Security Broker Registration' (21 November 2022) <https://www.goodwinlaw.com/en/insights/publications/2022/11/11_21-finra-sheds-light-on-path-to-digital-asset>

Lucas, Kawa, 'Stiglitz: Central Bank Independence Is Unnecessary and Impossible' (*Business Insider*, 3 January 2013) <https://www.businessinsider.com/stiglitz-on-central-bank-independence-2013-1?r=US&IR=T>

Macey, Jonathan and Maureen O'Hara, 'The Corporate Governance of Banks' (2003) 9 FRBNY EconPolRev 91

Mancini-Griffoli, Tommaso, Maria Soledad Martinez Peria, Itai Agur, Anil Ari, John Kiff, Adina Popescu, and Celine Rochon, 'Casting Light on Central Bank Digital Currency' (2018) IMF Staff Discussion Note 18/03 <https://www.imf.org/en/Publications/Staff-Discussion-Notes/Issues/2018/11/13/Casting-Light-on-Central-Bank-Digital-Currencies-46233>

Marous, Jim, 'The Future of Banking: Fintech or Techfin?' (*Forbes*, August 2018) <https://www.forbes.com/sites/jimmarous/2018/08/27/future-of-banking-fintech-or-techfin-technology/#5a44e415f2d5>

Martin, Katie, 'What Happens in Crypto May Not Stay in Crypto This Time Around' (*Financial Times*, 13 May 2022) <https://www.ft.com/content/6dcd0263-f974-4833-97a9-93b05be74f6e>

Massad, Timothy, 'Testimony before the U.S. Senate Committee on Agriculture, Nutrition & Forestry' (10 December 2014) <https://www.cftc.gov/PressRoom/SpeechesTestimony/opamassad-6>

Mathew, Gregory S., 'IEO vs STO vs ICO: A Comparison of Tokenized Fundraising. Which One Is Better? (*Medium*, 9 June 2014) <https://medium.com/hackernoon/ieo-vs-sto-vs-ico-a-comparison-of-tokenized-fundraising-which-one-is-better-ab71b1c2a32b>

Maues, Julia, 'Banking Act of 1933 (Glass-Steagall)' (*Federal Reserve History*, 22 November 2013) <https://www.federalreservehistory.org/essays/glass_steagall_act>

Mazzucato, Mariana, *The Entrepreneurial State: Debunking Public vs. Private Sector Myths* (Penguin 2015)

Mazzucato, Mariana, *The Value of Everything* (Penguin 2019)

Mazzucato, Mariana, Rainer Kattel, and Josh Ryan-Collins, 'Challenge-Driven Innovation Policy: Towards a New Policy Toolkit' (2020) 20 JIndCompTrade 421

Mcaffrey, David P. and David W. Hart, *Wall Street Polices Itself: How Securities Firms Manage the Legal Hazards of Competitive Pressures* (OUP 1998)

McDonald, Brian D., 'The Uniform Computer Information Transactions Act' (2001) 16 BTLJ 461

McDowell, Maghan, 'What Fashion Week Looks Like in the Metaverse' (*Vogue Business*, 1 February 2022) <https://www.voguebusiness.com/technology/what-fashion-week-looks-like-in-the-metaverse>

McIntosh, Donald, 'Max Weber as a Critical Theorist' (1983) 12 Th&Soc 69

McJohn, Stephen and Ian McJohn, 'The Commercial Law of Bitcoin and Blockchain Transactions' (2016) 47 UniformComCodeLJ 187

McLeay, Michael, Amar Radia, and Ryland Thomas, 'Money in the Modern Economy: An Introduction' (2014) Bank of England—Quarterly Bulletin 2014 Q1 <https://www.bankofengland.co.uk/quarterly-bulletin/2014/q1/money-in-the-modern-economy-an-introduction>

McLeay, Michael, Amar Radia, and Ryland Thomas, 'Money in the Modern Economy' (2014) Bank of England—Quarterly Bulletin 2014 Q1 <https://www.bankofengland.co.uk/-/media/boe/files/quarterly-bulletin/2014/money-creation-in-the-modern-economy.pdf?la=en&hash=9A8788FD44A62D8BB927123544205CE476E01654>

Mengoni, Luigi, *Ermeneutica e dogmatica giuridica* (Giuffre 1996)

Merrill, Ryan K., Simon J. D. Schillebeeckx, and Sofie Blakstad, 'DBS & Sustainable Digital Finance Alliance, Sustainable Digital Finance in Asia: Creating Environmental Impact through Bank Transformation' (2019) <https://greendigitalfinancealliance.org/wp-content/uploads/2019/11/SustainableDigitalFinanceinAsia.pdf>

Mersch, Yves, 'International Trends in Central Bank Independence: The ECB's Perspective' (Speech at the ECB Roundtable Discussion on Central Bank Independence, Frankfurt am Main, 12 November 2019) <https://www.ecb.europa.eu/press/key/date/2019/html/ecb.sp191112_1~f304b47e14.en.html>

Mettling, Stephen and David Cusic, *Principles of Real Estate Practice in North Carolina* (2nd edn, PPC 2020)

Meyer, Stephan D. and Benedikt Schluppi, '"Smart Contracts" und deren Einordnung in das schweizerische Vertragsrecht' (2017) 3 Recht 204

Michaels, Dave, 'Stablecoins Attract Scrutiny in SEC's Drive to Control Crypto' (*WSJ*, 22 February 2023) <https://www.wsj.com/articles/stablecoins-attract-scrutiny-in-secs-drive-to-control-crypto-12179e04>

Micheler, Eva, 'Custody Chains and Asset Values: Why Crypto-Securities Are Worth Contemplating' (2015) 74 CLJ 505

Miller, Gary, 'Blockchain Valley: Wyoming Is Poised to Become the Cryptocurrency Capital of America' (*Newsweek*, 2 March 2018) <http://www.newsweek.com/wyoming-cowboy-state-poised-today-become-blockchain-valley-828124>

Miller, John H. and Scott E. Page, *Complex Adaptive Systems: An Introduction To Computational Models of Social Life* (PUP 2007)

Mills, David, Kathy Wang, Brendan Malone, Anjana Ravi, Jeff Marquardt, Clinton Chen, Anton Badev, Timothy Brezinski, Linda Fahy, Kimberley Liao, Vanessa Kargenian, Max Ellithorpe,

Wendy Ng, and Maria Bair, 'Distributed Ledger Technology in Payments, Clearing, and Settlement' (2016) Finance & Economics Discussion Series Working Paper No. 095 <https://doi.org/10.17016/FEDS.2016.095>

Minsky, Hyman P., *Stabilizing an Unstable Economy* (McGraw-Hill 1986)

Mitchell, Melanie, *Complexity: A Guided Tour* (OUP 2009)

Miyazaki, Kumiko and Kyoichi Kijima, 'Complexity in Technology Management: Theoretical Analysis and Case Study of Automobile Sector in Japan' (2000) 64 TechForec&SocChange 39, 39

Modigliani, Franco and Merton H. Miller, 'The Cost of Capital, Corporation Finance and the Theory of Investment' (1958) 48 AmEconRev 261

Moloney, Niamh, 'MiFID II: Reshaping the Perimeter of EU Trading Market Regulation' (2012) 6 L&FinMktRev 327

Momtaz, Paul P., 'Initial Coin Offerings' (2020) 15 PLOS ONE 1

Momtaz, Paul P., 'The Pricing and Performance of Cryptocurrency' (2021) 27 EurJFin 367

Moody's, 'Moody's Downgrades El Salvador's Rating to Caa1, Maintains Negative Outlook' (30 July 2021) <https://www.moodys.com/research/Moodys-downgrades-El-Salvadors-rating-to-Caa1-maintains-negative-outlook--PR_450956>

Moore, Galen, 'Crypto Derivatives—What to Expect in a Changing World' (*CoinDesk*, October 2019) 6 <https://downloads.coindesk.com/crypto-investing/crypto_derivatives.pdf >

Moore, Galen, 'Custody—Crypto Assets' Unique Challenge and Opportunity' (*CoinDesk*, 2019) 6 <https://downloads.coindesk.com/crypto-investing/custody-report.pdf>

Morçöl, Göktuğ and Aaron Wachhaus, 'Network and Complexity Theories: A Comparison and Prospects for a Synthesis' (2009) 31 ATP 44

Morgan Stanley Capital International (MSCI), 'MSCI World ESG Leaders Index (USD)' (29 April 2022) <https://www.msci.com/documents/10199/db88cb95-3bf3-424c-b776-bfdcca67d460>

Morgan Stanley Capital International, 'MSCI ACWI ESG Leaders Index (USD)' (29 April 2022) <https://www.msci.com/documents/10199/9a760a3b-4dc0-4059-b33e-fe67eae92460>

Morris, David Z., 'Bitcoin Is Not Just Digital Currency. It's Napster for Finance' (*Fortune*, 21 January 2014) <https://fortune.com/2014/01/21/bitcoin-is-not-just-digital-currency-its-napster-for-finance/>

Morris, David Z. and Robert Hackett, 'Should "Fintech" Fear Big Tech's Push into Banking?' (*Fortune*, 20 November 2019) <https://fortune.com/2019/11/20/should-fintech-fear-big-techs-push-into-banking/>

Morrison & Foerster LLP, 'Federal Judge Upholds CFTC's Determination that Virtual Currencies Are Commodities' (*Lexology*, 9 March 2018) <https://www.lexology.com/library/detail.aspx?g=cf5d9eb6-7060-4aa4-bde2-81111e8d0ca6>

Moslein, Florian, 'Legal Boundaries of Blockchain Technologies: Smart Contracts as Self-Help?' in Alberto de Franceschi, Reiner Schulze, Michele Graziadei, and Oreste Pollicino (eds), *Digital Revolution—New Challenges for Law* (C. H. Beck 2019) 313–326

Mudgil, Sumi, 'How to Mint an NFT (Part 2/3 of NFT Tutorial Series)' (*Ethereum*, 22 April 2021) <https://ethereum.org/en/developers/tutorials/how-to-mint-an-nft/>

Mudgil, Sumi, 'How to Write & Deploy an NFT (Part 1/3 of NFT Tutorial Series)' (*Ethereum*, 22 April 2021) <https://ethereum.org/en/developers/tutorials/how-to-write-and-deploy-an-nft/>

Mui, Rachel, 'SGX-Backed iSTOX Lists Unicorn Fund with US$20,000 Minimum Investment' (*The Business Times*, 22 December 2020) <https://www.businesstimes.com.sg/garage/sgx-backed-istox-lists-unicorn-fund-with-us20000-minimum-investment>

Mulders, Michiel, 'Comparing ERC20, ERC223, and the New Ethereum ERC777 Token Standard' (*Cointelligence*, 19 February 2018) <https://www.cointelligence.com/content/comparison-erc20-erc223-new-ethereum-erc777-token-standard/>

Müller, Christoph (ed), *Berner Kommentar—Art.1-18 OR mit allgemeiner Einleitung in das Schweizerische Obligationenrecht* (Stämpfli 2018)

Müller, Christoph, 'Die Smart Contracts aus Sicht des Schweizerischen Obligationenrechts' (2019) 5 ZBJV 330

Muller, Lukas and Reto Seiler, 'Smart Contracts aus Sicht de Vertragsrechts' (2019) 3 AJP 317

Mulligan, Jessica and Bridgette Patrovsky, *Developing Online Games: An Insider's Guide* (New Riders 2003)

Murphy, Hanna and Kiran Stacey, 'Where It All Went Wrong for Facebook's Libra' (*The Irish Times*, 16 October 2019) <https://www.irishtimes.com/business/technology/where-it-all-went-wrong-for-facebook-s-libra-cryptocurrency-1.4055121>

Murphy, Hannah and Izabella Kaminska, 'Facebook's Libra Overhauls Core Parts of Its Digital Currency Vision' (*Financial Times*, 16 April 2020) <https://www.ft.com/content/23a33fcb-1342-4a18-be39-504e8507f752>

Nadex, 'Products and Markets' <https://www.nadex.com/product-market/>

Nadini, Matthieu, Laura Alessandretti, Flavio Di Giacinto, Mauro Martino, Luca Maria Aiello, and Andrea Baronchelli, 'Mapping the NFT Revolution: Market Trends, Trade Networks, and Visual Features' (2021) 11 Scientific Reports 20902 <https://www.nature.com/articles/s41598-021-00053-8.pdf>

Nakamoto, Satoshi, 'Bitcoin: A Peer-to-Peer Electronic Cash System' (31 October 2008) <https://bitcoin.org/bitcoin.pdf>

NASA, 'Second Law of Thermodynamics'<https://www.grc.nasa.gov/WWW/K-12/airplane/thermo2.html>

NASCIO, 'Digital Transformation in Government: The Illinois Blockchain Initiative' (1 June 2017) <https://www.nascio.org/resource-center/resources/digital-transformation-in-government-the-illinois-blockchain-initiative-webinar/>

Nasdaq, 'Nasdaq to Deliver Blockchain E-Voting Solution to Strate' (22 September 2017) <http://ir.nasdaq.com/news-releases/news-release-details/nasdaq-deliver-blockchain-e-voting-solution-strate>

Nash, Gerald, 'The Anatomy of ERC721' (*Medium*, 23 December 2017) <https://medium.com/crypto-currently/the-anatomy-of-erc721-e9db77abfc24>

Natarajan, Sridhar, 'Goldman Sachs Is Considering a Custody Offering for Crypto Funds' (*Bloomberg*, 6 August 2018) <https://www.bloomberg.com/news/articles/2018-08-06/goldman-is-said-to-consider-custody-offering-for-crypto-funds>

Nauman, Billy, 'S&P Acquires ESG Ratings Arm of RobecoSAM' (*Financial Times*, 21 November 2019) <https://www.ft.com/content/098258d6-0bc6-11ea-bb52-34c8d9dc6d84>

Nelaturu, Keerthi, 'Blockchain Interoperability—Sidechains' (*Medium*, 1 August 2018) <https://medium.com/coinmonks/blockchain-interoperability-sidechains-e8204b8c2a10>

Nelson, Danny, 'AlphaPoint's White Label Tech Now Lets Crypto Exchanges Offer Margin Trading' (*CoinDesk*, 12 November 2019) <https://www.coindesk.com/alphapoint-to-support-margin-trading-at-its-crypto-exchange-clients>

Nelson, Danny, 'E-Krona or Bust, Says Sweden's Chief Central Banker, Trying to Drag Swedish Govt into Digital Age' (*CoinDesk*, 16 October 2020) https://www.coindesk.com/riksbank-governor-calls-for-swedish-digital-currency>

Niedziela, Theresa A., 'Franklin D. Roosevelt and the Supreme Court' (1976) 6 PSQ 51

Noonan, Laura and Hannah Murphy, 'Facebook in Talks with US Regulator over Digital Currency' (*Financial Times*, 2 June 2019) <https://www.ft.com/content/3b2084fe-83c6-11e9-b592-5fe435b57a3b>

Norton Rose Fulbright and R3, 'Can Smart Contracts Be Legally Binding Contracts?' (2016) <https://www.nortonrosefulbright.com/-/media/files/nrf/nrfweb/imported/norton-rose-fulbright--r3-smart-contracts-white-paper-key-findings-nov-2016.pdf>

Nowzad, Bahram, 'The IMF and Its Critics' (1981) Princeton Essays in International Finance No. 146 <https://ies.princeton.edu/pdf/E146.pdf>

NY Attorney General, 'Attorney General James Announces Court Order against 'Crypto' Currency Company under Investigation for Fraud' (25 April 2019) <https://ag.ny.gov/press-release/2019/attorney-general-james-announces-court-order-against-crypto-currency-company>

O'Connor, Chris, 'What Blockchain Means for You, and the Internet of Things' (*IBM IoT Blog*, 10 February 2017) <https://www.ibm.com/blogs/internet-of-things/watson-iot-blockchain/>

O'Donnell, Ruaridh, 'In 2020, Will Decentralized Finance Finally Flourish in a Centralized World?' (*Nasdaq*, 27 November 2019) <https://www.nasdaq.com/articles/in-2020-will-decentralized-finance-finally-flourish-in-a-centralized-world-2019-11-27>

O'Reilly, 'Sidechains or Relays' <https://www.oreilly.com/library/view/blockchain-for-enterprise/9781788479745/6326eb12-e7d6-4752-be7c-edb74cb66b3d.xhtml>

OECD, 'Blockchain Technology and Corporate Governance' (6 June 2018) <http://www.oecd.org/officialdocuments/publicdisplaydocumentpdf/?cote=DAF/CA/CG/RD(2018)1/REV1&docLanguage=En>

Office of the Comptroller of the Currency, Treasury; Board of Governors of the Federal Reserve System; Federal Deposit Insurance Corporation; SEC; and Commodity Futures Trading Commission, 'Prohibitions and Restrictions on Proprietary Trading and Certain Interests in, and Relationships With, Hedge Funds and Private Equity Funds' (SEC Release No. BHCA-9, 1 October 2020) <https://www.sec.gov/rules/final/2020/bhca-9.pdf>

OKX Support, 'BTCUSD Options Now Available' (9 January 2020) <https://okexsupport.zendesk.com/hc/en-us/articles/360038631171?utm_source=twitter.com&utm_medium=social&utm_campaign=okexoptions-the-much-awaited-btc-usd-o>

Omarova, Saule T., 'New Tech v. New Deal: Fintech as a Systemic Phenomenon' (2019) 36 YaleJonReg 735

Omarova, Saule, 'The People's Ledger: How to Democratize Money and Finance the Economy' (2021) 74 VandLRev 1301

Ondrejka, Cory, 'Escaping the Gilded Cage: User Crated Content and Building the Metaverse' (2004) 49 NYLSchLRev 81

Onyx by J.P. Morgan, <https://www.jpmorgan.com/global/news/digital-coin-payments>

Ooi, Gene Yan, 'What Is an Initial Exchange Offering (IEO)?' (*Medium*, 13 March 2018) <https://medium.com/traceto-io/what-is-an-initial-exchange-offering-ieo-245a7cf72f28>

OpenANX, 'Real World Application of Decentralized Exchanges V2.3.8' (White paper, 2017) <https://cryptorating.eu/whitepapers/openANX/openANX_White_Paper_ENU.pdf>

OpenZeppelin Library, 'ERC-721' <https://docs.openzeppelin.com/contracts/3.x/erc721>

Osipovich, Alexander and Caitlin Ostroff, 'Crash of TerraUSD Shakes Crypto. "There Was a Run on the Bank"' (*WSJ*, 12 May 2022) <https://www.wsj.com/articles/crash-of-terrausd-shakes-crypto-there-was-a-run-on-the-bank-11652371839>

Overstock, 'Overstock.com Announces Key Dates and Provides Detailed Information Regarding Its Digital Series A-1 Preferred Stock Dividend' (7 April 2020) <https://www.sec.gov/Archives/edgar/data/1130713/000113071320000019/a991pressreleasedatedapril.htm>

Overstock.com, Inc., Prospectus (Form 424B3) (9 December 2015) <https://www.sec.gov/Archives/edgar/data/1130713/000104746915009167/a2226837z424b3.htm>

Oxford Dictionary, 'Complexity' <https://www.lexico.com/definition/complexity>

Oxford Learner's Dictionary, 'Complexity' <https://www.oxfordlearnersdictionaries.com/definition/english/complexity>

Ozair, Merav, 'Stablecoins, Are They Coins or Security Tokens?' (*Elev8*, 17 October 2018) <https://www.elev8con.com/stablecoins-are-they-coins-or-security-tokens/#_edn8>

Padoa-Schioppa, Tommaso, 'An Institutional Glossary of the Eurosystem' (*ECB*, 8 March 2000) <https://www.ecb.europa.eu/press/key/date/2000/html/sp000308_1.en.html>

Paech, Philipp, 'The Governance of Blockchain Financial Networks' (2017) 80 ModLRev 1073

Palmer, Daniel, 'CME Says It Will Launch Bitcoin Options in January' (*CoinDesk*, 12 November 2019) <https://www.coindesk.com/markets/2019/11/12/cme-says-it-will-launch-bitcoin-options-in-january/>

Palumbo, Jacqui, 'Ambitious Plans Unveiled for a Libertarian City in the Metaverse' (*CNN style*, 24 March 2022) <https://edition.cnn.com/style/article/liberland-metaverse-city-zaha-hadid-architects/index.html>

Pan, David, 'China's Crypto Czar: Facebook-Led Libra "Might Be Unstoppable"' (*CoinDesk*, 19 September 2019) <https://www.coindesk.com/chinese-crypto-czar-no-one-would-say-welcome-to-libra-but-it-might-be-unstoppable>

Panisi, Federico, Ross P. Buckley, and Douglas Arner, 'Blockchain and Public Companies: A Revolution in Share Ownership Transparency, Proxy Voting and Corporate Governance?' (2019) 4 StanJBlockchainL&Pol'y 189

Parenti, Radostina, 'FinTech: Regulatory Sandboxes and Innovation Hubs' (2020) https://www.europarl.europa.eu/RegData/etudes/STUD/2020/652752/IPOL_STU(2020)652752_EN.pdf

Partnoy, Frank, 'Barbarians at the Gatekeepers? A Proposal for a Modified Strict Liability Regime' (2001) 79 WashULQ 491

Partz, Helen, 'ERC-20 Co-Author Proposes New ICO Model to Protect Investors from Fraudulent Token Sales' (*Cointelegraph*, 31 October 2018) <https://cointelegraph.com/news/erc-20-co-author-proposes-new-ico-model-to-protect-investors-from-fraudulent-token-sales>

Patti, Giovanni, 'Prodotti finanziari e contratti con i consumatori. Una recente pronuncia della Corte di giustizia a confronto con la securities law Americana' (2011) 5 GC 1015 (on file with author)

Patti, Giovanni, 'The Regulation of Financial Product Innovation Typified by Bitcoin-Based Derivative Contracts' (2019) 38 RevBank&FinL 765

Payments Canada, 'Project Jasper—Outline' (January 2017) <https://payments.ca/sites/default/files/2022-09/project_jasper_primer_EN.pdf>

Payments Canada, 'Payments Canada, Bank of Canada and R3 Release Detailed Findings of Blockchain Experiment' (29 September 2017) <https://www.payments.ca/industry-info/our-research/payments-canada-bank-canada-and-r3-release-detailed-findings-blockchain>

Payne, Jennifer, 'The Role of Gatekeepers' in Niamh Moloney, Eilis Ferran, and Jennifer Payne (eds), *The Oxford Handbook of Financial Regulation* (OUP 2015) 254–279

Peck, Morgen E., 'Bitcoin: The Cryptoanarchists' Answer to Cash' (*IEEE Spectrum*, 30 May 2012) <https://spectrum.ieee.org/computing/software/bitcoin-the-cryptoanarchists-answer-to-cash>

Peel, Edwin, *Treitel—The Law of Contract* (15th edn, Sweet & Maxwell 2015)

Peirce, Hester M., 'Regulation: A View from Inside the Machine' (Speech at University of Missouri School of Law, Columbia, MO, 8 February 2019) <https://www.sec.gov/news/speech/peirce-regulation-view-inside-machine>

Peirce, Hester M., 'Running on Empty: A Proposal to Fill the Gap Between Regulation and Decentralization' (Speech at Chicago, IL, 6 February 2020) <https://www.sec.gov/news/speech/peirce-remarks-blockress-2020-02-06>

People's Bank of China, 'Progress of Research & Development of E-CNY in China' (*Law Info China*, 7 January 2021) <https://www.lawinfochina.com/display.aspx?id=302&lib=dbref&SearchKeyword=&SearchCKeyword=&EncodingName=big5>

Perez, Yessi Bello, 'Sweden's Nasdaq Exchange Approves Bitcoin-based ETN' (*CoinDesk*, 29 April 2019) <https://www.coindesk.com/swedens-nasdaq-exchange-approves-bitcoin-based-etn>

Perrin, Robert G., 'Herbert Spencer's Four Theories of Social Evolution' (1976) 81 AmJSoc 1339

Peters, Gareth and Efstathios Panayi, 'Understanding Modern Banking Ledgers Through Blockchain Technologies: Future of Transaction Processing and Smart Contracts on the Internet of Money' in Paolo Tasca, Tomaso Aste, Loriana Pelizzon, and Nicolas Perony (eds), *Banking Beyond Banks and Money* (Springer 2016) 239–278

Pichai, Sundar, 'COVID-19: $800+ Million to Support Small Businesses and Crisis Response' (*Google*, 27 March 2020) <https://blog.google/inside-google/company-announcements/commitment-support-small-businesses-and-crisis-response-covid-19>

Pick, Leon, 'UBS Chairman: Bitcoin Currency Will Fail, Has No Lender of Last Resort' (*Finance Magnates*, 12 November 2015) <https://www.financemagnates.com/cryptocurrency/news/ubs-chairman-bitcoin-currency-will-fail-has-no-lender-of-last-resort/>

Pilling, David, 'Central African Republic's Adoption of Bitcoin Is Mostly about Geopolitics' (*Financial Times*, 26 May 2022) https://www.ft.com/content/8b68b0cd-230c-4e9b-aa66-84bdbe98c9e0

Pinna, Andrea and Wiebe Ruttenberg, 'Distributed Ledger Technologies in Securities Post-Trading' (2016) European Cent. Bank Occasional Paper Series, Paper No. 172, 10 <https://www.ecb.europa.eu/pub/pdf/scpops/ecbop172.en.pdf>

Pistor, Katharina, 'A Legal Theory of Finance' (2013) 41 JCompEcon 315

Pistor, Katharina, *The Code of Capital* (PUP 2019)

Pistor, Katharina, 'Written Statement of Proposed Testimony for the Hearing entitled "Examining Facebook's Proposed Cryptocurrency and Its Impact on Consumers, Investors, and the American Financial System" before the Committee on Financial Services, U.S. House of Representatives' (17 July 2019) <https://financialservices.house.gov/uploadedfiles/hhrg-116-ba00-wstate-pistork-20190717.pdf>

Pistor, Katharina and Co-Pierre Georg, 'The Right Response to the Libra Threat' (*Project Syndicate*, 5 August 2019) <https://www.project-syndicate.org/commentary/regulating-private-money-facebook-libra-by-katharina-pistor-and-co-pierre-georg-2019-08>

Poletti, Therese, 'Opinion: Pinterest's IPO Filing: 5 Things Investors Should Know' (*Market Watch*, 14 April 2019) <https://www.marketwatch.com/story/pinterests-ipo-filing-5-things-investors-should-know-2019-03-22>

Pollock, Darryn, 'Ripple Hate: Is Ripple a Wolf in Sheep's Clothing?' (*Cointelegraph*, 18 January 2020) <https://cointelegraph.com/news/ripple-hate-is-ripple-a-wolf-in-sheeps-clothing>

Polymath Network, 'What Is a Security Token Offering (STO)?' (12 March 2018) <https://blog.polymath.network/what-is-a-security-token-offering-sto-4e5a92bf6bca>

Poole, William, 'Causes and Consequences of the Financial Crisis of 2007–2009' (2010) 33 HarvJL&PubPol'y 421

Posner, Cydney, 'What Happened at the SEC's Proxy Process Roundtable?' (*HLS Forum on Corporate Governance*, 21 November 2018) <https://corpgov.law.harvard.edu/2018/11/21/what-happened-at-the-secs-proxy-process-roundtable/>

Pozsar, Zoltan, 'The Rise and Fall of the Shadow Banking System' (*Economy*, 2008) <https://www.economy.com/sbs>

Pozsar, Zoltan, Tobias Adrian, Adam Ashcraft, and Hayley Boesky, 'Shadow Banking' (July 2010) Federal Reserve Bank of New York Staff Reports—Staff Report No. 458 <https://www.newyorkfed.org/medialibrary/media/research/staff_reports/sr458_July_2010_version.pdf>

President Biden's Executive Order on Ensuring Responsible Development of Digital Assets (9 March 2022)

President's Working Group on Financial Markets, the Federal Deposit Insurance Corporation, and the Office of the Comptroller of the Currency, *Report on Stablecoins* (November 2021)

Prigogine, Ilya and Isabelle Stengers, *Order Out of Chaos: Man's New Dialogue with Nature* (Verso 1984)

Proskauer LLP, 'A Proposed Statutory Framework for State Regulation of Virtual Currency Businesses: The Uniform Law Commission's "Uniform Regulation of Virtual-Currency Businesses Act"' (*Blockchain & the Law*, 4 April 2018) <https://www.blockchainandthelaw.com/2018/04/a-proposed-statutory-framework-for-state-regulation-of-virtual-currency-businesses-the-uniform-law-commissions-uniform-regulation-of-virtual-currency-businesses-act/>

PwC, *5th ICO/STO Report* (2019) <https://www.pwc.ch/en/publications/2019/ch-PwC-Strategy&-ICO-Report-Summer-2019.pdf>

PwC, 'Central Bank Digital Currency—Benefits and Drawbacks' (2019) <https://www.pwc.ch/en/publications/2019/Central%20Bank%20Digital%20Currency_EN-web.pdf>

PwC, 'IoT Makes Industrial Manufacturers "Smart"' (2019) <https://www.pwc.com/us/en/services/consulting/technology/emerging-technology/iot-pov/manufacturing-iot-snapshot.html>

PwC and Elwood Asset Management, *2019 Crypto Hedge Fund Report* (May 2019) <https://www.pwc.com/gx/en/financial-services/fintech/assets/pwc-elwood-2019-annual-crypto-hedge-fund-report.pdf>

Quiroz-Gutierrez, Marco, 'Someone Got a $1.25 Million Loan by Using NFTs as Collateral. Here's How You May Be Able to Do the Same Thing' (*Fortune*, 8 February 2022) <https://fortune.com/2022/02/07/nft-collateral-for-million-dollar-loans/>

R3, 'About R3' <https://www.r3.com/about/>

R3, 'Blockchain/DLT101' <https://www.r3.com/blockchain-101/>

R3, 'Illinois Becomes First State Level Regulator to Join R3 Distributed Ledger Group' (16 March 2017) <https://r3.com/press-media/illinois-becomes-first-state-level-regulator-to-join-r3-distributed-ledger-group/>

Rajan, Raghuram G. and Luigi Zingales, 'Power in a Theory of the Firm' (1998) 113 QJEcon 387

Ramaekers, Eveline, 'What is Property Law?' (2017) 37 OJLS 588

Raskin, Max, 'The Law and Legality of Smart Contracts' (2017) 1 GeoL&TechRev 305

Rasmussen, Robert K., 'The Uneasy Case against the Uniform Commercial Code' (2002) 62 LaLRev 4

Ray III, John J., 'Declaration in Support of FTX Trading LTD Chapter 11 Petitions and First Day Pleadings' (17 November 2022) <https://s3.documentcloud.org/documents/23310507/ftx-bankruptcy-filing-john-j-ray-iii.pdf>

Rechtschaffen, Alan N., *Capital Markets, Derivatives, and the Law: Positivity and Preparation* (OUP 2019)

Refinitiv, 'Meet Refinitiv' (1 October 2018) <https://www.refinitiv.com/perspectives/ai-digitalization/meet-refinitiv/>

Reidenberg, Joel R., 'Lex Informatica: The Formulation of Information Policy Rules Through Technology' (1997) 76 TexLRev 553

Report of Investigation Pursuant to Section 21(a) of the Securities Exchange Act of 1934: The DAO [2017] Release No. 81207, WL 7184670 <https://www.sec.gov/litigation/investreport/34-81207.pdf>

Reputaction, 'Google USD Stablecoin on Hedera Hashgraph Sooner than Libra?' (*Medium*, 12 February 2020) <https://medium.com/@reputaction/google-usd-stablecoin-on-hedera-hashgraph-sooner-than-libra-572b652a2ec2>

Reuters, 'China Says New Digital Currency Will Be Similar to Facebook's Libra' (6 September 2019) <https://www.reuters.com/article/us-china-cryptocurrency-cenbank/china-says-new-digital-currency-will-be-similar-to-facebooks-libra-idUSKCN1VR0NM>

Reyes, Carla L., 'Moving Beyond Bitcoin to an Endogenous Theory of Decentralized Ledger Technology Regulation: An Initial Proposal' (2016) 61 VillLRev 191

Reyes, Carla L., 'Conceptualizing Cryptolaw' (2017) 96 NebLRev 384
Reyes, Carla L., 'If Rockefeller Were a Coder' (2019) 87 GWashLRev 373
Reyes, Carla L., '(Un)Corporate Crypto-Governance' (2020) 88 FordhamLRev 1875
Reyes, Carla L., 'Creating Cryptolaw for the Uniform Commercial Code' (2021) 78 Wash&LeeLRev 1521
Reyes, Carla L., 'Emerging Technology's Unfamiliarity with Commercial Law' (2023) SMU Dedman School of Law Legal Studies Research Paper No. 590 <https://papers.ssrn.com/sol3/papers.cfm?abstract_id=4388919>
Reyes, Carla L. and Andrea Tosato, 'Crypto's Future Is at Stake in a Dispute Over Commercial Law's Definition of Money' (*Barron's*, 7 April 2023) <https://www.barrons.com/articles/crypto-commercial-laws-definition-of-money-5fbd8fe4>
Ribstein, Larry E., 'Accountability and Responsibility In Corporate Governance' (2006) 81 NotreDameLRev 1431
Ribstein, Larry, 'Market vs. Regulatory Responses to Corporate Fraud: A Critique of the Sarbanes-Oxley Act of 2002' (2002) 28 JCorpL 1
Richardson, Gary, 'Bank Distress during the Great Depression: The Illiquidity–Insolvency Debate Revisited' (2006) NBER Working Paper Series No. 12717 <https://www.nber.org/papers/w12717>
Richardson, Gary, 'Banking Crises and the Federal Reserve as a Lender of Last Resort during the Great Depression' (*The Reporter*, 2013) <https://www.nber.org/reporter/2013number3/banking-crises-and-federal-reserve-lender-last-resort-during-great-depression>
Richardson, Gary, 'The Great Depression' (*Federal Reserve History*, 22 November 2013) <https://www.federalreservehistory.org/essays/great_depression>
Rickles, Dean, Penelope Hawe, and Alan Shiell, 'A Simple Guide to Chaos and Complexity' (2007) 61 JEp&CommHeal 93
Ricks, Morgan, 'Shadow Banking and Financial Regulation' (2010) Columbia Law and Economics Working Paper No. 370 <http://ssrn.com/abstract=1571290>
Ricks, Morgan, John Crawford, and Lev Menand, 'FedAccounts: Digital Dollars' (2021) 89 GWashLRev 113
Ringe, Wolf-Georg, 'Building a European Market for Crypto-assets: Who's Afraid of Libra?' (*OBLB*, 27 October 2020) <https://www.law.ox.ac.uk/business-law-blog/blog/2020/10/building-european-market-crypto-assets-whos-afraid-libra>
Ritholtz, Barry, 'Black Monday Really Did Look Like 1929 Again' (*Bloomberg*, 19 October 2015) <https://www.bloomberg.com/opinion/articles/2015-10-19/1987-stock-market-crash-looked-like-1929-all-over-again>
Roberds, William and François R. Velde, 'Early Public Banks I' in David Fox and Wolfgang Ernst (eds), *Money in the Western Legal Tradition: Middle Ages to Bretton Woods* (OUP 2016) 321–356
Roberds, Willam and François R. Velde, 'Early Public Banks II' in David Fox and Wolfgang Ernst (eds), *Money in the Western Legal Tradition: Middle Ages to Bretton Woods* (OUP 2016) 465–488
Roberts, Daniel, 'CFTC Says Cryptocurrency Ether Is a Commodity, and Ether Futures Are Next' (*yahoo!finance*, 10 October 2019) <https://finance.yahoo.com/news/cftc-says-cryptocurrency-ether-is-a-commodity-and-is-open-to-ether-derivatives-133455545.html>
Robinson, Matt, 'SEC Scrutinizes NFT Market over Illegal Crypto Token Offerings' (*Bloomberg*, 2 March 2022) <https://www.bloomberg.com/news/articles/2022-03-02/sec-scrutinizes-nft-market-over-illegal-crypto-token-offerings>
Rock, Edward B., 'For Whom Is the Corporation Managed in 2020? The Debate over Corporate Purpose' (2021) 76 BusLaw 363

Rodriguez, Jesus, 'Collateralized Debt Positions for Security Tokens' (*Hackernoon*, 25 February 2019) <https://hackernoon.com/collateralized-debt-positions-for-security-tokens-28b7ec8f5522>

Roe, Mark J., 'Chaos and Evolution in Law and Economics' (1995) 109 HarvLRev 64

Roe, Mark J., 'Political Determinants of Corporate Governance' (2003) Discussion Paper no. 451, Harvard John M. Olin Discussion Paper Series <http://www.law.harvard.edu/programs/olin_center/papers/pdf/451.pdf>

Rohr, Jonathan and Aaron Wright, 'Blockchain-Based Token Sales, Initial Coin Offerings, and the Democratization of Public Capital Markets' (2019) 70 HLJ 463

Romano, Roberta, 'Law as a Product: Some Pieces of the Incorporation Puzzle' (1985) 1 JLEcon&Org 225

Romano, Roberta, 'Does the Sarbanes-Oxley Act Have a Future' (2009) 26 YaleJonReg 229

Rossi, Guido, *Il Gioco delle Regole* (Adelphi 2006)

Roubini, Nouriel, 'Why Central Bank Digital Currencies Will Destroy Cryptocurrencies' (*Project Syndicate*, 19 November 2018) <https://www.project-syndicate.org/commentary/central-banks-take-over-digital-payments-no-cryptocurrencies-by-nouriel-roubini-2018-11>

Roubini, Nouriel and Stephen Mihm, *Crisis Economics: A Crash Course in the Future of Finance* (Penguin 2010)

Rühl, Giesela, 'The Law Applicable to Smart Contracts, or Much Ado About Nothing?' (*OBLB*, 23 January 2019) <https://www.law.ox.ac.uk/business-law-blog/blog/2019/01/law-applicable-smart-contracts-or-much-ado-about-nothing>

Ruhl, J. B., 'Fitness of Law: Using Complexity Theory to Describe the Evolution of Law and Society and Its Practical Meaning for Democracy' (1996) 49 VandLRev 1406

Ruhl, J. B., 'Thinking of Environmental Law as a Complex Adaptive System: How to Clean Up the Environment by Making a Mess of Environmental Law' (1997) 34 HousLR 933

Ruhl, J. B., 'Managing Systemic Risk in Legal Systems' (2014) 89 IndLJ 559

Ruhl, J. B. and Daniel M. Katz, 'Measuring, Monitoring, and Managing Legal Complexity' (2011) 101 IowaLR 191

Ruhl, J. B. and Daniel M. Katz, 'Harnessing the Complexity of Legal Systems for Governing Global Challenges' in Victor Valz (ed), *Global Challenges, Governance, and Complexity—Applications and Frontiers* (Elgar 2019) 147–165

Ruhl, J. B., Daniel Martin Katz, and Michael J. Bommarito II, 'Harnessing Legal Complexity' (2017) 355 Science 1377

Rusch, Linda J., 'Summary of Amendments to UCC Article 2' (*Commercial Law Newsletter*, December 2003) <https://www.americanbar.org/content/dam/aba/administrative/business_law/newsletters/CL190000/full-issue-200312.pdf>

Ryan, Reade and Mayme Donohue, 'Securities on Blockchain' (2018) 73 BusLaw 85

SAFE Finance Blog, 'Wirecard—A Scandal at the Right Time' (20 August 2020) <https://safe-frankfurt.de/news-latest/safe-finance-blog/details/wirecard-a-scandal-at-the-right-time.html>

Sáinz de Vicuña, Antonio, 'An Institutional Theory of Money' in Mario Giovanoli and Diego Devos (eds), *International Monetary and Financial Law: The Global Crisis* (2010) 517–532

Sams, Robert, 'A Note on Cryptocurrency Stabilisation: Seigniorage Shares' (*BitMex blog*, 28 April 2015) https://blog.bitmex.com/wp-content/uploads/2018/06/A-Note-on-Cryptocurrency-Stabilisation-Seigniorage-Shares.pdf

Sandbox <https://www.sandbox.game/en/>

Sandner, Philipp, 'Liechtenstein Blockchain Act: How Can Nearly Any Right and Therefore Any Asset be Tokenized based on the Token Container Model?' (*Medium*, 9 October 2019) <https://philippsandner.medium.com/liechtenstein-blockchain-act-how-can-nearly-any-right-and-therefore-any-asset-be-tokenized-based-389fc9f039b1>

Sandner, Philipp, 'Understanding Libra 2.0: A Compliant Global Platform for the Digital Programmable EUR, USD, GBP & Co.' (*Medium*, 17 April 2020) <https://medium.com/@philippsandner/libra-2-0-a-compliant-global-platform-for-the-digital-programmable-eur-usd-gbp-co-67e1b8a2c0cb>

Sandor, Krisztian and Ekin Genç, 'Timeline of the Meteoric Rise and Crash of UST and LUNA' (*Coindesk*, 12 May 2022) <https://www.coindesk.com/learn/the-fall-of-terra-a-timeline-of-the-meteoric-rise-and-crash-of-ust-and-luna/>

SAS, 'Artificial Intelligence: What It Is and Why It Matters' <https://www.sas.com/en_us/insights/analytics/what-is-artificial-intelligence.html>

SAS, 'Big Data: What It Is and Why It Matters' <https://www.sas.com/en_us/insights/big-data/what-is-big-data.html>

SAS, 'Deep Learning—What It Is and Why It Matters' <https://www.sas.com/en_us/insights/analytics/deep-learning.html>

SAS, 'Machine Learning: What It Is and Why It Matters' <https://www.sas.com/en_us/insights/analytics/machine-learning.html>

SAS, 'Neural Networks—What Are They and Why They Matter' <https://www.sas.com/en_us/insights/analytics/neural-networks.html>

Schär, Fabian, 'Decentralized Finance: On Blockchain- and Smart Contract-based Financial Markets' (2020) 103 FedResBankStLRev 153

Schleiermaker, Friederich Daniel Ernst, *Hermeneutics and Criticism* (Andrew Bowie ed, CUP 1998)

Schneider, Lee, 'Blockchaingers Legal Deep Dive: Keynote by Lee Schneider' (30 November 2017) <https://www.youtube.com/watch?v=82S6NDzebFQ>

Schorr, Brian L., 'Remarks to the SEC Investor Advisory Committee' (*SEC*, 13 September 2018) https://www.sec.gov/spotlight/investor-advisory-committee-2012/iac091318-brian-schorr-opening-remarks.pdf

Schrepel, Thibault, 'Blockchain and Human Rights: Utopia, or Dystopia, or Both?' (*OBLB*, 4 December 2019) <https://www.law.ox.ac.uk/business-law-blog/blog/2019/12/blockchain-and-human-rights-utopia-or-dystopia-or-both>

Schroeder, Ralph and Rich Ling, 'Durkheim and Weber on the Social Implications of New Information and Communication Technologies' (2014) 16 NM&S 789

Schurr, Fransesco A., 'Anbahnung, Abschluss un Durchfuhrung von Smart Contracts im Rechtsvergleich' (2019) 118 ZVRW 257

Schuster, Edmund, 'Cloud Crypto Land' (2021) 84 ModLR 974

Schwarcz, Steven L., 'Rethinking the Disclosure Paradigm in a World of Complexity' (2004) UIllinoisLRev1

Schwartz, Robert F., 'Risk Distribution in the Capital Markets: Credit Default Swaps, Insurance and a Theory of Demarcation' (2007) 12 FJCFL 167

Schwarcz, Steven L., 'Systemic Risk' (2008) 97 GeoLJ 193

Schwarcz, Steven L., 'Regulating Complexity in Financial Markets' (2009) 87 WUnLRev 21

Schwarcz, Steven L., 'Regulating Shadow Banking' (2012) 31 RevBank&FinL 619

Schwarcz, Steven L., 'Banking and Financial Regulation' in Francesco Parisi (ed), *The Oxford Handbook of Law & Economics: Volume 2: Private and Commercial Law* (OUP 2017) 423–446

Scott, Hal S., 'The Reduction of Systemic Risk in the United States Financial System' (2010) 33 HarvJL&PubPol'y 671, 673

SEC, 'Key Points about Regulation SHO' <https://www.sec.gov/investor/pubs/regsho.htm#ftn1>

SEC, 'Money Market Funds' <https://www.sec.gov/spotlight/money-market.shtml>

SEC, 'Request Form for Fintech Related Meetings and Other Assistance' <https://www.sec.gov/finhub-form#no-back>

REFERENCES   421

SEC, 'Concept Release on the U.S. Proxy System' (Release No. 34-62495, 14 July 2010) <https://www.sec.gov/rules/concept/2010/34-62495.pdf>
SEC, 'Custody of Funds or Securities of Clients by Investment Advisers' (Release No. IA-2671, 5 November 2003) <https://www.sec.gov/rules/final/ia-2176.htm#P57_4850>
SEC, *Summary Report of Issues Identified in the Commission Staff's Examinations of Select Credit Rating Agencies* (July 2008) <https://www.sec.gov/news/studies/2008/craexamination070808.pdf>
SEC, 'President's Working Group Report on Money Market Fund Reform' (Release No. IC-29497, October 2010) <https://www.sec.gov/rules/other/2010/ic-29497.pdf>
SEC, 'Investor Bulletin: Measures to Address Market Volatility' (1 July 2012) <https://www.sec.gov/oiea/investor-alerts-bulletins/investor-alerts-circuitbreakersbulletinhtm.html>
SEC, 'Money Market Fund Reform; Amendments to Form PF' (Release No. 33-9616, 1 May 2014) <https://www.sec.gov/rules/final/2014/33-9616.pdf>
SEC, 'Report of Investigation Pursuant to Section 21(a) of the Securities Exchange Act of 1934: The DAO' (25 July 2017) 4 <https://www.sec.gov/litigation/investreport/34-81207.pdf>
SEC, 'Self-Regulatory Organizations; Bats BZX Exchange, Inc.; Order Setting Aside Action by Delegated Authority and Disapproving a Proposed Rule Change, as Modified by Amendments No. 1 and 2, to List and Trade Shares of the Winklevoss Bitcoin Trust' (Release No. 34-83723, 26 July 2018) <https://www.sec.gov/rules/other/2018/34-83723.pdf>
SEC, 'SEC Launches New Strategic Hub for Innovation and Financial Technology' (18 October 2018) <https://www.sec.gov/news/press-release/2018-240>
SEC, 'Framework for 'Investment Contract' Analysis of Digital Assets' (3 April 2019) <https://www.sec.gov/files/dlt-framework.pdf>
SEC, 'Joint Staff Statement on Broker-Dealer Custody of Digital Asset Securities' (8 July 2019) https://www.sec.gov/news/public-statement/joint-staff-statement-broker-dealer-custody-digital-asset-securities
SEC, 'Initial Exchange Offerings (IEOs)—Investor Alert' (14 January 2020) <https://www.sec.gov/oiea/investor-alerts-and-bulletins/ia_initialexchangeofferings>
SEC, 'SEC FinHub Staff Statement on OCC Interpretation' (21 September 2020) <https://www.sec.gov/news/public-statement/sec-finhub-statement-occ-interpretation#_ftn3>
SEC, 'SEC Announces Office Focused on Innovation and Financial Technology' (3 December 2020) <https://www.sec.gov/news/press-release/2020-303>
SEC, 'Custody of Digital Asset Securities by Special Purpose Broker-Dealers' (Release No. 34-90788, 23 December 2020) <https://www.sec.gov/rules/policy/2020/34-90788.pdf>
SEC Order Instituting Cease-and-Desist Prooceedings, Making Findings and Imposing a Cease-And-Desist Order *Re Zachary Coburn* [2018] Release No. 84553 (8 November 2018) https://www.sec.gov/litigation/admin/2018/34-84553.pdf
Sedgwick, Kai, 'Six Alternatives to an Initial Coin Offering' (*Bitcoin.com*, 18 June 2018) <https://news.bitcoin.com/six-alternatives-to-an-initial-coin-offering/>
Sedgwick, Kai, 'How Prime Brokerage Will Affect Crypto Markets' (*Bitcoin.com*, 14 November 2019) <https://news.bitcoin.com/how-prime-brokerage-will-affect-crypto-markets/>
Segal, Troy, 'Money Market Fund' (*Investopedia*, updated 7 April 2022) https://www.investopedia.com/terms/m/money-marketfund.asp>
Sergeenkov, Andrey, 'Number of STOs May Double while IEOs will Almost Triple by Q4 2019' (*Hackernoon*, 15 May 2019) <https://hackernoon.com/number-of-stos-may-double-while-ieos-will-almost-triple-by-q4-2019-a90a957d7c3f>
'Serving Documents—National Information and Online Forms Concerning Regulation No. 1393/2007' (*E-Justice.europa.eu*) <https://e-justice.europa.eu/373/EN/serving_documents>
Sexer, Nathan, 'State of Stablecoins 2018' (*Medium*, 24 July 2018) <https://media.consensys.net/the-state-of-stablecoins-2018-79ccb9988e63>

Shadab, Houman B., 'Regulating Bitcoin and Block Chain Derivatives' (2014) <https://papers.ssrn.com/sol3/papers.cfm?abstract_id=2508707>

Shadab, Houman B., 'What Are Smart Contracts, and What Can We do with Them?' (*Coincenter*, 15 December 2014) <https://www.coincenter.org/education/key-concepts/smart-contracts/>

Sherlock, Michael, 'Digital Securities: Overstock.com and Beyond' (*Law360*, 2016) <https://www.law360.com/articles/873790/overstock-issues-first-ever-blockchain-shares-in-11m-offer>

Shin, Laura, 'Here's the Man Who Created ICOs and this Is the New Token He's Backing' (*Forbes*, 21 September 2017) <https://www.forbes.com/sites/laurashin/2017/09/21/heres-the-man-who-created-icos-and-this-is-the-new-token-hes-backing/#108e76ad1183>

Shrimpy, 'What Are Crypto Synths? Synthetic Assets Explained' (28 October 2021) <https://academy.shrimpy.io/post/what-are-crypto-synths-synthetic-assets-explained>

Shuchman, Hedvah L., *Self-Regulation in the Professions: Accounting, Law, Medicine, Final Report* (Glastonbury 1981)

Sicard, Germain, *The Origins of Corporations* (YUP 2015)

Siekmann, Helmut (ed), *The European Monetary Union: A Commentary on the Legal Foundations* (Bloomsbury 2021)

Sigalos, MacKenzie, 'From $10 billion to zero: How a crypto hedge fund collapsed and dragged many investors down with it' (*CNBC*, 12 July 2022) <https://www.cnbc.com/2022/07/11/how-the-fall-of-three-arrows-or-3ac-dragged-down-crypto-investors.html>

Singh, J., 'Difference between Flow Variables and Stock Variables' (*Economic Discussion*) <https://www.economicsdiscussion.net/difference-between/difference-between-flow-variables-and-stock-variables/555>

Sirena, Pietro and Francesco Paolo Patti, 'Smart Contracts and Automation of Private Relationships' in Hans-W Micklitz, Oreste Pollicino, Amnon Reichman, Andrea Simoncini, Giovanni Sartor, and Giovanni De Gregorio (eds), *Constitutional Challenges in the Algorithmic Society* (CUP 2021) 315–330

SIX, 'SIX and SBI Digital Asset Holdings Announce Plans for Singapore-Based Joint Exchange Venture to Drive Institutional Digital Asset Liquidity' (8 December 2020) <https://www.six-group.com/en/newsroom/media-releases/2020/20201208-six-sbi-jev.html>

Smart, Adam R., 'E-Sign versus State Electronic Signature Laws: The Electronic Statutory Battleground' (2001) 5 NCBankInst 485

Smart Contracts Alliance and Deloitte, 'Smart Contracts: 12 Use Cases for Business & Beyond' (December 2016) <https://www.perkinscoie.com/images/content/1/6/v2/164979/Smart-Contracts-12-Use-Cases-for-Business-Beyond.pdf>

Smedinghoff, Thomas J., 'The Legal Challenges of Implementing Electronic Transactions' (2008) 41 UniformComCodeLJ 1

Smelser, Neil, *Karl Marx on Society and Social Change* (UCP 1973)

Smialek, Jeanna and Neil Irwin, 'Fed Slashes Rates to Near-Zero and Unveils Sweeping Program to Aid Economy' (*NYT*, 15 March 2020) <https://www.nytimes.com/2020/03/15/business/economy/federal-reserve-coronavirus.html>

Smith, Adam, 'E-Commerce in the New Century' (2002) 8 NewEngJIntl&CompL 1

Smith, Oliver, 'How to Short Sell Bitcoin, And Why More People Aren't' (*Forbes*, 12 June 2018) <https://www.forbes.com/sites/oliversmith/2018/07/12/how-to-short-sell-cryptocurrencies-and-why-more-people-arent/#5c9ee2b14e63>

Smith and Crown, 'What Is a Token Sale (ICO)?' (21 June 2016) <https://smithandcrown.com/research/what-is-a-token-sale-ico/>

SNB, 'Swiss National Bank and Six Announce Successful Wholesale Cbdc Experiment' (3 December 2020) <https://www.snb.ch/en/mmr/reference/pre_20201203/source/pre_20201203.en.pdf>

Société Générale, 'Société Générale réalise la première transaction financière réglée en Monnaie Digitale de Banque Centrale' (30 May 2020) <https://www.societegenerale.com/sites/defa ult/files/200023_cp_societe_generale_realise_la_premiere_transaction_financiere_reglee_ en_monnaie_digitale_de_banque_centrale.pdf>

Song, Wonnie, 'Bullish on Blockchain: Examining Delaware's Approach to Distributed Ledger Technology in Corporate Governance Law and Beyond' (*Harvard Business Law Review Online*, 2018) <http://www.hblr.org/2018/01/bullish-on-blockchain-examining-delawares-approach-to-distributed-ledger-technology-in-corporate-governance-law-and-beyond>

Spatt, Chester S., 'Complexity of Regulation' (*Harvard Business Law Review Online*, 16 June 2012) <https://www.hblr.org/2012/06/complexity-of-regulation/>

Speidel, Richard E., 'Revising UCC Article 2: A View from the Trenches' (2001) 52 HastingsLJ 607

Sraders, Anne, '4 Things Investors Need to Know about Slack's Direct Listing' (*Fortune*, 9 June 2019) <https://fortune.com/2019/06/19/slack-direct-listing-stock-ipo-investors/>

Stacey, Kiran and Hannah Murphy, 'How Facebook's Libra Went from World Changer to Just Another PayPal' (*Financial Times*, 17 April 2020) <https://www.ft.com/content/79376464-72b5-41fa-8f14-9f308acaf83b>

Stankiewicz, Kevin, 'Jim Cramer Says These 4 Companies Are the Best Ways to Invest in The Metaverse' (*CNBC*, 11 November 2021) <https://www.cnbc.com/2021/11/10/jim-cramer-says-these-4-companies-are-the-best-ways-to-invest-in-the-metaverse.html>

Stanley, Aaron, 'Just In Time? Winklevoss-Backed Crypto Self-Regulatory Effort Picks Up Steam?' (*Forbes*, 20 August 2018) <https://www.forbes.com/sites/astanley/2018/08/20/just-in-time-winklevoss-backed-crypto-self-regulatory-group-has-liftoff/#4a2cc0902ea5>

Stapczynski, Stephen, 'Goldman Sachs Explores Entering Crypto Market, CoinDesk Reports' (*Bloomberg*, 15 January 2021) <https://www.bloomberg.com/news/articles/2021-01-16/gold man-sachs-explores-entering-crypto-market-coindesk-reports>

State Secretariat for International Finance, 'SIF Launches Green Fintech Network' (5 November 2020) <https://www.sif.admin.ch/sif/en/home/dokumentation/fokus/fintech-network.html>

Steemit, 'Where Can You Trade Cryptocurrency? List of Crypto Exchanges' (2017) <https://stee mit.com/cryptocurrency/@dragonsteem/where-can-you-trade-cryptocurrency-list-of-cry pto-exchanges>

Stibbe, 'Blockchain and the Law—Regulation for Smart Contracts on the Way?' (October 2019) <https://www.stibbe.com/en/news/2019/october/blockchain-and-the-law---regulation-for-smart-contracts-on-the-way>

Stout, Lynn A., 'Risk, Speculation, and OTC Derivatives: An Inaugural Essay for Convivium' (2011) 1 AccountEconL: Conviv 1

Suberg, William, 'BitMEX to Compensate Users Affected by Unforeseen Auto-Deleveraging after Bitcoin Bullrun' (*Cointelegraph*, 4 April 2019) <https://cointelegraph.com/news/bitmex-to-compensate-users-affected-by-unforeseen-auto-deleveraging-after-bitcoin-bullrun>

Sustainalytics, <https://www.sustainalytics.com/about-us/#>

Sveriges Riksbank, 'The Riksbank's E-Krona Project—Report 2' (October 2019) <https://www.riksbank.se/globalassets/media/rapporter/e-krona/2018/the-riksbanks-e-krona-project-report-2.pdf>

Swanson, Tim, 'Consensus-as-a-Service: A Brief Report on the Emergence of Permissioned, Distributed Ledger Systems' (6 April 2015) <https://www.ofnumbers.com/2015/04/06/consensus-as-a-service-a-brief-report-on-the-emergence-of-permissioned-distributed-led ger-systems/>

Swint, Brian, 'Carney Urges Libra-Like Reserve Currency to End Dollar Dominance' (*Bloomberg*, 23 August 2019) <https://www.bloomberg.com/news/articles/2019-08-23/car ney-urges-libra-like-reserve-currency-to-end-dollar-dominance>

Swiss Blockchain Federation, 'About us' <https://blockchainfederation.ch/about-us/?lang=en>
Swiss Blockchain Federation, 'Guidelines for Issuers of Equity and Related Tokens' (12 December 2019) <http://blockchainfederation.ch/wp-content/uploads/2019/12/SBF-Circular-2019-01-Tokenized-Equity-1.pdf>
Swiss Federal Council, *Report on the Legal Framework for Distributed Ledger Technology and Blockchain in Switzerland* (14 December 2018) <https://www.newsd.admin.ch/newsd/message/attachments/55153.pdf>
Swiss Federal Council, 'Federal Council Informed of Current Status of Stablecoin Debate' (16 October 2019) <https://www.admin.ch/gov/en/start/documentation/media-releases.msg-id-76722.html>
Swiss Federal Council, 'Botschaft zum Bundesgesetz zur Anpassung des Bundesrechts an Entwicklungen der Technik verteilter elektronischer Register vom 27 November 2019' (BBl 2020 233) (27 November 2019)
Swiss Federal Council, 'Federal Council Wants to Further Improve Framework Conditions for DLT/Blockchain' (27 November 2019) <https://www.admin.ch/gov/en/start/documentation/media-releases.msg-id-77252.html>
Swiss Federal Council, 'Federal Council Takes Note of Current Stablecoin Developments' (15 January 2020) <https://www.admin.ch/gov/en/start/documentation/media-releases.msg-id-77785.html>
Swiss National Bank, BIS Innovation HUB and SIX, 'Project Helvetia Settling Tokenised Assets in Central Bank Money' (December 2020) https://www.bis.org/publ/othp35.pdf
Swiss National Bank, BIS Innovation HUB and SIX, 'Project Helvetia Phase II: Settling Tokenised Assets in Wholesale CBDC' (January 2022) <https://www.bis.org/publ/othp45.pdf>
Sygnum, 'Sygnum's Digital Asset Trading Facility (OTF) Gets Regulatory Clearance from FINMA' (1 September 2020) <https://www.insights.sygnum.com/post/sygnum-s-digital-asset-trading-facility-otf-gets-regulatory-clearance-from-finma>
Szabo, Nick, 'Smart Contracts' (1994) <https://www.fon.hum.uva.nl/rob/Courses/InformationInSpeech/CDROM/Literature/LOTwinterschool2006/szabo.best.vwh.net/smart.contracts.html>
Szabo, Nick, 'Smart Contracts: Building Blocks for Digital Markets' (1996) <https://www.fon.hum.uva.nl/rob/Courses/InformationInSpeech/CDROM/Literature/LOTwinterschool2006/szabo.best.vwh.net/smart_contracts_2.html>
Szabo, Nick, 'Formalizing and Securing Relationships on Public Networks' (*First Monday*, 1 September 1997) <https://firstmonday.org/ojs/index.php/fm/article/view/548/469>
Szabo, Nick, 'The Idea of Smart Contracts' (1997) <https://www.fon.hum.uva.nl/rob/Courses/InformationInSpeech/CDROM/Literature/LOTwinterschool2006/szabo.best.vwh.net/idea.html>
Szabo, Nick, 'BitGold' (*Unenumerated blogspot*, 27 December 2008) <http://unenumerated.blogspot.com/2005/12/bit-gold.html>
Szabo, Nick, 'Smart Contracts: From Vending Machines to Global Finance Machines' (*Swiss Re*, 2016) <https://www.swissre.com/dam/jcr:e1775ba6-2ad5-4aac-a1c5-e35d584fb59b/Presentation_Nick_Szabo.pdf>
Szalay, Eva, 'Crypto Lender Genesis Accepts NFTs as Collateral for Loans' (*Financial Times*, 28 January 2022) <https://www.ft.com/content/ce600e79-93cf-40c8-928c-e9bbd66072c7>
Szilagyi, Peter G. and Chong Wei Wong, 'The Board of Directors in Hedge Fund Governance' (2012) (unpublished manuscript) <https://pdfs.semanticscholar.org/319d/c4d3c4bf92ad949208138b733b44cd491cca.pdf?_ga=2.257922315.1814225679.1589206661-1203352850.1589206661>
Tafara, Ethiopis, 'Foreword: Observations about the Crisis and Reform' in Eilis Ferran, Niamh Maloney, Jennifer G. Hill, and John C. Coffee, Jr. (eds), *The Regulatory Aftermath of the Global Financial Crisis* (CUP 2012) xi–xxvi

Taleb, Nassim Nicholas, *The Black Swan* (2nd edn, Random House 2010)

Tanno, Alessandro, 'Italy Affirms Legal Effectiveness of DLTs and Smart Contracts' (*Linklaters*, 2019) <https://www.linklaters.com/en/insights/blogs/fintechlinks/2019/fintech-italy-affirms-legal-effectiveness-of-distributed-ledger>

Tassev, Lubomir, 'Liechtenstein Adopts Token Act to Attract Crypto Business' (*Bitcoin.com*, 6 October 2019) <https://news.bitcoin.com/liechtenstein-adopts-token-act-to-attract-crypto-business/>

Techopedia, 'What Does Scalability Mean?' (27 January 2017) <https://www.techopedia.com/definition/9269/scalability>

The Business of Crypto, 'List of Blockchain Custody Companies | Crypto Custody' <https://www.thebusinessofcrypto.com/company/markets/custody/>

The Diem Association, 'Diem Announces Partnership with Silvergate and Strategic Shift to the United States' (12 May 2021) <https://www.diem.com/en-us/updates/diem-silvergate-partnership/>

The Diem Association, 'Statement by Diem CEO Stuart Levey on the Sale of the Diem Group's Assets to Silvergate' (31 January 2022) <https://www.diem.com/en-us/updates/stuart-levey-statement-diem-asset-sale/>

The Economist, 'The Market in Initial Coin Offerings Risks Becoming a Bubble' (25 April 2017) <http://www.economist.com/news/finance-and-economics/21721425-it-may-also-spawn-valuable-innovations-market-initial-coin-offerings>

The Economist, 'Norway's Sovereign-Wealth Fund Passes the $1trn Mark' (23 September 2017) <https://www.economist.com/finance-and-economics/2017/09/23/norways-sovereign-wealth-fund-passes-the-1trn-mark>

The European Union Blockchain Observatory & Forum <https://www.eublockchainforum.eu/>

The European Union Blockchain Observatory & Forum, 'Legal and Regulatory Framework of Blockchains and Smart Contracts' (27 September 2019) <https://www.eublockchainforum.eu/sites/default/files/reports/report_legal_v1.0.pdf>

The High Level Group on Financial Supervision in the EU, *Report of the de Larosière Group* (2009) <https://ec.europa.eu/economy_finance/publications/pages/publication14527_en.pdf>

The Libra Association, 'Libra White Paper' (June 2019) https://web.archive.org/web/20190618094622/https://libra.org/en-US/white-paper/

The Libra Association, 'Libra White Paper v2.0' (April 2020) <https://web.archive.org/web/20221129004028/https://wp.diem.com/en-US/wp-content/uploads/sites/23/2020/04/Libra_WhitePaperV2_April2020.pdf>

The Writer's Lounge, 'Choosing the Right Blockchain for Your NFT' (*Medium*, 30 November 2020) <https://medium.com/phantasticphantasma/choosing-the-right-blockchain-for-your-nft-d1df2bebae91>

Thierer, Adam, '15 Years On, President Clinton's 5 Principles for Internet Policy Remain the Perfect Paradigm' (*Forbes*, 12 February 2012) <https://www.forbes.com/sites/adamthierer/2012/02/12/15-years-on-president-clintons-5-principles-for-internet-policy-remain-the-perfect-paradigm/?sh=4425ecb57170>

Thoma, Silvan, 'Switzerland Strengthens Fintech and Blockchain Sector' (*PwC*, 15 September 2020) <https://www.pwc.ch/en/insights/fs/amending-act-DLT-blockchain.html>

Thomas, Leigh and Michael Nienaber, 'G7 Finance Chiefs Pour Cold Water on Facebook's Digital Coin Plans' (*Reuters*, 17 July 2019) <https://www.reuters.com/article/us-g7-economy/g7-finance-chiefs-pour-cold-water-on-facebooks-digital-coin-plans-idUSKCN1UC0IC>

Thomson Reuters, 'Thomson Reuters Announces Closing of Sale of Refinitiv to London Stock Exchange Group' (29 January 2021) <https://www.thomsonreuters.com/en/press-releases/2021/january/thomson-reuters-announces-closing-of-sale-of-refinitiv-to-london-stock-exchange-group.html>

Timiraos, Nick and Julia-Ambra Verlaine, 'Fed to Inject $1.5 Trillion in Bid to Prevent "Unusual Disruptions" in Markets' (*WSJ*, 12 March 2020) https://www.wsj.com/articles/fed-to-inject-1-5-trillion-in-bid-to-prevent-unusual-disruptions-in-markets-11584033537>

Tinianow, Andrea and Caitlin Long, 'Delaware Blockchain Initiative: Transforming the Foundational Infrastructure of Corporate Finance' (*HLS Forum on Corporate Governance*, 16 March 2017) <https://corpgov.law.harvard.edu/2017/03/16/delaware-blockchain-initiative-transforming-the-foundational-infrastructure-of-corporate-finance/#more-80025>

Toth, Orsolya, *The Lex Mercatoria in Theory and Practice* (OUP 2014)

Travis Laster, J., 'The Block Chain Plunger: Using Technology to Clean Up Proxy Plumbing and Take Back the Vote' (*Cii*, 2016) <https://www.cii.org/files/09_29_16_laster_remarks.pdf>

Treitel, Guenter H., *The Law of Contract* (Sweet & Maxwell 1995)

Tuch, Andrew F., 'Multiple Gatekeepers' (2010) 96 VaLRev 1583

Tucker, Paul, 'The Lender of Last Resort and Modern Central Banking: Principles and Reconstruction' (2014) BIS Papers No. 79 <https://www.bis.org/publ/bppdf/bispap79.pdf>

TwobitIdiot, 'Introducing Messari: An Open-Source EDGAR Database for Cryptoassets' (*Medium*, 26 October 2017) <https://medium.com/tbis-weekly-bits/introducing-messari-an-open-source-edgar-database-for-cryptoassets-46fec1b402f6>

Tymoigne, Eric and Randall L. Wray, 'Money: An Alternative Story' in Philip Arestis and Malcolm Sawyer (eds), *A Handbook of Alternative Monetary Economics* (Elgar 2007) 1–16

UK Government Chief Scientific Adviser, 'Distributed Ledger Technology: Beyond Block Chain' (2016) <https://assets.publishing.service.gov.uk/government/uploads/system/uploads/attachment_data/file/492972/gs-16-1-distributed-ledger-technology.pdf>

UK Jurisdictional Taskforce, 'Legal Statement on the Status of Cryptoassets and Smart Contracts' (18 November 2019) 31 https://35z8e83m1ih83drye280o9d1-wpengine.netdna-ssl.com/wp-content/uploads/2019/11/6.6056_JO_Cryptocurrencies_Statement_FINAL_WEB_111119-1.pdf

UN Convention on Contracts for the International Sale of Goods 1980 <https://uncitral.un.org/sites/uncitral.un.org/files/media-documents/uncitral/en/19-09951_e_ebook.pdf>

UN Environment Inquiry, 'Green Digital Finance: Mapping Current Practice and Potential in Switzerland and Beyond' (September 2018) <https://www.greengrowthknowledge.org/sites/default/files/downloads/resource/Green_Digital_Finance_Mapping_in_Switzerland_and_Beyond.pdf>

UN Environment Programme (20 January 2017) <https://web.unep.org/revolutionary-digital-platform-boost-green-finance>

UN Res 70/1 'Transforming Our World: The 2030 Agenda for Sustainable Development' (25 September 2015) UN A/RES/70/1 <https://sustainabledevelopment.un.org/post2015/transformingourworld>

UN Task Force on Digital Financing of the Sustainable Development Goals, 'People's Money: Harnessing Digitalization to Finance a Sustainable Future' (2020) <https://unsdg.un.org/resources/peoples-money-harnessing-digitalization-finance-sustainable-future>

UNCITRAL Model Law on Electronic Signatures with Guide to Enactment 2001 <https://uncitral.un.org/sites/uncitral.un.org/files/media-documents/uncitral/en/ml-elecsig-e.pdf>)

Uniform Law Commission, 'A Few Facts about the Uniform Electronic Transactions Act' <https://www.uniformlaws.org/HigherLogic/System/DownloadDocumentFile.ashx?DocumentFileKey=c5976d91-07e2-b3f8-9b1e-4450fe809c21&forceDialog=0>

U.S. Bureau of Economic Analysis, 'Gross Domestic Product, Fourth Quarter and Year 2019 (Advance Estimate)' (30 January 2020) <https://www.bea.gov/news/2020/gross-domestic-product-fourth-quarter-and-year-2019-advance-estimate>

U.S. Bureau of Economic Analysis, 'Gross Domestic Product, Fourth Quarter and Year 2021 (Advance Estimate)' (27 January 2022) <https://www.bea.gov/news/2022/gross-domestic-product-fourth-quarter-and-year-2021-advance-estimate>

U.S. Department of the Treasury, 'Financial Stability Oversight Council' <https://home.treasury.gov/policy-issues/financial-markets-financial-institutions-and-fiscal-service/fsoc>
Van der Elst, Christoph and Anne Lafarre, 'Blockchain and Smart Contracting for the Shareholder Community' (2019) 20 EBOR 111
Vaugh, Douglas and Anna Outzen, 'Understanding How Block Chain Could Impact Legal Industry' (*Law360*, 11 January 2017) <https://www.law360.com/articles/879810/understanding-how-blockchain-could-impact-legal-industry>
Veerpalu, Anne, Liisi Jürgen, Eduardo da Cruz e Silva, and Alex Norta, 'The Hybrid Smart Contract Agreement Challenge to European Electronic Signature Regulation' (2020) 28 IJLIT 39
Vidal-Tomas, David, 'The Entry and Exit Dynamics of the Cryptocurrency Market' (2021) 58 ResIntlBus&Fin 1 (101504)
Vigna, Paul, 'Winklevoss Effort to Self-Regulate Cryptocurrency Gets Members' (*WSJ*, 20 August 2018) <https://www.wsj.com/articles/winklevoss-effort-to-self-regulate-cryptocurrency-gets-members-1534804308>
Vuong, Madeline, 'This Smart Water Pitcher Orders Its Own Filters: Amazon and Brita Unveil the "Infinity Pitcher"' (*GeekWire*, 29 February 2016) <https://www.geekwire.com/2016/amazon-dash-replenishment-powers-first-brita-smart-pitcher-that-orders-its-own-filters/>
Wackerow, Paul, 'ERC-20 Token Standard' (*Ethereum*, 3 December 2021) <https://ethereum.org/en/developers/docs/standards/tokens/erc-20/>
Walch, Angela, 'Bitcoin as a Market Infrastructure' (2015) 18 NYUJL&PubPol'y 837
Walch, Angela, 'The Patch of the Blockchain Lexicon (and the Law)' (2017) 36 RevBank&FinL 713
Walch, Angela, 'Intermediaries Who Must Not Be Named? A Legal & Policy Research Agenda for Crypto Miners' (21 November 2019) <https://www.youtube.com/watch?v=jywZcWoinVU>
Waller, Matthew Alan and Stanley E. Fawcett, 'Data Science, Predictive Analytics, and Big Data: A Revolution that Will Transform Supply Chain Design and Management' (2013) 34 JBusLog 77
Wandhöfer, Ruth, 'The Future of Digital Retail Payments in Europe: A Role for Central Bank Issued Crypto Cash?' (*ECB*, 1 October 2017) https://www.ecb.europa.eu/pub/conferences/shared/pdf/20171130_ECB_BdI_conference/payments_conference_2017_academic_paper_wandhoefer.pdf>
Wang, Kyle, 'Ethereum: Turing-Completeness and Rich Statefulness Explained' (*Hackernoon*, 6 July 2017) <https://hackernoon.com/ethereum-turing-completeness-and-rich-statefulness-explained-e650db7fc1fb>
Wang, Qin, Rujia Li, Qi Wang, and Shipping Chen, 'Non-Fungible Token (NFT): Overview, Evaluation, Opportunities and Challenges' (*arXiv*, 16 May 2021) <https://arxiv.org/abs/2105.07447>
Weber, Rolf H. and Douglas W. Arner, 'Toward a New Design for International Financial Regulation' (2007) 29 UPaJIntL 391
Weber, Rolf H., 'Multilayered Governance in International Financial Regulation and Supervision' (2010) 13 JIntlEconL 683
Weber, Rolf H., 'The Legitimacy of the G20 as a Global Financial Regulator' (2013) 28 Bank&FinLRev 389
Weber, Rolf H., 'Leistungsstörungen und Rechtsdurchsetzung bei Smart Contracts: Eine Auslegeordnung möglicher Problemstellungen' (*Jusletter*, 2017) <https://jusletter.weblaw.ch/juslissues/2017/917/leistungsstorungen-u_3e7a005a8f.html__ONCE&login=false>
Weber, Rolf H., '"Rose Is a Rose Is a Rose Is a Rose"—What about Code and Law?' (2018) 34 CompL&SecRev 704
Weber, Rolf H., 'Smart Contracts: Vertrags-und verfügungsrechtlicher Regelungsbedarf?' (2018) 22 ZIIW 291

Weber, Rolf H., 'Smart Contracts: Do we need New Legal Rules?' in Alberto De Franceschi and Reiner Schulze (eds), *Digital Revolution—New Challenges for the Law* (Verlag C. H. Beck 2019) 299–312

Weiler, Bob, 'How Digital Disruption Transcends Industry Borders' (*Forbes*, 23 March 2017) <https://www.forbes.com/sites/ciocentral/2017/03/23/how-digital-disruption-transcends-industry-borders/#5eeb4d7d4d00>

Werbach, Kevin, 'The Centripetal Network: How the Internet Holds Itself Together, and the Forces Tearing it Apart' (2009) 42 UCDavisLRev 343

Werbach, Kevin, *The Blockchain and the New Architecture of Trust* (MIT Press 2018)

Werbach, Kevin and Nicolas Cornell, 'Contracts Ex Machina' (2017) 67 DukeLJ 313

Werner, Richard A., 'Can a Bank Create Money out of Nothing? Using Accounting Information to Test the Three Theories of Banking Empirically' (2014) 36 IntlRevFinAn 1

Werner, Richard A., 'How Do Banks Create Money, and Why Can Other Firms Not Do the Same? An Explanation for the Coexistence of Lending and Deposit-Taking' (2014) 36 IntlRevFinAn 71

Westerkamp, Martin and Jacob Eberhardt, 'zkRelay: Facilitating Sidechains using zkSNARK-based Chain-Relays' (2020) <https://eprint.iacr.org/2020/433.pdf>

Whaley, Douglas and Stephen McJohn, *Problems and Materials on Commercial Law* (11th edn, Wolters Kluwer 2016)

White, Larry, 'The World's First Central Bank Electronic Money Has Come—And Gone: Ecuador, 2014–2018' (*Alt-M*, 29 March 2018) <https://www.alt-m.org/2018/03/29/the-worlds-first-central-bank-electronic-money-has-come-and-gone-ecuador-2014-2018/>

White, Lawrence H., 'Competitive Payments Systems and the Unit of Account' (1984) 74 AmEconRev 699

White House, 'FACT SHEET: President Biden to Sign Executive Order on Ensuring Responsible Development of Digital Assets' (9 March 2022) <https://www.whitehouse.gov/briefing-room/statements-releases/2022/03/09/fact-sheet-president-biden-to-sign-executive-order-on-ensuring-responsible-innovation-in-digital-assets/>

Whitehead, Charles K., 'The Evolution of Debt Covenants, the Credit Market, and Corporate Governance' (2009) 34 JCorpL 641

Whitehead, Charles K., 'Destructive Coordination' (2011) 96 CornellLRev 323

Whitehead, Charles K., 'The Volcker Rule and Evolving Financial Markets' (2011) 1 HarvBusLRev 39

Whitehead, Charles K., 'Size Matters: Commercial Banks and the Capital Markets' (2015) 76 OhioStLJ 765

Whitt, Richard S. and Stephen J. Schultze, 'The New "Emergence Economics" of Innovation and Growth, and What It Means for Communications Policy' (2009) 7 JTHTL 217

Willett, J. R. 'The Second Bitcoin Whitepaper' (2012) <https://cryptochainuni.com/wp-content/uploads/Mastercoin-2nd-Bitcoin-Whitepaper.pdf>

Wilmarth Jr., Arthur E., 'It's Time to Regulate Stablecoins as Deposits and Require Their Issuers to Be FDIC-Insured Banks' (2022) 41 Banking & Financial Services Policy Report No. 2 <https://scholarship.law.gwu.edu/cgi/viewcontent.cgi?article=2834&context=faculty_publications>

Winn, Jane K. and Benjamin Wright, *Law of Electronic Commerce* (4th edn, Wolters Kluwer 2019)

Wolff, Lutz-Christian, 'The Relationship between Contract Law and Property Law' (2020) CLWR 49

World Bank, 'Distributed Ledger Technology & Secured Transactions: Legal, Regulatory and Technological Perspectives—Guidance Notes Series' (May 2020) <https://openknowledge.worldbank.org/bitstream/handle/10986/34007/Collateral-Registry-Secured-Transactions-Law-and-Practice.pdf?sequence=5>

World Economic Forum, 'What Is the Metaverse? And Why Should We Care?' (29 October 2021) <https://www.weforum.org/agenda/2021/10/facebook-meta-what-is-the-metaverse/>

World Economic Forum, 'Norway's Massive Sovereign-Wealth Fund Sets Net-Zero Goals' (23 September 2022) <https://www.weforum.org/agenda/2022/09/norways-massive-sovereign-wealth-fund-sets-net-zero-goal/>

Wray, Randall, 'From the State Theory of Money to Modern Money Theory: An Alternative to Economic Orthodoxy' in David Fox and Wolfgang Ernst (eds), *Money in the Western Legal Tradition: Middle Ages to Bretton Woods* (OUP 2016) 631–652

Wright, Aaron and Primavera De Filippi, 'Decentralized Blockchain Technology and the Rise of Lex Cryptographia' (2017) <https://www.ssrn.com/abstract=2580664>

WSJ, 'Lehman Makes It Official in Overnight Chapter 11 Filing' (15 September 2008) <https://blogs.wsj.com/wallstreetcrisis/2008/09/15/lehman-makes-it-official/>

Wu, Tim, 'Agency Threats' (2011) 60 DukeLJ 184

Yadav, Yesha, 'The Problematic Case of Clearinghouses in Complex Markets' (2013) 101 GeoLJ 387

Yadav, Yesha, 'Too-Big-to-Fail Shareholders' (2018) 103 MinnLRev 587

Yakubowski, Max, 'What's Next for the Industry as "Crypto Winter" Thaws?' (*Cointelegraph*, 5 October 2019) <https://cointelegraph.com/news/whats-next-for-the-industry-as-crypto-winter-thaws>

Yates, Tony, 'Bitcoin and the Lender of Last Resort Function' (*longandvariable*, 18 September 2017) <https://longandvariable.wordpress.com/2017/09/18/bitcoin-and-the-lender-of-last-resort-function/>

Yee, Robert, 'Financial Innovation and Commenda Contracts in Medieval Europe' (*The Vanderbilt Historical Review*, updated 21 December 2019) <https://www.vanderbilthistoricalreview.com/post/financial-innovation-and-commenda-contracts-in-medieval-europe>

Yermack, David, 'Corporate Governance and Blockchains' (2017) 21 RevFin 7

Yeyati, Eduardo Levy, 'Covid, Fed Swaps and the IMF as Lender of Last Resort' (*Vox*, 31 March 2020) <https://voxeu.org/article/covid-fed-swaps-and-imf-lender-last-resort>

Young, Joseph, 'Big Banks Are Investing Heavily in Blockchain and Crypto: $364 Billion Investment Firm' (*CNN*, 12 May 2018) <https://www.ccn.com/big-banks-are-investing-heavily-in-blockchain-and-crypto-364-billion-investment-firm/>

Young, Joseph, 'Why New Generation Stablecoins Are Crucially Based on Ethereum' (*yahoo!finance*, 24 October 2018) <https://finance.yahoo.com/news/why-generation-stablecoins-crucially-based-152605210.html>

Zanki, Tom, 'Overstock Issues First-Ever Blockchain Shares in $11M Offer' (*Law360*, 16 December 2016) <https://www.law360.com/articles/873790/overstock-issues-first-ever-blockchain-shares-in-11m-offer>

Zapotochnyi, Andrew, 'What Are Smart Contracts' (*Blockgeeks*, updated 11 April 2016) <https://blockgeeks.com/guides/smart-contracts/>

Zaring, David, 'Litigating the Financial Crisis' (2014) 100 ValLRev 1405

Zec, Jelena, 'The Metaverse Mall: From Science Fiction to Retail Reality' (*citiVentures*, 22 November 2021) <https://www.citi.com/ventures/perspectives/opinion/metaverse-mall.html>

Zellweger-Gutknecht, Corinne and Rolf H. Weber, 'Private Zahlungsmittel und Zahlungssysteme' (*Jusletter*, 2021) <https://jusletter.weblaw.ch/juslissues/2021/1050/private-zahlungsmitt_a7ce9d6728.html__ONCE&login=false>

Zellweger-Gutknecht, Corinne, Benjamin Geva, and Seraina Neva Grünewald, 'Digital Euro, Monetary Objects, and Price Stability: A Legal Analysis' (2021) 7 JFinRegul 284

Zetzsche, Dirk A., 'Hidden Ownership in Europe: BAFin's Decision in Schaeffler v. Continental' (2009) 10 EBOR 115

Zetzsche, Dirk A., Ross P. Buckley, Douglas W. Arner, and Janos N. Barberis, 'Regulating a Revolution: From Regulatory Sandboxes to Smart Regulation' (2017) 23 FordhamJCorp&FinL 3

Zetzsche, Dirk A., Ross P. Buckley, and Douglas W. Arner, 'The Distributed Liability of Distributed Ledgers: Legal Risks of Blockchain' (2018) 4 IllinoisLRev 1361

Zetzsche, Dirk A., Ross P. Buckley, Douglas W. Arner, and Janos N. Barberis, 'From FinTech to TechFin: The Regulatory Challenges of Data-Driven Finance' (2018) 14 NYUJL&Bus 393

Zetzsche, Dirk A., Ross P. Buckley, Douglas W. Arner, and Linus Föhr, 'The ICO Gold Rush: It's a Scam, It's a Bubble, It's a Super Challenge for Regulators' (2019) 60 HarvIntlLJ 267

Zetzsche, Dirk A., Douglas Arner, and Ross P. Buckley, 'Decentralized Finance' (2020) 6 JFinReg 172

Zetzsche, Dirk A., Douglas W. Arner, Ross P. Buckley, and Rolf H. Weber, 'The Evolution And Future Of Data-Driven Finance In The EU' (2020) 57 CMLRev 33

Zetzsche, Dirk A., Filippo Annunziata, Douglas W. Arner, and Ross P. Buckley, 'The Markets in Crypto-Assets Regulation (MiCA) and the EU Digital Finance Strategy' (2021) 16 CMLJ 203

Zetzsche, Dirk A., Ross P. Buckley, and Douglas W. Arner, 'Regulating LIBRA: The Transformative Potential of Facebook's Cryptocurrency and Possible Regulatory Responses' (2021) 41 OJLS 80

Zheng, Steven, 'Bakkt's Monthly Bitcoin Futures Hit All-Time-High of $15M' (*The Block Crypto*, 9 November 2019) <https://www.theblockcrypto.com/linked/46523/bakkts-monthly-bitcoin-futures-hit-all-time-high-of-15m>

Zimmerman, Brenda, Curt Lindberg, and Paul Plsek, 'A Complexity Science Primer: What Is Complexity Science and Why Should I Learn about It?' (*napcrg.org*, adapted from: Brenda Zimmerman, Curt Lindberg, and Paul Plsek, *Edgeware: Lessons From Complexity Science for Health Care Leaders* (VHA 1998) <https://www.napcrg.org/media/1278/beginner-complexity-science-module.pdf>

Zimmermann, Claus D., 'Monetary Policy in the Digital Age' in Ioannis Lianos, Philipp Hacker, Stefan Eich, and Georgios Dimitropoulos (eds), *Regulating Blockchain: Techno-Social and Legal Challenges* (OUP 2019) 99–335.

Zuckerman, Molly Jane, 'Wyoming Introduces New Bill to Exempt Crypto from Property Taxation' (*Cointelegraph*, 19 February 2018) <https://cointelegraph.com/news/wyoming-introduces-new-bill-to-exempt-crypto-from-property-taxation>

Index

For the benefit of digital users, indexed terms that span two pages (e.g., 52-53) may, on occasion, appear on only one of those pages.

Abacus 45, 47
accountability 73, 231, 284-86
Agenzia per l'Italia Digitale (AgID) 113
AIFMD 47, 48-49, 131, 223, 282
algorithmic stablecoins 127-28, 236, 250, 306
Anti-Money Laundering (AML) 155, 273, 278, 298-99, 329-30
Anti-Money Laundering Act (AMLA) 155, 160-61
Apple 88, 312
Arizona (State of) 102, 187
Article 128 TFEU 275
artificial intelligence 26-27
Autorité des Marchés Financiers (AMF) 124-25

Banco de España 229
Bank for International Settlements (BIS) 237, 268, 278
Bank of Amsterdam 229
Bank of Canada 263-64, 277
Bank of England 222-23, 225-26, 229, 243, 264, 265-66, 277, 295
Bank of Thailand 263-64
Banking Act 1933 (Glass-Steagall Act) 48, 288
Banking Act 1934 (*Bundesgesetz über die Banken und Sparkassen*) 160-61
Banque de France 229, 270-71, 272-45
Basel Agreements 40, 227-28
Bell, Jim 50, 238
Big Data 25-26
Bitcoin 49-56, 57, 59, 70-72, 92, 130-31, 140-41, 146, 223-24, 239-40, 279-80, 293-94, 301-2, 318-20
Bitcoin derivatives 319, 320-21
blockchain 25, 32, 52-56, 299-300, *see also* bitcoin; consensus; crypto-assets; crypto-financial products; cryptocurrencies; digital securities; digital tokens; distributed ledger technology (DLT); ethereum, F-NFTs; initial coin offerings (ICOs); NFTs; smart contracts; tokenization
board of directors 200
Broadridge 103, 196, 205
broker dealers 44, 181-82, 201-2, 329, 349-50
Bundesanstalt für Finanzdienstleistungsaufsicht (Bafin) 161

California (State of) 187
central bank 58-59, 225-31, 281-82, 283-84, 290, 293-97, 300-2, 305-6
central bank digital currencies (CBDC) 259-68, 271-72, 273-75, 276-78, 304-6, *see also* Helvetia (project); multiple CBDCs (mCBDCs); Project Jasper
central bank independence 230-31, 285-86, 287

central bank money 231-32 *see also* Central Bank Digital Currencies (CBDC)
central securities depositors (CSDs) 191, 205-6
Chamber of Digital Commerce 125, 126
chartalist approach 233
Clayton, Jay 143-44, 165
clearing houses 190-91, 235-36, 283, 292, 300, 336
clearing *see* clearing houses
Code is Law 84-85, 121-22, 124
collateral 44-45, 162-63, 216-17, 241-42, 250, 257, 292, 314, 315-16, 324-25, 336, 338
collateralized debt obligation (CDO) 18, 321-22
Collective Investment Scheme Act 2021, 155
Commenda 22, 115
commercial bank money 231-32, 243
Commodities and Futures Commission (CFTC) 140-41, 149, 158, 164-65, 251, 336
commodity 140-41, 150-51, 163, 164-65, 220, 232-33, 250-52, 255-56
complex adaptive systems (CAS) 7-10, 12-14, 20-21
complexity science 7-14
Comte, Auguste 11-12
consensus 51, 54-55, 60-61, 146, 340
CONSOB 161
corporate governance 20, 45-46, 192-208, 282-84, 290-91
CorpTech 192, 200
Covid-19, 74, 225-26, 295-97
credit ratings 340
credit transformation 39-40
crypto hedge funds 241-42, 326-27
Crypto Valley Association *see* Crypto Valley
Crypto Valley 167
crypto-assets 209-11, 256-57, 286, *see also* blockchain; crypto-lending; crypto-exchanges; digital securities; digital tokens; distributed ledger technology (DLT); F-NFTs; initial coin offerings (ICOs); initial exchange offerings (IEOs); NFTs; rating in crypto-assets; security tokens; shadow central banking
cryptocurrencies 51, 59, 61-62
cryptoeconomy 59-60, 61-62, 68-69, 166-67, 173-74, 302, 309-10, 317-18, 321-22, 343-45, 346, 347-48, 351-52, 356-57, 373, 374-75
crypto-exchanges 137, 172-73, 174, 318, 348
crypto-financial products 350
crypto-lending 314-16, 323-24, 348
CryptoUK 168
currency *see* bitcoin; cryptocurrencies; fiat currency; legal tender; money

432 INDEX

custodians *see* custody
custody 191-92, 327-30, 349-50
cyberattacks 201, 202-3, 339
cybersecurity 293, 354

dark pools 173-74
de Larosière Report 48-49
de Larosière, Jacques *see* de Larosière Report
Debt Enforcement and Bankruptcy Act 1889 (*Bundesgesetz über Schuldbetreibung und Konkurs*) 209
decentralized applications (DApps) 60-61
decentralized exchanges (DEXs) 172
Delaware (State of) 101, 103, 186-87, 195
Depository Trust & Clearing Corporation (DTCC) 58, 191
derivatives 19-20, 41, 140-41, 154-55, 216-17, 318-21, 323-24, 334, 336, 338, 347-48, *see also* bitcoin derivatives; on-chain derivatives
Diem Association 246-48
DigiCash 50
digital assets 209-10
digital commodity 149, 349
Digital Commodity Exchange Act (DCEA) 148-49, 349
Digital Finance 62-63
Digital Operational Resilience Act (DORA) 293
digital securities 179-87, 188-92, 193-94, 201-2, 219
digital tokens 59-60, 131-32, 141-44, 152-53, 179-80, 192, *see also* digital assets; initial coin offerings (icos); tokenization
disruptive technology 5, 22-33, 37-38, 57-58
Distributed Autonomous Organization (DAO) 89-90, 193, *see also* The DAO
distributed ledger technology (DLT) 24, 52-56, 86, 113, 176, 206, *see also* blockchain; crypto-assets; decentralized applications (dapps); decentralized exchanges (dexs); smart contracts
DLT Law (*Bundesgesetz zur Anpassung des Bundesrechts an Entwicklungen der Technik verteilter elektronischer Register*) 154, 176, 185, 186
Dnick Holding 196
Do No Harm Approach 29-30, 98-99, 122
Dodd-Frank Act 2010, 48, 228, 351
Draghi, Mario 225-26
Durkheim, Émile 11-12
dynamic regulation 35-38

E-Gold 50
El Salvador 301-2
Electronic Identification and Trust Services Regulation (eIDAS) 107, 108-9
Electronic Signature in Global and National Commerce Act (ESIGN) 99, 100-1
emergence economies 2
e-money 237-38, 253-55, 260
Enron 46
entrepreneurial state 29
equilibrium (Far-From) 9, 21
ERC-20 (ERC20) 216, 240-41
ERC-721 (ERC721) 213-14, 216
ESG ratings 340-42
Estonia 189
Ethereum 60-61, 87-139, 204, 213-14, 345
EU Data Act 109-10

European Banking Authority (EBA) 151, 254, 255
European Central Bank (ECB) 273-76, 295-96
European Electronic Communications Code 205-6
European Market Infrastructure Regulation (EMIR) 48-49, 351
European Securities and Markets Authority (ESMA) 149, 151, 206
European Systemic Risk Board (ESRB) 49, 228, 351
evolutionism 12
exchange-traded fund (ETF) 319-20
exchange-traded note (ETN) 319
Executive Order on Ensuring Responsible Development of Digital Assets 147, 267-68
Ex-Post Facts-Based Rule-Making 231

Facebook 166, 246-47, 248-49, 251, 291
Federal Intermediated Securities Act (*Bundesgesetz über Bucheffekten*) (FISA) 186
Federal Reserve 125-26, 226-27, 229-31, 266-67, 281-82, 295-97
fiat currency 292
Financial Conduct Authority (FCA) 218
financial conglomerates 45, 287, 345, 350-53
financial crisis 3-4, 15, 44-46, 47-50, 288, 336, *see also* Covid-19; collateralized debt obligation (CDO); credit ratings, leverage; liquidity risk
financial inclusion 73, 168-70, 245-46, 264-65, 267
financial innovation 19-20, 21-22, 30, 38-63, 78-80, 115-16, 313-14, 353
Financial Market Infrastructure Act (*Bundesgesetz über die Finanzmarktinfrastrukturen und das Marktverhalten im Effekten- und Derivatehandel*) (FMIA) 153-54, 163, 176, 186, 283, 348
financial services agency (FSA) 168
Financial Stability Board (FSB) 292, 300
Financial Stability Oversight Committee (FSOC) 49, 228
Fintech Association of Hong Kong 168
fintech hub 34, *see also* Switzerland; Singapore; Malta; United Kingdom
F-NFTs 139-218, 372
France 156, 183, 209, 229, 238-39, 270-71
FTX, right after 47, 173-74, 347-48
Full-Faith-And-Credit 234, 280

G20, 49-50, 286, 300
G7, 52, 242, 265, 278
gatekeepers 174-75, 182-83, 199-200, 201, 202-3, 208, 337-38
Germany 110, 209, 217-18, 330
Giancarlo, Christopher 122, 165
Goldman Sachs 47, 276-77, 328, 345
Google 205, 221-22, 295-96, 345
Great Depression 43, 160, 293-94

Helvetia (Project) 268-70
historicism 12
history dependency 21, 38
Hong Kong 34-35, 156, 220
Hong Kong Monetary Authority 278
Howey test 120, 143, 145-46, 148, 160, 249

ICO tokens *see* digital tokens
Illinois (State of) 103-4

INDEX

Initial Coin Offerings (ICOs) 33, 51–52, 59–60, 81, 131–55, 156–62, 163–64, 165–66, 167–92, 218–20, 221, 234, 249, 251–52, 255, 317–18, 326, 343, 359–60, 361
initial exchange offerings (IEOs) 137, 139, 171, 173–74
initial game offerings (IGOs) 213
initial public offerings (IPOs) 131, 134, 135–36, 178
institutional investors 170, 197–98, 321, 326, 327
institutional theory of money 233
interactive initial coin offerings (IICOs) 138
International Monetary Fund (IMF) 51, 286, 293–94, 301–2, 305, 325, 338–39
Internet of Things (IoT) 27, 117
interoperability 31, 203–6, 297–98
Investment Advisers Act 1940, 299
IOSCO 53, 60, 243–44, 286

J.P. Morgan Coin 244
Japan Virtual Currency Exchange Association 168
Japanese Financial Services Agency 168

Kenya 301
know your customer (KYC) 138, 329-30

Law, John 287–88
legal tender 209, 274, 275–76, 301–2, 303–4
Lehman Brothers 49–50
Lender of Last Resort 294–95, 296–97
lending platforms 315–16, 323–24, 337, 340, 345
leverage 317–24, 335–37, *see also* margin trading
lex cryptographia *see* Law is Code
Liberty Reserve 50, 237–38
Libra 165–66, 221–23, 245–46, 247–48, 285, 352–53
Libra Foundation 245
Liechtenstein 183, 210
liquidity 210, 216–17, 225–27, 254–55, 292, 294–95, 296–97, 318, 330–31, 336, 337
liquidity pools 315–16, 338–39
liquidity risk 44–45, 93, 138, 289, 290, 337–39, 346–47
liquidity transformation 39–40, 232
Loi Pacte 209
London Stock Exchange Group (LSEG) 189–90, 342

machine learning 26–27
macroprudential supervision 48–49, 227–28
Madoff, Bernie 47
Malta 114–15
Malta Digital Innovation Authority (MDIA) 114
margin trading 323
Market in Financial Instruments Directive (MiFID) 48–49
Market in Financial Instruments Directive II (MiFID II) 48–49, 149, 150–51, 251–52
market infrastructures 172–76, 347–50, *see also* Broker dealers; clearing houses; crypto-exchanges; custodians; decentralized exchanges (DEXs); lending platforms; London Stock Exchange Group (LSEG); money market funds (MMFs); pension funds, prime brokers; private funds; SIX Digital Exchange; stablecoins; stock exchanges; Tokyo Stock Exchange, Inc (TSE); trading platforms
market manipulation 140, 172–73, 287–88, 319–20, 334
Marx, Karl 12
maturity transformation 39–40, 232, 243

May, Timothy 50, 246
medium of exchange 132, 232–33, 260, 361
Meta 373
metalist approach 233, 238–39
metaverse 27–28, 212–13, 369–75
MiCA (Market in Crypto-Assets Regulation) 151–52, 252–55, 306, 330, 349
microprudential supervision 227–28
Monetary Authority of Singapore (MAS) 264, 298
Money (Functions) 232–34
money 237–49, 280–81
money market funds (MMFs) 290–91, 299–300, 324–26, 346–47
multiple CBDCs (mCBDCs) 278

Nakamoto, Satoshi 49–50, 223
Netherlands 110, 112–13
network growth economies 2–3
Network of Central Banks and Supervisors for Greening the Financial System (NGFS) 228
Nevada (State of) 102
New Deal 160
new monetary economics (NME) 238–39
New York (State of) 103
NFTs (non-fungible tokens) 211–18, 252, 331, *see also* F-NFTs
nonlinearity 9

off-chain stablecoins 250
on-chain derivatives 322–23
on-chain stablecoins *see* stablecoins
Orderly Resolution Authority 49
Overstock 181–83, 201–2

Paris Agreement 228
Parmalat 46, 199
Peltz, Nelson 196
pension funds 40–41, 340–41
People's Bank of China 276–77, 303
People's Republic of China 190, *see also* People's Bank of China
Ponzi scheme 47, 169
post-trading phase 54, 190–92, *see also* clearing; settlement
President's Working Group (PwG) 288–89
prime brokers 327–28, 356–57
principal–agent 199, 200
principle-based regulation 33, 152–53, 159, 160–61
private central banking 235–36, 279–80, 281–82
private funds 344
Project Jasper 263–64
Project Ubin 264, 298
proof-of-stake (PoS) 54–55, *see also* consensus
proof-of-work (PoW) 54–55, *see also* consensus
proxy fights 196, 197
proxy voting 103, 197–98, 205
public regulation 77, 127, 156

quantitative easing 225–26

R3 Corda 58, 88, 263–64
rating in crypto-assets 343–44, 353–54
Re Appraisal of Dell, Inc., 195

Re Dole Food Co., 195
Reg. A+, 138
Reg. D, 138
Reg. S, 138
regulated markets 40–41, *see also* exchange-traded notes (ETN); stock exchanges; maturity transformation; liquidity transformation; credit transformation; public regulation; private regulation; self-regulation
regulatory disruption 35–38
regulatory sandboxes 34–35, 363–64
Restatement of Contracts 94
retail investors 175–76, 197–98
Ripple (XRP) (case) 146–47, 157–58
Roosevelt, Franklin Delano 160

sandboxes 34–35, 363–64
Sarbanes–Oxley Act 46
SEBA 210, 332
Section 2 (UCC) 96, 97–98, 101, 119
Securities Act 1933, 141–42, 145–46, 148, 192, 249
Securities Clarity Act (SCA) 148–49
Securities Exchange Act 1934, 144, 148, 349–50
Securities Exchange Authority (SEC) 33, 89, 140, 141–47, 157–58, 159, 161–62, 166, 192, 319–20, 324, 329–30, 349–50, *see also* The DAO Report
securities *see* bitcoin derivatives; collateralized debt obligation (CDO); derivatives; digital securities; exchange-traded fund (ETF); exchange-traded note (ETN); F-NFTs; securitization; structured products; synthetic assets; uncertificated securities
securitization 44–45, 330–31
security token offerings (STOs) 138, 139, 171
self-regulation 77–78, 124, 127, 167, 284, 347
self-regulatory organizations (SROs) 124–27, 347
settlement 54, 61, 190–91, 264, 268–69, 277–78, 289
shadow banking 236–37, 257–59, 287–88, 345
shadow central banking 234–37, 257–59, 278–80, 282–85, 286–88, 290–93, 296, 300–8, 332–40, 355–56
shareholder voting 194–99, 202
Short Selling Regulation (SSR) 48–49, 351
short-selling 195, 323–24
Simple Agreement for Tokens (SAFT) 137–38
Singapore 34–35, 156, 220
Single Resolution Board 49, 351
Six Digital Exchange 222–23, 268, 332, 347
smart contracts 60–61, 81–98, 100–5, 106–15, 116, 117–21, 122, 123–24, 125–26, 127–29, 316–17, 322, *see also* blockchain; distributed autonomous organizations (DAO); distributed ledger technology (DLT); NFTs; synthetic assets
Societé Générale—Forge 270–71
stablecoins 52, 132–33, 151–52, 158–59, 162–64, 174, 187–88, 223, 235, 240–56, 260, 280–81, 286, 288, 289, 290–91, 292, 293, 296, 306, 312, 324–26, 333, 338, 346, 347, 350, 361–62, *see also* algorithmic stablecoins; initial coin offerings (ICOs); J.P Morgan Coin; Libra; Terra Stablecoin; Tether (USDT)
Stock Exchanges 188–90, 347
store of value 132, 232–33, 260, 361
structural functionalism 11–12

structured products 22, 41
sustainability 73–74, 228, 340–42, 353
Sustainable Development Goals (SDGs) 365
Sveriges Riksbank 228–29, 263
swap lines 226–27, 296–97
Sweden 263, 319
Swiss Code of Obligations (CO) 81–82, 111, 158–59
Swiss Financial Market Supervisory Authority (FINMA) 33, 34–35
Swiss National Bank (SNB) 227, 228, 268–69, 270, 277, 281–82
Switzerland 80–81, 110–13, 121, 152–55, 158–59, 160–61, 163, 167, 184–86, 194, 210, 255–56, 268–70
Sygnum 210, 332
synthetic assets 322
systemic risk 44–45, 49, 286–93, 335–36, 340
systemically important financial institution (SIFI) *see* financial conglomerates
Szabo, Nick 50, 83–85, 238

technological risk 339, 353, 354–55
Telegram (case) 164–66
Terra Luna Crash 241–42
Terra Stablecoin 302, 338, 346
Tether (USDT) 172–73, 174, 241, 302, 304, 346, 352
The DAO 89–90, 192, 207, 354, 374
The DAO Report 143, 145, 249
Token Taxonomy Act 147–49
tokeneconomy 59–60, 61–62, 63, 68, 309–10
tokenization 179–80, 209–10, 219, 264, 271–72, 331–33, 337–38 *see also* NFTs; Societé Générale—Forge
Tokyo Stock Exchange, Inc (TSE) 205
too big to fail (TBTF) 45, 286, 345, 350–51
trading platforms 149, 172–73, 176, 181–82, 190, 349, 355
trial-and-error rule-making 30
Trust Service Provider (TSP) 108

uncertificated securities 153–54, 184, 185–86
Uniform Commercial Code (UCC) 93–98, 101, 118, 119, 120, 122
Uniform Computer Information Transaction Act (UCITA) 101
Uniform Electronic Transaction Act (UETA) 99–101
unit of account 52, 130, 232–33, 238–40, 260, 263–64
United Kingdom 40–41, 110, 112–13, 168, 218, 229–30, 265–66

Venezuela 188
venture capital 133, 170–71, 177, 326
Vermont (State of) 102

wait and see (approach) 32–33
Web 2.0, 371
Web 3.0, 371
Weber, Max 11–12
Wirecard, para after 47
Worldcom 46, 199
Wyoming (State of) 104–5